Social Networking Communities and E-Dating Services:
Concepts and Implications

Celia Romm-Livermore
Wayne State University, USA

Kristina Setzekorn
Smith Barney Ltd., USA

Information Science REFERENCE

INFORMATION SCIENCE REFERENCE

Hershey · New York

Director of Editorial Content:	Kristin Klinger
Senior Managing Editor:	Jennifer Neidig
Managing Editor:	Jamie Snavely
Managing Development Editor:	Kristin M. Roth
Assistant Managing Editor:	Carole Coulson
Assistant Development Editor:	Deborah Yahnke
Typesetter:	Chris Hrobak
Copy Editor:	Ashley Fails
Editorial Assistant:	Rebecca Beistline
Cover Design:	Lisa Tosheff
Printed at:	Yurchak Printing Inc.

Published in the United States of America by
Information Science Reference (an imprint of IGI Global)
701 E. Chocolate Avenue, Suite 200
Hershey PA 17033
Tel: 717-533-8845
Fax: 717-533-8661
E-mail: cust@igi-global.com
Web site: http://www.igi-global.com

and in the United Kingdom by
Information Science Reference (an imprint of IGI Global)
3 Henrietta Street
Covent Garden
London WC2E 8LU
Tel: 44 20 7240 0856
Fax: 44 20 7379 0609
Web site: http://www.eurospanbookstore.com

Library of Congress Cataloging-in-Publication Data

Social networking communities and e-dating services : concepts and implications / Celia Romm and Kristina Setzekom, editors.

p. cm.

Includes bibliographical references and index.

Summary: "This book provides an overview of the major questions that researchers and practitioners in this area are addressing at this time and by outlining the possible future directions for theory development and empirical research on social networking and eDating"--Provided by publisher.

ISBN 978-1-60566-104-9 (hardcover) -- ISBN 978-1-60566-105-6 (ebook)

1. Online social networks. 2. Social networks. 3. Online dating. 4. Dating services. 5. Internet--Social aspects. I. Romm, Celia T., 1954- II. Setzekom, Kristina.

HM742b.S63 2009

306.730285'4678--dc22

2008022552

British Cataloguing in Publication Data
A Cataloguing in Publication record for this book is available from the British Library.

Table of Contents

Section II
Social Networking Sites for Teenagers and Young Adults

Section III
E-Dating Services

Detailed Table of Contents

Section I
Social Networking Communities

This chapter focuses on detailing the role of five individual level factors—Internet self-efficacy, self-esteem, need to belong, need for information, and gender—in influencing the attitudes toward social networking sites (SNS) and the adoption of such sites. First, the growing importance of social networking sites in business is discussed, and their usage as advertising vehicles is outlined. Individual differences in SNS adoption are presented from a technology acceptance model framework. A paper-based survey is conducted and data obtained is used to test a structural model that explains the role of individual-level factors in influencing individuals' attitudes toward SNS, their willingness to join SNS, and their actual membership on SNS. Results are presented and managerial implications are drawn.

Popular online social networks such as Friendster and MySpace do more than simply reveal the superficial structure of social connectedness; the rich meanings bottled within social network profiles themselves imply deeper patterns of culture and taste. If these latent semantic fabrics of taste could be harvested formally, the resultant resource would afford completely novel ways for representing and reasoning about Web users and people in general. This chapter narrates the theory and technique of such a feat; the natural language text of 100,000 social network profiles were captured, mapped into a diverse ontology of music, books, films, foods, and so forth, and machine learning was applied to infer a semantic fabric of taste.

Taste fabrics bring us closer to improvisational manipulations of meaning, and afford us at least three semantic functions: the creation of semantically flexible user representations, cross-domain taste-based recommendation, and the computation of taste-similarity between people, whose use cases are demonstrated within the context of three applications; the InterestMap, Ambient Semantics, and IdentityMirror. Finally, we evaluate the quality of the taste fabrics, and distill from this research reusable methodologies and techniques of consequence to the semantic mining and Semantic Web communities.

This chapter discusses how virtual social networks have evolved from their original purpose of being online meeting places where people interact with one another to becoming an important locus for innovation. It delineates the salient characteristics of these networks (both Web-based and mobile) and suggests that the advent of these networks has shifted the balance of value creation away from traditional companies and towards the creation of companies which provide technology platforms and services for user-centric innovation. The chapter discusses how users on these virtual networks have become important sources of innovation in a variety of ways: they develop content which they share with others and participate in virtual community centers; they interact with companies who are developing products and provide valuable feedback; and they are the impetus for the creation of new kinds of marketing tools as businesses try to tap into these virtual networks in order to better understand what products will sell to these users. In addition, the chapter discusses the implications of these developments for managers, especially those in content-intensive industries such as financial services and media. Examples will be given to support these ideas from case studies on Upoc, a New York City-based mobile services company which hosts social networks for a wide variety of users; Dodgeball, another New York City-based company (recently acquired by Google) which is one of the pioneers in the mobile social networking arena; and Tapuz Mobile, an Israeli-based social network.

Chapter IV

The rise of online communities in Internet environments has set in motion an unprecedented shift in power from vendors of goods and services to the customers who buy them, with those vendors who understand this transfer of power and choose to capitalize on it by organizing online communities and being richly rewarded with both peerless customer loyalty and impressive economic returns. A type of online community, the virtual world, could radically alter the way people work, learn, grow, consume, and entertain. Understanding the exchange of social and economic capital in online communities could involve looking at what causes actors to spend their resources on improving someone else's reputation. Actors' reputations may affect others' willingness to trade with them or give them gifts. Investigating online communities reveals a large number of different characters and associated avatars. When an actor looks at another's avatar, they will evaluate them and make decisions that are crucial to creating interaction between customers and vendors in virtual worlds based on the exchange of goods and services. This chapter utilizes the ecological cognition framework to understand transactions, characters and avatars in virtual worlds and investigates the exchange of capital in a bulletin board and virtual. The chapter finds strong evidence for the existence of characters and stereotypes based on the Ecological Cognition Framework and empirical evidence that actors using avatars with antisocial connotations are more likely to have a lower return on investment and be rated less positively than those with more sophisticated appearing avatars.

This chapter investigates the nature and structure of social networks formed between the players of massively multiplayer online games (MMOGs), an incredibly popular form of Internet-based entertainment attracting millions of subscribers. To do so, we use data collected about the behavior of more than 300,000 characters in World of Warcraft (the most popular MMOG in America). We show that these social networks are often sparse and that most players spend time in the game experiencing a form of "collective solitude": they play surrounded by, but not necessarily with, other players. We also show that the most successful player groups are analogous to the organic, team-based forms of organization that are prevalent in today's workplace. Based on these findings, we discuss the relationship between online social networks and "real world" behavior in organizations in more depth.

Chapter VI

This chapter reviews the literature on networks and more specifically on the development of community telecommunication networks. It strives to understand the collaboration needed for innovative projects such as intelligent networks. Guided by a change management framework, collaboration within a community network is explored in terms of the formation and performance phases of its development. The context, content, and process of each phase is analyzed, as well as the interaction of the two phases. User involvement and technology appropriation are discussed. Collaboration challenges are identified and linked to the sustainability of the community network. Policy makers are presented with a model that gives some insight into planning and managing a community network over time.

The core issue for this study concerns less the social than the political consequences of the rise of knowledge societies; in particular, the capacity of the Internet for strengthening democratic participation and civic engagement linking citizens and government. To consider these issues, Part I summarizes debates about the impact of the Internet on the public sphere. The main influence of this development, as it is theorized in a market model, will be determined by the "supply" and "demand" for electronic information and communications about government and politics. Demand, in turn, is assumed to be heavily dependent upon the social characteristics of Internet users and their prior political orientations. Given this understanding, the study predicts that the primary impact of knowledge societies in democratic societies will be upon facilitating cause-oriented and civic forms of political activism, thereby strengthening social movements and interest groups, more than upon conventional channels of political participation exemplified by voting, parties, and election campaigning. Part II summarizes the sources of survey data and the key measures of political activism used in this study, drawing upon the 19-nation European Social Survey, 2002. Part III examines the evidence for the relationship between use of the Internet and indicators of civic engagement. The conclusion in Part IV summarizes the results and considers the broader implications for governance and democracy

Chapter VIII

Malte Geib, University of St. Gallen, Switzerland
Christian Braun, University of St. Gallen, Switzerland
Lutz Kolbe, University of St. Gallen, Switzerland
Walter Brenner, University of St. Gallen, Switzerland

In this chapter, we analyze the design factors of community systems in two real-world professional communities: a learning network and an expert network that employ a mix of communication modes, that is, face-to-face communication and computer-mediated communication. Our objectives are to determine which design factors influence community activity and therefore community output. We furthermore intend to make recommendations to improve the design of community systems that support professional communities using a mix of communication modes. Our study is exploratory and based on action research given the lack of studies on the design of community-supporting systems in professional communities that employ a mix of communication modes. To illustrate similarities and to enhance the generalizability of our findings, we analyzed two real-world professional communities in depth, namely, a learning network and an inter-organizational expert network. Our study shows that face-to-face communication is the primary mode of communication in these communities; the community systems that they employ only have a supporting function. This leads us to a few design guidelines for the systems that support such communities. Generally, community systems have to support professional communities' work processes and relationship development. Important functions for work-process support are those that support face-to-face meetings (for the preparation and wrap-up of meetings) and that explicitly support specific work processes. Important functions for relationship development are functions that enable or facilitate face-to-face meetings, for example, member profiles.

Chapter IX

Maryann Mori, Evansville Vanderburgh Public Library, USA

Teens are active users of social networking sites, and the implications of this usage affect and/or cross social, moral, educational and political lines. By reviewing the works of D. Boyd, C. Kelsey, A. Lenhart, M. Madden, D. Oblinger, J. Oblinger and D.Tapscott, as well as current trends and statistics from various other sources, this chapter provides background information to understanding the growth and importance of online social networking among the Internet generation. Topics include demographics, ramifications on social behavior, adult concerns, restrictions, educational benefits and future directions of teens' use of social networking services.

Section II
Social Networking Sites for Teenagers and Young Adults

This chapter presents information on the usages and intent of social media by college students and administrators. Primary and secondary quantitative data is provided, as well as qualitative information obtained from interviews of multiple constituents. Researchers and postsecondary employees can more effectively examine technological trends in regard to online social networking for non-academic purposes after considering this data. Theories of self-esteem, interpersonal communication, decision making, and innovation diffusion are integrated throughout the chapter.

The purpose of this study was to examine the relative impact of "inappropriate" postings on job candidates' Facebook profiles on hiring decisions. Such postings included negative work-related attitudes, the use of profanity, and comments regarding alcohol abuse, use of drugs and sexual activities. Respondents indicated that all five types of information were relevant to such decisions and that they would be unlikely to pursue candidates who posted such information. However, female candidates were more likely to suffer negative consequences in terms of hiring, given that such information was viewed as being more relevant for female job candidates. In addition, respondents were more likely to pursue male candidates than female candidates who posted such information. Although negative work-related attitudes and drug use were considered more relevant to hiring decisions than the other types of information, respondents were more likely to pursue candidates with Facebook profiles containing information related to sexual activities, drug use and profanity as opposed to those with comments regarding negative work-related attitudes and alcohol use. Implications and suggestions for future research are presented.

Chapter XII

This chapter attempts to understand the trust in social network services, where users post their personal information online to everyone with or without any specific relationships. Many definitions of trust were examined through a literature review in electronic commerce and virtual community areas, and it was found that most of them were based on a specific relationship, such as a buyer-seller relationship. However, one concept of trust—generalized trust, also known as dispositional trust—was found to best fit the situation of social networking. Generalized trust in social networking is further discussed from a cultural viewpoint. As an example, a Japanese SNS, Mixi, was analyzed in detail. Future research direction on trust in social networking is discussed as well.

Chapter XIII

Celia Romm-Livermore, Wayne State University, USA
Gail Livermore, Spin Master Ltd., Canada

This conceptual chapter explores the distinction between virtual and real environments, the situations when they might clash and the implications from this clash. We start by categorizing virtual environments. Next, we present a framework for comparing the rules that govern behavior in different virtual and real environments. We list a number of situations where virtual and real environments can collide and explore the characteristics of such situations. Finally, we discuss the implications from clashes between virtual and real environments and what society can or should do about such potential and actual clashes.

Section III
E-Dating Services

Chapter XIV

Linda Jane Coleman, Salem State College, USA
Nisreen Bahnan, Salem State College, USA

This chapter investigates the current practices and strategies used by marketers of electronic dating services. This chapter does not develop or test a model, but rather is centered round an analysis of secondary data sources. Specific focus is placed on documenting the various demographic and psychographic segmentation basis and niche targeting strategies utilized by providers. An enormous ground swell is occurring of consumers participating in meeting a "significant other" through e-dating Web sites. People are increasingly relying on such services to meet people via the Internet: older, younger, black, white, pet lovers, religious, spiritual, and gay or straight individuals seeking partners for fun, companionship, commitment or conversation. This trend continues to grow. This chapter will cite a variety of networks that have blossomed over the years indicative of the interest and ideas related to this phenomenon. It also provides details of the nuances in the marketing and consumption of electronic-based personal relationships.

Chapter XV

Online dating is a big business, allowing people from the comfort of their own home to view and read about potential mates all around the world. Different dating sites offer different services. However, it is not yet commonplace for Web sites dedicated to dating to use the social networking tools used by popular online communities, such as those that use the personal homepage and message board genres. The Ecological Cognition Framework (ECF) provides a theoretical model regarding online dating communities' behavior and relationship development. A model based on the ECF is proposed and provides a basis for developing online dating services that effectively support relationship development. Two investigations are presented in this chapter, one that uses a case study approach to identify and describe online dating services from the perspective of a specific case and another that assess the effectiveness of existing online dating services based on the guidelines developed from the case study. The case study provides a useful insight into the nature of social networking from the perspective of a specific case, which led to guidelines for developing e-dating systems that when evaluated showed that the most popular social networking services also score well against the criteria proposed in those guidelines.

Online dating continues to grow in popularity as a way for individuals to locate a potential romantic partner. Researchers have examined how people present themselves on these sites, which presentations are more likely to lead to success, the effectiveness of the matchmaking tools that some companies employ, the stigma attached to using these sites and the types of people who are drawn to online dating. However, there is an absence of scholarly work on how these relationships progress compared to traditional models of courtship. This chapter sets out a model for the phases of online dating and compares this model with Givens' (1979) work on a traditional model of courtship. It is argued here the phases of online dating are very different to other courtship models. These differences pose new challenges and create new benefits to those who elect to find a partner via one of these sites.

Chapter XVII

Online dating continues to grow in popularity as a way for individuals to locate a potential romantic partner. Researchers have examined how people present themselves on these sites, which presentations are more likely to lead to success, the effectiveness of the matchmaking tools that some companies employ, the stigma attached to using these sites and the types of people who are drawn to online dating.

However, there is an absence of scholarly work on how these relationships progress compared to traditional models of courtship. This chapter sets out a model for the phases of online dating and compares this model with Givens' (1979) work on a traditional model of courtship. It is argued here the phases of online dating are very different to other courtship models. These differences pose new challenges and create new benefits to those who elect to find a partner via one of these sites.

More than half a billion users across the globe have availed themselves of e-dating services. This chapter looks at the marketing and cross-cultural aspects of mate-seeking behavior in e-dating. We content analyzed 238 advertisements from online matrimonial sites in three countries: India (n=79), Hong Kong (n=80), and Australia (n=79). Frequencies of mention of the following ten attribute categories in the advertiser's self-description were established using post hoc quantitative analysis: love, physical status, educational status, intellectual status, occupational status, entertainment services, money, demographic information, ethnic information, and personality traits. Past research on mate selection using personal ads and the three countries' positions on Hofstede's dimensions of culture were used in hypotheses generation. The results support several culture-based differences in people's self-description in online personal ads; however, some anticipated differences were not realized, suggesting that some cultural differences may not be as strong as Hofstede (2001) suggests.

Chapter XIX

Online personals have been remarkably successful in the western world and have been emulated in other cultural contexts. The introduction of the Internet can have vastly different implications on traditional societies and practices such as arranged marriages in India. This chapter seeks to investigate using an ethnographic approach the role of matrimonial Web sites in the process of arranging marriages in India. It seeks to explore how these Web sites have been appropriated by key stakeholders in arranging marriage and how such appropriation is changing the process and traditions associated with arranged marriage. The key contributions of this study are in that it is an investigation of complex social processes in a societal context different from traditional western research contexts and an exploration of how modern technologies confront societal traditions and long-standing ways of doing things. Our investigation suggests that the use of matrimonial Web sites have implications for family disintermediation, cultural convergence, continuous information flows, ease of disengagement, virtual dating and reduced stigma in arranged marriages in India.

Foreword

In *Social Networking Communities and E-Dating Services,* editors Celia Romm-Livermore and Kristina Setzekorn have gathered a remarkably diverse group of researchers whose articles cover a wide range of topics. This book advances our thinking about how and why people meet and interact online within various contexts, settings or places. The framework is a typology of social networking communities, with e-dating services emerging as one thriving type of place within those communities, attracting members from around the world.

The book collects authors of different disciplines, both academic and more practically oriented, from fields including political science, psychology, linguistics, management, marketing, information systems, and media studies. Using various research methodologies from content analysis to ethnography, they reside in Australia, Canada, Switzerland, the United Kingdom, and the United States. While the authors work in countries with predominantly Western cultures, some of the chapters contain data sets from China, India, Japan and India to offer a more truly global perspective.

The chapters of the book's first half address the motives for joining social networks and tell us methods that people employ to create a community within them. Authors describe how such varied constituents as learners and experts, workers and managers, gamers, and political activists collaborate in social networks to affect the social worlds they inhabit both online and off-line. This section of the book also highlights the interaction of young people, who currently dominate those who interact within the most popular social networking sites. Researchers go beyond the surfaces of MySpace and Facebook to analyze both the benefits and drawbacks of participation. For example, education of users can show them how older adults may use information gathered from social networking sites in their hiring decisions. An included chapter on the game play of animated avatars in the World of Warcraft describes how members often explore online territories alone, as well as by joining with others, adding to the understanding of virtual world dynamics.

With the e-dating chapters, this book builds upon the research up to now. Considering that Match. com started in 1994, the relative dearth of research-oriented publications on the topic is surprising. While scholarly books devoted solely to the area of online dating and intimate relationships in cyberspace have started to appear, this collection adds to those works about people who first meet through computer-mediated communication. The chapters here provide much needed elaboration upon the behaviors of daters in the online dating services, and outline theories to explain them. They explore dimensions such as the development of special markets for different types of e-daters and how e-dating may affect relationships off-line. A unique piece ties together the first section on "Social Networking Communities" to the "e-Dating Services" section that follows. It links the larger area of social networking sites and the online dating sites by classifying groups into two major categories of intent, the social and commercial.

In sum, this book engages the reader with practical and theoretical ideas about the processes of collaboration and competition among people forming work relationships and more playful, personal connections in cyberspace. With the increase of mobile technologies, and growth of the number of relationships either started or developed online, the lines between online and "real-life" worlds have blurred. This book advances our knowledge of everyday happenings that are harbingers of our futures, both online and off-line.

Andrea Baker
Ohio University

Preface

Social networking communities have been around since the 1980s and are among the largest e-commerce sectors in terms of sales revenue, participant numbers and social impact. The industry provides opportunities for people to exchange ideas, meet, date, and possibly marry—much more efficiently than through chance face-to-face meetings.

We define social networking communities as online communities that focus on the building and verifying of social networks for whatever purpose. Indeed, social networking communities offer a range of services. Some are merely blog hosting services, some offer the option of joining groups temporarily (through chat rooms) or for longer periods of time (through electronic bulletin boards, newsgroups or online groups). Some social networking communities encourage their members' creativity through sharing of music and video clips, while others enable members to meet, develop relationships, and possibly marry (e-dating services).

While the social networking industry (and its sub-category, e-dating) started in North America, it is now a global phenomenon, as it includes services in South America, Asia, Australia, Europe, the Middle East and Africa. Indeed, recent research on the proliferation of social networking services shows that the biggest growth areas for the industry at this time are outside North America and particularly in Europe, South America and Asia. As for social networking being a global phenomenon, this is not just a result of the geographical location of social networking services but also of the fact that many users of these services interact and possibly marry users from other countries.

The best indication that social networking Web sites are becoming big business is the acquisition in 2006 of YouTube by Google for 1.6 billion dollars. The social networking video Web site, developed by its 29-year-old CEO, Chad Hurley, and its 28-year-old chief technology officer, Steve Chen, in their garage in 2005, has managed to increase its hit rate from zero to over 100 million visitors per month in one single year.

Most commentators agree that the reason for this phenomenal growth is that social networking Web sites provide an entry point into the Web for consumers who otherwise would not be members of online communities. By playing the role of gate keepers of the Internet, social networking Web sites are helping to expand the scope of cyberspace, as well as revolutionize society as we know it today.

As for the reasons for establishing social networking communities, some of the earliest services have been created by companies as virtual communities of customers. They were intended to serve as platforms for conducting market research, venues for customer support, and means for promoting customer loyalty. Some companies (e.g., Amazon.com) used their social networking services for selling their products by enabling customers to read other customers' comments about the products and services that the company sells. Some companies, for example, eBay, took the concept of community one step further by inviting their users to buy and sell from each other through the biggest auction house in the world.

Recently, corporations have been establishing social network Web sites as a means for connecting employees within and beyond the company boundaries. The Web sites are intended to enhance employees' social connectivity with the hope that better connected employees are more effective managers of the company's environment. Business associations are creating similar networks to connect business professionals by industry, functions, geographic areas and areas of interest.

The new social and business reality created by social networking services calls for appropriate research and scholarship. Instead of playing a catch-up game with this unknown monster, it is necessary that conscious and deliberate initiatives be made by academics and leaders of industry to understand and tame it. It is also necessary that appropriate texts be created to teach students and the general public how to understand and cope with the new reality that social networking communities have created.

Our book, *Social Networking Communities and E-Dating Services: Concepts and Implications,* addresses this goal. By providing an overview of the major questions that researchers and practitioners in this area are addressing at this time and by outlining the possible future directions for theory development and empirical research on social networking and e-dating, this volume contributes toward closing the gap that currently exists in this area.

Before we consider the specific issues that are covered by the authors of this volume, it is important to discuss how the two focus areas for our book, social networking communities and e-dating services, relate to each other.

A useful theoretical concept that can help us chart the social networking terrain is that of the business model. Thus, we can think of the different sub-categories of social networking communities, one of which is e-dating services, as different business models. All the business models that fit under the category of social networking communities share the same purpose, namely, they all provide electronic platforms for social networking among their users. However, the services differ in the manner in which they provide support for their users and in the type of users that they attract.

Considered from this perspective, the social networking arena can be divided into four major sub-categories or "types" of communities. These subcategories can be seen as a continuum, where each type represents a different level of involvement on the part of the company that provides the service. Thus, while the first type in our categorization, (sub-category 1), represents a relatively low level of involvement on the part of the company that provides the service, the last type of in the categorization (sub-category 4) represents a high level of involvement of the company in the interactions that take place on its Web site.

Based on this logic, we distinguish between the following four types of social networking communities or services:

1. **The blogging service:** Examples of this type of social networking community would be MySpace or Facebook. These services provide a space for bloggers to set up a presence on the company Web site. Even though bloggers can join groups and can contact individuals that are members of the service, the company does not get involved in these interactions in any active way. YouTube is another example of this type of service. Even though the company does provide an added service, the ability to display one's home videos and to see videos of other members, the company does not actively "match" users with other users. A similar concept is also demonstrated by SecondLife, a virtual reality Web site that offers customers the opportunity to create a "home" and interact (through avatars) with other users. Here again, even though the company offers users "space" and enables them to interact with each other, it does not actively match them to each other.

2. **The groups creating service:** An example of this type of social networking community would be YahooGroups. Even though the company invites users to select the groups that they wish to join and/or establish, and even though users can be contacted by other users through the service (if they choose to make their Web site public), the company's involvement in the activities that take

place within the groups is minimal and the benefits that it reaps from helping individuals match themselves with appropriate groups are minimal too.

3. **The support service:** An example of this type of social networking community would be the virtual communities established by companies for their customers. The virtual communities serve different purposes ranging from customer support (Del.com), to active selling of the company's products (Amazon.com). The principle in all cases is that new prospective buyers are invited to interact directly or indirectly with a group of people who share their interests in the company's products and services. We consider this an example of a relatively high level of involvement by the company because the company developed unique "matching" algorithms to create the group(s) and to match individuals with the pre-existing group. The major contribution of the company here is in the matching process. And, yes, the matching process is not intended just for social networking but for selling the company's products and services.

4. **The e-dating service:** All e-dating communities would fit this category because they are all examples of communities where individuals are matched with other individuals based on criteria that the users specify and/or on criteria that the company gleans from information that is provided by users. We consider the fourth sub-category of the model an example of the highest level of involvement by the company because the company does not just set up the platform that enables the social interaction between users but actually provides value adding matching services. Thus, even though users are expected to establish a Web page (or a profile) and even though some services do provide discussion forums or chat-rooms, the major service that the company provides is the matching of individual users to each other. And, yes, just like the previous type of social networking service, here too, the company is making a profit by charging both parties a fee for its matching service.

It should be noted that even though the above categorization suggests that the four types are distinct, this may not always be the case. Thus, SecondLife, a relatively new player in the social network arena, demonstrates that several of the above types can be combined into one service. The uniqueness of SecondLife is that while offering users "space" to build their virtual home (which appears to represent the first sub-category in our categorization), it also encourages users to engage in buying and selling among each other, which can be seen as a variation of the fourth category in our categorization, where individual users are matched to each other.

To reflect the double foci of this book, we organized it in two major parts: the first part deals with social networking communities and the second part deals with e-dating services. Each part follows a similar internal structure in that the discussion moves from the individual level of analysis (in the very first sub-sections) to the group level, and, then, to the global or societal level of analysis.

Each of the two major parts of the book is further sub-divided into a number of sub-sections. In the following sections, we present each of these sub-sections with some detail on the issues that are discussed in them.

SOCIAL NETWORKING COMMUNITIES

Why People Join Social Networking Communities

The first section in the social networking part of the book presents two chapters that focus on individual aspects that motivate people to join social networking communities or explain their behavior once they have joined.

In Chapter I, Harsha Gangadharbatla discusses the impact of five individual level factors, Internet self-efficacy, self-esteem, need to belong, need for information and gender on users' attitudes to social networking sites and their inclination to join such sites. The most important finding from this research was that females' attitude toward social networking sites is dependent on their need to belong and on their self-esteem while males' attitude toward SNS is only dependent on their Internet self-efficacy level. Furthermore, while females' attitudes toward social networking Web sites predict their behavior, this link is not as strong for males.

In Chapter II, Hugo Liu, Pattie Maes, and Glorianna Davenport discuss a technical facet of the interaction between individuals and social networking services, namely, the algorithms that enable matching of individuals based on their self-reported tastes. The data source for this investigation was the text of over 100,000 social profiles in which users described their taste in music, books, films, food, and so forth. The researchers inferred from the data "a semantic fabric of taste," demonstrating that this mechanism can help "sanitize" knowledge resources from personal idiosyncrasies, thus enabling a system to match individuals to each other without "knowing" who they are.

Social Networking as a Community Building Experience

The second section in the social networking part of the book, which is the heart of the book and its longest section, presents six chapters that cover different types of social networking communities, including: (1) mobile communities networks, (2) virtual reality networks, (3) war-game networks, (4) community building networks, (5) political activism networks, and (6) professional communities networks.

In Chapter III, Nina Ziv discusses the ways in which users of mobile virtual networks have become important sources of innovation rather than simply users of a technology that is provided by a service. The basis for this chapter is data gleaned from three case studies of mobile social networking services, Upoc, Dodgeball and Tapuz. Based on the three case studies, the author demonstrates that by participating in these networks, users provide feedback to the companies on the performance of existing products, the development of new products, and the marketing of products to potential new users.

In Chapter IV, Jonathan Bishop analyzes a fascinating phenomenon, the use of avatars for social interactions between members of social networking communities and the degree to which selecting one's avatar influences one's status in the community. As noted by the author of this chapter, members of social networking communities can select appealing or repelling avatars to represent them in the community. Utilizing an ecological cognition framework, the author demonstrates that members of social networking communities who use avatars with anti-social connotations are more likely to be rated less positively than those who use more sophisticated avatars with positive connotations.

In Chapter V, Nicolas Ducheneaut and Nicholas Yee explore the social dynamics of the players of Massively Multiplayer Online Games (MMOGs), an incredibly popular form of Internet-based entertainment attracting millions of subscribers. The authors use data collected about the behavior of more than 300,000 characters in World of Warcraft (the most popular MMOG in America) to show that most players spend time in the game experiencing a form of "collective solitude," namely, they play surrounded by, but not necessarily with, other players. They also demonstrate that just like in work-related organizations, the most successful player groups are cohesive, well-managed entities that expect their members to adhere to their rules of behavior.

In Chapter VI, Sylvie Albert and Rolland Labrasseur discuss community development networks and the impact that collaboration has on innovative projects. The theoretical basis for this chapter was a change management framework, which denotes the role that the researchers played as change agents in the projects that they describe. The chapter considers the phases in the project development in terms of both content and process, exploring the effect that user involvement had on technology appropriation. The chapter concludes with insights for policy makers on how to plan and manage successful community networks over time.

In Chapter VII, Pippa Norris describes the impact of electronic-based social networks on cause-oriented and civic forms of political activism. The chapter is based on a model that links the use of Internet-based social networks with the propensity to engage in social movements and interest groups. Survey data and key measures of political activism are used as the data source for this chapter, drawing upon the 19-nation European Social Survey, 2002 to examine the relationship between the use of the Internet and indicators of civic engagement. The findings indicate that the most important factors predicting political activism are political efficacy (a feeling that the person could influence the political process), age, education, region and civic duty. As expected, after these factors, the use of the Internet proved the next strongest predictor of political activism.

In Chapter VIII, Malte Geib, Christian Braun, Lutz Kolbe, and Walter Brenner analyze the design factors of community systems in two real-world professional communities—a learning network and an expert network—that employ a mix of communication modes, that is, face-to-face communication and computer-mediated communication. The objectives of this action research study were to determine which design factors influence community activity and therefore community output. The findings demonstrated that since the interactions in these communities started in the face-to-face mode and only at a later stage migrated to the online environment, that systems that would support community output had to improve both face-to-face communication and online work processes

Social Networking Sites for Teen Agers and Young Adults

The third section of the social networking part of the book discusses one of the most important growth areas for social networking services, the teenagers and young adults market. While the first two chapters in this sub-section focus primarily on the positive aspects of the utilization of social networking by teenagers and young adults, the third chapter elaborates on the risks that are associated with social networking, including the way in which adults (particularly employers) take advantage of young people's self-exposure through social networking sites.

In Chapter IX, Maryann Mori reviews a number of key papers and statistics on the use of social networking by teenagers. The chapter discusses the ramifications of social networking on teenagers' behavior, adult concerns, possible restrictions on teenage use of social networking services, potential educational benefits of social networking participation by teenagers, and future directions of teenagers' use of social networking services.

The discussion of young people's use of social networking Web sites continues in Chapter X, in which Tamara L. Wandel presents information on the usages and intent of social media by college students and university administrators. The author utilizes primary and secondary quantitative data, as well as qualitative information obtained from interviews with multiple constituents. Theories of self-esteem, interpersonal communication, decision making, and innovation diffusion are integrated throughout the chapter to present a coherent set of recommendations to university policy makers on how to utilize social networks in the university environment.

The section concludes with Chapter XI, in which Katherine Karl, and Joy Peluchette examine the relative impact of "inappropriate" postings on job candidates' Facebook profiles on hiring decisions by employers. Such postings included negative work-related attitudes, the use of profanity, and comments regarding alcohol abuse, use of drugs and sexual activities. Respondents to the survey employed in this study indicated that all five types of information were relevant to hiring decisions and that they would be unlikely to pursue candidates who posted such information. However, female candidates were more likely to suffer negative consequences in terms of hiring than were male candidates. Also, although negative work-related attitudes and drug use were considered relevant to hiring decisions, respondents were more likely to pursue candidates with profiles containing information related to sexual activities, drug use and profanity than candidates whose profiles contained negative work-related attitudes and alcohol use.

Social Networking in a Global Context

This section concludes the first part of the book with a discussion of the cultural and philosophical aspects of social networking.

In Chapter XII, Max Kennedy and Toru Sakaguchi develop a conceptual model that relates culture to trust in social networking services. The authors propose that trust in the context of social networking communities is associated with the degree to which the culture is high (or low) on individualism and uncertainty avoidance. It suggests that members of cultures that are relatively high on individualism and low on uncertainty avoidance (the U.S.) are more likely to trust social networking services and accept the exposure that social networking services imply than members of cultures that are low on individualism and high on uncertainty avoidance (Japan). The chapter proceeds to explain, based on case study data from Japan, what features need to be introduced to a social networking service in Japan in order to make it acceptable to members of the culture.

In Chapter XIII, Celia Romm-Livermore and Gail Livermore discuss the differences between virtual and real worlds and how these differences can predict clashes between the two. This last chapter of the first part of the book uses examples from a range of different types of social networking and e-dating services, thus, linking the two parts of the book and introducing the second part that focuses on e-dating. Because of its wide-scope, this chapter also introduces philosophical issues such as the nature of reality and virtuality that are central to the book as a whole.

E-DATING SERVICES

Exploring the Individual Aspects of E-Dating

The second part of the book, which focuses on e-dating, is organized in a similar way to the first part. Here too, we move from the individual level of e-dating to the dyad and then to the societal and international aspects of this phenomenon.

The very first section in the e-dating part of the book deals with the individual perspective of e-dating in that both address the relationship between individuals and the e-dating industry. The first chapter in this section discusses segmentation practices in e-dating, while the second chapter looks at how individual e-daters experience the different types of services offered by the e-dating industry.

In Chapter XIV, Linda Jane Coleman and Nisreen Bahnan present an investigation of the current practices and strategies used by marketers of electronic dating services. The chapter uses secondary data sources to document the segmentation basis and niche targeting strategies utilized by providers of e-dating services, including the various sub-categories of services for older adults, younger adult, blacks, whites, pet lovers, religious, spiritual, gay, straight and other niche markets of individuals seeking relationships. The chapter discusses the major players in the industry and the nuances of their business strategy as it relates to provision of e-dating services.

In Chapter XV, Jonathan Bishop uses the Ecological Cognition Framework (ECF) as the basis of a study of the individual aspects of e-dating. Two investigations are presented in this chapter. The first uses a case study approach to identify and describe online dating services from the perspective of a specific individual e-dater. The second investigation assesses the effectiveness of existing online dating services based on guidelines developed from the case study.

How E-Daters Behave and Evolve

The second section in the e-dating part of the book focuses on the developmental process that takes place when e-daters interact with each during the e-dating process. The first chapter in this section presents a five-phase model of e-dating development, while the second chapter focuses on the differences between males and females in how they experience e-dating.

In Chapter XVI, Monica Whitty examines the differences between the development of online relationships and the more traditional face-to-face courtships. The chapter presents a model for the phases of online dating and compares this model with Givens' (1979) work on a traditional model of courtship. It argues that e-dating follows different "phases" than other courtship models and that these differences pose challenges and create benefits that are different from the challenges and benefits that traditional daters face.

The second section concludes with Chapter XVII, in which Celia Romm-Livermore, Toni Somers, Kristina Setzekorn, and Ashley King introduce the e-dating development model. The model focuses on the changes that male and female e-daters undergo during the process of e-dating. The discussion in the chapter focuses on findings from a preliminary empirical research undertaken by the authors. The findings supported all of the model's hypotheses, indicating that: (1) male and female e-daters follow different stages in their e-dating evolvement; (2) the behaviors that males and females exhibit as e-daters are different; and (3) the feedback that male and female e-daters receive from the environment is different too.

E-Dating as a Global Phenomenon

This section concludes the discussion of e-dating by introducing one of the most important growth areas for the industry: the matrimonial e-dating sector in developing countries. The first chapter in this section deals with how e-daters present themselves online and how culture influences e-daters' self-presentation. The second chapter discusses changing practices of e-dating in India, exploring the interactions between the tradition of arranged marriage and the modern use of e-dating by parents to facilitate the marriages of their offspring.

In Chapter XVIII, Sudhir H. Kale and Mark T. Spence consider the marketing and cross-cultural aspects of mate-seeking behavior in e-dating. The study that is presented in this chapter is based on a content analysis of 238 advertisements from online matrimonial sites in three countries: India (n=79), Hong Kong (n=80), and Australia (n=79). Frequencies of the following ten attribute categories in the advertiser's self-description were established, including, love, physical status, educational status, intellectual status, occupational status, entertainment services, money, demographic information, ethnic information, and personality traits. The results support several culture-based differences in people's self-description in online personal ads.

And, finally, in Chapter XIX, Nainika Seth and Ravi Patnayakuni use an ethnographic approach to examine the role of matrimonial Web sites in the process of arranging marriages in India. The chapter explores how e-dating Web sites have been appropriated by key stakeholders in arranging marriages and how such appropriation is changing the process and traditions associated with arranged marriages in India. The investigation undertaken by the authors suggests that the use of matrimonial Web sites have implications for family disintermediation, cultural convergence, continuous information flows, ease of disengagement, virtual dating and reduced stigma in arranged marriages in India.

Acknowledgment

This book has been an interesting, emotional, and intellectual journey of self-discovery for me. It started with a several-hour long conversation with my co-editor, Dr. Kristina Setzekorn, at the GITM conference in Florida. This conversation made us both aware of the need for a "scientific" book on social networking and e-dating. This book is a tribute to Dr. Setzekorn's enthusiasm and foresight. The book would not have been written if it were not for her.

Next, I would like to take this opportunity to thank IGI Global, the publisher of this book, and in particular, I would like to extend my sincere gratitude to Ms. Kristin Klinger, the acquisitions editor, Ms. Corrina Chandler, the business assistant, and Mr. Ross Miller, Ms. Deborah Yahnke, and Ms. Rebecca Beistline, the three editorial assistants at IGI Global who have supported us tirelessly throughout this book project.

The contributions of the team at IGI Global go above and beyond the technical assistance usually offered by a publisher to its authors. The team at IGI Global was actively involved in this book project from the very beginning. They offered many insights on how to convert our initial idea to write a special issue for a journal into a full fledged book proposal on social networking and e-dating. It was their insistence to include in the book both social networking and e-dating that resulted in a much wider and theoretically more significant scope for this book than we initially envisaged.

This book would not have been written if it were not for the pioneers of research on social networking and e-dating whose work has inspired us to initiate this project in the first place. The list of authors who made important contributions to the emerging body of research on social networking and e-dating is long. Many of them are quoted in the book and some of them were gracious enough to contribute chapters to our book.

There is, however, one author that I would like to single out, Dr. Andrea Baker, the author of the very first theoretically-based book on e-dating, *Double Click: Romance and Commitment Among Online Couples* (Hampton Press, 2005). Dr. Baker is also the author of the Foreword to our book. Dr. Baker's book was preceded by at least a dozen books and many articles on social networking and e-dating. However, it was her book that was the very first to take a systematic, theory-based, approach to e-dating. As such, it was a very important inspiration to our project.

Finally, I would like to take this opportunity to thank the members of my family, my husband, the Honorable Bill Callahan, and my children, David, Jonathan and Gail. It was their love and support, as well, as their enthusiasm about social networking and e-dating that made this book project an enjoyable experience for me.

Celia Romm-Livermore

Section I
Social Networking Communities

Chapter I
Individual Differences in Social Networking Site Adoption

Harsha Gangadharbatla
University of Oregon, USA

ABSTRACT

This chapter focuses on detailing the role of five individual level factors—Internet self-efficacy, self-esteem, need to belong, need for information, and gender—in influencing the attitudes toward social networking sites (SNS) and the adoption of such sites. First, the growing importance of social networking sites in business is discussed, and their usage as advertising vehicles is outlined. Individual differences in SNS adoption are presented from a technology acceptance model framework. A paper-pencil-based survey is conducted and data obtained is used to test a structural model that explains the role of individual-level factors in influencing individuals' attitudes toward SNS, their willingness to join SNS, and their actual membership on SNS. Results are presented and managerial implications are drawn.

INTRODUCTION

The Internet has radically changed the way people shop, transact, bank, and communicate with others in the recent years. With an estimated 73% of all American adults now online (Madden, 2006), the impact of the Internet on communication, commerce, and society in general continues to grow. One such impact is the proliferation of social networking sites (SNS) that are particularly popular with teens and young adults. It is estimated that over 55% of online teens use social networks and at least 48% of them visit social networking Web sites daily or more often (Lenhart & Madden, 2007). However, very little research has been done to understand the process of social networking site (SNS) adoption.

The success of social networking sites and communication on such sites depends a lot on the innovation and adoption of such sites (Ridings & Gefen, 2004). With more and more businesses implementing these social networking sites, it becomes important to understand how and why people are deciding to use sites such as MySpace and Facebook (Wellman & Gulia, 1999). As with the successful adoption of any new consumer technology, the success of social networking sites also depends on numerous factors of which individual-level factors are often ignored in this area of research. Agarwal and Prasad (1999) suggest that individual differences are important in information technology acceptance and are often not included in technology acceptance models. Therefore, the current chapter fills the gap in literature by examining individual differences in SNS adoption from a technology acceptance model perspective.

The following section explains the concept and types of social networking sites before discussing the role of such sites in creating and adding value to businesses and their usage as advertising vehicles.

Social Networking Sites (SNS)

Social networking sites (SNS) have existed in some form or another since the advent of the Internet. Bulletin boards, user and discussion groups, multi user dungeons (MUDs), and other forms of online communities are predecessors to the present generation of networking sites like Facebook, Friendster, and MySpace. Advances in Internet technology have made it much easier for individuals to connect and communicate online through a new wave of technology often collectively referred to as Web 2.0 tools. Social networking sites are a type of online or virtual communities (such as Yahoogroups or Google Groups) with a few differences. The emphasis in social networking sites is on (1) the individual and his or her profile information, (2) the people that the individual is connected to, (3) the groups that he or she is part of, and (4) the explicit representation of relationships. These factors determine the individual's role, involvement, and usage of SNS in contrast to traditional virtual communities where the emphasis is on public discussions and the commonality that underlies the very existence of such communities. In other words, the emphasis in the case of social networking sites is on the

user and his or her network of friends whereas in virtual communities and online discussion groups the emphasis is on the content generated by members. Social networking sites are about people and their network of relationships.

Networking sites can be classified into many types. For an excellent review of classifications, readers are advised to refer to Murchu, Breslin, and Decker (2004). Depending on the type of user profiles, networking sites can be either classified as business-oriented (Ecademy, LinkedIn, or Spoke) or as social networks (Friendster, MySpace, Friendzy, Meetup, Orkut, Tickle, or Tribe). However, some networks have transcended their original purposes to extend into the other category over the years. For example, Ryze was originally intended to serve online business networking purposes but members have ever since used it for dating and other social networking purposes. Members can join social networking sites in one of the two ways—via registration or via connection. In the registration-based model, individuals sign in with a valid e-mail address and the site is open to everyone without any sort of approval or moderation, whereas in the connection-based model, individuals can only become members if they know someone who is already a member of that social networking site (Murchu, Brestlin, & Decker 2004).

The usage of social networking sites has grown from 5% of American households in 2005 to over 10% in just one year. According to a recent survey by iProspect, over 25% of all Internet users visit social networking sites at least once a month (Lewis, 2007). MySpace, for example, has over 22 million members and is growing at a rate of 2 million users a month (Rosenbush, 2005). Social networking sites are not only becoming the hottest destination spots on the World Wide Web, but are also building huge databases of user information in the process. When registering with such sites, users voluntarily provide information about their choice of movies, books, television shows, radio stations, hobbies, political leanings, and music.

Most sites also display users' demographics in terms of income level, location, education, and work information. Other kinds of information usually captured (and often displayed on users' profiles) include contact information such as phone numbers, e-mail addresses, and instant message ids, and personal information such as relationship status, sexuality, favorite activities, quotes, photos, conversations with friends, groups users belong to, and discussions users are taking part in. Different sites have different ways in which members can display their networks and connections with other members. Some allow members to rank their friends (Friendster and Facebook) while others allow for categorizing their friends (Orkut).

Social Networking Sites and Revenue

The business of social networking has grown into a multi-billion dollar sector even though it is still somewhat unclear as to what a viable business model should be for these sites to generate revenue. Broadly speaking, there are two operating business models for social networking sites: subscription-based and advertising revenue. Some sites, especially e-dating sites, have turned to a subscription-based business model while many social networking sites are still looking for a viable business model. Murchu, Breslin, and Decker (2004) suggest that social networking sites may be perfect vehicles for targeted advertising given the large amounts of valuable data these sites contain in terms of profile information. The success of both models requires that users register and sign up with these sites in large numbers. Therefore, it becomes crucial and important to understand usage and adoption of SNS.

Social networking sites are being increasingly used in advertising and marketing campaigns given the clutter problems associated with other advertising media, audience fragmentation and increased usage of newer media, and the threat of new technologies such as DVRs. The amount of money spent on social networking site for advertising in 2006 was $350 million, which increased to over twice that amount ($865 million) in just one year. Overall, advertising spending is expected to increase to $1.8 billion by 2010 and $2.1 billion by 2011 (eMarketer, 2006a). It is no surprise that a major share of the advertising dollars has gone to MySpace (roughly $525 million out of the total $865 in the year 2007) given that this SNS drew over 55 million unique visitors in September 2006 which is an increase from 21 million just a year before (Advertising Age, 2007).

There are also examples of how advertisers and media firms have begun to leverage the potential of social networking sites. For instance, Starcom Media Group (SMG) ran a MySpace campaign for one of its clients, Fanta®. SMG created a profile page "*The Fantanas*" that several of MySpace members added to their buddy list. Facebook features several classified and highly targeted advertisements that show up on users' home pages when they sign in. Social networking sites like MySpace make over $25 million per month in advertising (Cashmore, 2007), and it is for the same reason that MySpace was recently bought by Rupert Murdoch's New Corp.

The trend to use social networking sites for advertising and adding value to businesses is only expected to escalate given that almost half the people recently surveyed by eMarketer (2006b) claim that they would seek out shopping information including coupons and discounts on social networking sites if they were made available. Social networking sites can also let members link to other sites such as Amazon.com and attach an image of a CD they are listening to or a book they are reading or a videogame they are playing (Rapacki, 2007). This presents great opportunities for marketers to link with social networking sites and tap into the power of key influencers or opinion leaders. There are also instances where advertisers have created viral content to be transmitted by key influencers—identified by their network size and their activity on social networking sites—or created brand-related communities that members could be a part of and participate in discussions in a more advertiser-content environment (Smith, 2006).

With revenue of social networking sites tied to the number of users registered, it becomes imperative to study and understand the factors that influence adoption of SNS. Therefore, the current study focuses on individual differences in SNS usage and adoption. The following section examines literature on SNS adoption and usage from a technology acceptance model perspective.

THEORETICAL FRAMEWORK

Research Exploring SNS Adoption and Usage

The success or failure of any innovation is often linked to its ultimate adoption (DeLone & McLean, 1990; Agarwal & Prasad, 1999). This is true for social networking sites as well given that the success of both the revenue models discussed in the previous section depends largely on the number of users registered. However, understanding why users accept or reject technological innovations (such as social networking sites) is a difficult and challenging research problem (Swanson, 1988; Davis, Bagozzi, & Warshaw, 1989)

In order to better understand SNS adoption and usage, one needs to examine literature on the technology acceptance model and draw from attitude-intention-behavior models from social psychology. Technology acceptance model (TAM) suggests that the ultimate adoption of any innovation depends on two key factors: perceived usefulness and perceived ease of use (Davis et al., 1989; Venkatesh et al., 2003). Social networking sites fulfill various needs such as an individuals' need to stay in touch and keep tabs on friends,

make plans with friends, make new friends and to even flirt with someone (Lenhart & Madden, 2007). Other factors motivating SNS adoption mentioned in the literature include feelings of affiliation and belonging, need for information, goal achievement, self-identity, values, and notions of accepted behavior (Ridings & Gefen, 2004). All of these factors relate to the perceived usefulness of social networking sites. The perceived ease of use is often conceptualized in SNS literature as Internet self-efficacy. Internet self-efficacy is defined as the personal confidence in one's ability to successfully understand, navigate, and evaluate content should alleviate doubts and suspicions when dealing with social networking sites (Daugherty, Eastin, & Gangadharbatla, 2005).

The technology acceptance model (TAM) draws extensively from attitude-intention-behavior models in social psychology. For instance, Fishbein and Ajzen's (1975) theory of reasoned action (TRA) suggests that attitudes are good predictors of behavioral intentions, which in turn successfully predict behavior across a wide variety of fields. This attitude-intention-behavior model is "designed to explain virtually any human behavior" (Ajzen & Fishbein, 1980, p.4) and could therefore be used to explain SNS adoption and usage as well. Individuals' attitudes toward social networking sites influence their intentions to join such sites, which in turn predict their actual adoption and usage. This basic TRA model when combined with technology acceptance model (TAM) explains the adoption process of almost all innovations and technological services (Gefen & Straub, 1997). However, a number of individual-level factors (e.g., gender) have not been included in this technology adoption model (Gefen & Straub, 1997; Agarwal & Prasad, 1999; Venkatesh & Morris, 2000). The following section examines individual differences frequently mentioned in technology adoption literature that can potentially influence SNS adoption and usage.

Individual-Level Differences in SNS Adoption

Researchers have frequently lamented that a "set of constructs not specifically included in TAM are variables related to individual differences" (Agarwal & Prasad, 1999, p. 362). These individual factors range from cognitive and personality traits to demographic and situational variables such as training and expertise (Zmud, 1979; Agarwal & Prasad, 1999). Many researchers acknowledge the importance of individual differences in technology adoption (Agarwal & Prasad, 1999). Although a wide spectrum of individual-level variables are frequently mentioned in the technology adoption literature, only a few that are relevant to social networking site adoption and usage will be considered here.

Need to Belong

A commonly expressed motivation to join virtual communities is an individual's need to belong (Watson & Johnson, 1972; Ridings & Gefen, 2004). Need to belong is a personality variable that is considered a fundamental human motivation that all human beings posses (Baumeister & Leary, 1995). Over 90% of teens that visit social networking sites do so to stay in touch with friends, something that suggests the importance of need to belong. Other related reasons often mentioned in the literature include social support, friendship, and common interests (Ridings & Gefen, 2004). Furlong (1989) suggests that virtual communities are places where individuals go for emotional support, sense of belongingness, and encouragement in times of need. One of the main reasons for individuals joining virtual networks is finding social support on such sites (Herring, 1996) and making friends (Horrigan et al., 2001). Connections made online go beyond receiving support, as Ridings and Gefen (2004) suggest "the feeling of being together and being a member of a group of friends comes with the notions of being part of a group, spending time together, companionship, socializing, and networking" (p. 5). Online friendships go beyond just social support exchange. Internet makes it easy for individuals to connect to others in today's busy world. Social networking sites allow for individuals to reconnect with high school and college friends, ex-lovers, past and current colleagues, and sometimes even random strangers. This need to belong motivation is also related to individual usage of virtual communities. Leung (2001) found in a survey of 576 college students that students who were motivated by affection and sociability were the heaviest users of ICQ whereas light users were motivated by fashion.

Individuals have a strong motivation to "form and maintain at least a minimum quantity of lasting, positive, and significant interpersonal relationships" (Baumeister & Leary, 1995, p. 497). Due to this natural pursuit of maintaining belongingness, they propose that the strength and intensity would vary among individuals but that it would be "difficult or impossible for culture to eradicate the need to belong" (Baumeister & Leary, 1995, p. 499). Given that individuals vary in their levels of belongingness, it is only logical to except the effect of this "need to belong" on their SNS adoption and usage to also vary accordingly.

Internet Self-Efficacy

One of the chief determining factors of technology acceptance in TAM is individual's perceived ease of use of the technology. Perceived use of ease translates to Internet self-efficacy when dealing with social networking sites, which is represented in reasons such as "interface being ease to use" and "the search functionality being really cool" (Ridings & Gefen, 2004). Self-efficacy has been shown to have a significant impact on individuals' adoption of technology (Eastin & LaRose, 2000; Eastin, 2002). Self-efficacy is a person's ability to perform a task, a person's judgment about a future event, or even one's belief in their own ability (i.e., self-confidence) (Barbalet, 1998). This belief is a known predictor of involvement, intrinsic motivation, and task completion in a variety of domains (Ellen, Bearden, & Sharma, 1991). The effect of self-efficacy on consumer decision-making and behavior has been well documented in marketing literature (see Fleming & Courtney, 1984; Bettman, Johnson, & Payne, 1991; Bearden, Hardesty, & Rose, 2001) and information technology (Compeau & Higgins, 1995). However, none have directly examined the role of Internet self-efficacy on attitudes toward social networking sites and individuals' likelihood of adopting such Web sites.

Internet self-efficacy can be defined as the personal confidence in one's ability to successfully understand, navigate, and evaluate content, which should alleviate doubts and suspicions when dealing with social networking sites. Ajzen and Sexton (1999) suggest that as self-efficacy (i.e., beliefs) increases, attitudes toward the object of those beliefs will also increase. In other words, as individuals' levels of Internet self-efficacy increase their attitudes toward joining social networking sites should also increase.

Self-Esteem

A variable similar to self-efficacy is the individual's level of self-esteem. Rapacki (2007) argues that teens need places like MySpace as they help them express their ever-changing liquid self-concept in a non-permanent way as opposed to "permanent reminders like scares, bad credit, and tattoos" (p. 28). And self-esteem is an evaluative dimension of self-concept. The impact of self-esteem on technology adoption—in this case, adoption of social networking sites—has never been examined before. Given the expected positive relationship between self-efficacy and attitude toward SNS, one could also assume a positive influence of individual's self-esteem level on SNS adoption.

Need for Cognition

According to TAM, perceived usefulness of an innovation plays an important role in its ultimate adoption. Both need to belong and need for cognition in an individual can be linked to the perceived usefulness of social networking sites. Need to exchange information and goal achievement are often cited as reasons why individuals join virtual communities (Ridings & Gefen (2004). Need to exchange information relates to need for cognition or the desire to obtain information about a topic, educate oneself or learn new things. The successful adoption of virtual communities often depends on two key factors: individuals' need to access information and member-generated content (Furlong, 1989; Hagel & Armstrong, 1997; Ridings & Gefen, 2004). Many individuals join virtual groups mainly to obtain information and this is particularly true in the case of groups that are formed around special topics (Rheingold, 1993; Herring, 1996).

With social networking sites that allow for friends to keep tabs on each other, learn about each other's interests and groups, discuss and gather information on a wide variety of topics, the need for cognition should influence the usage and adoption. If an individual exhibits a high desire to gather this information, the likelihood of his or her adoption of SNS to serve such needs should also be high.

Gender

A number of demographic variables have been shown to influence technology adoption including age, income, education, occupation, and sex. The current study is limited to examining the effect of only one demographic variable—gender. Several studies examined the role of gender in technology adoption and usage (Gefen & Straub, 1997; Agarwal & Prasad, 1999; Venkatesh & Morris, 2000). Hawkins (1987) categorized various factors that are possible reasons for existing inequalities in computer usage between males and females. The first is the presence of a biological disadvantage in that girls find spatial and manipulative tasks required for interacting with a computer difficult and unappealing. The second reason suggests that usage of computers is incompatible with females' learning styles. Hawkins explains this further by saying that boys are more likely to attribute failure to external factors whereas girls tend to attribute failure to their own inability to succeed. The third reason is boarder and cultural in context in that most societies reinforce sexual stereotypes and prescribe gender-appropriate interests. Gender differences in computer skills and usage were found to transcend cultures as shown by Lowe and Krahn (1989) in their study of computer usage in Canada.

Gefen and Straub (1997) cite socio-linguistic literature to suggest that men tend to focus on hierarchy and independence, while females focus on intimacy and solidarity. This suggests gender differences in how individuals approach social networking sites. Self-efficacy and need for cognition might have a stronger say in SNS adoption for men whereas the need to belong might play a bigger role in SNS adoption for women. Lewis (2007) suggests the same in that social network-

ing sites are primarily places to reconnect with friends from past for girls whereas for boys, the attraction to SNS is more geared toward making new friends (Lewis, 2007). In another study, it was found that female ICQ users spend more time on ICQ and chat longer for reasons of sociability and need to belong than males who tend to spend time chatting for recreation (Leung, 2001).

To summarize, the role of five individual-level factors in influencing an individuals' SNS adoption is examined. More precisely, the role of need to belong, need for cognition, Internet self-efficacy, self-esteem, and gender in influencing individuals' attitudes toward social networking sites and their willingness to join such sites is examined.

PRIMARY RESEARCH

Research Proposition

In order to better understand the role of Internet self-efficacy, need to belong, need for cognition, self-esteem, and gender in social networking site adoption, the following theoretical model is proposed based on the discussion in the earlier

Figure 1. Proposed model with gender as grouping variable

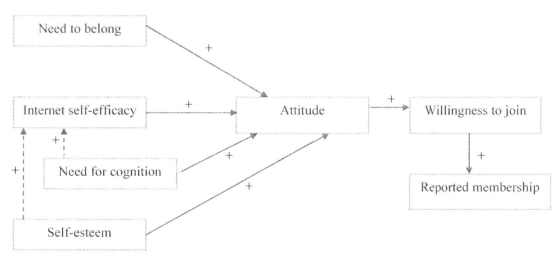

section. Although the model is the same for both genders, the magnitude of co-efficient estimates is expected to be different for males and females. Therefore, the grouping variable for the proposed model in Figure 1 is gender.

The principle research proposition is that individuals' need to belong, level of Internet self-efficacy, need for cognition, and self-esteem all positively affect their attitude toward social networking sites, which in turn positively affects their willingness to join such sites. Furthermore, this reported level of willingness to join SNS is positively related to their actual membership. This is reflected with solid line with + signs on top of them in the proposed model. Intuitively, Internet self-efficacy is expected to be dependent on individuals' need for cognition and their level of self-esteem. However, there were no direct studies found to support the directionality of this link, hence these relationships are represented by dotted lines with + signs on them.

Sample and Procedure

To test the proposed model, data was collected using a paper-pencil-based survey. An online version was not used to include both social networking site users and non-users. Furthermore, a paper-pencil-based survey would also ensure that non-users of the Internet are captured in the sample. A total of 237 undergraduate students (N=237) were recruited from a large southwestern university to participate in the study. Students were recruited to participate for extra credit during class time via an oral presentation given by the principal investigator. A student sample is justified given that social networking site users fit the demographics of college students between the ages 18 to 30 and that is the demographic of interest for the current study. Respondents took approximately 20 minutes to complete the entire survey. To maintain anonymity, no names were collected on the questionnaire.

Questionnaire

A 65-item questionnaire was developed and pre-tested on a small sample of academic professionals and graduate students to insure clarity (additional data was collected but not analyzed for this study). Attitude was measured using an established six-item semantic differential scale (bad/good, foolish/clever, unpleasant/pleasant, useful/useless, boring/interesting, and negative/positive) (Bruner, James, & Hensel, 2001, p. 84). Willingness to join social networking sites was measured using four established semantic differential items (unlikely/likely, probably/probably not, impossible/possible, and definitely would/definitely would not) (MacKenzie & Spreng, 1992). Need to belong was measured using a seven-item Likert scale. Scale items included statements such as "I want other people to accept me," "I do not like being alone," and "I try hard to stay in touch with my friends" (Leary, 1957; Leary, Kelly, & Schreindorfer, 2001). Need for cognition was measured using Likert scale items such as "I prefer complex to simple problems" and "Thinking is not my idea of fun" (Cacioppo & Petty, 1982; Cacioppo, Petty, & Kao, 1984). Self-esteem was measured using six Likert scale items such as "On the whole, I am satisfied with myself," "I feel that I have a number of good qualities," and "I take a positive attitude toward myself" (Rosenberg, 1965). Finally, the Internet self-efficacy scale consisted of 10 items such as "I often surf the web for information," "I feel confident troubleshooting Internet problems," and "I am familiar with computers" (Eastin & LaRose, 2000). The questionnaire also asked about the number of hours subjects spent surfing the Web, the number of social networking sites they belonged to, the average number of times they signed on to their account on a social networking site, and the number of hours per week they spent on these sites. The survey concluded with demographic questions.

Table 1. Mean, variance, and Cronbach's alpha coefficients for scales.

Scale	Mean	Variance	α
Attitude toward social networking sites (6 items)	4.90	0.12	0.84
Willingness to join SNS (4 items)	5.19	0.07	0.89
Need for cognition (7 items)	4.00	0.21	0.75
Need to belong (7 items)	4.68	0.71	0.63
Self-esteem (6 items)	5.50	0.29	0.77
Internet self-efficacy (10 items)	4.74	0.42	0.91

Results

The sample (N=237) consisted of 56% females (133) and 44%t males (104) with majority of subjects being Anglo (75%), followed by Hispanic American (8.4%). The mean age of the sample was 22.6 with ages ranging from 18 to 46. Reliability analysis was conducted using Cronbach's Alpha. Table 1 lists the average scores, variances, and reliability indices for each scale used in the model. All scales had a Cronbach's Alpha of over 0.70 (Hair, Anderson, Tatham, & Black, 1998, p. 118) except for one (need to belong). However, need to belong was still used in the model given that it was over 0.60 and somewhat close to the prescribed limit.

The proposed model was estimated using AMOS software. Gender was used as a grouping variable in the model. In other words, the model was estimated twice, once for males in the sample and once for females. Table 2 depicts the correlation matrix of variables used in the model. The fit statistics for both models suggest that data fits the model very well. Both CFI (Comparative Fit Index= 0.984) and GFI (Goodness of Fit Index=0.967) are well above the prescribed limit of 0.90 (Tanaka & Huba, 1985; McDonald & Marsh, 1990), chi-square is not significant, and RMSEA (0.021) is below the limit of 0.80.

The various factors that influence individuals' attitude toward social networking sites are different for both genders as suggested by Figures 2 (a) and (b). For females in the sample, need to belong and self-esteem seem to play a part in influencing their attitudes toward social networking sites, whereas for males, only Internet self-efficacy seems to influence the attitudes. For both genders, attitude toward social networking site positively affects their willingness to join such sites, which in turn positively affects their actual membership.

Table 2. Correlation matrix

	Attitude	Willingness	Internet self-efficacy	Need for cognition	Need to belong	Self-esteem
Attitude	1.00					
Willingness	0.53*	1.00				
Internet self-efficacy	0.17*	0.11	1.00			
Need for cog	0.01	-0.07	0.30*	1.00		
Need to belong	0.23*	0.20*	0.08	-0.05	1.00	
Self-esteem	0.15*	0.10	0.16*	0.03	0.03	1.00

*p< 0.01, N=237

Figure 2.a Structural model with fit statistics and standardized estimates for group 1-females

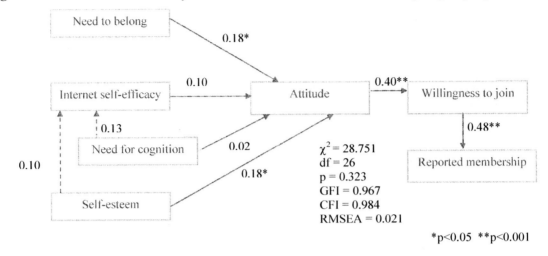

Figure 2.b Structural model with fit statistics and standardized estimates for group 2-males

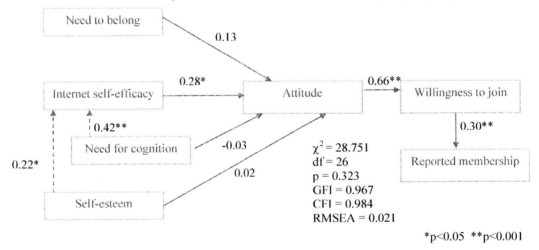

Table 3(a). Unstandardized regression weights (maximum likelihood estimation)-females

			Estimate	S.E.
Internet self-efficacy	<---	Need for cognition	0.148	0.097
Internet self-efficacy	<---	Self-esteem	0.123	0.104
Attitude	<---	Need for cognition	0.021	0.102
Attitude	<---	Need to belong	0.251*	0.119
Attitude	<---	Internet self-efficacy	0.104	0.091
Attitude	<---	Self-esteem	0.226*	0.108
Willingness	<---	Attitude	.498**	0.099
Reported membership	<---	Willingness	.093**	0.015
*p<0.05 **p<0.001				

Table 3b. Standardized regression weights (maximum likelihood estimation)-females

			Estimate
Internet self-efficacy	<---	Need for cognition	0.131
Internet self-efficacy	<---	Self-esteem	0.102
Attitude	<---	Need for cognition	0.018
Attitude	<---	Need to belong	0.176*
Attitude	<---	Internet self-efficacy	0.098
Attitude	<---	Self-esteem	0.176*
Willingness	<---	Attitude	.402**
Reported membership	<---	Willingness	.479**
*p<0.05 **p<0.001			

Table 4a. Unstandardized regression weights (maximum likelihood estimation)-males

			Estimate	S.E.
Internet self-efficacy	<---	Need for cognition	0.595**	0.124
Internet self-efficacy	<---	Self-esteem	0.264*	0.106
Attitude	<---	Need for cognition	-0.044	0.134
Attitude	<---	Need to belong	0.214	0.152
Attitude	<---	Internet self-efficacy	0.253*	0.096
Attitude	<---	Self-esteem	0.026	0.106
Willingness	<---	Attitude	0.893**	0.100

Table 4b. Standardized regression weights (maximum likelihood estimation)-males

			Estimate
Internet self-efficacy	<---	Need for cognition	0.417**
Internet self-efficacy	<---	Self-esteem	0.217*
Attitude	<---	Need for cognition	-0.034
Attitude	<---	Need to belong	0.132
Attitude	<---	Internet self-efficacy	0.280*
Attitude	<---	Self-esteem	0.024
Willingness	<---	Attitude	0.661**
Reported membership	<---	Willingness	0.303**
*p<0.05 **p<0.001			

However, the magnitude of these effects is different for males and females.

Tables 3 (a) and (b) list the unstandardized and standardized co-efficients for females and tables 4 (a) and (b) list the same for males.

For females, attitude toward social networking sites is dependent on their need to belong and self-esteem levels, whereas for males, attitude toward SNS is only dependent on their Internet self-efficacy level. To interpret the standardized co-efficient estimates, each value represents the amount of change in "attitude toward SNS" given a standard deviation unit change in X (X being Internet self-efficacy or need to belong or self-esteem). More precisely, attitude toward SNS changes by 0.28 given a standard deviation unit change in Internet self-efficacy level for men. Similarly, attitude toward SNS changes by 0.18 and 0.18 for each standard deviation unit changes in need to belong and self-esteem, respectively for females. The parameters can also be interpreted using the unstandardized co-efficient estimates. In this case, each unstandardized value represents the amount of change in "attitude toward SNS" given a single raw score unit change in X (again, X being Internet self-efficacy or need to belong or self-esteem). Attitude toward SNS (on a scale of 1 to 7) increases by 0.253 for a unit increase in the value of Internet self-efficacy for men and by 0.251 and 0.226 for a unit increase in the values of need to belong and self-esteem, respectively for women.

Next, it is interesting to note the differences in attitude-intention-behavior relationship by gender. From the standardized co-efficient estimates, the link between attitude-intention is stronger for males than females, and the link between intention-behavior is stronger for females than males. In other words, men are more likely to report a willingness to join SNS if they have a favorable predisposition toward SNS but women are more likely to actually join SNS if they report a willingness to join SNS.

DISCUSSION

Social networking sites (SNS) are growing in importance not just as places for individuals to communicate, network, and express themselves but also as advertising/marketing vehicles. Of all the existing revenue models for SNS, the most viable so far seems to rely on advertising and use of SNS as vehicles for branding. And with

expected advertising spending on such sites to be around $2 billion by 2010 (eMarketer, 2006a) it is imperative that researchers focus on SNS and SNS adoption. The present chapter presents a framework for understanding SNS adoption based on five individual-level factors: need to belong, need for cognition, Internet self-efficacy, self-esteem, and gender.

Researchers in the past have registered gender differences in technology acceptance. For instance, Gefen and Straub (1997) found that females view e-mail as being higher in social presence than men. Consistent with gender differences in TAM literature, the current study also found differences in the way males and females adopt social networking sites. For females, the need to belong and self-esteem level were significant predictors of SNS adoption whereas for males, only Internet self-efficacy was significant in predicting SNS adoption. Surprisingly, the need for cognition did not predict SNS adoption for both genders. This may be due to the fact that social networking sites are geared more toward building networks and appealing to other social needs more so than virtual communities and discussion groups such as Yahoogroups where the focus is on information access and the member-generated content.

Consistent with TRA literature, the current study provides more evidence for attitudes-intention-behavior model. For both genders, attitudes significantly predicted their willingness and intention to join social networking sites, which in turn positively predicted their actual usage. In other words, if individuals report a favorable attitude toward social networking sites they are more likely to express a willingness to join such sites, which in turn is significantly related to their actual usage and adoption of SNS. However, the magnitude of attitude-intention-behavior relationship seems to differ by gender for SNS. This is surprising and suggestive of individual differences in the TRA model itself based on gender. Attitudes-intention-behavior relationships in TAM have been tested and supported extensively, but the influence of individual-level factors on attitudes is yet to be detailed (Agarwal & Prasad, 1999). Future research should address this.

LIMITATIONS

The current study presents numerous limitations. First, the sample drawn is a convenience sample of college students. Although majority users of social networking sites are between the age groups 18 to 30, a convenience sample does limit the validity of findings. Second, a number of individual factors (age, income, education, and occupation) that potentially influence SNS adoption were not included in the current study. This is again due to the convenience sample that was used where variation in terms of age, education, income, and occupation was not much. Third, the low score in Cronbach's Alpha for need to belong also limits the overall reliability of the study. That said, individual differences in social networking site (SNS) adoption has never been investigated before and the author feels that the present study is a right step in the direction of furthering our initial understanding of social networking site adoption even with its limitations.

MANAGERIAL IMPLICATIONS

The focus on only individual factors might lead one to question the practical significance of the current study. One could argue that individual-level factors are beyond the control of brand managers, and therefore the current findings hold no managerial implications. Nonetheless, the author strongly believes that our understanding of the role of individual-level factors does help in devising effective strategies to increase membership of SNS as well as target individuals on such sites with relevant and effective promotional messages. Furthermore, the establishment of a relationship between individual level factors, brand attitude

and behavior for social networking sites is of importance to academic scholars interested in theoretical research. The study's findings present many implications for social networking site (SNS) owners and advertisers looking to use these sites as advertising vehicles. For both parties, the common objective is to increase usage and membership and enable brand managers to develop new markets and improve their competitive positions. The following are some such strategies.

The success of a social networking site is directly related to the number of individuals registered with a particular SNS as higher membership translates to an increased number of eyeballs that could be potentially reached with a promotional message. The current study suggests that SNS adoption is significantly influenced by gender. The underlying factors that drive female membership—and this becomes relevant when dealing with social networking sites devoted to women or e-dating sites that typically have fewer women registered than men—are their levels of self-esteem and need to belong. Designing advertising campaigns around these two factors can significantly increase female membership. For instance, designing a TV commercial for an e-dating site that taps into a single woman's need to belong while at the same time emphasizing and applauding her individuality and independence (self-esteem factor) should evoke positive feelings toward that particular e-dating site, which in turns translates to a willingness to join such a network resulting in an actual registration, ultimately.

When the objective is to increase male membership, which is dependent on Internet self-efficacy, social networking site owners can design sites that are easier to navigate, and thereby influence the perceived level of confidence. Social networking sites that enhance members' sense of control by providing highly interactive environments and allow users to upload multimedia files, link to their blogs on others sites, link to videos on YouTube®, and provide Web 2.0 tools extensively are more likely to appeal to men. An increased sense of control translates to an increase in perceived level of self-efficacy, which leads to a favorable predisposition toward a SNS leading ultimately to its adoption.

Gender differences also exist in the strength of relationship of the attitude-intention-behavior in the proposed structural model. Based on the co-efficients in the model, females are more likely to do something if they say they would as opposed to men who might be more willing to do something if they had a favorable predisposition toward it. A plausible strategy that exploits this finding is to attempt to increase men's attitudes toward SNS and for women, stress more on their willingness to join SNS. For example, promotional messages devoted to increasing the membership of an e-dating site should concentrate on changing the attitudes of men (by advertising) and in providing incentives to join for women (by offering discounts).

For brand managers and marketers looking to use social networking sites as advertising vehicles, it pays to note that men and women choose to register and be a part of a SNS for different reasons. This difference in motivations can become the basis for designing campaigns on social networking sites that appeal to different genders. If indeed women increasingly choose to become members of SNS owing to high levels of need to belong then ads placed on SNS should carry emotional appeals that tap into this need. Along the same lines, ads targeting women on SNS should also consider appealing to the self-esteem of members. Moreover, social networking sites may be best suited for products that can easily appeal to individual's need to belong and self-esteem (such as beauty-related products). As an example, when targeting women on an e-dating site with an ad for a beauty product, the emphasis of the creative could be on how the product enhances the individuals' personality and looks (and indirectly her self-esteem), which in turn makes her more desirable to others (need to belong).

Despite the model investigated in the current study being overly simplistic, it does present some theoretical implications for researchers interested in understanding SNS adoption. A number of other factors could potentially impact SNS adoption (factors such as type and genre of SNS, relevance, socio-economic factors of members, context, mood, influence of peers and relationships with members on one's network, perceived risk and privacy issues, parental influence and success) and future research should include these factors and test a modified version of the model presented in this chapter.

REFERENCES

Advertising Age. (2007). *Digital marketing and media fast pack.* Retrieved October 22, 2007, from http://www.adage.com/images/random/digitalfactpack2007.pdf.

Agarwal, R., & Prasad, J. (1999). Are individual differences germane to the acceptance of new information technologies?. *Decision Sciences, 30*(2), 361-391.

Ajzen, I., & Fishbein, M. (1980).*Understanding attitudes and predicting social behavior.* Englewood Cliffs, NJ: Prentice-Hall, Inc.

Ajzen, I., & Sexton, J. (1999). Depth of processing, belief congruence, and attitude-behavior correspondence. In: S. Chaiken, & Y. Trope (Eds.), *Dual-process theories in social psychology* (pp. 117-138). New York, NY: The Guilford Press.

Barbalet, J. (1998). *Emotions, social theory, and social structure: A macro-sociological approach.* Cambridge: Cambridge University Press.

Baumeister, R., & Leary, M. (1995). The need to belong: Desire for interpersonal attachments as a fundamental human motivation. *Psychological Bulletin, 117,* 497-529.

Bearden, W., Hardesty, D., & Rose, R. (2001). Consumer self-confidence: Refinements in conceptualization and measurement. *Journal of Consumer Research, 28*(June), 121-134.

Bettman, J., Johnson, E., & Payne, J. (1991). Consumer decision-making. In: S. Robertson Thomas, & H. Kasssarjian (Ed.), *Handbook of consumer behavior* (pp. 54-80). Englewood Cliffs, NJ: Prentice Hall.

Bruner II, G., James, K., & Hensel, P. (2001). *Marketing scales handbook, Vol. III.* Chicago, IL: American Marketing Association.

Cacioppo, J., & Petty, R. (1982). The need for cognition. *Journal of Personality and Social Psychology, 42,* 116-131.

Cacioppo, J., Petty, R., & Kao, C. (1984). The efficient assessment of need for cognition. *Journal of Personality Assessment, 48*(3), 306-307.

Cashmore, P. (2007). *MySpace makes $25 Million a month in ads.* Retrieved August 29, 2007, from http://mashable.com/2007/02/09/myspace-makes-25-million-a-month-in-ads/.

Compeau, D., & Higgins, C. (1995). Application of social cognitive theory to training for computer skills. *Information Systems Research, 6*(2), 118-143.

Daugherty, T., Matthew S., & Gangadharbatla, H. (2005). E-CRM: Understanding Internet confidence and implications for customer relationship management. In: Clarke III & Flaherty (Eds.), *Advances in electronic marketing.* James Madison University, Harrisonburg, VA: Idea Group Publishing, Inc.

Davis, F., Bagozzi, R., & Warshaw, P. (1989). User acceptance of computer technology: A comparison of two theoretical models. *Management Science, 35*(8), 982-1003.

DeLone, W., & McLean, E. (2003). The DeLone and McLean model of information systems success: A ten-year review. *Journal of Management Information Systems, 19*(4), 9-30.

Eastin, M. (2002). Diffusion of e-commerce: An analysis of the adoption of four e-commerce activities. *Telematics and Informatics, 19*(3), 251-267.

Eastin, M., & LaRose, R. (2000). Internet self-efficacy and the psychology of the digital divide. *Journal of Computer-Mediated Communication, 6.* Retrieved August 27, 2007, from http://www.ascusc.org/jcmc/vol6/.

Ellen, P., Bearden, W., & Sharma, S. (1991). Resistance to technological innovations: An examination of the role of self-efficacy and performance satisfaction. *Journal of the Academy of Marketing Science, 19,* 297-307.

E-Marketer. (2006a). *Brands to spend $1.8 billion on social networking sites by 2010.* Retrieved August 29, 2007, from http://www.emarketer.com/Article.aspx?id=1004085.

E-Marketer. (2006b). *Social networking online boosts bottom line.* Retrieved August 29, 2007, from http://www.emarketer.com.

Fishbein, M., & Ajzen, I. (1975). *Belief, attitude, intention and behavior: An introduction to theory and research.* Reading, MA: Addison-Wesley.

Fleming, J., & Courtney, B. (1984). The dimensionality of self-esteem II: Hierarchical facet model for revised measurement scales. *Journal of Personality and Social Psychology. 46*(February), 404-421.

Forrester Research. (2006). *North American Consumer Technographics (NACTAS) 2006 Benchmark Survey.* Retrieved August 30, 2007, from http://www.forrester.com.

Franz, R., & Wolkinger, T. (2003). Customer integration with virtual communities. Case study: The online community of the largest regional newspaper in Austria. *Proceedings of the Hawaii International Conference on System Sciences.* Big Island, Hawaii.

Furlong, M. (1989). An electronic community for older adults: The senior network. *Journal of Communication, 39*(3), 145-153.

Gefen, D., & Straub, D. (1997). Gender differences in perception and adoption of e-mail: An extension to the technology acceptance model. *MIS Quarterly, 21*(4), 389-400.

Gross, R., Acquisti, A., & Heinz, A. (2005). Information revelation and privacy in online social networks. *Proceedings of the 2005 ACM workshop on Privacy in electronic society,* (71-80).

Hagel, J., & Armstrong, A. (1997). *Net gain: Expanding markets through virtual communities.* Boston, MA: Harvard Business School Press.

Hair, J., Anderson, R., Tatham, R., & Black, W. (1998). *Multi-variate data analysis (5th ed.).* Upper Saddle River, NJ: Prentice Hall.

Hawkins, J. (1987). Computers and girls, rethinking the issues. *Sex Roles, 13*(3-4), 165-179.

Herring, S. (1996). Two variants of an electronic message schema. In: S. Herring (Ed.), *Computer-mediated communication: Linguistic, social and cross-cultural perspectives* (pp. 81-106). Philadelphia, PA: John Benjamins.

Horrigan, J., Rainie, L., & Fox, S. (2001). *Online communities: Networks that nurture long-distance relationships and local ties.* Retrieved October 17, 2003, from http://www.pewinternet.org/pdfs/Report1.pdf.

Leary, T. (1957). *Interpersonal diagnosis of personality.* New York, NY: Ronald Press.

Leary, M., Kelly, K., & Schreindorfer, L. (2001). *Individual differences in the need to belong.* Unpublished manuscript. Wake Forest University, Winston-Salem, NC.

Lenhart, A., & Madden, M. (2007). *Social networking Web sites and teens: An overview.* Pew Internet & American Life Project. Retrieved August 27, 2007 from, http://www.pewinternet.org/PPF/r/198/report_display.asp.

Leung, L. (2001). College student motives for chatting on ICQ. *New Media and Society, 3*(4), 483-500.

Lewis, J. (2007). *Social networking: Examining user behavior.* Retrieved August 29, 2007, from http://www.webpronews.com/topnews/2007/04/10/social-networking-examining-user-behavior.

Lowe, G., & Krahn, H. (1989). Computer skills and use among high school and university graduates. *Canadian Public Policy, 15*(2), 175-188.

Madden, M. (2006). *Internet penetration and impact.* Pew Internet & American Life Project, April 2006. Retrieved August 27, 2007, from http://www.pewinternet.org/PPF/r/182/report_display.asp.

MacKenzie, S., & Richard A. (1992). How does motivation moderate the impact of central processing on brand attitudes and intentions?. *Journal of Consumer Research, 18*(March), 519-529.

McDonald, R., & Marsh, H. (1990). Choosing a multi-variate model: Non-centrality and goodness of fit. *Psychological Bulletin, 707*(2), 247-255.

Morrison, E. (2002). Newcomers' relationships: The role of social network ties during socialization. *Academy of Management Journal, 45*(6), 1149.

Murchu, I., Breslin, J., & Decker, S. (2004). *Online social and business networking communities.* DERI Technical Report, August.

Preece, J., Nonnecke, B., & Andrews, D. (2004). The top five reasons for lurking: Improving community experiences for everyone. *Computers in Human Behavior, 20*(2), 201-223.

Rapacki, S. (2007). Social networking sites: Why teens need places like MySpace. *Young Adult Library Services, 5*(2), 28-30.

Rheingold, H. (1993). A slice of life in my virtual community. In: L. Harasim (Ed.), *Global networks: Computers and international com-*

munication (pp. 57-80). Cambridge, MA: The MIT Press.

Ridings, C., & Gefen, D. (2004). Virtual community attraction: Why people hang out online. *Journal of Computer-Mediated Communication, 10*(1).

Rosenberg, M. (1965). *Society and the adolescent self-image*. Princeton, NJ: Princeton University Press.

Rosenbush, S. (2005). News Corp.'s Place in MySpace. *BusinessWeek*, July 19. Retrieved August 22, 2007, from http://www.businessweek.com/technology/content/jul2005/tc20050719_5427_tc119.htm.

Smith, J. (2006). *Becoming a part of the community*. WARC Report, October 2006.

Swanson, E. (1988). *Information system implementation: Bridging the gap between design and utilization*. Homewood, IL: Irwin.

Tanaka, J., & Huba, G. (1985). A fit index for covariance structure model under arbitrary GLS estimation. *British Journal of Mathematical and Statistical Psychology, 38*(2), 197-201.

Valkenburg, P., Peter, J., & Schouten, A. (2006). Friend networking sites and their relationship to adolescents' well-being and social self-esteem. *CyberPsychology & Behavior, 9*(5), 584-590.

Venkatesh, V., & Morris, M. (2000). Why don't men ever stop to ask for directions? Gender, social influence, and their role in technology acceptance and usage behavior. *MIS Quarterly, 24*(1), 115-139.

Watson, G., & Johnson, D. (1972). *Social psychology: Issues and insights*. Philadelphia, PA: J. B. Lippincott.

Watts, D., Dodds, P., & Newman, M. (2002). Identity and search in social networks. *Science, 296*(5571), 1302-1306.

Wellman, B., & Gulia, M. (1999). The network basis of social support: A network is more than the sum of its ties. In: B. Wellman (Ed.), *Networks in the global village: Life in contemporary communities* (pp. 83-118). Boulder, CO: Westview Press.

Zmud, R. (1979). Individual differences and MIS success: A review of the empirical literature. *Management Science, 25*(10), 966-979.

Chapter II
Unraveling the Taste Fabric of Social Networks

Hugo Liu
The Media Laboratory, USA

Pattie Maes
The Media Laboratory, USA

Glorianna Davenport
The Media Laboratory, USA

ABSTRACT

Popular online social networks such as Friendster and MySpace do more than simply reveal the superficial structure of social connectedness — the rich meanings bottled within social network profiles themselves imply deeper patterns of culture and taste. If these latent semantic fabrics of taste could be harvested formally, the resultant resource would afford completely novel ways for representing and reasoning about web users and people in general. This paper narrates the theory and technique of such a feat — the natural language text of 100,000 social network profiles were captured, mapped into a diverse ontology of music, books, films, foods, etc., and machine learning was applied to infer a semantic fabric of taste. Taste fabrics bring us closer to improvisational manipulations of meaning, and afford us at least three semantic functions — the creation of semantically flexible user representations, cross-domain taste-based recommendation, and the computation of taste-similarity between people — whose use cases are demonstrated within the context of three applications — the InterestMap, Ambient Semantics, and IdentityMirror. Finally, we evaluate the quality of the taste fabrics, and distill from this research reusable methodologies and techniques of consequence to the semantic mining and Semantic Web communities.

INTRODUCTION

Recently, an online social network phenomenon has swept over the Web — MySpace, Friendster, Orkut, thefacebook, LinkedIn — and the signs say that social networks are here to stay; they constitute the *social Semantic Web*. Few could have imagined it — tens of millions of Web users joining these social network sites, listing openly their online friends and enlisting offline ones too, and more often than not, specifying in great detail and with apparent exhibitionism tidbits about who they are, what music they listen to, what films they fancy. Erstwhile, computer scientists were struggling to extract user profiles by scraping personal homepages, but now, the extraction task is greatly simplified. Not only do self-described personal social network profiles avail greater detail about a user's interests than a homepage, but on the three most popular sites, these interests are distributed across a greater spectrum of interests such as books, music, films, television shows, foods, sports, passions, profession, etc. Furthermore, the presentation of these user interests is greatly condensed. Whereas interests are sprinkled across hard-to-parse natural language text on personal homepages, the prevailing convention on social network profiles sees interests given as punctuation-delimited keywords and keyphrases (see examples of profiles in Figure 1), sorted by interest genres.

It could be argued that online social networks reflect — with a great degree of insight — the social and cultural order of offline society in general, though we readily concede that not all social segments are fairly represented. Notwithstanding, social network profiles are still a goldmine of information about people and socialization. Much computational research has aimed to understand and model the surface connectedness and social clustering of people within online social network through the application of graph theory to friend-relationships (Wasserman, 1994; Jensen & Neville, 2002; McCallum, Corrada-Emmanuel,

& Wang, 2005); ethnographers are finding these networks new resources for studying social behavior in-the-wild. Online social networks have also implemented site features that allow persons to be searched or matched with others on the basis of shared interest keywords.

Liminal semantics. However, the full depth of the semantics contained within social network profiles has been under-explored. This paper narrates one such deep semantic exploration of social network profiles. Under the keyword mediation scheme, a person who likes "rock climbing" will miss the opportunity to be connected with a friend-of-a-friend (foaf) who likes "wakeboarding" because keyword-based search is vulnerable to the *semantic gap* problem. We envision that persons who like "rock climbing" and "wakeboarding" should be matched on the basis of them both enjoying common *ethoi* (characteristics) such as "sense of adventure," "outdoor sports," "and "thrill seeking." A critic might at this point suggest that this could all be achieved through the semantic mediation of an organizing ontology in which both "rock climbing" and "wakeboarding" are subordinate to the common governor, "outdoor sports." While we agree that *a priori* ontologies can mediate, and in fact they play a part in this paper's research, there are subtler examples where *a priori* ontologies would always fail. For example, consider that "rock climbing," "yoga," the food "sushi," the music of "Mozart," and the books of "Ralph Waldo Emerson" all have something in common. But we cannot expect *a priori* ontologies to anticipate such ephemeral affinities between these items. The common threads that weave these items have the qualities of being liminal (barely perceptible), affective (emotional), and exhibit shared identity, culture, and taste. In short, these items are held together by a liminal semantic force field, and united they constitute a *taste ethos*.

What is a taste ethos? A taste ethos is an ephemeral clustering of interests from the taste fabric. Later in this paper we will formally explain and justify inferring a taste fabric from social network profiles, but for now, it suffices to say that the taste fabric is an *n* by *n* correlation matrix, for all *n* interest items mentioned or implied on a social network (e.g., a book title, a book author, a musician, a type of food, etc.). Taste fabric specifies the pairwise affinity between *any* two interest items, using a standard machine learning numeric metric known as pointwise mutual information (PMI) (Church & Hanks, 1990). If a taste fabric is an oracle which gives us the affinity between interest items as $a(x_i, x_j)$, and a taste ethos is some set of interest items $x_1, x_2, \ldots x_k$, then we can evaluate quantitatively the strength, or *taste-cohesiveness*, of this taste ethos. While some sets of interest items will be weakly cohesive, other sets will demonstrate strong cohesion. Using *morphological opening* and *thresholding* (Serra, 1982; Haralick, Sternberg, & Zhuang, 1987), standard techniques for object recognition in the image processing field, we can discover increasingly larger sets of strong cohesiveness. The largest and most stable of these we term *taste neighborhoods* — they signify culturally stable cliques of taste. Visualizing these interconnected neighborhoods of taste, we see that it resembles a topological map of taste space!

Taste neighborhoods and taste ethoi, we suggest, are novel and deep mechanisms for taste-based intrapersonal and interpersonal semantic mediation. Rather than mapping two persons into interest keyword space, or into *a priori* ontological space, the approach advocated in this paper is to map the two persons first into taste-space, and then to use their shared *ethoi* and *neighborhoods* to remark about the taste-similarity of these persons.

Emergent and implicit semantics. While our work builds directly upon age-old language modeling techniques in Computational Linguistics, and graph-based associative reasoning in Artificial Intelligence (Collins & Loftus, 1975; Fellbaum, 1998; Liu & Singh, 2004), it is also sympathetic to trends in the Semantic Web literature — away from formal semantics, and toward an embrace of emergent and implicit semantics. In Volume 1 of this journal, Sheth, Ramakrishnan, and Thomas (2005) distinguish between formal, implicit, and powerful (soft) semantics for the Semantic Web movement. Whereas formal semantics must be manually specified, implicit semantics can be readily mined out of the unstructured Web using statistical approaches. Upon further refinement, implicit semantic resources can be transformed into powerful (soft) semantic resources that afford the ability to mediate informal and formal entities. Related to implicit semantics, emergent semantics is an evolutionary approach to knowledge management (Staab et al., 2002; Aberer et al., 2004) that advocates semantic organization to be shaped from the ground-up, *a posteriori*, and in accordance with the natural tendencies of the unstructured data — such a resource is often called a *folksonomy*. We suggest that online social network profiles give an implicit semantics for cultural taste-space, and that taste fabrics afford a semi-formal, soft semantics appropriate for semantic mediation between informal and formal entities. Finally, arising out of correlation analysis, topological features of the taste fabric — such as taste neighborhoods, identity hubs, and taste cliques — constitute an emergent semantics for taste-space.

Paper's organization. The rest of the paper has the following organization. Section Two lays out a theoretical foundation for representing and computing taste, framed within theories in the psychological and sociological literatures. In particular, it addresses a central premise of our taste-mining approach — "is the collocation of interest keywords within a single user's profile meaningful; how does that tell us anything about the fabric of taste?" The section titled "Weaving the Taste Fabric" narrates the computational architecture of the implementation of taste fabric, including techniques for ontology-driven natural language normalization, and taste neighborhood discovery. The section "What Is a Taste Fabric

Good For?" describes three semantic functions of a taste fabric — semantically flexible user modeling, taste-based recommendation, and interpersonal taste-similarity — within the context of three applications — InterestMap (Liu & Maes, 2005a), ambient semantics (Maes et al., 2005), and IdentityMirror. The following section evaluates the quality of the taste fabric by examining its efficacy in a recommendation task, and also entertains an advanced discussion apropos related work and reusable methodologies distilled from this research. The final section in the paper is the conclusion.

THEORETICAL BACKGROUND

This section lays a theoretical foundation for how taste, identity, and social network politics are approached in this work. For the purposes of the ensuing theoretical discussion, social network profiles of concern to this project can be conceptualized as a bag of interest items which a user has written herself in natural language. In essence, it is a self-descriptive free-text user representation, or harkening to Julie Andrews in *The Sound of Music*, "these are a few of my favorite things." A central theoretical premise of mining taste fabric from social network profiles by discovering latent semantic correlations between interest items is that "the collocation of a user's bag of interest items is meaningful, structured by his identity, closed within his aesthetics, and informs the total space of taste." Next, the paper argues that a user's bag of interests gives a true representation of his identity, and enjoys unified ethos, or, *aesthetic closure*. This is followed with a section which plays devil's advocate and betrays some limitations to our theoretical posture. The section theorizes a segregation of user's profile keywords into two species — identity-level items vs. interest-level items. This distinction has implications for the topological structure of the taste fabric.

Authentic Identity and Aesthetic Closure

In the wake of this consumer-driven contemporary world, the proverb "you are what you eat" is as true as it has ever been — we are what we *consume*. Whereas there was a time in the past when people could be ontologized according to social class, psychological types, and generations — the so-called demographic categories—today's world is filled with multiplicity, heterogeneity, and diversity. The idea that we now have a much more fine-grained vocabulary for expressing the self is what ethnographer Grant McCracken, echoing Plato, calls *plenitude* (McCracken, 1997). In a culture of plenitude, a person's identity can only be described as the sum total of what she likes and consumes. Romantic proto-sociologist Georg Simmel (1908/1971) characterized identity using the metaphor of our life's materials as a broken glass — in each shard, which could be our profession, our social status, our church membership, or the things we like, we see a partial reflection of our identity. These shards never fully capture our individuality, but taken together, they do begin to approach it. Simmel's fundamental explanation of identity is Romantic in its genre. He believed that the individual, while born into the world as an unidentified *content*, becomes over time reified into identified *forms*. Over the long run, if the individual has the opportunity to live a sufficiently diverse set of experiences (to ensure that he does not get spuriously trapped within some local maxima), the set of forms that he occupies — those shards of glass — will converge upon an authentic description of his underlying individuality. Simmel believes that the set of shards which we collect over a lifetime sum together to describe our true self because he believes in authenticity, as did Plato long before him, and Martin Heidegger after him, among others.

While Simmel postulated that earnest self-actualization would cause the collection of a person's shards to converge upon his true individuality, the post-Freudian psychoanalyst Jacques Lacan went so far as to deny that there could be any such true individual — he carried forth the idea that the ego (self) is always constructed in the Other (culture and world's materials). From Lacan's work, a mediated construction theory of identity was born — the idea that who we are is wholly fabricated out of cultural materials such as language, music, books, film plots, etc. Other popular renditions of the idea that language (e.g., ontologies of music, books, etc.) controls thought include the Sapir-Whorf hypothesis, and George Orwell's *newspeak* idea in his novel *1984*. Today, mediated construction theory is carried forth primary by the literature of feminist epistemology, but it is more or less an accepted idea.

At the end of the day, Simmel and Lacan have more in common than differences. Csikszentmihalyi and Rochberg-Halton (1981), succeed in the following reconciliation. Their theory is that the objects that people keep in their homes, plus the things that they like and consume, constitute a "symbolic environment" which both echoes (Simmel) and reinforces (Lacan) the owner's identity. In our work, we take a person's social network profile to be this symbolic environment which gives a true representation of self.

If we accept that a user profile can give a true representation of self, there remains still the question of closure. Besides all being liked by a person, do the interests in his bag of interests have coherence amongst themselves? If it is the case that people tend toward a tightly unified ethos, or *aesthetic closure*, then all the interests in a person's bag will be interconnected, interlocked, and share a common aesthetic rationale. If there is aesthetic closure, then it will be fair for our approach to regard every pair of interest co-occurrences on a profile to be significant. If we know there is not any closure, and that people are more or less arbitrary in what interests they choose, then our approach would be invalid.

Our common sense tells us that people are not completely arbitrary in what they like or consume,

they hold at least partially coherent systems of opinions, personalities, ethics, and tastes, so there should be a pattern behind a person's consumerism. The precise degree of closure, however, is proportional to at least a person's ethicalness and perhaps his conscientiousness. In his *Ethics* (350 B.C.E.), Aristotle implied that a person's possession of ethicalness supports closure because ethics lends a person *enkrasia* or continence, and thus the ability to be consistent. Conscientiousness, a dimension of the Big Five personality theory (John, 1990), and perhaps combined with neuroticism, a second dimension in the same theory, would lead a person to seek out consistency of judgment across his interests. They need not all fall under one genre, but they should all be of a comparable quality and enjoy a similarly high echelon of taste. Grant McCracken (1991) coined the term Diderot Effect to describe consumers' general compulsions for consistency — for example, John buys a new lamp that he really loves more than anything else, but when he places it in his home, he finds that his other possessions are not nearly as dear to him, so he grows unhappy with them and constantly seeks to upgrade all his possessions such that he will no longer cherish one much more than the others. Harkening to the Romantic hermeneutics of Friedrich Schleiermacher (1809/1998), we might seek to explain this compulsion for uniformity as a tendency to express a unified emotion and intention across all aspects of personhood. Indeed, McCracken termed this uniformity of liking the various things we consume, Diderot Unity. Diderot Unity Theory adds further support to our premise that *for the most part*, a person's bag of interests will have aesthetic closure.

Upper Bounds on Theoretical Ideal

From the above discussion, we could conclude a theoretically ideal situation for our taste-mining approach – (1) a user's bag of interests is an authentic and candid representation of what the user really likes, and (2) none of the interests are out-of-place and there is strong aesthetic closure and share taste which binds together all of the interests in the bag. Here, we raise three practical problems which would degrade the theoretically ideal conditions, thus, constituting an upper bound; however, we suggest that these would degrade but not destroy our theoretical premise, resulting in noise to be introduced into the inference of the taste fabric.

A first corruptive factor is performance. Erving Goffman (1959) posed socialization as a theatrical performance. A social network is a social setting much like Goffman's favorite example of a cocktail party, and in this social setting, the true self is hidden behind a number of personae or masks, where the selection of the mask to wear is constrained by the other types of people present in that setting. Goffman says that we pick our mask with the knowledge of those surrounding us, and we give a rousing performance through this mask. In other words, the socialness of the social network setting would rouse us to commit to just one of our personae, and to give a dramatic performance in line with that persona. Performance might strength aesthetic closure, but

it could also be so overly reductive that the bag of interests no longer represent all of the aspects of the person's true identity.

A second corruptive factor is publicity. In her ethnographic review of the Friendster social networking site, Danah Boyd (2004) raises concerns over the quality and truth of profiles in light of the fact that a personal profile is public, not only to strangers, but also to one's high school friends, college friends, professors, ex-girlfriends, and coworkers alike. Because social networking sites generally make a profile visible to all these different social circles at once, Boyd suggests that some users are cowed to the fear of potentially embarrassing exposure — for example, teacher exposing to his students, or teenager exposing to his mother. As a result, users may be cowed into a lowest-common-denominator behavior, sanitizing the personal profile of all potentially embarrassing, incriminating, or offensive content.

Finally, a third corruptive factor also raised by Boyd, concerns the integrity and timeliness of social networks themselves. Boyd claims that Friendster profiles and friend connections are not frequently updated, leading to stale information which could distort the taste fabric if we were

Figure 1. Examples of social network profile formats, on Orkut (left) and Friendster (right). Note the similarity of categories between the two.

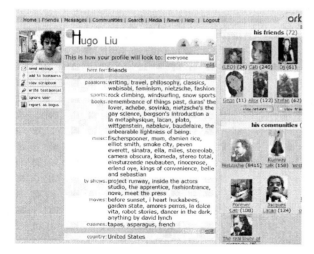

interested in looking at the temporal animation of the fabric. Boyd also writes about a phenomenon known as Fakesters — the creation of bogus user profiles such as for celebrities. However, the scope of Fakesters is arguably limited, and since Fakesters are chiefly imitations of actual people, aesthetic closure should still be observed and learning over Fakester profile examples should not greatly compromise the integrity of the meaning implied by the taste fabric.

Identity Keywords vs. Interest Keywords

While each social network has an idiosyncratic representation, the common denominator across all the major web-based social networks we have examined is the representation of a person's broad interests (e.g., hobbies, sports, music, books, television shows, movies, and cuisines) as a set of keywords and phrases. But in addition, more than just interests, higher-level features about a person such as cultural identities (e.g., "raver," "extreme sports," "goth," "dog lover," "fashionista") are also articulated via a category of special interests variously named, "interests," "hobbies & interests," or "passions."

As shown in the web page layout of the personal profile display (Figure 1), the *special interests* category appears above the more specific interest categories. We suggest that this placement encourages a different conceptualization for the special interests category—as a container for descriptions more central to one's own self-concept and self-identification. Of course, syntactic and semantic requirements are not enforced regarding what can and cannot be said within any of these profile entry interfaces, but based on our experiences, with the exception of those who are intentionally tongue-and-cheek, the special interests category is usually populated with descriptors more central to the self than other categories. For example, a person may list "Nietzsche" and "Neruda" under the "books" category, and "reading," "books," or

"literature" under the special interests category. In the profile normalization process, identity descriptors are inferred from descriptors listed under the special interests category (e.g., "dogs" → "Dog Lover," "reading" → "Book Lover", "deconstruction" → "Intellectual").

Theoretically speaking, it is desirable to have two different granularities of description for a person. Identity descriptors are more general and constitute a far smaller ontology than interest descriptors, thus, the resulting effect is to create a taste fabric structured according to a hub-and-spoke topology. Identity descriptors serve as hubs and interest descriptors serve as spokes. The advantages to such an organization are revealed in a later section on applications, and in the evaluation of the taste fabric in a recommendation task.

Having established a theoretical premise for mining taste fabric from social network profiles, and having argued for identity descriptors to be separate from interest descriptors, the following section dives into the architecture and techniques of the taste fabric implementation.

WEAVING THE TASTE FABRIC

The implementation of the taste fabric making system was completed in approximately 3,000 lines of Python code. As depicted in Figure 2, the architecture for mining and weaving the taste fabric from social network profiles can be broken down into five steps: (1) acquiring the profiles from social networking sites, (2) segmentation of the natural language profiles to produce a bag of descriptors, (3) mapping of natural language fragment descriptors into formal ontology, (4) learning the correlation matrix, and (5) discovering taste neighborhoods via morphological opening, and labeling the network topology. The following subsections examine each of these phases of processing more closely. A condensed description of the mining process, sans neighborhood discovery, can be found in Liu and Maes (2005a).

Figure 2. Implemented architecture of the taste fabric maker

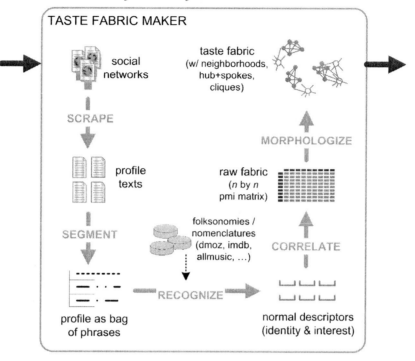

Acquiring Profiles from Social Networking Sites

The present implementation of the taste fabric sources from a one-time crawl of two Web-based social network sites, which took place over the course of six months in 2004. The shortcoming of this approach is that we were only able to mine 100,000 personal profiles from the sites, and only approximately 80% of these profiles contained substantive content because about 20% of users elected to not make their profile details publicly visible to our robotic crawler. Also, the one-time crawls prevents us from being able to engage in more interesting dynamic tracking of profiles which would potentially allow us to animate taste fabrics through time. At press time, we are in discussions with two social network Web sites to gain research access to their user profiles, which should allow for the implementation that we discuss in this paper to be deployed on a larger scale.

At every step of mining, we are careful not to compromise the anonymity or personal information of social network users. In fact, in the end product, all traces of individual users, as well as their idiosyncratic speech, are purged from the taste fabric. From our 100,000 seed profiles, we used only the text of the categorical descriptors and none of the personal information including names and screen names. We chose two social networks rather than one, to attempt to compensate for the demographic and usability biases of each. One social network has its membership primarily in the United States, while the other has a fairly international membership. Both however, have nearly identical descriptor categories, and both sites elicit users to specify punctuation-delimited descriptors rather than sentence-based descriptors. One cost to mining multiple social networks is that there is bound to be some overlap in their memberships (by our estimates, this is about 15%), so these twice-profiled members may have disproportionately greater influence on the produced fabric.

Segmenting Profiles

Once profile texts are acquired, these texts need to be segmented. First, texts are easily segmented based on their interest categories. Recall in Figure 1 that texts are distributed across templated categories, e.g., passions/general interests, books, music, television shows, movies, sports, foods, "about me." Experience with the target social network websites tell us that most users type free-form natural language text into "about me," and natural language fragments for the specific interest categories. For the passions/general interest category, text is likely to be less structured than for specific interest categories, but still more structured than "about me." Perhaps this is due to the following psychology — for specific interests, it is clear what the instances would be, e.g., film names, director names, and film genres for the films category, yet for the general interest category, the instance types are more ambiguous — so that field tends to elicit more idiosyncratic speech.

For each profile and category, its particular style of delimitation is heuristically recognized, and then applied. Common delimitation strategies were: comma-separated, semicolon-separated, stylized character sequence-separated (e.g. "item 1 \../ item 2 \../ …"), new line –separated, commas with trailing 'and', and so on. Considering a successful delimitation as a category broken down into three or more segments, approximately 90% of specific categories were successfully delimited, versus about 75% of general categories. We did not attempt to segment "about me." Unsegmentable categories were discarded.

Ontology-Driven Natural Language Normalization

After segmentation, descriptors are normalized by mapping them into a formal ontology of identity and interest descriptors (Figure 3). Newly segmented profiles are represented as lists containing casually-stated natural language fragments referring to a variety of things. They refer variously to authorships like a book author, a musical artist, or a filmmaker; to genres like "romance novels," "hip-hop," "comedies," "French cuisine"; to titles like a book's name, an album or song, a television show, the name of a sport, a type of food; or to any combination thereof, e.g., "Lynch's Twin

Figure 3. Table of instance type ontology and data sources

TASTE FABRIC'S INSTANCE TYPES

category	types	ontology sources
identities	subculture, __ lover, taste echelon	wikipedia's "list of subcultures", dmoz
films	filmmaker, film title, film genre	imdb, dmoz
books	author, title, genre	amazon, wikipedia, dmoz
music	artist, album, song, genre/decade	allmusic, amazon, dmoz
foods	dish name, ethnicity, ingredient, course	allrecipes, foodsubs
sports	name, genre	dmoz, amazon
television	show name, genre	tvguide's "showguide", dmoz

Peaks," or "Romance novels of Danielle Steele." To further complicate matters, sometimes only part of an author's name or a title is given, e.g., "Bach," "James," "Miles," "LOTR," "The Matrix trilogy." Then of course, the items appearing under the general interest categories can be quite literally anything.

Figure 3 presents the ontology of descriptor instance types for the present taste fabric. At the top-level of the ontology are six specific interest categories plus one general interest category (i.e., "identities"). Also, as shown, there are roughly 25 second-level ontological types. There are a total of 21,000 recognizable interest descriptors, and 1,000 recognizable identity descriptors, sourcing from ontologies either scraped or XML-inputted from The Open Directory Project (dmoz)[1], the Internet Movie Database (imdb)[2], TV Tome[3], TV Guide[4], Wikipedia[5], All Music Guide[6], AllRecipes[7], and The Cook's Thesaurus[8]. Figure 3 only lists the primary sources, and lists them in order of descending saliency. The diversity and specificity of types ensures the maximal recognition capability over the free-form natural language in the profiles.

Ontologizing identity. The ontology of 1,000 identity descriptors required the most intensive effort to assemble together, as we wanted them to reflect the types of general interests talked about in our corpus of profiles; this ontology was hand-engineered out of a few nomenclatures and folksonomies — most prominently Wikipedia's extensive list of subcultures and The Open Directory Project's hierarchy of subcultures and hobbies. We also generated identity descriptors in the form "(blank) lovers" where blank was replaced with major genres in the rest of our ontology, e.g., "book lovers," "country music lovers," etc. Some profiles simply repeat a select subset of interest descriptors in the identity descriptors category, so having the "(blank) lovers" template would facilitate the system in recognizing these examples. The mapping from the general interest category into the identity descriptors ontology is

far more indirect a task than recognizing specific interests because the general interest category does not insinuate a particular ontology in its phrasing. Thus, to facilitate indirect mapping, each identity descriptor is annotated with a bag of keywords which were also mined out from Wikipedia and The Open Directory Project — so for example, the "Book Lover" identity descriptor is associated with, inter alia, "books," "reading," "novels," and "literature." Because we employed two parallel mechanisms for identity descriptors, i.e., cultures versus "(blank) lovers," we cannot be completely assured that these do not overlap — in fact, they are known to overlap in a few cases, such as "Book Lovers" and "Intellectuals" or "Indie Rock Music Lovers" (genre of music) and "Indie" (subculture). Most cases of overlap, however, are much more justified because the cultural lexicon, just as natural language, cannot be flattened to a canon. Perhaps the most debatable choice we made was — for the sake of bolstering recognition rates — up-casting descriptors until they could be recognized in the identity ontology. For example, while "Rolling Stones" is not in the ontology of identity descriptors, we automatically generalize it until it is recognized, or all generalizations are exhausted — in the case of "Rolling Stones," it is up-cast into "Classic Rock Music Lovers."

Popularity-driven disambiguation. To assist in the normalization of interest descriptors, we gathered aliases for each interest descriptor and statistics on the popularity of certain items (most readily available in The Open Directory Project) that the system uses for disambiguation. For example, if the natural language fragment says simply "Bach," the system can prefer the more popular interpretation of "JS Bach" over "CPE Bach."

Situated semantic recognition. Once a profile has been normalized into the vocabulary of descriptors, they are relaxed semantically using a spreading activation (Collins & Loftus, 1975) strategy over the formal ontology, because more than simply being flat wordlists, the ontological instances are cross-annotated with each other to constitute a fabric of metadata. For example, a musical genre is associated with its list of artists, which in turn is associated with lists of albums, then of songs. A book implies its author, and a band implies its musical genre. Descriptors generated through metadata-association are included in the profile, but at a spreading discount of 0.5 (read: they only count half as much). This ensures that when an instance is recognized from free-form natural language, the recognition is situated in a larger semantic context, thus increasing the chances that the correlation learning algorithm will discover latent semantic connections.

In addition to popularity-driven disambiguation of, e.g., "Bach" into "JS Bach," we also leverage several other disambiguation strategies. Levenshtein (1965/1966) edit distance is used to handle close misspellings such as letter deletions, consecutive key inversions, and qwerty keyboard near-miss dislocations, e.g., "Bahc" into "Bach." Semantically empty words such as articles are allowed to be inserted or deleted for fuzzy matching, e.g. "Cardigans" into "The Cardigans" (band).

Using this crafted ontology of 21,000 interest descriptors and 1,000 identity descriptors, the heuristic normalization process successfully recognized 68% of all tokens across the 100,000 personal profiles, committing 8% false positives across a random checked sample of 1,000 mappings. Here, "tokens" refer to the natural language fragments outputted by the segmentation process; a recognition is judged successful if after stripping away semantically empty words, the token finds correspondence with an instance in the ontology, while remaining within the heuristically-specified tolerances for misspelling and popularity-driven disambiguation. We suggest that this is a good result considering the difficulties of working with free text input, and with an enormous space of potential interests and identities.

Correlation: Weaving the Raw Fabric

From the normalized profiles now each constituted by normalized identity and interest descrip-

tors, correlation analysis using classic machine learning techniques reveals the latent semantic fabric of interests, which, operationally, means that the system should learn the overall numeric strength of the semantic relatedness of every pair of descriptors, across all profiles. In the recommender systems literature, our choice to focus on the similarities between descriptors rather than between user profiles reflects an item-based recommendation approach such as that taken by Sarwar et al. (2001).

Technique-wise, the idea of analyzing a corpus of profiles to discover a stable network topology for the interrelatedness of interests is similar to how *latent semantic analysis* (Landauer, Foltz, & Laham, 1998) is used to discover the interrelationships between words in the document classification problem. For our task domain though, we chose to apply an information-theoretic machine learning technique called *pointwise mutual information* (Church & Hanks, 1990), or PMI, over the corpus of normalized profiles. For any two descriptors f_1 and f_2, their PMI is given in equation (1). The probability of a descriptor, $\Pr(f)$, is defined here as the frequency of global occurrences of f divided by the summed frequency of global occurrences for all descriptors.

$$PMI(f_1, f_2) = \log_2\left(\frac{\Pr(f_1, f_2)}{\Pr(f_1)\Pr(f_2)}\right) \qquad (1)$$

Looking at each normalized profile, the learning program judges each possible pair of descriptors in the profile as having a correlation, and updates that pair's PMI. What results is a 22,000×22,000 matrix of PMIs, because there are 21,000 interest descriptors and 1,000 identity descriptors in the ontology. After filtering out descriptors which have a completely zeroed column of PMIs, and applying thresholds for minimum connection strength, we arrive at a 12,000×12,000 matrix (of the 12,000 descriptors, 600 are identity descriptors), and this is the raw interest fabric. This is too dense to be visualized as a semantic network, but we have built less dense semantic networks by applying higher thresholds for minimum connection strength, and this is the reason why small clusters seem to appear in the InterestMap taste fabric visualization.

Criticism and limitations. A common critique heard about our approach is one that questions the efficacy of using the PMI metric for association. It has been suggested that we should look at collocations of greater rank than binary. Following our initial InterestMap publication, we extended the work by using morphological opening plus thresholding, as is done in image processing, to try to discover larger blocks of collocations which we call neighborhoods. This is to be discussed imminently. Additionally, another suggestion we are considering at press is negative collocation, that is, the collocation of a descriptor's absence with other descriptors. This would address an apparent flaw of pointwise mutual information, which is that it "overvalues frequent forms" (Deane, 2005), and would shed a new interpretation on the Semiotician Ferdinand de Saussure's structuralist enouncement that meaning must be 'negatively defined' (1915/1959).

Looking at Topological Features

The raw fabric has two extant topological features worthy of characterization — *identity hubs* and *taste cliques.* In addition, we describe what we believe to be a novel application of mathematical morphology (Serra, 1982; Haralick, Sternberg, & Zhuang, 1987) in conjunction with spreading activation (Collins & Loftus, 1975) to discover the taste neighborhoods we hinted at in Section 1.

Identity hubs behave like seams in the fabric. Far from being uniform, the raw fabric is lumpy. One reason is that identity hubs "pinch" the network. Identity hubs are identity descriptor nodes which behave as "hubs" in the network, being more strongly related to more nodes than the typical interest descriptor node. They exist because the ontology of identity descriptors is smaller and less sparse than the ontology of interest descriptors; each identity descriptor occurs in the corpus on the average of 18 times more frequently than the typical interest descriptor. Because of this ratio, identity hubs serve an indexical function. They give organization to the forest of interests, allow interests to cluster around identities. The existence of identity hubs allows us to generalize the granular location of what we are in the fabric, to where in general we are and what identity hubs we are closest to. For example, it can be asked, what kinds of interests do "Dog Lovers" have? This type of information is represented explicitly by identity hubs.

Taste cliques as agents of cohesion. More than lumpy, the raw fabric is denser in some places than in others. This is due to the presence of taste cliques. Visible in Figure 5, for example, we can see that "Sonny Rollins," is straddling two cliques with strong internal cohesion. While the identity descriptors are easy to articulate and can be expected to be given in the special interests category of the profile, tastes are often a fuzzy matter of aesthetics and may be harder to articulate using words. For example, a person in a Western European taste-echelon may fancy the band "Stereolab" and the philosopher "Jacques Derrida," yet there may be no convenient keyword articulation to express this. However, when the taste fabric is woven, cliques of interests seemingly governed by nothing other than taste clearly emerge on the network. One clique for example, seems to demonstrate a Latin aesthetic: "Manu Chao," "Jorge Luis Borges," "Tapas," "Soccer," "Bebel Gilberto," "Samba Music." Because the cohesion of a clique is strong, taste cliques tend to behave much like a singular identity hub, in its impact on network flow. In the following Section, we discuss how InterestMap may be used for recommendations, and examine the impact that identity hubs and taste cliques have on the recommendation process.

Figure 4. Two Ptolemaically-centered taste neighborhoods, computer generated with the follow parameters — a maximum of 50 nodes in each neighborhood, up to the first three instances of any category type are shown. Spatial layout is not implied by the neighborhood; nodes are manually arranged here.

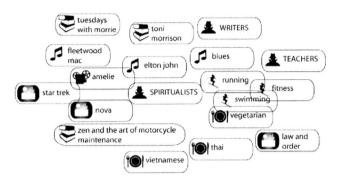

SPIRITUALISTS Taste Neighborhood

EXTREME SPORTS LOVERS Taste Neighborhood

Carving Out Taste Neighborhoods with Mathematical Morphology

From the raw fabric, another step of processing is needed to reveal *taste neighborhoods* — patches of taste cohesion that are larger than taste cliques and more stable than ephemeral taste ethoi. Taste neighborhoods of course, overlap with one another, and the discovery and definition of taste neighborhoods seems even prone to the Ptolemaic dilemma — some nodes must be designated as "center of the universe," and the choice of these centric nodes can greatly affect the resultant neighborhood definition. Two taste neighborhoods with different Ptolemaic centers are shown in Figure 4.

Taste ethos from spreading activation. While the technical details for the discovery process are potentially lengthy, we sketch a conceptual overview of the implementation here. The raw n by n correlation matrix is reviewed as a classic spreading activation network (Collins & Loftus, 1975). That is to say, activation spreads outward from an origin node to all the connected nodes, then from all connected nodes to each of their connected nodes. The obvious observation here is that in our correlation situation, all nodes are connected to a large percentage of the graph, so our graph is super-connected. However, what makes the spreading activation meaningful is that the strength of the spread activation is proportional to the strength of the PMI along any edge in the graph. The energy of the spreading is also inhibited as the number of hops away from the origin grows, according to a per hop discount rate (e.g., 50%) So, spreading with a low tolerance (or, a high threshold for activation), and outward from "Jazz," "Yoga" (two-hops away) is reachable, but the energy attenuates before the "Football" (also, two-hops away) node can be activated.

Spreading activation outward from an origin node, the result can be likened to that node's defeasible (default, in the absence of other inputs or biases) taste ethos. This taste ethos is too small when spreading activation is configured with a modest tolerance. On the other hand, if the tolerance is increased too dramatically, the taste ethos will grow in size but its stability will be undermined due to this well-known problem in graph-based inference: beginning at two hops away, reached nodes lose their semantic relevance to the origin node very rapidly. Think of this as the *telephone game effect* — playing the childhood game of telephone, the first couple of hops are still recognizable, but recognition often rapidly tapers off after the first couple of hops. The effect is also observed by Google in their PageRank algorithm (Brin & Page, 1998) for scoring the salience of web pages by voting. They noted that high-rank pages tended to link to high-quality pages, and those to other high-quality pages, but after distance=2, reliability tapered off rapidly.

Mathematical morphology. To discover neighborhoods of taste which are larger than particular node-centric ethoi, but which are still nonetheless stable, we borrow two techniques from the field of mathematical morphology (Serra, 1982; Haralick, Sternberg & Zhuang, 1987) and that are widely used in the image processing literature which appropriates them for object segmentation —morphological opening and thresholding. Morphological opening is the mathematical composition of two operators erosion and dilation, in that order. The intuition is that erosion 'eats away' at the boundaries of an object, whereas dilation 'grows' the boundaries of the object. However, erosion and dilation are not inverses because both erosion and dilation are injective, that is, they are many-to-one and lossful transformations. The effect of morphological opening is also quite intuitive — it removes small objects 'disturbances' and opens up gaps when they are located near a boundary. There is morphological opening and there is also morphological closing which is dilation composed with erosion; closing fills in holes and around boundaries more than opening. We employ opening because it is a bit crisper. Opening eliminates blemishes while closing magnifies blemishes. The other technique, thresholding, is frequently used to post-process an opened image. Applying a fixed threshold to an opened image simply turns every pixel above the threshold to 1, and below the threshold to 0.

Erosion and dilation over spread activations. We choose identity nodes as the centric origins for spreading because they are in general more stable places to start from. This follows the rationale that identities are stronger cultural fixtures than a book or a music album, generally speaking. From the identity nodes, we apply a relatively lenient discount, e.g., 0.8, and spread to define a fairly relevant neighborhood. This is repeated over all identity nodes, begetting an ethos for each identity node. Where ethoi overlap, the max of the node's energy is taken, rather than the sum of the node's energies. Now, erosion is applied, trimming back the weakest boundary nodes, followed by a dilation, growing the boundary by adding some energy to all nodes connected to the boundary, pushing some of them over the activation threshold and thus growing the mass. In the current implementation, two iterations of opening are performed, though the meaning of this varies widely with the choice of thresholds and other considerations.

In this manner, larger stable masses of nodes, termed taste neighborhoods, are discovered. Thresholding can help us trim a neighborhood to an arbitrary node-size. For visualizations such as InterestMap, neighborhoods comprised of up to thirty nodes seem visually appropriate. We believe that the application of morphological opening and thresholding to a spreading activation network in order to discover larger stable neighborhoods is a novel use, though we do not evaluate this claim within this paper's scope.

Summary. This section discussed an implementation of weaving the interest fabric out of social networks. Profiles mined from two social network websites were heuristically segmented and normalized according to a heterogeneous ontology assembled together from a variety of data sources. After normalization, correlation analysis learned the affinities between descriptors, and mathematical morphology over the "raw" fabric enabled taste neighborhoods to be discovered and overlaid onto the fabric. Next, we demonstrate the semantic uses of the taste fabric within application contexts.

Figure 5. Two screenshots of the InterestMap interactive visualization. 5a (top) depicts a user browsing neighborhoods of taste visually. 5b (bottom) depicts a user visualizing his own taste ethos by dragging and connecting interesting nodes to the "who am i?" node

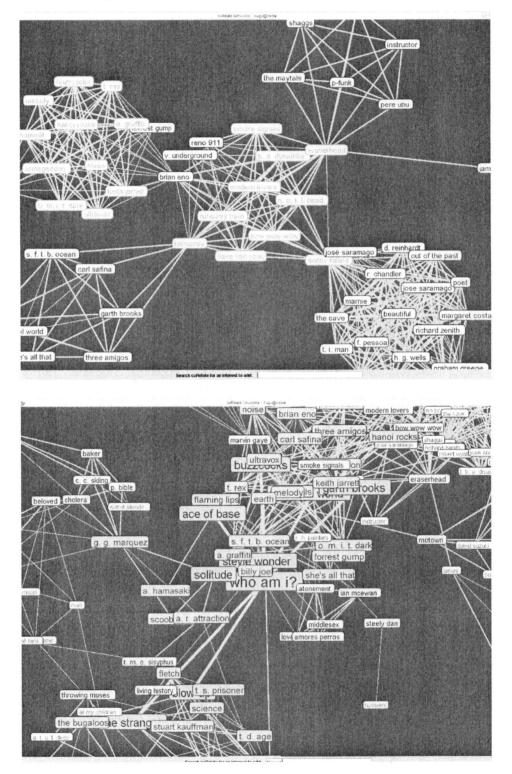

WHAT IS A TASTE FABRIC GOOD FOR?

As a rich tapestry of interconnected interests and identities, the taste fabric brings us closer to improvisational manipulations of meaning, and affords us at least three semantic functions — the creation of semantically flexible user representations, cross-domain taste-based recommendation, and the computation of taste-similarity between people. This section explores these three basic semantic functions in the context of a survey of three applications we have developed. InterestMap is a taste-based recommendation system that leverages interactive visualization of neighborhoods to make the recommendation mechanism transparent, thereby enhancing users' trust perceptions of the recommender. Ambient semantics uses the taste fabric to facilitate social introductions between two strangers, based on their shared taste. IdentityMirror is a digital mirror for identity self-management. Whereas a real mirror shows you what you look like, IdentityMirror shows you who you are. It explores semantically flexible user representations by allowing time, orderliness, and current events in the world to nuance the representation of the viewer.

InterestMap

InterestMap (Liu & Maes, 2005a) visualizes the topology of the taste fabric, and in particular it depicts taste cliques, identity hubs, and taste neighborhoods as a navigatable map. As shown in Figure 5a, users can browse InterestMap's tapestry of neighborhoods, cliques and identity hubs, or, as depicted in Figure 5b, they can interactively build up their own taste ethoi, by searching for and attaching descriptors to a stationary "who am i?" node. The act of connecting a descriptor to the self is deeper than making a mere superficial keyword association since each descriptor is actually something more like a semantic cloud. Once a user has connected several descriptors to

his self, those semantic clouds begin to intersect, overlap, and mingle. They begin to imply that other descriptors, which the user has not selected himself, *should* be within the user's taste. Hence, the notion of a visual recommendation.

Taste-based recommendation. InterestMap can, given a profile of the user's interests, recommend in a cross-domain way, books, songs, cuisines, films, television shows, and sports to that user based on taste. The user's interests are normalized according to aforementioned processes and mapped into the taste fabric. These nodes in the fabric constitute a particular activation configuration that is unique to the user, and the total situation described by this configuration is the fuzzy taste model of the user. To make recommendations, activation is spread outward from this configuration, into the surrounding nodes. Some nodes in the surrounding context will be activated with greater energy because they are more proximal to the taste signature of the starting configuration. The nodes activated with the highest energy constitute the user's recommendation. Figure 5b shows a visualization of the recommendation process. The user's self-described interests are the descriptors directly connected to the "who am i?" node. Each of these interests automatically entails other strongly connected descriptors. This is visually expressed well in the InterestMap visualization because a node getting pulled toward "who am i?" will tug a whole web of nodes behind it. Since the visualization starts with just the "who am i?" node visible on the screen, specifying just a couple of interests can literally fill up the screen with its taste entailments. To visualize the spreading activation mechanism, the size and yellowness of nodes diminishes as activation spreads outward from the "who am i?" node.

Visual recommendation enhances transparency and trust. That a user trusts the recommendations served to him by a recommender system is important if the recommender is to be useful and adopted. Among the different facilitators of trust, Wheeless and Grotz (1977) identify transparency as a prominent desirable property. When a human or system agent discloses its assumptions and reasoning process, the recipient of the recommendation is likely to feel less apprehensive toward the agent and recommendation. Also in the spirit of transparency, Herlocker, Konstan, and Riedl (2000) report experimental evidence to suggest that recommenders which provide explanations of its workings experience a great user acceptance rate than otherwise.

Unlike opaque statistical mechanisms like collaborative filtering (Shardanand & Maes, 1995), InterestMap's mechanism for recommendation can be communicated visually. The idiosyncratic topology of this taste fabric symbolizes the common taste tendencies of a large group of people. For example, in Figure 5a, it is plain to see that "Sonny Rollins" and "Brian Eno" are each straddling two different cliques of different musical genres. The rationale for each recommendation, visually represented as the spreading of flow across the network, is easily intelligible. Thus it may be easier for a user to visually contextualize the reasons for an erroneous recommendation, e.g., "I guess my off-handed taste for Metallica situated me in a group of metal heads who like all this other stuff I hate."

Although we have not yet implemented such a capability, the ability to interact with the Interest-Map network space would also afford the system an opportunity to *learn* more intelligently from user feedback about erroneous recommendations. Rather than a user simply stating that she did not like a particular recommendation, she could black out or deprecate particular clusters of the network which she has diagnosed as the cause of the bad recommendation, e.g., "I'll black out all these taste cliques of heavy metal and this identity hub of "Metal Heads" so the system will not make *that* mistake again."

Ambient Semantics

Ambient Semantics (Maes et al., 2005) is a wearable contextual information system that supports users in discovering objects and meeting people through pithy *just-in-time feedback* given in the crucial first moments of an encounter. Here is an example of a use case involving the discovery of a new book: Wearing the Ambient Semantics RFID reader wristband, you pick up a copy of Marvin Minsky's "Society of Mind" book. Through your cell phone display, the system tells you that you would be particularly interested in section 3 because it is relevant to your current research topics. It would tell you that your friends Henry and Barbara listed this book among their favorites, and that the author's expressed opinions seem sympathetic to your own, based on semantic analyses of both your writings. The system can indicate that you would find the book tasteful because it can use taste fabric to detect that it is indeed within close proximity to your taste ethos, translating to a strong taste-based recommendation.

Exposing shared taste-context between two strangers. The second use case concerns the system facilitating social introductions by breaking the ice. This scenario demonstrates using the taste fabric for the quantification and qualification of the taste-similarity between two strangers. First, a scenario. You are at a business networking event where Ambient Semantics wristwatches have been given to the attendees. You are tired of the same old conversation starters — what's your name — who do you work for — how do you like it here? — so you head to the Ambient Semantics kiosk where people are meeting each other in a new way. You introduce yourself to a lady standing next to you. By virtue of your handshake, the physical surroundings are transformed. The music and lighting in the area change to suit the shared aspects of yours and the lady's tastes. Some graphics of kayaking are thrown up on the kiosk display, as well as the faces of some people. The lady says to you, 'so you know Bob and Terry too? Are you in the Boston Outdoor Society too?'

Calculating taste-similarity: quantitatively vs. qualitatively. There is more than one good way to use taste fabric to calculate the taste-similarity of two people. The more direct way is to measure the intersection of two spread activations. Taking each person's seed profile of interests and mapping it into the taste fabric, we arrive at an initial configuration. Spreading activation outward from this configuration defines a semantic neighborhood, which earlier in the paper we referred to as a person's taste ethos. Taking the semantic intersection of two or more persons' ethoi, we arrive at the quantitative calculation of taste-similarity.

However, another intriguing possibility is to make a qualitative calculation about taste-similarity. Although the intersection of two taste ethoi is mathematically satisfying, it is not easily explainable and articulated. In other words, having the system explain that "the two of you share taste because you both have interests x, y, and z in your spreading activation clouds" is inappropriate. More articulate would be to cite a shared habitation of taste neighborhoods, for example, this explanation — "the two of you share taste because both of you are adventurers and lovers of wine." Here, the mechanism of the recommendation feels more transparent. To calculate qualitative similarity, each person's taste ethos would be used to score the degree of a person's habitation across the various taste neighborhoods, which as you recall, are centered around identity nodes. Like the classic k-nearest neighbors classification scheme, here we classify persons by their k-nearest taste neighborhoods. Having completed this mapping, the subset of neighborhoods shared among the two or more persons become those persons' shared situation. To communicate shared neighborhoods to the persons, the neighborhoods could be effectively

visualized on a screen, or, neighborhoods are safely summarized by stating the identity nodes which live within that neighborhood.

IdentityMirror

What if you could look in the mirror and see not just what you look like, but also who you are? Identity mirror (Figure 6) is an augmented evocative object that reifies its metaphors in the workings of an ordinary mirror. When the viewer is distant from the object, a question mark is the only keyword painted over his face. As he approaches to a medium distance, larger font sized identity keywords such as "fitness buffs", "fashionistas", and "book lovers" identify him. Approaching further, his favorite book, film, and music genres are seen. Closer yet, his favorite authors, musicians, and filmmakers are known, and finally, standing up close, the songs, movies, and book titles become visible.

The Identity Mirror learns and visualizes a dynamic model of a user's identity and tastes. Looking into it, the viewer's face is painted over with identity and keywords, sourced from this dynamic user model. Taste fabric is used to interpret an initial seed profile into a semantic situation within the fabric. For instance, the viewer specifies that he listens to "Kings of Convenience" and enjoys the fiction of Vladmir Nabakov, and using this, taste fabric situates the viewer within its multiple neighborhoods of taste. The keywords which paint over the viewer's face represent his context within taste-space.

Dynamic model of taste. The richness of connections in the taste fabric allow for a truly dynamic model of a user's taste — one that can evolve over time, and can absorb the influence of each morning's world events. First, we explain how world events effect the dynamic user model. In Liu (2003), one of the authors gave a model of context-sensitive semantic interpretation for noun phrases. The phrase "fast car," under a default context, would mean "a car that is moving fast," but uttered at a carwash, it could also mean "a car that is washed fast." Similarly, a person's identity can be interpreted differently based on each morning's news. For example, supposing that the morning news reveals an international conspiracy, that event could tease out from the user's taste ethos her one-time penchant for Tom Clancy mystery and suspense novels, even though on any other day, that part of her taste would not have been visible. IdentityMirror implements a feature to allow world events to bias who you look like. It operationalizes this by parsing each morning's news feeds for major topics, and activating those topics in the taste fabric as contextual biases. When the user's taste ethos is generated by spreading activation away from a starting configuration, the activation would now flow in an unusual way because of the new contextual biases. Thus, the image of the user's identity has been biased by world events.

Second, we explain how the user's model can evolve over time by recording the history of changes that a viewer makes to himself in the mirror. By gazing into IdentityMirror, a viewer can glean his identity-situation. Is his hair out of place? Are one of his *interests* out of place? How do his facial features combine to compose a gestalt? How do his various interests come together to compose an identity or *aesthetic gestalt*? We implement a feature called Identity Fixing which allows a viewer to "fix" himself as he would fix his hair. Keywords are distributed between a hearth (keywords that are taste-cohesive) and a periphery (outlier keywords seemingly out-of-place about a person); the hearth covers the face, the periphery covers the hair. A person with a strong degree of taste-coherence has ruly hair, whereas a postmodernist with scattered interests has unruly hair. The viewer can use his hands to adjust his hair — he can dishevel those unwanted peripheral keywords, or accept them by packing them into his hair. In the user model, rejecting a keyword de-energizes that keyword in the user's taste ethos, whereas affirming the keyword energizes that keyword

in the user's taste ethos. As world events tease out new and hidden aspects to the viewer's taste over time, and as the viewer continues to fix his identity, over time, the viewer's identity will be well groomed and even well vetted.

ADVANCED DISCUSSION

In this section, we present an evaluation of the taste fabric, present related work, and discuss other ways in which this work is of consequence to the semantic mining and Semantic Web communities.

Evaluation

We evaluate the quality of the taste fabric apropos a *telos* of recommendation, scrutinizing the performance of recommending interests via spreading activation over the taste fabric, as compared with a classic collaborative filtering recommender. Much of this discussion is adapted from (Liu & Maes, 2005a).

In this evaluation, we introduced three controls to assess two particular features: (1) the impact that identity hubs and taste cliques have on the quality of recommendations; and (2) the effect of using spreading activation rather than a simple tally of PMI scores. Notably absent is any evaluation for the quality of the produced taste neighborhoods, because here we consider only quantitative and not qualitative recommendation. Qualitative recommendation is not claimed to outperform quantitative recommendation in terms of accuracy — our suggestion was that linguistically identifying and visually illustrating two persons' cohabitations of taste neighborhoods should facilitate trust and transparency in the recommender's process.

In the first control, identity descriptor nodes are simply removed from the network, and spreading activation proceeds as usual. In the second control, identity descriptor nodes are removed, and n-cliques[9] where $n>3$ are weakened[10]. The third control does not do any spreading activation, but rather, computes a simple tally of the PMI scores generated by each seed profile descriptor for each of the 11,000 or so interest descriptors. We believe that this successfully emulates the mechanism of a typical non-spreading activation item-item recommender because it works as a pure information-theoretic measure.

We performed five-fold cross validation to determine the accuracy of the taste fabric in recommending interests, versus each of the three control systems. The corpus of 100,000 normalized and metadata-expanded profiles was randomly divided into five segments. One-by-one, each segment was held out as a test corpus and the other four used to train a taste fabric using PMI correlation analysis. The final morphological step of neighborhood discovery is omitted here.

Within each normalized profile in the test corpus, a random half of the descriptors were used as the "situation set" and the remaining half as the "target set." Each of the four test systems uses the situation set to compute a *complete recommendation* — a rank-ordered list of all interest descriptors; to test the success of this recommendation, we calculate, for each interest descriptor in the target set, its percentile ranking within the complete recommendation list. As shown in (2), the overall accuracy of a complete recommendation, *a(CR)*, is the arithmetic mean of the percentile ranks generated for each of the *k* interest descriptors of the target set, t_i.

$$a(CR) = \tfrac{1}{k} \sum_{i=1}^{k} percentile(t_i, CR) \qquad (2)$$

We opted to score the accuracy of a recommendation on a sliding scale, rather than requiring that descriptors of the target set be guessed exactly within *n* tries because the size of the target set is so small with respect to the space of possible guesses that accuracies will be too low and standard errors too high for a good performance assessment. For the TASTEFABRIC test system and control test systems #1 (Identity OFF) and

#2 (Identity OFF and Taste WEAKENED), the spreading activation discount was set to 0.75). The results of five-fold cross validation are reported in Figure 7.

The results demonstrate that on average, the full taste fabric recommended with an accuracy of 0.86. In control #1, removing identity descriptors from the network not only reduced the accuracy to 0.81, but also increased the standard error by 38%. In control #2, removing identity descriptors and weakening cliques further deteriorated accuracy slightly, though insignificantly, to 0.79. When spreading activation was turned off, neither identity hubs nor taste cliques could have had any effect, and we believe that is reflected in the lower accuracy of 73%. However, we point out that since control #3's standard error has not worsened, its lower accuracy should be due to overall weaker performance across all cases rather than being brought down by exceptionally weak performance in a small number of cases.

We suggest that the results demonstrate the advantage of spreading activation over simple one-step PMI tallies, and the improvements to recommendation yielded by identity and taste influences. Because activation flows more easily and frequently through identity hubs and taste cliques than through the typical interest descriptor node, the organizational properties of identity and taste yield proportionally greater influence on the recommendation process; this of course, is only possible when spreading activation is employed.

Related Works

A cultural metadata approach to musical taste. Whitman and Lawrence (2002) developed a metadata model for characterizing the taste coherence of musical genres. Mining adjectival and noun phrases collocated with musical artist discussions in newsgroups and chatrooms, they applied machine learning to automatically annotate music artists with what they termed "community

Figure 7. Results of five-fold cross-validation of taste-fabric recommender and three control systems on a graded interest recommendation task.

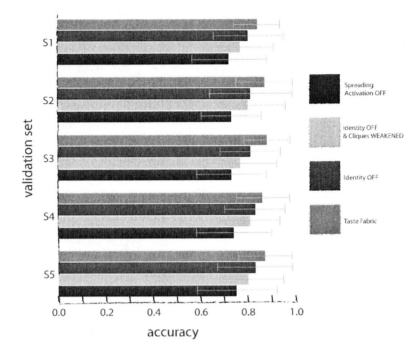

taste-fabric recommender results

metadata." Then Whitman and Smaragdis (2002) applied community metadata to build cultural signatures for music genres that could be used, in conjunction with the auditory signal, to classify unknown artists based on style similarity. Their notion of a metadata signature for musical styles is sympathetic to our notion of taste ethos and taste neighborhood, and both systems take a bottom-up metadata-driven view of meaning definition. A chief difference between our two works is that taste knowledge is located in descriptive word-choice in their system (e.g., "wicked," "loud"), and located in interest-choice in our system, that is, the choices of what people consume (e.g., "Britney Spears", "Oreo cookies").

Social information filtering. In prior work, one of the authors co-developed a well-known technique for item recommendation based upon nearest taste-neighbor, the approach known variously as social filtering, or collaborative filtering.

Shardanand and Maes (1995) represent users as vectors of (item, rating) pairs, and compute taste-similarity as statistical correlation between user vectors, or alternatively as cosine similarity of vectors in n-dimensional item space. In their Ringo social music browsing system, users were recommended a list of potential 'tastemates' on the basis of taste-similarity. One difference between our two approaches is that social filtering maintains distinct user profiles, whereas taste fabrics dissolves user boundaries, and is, in their terminology, a 'content-based filtering' approach. In distilling a reusable knowledge resource out of social network profiles that can be reappropriated for a variety of other purposes not concerned with the original social network community, it is necessary to protect the privacy of the original users, and we suggest that taste fabrics serves as a model for doing so. Also relevant is Sarwar et al.'s (2001) item-based collaborative filtering approach to recommendation, which, like taste fabrics, relies upon item-item correlation rather than user-user correlation. Taste fabric exceeds item-based filtering by use of extensive metadata to 'relax' the meaning from the item itself, by defining identity descriptors as supernodes, and by representing users as k-nearest neighborhoods. In general, collaborative filtering is more representation-opaque whereas spreading activation over neighborhoods can be visualized and more easily debugged.

Social network analysis and relational mining. Much research has examined the explicit structure of social networks, and studied their topologies via graph theory. Newman (2001) mined scientific coauthorship networks and found that collaborations 'funneled' through gatekeeper scientists. In taste fabrics, identity hubs, and hubs created around particularly salient interest descriptors constitute a similar topological feature. Jensen and Neville (2002) mined structured metadata relations from the Internet Movie Database (imdb.com) called 'schema' and learned a Bayesian network model to represent and predict item distances probabilistically. They also model the relational semantics of social network relations implied between movie actors from the Internet Movie Database and the Hollywood Stock Exchange (www.hsx.com). Finin et al. (2005) examine how the FOAF ("friend-of-a-friend") ontology applies Semantic Web concepts to enable efficient exchange of and search over social information, illustrating how social networks could develop with its semantics already explicit. Finally one work which considers the semantic content entailments of social network users is Mc-Callum, Corrada-Emmanuel, and Wang's (2005) modeling of Author-Recipient-Topic correlations in a social network messaging system. Given the topic distributions of email conversations, the ART model could predict the role-relationships of author and recipient. The work considers group clusters and dyadic relationship dynamics but does not consider cultural aggregates as is the concern of our present work.

Large-scale commonsense knowledge networks. Taste fabrics are a rich tapestry which define the meaning space of taste and interests. They are represented as semantic networks and reasoning is performed via spreading activation over this network. This approach to knowledge representation and reasoning builds upon previous work in large-scale semantic knowledge bases such as WordNet (Fellbaum, 1998) and ConceptNet (Liu & Singh, 2004). WordNet is a semantic network whose nodes are words, and edges are various nymic lexical relations between the words, e.g. a "dog" has the hypernym of "canine." ConceptNet is a semantic network of commonsense knowledge whose 200,000 nodes are verb phrases ("eat burger", "take shower"), and 1.6 million edges are one of 20 kinds of world semantic relations (e.g., "EffectOf," "PropertyOf," "DesireOf"), e.g., (EffectOf "be hungry" "cook food"). ConceptNet and taste fabrics reason similarly by activating a seed configuration of nodes, and spreading activation outward to define a semantic context. Both resources are densely connected, semantically extensive within their respective domains, and allow for improvisational manipulations of meaning to take place atop them.

Reusable Methodologies

Sanitary semantic mining. The sanitariness of a mined knowledge resource is the degree to which it is purged of idiosyncrasy, especially idiosyncratic traces of user-specific information, and also idiosyncrasies which implicate the original application domain from which the resource was mined. When a knowledge resource is sanitary, assurances can be made that private user data is not recoverable, and that the resource is sufficiently context-free so that it could potentially be used to solve problems across a variety of domains. Taste fabrics are an illustration of how a sanitary knowledge resource can be mined out of a highly idiosyncratic and application-specific data source such as self-descriptive social network profiles.

Because it is sanitized, taste fabrics can be publicly distributed and used to power applications living in other domains.

When mining social network data, concern for privacy and copyrights of user data make derivative works especially problematic; yet there is a great need and opportunity to infer valuable semantic knowledge from these sources. Ensuring data anonymity in the produced knowledge resource is a particularly sensitive issue. An early phase of the taste fabric construction process is to normalize the casually-stated keywords and phrases into formal ontologies of non-idiosyncratic form (e.g., "Nietzsche" into "Friedrich Nietzsche", "dogs" appearing under the "passions" category into "Dog Lover"). Already, the unrestricted idiosyncratic language which bears traces of an authorship are beginning to be wiped away. In contrast, collaborative filtering systems maintain ratings for each user, and while users do not have to be named, even unnamed users are not anonymous, they are only pseudonymous. A user's name is simply wiped away and replaced with a unique id (renamed from "John Smith" to "User #123"), but the profile's integrity is intact. Because the number of instances is quite large in the space of tastes, it may be possible to recover the identities of pseudonymized users because the constitution of profiles are quite unique. At the very least, maintaining any information structured around the notion of a user lends itself to the perception that privacy of the source data may be violated.

Rather than preserving individual profiles, the taste fabric simply uses these profiles to learn the strengths of connections on a network whose nodes already exist (they are simply an exhaustively enumeration of all features in the ontology). The method of the learning is non-linear so explicit frequency counts cannot easily be recovered. Thresholding and neighborhood definition are further lossful transformations which make details of the original application data virtually unrecoverable. The final structure

is sanitary — it assures the anonymity of the data source, and is much easier to distribute.

Instance-based semantic webs and ethotic representation. In the Semantic Web community, ontology and metadata systems are often seen as top-down and bottom-up approaches to knowledge representation, respectively. To draw parallels with the artificial intelligence literature, ontology is a category-based representation, and metadata is a feature-based representation. However, taste fabrics introduces the notion of an instance-based representation, which we feel to be a promising methodology for the Semantic Web community that warrants further study, especially into the issue of scalability. An instance-based representation lacks categories or features, having only items and dense numerical connections between them. Knowledge is thus unpacked from the linguistic symbolism of a category or feature's name, and instead, is found in connectionism — the flow of semantics through a graph of items. The shift from symbolic interpretation toward continuous interpretation parallels Zadeh's efforts in attempting to soften the bivalence of logic representation by giving a fuzzier, more continuous account of meaning (Zadeh, 2004).

Instance-based representations are more appropriate for semantic recognition and semantic mediation because they offer continuous numerical interpretation of entity similarity. In taste fabrics, users, groups of users, and cultures can all be represented uniformly as clouds of node activations in the fabric. A taste fabric allows the meaning of a user's keyword profile to be 'relaxed' into a semantic cloud which we term an ethos. Using ethotic representation, semantic mediation between two users or entities in the fabric can be computed quite easily as shared activation, and even effectively visualized. By interpreting an ethos as a membership into k-neighborhoods, the resource can be used to classify users or entities into an ontology of neighborhoods (the organizing force of ontology, in fact, is still present in the resource via neighborhoods and identity descriptors). Instance-based representations and ethotic representations would be well-suited for semantic resources meant for mediation and classification in the Semantic Web.

CONCLUSION

This paper presented a theory and implementation of taste fabrics — a semantic mining approach to the modeling and computation of personal tastes for lifestyle, books, music, film, sports, foods, and television. Premised on philosophical and sociological theories of taste and identity, 100,000 social network profiles were mined, ontologically-sanitized, and a semantic fabric of taste was weaved. The taste fabric affords a highly flexible representation of a user in taste-space, enabling a keyword-based profile to be 'relaxed' into a spreading activation pattern on the taste fabric, which we termed a *taste ethos*. *Ethotic representation* makes possible many improvisational manipulations of meaning, for example, the taste-similarity of two people can be computed as the shared activation between two ethoi. Taste-based recommendation is already implied by a taste ethos, as all items within an ethos are intrinsically relevant to the taste of the individual. Indeed, an evaluation of recommendation using the taste fabric implementation shows that it compares favorably to classic collaborative filtering recommendation methods, and whereas collaborative filtering is an opaque mechanism, recommendation using taste fabrics can be effectively visualized, thus enhancing transparency and cultivating user trust.

Two models of taste-based recommendation — one quantitative based on shared activation, and one qualitative based on *k-nearest neighborhoods* — were presented. Recommendation, time and world-sensitive user representation, and interpersonal taste-similarity, were illustrated within a survey of three applications of taste fabrics.

This paper makes three contributions to the literature. First, it presents a novel mechanism for mining and modeling the taste-space of personal identities and interests. Second, the mining and weaving of taste fabrics from idiosyncratic social network profiles raises the issue of *sanitation* of knowledge resources, and this paper illustrated how ontology and non-linear correlation learning can be used to purge idiosyncrasy and prepare a general-purpose grade knowledge resource. Finally and third, in addition to ontology-based and metadata-based knowledge resources, taste fabrics introduces a novel third approach to the literature — instance-based fabrics, where the notion of 'knowledge' is a purely relational one. Fabrics, we suggest, excel at semantic mediation, contextualization, and classification, and may play a valuable role as a context mediator in a recently complicated Semantic Web of formal, semi-formal, and now, informal, entities.

ACKNOWLEDGMENT

This research was supported by a British Telecom Fellowship, an AOL Fellowship, and by the research consortia sponsors of the MIT Media Lab.

REFERENCES

Aberer K., et al. (2004). Emergent semantics. *Proc. of 9th International Conference on Database Systems for Advanced Applications (DASFAA 2004),* LNCS 2973 (pp. 25-38). Heidelberg.

Aristotle. (350 BCE). *Nichomachean Ethics.*

Boyd, D. (2004). Friendster and publicly articulated social networks. *Conference on Human Factors and Computing Systems (CHI 2004).* ACM Press.

Brin, S., & Page, L. (1998). The anatomy of a large-scale hypertextual Web search engine. *Computer Networks and ISDN Systems, 30*(1-7), 107-117.

Church, K.W., & Hanks, P. (1990). Word association norms, mutual information, and lexicography. *Computational Linguistics, 16*(1), 22-29.

Collins, A.M., & Loftus, E.F. (1975). A spreading-activation theory of semantic processing. *Psychological Review, 82*, 407-428.

Csikszentmihalyi, M., & Rochberg-Halton, E. (1981). *The meaning of things: Domestic symbols and the self.* Cambridge, UK: Cambridge University Press.

Deane, P. (2005). A nonparametric method for extraction of candidate phrasal terms. *Proceedings of ACL2005.*

Fellbaum, C. (Ed.). (1998). *WordNet: An electronic lexical database.* MIT Press.

Finin, T., Ding, L., Zhou, L., & Anupam J. (2005) Social networking on the Semantic Web. *The Learning Organization: An International Journal, 12*(5), 418-435.

Goffman, E. (1959). *The presentation of self in everyday life.* Garden City, NY: Doubleday.

Haralick, R.M., Sternberg, S.R., & Zhuang, X. (1987). Image analysis using mathematical morphology. *IEEE Transactions on Pattern Analysis and Machine Intelligence, 9*(4), 532-550.

Herlocker, J., Konstan J., & Riedl, J. (2000). Explaining collaborative filtering recommendations. *Conference on Computer Supported Cooperative Work* (pp. 241-250).

Jensen, D., & Neville, J. (2002). Data mining in social networks. *National Academy of Sciences Symposium on Dynamic Social Network Analysis.*

John, O.P. (1990). The "Big Five" factor taxonomy: Dimensions of personality in the natural language and in questionnaires. In L. A. Pervin (Ed.), *Handbook of personality: Theory and research* (pp. 66-100). New York: Guilford.

Landauer, T.K., Foltz, P.W., & Laham, D. (1998). An introduction to latent semantic analysis. *Discourse Processes, 25*, 259-284.

Levenshtein, V. (1965/1966). Binary codes capable of correcting deletions, insertions, and reversals, *Doklady Akademii Nauk SSSR, 163*(4), 845-848, 1965 (Russian). English translation in *Soviet Physics Doklady, 10*(8), 707-710.

Liu, H. (2003). Unpacking meaning from words: A context-centered approach to computational lexicon design. In Blackburn et al. (Eds.), *Modeling and Using Context, The 4th International and Interdisciplinary Conference, CONTEXT 2003,* LNCS 2680 (pp. 218-232). Springer.

Liu, H., & Maes, P. (2005a, Jan 9). InterestMap: Harvesting social network profiles for recommendations. *Proceedings of IUI Beyond Personalization 2005: A Workshop on the Next Stage of Recommender Systems Research,* San Diego, CA (pp. 54-59).

Liu, H., & Singh, P. (2004). ConceptNet: A practical commonsense reasoning toolkit. *BT Technology Journal, 22*(4), 211-226.

Maes, P., et al. (2005). Ambient semantics and reach media. *IEEE Pervasive Computing Magazine.* Submitted.

McCallum, A., Corrada-Emmanuel, A., & Wang, X. (2005). Topic and role discovery in social networks. *Proceedings of 19th International Joint Conference on Artificial Intelligence* (pp. 786-791).

McCracken, G. (1991). *Culture and consumption: New approaches to the symbolic character of consumer goods and activities.* Indiana University Press.

McCracken, G. (1997). *Plenitude.* Toronto: Periph: Fluide.

Newman, M. (2001). Who is the best connected scientist? A study of scientific coauthorship networks. *Phys. Rev., E 64.*

Sarwar, B.M., et al. (2001). Item-based collaborative filtering recommendation algorithms. *The 10th Int'l World Wide Web Conference* (pp. 285-295). ACM Press.

Saussure, Ferdinand de (1915/1959). *Course in general linguistics* (W. Baskin, Trans.). New York: McGraw-Hill.

Schleiermacher, F. (1809/1998). General hermeneutics. In A. Bowie (Ed.), *Schleiermacher: Hermeneutics and criticism* (pp. 227-268). Cambridge University Press.

Serra, J. (1982). *Image analysis and mathematical morphology.* London: Academic Press.

Shardanand, U., & Maes, P. (1995). Social information filtering: Algorithms for automating 'word of mouth'. *Proceedings of the ACM SIGCHI Conference on Human Factors in Computing Systems* (pp. 210-217).

Sheth, A., Ramakrishnan, C., & Thomas, C. (2005). Semantics for the Semantic Web: The implicit, the formal and the powerful. *International Journal on Semantic Web and Information Systems, 1*(1), 1-18.

Simmel, G. (1908/1971). How is society possible? In D. N. Levine (Ed.), *On individuality and social forms: Selected writings.* University of Chicago Press.

Staab, S., Santini, S., Nack, F., Steels, L., & Maedche, A. (2002). Emergent semantics. *IEEE Intelligent Systems, 17*(1), 78-86.

Wasserman, S. (1994). *Social network analysis: Methods and applications.* Cambridge University Press.

Wheeless, L., & Grotz, J. (1977). The measurement of trust and its relationship to self-disclosure. *Communication Research, 3*(3), 250-257.

Whitman, B., & Lawrence, S. (2002). Inferring descriptions and similarity for music from community metadata. In *"Voices of Nature," Proceedings of the 2002 International Computer Music Conference* (pp. 591-598).

Whitman, B., & Smaragdis, P. (2002). Combining musical and cultural features for intelligent style detection. *Proceedings of the 3rd International Conference on Music Information Retrieval.*

Zadeh, L.A. (2004, Fall). Precisiated natural language. *AI Magazine.*

ENDNOTES

1. http://www.dmoz.org
2. http://www.imdb.com
3. http://tvtome.com
4. http://tvguide.com
5. http://www.wikipedia.org
6. http://www.allmusic.com
7. http://allrecipes.com
8. http://www.foodsubs.com
9. A qualifying clique edge is defined here as an edge whose strength is in the 80th percentile, or greater, of all edges.
10. By discounting a random 50% subset of the clique's edges by a Gaussian factor (0.5 mu, 0.2 sigma).

This work was previously published in International Journal on Semantic Web & Information Systems, Vol. 2, Issue 1, edited by A. Sheth, M. Lytras, pp. 42-71, copyright 2006 by IGI Publishing, formerly known as Idea Group Publishing (an imprint of IGI Global)

Chapter III
Mobile Social Networks:
A New Locus of Innovation

Nina D. Ziv
New York University, USA

ABSTRACT

This chapter discusses how virtual social networks have evolved from their original purpose of being online meeting places where people interact with one another to becoming an important locus for innovation. It delineates the salient characteristics of these networks (both Web-based and mobile) and suggests that the advent of these networks has shifted the balance of value creation away from traditional companies and towards the creation of companies which provide technology platforms and services for user-centric innovation. The chapter discusses how users on these virtual networks have become important sources of innovation in a variety of ways: they develop content which they share with others and participate in virtual community centers; they interact with companies who are developing products and provide valuable feedback; and they are the impetus for the creation of new kinds of marketing tools as businesses try to tap into these virtual networks in order to better understand what products will sell to these users. In addition, the chapter discusses the implications of these developments for managers, especially those in content-intensive industries such as financial services and media. Examples will be given to support these ideas from case studies on Upoc, a New York City-based mobile services company which hosts social networks for a wide variety of users; Dodgeball, another New York City-based company (recently acquired by Google) which is one of the pioneers in the mobile social networking arena; and Tapuz Mobile, an Israeli-based social network.

INTRODUCTION

During the mid-1990s, the Internet emerged as a robust technological platform and almost immediately gained traction as a value creation engine. Firms in such diverse industries as financial services, media, and healthcare, began to invest their resources in generating unique digital-based products and services into their cadre of physically-based businesses (Andal-Ancion, Cartwright, & Yip, 2003). Indeed, managers at such firms recognized that technology-enabled innovation was now an essential part of their firm's strategy (Freeman & Soete, 1999). These new users of technology also realized that in order to compete with companies that were basing their business models on digital products, they would have to venture beyond their traditional, circumscribed organizational structures which resided in brick and mortar environments and tap into the resources that existed in a larger more networked business environment (Gemunden, Ritter, & Heydebreck, 1996).

As the locus of innovation shifted from so-called 'brick and mortar' delineated companies to a more networked ecological model, a further organizational shift occurred toward a more powerful user presence within these networks. Various types of online communities appeared including special interest groups such as usenet groups; professional associations and online forums where people could exchange ideas on specific topics of interest to them; portals which provided a single point of entry for individuals and businesses to interact with one another; chat rooms, where users sought new communities and contacts; and short-term groups where users participated in one time events such as online competitions, quizzes and polls (Hamman, 2001). These communities consisted of individuals who might be scattered geographically but used the Internet as a platform for discussion. Howard Rheingold, who pioneered such online communities, defined them as "...cultural aggregations that emerge when enough people bump into each other often enough in cyberspace" (Rheingold, 1994). Some of these communities had moderators and others were more dependent on users to keep them going. For example, The Well which still exists, is essentially an online set of forums which are available to users who pay a monthly fee to participate in discussions on such wide-ranging topics as entertainment and media, computer tools, and politics (www.well.com/aboutwell.html).These online communities were initially only accessible through Web sites and therefore uni-dimensional from a technological point of view.

More recently, there has been growth in companies on the Internet which have focused on the development of virtual social networks. Such networks range in purpose from being purely social in nature to those which are commercially oriented with content development being a key purpose for these networks. Thus, such companies as Facebook and MySpace have reached out to users in the 18-24 year-old range who create their own content, for example, personal profiles, photos, blogs, and journals and share it as well as other aspects of their lives with their friends as well as with the rest of the world (Hansell, 2006). Ryze and LinkedIn have enabled business users to establish networks of business associated and potential clients. While these virtual social networks are intrinsically interesting as places where young people socialize with one another in an online setting and are seen by marketeers as a perfect target for advertising products and services designed specifically for this population (Elliott, 2007), more importantly, they have become a new and fertile locus for innovation.

This chapter will explore the development of mobile social networks, a subset of virtual social networks. In an initial study of online social networks (Ziv & Mulloth, 2006) social networking companies were plotted along two matrices: technological and purpose (Figure 1). On the technological matrix, social networks were plotted along an axis which ranged from Web-based

Figure 1. Social network matrix (partial list)

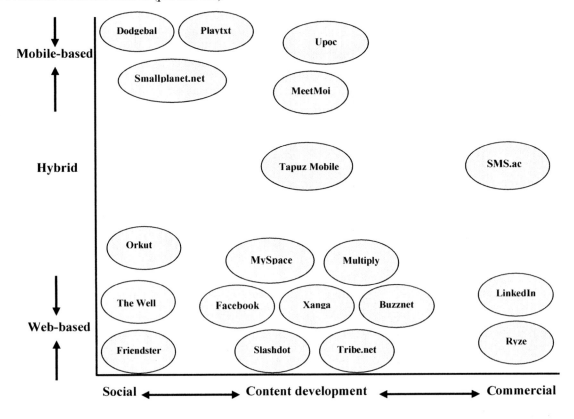

to mobile-based and included a middle ground, that is, a hybrid scenario where social networking companies incorporated both the Web and the mobile platform.

It is clear from this chart that mobile social networks are in the minority in the overall social networking industry as presently constituted. However, this chapter will discuss how this subset of companies is at the forefront of innovation in social networking. It will delineate the salient characteristics of these networks and discuss how users who populate these networks have become significant sources of innovation in several ways: they have begun to shift the balance of value creation away from traditional companies and toward the creation of companies which provide technology platforms and services for user-centric innovation; as they engage in community build-

ing, these users develop new business content and knowledge; and they have been the catalyst for transforming organizations and rethinking managerial competencies.

The chapter is divided into four sections. The first section provides a brief overview of the effect of digital-based innovation on the business environment especially with regard to the changing role of customer/users and the transformation of firms into more networked, ecological organizations. These trends in the business environment have played a significant part in the establishment of virtual social networks. The second section discusses the emergence of the mobile platform and other technologies which enabled mobile social networks to develop. The third section focuses on three mobile social networking companies, Dodgeball and Upoc, New York City-based companies and Tapuz Mobile, an Israeli-based company, and defines the salient characteristics of these companies. Field research was conducted on all three companies. In the final part of the chapter, some conclusions are drawn about mobile social networking organizations, which can serve as a beginning point for further research on the entire universe of social networking organizations. Moreover, these conclusions have implications for managers in technology-enabled organizations who wish to foster an innovative environment in their companies.

The Impact of Digital-Based Innovation

As background for the development of virtual social networks, three major ideas on the nature of innovation with relation to managerial competencies and the development of the firm will be discussed. The first idea concerns business networks of innovation which have emerged as a result of the Internet and have enabled companies to go beyond their traditional 'brick and mortar' boundaries in order to access innovative capabilities from sources such as partners, vendors, experts, universities and most significantly customers/users. Indeed, until recent developments in digital-based innovation, which have led to a redefinition of how firms compete and are configured, firms were defined by how they made use of "productive resources for the purpose of supplying goods and services to the economy in accordance with plans developed and put into effect within the firm" (Penrose, 1959). The resources that the firm had within its span of control were physical in nature, that is, they consisted of tangible things such as plants, equipment, land and natural resources, and raw materials as well as human resources (Penrose, 1959). This view of the firm also posited that firms had very clear administrative structures with a central management structure which was responsible for the general policies under which

the firm's hierarchy operated (Penrose, 1959) and well-defined reporting relationships and job responsibilities (Schoonhoven & Jelinek, 1997). Moreover, firms were thought of as isolated "islands of hierarchical control embedded in a market structure and interacting with each other through the price mechanism" (Teece, 1998).

In the post-industrial business environment, which is characterized by an emphasis on digital-based innovation and hybrid (digital and physical) innovation, the role of the firm and consequently its structure has had to change dramatically. Huber forecasted that this new business environment would be one where there will be more available knowledge, increasing complexity, and increasing turbulence (Huber, 1984). He suggests that because of these three factors, organizational decision making will be faster and more complex and therefore organizational structures will have to change to accommodate this new kind of decision making (Huber, 1984). In this new environment, innovation is characterized by uncertainty, interrelatedness between various sub-systems, and often relies on tacit knowledge accumulated by various members of the organization who may reside in different structural units (Teece, 1998). Instead of residing in a structured hierarchical organization, innovation now takes place with a larger networked environment (Benkler, 2006).

Therefore, for firms to be successful and differentiate themselves in the marketplace, it has become increasingly clear that along with having a set of core competencies, such firms would also need to acquire a network competence, which would enable them to exploit the set of relationships among customers, suppliers, vendors, and other so-called 'nodes' on the network (Ritter, 1999). Managers now understand that developing such relationships is crucial for enabling the continuous transfer of knowledge to their firms thereby providing a richer environment for the creation of innovative products and services (Kodama, 2005; (Rothschild & Darr, 2005). Such networks have enabled various constituencies to become nodal points on the technological platform and interact continually with one another in order to create value.

The second major idea is related to the development of these business networks: it is the ability of customers to provide instantaneous feedback to firms and be so-called co-creators with the members of these firms. While traditional firms had always 'pushed' their products to customers, the Internet has suddenly enabled such customers/users to become significant nodes in the business network of many firms. Thus along with communicating in a new way with businesses, users themselves have become an important source of innovation.

The notion of users as sources of innovation is not new. In his landmark book, *The Sources of Innovation*, Eric Von Hippel discusses how the users he studied had a great advantage over manufacture-centered development because they could create exactly what they wanted and could benefit from exchanges of ideas with other users in the community (von Hippel, 1988). Such users developed new products in order to satisfy their own needs and ultimately offered their innovations to companies who then marketed them. Improvements in software and hardware as well as cheaper tools that enable users to create new products, led to a 'democratization of innovation' in which users not only have the opportunity to make exactly the right products for themselves but also create communities which foster an environment in which creativity and continuous learning take place (von Hippel, 2005). Such communities of user-innovators have been very important especially in the beginning stages of new industries. For example, in the early days of Silicon Valley, informal networks of engineers and other like-minded affinity groups traded ideas with each other in settings outside of the workplace. The ideas which came out of these networks had a significant impact on the development of some of the hardware and software products which made Silicon Valley a hotbed of innovation in the 1990s (Saxenian, 1994).

The third major idea concerns the development of user communities. As the technological platform underlying the World Wide Web became more robust, such communities have become important entities not only with regard to the business networks described above but also as seedbeds of innovation. A prime example of community-based innovation is Linux. In 1991, Linus Torvalds, a computer programmer in Finland, released an operating system kernel and made it available on the World Wide Web for anyone who wanted to view it and/or add to it. Thousands of computer programmers around the world began to contribute to the kernel and the Linux operating system evolved into an alternative to proprietary operating systems such as Windows. Torvalds became the moderator/facilitator of the Open Source project and the Open Source software movement has developed into a global community of software developers who contribute freely and voluntarily to an operating system kernel known as Linux because they derive personal satisfaction and enhance their reputations as software developers from making such contributions (von Hippel, 2001). A recent manifestation of the Open Source network structure is Wikipedia, which is an online encyclopedia to which users contribute voluntarily (Levine, 2006). Another well-known technologically- based user community was started by Shawn Fanning, a college student, whose original aim was to share his music with his circle of friends. His development of a peer-to-peer platform enabled Napster to become an application on which users could send each other music files (Menn, 2003). Later, other companies such as Apple, developed ancillary services to supplement the original file sharing application (Fried, 2003).

In summary, digital-based innovations, in particular the Internet, have led to a significant change in how some industries and firms conduct business. Along with fostering a new mindset among managers about how to create value, the development of networks of innovation has shifted to some degree, the center of creativity and product development into the hands of users who can now drive innovation and play a key role in successful value creation. As users became active participants in networks of innovation, they have formed virtual communities like those in the physical world in which they have created new kinds of knowledge and content. Such communities are slated to play a more significant role in the future of organizations as they become more networked and access a variety of constituents as sources of innovation.

The Emergence of the Mobile Platform

This section will focus on the emergence of the mobile platform and other related technologies which enabled the development of mobile social networks. In the early stages of the social networking arena, mobile social networking did not develop at the pace of Web-based applications. This was in large part due to the static nature of innovation on the mobile platform. Historically, much of the innovation on the mobile platform focused on the development of infrastructure and devices. In the United States, telecommunications carriers such as Verizon, Sprint and AT&T all invested significant resources into wireless technologies, primarily by building out the telecommunications infrastructure to accommodate the increasing demand for wireless services, and acting as service providers. Other technology companies such as Nokia and Ericsson in Europe and Samsung in Korea developed handsets. Indeed, in the early days of the mobile platform, the emphasis was almost exclusively on technology and making sure that a user could complete a phone call without being 'dropped' in the middle of it (Cook & Ghosh, 2001).

Because of the emphasis on technology, there was not much content available to the general user population and usage was limited to cell phone calls. In many ways, the process of adoption of this technological innovation was very similar to what occurred with the World Wide Web, where initially there was also a dearth of content available to mainstream users. In fact, some analysts contended that the wireless platform was just a 'watered down Web' with little content that users wanted to access or pay for (Mobile content, 2000).

As the mobile platform developed, voice traffic became more and more of a commodity and mobile operators looked to new sources of revenue. One of most lucrative appeared to be in the area of content provisioning. Realizing this was an important new trend, mobile operators became the center of a paradigm of innovation in which content providers and handset manufacturers were providing their products to the mobile operators and users of these services had no choice but to access services and content from the operators. In this paradigm, the carriers provide the content and devices and the users have little contact with handset/device manufacturers or content providers. While this paradigm presumably worked in the early days of the platform when technology drove the business, with the development of new kinds of content for mobile devices, it was suggested that this paradigm may stifle innovation for all constituencies and what was needed is a new paradigm that is more networked and porous in structure and is characterized by continual interaction between content providers, handset manufacturers, other device manufacturers, for example, Nokia, Apple and most importantly, users. In addition, so-called content integrators/infomediaries who provide technical- and content-related services to both content providers and carriers as well create their own portfolios of content were deemed to be important constituents in the paradigm (Ziv, 2005).

This shift toward a more ecological and fluid model began to occur. Carriers began to create more equitable partnerships with content providers and allow small companies to use their network for distributing a variety of applications

Figure 2. Networked model of innovation on the mobile platform

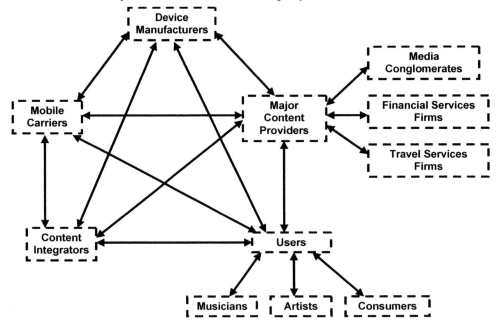

to users. Large content providers also recognized the need to access the expertise of content developers outside of the traditional boundaries of their organizations in order to find creative ways of using the premium content that is their most important asset. Users began to assume a more active role in content creation and the use of the mobile platform (Figure 2).

Along with the advent of an increasingly stable mobile platform and the rapid adoption of mobile devices such as cell phones, gaming machines and handheld computers by a wide variety of users, a new set of technologies, that is, Location-Based Services (LBS) emerged which further provided the impetus for the creation of mobile social networking applications and companies. LBS technologies allow programmers to capture the location of a particular user and integrate the position information into a wide variety of applications (Geier, 2004). Such technologies include GPS (Global Positioning Systems) which

allow customers to find their way to their destinations and alert friends and colleagues to their whereabouts and Wi-Fi, which can be used as the basis for determining position and acts like an indoor form of GPS, with access points acting as satellites. With this approach, the server software keeps track of client device positions and also transmits this information to specific clients (Geier, 2004).

The availability of LBS applications transformed virtual social networking from being a people-to-people phenomenon which exists irrespective of geographical place to one in which individuals use technology to maintain a network of strong social ties within a local geographical context such as a city or a university community (Jones & Grandhi, 2005). Coupled with a more robust mobile platform and better devices, mobile applications began to proliferate. The next section will describe the characteristics of mobile social networks.

Characteristics of Mobile Social Networks

From an analysis of three mobile social networking companies—Dodgeball, Tapuz Mobile, and Upoc—a number of salient characteristics emerged. One of these characteristics in a larger sense defines the entire genre of these companies. It is the overall notion that unlike other organizations whose core competency is based on the development of products which the company decides is important for its customers (Prahalad, 1997), these companies' core competency is to provide services for users who 'create the products'. Thus value creation depends almost entirely on the users themselves and their co-creation with the company which hosts them. A prime example is Dodgeball, a New York-based subsidiary of Google, an early instance of a company which provided a technological platform and some services to its users. Essentially, the service that Dodgeball offers to users is the ability to connect to one another while on the go in an urban environment. In order to make it simple for users to connect to one another, each bar, coffee shop and major place of interest, for example, museum, sports arena, restaurant in a particular city was geo-coded by the company. The major 'product' of the company is the user profiles which are listed on the Web site. Users fill out profiles, post photographs and list their friends and their cell phone numbers. When Dodgeball users 'check in' at a given locale, they send a text message which goes to all their preselected friends as well as any friends of friends in a ten block radius telling all these people where the message sender is located. The system then finds other users who have checked in during the last three hours and compares their locations on a virtual map to see if these users are within a 0.8 kilometer radius. Another major 'product' of Dodgeball is the interaction that occurs between the users when they meet or exchange information about one another. In addition, the users themselves create mini Web sites which contain not only their own profiles and pictures of their friends and friends of friends, but also a listing of the places they frequent and their own personal commentary about particular places such as a review of a restaurant (Ziv, 2006).

For Tapuz Mobile, which is based in Ramat Gan, Israel, the major goal is to provide services for its users which they can employ to develop new 'products' and participate in online communities. Thus, the company offers services which enable its users to create communities where they can discuss topics of interest to them. Tapuz has over 1,100 managed forums as well as 5,000 private forums called communas which focus on particular topics related to Israeli politics, culture and society. The company has over 1.6 million unique users per month who participate in the communities. Along with providing platforms for community building, Tapuz also provides its users with a variety of mobile and Web-based applications. One such application is BLOGTV, which enables users to create a live TV show and broadcast it on the Web and on mobile phones. A user entering the BLOGTV site can interact with the broadcaster and contribute to the ongoing text chat. Other applications include Getit, a mobile auction site, and Flix, a video sharing platform, has a Web site which has a video channel with continuously running videos created by users (Ziv, 2006).

Upoc is a subsidiary of Dada, an Italian-based provider of Web and mobile entertainment services. Dada is a fairly large public company based in Florence, Italy which packages and distributes ring tones, wallpapers and Java games in 12 different countries around the world. In addition, they own the equivalent of the online dating personals service, Match.com in Italy and they also own a blogging company—Life—which compares with the U.S.-based company MySpace.com. Upoc hosts social networking groups for New York City-based users, as well as provides ISP services on the mobile platform. Upoc was one of the first mobile social networks established in the United States and today has a user base of 4 million unique users. Upoc has positioned itself as a multi-faceted mobile services provider and has developed a cohesive approach for mobile media, community, marketing and third-party services for its customers and business partners (Ziv, 2007).

The core of Upoc (which means Universal Point of Contact) is the social networking service which enables users to send text messages to their friends and start any number of mobile groups for friends or family on an unlimited range of topics. Currently at Upoc, there are around 40,000 groups with categories such as music and dating being the most popular. There are also religious groups, and groups which discuss controversial topics. Like other mobile social networking organizations, Upoc is very user-centric especially with regard to the products which define the company. In Upoc's case, users define their mobile identities and participate in creating content and establishing permanent communities. Upoc's services are designed to enable the creation of user-based output. For example, Upoc provides a service called Up2 which enables users to microblog and share their thoughts on a real-time basis with their friends and others. In addition, there are subscription services available to users, for example, dating services, which enhance the mobile social networking user experience.

Thus, mobile social networks such as Dodgeball, Tapuz and Upoc provide tools that enable people to collectively construct a range of resources that were too difficult or expensive, or simply impossible to develop previously (Terdiman, 2004). Users who participate in these networks have the opportunity to generate personalized content such as mobile blogs and/or collaborate on the mobile platform to develop exciting new kinds of content.

A second major characteristic of these companies and related to the notion of user-centricity, is that users are not only active members of their communities and participate in them, they also

give valuable feedback to their organizations which enables innovation to occur. Tapuz for example, attributes its success to not only offering superior technology but also being very attentive to the requests and needs of their users. The majority of Tapuz users are young people (the average age is 22) who are early adopters of technology and provide continual feedback to the company on a regular basis on Tapuz's applications and services. The Tapuz management team considers these users a prime source of innovation and often implements suggestions from users into the suite of applications on the Web site. Indeed, Tapuz is an example of a new kind of firm which exists in complete partnership with its users.

In addition, Tapuz's communities while overwhelmingly social in nature, have sparked the interest of firms in the mobile product development arena who participate in some of these communities in order to get feedback about the mobile technology arena. Thus, one community which is a group devoted to a discussion of cell phones has among its users members of the cell phone manufacturing industry who listen to the dialogue and incorporate the suggestions and ideas they hear from the community in their designs of mobile devices for the marketplace.

Given that the users are central to the strategy of these companies, one of the most important aspects of these social networking companies is that they are able to provide the technological infrastructure for product development as well as services which will enable such development. Thus, a third major characteristic of these companies is that they are techno-centric, that is, these companies could not exist or provide services without developing a sophisticated technology strategy. For both Dodgeball and Tapuz, this strategy consists of using the mobile platform exclusively or a hybrid model in which a company provides a Web-based product which enables users to sign up for a particular service and then use the mobile platform. Dodgeball, for example, uses mobile services such as Location-Based Services and short messaging services (SMS) in order to reach their customer base. Dodgeball's services include a Web site which was built using off-the-shelf open source tools which were cobbled together to provide a platform that is accessible to everyone who owns a cell phone. While users may sign up initially via a Web site, once they are signed up, the service exists entirely on the mobile technology platform (Geier, 2004).

Tapuz has developed an advanced mobile platform which enables users to interact seamlessly with one another and also has partnered with Israeli telecommunications operators such as Cellcom, Pelephone, and Orange to develop robust applications and enable subscribers of these operators access Tapuz's applications through operator portals which are available on their handsets. However, as the mobile platform has become more robust, hybrid online/mobile communities have emerged with users participating both through a Web site and by using their mobile devices, for example, PDAs, and cell phones. Indeed, Tapuz offers full synergy between the web and mobile devices. Thus, users who are on the web-based chat platform can talk with users who are surfing from their mobile phones as well as send them messages. An example of a major service of Tapuz is Panet, an Arabic Internet portal which has more than 500,000 daily visitors. Tapuz constructed the application so that the mobile portal is a mirror site of the Web-based portal (www.tapuz.co.il).

Upoc is also techno-centric and has a complex technology strategy for servicing both its users and also its partners, for example, the carriers, media companies and marketing organizations As a multi-faceted mobile services provider, Upoc has developed a comprehensive mobile technology solution for carriers, consumers, media companies and marketers to communicate through various applications including SMS (text messaging), WAP (wireless Internet), voice, and MMS (multimedia messaging). Upoc's technology platform integrates text, voice, Web, and wireless Internet and works on any mobile phone, Internet-enabled

phone, wireless PDA, two-way or text pager. Upoc was the first company in North America to have direct connections to all the carriers for facilitating text messaging and in the early days of mobile text messaging, the company was actually generating a significant percentage of the SMS traffic in the United States.

In developing their technology platforms, both Upoc and Tapuz recognized that they would need to integrate the capabilities of their organizations with those of the mobile carriers in their respective countries. This integration enabled both organizations to have viable business models which could sustain them and enable them to provide top notch services for their clients. Thus Tapuz has partnerships with Cellcom and other carriers in Israel and has developed revenue sharing models with these companies. Upoc has a complex business model. It has partnerships with all the major carriers including Verizon, Sprint, T-Mobile and Cingular and is the only company in the United States which actually gets paid by the carriers for generating SMS messages. In addition, Upoc provides local subscription services in which users can download Bible quotes and dating services using premium SMS and also provides advertising services for the carriers.

As a result of its acquisition by Dada, Upoc has become the proprietary aggregator of Dada's billing services for Cingular in the United States and for Dada's local TV promotions. As the intermediary services provider, Upoc gets a percentage of the overall profits. Clearly, the role which Upoc plays as a technology intermediary to the carriers as well as a partner to them in revenue generation extends the model of the mobile social networking organizations beyond simply being a platform for its users to create content and communities.

While users participate as individuals in communities or generate their own content using the various services of the companies, they also are members of communities and engage in continual community building. This virtual community building is another very important characteristic of mobile social networking organizations. Each organization tends to attract a different demographic for its communities. Thus Dodgeball's constituents are mostly young urbanites in the 18-24 year-old age range while at Upoc, the service attracts blue collar workers such as truck drivers, firemen, and police officers who do not necessarily spend a lot of time in front of a computer but do see the need to communicate in the mobile environment for a variety of reasons. Upoc's users are generally Black and Hispanic people in the 20 to 40 year-old age group and remain part of the community for an extended period of time. Tapuz attracts a wide range of people who span various ages, interests, and demographics throughout the Israeli community.

Along with socially-oriented communities, a number of business environments have established mobile social networking communities to enhance their employees' communication with one another and build new knowledge. Thus Upoc's multi-platform cross-carrier group SMS capabilities enable groups of real estate agents and sales teams to be in constant communication with one another. Professionals such as doctors and lawyers have also created these on-the-go communities to exchange and share their knowledge with one another (www.upocnetworks.com). Many of these professionals are not necessarily able to access their Web-based fixed line computers but are able to participate in dialogues with fellow professionals while out in the field.

Community building for these different groups of people is challenging. Most mobile social networking communities are self-policing and support open communication among their members. Users have complete control of how they communicate with one another and what type of content they access. Thus users can change their messaging options at any time, block messages from members they do not like, remove people from messaging groups and unsubscribe from any content they do not want.

A key aspect of community building entails having a community manager who moderates the discussions of these communities, keeps the conversation going and makes sure that there is nothing fraudulent or illegal occurring. Mobile social networking services do vary in how they approach the issue of community managers. At Tapuz, after an incident in which a community moderator who was a woman turned out to be a male, the management at Tapuz decided to meet with each moderator in order to make sure they are aware of their responsibilities and guard against misrepresentation (Ziv, 2006a). At Upoc, any user can create a community on any topic and then become the owner and moderator of the community. However, Upoc maintains a staff of community managers who check in on groups to ensure that the discussions are proceeding appropriately. If a person becomes offensive, the company's community managers can step in and either ask the person to leave or blacklist the person from ever joining the community again. An example of someone who could be blacklisted is a person who tries to sell drugs to community members or makes offensive remarks. Unlike a PC, where a user can assume a different identity, the interaction on a mobile phone can be traced to a network identifiable device so it is easy to track down a person and exclude him or her from the conversation.

The importance of community managers in the life of the communities has become apparent to the management team at Upoc. Steve Spencer, the CEO of the company, suggested that without these managers, many of the communities would not be viable. During the 2007 holiday season, themed communities with Upoc community managers were created around such subjects as Thanksgiving, Hanukkah, and Christmas. Community managers moderated these groups to ensure that anti-social behavior was not tolerated. In fact, about 100 people were expelled from the community because of inappropriate behavior. As a result, these communities became social safety nets for new users who knew that the communities would welcome them. For the Christmas themed community, which was entitled 'What do you want from Santa Claus?', the CEO of the company became the community manager and assumed the identity of Santa Claus. He was able to reach out to people across the United States who shared their stories of heartbreak and joy during the season (Ziv, 2008) .Other functions served by community managers include helping people to understand how to use the functions on their mobile phones and reporting errors and glitches in the system (Alleven, 2007).

By participating in the communities, which are the core service of their company, community managers at Upoc and at Tapuz have begun to change the nature of their companies' organizations.

Rather than the usual management team being the focus of the organization's hierarchical structure, the communities of users who populate the technological platforms of each of these companies have in effect, became the most important nodes on a network which includes the management team. Indeed, all three of the companies that were researched had lean management teams. At Upoc for example, the management team consists of the CEO and a small team of managers who oversee operations, engineering, quality assurance, customer service, and business development.

A final characteristic of mobile social networks is that they are multi-locational. By taking advantage of the mobile platform, they can be intensely urban-centric and operate in a very localized manner or they can connect users on a national level who are subscribers in a national wireless network. Thus Dodgeball's social networks are made up of people who interact in densely packed urban environments. Indeed, in New York City and other large metropolises in the United States, the young generation, largely referred to as Generation @, increasingly looks at such networks as a medium through which they can establish their social identities. These social networks act as virtual community centers, a place for the Generation @ to socialize online as well as use it to tap into information, buy books, send flowers or even breakup with a boyfriend. Dodgeball and other services like it depend on people wanting to meet with one another at particular locations in an urban setting.

Tapuz and Upoc operate on multiple levels. Upoc's communities are sometimes localized in one city where local nurses, for example, may communicate regularly with one another. Other times they operate on a national level across the wireless network which enables users whose mobile phones are tied to different carriers to interact with one another. In the case of the themed Christmas community, some of the users were in rural locations and used pre-paid phone cards as a way of communicating with those in urban environments. For Tapuz, there are local communities as well as national communities and because community members can interact with one another through the company's Web site, many Israelis abroad participate in the communities thus enabling such communities to assume a global stance.

CONCLUSION

As demonstrated by the discussion of mobile social networking organizations such as Dodgeball, Tapuz Mobile and Upoc, the mobile social networking arena is a burgeoning one and poised to evolve into a more robust and developed industry sub-sector in the near future. Of the three companies studied, Upoc is most advanced in terms of providing a comprehensive set of services and also having a sustainable business model. It may be that some companies which provide social networking services such Tapuz Mobile will choose to remain purely social and influence the development of the sector in less tangible ways while others will become more commercialized in nature. Indeed, as the sub-sector evolves, there may be a spectrum of social networking organizations ranging from those established purely by users for their own needs to those which offer more substantial products and services.

For managers, it is clear that in this new business environment, where users are a key component of value creation and user-centric companies are proliferating, it is essential to reach out into the larger networked environment in which these users thrive and seek the sources of innovation outside of the traditional organizational structures. While user-based innovation overall is not new, what is new is the increasing importance and centrality of users with regard to the competitive strategy of these companies. Managers need to rethink the core competency of their companies to include a significant set of user-based innovations. Indeed, they may also have to restructure their organizations to incorporate such user communities and the range of innovation that occurs in them. Thus, users may share products that they have developed with the community at large, for example, Upoc, and Dodgeball users generate profiles of themselves which contain personal information that they upload to the technological platform for sharing with the rest of the community. Innovation in this case takes place on an individual level as individual users create value for others. On the community level, users who interact with one another build new knowledge and content which contributes to the overall knowledge base of the community members.

In addition to the social nature of many of these communities, those communities established by professionals become laboratories for learning about how groups of people interact with one another and how knowledge sharing in a corporate setting can be enhanced. In a sense, community building and sharing of ideas and knowledge becomes a new form of R&D in the corporate environment where users/customers who represent another community node on the larger network interact with internal communities of the organization and continually create new

knowledge and ideas. As the economy becomes more service-based, such interaction between external and internal communities becomes essential for the optimal development and deployment of products and services.

Beyond providing a source of innovation, these user communities also provide excellent opportunities for the business community as they enable firms to directly tap into markets and better understand what products will be successful for particular customers. Companies that recognize the importance of community-based innovation include Proctor and Gamble which recently launched two Web sites which are designed to serve as platforms for the creation of user communities made up of their customers (Vranica, 2007) and Cisco, which is providing a variety of services for its customers aimed at helping them bring their users together in online communities (Stone, 2007). The recent partnership forged by Microsoft to provide advertising services for Facebook.com and Google's deal to be the exclusive provider of search capabilities for MySpace.com indicates that major players in the software arena have recognized the importance and potentially lucrative nature of these user communities (Seelye, 2006).

Along with recognizing the value creation done by users, this chapter suggests that these mobile social networking companies represent a significant change in how companies organize themselves and that they are at the leading edge of organizational transformation. Formed to service communities, such companies have a minimalist organizational structure, and a rich technological environment which is designed to encourage customers, that is, the members of these user communities, to innovate. In the future, managers who once headed traditional hierarchical organizations may have to assume new roles which are more in line with the community manager of these social networks who acts as a facilitator of the members of the organization. While making sure the community functions properly, the 'manager' lets the members of the community freely interact with one another to create innovative products and services. For many companies such radical changes may come about in incremental stages. For example, one way such user-centric organizations can help larger organizations become more innovative and competitive is to become an important 'subsidiary' within a larger organization. Companies such as Newscorp have recognized the power of these user-centric organizations and have acquired MySpace.com, a social networking site (Siklos, 2007).

One aspect of mobile social networking which needs further exploration is the locational issue. Services such as Dodgeball show that digital networks actually make cities more attractive than ever before, as opposed to a widely held belief that the technology platform now in place which provides connectivity for vast numbers of users who are not necessarily in the same place or even time zone, and especially the mobile platform which encourages people to be dispersed, were going to make the whole idea of densely packed urban locations obsolete. Instead, such mobile social networks promote the positive aspects of interaction and add credence to the Porterian notion of clustering of individuals and businesses in geographical proximity in order to achieve economic success (Porter, 1998) as well as to the idea that groups of people using mobile social networks will find new ways of organizing and interacting, and in doing so, will in some way change the nature of the social order (Rheingold, 2002). In the spectrum of mobile social networking organizations, more dispersed communities especially on the national level, can bring various people together in powerful groups which can unite for a common purpose or serve as a national sounding board for a company seeking to reach a customer base that is nation-wide and solicit ideas from this base in order to create products and services that will be successful beyond the local business environment.

While mobile social networking companies as described above continue to develop on the national level, it is clear that innovation is now viewed as a global endeavor and companies which want to compete successfully must learn to operate within this new environment. This is especially true in industries which rely on the collection, distribution and processing of information such as the music industry where the value chain has been reconfigured to reflect new modes of delivering products and services (Mol, Winjberg, & Carroll, 2005). Such reconfiguration calls for firms to have new approaches to creating value and to use the technology platform, that is, the Internet, as a tool for developing and accessing sources of innovation around the world. This might entail reaching out beyond the bounds of the traditional corporation to access the R&D talent that is dispersed globally in order to solve technological problems (Moitra & Krishnamoorthy, 2004) or restructuring the process of gathering knowledge about a new product or service by creating a 'web of innovation' which will facilitate the optimal interchange of ideas from experts in various locations (Farris, Hartz, & Whitwell, 2003). As a result of its acquisition by Dada, Upoc has ventured into globalizing its offerings. Its plans include developing mobile social networking applications in Brazil, Italy, and Spain (Ziv, 2008).

As the mobile social networking arena evolves, challenges clearly remain. Although a variety of personal computing devices enable users to stay connected to the community through the Web, limitations such as small screens on mobile devices, poor connectivity and issues of privacy and security will continue to be of concern to users who employ the mobile platform exclusively. New advances in technology both on the infrastructure side and the device side are needed in order for the mobile social networking industry to advance. Clearly more research needs to be done to understand how the mobile social networking arena is evolving, and its potential impact on the future environment of a variety of industries and on managerial imperatives.

REFERENCES

Alleven, M. (2007, May 15). Help wanted: Community managers. *Wireless Week.*

Andal-Ancion, A.., Cartwright, P., & Yip, G. (2003). The digital transformation of traditional businesses. *MIT Sloan Management Review, 44*(4).

Benkler, Y. (2006). *The wealth of networks: How social production transforms markets and freedom.* Retrieved on July 14, 2007, from http://www.benkler.org/wealth_of_networks/index.php.

Cook, T., & Gosh, A. (2001). The wireless data industry and the birth of m-commerce. *European Case Clearing House Case #2-101-039.*

Elliott, S. (2007, February 28). A CBS take on the YouTube madness. *The New York Times.*

Farris, G., Hartz, C., Krishnamurthy, K., McIlvaine, B., Postle, S., Taylor, R., Whitwell, G. (2003, November/December). Web-enabled innovation in new product development. *Research Technology Management Journal,* 24-35.

Freeman, C., & Soete, L. (1999). *The economics of industrial innovation.* Cambridge, MA: MIT Press.

Fried, I. (2003). *Apple limits tunes file sharing.* Retrieved May 10, 2007, from CNET News.com.

Geier, J. (2004). *Location-based services realize benefits.* Retrieved May 10, 2006, from Mobilizedsoftware.com.

Gemunden, H., Ritter, T., & Heydebreck, P. (1996). Network configuration and innovation success: An empirical analysis in German high-tech industries. *International Journal of Research in Marketing, 5*(13), 449-462.

Hamman, R. (2001). Granada broadband. *Presentation given at the 4th International Conference on Virtual Communities.* London.

Huber, G. (1984). The nature and design of post-industrial organizations. *Management Science, 30*(8), 928-951.

Mobile content and applications: Monetizing popular interactive services. (2000). *Jupiter Research Vision Report on Broadband and Wireless, 8.*

Jones, Q., & Grandhi, S. (2005, September/October). A. P3 systems: Putting the place back into social networks. *IEEE Internet Computing,* 38-46.

Kodama, M. (in press). Innovation and knowledge creation through leadership-based strategic community: Case study on high-tech company in Japan. *Journal of Technovation.*

Levine, R. (2006, August 7). The many voices of Wikipedia, heard in one place. *The New York Times.*

Menn, J. (2003). *All the rave: The rise and fall of Shawn Fanning's Napster.* New York, NY: Crown Business.

Moitra, D., & Krishnamoorthy, M. (2004, July/August). Global innovation exchange. *Research Technology Management Journal,* 32-38.

Mol, J., Wijnberg, N., & Carroll, C. (2005). Value chain envy: Explaining new entry and vertical integration in popular music. *Journal of Management Studies, 42*(2), 251-282.

Penrose, E. (1959). *The theory of the growth of the firm.* New York, NY: Oxford University Press.

Porter, M. (1998, November/December). Clusters and the new economics of competition. *Harvard Business Review.*

Prahalad, C. (1997). The role of core competencies in the corporation. In: M. Tushman & P.

Anderson (Eds.), *Managing strategic innovation and change* (pp. 172-182). New York, NY: Oxford University Press.

Rheingold, H. (1994). *The virtual community: Surfing the Internet.* London: Minerva.

Rheingold, H. (2002). *Smart mobs: The next social revolution.* Cambridge, MA: Perseus Books.

Ritter, T. (1999). The networking company. *Industrial Marketing Management, 28,* 467-479.

Rothschild, L., & Darr, A. (2005). Technological incubators and the social construction of innovation networks: An Israeli case study. *Technovation, 25,* 59-67.

Saxenian, A. (1994). *Regional advantage: Culture and competition in Silicon Valley and Route 128.* Cambridge, MA: Harvard University Press.

Schoonhoven, C., & Jelinek, M. (1997). Dynamic tension in innovative, high-technology firms: Managing rapid technological change through organizational structure. In: M. Tushman & P. Anderson (Eds.), *Managing strategic innovation and change* (pp. 233-254) New York, NY: Oxford University Press.

Seelye, K. (2006, August 23). Microsoft to provide and sell ads on Facebook, the Web site. *The New York Times.*

Siklos, R. (2007, January 21). Big media's crush on social networking. *The New York Times.*

Stone, B. (2007, March 3). Social networking's next phase. *The New York Times.*

Tapuz Website: www.tapuzmobile.com/about.

Teece, D. (1998). Design issues for innovative firms: Bureaucracy, incentives and industrial structure. In: A. Chandler Jr., P. Hagstrom, & O. Solvell (Eds.), *The dynamic firm: The role of technology, strategy, organization and regions* (pp. 134-165). New York, NY: Oxford University Press.

Terdiman, D. (2004, July 22). Open arms for open source news. *Wired News.*

Upoc Networks Website. www.upocnetworks. com.

von Hippel, E. (2005). *Democratizing innovation.* Cambridge, MA: MIT Press.

von Hippel, E. (2001). Innovation by user communities: Learning from open-source software. *MIT Sloan Management Review, 42*(4) 82-86.

von Hippel, E. (1988). *The sources of innovation.* New York, NY: Oxford University Press.

Vranica, S. (2007, January 8). P&G boosts social-networking phenomenon. *The Wall Street Journal.*

The Well website. www.well.com/aboutwell. html.

Ziv, N. (2008). Interview with Steve Spencer, CEO of Upoc on January 15, 2008 in New York City.

Ziv, N., & Mulloth, B. (2007). The evolution of a mobile services provider in a global context: Upoc as a case in point. *Proceedings of the Mobile Business Conference.* Toronto, Ontario.

Ziv, N., & Mulloth, B. (2006). An exploration on mobile social networking: Dodgeball as a case in point. *Proceedings of the Mobile Business Conference.* Copenhagen, Demark.

Ziv, N. (2005). Toward a new paradigm of innovation on the mobile platform: Redefining the roles of content providers, technology companies, and users. *Proceedings of the Mobile Business Conference.* Sydney, Australia.

Chapter IV
Increasing Capital Revenue in Social Networking Communities:
Building Social and Economic Relationships through Avatars and Characters

Jonathan Bishop
Glamorgan Blended Learning Ltd. & The GTi Suite & Valleys Innovation Centre & Navigation Park & Abercynon, UK

ABSTRACT

The rise of online communities in Internet environments has set in motion an unprecedented shift in power from vendors of goods and services to the customers who buy them, with those vendors who understand this transfer of power and choose to capitalize on it by organizing online communities and being richly rewarded with both peerless customer loyalty and impressive economic returns. A type of online community, the virtual world, could radically alter the way people work, learn, grow consume, and entertain. Understanding the exchange of social and economic capital in online communities could involve looking at what causes actors to spend their resources on improving someone else's reputation. Actors' reputations may affect others' willingness to trade with them or give them gifts. Investigating online communities reveals a large number of different characters and associated avatars. When an actor looks at another's avatar they will evaluate them and make decisions that are crucial to creating interaction between customers and vendors in virtual worlds based on the exchange of goods and services. This chapter utilizes the ecological cognition framework to understand transactions, characters and avatars in virtual worlds and investigates the exchange of capital in a bulletin board and virtual. The chapter finds strong evidence for the existence of characters and stereotypes based on the ecological cognition framework and empirical evidence that actors using avatars with antisocial connotations are more likely to have a lower return on investment and be rated less positively than those with more sophisticated appearing avatars.

INTRODUCTION

The rise of online communities has set in motion an unprecedented power shift from goods and services vendors to customers according to Armstrong and Hagel (1997). Vendors who understand this power transfer and choose to capitalize on it are richly rewarded with both peerless customer loyalty and impressive economic returns they argue. In contemporary business discourse, online community is no longer seen as an impediment to online commerce, nor is it considered just a useful Web site add-on or a synonym for interactive marketing strategies. Rather, online communities are frequently central to the commercial development of the Internet, and to the imagined future of narrowcasting and mass customization in the wider world of marketing and advertising (Werry, 2001). According to Bressler and Grantham (2000), online communities offer vendors an unparalleled opportunity to really get to know their customers and to offer customized goods and services in a cost executive way and it is this recognition of an individual's needs that creates lasting customer loyalty. However, if as argued by Bishop (2007a) that needs, which he defines as pre-existing goals, are not the only cognitive element that affects an actor's behavior, then vendors that want to use online communities to reach their customers will benefit from taking account of the knowledge, skills and social networks of their customers as well.

According to Bishop (2003) it is possible to effectively create an online community at a click of a button as tools such as Yahoo! Groups and MSN Communities allow the casual Internet user to create a space on the Net for people to talk about a specific topic or Interest. Authors such as Bishop have defined online communities based on the forms they take. These forms range from special interest discussion Web sites to instant messaging groups. A social definition could include the requirement that an information system's users go through the membership lifecycle identified by Kim (2000). Kim's lifecycle proposed that individual online community members would enter each community as visitors, or "Lurkers." After breaking through a barrier they would become "Novices," and settle in to community life. If they regularly post content, they become "Regulars." Next, they become "Leaders," and if they serve in the community for a considerable amount of time, they become "Elders." Primary online community genres based on this definition are easily identified by the technology platforms on which they are based. Using this definition, it is possible to see the personal homepage as an online community since users must go through the membership lifecycle in order to post messages to a 'guestbook' or join a 'Circle of Friends'. The Circle of Friends method of networking, developed as part of the VECC Project (see Bishop, 2002) has been embedded in social networking sites, some of which meet the above definition of an online community. One of the most popular genres of online community is the bulletin board, also known as a message board. According to Kim (2000), a message board is one of the most familiar genres of online gathering place, which is asynchronous, meaning people do not have to be in the same place at the same time to have a conversation. An alternative to the message board is the e-mail list, which is the easiest kind of online gathering place to create, maintain and in which to participate (ibid). Another genre of online community that facilitates discussion is the Chat Group, where people can chat synchronously, communicating in the same place at the same time (Figallo, 1998). Two relatively new types of online community are the Weblog and the Wiki. Weblogs, or blogs are Web sites that comprise hyperlinks to articles, news releases, discussions and comments that vary in length and are presented in chronological order (Lindahl & Blount, 2003). The community element of this technology commences when the owner, referred to as a 'blogger', invites others to comment on what he/she has written. A Wiki, which is so named

Table 1. Advantages and disadvantages of specific online community genres

Genre	Advantages/Disadvantages
Personal Homepage	Advantages: Regularly updated, allows people to re-connect by leaving messages and joining circle of friends Disadvantage: Members often need to re-register for each site and cannot usually take their 'Circle of Friends' with them.
Message Boards	Advantages: Posts can be accessed at any time. Easy to ignore undesirable content. Disadvantages: Threads can be very long and reading them time consuming
E-mail Lists and News-letters	Advantages: Allows a user to receive a message as soon as it is sent Disadvantages: Message archives not always accessible.
Chat Groups	Advantages: Synchronous. Users can communicate in real time. Disadvantages: Posts can be sent simultaneously and the user can become lost in the conversation.
Virtual Worlds and Simulations	Advantages: 3-D metaphors enable heightened community involvement Disadvantages: Requires certain hardware and software that not all users have
Weblogs and Direc-tories	Advantages: Easily updated, regular content Disadvantages: Members cannot start topics, only respond to them
Wikis and Hypertext Fiction	Advantages: Can allow for collaborative work on literary projects Disadvantages: Can bring out the worst in people, for example, their destructive natures

through taking the first letters from the axiom, 'what I know is', is a collaborative page-editing tool with which users may add or edit content directly through their Web browser (Feller, 2005). Despite their newness, Wikis could be augmented with older models of hypertext system. A genre of online community that has existed for a long time, but is also becoming increasingly popular is the Virtual World, which may be a multi-user dungeon (MUD), a massively multiplayer online role-playing game (MMORG) or some other 3-D virtual environment.

Encouraging Social and Economic Transactions in Online Communities

According to Shen et al. (2002), virtual worlds could radically alter the way people work, learn, grow, consume and entertain. Online communities such as virtual worlds are functional systems that exist in an environment. They contain actors, artifacts, structures and other external representations that provide stimuli to actors who respond (Bishop, 2007a; 2007b; 2007c). The transfer of a response into stimuli from one actor to another is

social intercourse and the unit of this exchange is the transaction (Berne, 1961; 1964). A transaction is also the unit for the exchange of artifacts between actors and is observed and measured in currency (Vogel, 1999). Transactions can be observed in online communities, most obviously in virtual worlds, where actors communicate with words and trade goods and services. Research into how consumers trade with each other has considered online reputation, focusing on how a trader's reputation influences trading partner's trust formation, reputation scores' impact on transactional prices, reputation-related feedback's effect on online service adoption and the performance of existing online reputation systems (Li et al., 2007). According to Bishop (2007a), encouraging participation is one of the greatest challenges for any online community provider. There is a large amount of literature demonstrating ways in which online communities can be effectively built (Figallo, 1998; Kim, 2000; Levine-Young & Levine, 2000; Preece, 2000). However, a virtual community can have the right tools, the right chat platform and the right ethos, but if community members are not participating the community will not flourish and encouraging members to change from lurkers into elders is proving to be a challenge for community providers. Traditional methods of behavior modification are unsuitable for virtual environments, as methodologies such as operant conditioning would suggest that the way to turn lurkers into elders is to reward them for taking participatory actions. The ecological cognition framework proposed Bishop (2007a; 2007c) proposes that in order for individuals to carry out a participatory action, such as posting a message, there needs to be a desire to do so, the desire needs to be consistent with the individual's goals, plans, values and beliefs, and they need to have to abilities and tools to do so. Some individuals such as lurkers, may have the desire and the capabilities, but hold beliefs that prevent them from making participatory actions in virtual communities. In order for them to do so, they need to have the desire to do so and their beliefs need to be changed. Traditional methods, such as operant conditioning may be able to change the belief of a lurker that they are not being helpful by posting a message, but it is unlikely that they will be effective at changing other beliefs, such as the belief they do not need to post. In order to change beliefs, it is necessary to make an actor's beliefs dissonant, something that could be uncomfortable for the individual. While changing an actor's beliefs is one way of encouraging them to participate in a virtual community, another potential way of increasing their involvement is to engage them in a state of flow which might mean that they are more likely to act out their desires to be social, but there is also the possibility that through losing a degree of self-consciousness they are also more likely to flame others (Orengo Castellá et al., 2000).

A CHARACTER THEORY FOR ONLINE COMMUNITIES

Kim's membership lifecycle provides a possible basis for analyzing the character roles that actors take on in online communities. Existing character theories could be utilized to explore specific types of online community (e.g., Propp, 1969) or explain to dominance of specific actors in online communities (e.g., Goffman, 1959). Propp suggested the following formula to explain characters in media texts:

$$\alpha a^5 D^1 E^1 M F^1 T a^5 B K N ToQW$$

Propp's character theory suggests that in media texts eight characters can be identified; the villain who struggles against the hero; the donor who prepares the hero or gives the hero an artifact of some sort; the helper who helps the hero in their expedition; the princess who the hero fights to protect or seeks to marry; her father the dispatcher; and the false hero who takes credit for the hero's actions or tries to marry the princess. While Propp's theory might be acceptable for analyzing multi-user dungeons or fantasy adventure games, it may not be wholly appropriate for bulletin board-based online communities. Goffman's character theory according to Beaty et al. (1998) suggests that there are four main types of characters in a media text: the protagonists who are the leading characters; the deuteragonists who are the secondary characters; the bit players who are minor characters whose specific background the audience are not aware of; and the fool who is a character that uses humor to convey messages. Goffman's model could be useful in explaining the dominance of specific types of online community members, but does not explain the different characteristics of those that participate online, what it is that drives them, or what it is that leads them to contribute in the way they do.

Bishop's (2007a; 2007c) ecological cognition framework (ECF) provides a theoretical model for developing a character theory for online communities based on bulletin board and chat room models. One of the most talked about types of online community participant is the troll. According to Levine-Young and Levine (2000), a troll posts provocative messages intended to start a flame war. The ECF would suggest that chaos drives these trolls, as they attempt to provoke other members into responding. This would also suggest there is a troll opposite, driven by order, which seeks to maintain control or rebuke obnoxious comments. Campbell et al. (2002) found evidence for such a character, namely the big man, existing in online communities. Salisbury (1965) suggests big men in tribes such as the Siane form a de facto council that confirms social policy and practices. Campbell et al. (2002) point out that big men are pivotal in the community as, according to Breton (1999), they support group order and stability by personally absorbing many conflicts. Actors susceptible to social stimuli activate one of two forces, either social forces or anti-social forces. Actors who are plainly obnoxious and offend other actors through posting flames, according to Jansen (2002) are known as snerts. According to Campbell, these anti-social characters are apparent in most online communities and often do not support or recognize any of the big men unless there is an immediate personal benefit in doing so. Campbell et al. (2002) also point out that the posts of these snerts, which they call sorcerers and trolls, which they call tricksters, could possibly look similar. Differentiating between when someone is being a troll and when they are being a snert although clear using the ECF, may require interviewing the poster to fully determine. Someone whose intent is to provoke a reaction, such as through playing 'devil's advocate' could be seen theoretically to be a troll, even if what they post is a flame. An actor who posts a flame after they were provoked into responding after interacting with another, could be seen theoretically to be a snert, as their intention is to be offensive. Another actor presented with the same social stimuli may respond differently. Indeed, Rheingold (1999) identified that members of online communities like to flirt. According to Smith (2001), some online community members banned from the community will return with

new identities to disrupt the community. These actors could be labeled as e-venegers, as like Orczy's (1904) character the scarlet pimpernel, they hide their true identities. Driven by their emotions, they seek a form of personal justice. A character that has more constructive responses to their emotions exists in many empathetic online communities according to Preece (1998), and may say things such as "MHBFY," which according to Jansen (2002) means "My heart bleeds for you," so perhaps this character type could be known as a MHBFY Jenny. Using the ecological cognition framework there should be also those actors that are driven by gross stimuli, with either existential or thanatotic forces acting upon them. Jansen (2002) identified a term for a member of an online community that is driven by existential forces, known to many as the chat room Bob, who is the actor in an online community that seeks out members who will share nude pictures or engage in sexual relations with them. While first believed to be theoretical by Bishop (2006), there is evidence of members of online communities being driven by thanatotic forces, as reported by the BBC (Anon., 2003). Brandon Vedas, who was a 21-year-old computer expert, killed himself in January 2003. This tragic death suggests strongly that those in online communities should take the behavior of people in online communities that may want to cause harm to themselves seriously. The existence of this type of actor is evidence for the type of online community member who could be called a Ripper, in memory of the pseudonym used by Mr Vedas.

There are two more characters in online communities, driven by action stimuli that results in them experiencing creative or destructive forces. Surveying the literature reveals a type of actor that uses the Internet that are prime targets for "sophisticated technical information, beta test software, authoring tools [that] like software with lots of options and enjoy climbing a learning curve if it leads to interesting new abilities" (Mena, 1999), who are referred to as wizards. There is also the opposite of the wizard who according to Bishop (2006) seeks to destroy content in online communities, which could be called the iconoclast, which according to Bernstein and Wagner (1976) can mean to destroy and also has modern usage in Internet culture according to Jansen (2002) as a person on the Internet that attacks the traditional way of doing things, supporting Mitchell's (2005) definition of an iconoclast being someone that constructs an image of others as worshippers of artifacts and sets out to punish them by destroying such artifacts.

These eleven character types, summarized in Table 2, should be evident in most online communities, be they virtual worlds, bulletin boards, or wiki-based communities.

Investigating the Proposed Character Theory

Some of the most widely used methods for researching online are interviewing, observation and document analysis (Mann & Stewart, 2000). Ethnography offers a rigorous approach to the analysis of information systems practices using observational techniques, with the notion of context being one of the social construction of meaning frameworks and as a research method, ethnography is well suited to providing information systems researchers with rich insights into the human, social and organizational aspects of information systems development and application because as ethnography deals with actual practices in real-world situations, it allows for relevant issues

Table 2. A character theory for online communities based on the ecological cognition framework

Label	Typical characteristics
Lurker	The lurker may experience a force, such as social, but will not act on it, resulting in them not fully taking part in the community.
Troll	Driven by chaos forces as a result of mental stimuli, would post provocative comments to incite a reaction.
Big Man	Driven by order forces as a result of mental stimuli, will seek to take control of conflict, correcting inaccuracies and keeping discussions on topic.
Flirt	Driven by social forces as a result of social stimuli, will seek to keep discussions going and post constructive comments.
Snert	Driven by anti-social forces as a result of social stimuli, will seek to offend their target because of something they said.
E-venger	Driven by vengeance forces as a result of emotional stimuli, will seek to get personal justice for the actions of others that wronged them.
MHBFY Jenny	Driven by forgiveness forces, as a result of experiencing emotional stimuli. As managers they will seek harmony among other members.
Chat Room Bob	Driven by existential forces as a result of experiencing gross stimuli, will seek more intimate encounters with other actors.
Ripper	Driven by thanatotic forces as a result of experiencing gross stimuli, seeks advice and confidence to cause self-harm.
Wizard	Driven by creative forces as a result of experiencing action stimuli, will seek to use online tools and artifacts to produce creative works.
Iconoclast	Driven by destructive forces as a result of experiencing action stiumli, will seek to destroy content that others have produced.

to be explored and frameworks to be developed which can be used by both practitioners and researchers and also means that researchers can deal with real situations instead of having to contrive artificial situations for the purpose of quasi-experimental investigations (Harvey & Myers, 1995). While Yang (2003) argues that it is not feasible to spend a year or two investigating one online community as part of an ethnography, this is exactly the type of approach that was taken to evaluate the proposed character theory, partially due to the author receiving formal training in this method. Yang's approach, while allowing the gathering of diverse and varied information, would not allow the research to experience the completeness of Kim's (2000) membership lifecycle, or be able to fully evaluate the character theory and whether the characters in it can be identified.

Location and Participants

An online community was selected for study, this one serving Wales and those with an interest in the geographical locations of Pontypridd and the Rhondda and Cynon Valleys in South Wales. Its members consist of workers, business owners, elected members, and expatriates of the area the online community serves. This online community, known to its members as 'Ponty Town', with 'Ponty' being the shortened term for Pontypridd, was chosen by the author due to his cognitive interest in the Pontypridd constituency and his belief that he would be a representative member of the community and fit in due to holding similar personal interests to the members. This is in line with Figallo (1998), who argues that similar interests is what convinces some members of online communities to form and maintain an Internet presence. The members of the community each had their own user ID and username that they used to either portray or mask their identity. They ranged from actual names, such as 'Mike Powell' and 'Karen Roberts' that

were used by elected representatives, names from popular culture, such as 'Pussy Galore', to location-based and gendered names, such as 'Ponty Girl', 'Bonty Boy' and 'Kigali Ken'.

Equipment and Materials

A Web browser was used to view and engage with the online community, and a word processor used to record data from the community.

Procedure

The author joined the online community under investigation and interacted with the other members. The community members did not know the author personally, however, he utilized his real name. Even though the author could have posted under a pseudonym it would have made the study less ecologically valid and more difficult for the author to assess the reaction of the participants. The author carried out activities in the online community by following the membership lifecycle stages, which manifested in not posting any responses, posting a few responses on specific topics to regularly posting as an active member of the community. Additionally, data collected by Livingstone and Bober (2006) was used to understand the results.

Results

Undertaking the ethnography proved to be time consuming, though revealing about the nature of online communities and the characteristics of the actors that use them. Of the eleven characters identified in the proposed character theory, eight were found in the investigated online community.

Lurkers could be identified by looking at the member list, where it was possible to find that 45 of the 369 members were lurkers in that they did not post any messages.

The Troll

The troll was easily identified as an actor that went by the pseudonym Pussy Galore, who even managed to provoke the author.

This Bishop baiting is so good I'm sure there will soon be a debate in the Commons that will advocate abolishing it. – Pussy Galore, Female, Pontypridd

Some of the troll's comments may be flames, but their intention is not to cause offence, but to present an alternative and sometimes intentionally provocative viewpoint, often taking on the role of devil's advocate by presenting a position that goes against the grain of the community.

There is some evidence of the troll existing in the data collected by Livingstone and Bober (2006), as out of a total of 996 responses, 10.9% (164) of those interviewed agreed that it is 'fun to be rude or silly on the internet'.

The Big Man

Evidence of actors being driven by order forces was also apparent, as demonstrated by the following comment from a big man.

I don't think so. Why should the actions of (elected member) attacking me unprovoked, and making remarks about my disability lead to ME getting banned? I am the victim of a hate crime here. – The Victim, Male, Trefforest

The example above clearly demonstrates the role of the big man as absorbing the conflicts of the community and having to take responsibility for the actions of others. While the big man may appear similar to the snert by challenging the actions of others, their intention is to promote their own worldview, rather than to flame and offend another person. The big man may resemble the troll by continually presenting alternative view-points, but their intention is not to provoke a flame war based on a viewpoint they do not have, but to justify a position they do have.

The importance of the big man to the community was confirmed approximately a year after the ethnography was completed when during additional observations, a particular actor, ValleyBoy, appeared to take over the role from the big man that was banned, and another member, Stinky, called for banned members to be allowed to return, suggesting the community was lacking strong and persistent characters, such as the big man.

The Flirt

In the studied online community, there was one remarkable member who posted mostly constructive posts in response to others' messages, known by her pseudonym Ponty Girl who was clearly identifiable as a flirt. Her comments as a whole appear to promote sociability as she responds constructively to others' posts. The flirt's approach to dealing with others appears to differ from the big man who absorbs conflict as it seems to resonate with the constructive sides of actors leading them to be less antagonistic towards the flirt than they would be the big man.

Yes, I've seen him at the train station on quite a few occasions," "A friend of mine in work was really upset when she had results from a feedback request from our team - I'd refused to reply on the principle that she is my friend and I would not judge her, but a lot of the comments said that she was rude, unsympathetic and aloof. She came to me to ask why people thought so badly of her. – Ponty Girl, Female, Graig

The Snert

There were a significant number of members of the community that responded to posts in an anti-social manner, characteristic of snerts.

While members like Stinkybolthole frequently posted flames, the online community studied had one very noticeable snert, who went by the name of JH, whom from a sample of ten of his posts, posted six flames, meaning 60% of his posts were flames.

Nobody gives a shit what you want to talk to yourself about. Get a life," "I'm getting the picture. 'Fruitcake Becomes Councilor' is such an over-used newspaper headline these days," "Sounds like you've won the lottery and haven't told us. Either that or your husband is a lawyer, accountant or drug dealer,, "The sooner we start to re-colonize ooga-booga land the better, then we'll see Britains (sic) prosperity grow. Bloody pc wimps, they need to get laid. – JH, Male, Trallwn

The existence of the snert is evident. The data collected by Livingstone and Bober (2006) reveals that from a sample of 1,511, 8.5% (128) of individuals have received nasty comments by e-mail and 7% (105) have received nasty comments in a chat room. Of the 406 that had received nasty comments across different media, 156 (38.42%) deleted them straight away. A total of 124 (30.54%) tried to block messages from the snert, 84 (20.69%) told a relative, 107 (26.35%) told a friend, 74 (18.23%) replied to ask the snert to stop their comments, and 113 (27.83%) engaged in a flame war with the snert.

The e-Venger

Evident in the online community investigated was the masked e-venger, who in the case of this particular community was an actor who signed up with the pseudonym elected member, claiming to be an elected representative on the local council, who the members quickly identified to be someone who had been banned from the community in the past. This user appeared to have similar ways of posting to the snert, posting flames and harassing other members. The difference between the

e-venger and the snert is that the former is driven by wanting to get even for mistreatment in the past whereas the latter responds unconstructive to the present situation.

Poor sad boy, have you met him? He's so incompitent (sic). His dissabilty (sic) is not medical it's laughable. The lad has no idea about public perception," "Don't give me this sh#t, she and they cost a fortune to the taxpayer, you and I pay her huge salary. This is an ex-education Cabinet Member who was thrown out by the party, un-elected at the next election and you STILL pay her wages!", "I'll see you at the Standards meeting [Mellow Pike]. 'Sponsor me to put forward a motion'! Bring it on. – Elected Member

The member appeared to be driven by emotional stimuli activating vengeance forces, seeking to disrupt the community and even making personal attacks on the members including the author. As outlined above, the data collected by Livingstone and Bober (2006) reveals that 27.83% of people that are flamed will seek revenge by posting a flame back.

The MHBFY Jenny

Sometimes the remarks of members such as flirts and big men are accepted, which can lead other actors to experience emotional stimuli activating forgiveness forces as was the case with Dave, the investigated online community's MHBFY Jenny.

Mind you it was funny getting you to sign up again as 'The Victim'. – Dave, Male, Pontypridd

While many of the MHBFY Jenny's comments are constructive like the flirt, they differ because the former responds to their internal dialogue as was the case with Dave above, whereas the flirt responds to external dialogue from other actors, as Ponty Girl clearly does.

The Chat Room Bob

The online community investigated, like many, had its own chat room Bob. The actor taking on this role in the investigated online community went by the name of Kigali Ken, and his contributions make one wonder whether he would say the same things in a real-world community.

Any smart women in Ponty these days? Or any on this message board? I've been out of the country for a while but now I'm back am looking for some uncomplicated sex. Needless to say I am absolutely lovely and have a massive... personality. Any women with an attitude need not apply. – Kigali Ken, Male, Pontypridd

While their action of seeking out others may appear to be flirting using the vernacular definition, the intention of the chat room Bob differs from the flirt who based on Heskell's (2001) definition is someone who feels great about themselves and resonates this to the world to make others feel good, as they will make pro-social comments about others and in response to others. The chat room Bob on the other hand, appears to be only after their own gratification, responding to their physical wants.

The existence of the chat room Bob is evident. The data collected by Livingstone and Bober (2006) reveals that 394 people from a sample of 1,511 have reported that they have received sexual comments from other users. Of these 238 (60.4%) deleted the comment straight away, 170 (43.14%) attempted to block the other person, 49 (12.44%) told a relative, 77 (19.54%) told a friend, and 75 (19.04%) responded to the message. This suggests that the chat room Bob is an unwanted character in online communities whose contributions people will want to delete and whom they may try to block.

The Ripper, Wizard, and Iconoclast

Despite studying the online community for over a year, there was no evidence of there being a ripper, a wizard or an iconoclast in the community, beyond the administrators of the site posting and deleting content and adding new features, such as polls. The closest an actor came to being a ripper was an actor called choppy, who faked a suicide and then claimed a friend had hijacked their account. Fortunately, it might be argued that a true ripper who was seeking to cause self-harm was not present, but the existence of this type of online community member should lead online community managers to show concern for them, and members should not reply with comments such as "murder/suicide" when they ask for advice, as happens in some online communities.

While visual representations are often absent from bulletin board communities, actors will often make their first interpretations of others in virtual worlds when they book at another's avatar and evaluates them based on their worldview, which may provoke a relation leading to the actor developing an interest in the other actor. In the context of online communities, an avatar is a digital representative of an actor in a virtual environment that can be an icon of some kind or an animated object (Stevens, 2004). According to Aizpurua et al. (2004), the effective modeling of the appearance of an avatar is essential to catch a consumer's attention and making them believe that they are someone, with avatars being crucial to creating interaction between customers and vendors. According to Puccinelli (2006), many vendors understand that customers' decisions to engage in economic transactions are often influenced by their reactions to the person who sells or promotes it, which seems to suggest that the appearance of an avatar will affect the number of transactions other actors will have with it.

A STEREOTYPE THEORY FOR INTERPRETING AVATARS IN ONLINE COMMUNITIES

Technology-enhanced businesses led by business leaders of a black ethnicity have been some of the most innovative in the world, with companies like Golden State Mutual ending the 1950s with electronic data processing systems in place, $133 million of insurance in force and $16 million in assets (Ingham & Feldman, 1994). Representations of black actors have also been some of the most studied, with potential applications for studying avatars in online communities. Alvarado et al. (1987) argue that black actors fit into four social classifications: the exotic, the humourous, the dangerous and the pitied. Furthermore, Malik (2002) suggests that male black actors are stereotyped as patriarchal, timid, assiduous, and orthodox. Evidence for these can easily be found in contemporary print media, such as Arena magazine (Croghton, 2007) where an advertisement for an electronic gaming system displays a black individual as pitied. In the same publication Murray and Mobasser (2007) argue that the Internet is damaging relationships, where images of women are of those in 'perfect' bodies, and although they do not define what a perfect body is, it would be safe to assume they mean those depicted in the publication, such as Abigail Clancy and Lily Cole, the later of which described herself as 'hot stuff', and perhaps depictions of this sort could be iconographic of an exotic avatar. Alvarado et al. (1987) supported by Malik (2002) have argued that these stereotypes have been effective in generating revenue for advertisers and not-for-profit organizations. While these stereotypes may be useful for developing an understanding of avatars and how they can generate both social and economic capital for individuals, they need to be put into the context of a psychological understanding of how actors behave and interact with others.

Utilizing the ecological cognition framework (Bishop, 2007a; 2007c); it can be seen that the visual appearance of an actor's avatar could be based on the five binary-opposition forces, with some of the stereotypes identified earlier mapping on to these forces. The image of actors as orthodox and pariahs can be seen to map onto the forces occupied by the flirts and snerts, respectively; the assiduous and vanguard stereotypes appear to be in harmony with the forces occupied by the wizard and iconoclast, respectively, the dangerous and timid stereotypes are consistent with the forces connected with the e-venger and MHBFY Jenny, the exotic and pitied stereotypes can be seen to map on to the forces used by the chat room Bob and ripper, respectively, and the patriarchal and humourous stereotypes appear to be consistent with the forces, respectively, used by the big man and troll. The stereotype theory provides a useful basis for investigating the role of avatars in online communities and the effect they have on social and economic transactions.

Location and Participants

A study was carried out in the second life virtual world and involved analyzing the avatars used to create a visual representation of the actor and profile pages displaying their personal details and avatar of 189 users, known as residents, of the community who met the criteria of having given at least one rating to another actor, a feature that has since been discontinued in the system despite it showing how popular a particular actor was.

Equipment and Materials

The Second Life application was used to view and engage with the online community, and a word processor and spreadsheet was used to record data from the community in the form of the number of times a person had received a gift or response from another.

Table 2. Mean (M) dollars ($) given and received by actors of specific avatars and their ROI (%)

Stereotype	Character	N	M Given $	M Received $	M ROI %
Exotic	Chat Room Bob	30	1171.67	1731.67	237.26
Pitied	Ripper	11	1743.18	2534.09	141.19
Humourous	Troll	48	362.5	446.35	120.69
Patriarchal	Big Man	17	4500	4588.24	428.43
Orthodox	Flirt	16	4393.75	4575	49.48
Pariah	Snert	26	149.04	107.69	-1.24
Assiduous	Wizard	16	267.19	159.38	-12.63
Vanguard	Iconoclast	4	75	162.5	233.33
Dangerous	E-venger	6	2587.5	2095.83	0.62
Timid	MHBFY Jenny	15	6150	4395	101.82

Procedure

The author became a member of the online community under investigation and interacted with the other members over a period of three months. The members of the community did not know the author, especially as a pseudonym was adopted, as is the norm with Second Life. The author carried out activities in the online community by following the membership lifecycle stages that each individual member of an online community goes through as discussed earlier in the chapter. A search was done for actors and possible locations and groups of specific avatars identified. After an avatar was categorized, data from their profile was recorded and the return on investment (ROI) calculated. According to Stoehr (2002), calculating the ROI is a way of expressing the benefit-cost ratio of a set of transactions, and can be used to justify an e-commerce proposal.

Results

The results, as summarized in Table 2, reveal that the avatar with greatest return on investment was the patriarchal stereotype with a 428.43% return and the one with the least ROI was the assiduous

with a 12.63% loss. The most common avatar was the humorous, followed by exotic and pariah. The least common avatar was the vanguard, followed by the dangerous and pitied.

An independent samples test using the Mann-Whitey method was carried out on one of the highest ROI avatars, the patriarchal, with one of the lowest, the pariah. It revealed, as expected, a significant difference in the return on investment ($Z=-3.21$, $p<0.002$). Also interesting was the difference between the specific attributes rated. The mean appearance rating for the patriarchal stereotype was 29.24 compared to 17.27 for the pariah ($Z=-3.10$, $p<0.003$), the mean building rating for the patriarchal was 29.03 compared to 17.40 for the pariah ($Z=-3.06$, $p<0.003$), and the mean behavior rating was 30.62 for the patriarchal stereotype and 16.37 for the pariah ($Z=-3.68$, $p<0.001$). This would seem to suggest that as well as not getting as high a return on investment, other actors will not judge the more antisocial-looking pariah as well as they judge the more sophisticated-looking patriarchal avatar. Examples of the avatars are presented in Figure 3. Studies such as those by Zajonc (1962) and Goldstein (1964) have demonstrated that actors will seek to avoid the uncovering of beliefs and other thoughts that

Figure 1. Examples of avatars in order top-bottom, left-right as Table 2

come about when an actor experiences threatening behavior from others or uncomfortable emotions. This being the case, it could be that when an actor is presented with an avatar that causes them discomfort or 'dissonance', then they will seek to resolve the conflict created by avoiding that particular avatar. This would explain why the pariah stereotype produces a limited number of economic transactions and has the one of the worst returns on investment, which would seem to support the findings of Eagly et al. (1991) that people that appear less discomforting are more popular with peers and receive preferential treatment from others.

THE FUTURE OF SOCIAL NETWORKING COMMUNITIES

In science fiction, the future is often portrayed as utopian or dystopian, where possible future outcomes of social trends or changes that are the result of scientific discoveries are depicted and the implications of them assessed (Csicsery-Ronay, 2003). In the cyberpunk genre of science fiction, the dystopian future is often made up of corporations, who ruthlessly corrupt, corrode, exploit and destroy (Braidotti, 2003). Social networking communities are quickly being subsumed into corporate structures. In July 2005, News Corporation bought Myspace.com, which is a social

networking service that integrates message boards with personal homepages and utilizes the Circle of Friends social networking technique, and in December of that year, the British broadcaster ITV bought the old school tie-based Friends Reunited social networking service (BBC, 2005; Scott-Joynt, 2005).

The ecological cognition framework has the potential to radically transform minor Web sites into highly persuasive and engaging communities where relationships between vendors and customers can be enhanced and the goals of each can be met. While there is also the possibility that a corporation that understands online communities can manipulate its members in such a way that it can easily exploit them, the model could be used by vendors with more of an interest in helping customers meet their goals to market their products and services effectively. Vendors that understand the stage of Kim's (2000) lifecycle they are at and the stage the consumer is at can more effectively target their messages in such a way that they are persuasive. Using the model, vendors can design avatars that provoke the particular responses they want from customers and continue that initial appeal by adopting the appropriate character type. This works well in some media texts where according to Kress (2004) media producers can use the appearance of their characters to convey that character's personality and build on that throughout the text.

DISCUSSION

The rise of online communities in Internet environments has set in motion an unprecedented shift in power from vendors of goods and services to the customers who buy them, with those vendors who understand this transfer of power and choose to capitalize on it by organizing online communities and being richly rewarded with both peerless customer loyalty and impressive economic returns. A type of online community, the virtual world, could radically alter the way people work, learn, grow consume, and entertain. Understanding the exchange of social and economic capital in virtual worlds could involve looking at what causes actors to spend their scarce resources on improving someone else's reputation. Actors' reputations may affect how willing others are to trade with them or even give them gifts, and their reputation is in part influenced by their appearance and how they interact with other actors and often feedback from other actors are displayed on their profile.

The ecological cognition framework provides a theoretical model for developing a character theory for online communities based on bulletin board and chat room models. The five forces and their opposites can be used to develop the types, and the judgments of ignorance and temperance can be used to explain the behavior of those that do not participate, namely lurkers, which were accounted for in the investigated online community where it was possible to find that 45 of the 369 members were lurkers for the reason that they did not post any messages. The ECF would suggest that chaos forces drive trolls, as they attempt to provoke other members into responding as a result of experiencing mental stimuli. The troll was easily identified in the investigated online community as an actor that went by the pseudonym Pussy Galore, who even managed to provoke the author. Order forces can be seen to drive the big man and was represented in the investigated online community by the victim. Those actors who are plainly obnoxious and offend or harass other actors through posting flames are known as snerts, who were most obviously represented in the investigated online community by a user called JH. Flirts are members that respond to the text posted by other members as social stimuli, and will respond to it after activating their social forces and in the studied online community there was one remarkable member who posted mostly constructive posts in response to others' messages, know by her pseudonym Ponty Girl. There are actors driven by their vengeance forces, which could be labeled as e-venegers, represented in the investigated online community by elected member and those actors driven by forgiveness forces could be called MBHFY Jenny, represented in the studied online community by Dave. An actor in an online community that is driven by existential forces, known to many as the chat room Bob, who seeks out members who will share nude pictures or engage in sexual relations with them, was apparent in the investigated online community using the name Kigali Ken. There is evidence for an online community member driven by thanatotic forces, who could be called a ripper, but this member was not found in the investigated online community beyond an actor called Choppy. There are also theoretically two more characters in online communities, driven by action stimuli that results in them experiencing creative or destructive forces, with the one driven by creative forces being the wizard, and the opposite of iconoclast being the one that seeks to destroy content in online communities.

These character types are particularly evidenced in bulletin board communities, but in the virtual world it is likely that an actor's avatar will have some effect on how others perceive them before they are spoken to. The extent to which an actor is able to sustain an appeal to another could be analyzed as seduction. An actor's avatar forms an important part of the intimacy stage of seduction, as the visual appearance of an actor could possibly have an impact on how others perceived them, and an actor may construct an image based on their identity or the image they want to project and the relationship between an actor's avatar and their identity can be understood as elastic as even the best and strongest elastic can break, with there being the possibility that avatars can develop to the point where connection between them and the identities of the actors using them can be stretched so far that they cease to exist. There has been a debate over whether identity is unitary or multiple with psychoanalytic theory playing a complicated role in the debate. If there is a lifecycle to an actor's membership in an online community, then it is likely that they will develop different cognitions, such as beliefs and values at different stages that may become 'joindered'. This would mean that an actor's behavior would be affected by the beliefs and values they developed when joining the community when they are at a more advanced stage in their membership of the community. Utilizing the ecological cognition framework, it can be seen that the visual appearance of an actor's avatar could be based on the five binary-opposition forces, with some of the stereotypes identified earlier mapping on to these forces. The investigation found that the avatar with the greatest return on investment was the patriarchal stereotype with a 428.43% return and the one with the least ROI was the assiduous with a 12.63% loss. The most common avatar was the humorous, followed by exotic and pariah. The least common avatar was the vanguard, followed by the dangerous and pitied. An independent samples test revealed, as expected, a significant differences between the pariah and the patriarchal stereotype with the later having a greater return on investment, and higher ratings on appearance, building and behavior, suggesting that as not getting as high a return on investment, other actors will not judge the more antisocial-looking pariah as well as they judge the more sophisticated-looking patriarchal avatar.

The research methods used in this study were an ethnographical observation and document analysis. These methods seem particularly suited to online communities, where behavior can be observed through participation and further information can be gained through analyzing user profiles and community forums. The study has demonstrated that online communities, in particular virtual worlds, can be viewed as a type of media, and traditional approaches to media, such as investigating stereotypes, can be applied to Internet-based environments.

ACKNOWLEDGMENT

The author would like to acknowledge all the reviewers that provided feedback on earlier drafts of this chapter. In addition the author would like to thank S. Livingstone and M. Bober from the Department of Media and Communications at the London School of Economics and Political Science for collecting some of the data used in this study, which was sponsored by a grant from the Economic and Social Research Council. The Centre for Research into Online Communities and E-Learning Systems is part of Glamorgan Blended Learning Ltd., which is a Knowledge Transfer Initiative, supported by the University of Glamorgan through the GTi Business Network of which it is a member.

REFERENCES

Aizpurua, I., Ortix, A., Oyarzum, D., Arizkuren, I., Ansrés, A., Posada, J., & Iurgel, I. (2004). Adaption of mesh morphing techniques for avatars used in Web applications. In: F. Perales & B. Draper (Eds.), *Articulated motion and deformable objects: Third international workshop*. London: Springer.

Anon. (2003). *Net grief for online 'suicide'*. Retrieved from http://news.bbc.co.uk/1/hi/technology/2724819.stm

Armstrong, A., & Hagel, J. (1997). *Net gain: Expanding markets through virtual communities.* Boston, MA: Harvard Business School Press.

BBC. (2005). *ITV buys Friends Reunited Web site.* London: BBC Online. Retrieved from http://news.bbc.co.uk/1/hi/business/4502550.stm.

Beaty, J., Hunter, P., & Bain, C. (1998). *The Norton introduction to literature.* New York, NY: W.W. Norton & Company.

Berne, E. (1961). *Transactional analysis in psychotherapy.* New York, NY: Evergreen.

Berne, E. (1964). *Games people play: The psychology of human relationships.* New York, NY: Deutsch.

Bernstein, T., & Wagner, J. (1976). *Reverse dictionary.* London: Routledge.

Bishop, J. (2002). *Development and evaluation of a virtual community.* Unpublished dissertation. http://www.jonathanbishop.com/ publications/display.aspx?Item=1.

Bishop, J. (2003). Factors shaping the form of and participation in online communities. *Digital Matrix, 85,* 22-24.

Bishop, J. (2005). The role of mediating artefacts in the design of persuasive e-learning systems. In: *Proceedings of the Internet Technology & Applications 2005 Conference.* Wrexham: North East Wales Institute of Higher Education.

Bishop, J. (2006). Social change in organic and virtual communities: An exploratory study of bishop desires. *Paper presented to the Faith, Spirituality and Social Change Conference.* University of Winchester.

Bishop, J. (2007a). The psychology of how Christ created faith and social change: Implications for the design of e-learning systems. *Paper presented to the 2nd International Conference on Faith, Spirituality, and Social Change.* University of Winchester.

Bishop, J. (2007b). Increasing participation in online communities: A framework for human-computer interaction. *Computers in Human Behavior, 23,* 1881-1893.

Bishop, J. (2007c). Ecological cognition: A new dynamic for human computer interaction. In: B. Wallace, A. Ross, J. Davies, & T. Anderson (Eds.), *The mind, the body and the world* (pp. 327-345). Exeter: Imprint Academic.

Braidotti, R. (2003). Cyberteratologies: Female monsters negotiate the other's participation in humanity's far future. In: M. Barr (Ed.), *Envisioning the future: Science fiction and the next millennium.* Middletown, CT: Wesleyan University Press.

Bressler, S., & Grantham, C. (2000). *Communities of commerce.* New York, NY: McGraw-Hill.

Campbell, J., Fletcher, G., & Greenhil, A. (2002). Tribalism, conflict and shape-shifting identities in online communities. *Proceedings of the 13th Australasia Conference on Information Systems.* Melbourne, Australia.

Chak, A. (2003). *Submit now: Designing persuasive Web sites.* London: New Riders Publishing.

Chan, T-S. (1999). *Consumer behavior in Asia.* New York, NY: Haworth Press.

Croughton, P. (2007). *Arena: The original men's style magazine.* London: Arena International.

Csicsery-Ronay, I. (2003). Marxist theory and science fiction. In: E. James & F. Mendlesohn (Eds.), *The Cambridge companion to science fiction.* Cambridge: Cambridge University Press.

Eagly, A., Ashmore, R., Makhijani, M., & Longo, L. (1991). What is beautiful is good, but…: A meta-analytic review of research on the physical attractiveness stereotype. *Psychological Bulletin, 110*(1), 109-128.

Feller, J. (2005). *Perspectives on free and open source software.* Cambridge, MA: The MIT Press.

Figallo, C. (1998). *Hosting Web communities: Building relationships, increasing customer loyalty and maintaining a competitive edge.* Chichester: John Wiley & Sons.

Freud, S. (1933). *New introductory lectures on psycho-analysis.* New York, NY: W.W. Norton & Company, Inc.

Givens, D. (1978). The non-verbal basis of attraction: Flirtation, courtship and seduction. *Journal for the Study of Interpersonal Processes, 41*(4), 346-359.

Goffman, E. (1959). *The presentation of self in everyday life.* Garden City, NY: Doubleday.

Goldstein, M. (1964). Perceptual reactions to threat under varying conditions of measurement. *Journal of Abnormal and Social Psychology, 69*(5), 563-567.

Harvey, L., & Myers, M. (1995). Scholarship and practice: The contribution of ethnographic research methods to bridging the gap. *Information Technology and People, 8*(3), 13-27.

Heskell, P. *Flirt Coach: Communication tips for friendship, love and professional success.* London: Harper Collins Publishers Limited.

Ingham, J., & Feldman, L. (1994). *African-American business leaders: A biographical dictionary.* Westport, CT: Greenwood Press.

Jansen, E. (2002). *Netlingo: The Internet dictionary.* Ojai, CA: Independent Publishers Group.

Jordan, T. (1999). *Cyberpower: An introduction to the politics of cyberspace.* London: Routledge.

Kiesler, S., & Sproull, L. (1992). Group decision making and communication technology. *Organizational Behavior and Human Decision Processes, 52*(1), 96-123.

Kim, A. (2000). *Community building on the Web: Secret strategies for successful online communities.* Berkeley, CA: Peachpit Press.

Kress, N. (2004). *Dynamic characters: How to create personalities that keep readers captivated.* Cincinnati, OH: Writer's Digest Books.

Kyttä, M. (2003). *Children in outdoor contexts: Affordances and independent mobility in the assessment of environmental child friendliness.* Doctoral dissertation presented at Helsinki University of Technology, Espoo, Finland.

Li, D., Li, J., & Lin, Z. (2007). Online consumer-to-consumer market in China—a comparative study of Taobao and eBay. *Electronic Commerce Research and Applications,* doi:10.1016/j.elerap.2007.02.010.

Lindahl, C., & Blount, E. (2003). Weblogs: Simplifying Web publishing. *IEEE Computer, 36*(11), 114-116.

Livingstone, S., & Bober, M. (2006). *Children go online, 2003-2005.* Colchester, Essex: UK Data Archive.

Malik, S. (2002). *Representing black Britain: A history of black and Asian images on British television.* London: Sage Publications.

Mantovani, F. (2001). Networked seduction: A test-bed for the study of strategic communication on the Internet. *CyberPsychology & Behavior, 4*(1), 147-154.

Mena, J. (1999). *Data mining your Web site.* Oxford: Digital Press.

Mann, C., & Stewart, F. (2000). *Internet communication and qualitative research: A handbook for Research Online.* London: Sage Publications.

Mitchell, W. (2005). *What do pictures want?: The lives and loves of images.* Chicago, IL: University of Chicago Press.

Murray, S., & Mobasser, A. (2007). Is the Internet killing everything?. In: P. Croughton (Ed.), *Arena: The original men's style magazine.* London: Arena International.

Orengo Castellá, V., Zornoza Abad, A., Prieto Alonso, F., & Peiró Silla, J. (2000). The influence of familiarity among group members, group atmosphere and assertiveness on uninhibited behavior through three different communication media. *Computers in Human Behavior, 16,* 141-159.

Orczy, E. (1905). *The scarlet pimpernel.* Binding Unknown.

Propp, V. (1969). *Morphology of the folk tale.* Austin, TX: University of Texas Press.

Puccinelli, N. (2006). Putting your best face forward: The impact of customer mood on salesperson evaluation. *Journal of Consumer Psychology, 16*(2), 156-162.

Rhiengold, H. (2000). *The virtual community: Homesteading on the electronic frontier.* London: The MIT Press.

Scott-Joynt, J. (2005). *What Myspace means to Murdoch.* London: BBC Online. Retrieved from http://news.bbc.co.uk/1/hi/business/4697671. stm.

Shen, X., Radakrishnan, T., & Georganas, N. (2002). vCOM: Electronic commerce in a collaborative virtual worlds. *Electronic Commerce Research and Applications, 1,* 281-300.

Smith, C. (2000). Content analysis and narrative analysis. In: H. Reis & C. Judd (Eds.), *Handbook of research methods in social and personal psychology.* Cambridge: Cambridge University Press.

Sternberg, R. (1986). A triangular theory of love. *Psychological Review, 93*(2), 119-135.

Stevens, V. (2004). Webhead communities: Writing tasks interleaved with synchronous online communication and Web page development. In: J. Willis & B. Leaver (Eds.), *Task-based instruction in foreign language education: Practices and programs.* Georgetown, VA: Georgetown University Press.

Stoehr, T. (2002). *Managing e-business projects: 99 key success factors.* London: Springer.

Turkle. (1997). *Life on the screen: Identity in the age of the Internet.* New York, NY: Touchstone.

Vogel, D. (1999). *Financial investigations: A financial approach to detecting and resolving crimes.* London: DIANE Publishing.

Wallace, P. (2001). *The psychology of the Internet.* Cambridge: Cambridge University Press.

Werry, C. (2001). Imagined electronic community: Representations of online community in business texts. In: C. Werry & M. Mowbray (Eds.), *Online communities: Commerce, community action and the virtual university.* Upper Saddle River, NJ: Prentice Hall.

Yang, G. (2003). The Internet and the rise of a transnational Chinese cultural sphere. *Media, Culture & Society, 25,* 469-490.

Zajonc, R. (1962). Response suppression in perceptual defense. *Journal of Experimental Psychology, 64,* 206-214.

Chapter V
Collective Solitude and Social Networks in World of Warcraft*

Nicolas Ducheneaut
Palo Alto Research Center, USA

Nicholas Yee
Palo Alto Research Center, USA

ABSTRACT

This chapter investigates the nature and structure of social networks formed between the players of massively multiplayer online games (MMOGs), an incredibly popular form of Internet-based entertainment attracting millions of subscribers. To do so, we use data collected about the behavior of more than 300,000 characters in World of Warcraft (the most popular MMOG in America). We show that these social networks are often sparse and that most players spend time in the game experiencing a form of "collective solitude": they play surrounded by, but not necessarily with, other players. We also show that the most successful player groups are analogous to the organic, team-based forms of organization that are prevalent in today's workplace. Based on these findings, we discuss the relationship between online social networks and "real-world" behavior in organizations in more depth.

INTRODUCTION

Online gaming has become a phenomenon of growing social, cultural, and economic importance. From the pioneering, text-only MUDs of the 1990s (Curtis, 1992; Cuciz, 2001) to today's rich, graphical 3-D environments, the market has grown to more than 13 million players (Woodcock, 2005) and generated revenues of more than 5 billion dollars in 2007. Growth is still considerable and estimated at about 25% per year for the foreseeable future (Olausson, 2007).

Figure 1. A night elf priest riding his mount

One behemoth stands out among all these lucrative massively multiplayer online games (MMOGs): World of Warcraft (WoW). As of today, more than 8 millions subscribers worldwide (Blizzard, 2007) are interacting, competing, and collaborating in WoW's online world. WoW was designed around a template broadly similar to other games in the same genre, itself inspired by the more traditional pen-and-paper role-playing games like Dungeons and Dragons (Fine, 1983). Like its predecessors, the game takes place in a persistent universe where there is no clear beginning and end and no set schedule. To enter the game players first create one or several "avatars" from a set of classes (e.g., magician, warrior) and races (e.g., night elves, orcs) as digital representations of themselves. Once this character is created, players can begin questing in a medieval-fantasy world broadly inspired from the works of authors such as J.R.R. Tolkien.

Azeroth (the world of WoW) is an extremely vast and richly detailed 3-D environment (see Figure 1). Players can fight dangerous creatures (which may include other players) and explore the game's two continents alone or in the company of others while undertaking quests. This allows them to earn "experience points" and reach progressively higher "levels" (60 was the maximum at the time of our analyses[1]), improving the abilities of their character and acquiring powerful items along the way.

Like its predecessors in the same genre, WoW is highly collaborative by design (Taylor, 2006): players often have to band together to accomplish the game's objectives, and trading items and information is essential to a player's advancement (Nardi & Harris, 2006). While some player groups can be short-lived (e.g., ad-hoc "pick up groups" formed by strangers to accomplish a difficult quest, and disbanded afterwards), many crystallize into more stable social networks of various size and complexity. The need for repeated collaboration in online games therefore translates into formal, persistent groups that are supported out-of-the box by nearly all MMOGs: guilds (Figure 2).

Guilds are essential elements in the social life of online gaming communities. They frame a player's experience (Seay, Jerome, Lee, & Kraut, 2004) by providing a stable social backdrop to many game activities, and their members tend to group with others more often and play longer than non-affiliated players (Ducheneaut, Yee, Nickell, & Moore, 2006a). At the "endgame" (when players have reached level 60 and cannot

Figure 2. A guild about to attack a powerful dragon

earn experience points—and levels—anymore), guilds even become indispensable. Indeed, the game's objectives change significantly at this stage. Since players cannot earn points to progress, the only way for them to increase their power is to gain access to powerful items (weapons, sets of armor) guarded by dangerous monsters in complex dungeons ("instances" in WoW's parlance). By design, these instances require a "raid" party of 10, 20, or sometimes up to 40 players at a time. Quite obviously it is almost impossible to assemble a pick-up group of this size—some formal coordination mechanisms are required, and the guilds provide such an environment. Being a member of an "elite" or "uber" guild, renowned for its ability to tackle the hardest challenges, is therefore a badge of honor and essential to progress at the endgame. Admission to these prestigious social groups often requires going through a "trial period," as well as being sponsored by one of the members (Taylor, 2006).

Interestingly, the game's software often provides only very limited tools to support these important player associations: members most commonly have access to an in-game roster showing who is currently logged on and a private chat channel to broadcast messages to them. Guilds, therefore, rely also on an array of important Web-based resources such as forums, Web sites, calendaring tools, and so forth, to organize their activities.

All the elements mentioned above demonstrate that, by design, MMOGs are essentially social engineering experiments. While it would be easy to dismiss them because of their deceivingly simplistic objectives (a comment we often hear: "It's just a game where you kill monsters, right?"), they are in fact social network engines: by casting strangers into an exciting environment filled with complexity and uncertainty, MMOGs offer conditions where players will naturally adopt different roles and responsibilities in order to get things done collaboratively. As such, MMOGs can be fascinating laboratories to observe group dynamics online. Observing the nature and structure of interactions between players in the game world could help us understand some fundamental properties of Internet-based social networks, which could in turn have practical implications for the creation and management of teams in other digital spaces.

In this chapter, we use data we collected over two years about the behavior of more than 300,000 characters in WoW to map the structure and evolution of social networks in this multiplayer game. Using automated "bots" constantly connected to WoW's game servers, we were able to estimate how often and how long players interact with each other in a variety of circumstances. This data lets us easily construct social network graphs representative of these connections, which we can then use to compute various metrics reflecting their most salient properties (e.g., a network's density, that is, how tightly interconnected people are; or a network's number of disconnected subgroups, indicative of fragmentation, etc.). Coupled with other data gathered by our bots (e.g., a character's class, its rate of advancement in the game, etc.), this also lets us assess how one's social relations affect (or are affected by) one's status in the game.

Our findings and analyses focus on two main areas. First, looking at the average structure of social networks across the entire game world, we discuss the reasons behind a surprisingly low level of network density in guilds. Indeed, it looks as if most players spend time in the game experiencing a form of "collective solitude" (Malaby, 2003): they play surrounded by, but not necessarily with, other players and guild members. Second, we examine the structural social network variables reflecting how organized guilds can be. Looking at these variables over time, we can see which properties of a guild's organization can help the group survive (or not). It turns out the most successful guilds are analogous to the organic, team-based forms of organization that are prevalent in today's workplace. We discuss this relationship between online social networks and "real-world" behavior in organizations in more depth.

To better understand how we were able to reach these conclusions, we begin below by presenting some additional background information about WoW and games research more generally, as well as describing our methods in more detail.

BACKGROUND AND METHODS

The Need for New Approaches to Online Gaming Research

Due to their increasing popularity and visibility in the mainstream media, online games have become a topic of active research in recent years. A great deal of work has been concerned with the social and cultural dimensions of these games: authors such as Yee (2001; 2002), Castranova (2003), Jakobson and Taylor (2003), and Bartle (2004) have all contributed early insights about the social dynamics of these entertainment communities. However, most of this research tends to be based on self-reports obtained from the players using interviews (Yee, 2001), surveys (Seay, Jerome, Lee, & Kraut, 2004), or ethnographic observations (Taylor, 2003; B. Brown & Bell, 2004). Except for the project we are about to describe in this chapter, until now no studies were based on data obtained directly from the game's software.

To address this limitation, we therefore decided to study social activities in MMOGs based on longitudinal data collected directly from games. We use this data to compute "social accounting" (Bernheim Brush, Wang, Combs Turner, & Smith, 2005) metrics allowing us to assess, for instance, how often players group with each other and how this affects their progress in the game. This provides us with a solid empirical foundation to better understand these complex social worlds. Of course, these metrics would be of little value if we did not have direct experience with the game world to put them into context. Our research is therefore complemented by hundreds of hours of playtime: all the contributors to this project have created characters on several different servers, joined guilds, big and small, successful and doomed to failure, since the launch of the game in November 2004. This deep, personal experience with the game's environment frames our analyses and allows us to make sense of our numbers in a contextualized manner.

Our current approach was influenced in great part by an interesting design choice made by Blizzard Entertainment, producers of WoW. Indeed, WoW was built such that its client-side user interface is open to extension and modification by the user community. Thanks to this open interface, we have been able to develop custom applications to collect data directly from the game. In particular, we rely on WoW's "/who" command, which lists the characters currently being played on a given server[2]. We created a "robot" software to periodically issue "/who" requests and take a census of the entire game world every 5 to 15 minutes, depending on server load. Each time a character is observed our software stores an entry of the form:

Alpha,2005/03/4,Crandall,56,Ni,id,y,Felwood,AntKillers.

The above represents a level 56 Night Elf Druid on the server Alpha, currently in the Felwood zone, grouped ("y"), and part of the Ant Killers guild. Using this application we have been collecting data continuously since June 2005 on five different servers: PvE(High) and PvE(Low), respectively high- and low-load player-versus-environment servers; PvP(High) and PvP(Low), their player-versus-player equivalents; and finally RP, a role-playing server. Overall, we have observed more than 300,000 unique characters to date. We then used the accumulated data to compute a variety of metrics reflecting these characters' activities (Ducheneaut, Yee, Nickell, & Moore, 2006a) and, in particular, the structure of their social networks.

To do so, we rely on three variables: the "zone" information, the "grouped" flag, and finally the "guild" data. We assume that characters that are grouped in the same zone are highly likely to be playing together. If so, we create a tie between them, where the strength of the tie is proportional to the cumulative time these characters have spent together. This lets us assess social networks in the game irrespective of formal group membership.

To take the latter into account, we simply enable connections between players only if they belong to the same guild, giving us a picture of social relations in these more formal groups (Figure 3). We then use the accumulated data to compute a variety of social network analysis metrics for each character and each guild, such as their density and fragmentation (Wasserman & Faust, 1994).

The Limitations of Automated Data Collection

Before going any further, it is important to mention some inherent limitations of our data and methods. First, note that we are collecting information about characters, not players. Players often create several characters or "alts" (some actively played, some acting as "mules" for storage and trading). We believe, however, that this does not affect the validity of our analyses for two reasons: 1) our observations show that all the "alts" of a player are generally members of the same guild; 2) except for a few "altoholics," players tend to focus on developing one character exclusively

Figure 3. Social network for a typical small guild. Note the core group and the two isolated triads, as well as the varying strengths of the ties connecting the players. Player nodes are colored based on their class (mages in blue, hunters in green, etc.)

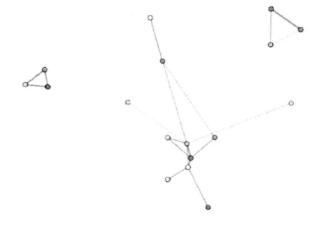

for a reasonably long stretch of time instead of constantly switching between many, simply because WoW's design makes the latter very unproductive—players cannot keep up with the "grind" required to advance and fall behind the rest of their guild. Considering that our sample periods are quite short (one month or less; see next section), it is therefore highly probable that each sample contains on average data limited to a player's current "main," their mule, and perhaps an additional "alt" leveled at the same time. Since we are looking at aggregate, group-level structural measures, not individual patterns of behavior, this relatively uniform spread of the number of characters played at any given time should therefore not skew our analyses too much.

We also rely heavily on a character's location to construct our social networks, which is not immune to distortion. For instance, characters are often left "AFK" (away from keyboard) in the game's main cities before or at the end of a play session—their physical proximity there does not necessarily reflect any kind of joint activity. We therefore exclude cities from our sample when computing social networks. It is also entirely possible for characters from the same guild to be in the same zone and not playing together—they could each be grouped with strangers. While this can be a common occurrence in the "entry level" zones of the games that are densely populated, our experience shows this clearly tapers off as characters gain in level. We therefore believe that while our social networking data might be a bit noisy and possibly creates more (or stronger) ties between guild members than really exist, this effect is not overwhelming.

Finally, while we believe the statistical treatment of large populations of characters yields interesting insights into their collective behavior, it also entirely ignores differences between the individuals controlling each character (Yee, 2006a). It is reasonable to assume, for instance, that players from different demographic segments of the population behave differently in the game (gender

seems like an obvious factor). But since this data was not publicly visible at the game's interface level, we had no choice but to proceed without it. Only a game publisher would be able to correlate demographic factors to in-game behaviors on a large scale since they collect the former as part of their sign-up process. We hope companies in this industry will one day be willing to share such data with the research community.

With this background in mind, we now turn to the analysis of our data.

SOCIAL NETWORKS IN WORLD OF WARCRAFT

Grouping Patterns: A Look at the Prevalence of Social Activities

For many MMOG players "it's the people that are addictive, not the game" (Lazzaro, 2004). Indeed, most of the activities they offer (e.g., developing a character, fighting monsters) are already present in single player games. What makes a difference for many is apparently the shared experience, the collaborative nature of most activities and, most importantly, the reward of being socialized into a community of gamers and acquiring a reputation within it (Yee, 2002; Jakobson & Taylor, 2003). In response to this perceived player need, game developers have therefore designed multiplayer games such that opportunities for interacting with others abound.

WoW encourages players to form groups using two classic mechanisms that were refined in EverQuest, the first widely successful MMOG in the U.S. (EverQuest's game mechanics were inspired in turn by tabletop, pen-and-paper role-playing games such as Dungeons and Dragons (Fine, 1983)). First, character classes have specific abilities that complement each other (e.g., priests are the best healers, warriors the best melee fighters, etc.). As such, grouping with players of a different class should increase efficiency. Second,

Figure 4. Average time spent in a group, by class (color added to facilitate comparison with Figure 5)

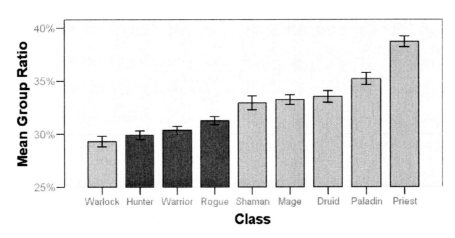

Figure 5. Percentage of the total population playing each class

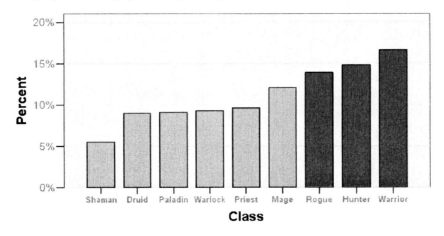

Figure 6. Fraction of time spent in groups, by level

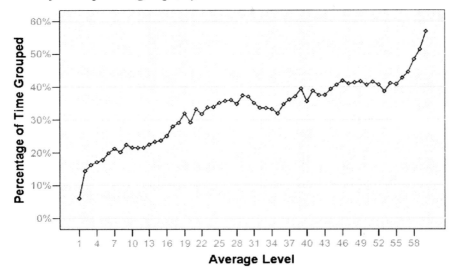

many quests and dungeons in the game are simply too difficult to be tackled alone. Players have to form either a party (5 players maximum) or even a raid (40 players maximum) to have a chance to win the powerful items available in these difficult locations. As players gain levels, an increasing amount of game content requires such groups, up to the "endgame" (level 60) where no dungeons are accessible without a strong party of at least 5 players (and often more).

Despite the complementarity of classes however, some stand a better chance of survival alone than others. For instance, Hunters are accompanied by a powerful pet, effectively allowing a single player to control a two-character unit. In the words of the players we talked to, this makes hunters a more "soloable" class. We computed the average time spent in a group for each class and the numbers clearly reflect their "soloability" (or lack thereof)—see Figure 4. The differences are significant, $F(8,129372) = 152.99$, $p < .001$, with the most soloable class (warlocks) spending about 30% of their time grouped versus the 40% spent by priests at the other end of the distribution. Interestingly, the more "soloable" classes tend to be the most popular. When we computed the

class distribution over the entire population, the three most-played classes (warrior, hunter, and rogue) were among those spending the least time in groups (less than 32%; see Figure 5).

We wondered, however, if grouping behavior changed as characters gained in level. It appears time spent in groups increases about linearly with levels to stabilize at around 40%. There is then a strong increase in grouping starting after level 55 and, starting at level 59, more than half of play time is spent in a group (Figure 6). This reflects the increasing difficulty in fighting the "mobs" (monsters) encountered in high-end dungeons: while soloable classes have an advantage in the early stages of the game where individual quests abound, the progressive emphasis on group tasks mitigates it somewhat later on.

Another interesting aspect to consider is the impact of grouping on progress in the game. We split characters into four bands of grouping ratio (e.g., characters in the 0-1% band were almost never observed to be in a group) and then plotted the average time it took them to complete a level across all the levels. As Figure 7 shows, characters that are never in a group consistently level faster than characters that group at any

Figure 7. Impact of grouping on leveling time

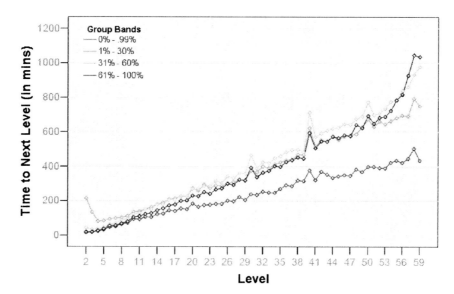

frequency. In fact, the former are about twice as efficient in leveling as the latter. This can probably be explained by the "overhead" induced by grouping: party members have to be recruited and assembled; responsibilities have to be discussed and assigned, and so forth. This significantly cuts into the "productive" time that can be spent killing monsters and earning the experience points needed to progress. For achievement-oriented players (Bartle, 1996; Yee, 2005), this grouping overhead is simply a nuisance and they simply dispense with it, completing most of the early game tasks alone instead. But as we mentioned above, groups cannot be ignored forever and players will have to form parties if they want to enjoy the endgame's content.

This data paints a more nuanced picture of the social nature of MMOGs than was previously available. Grouping is apparently an inefficient way to progress in the beginning stages of the game and many players are not observed to be in a group until they are past level 55. Players prefer "soloable" classes and it is only in the very late stages of the game, where dungeons are simply too difficult to enter alone, that the grouping rate rises. Therefore, WoW seems like a game where the endgame is social, not the game as a whole. One player summarized this situation nicely by saying that, during their first few months in the game world, WoW's subscribers tend to be "alone together": they play *surrounded by* others instead of *playing with* them—a phenomenon we explore in more depth below with the help of social network data.

Collective Solitude: Social Networks in Guilds

The grouping behaviors we just reported indicate that players spend, on average, little time in groups when they first enter WoW, but the metrics we used also tell only one part of the story. Indeed, a player can group with others in a variety of contexts: from pick-up groups quickly formed on the spot

to tackle a tough monster and rapidly disbanded afterwards, to permanent player associations like the guilds we described earlier in this chapter. We wanted to see whether collaborative play was more prevalent in these formal, persistent player groups than in others.

To evaluate the kind of social environment provided by a guild, we built social networks connecting the players in our sample using two different methods: one to assess the guild's *potential for sociability* and the other to quantify *joint activities*. With the first approach, players are connected to each other if they are observed online at the same time, irrespective of their game location (the strength of the tie is proportional to the time two characters overlap). The resulting network reflects the range of opportunities for social interaction in a guild. Indeed, it connects players who have the opportunity to chat using the "guild" channel and who are listed in the "guild members" window each time a player logs on. In other words, it lists the range of guildmates known (but not necessarily talked to or played with) by each player. In social networking terms, these connections could be called weak (Granovetter, 1973) or "bridging" (Putnam, 2000) ties.

Our second type of social network connects players who are observed to be in the same zones of the game, excluding the major cities. Such a network highlights players who are spending time together, grouping with guildmates to run quests and visit dungeons. These are stronger, "bonding" (Putnam, 2000) ties based on mutual interest in the same game activities.

We computed each guild's social network degree density (Table 1) (Wasserman & Faust, 1994). We limited this analysis to guilds having six members or more (densities in small networks can often be unreliable (Wasserman & Faust, 1994)). On average, it seems that players know at most 1 out of 4 members of their guilds, and play only with 1 out of 10 (Table 1, row 1). Guilds are therefore sparsely knit networks—a surprising finding, considering the effects they have

Table 1. Social network densities

Guild size		Co-Presence	Co-Location
All > 6	N	4205	4205
	Mean	0.27	0.09
	Median	0.23	0.06
6 – 15	N	1779	1779
	Mean	0.31	0.12
	Median	0.29	0.08
16 – 30	N	889	889
	Mean	0.27	0.08
	Median	0.25	0.07
31 – 60	N	618	618
	Mean	0.22	0.05
	Median	0.20	0.04
61 – 120	N	367	367
	Mean	0.18	0.03
	Median	0.17	0.02
> 120	N	244	244
	Mean	0.17	0.04
	Median	0.14	0.01

on play patterns. Moreover, density is inversely correlated with size (-.15): as guilds grow, it becomes more difficult to know and play with most of the members.

Since guilds tend to be sparsely knit, we then tried to identify cohesive sub-groups within them. We performed a k-core decomposition (Wasserman & Faust, 1994) for each guild in our five size categories, using the co-location networks. Each k-core is a sub-graph where each player is adjacent to at least k others. The main core (the k-core with the largest k) gives the size of the most cohesive subgroup (Table 2).

The ratio of main core size to guild size is inversely correlated with size (-.17), decreasing from 37% to 12%. In other words, growing a guild

has diminishing returns as far as forming tight play groups is concerned: a smaller and smaller fraction of the additional recruits will join the core. Still, our data illustrates why having a large guild can remain beneficial. Note that, for guilds with 16 to 60 members, the average main core is between 6 and 9. Considering that the basic quest party size in WoW is 5, this probably means that the core players in these guilds can form at least one, sometimes two stable quest groups. Guilds with 61 to 120 members probably have three such groups. And finally, guilds with more than 120 members have a large enough core (about 22) to form a credible raid group in order to tackle the toughest dungeons at the endgame.

We also observed that players belonging to the core of a guild do not simply play with many guildmates, they play with them longer. We computed that, on average, any two members in a guild spend 22.8 minutes playing together over a 30-day period, while for core members the average is 154 minutes. Guild cores are "tight" sub-groups. Finally, our data shows that a large majority (65%) of guilds have a single core group. A few guilds (13%) have two cores, and fewer still (4%) have three.

Figure 8 illustrates the co-location network for a typical, medium-sized guild. Out of the 41 members, 17 were never observed in the same zone as another guildmate. Among the 24 remaining there is a main core of eight players actively playing together, with a really active central trio (their thick ties show they spend a lot of time together). The other 13 players are only peripherally connected and play with two or fewer guildmates.

Table 2. Main core size for the five guild categories

sizeband	N	Minimum	Maximum	Mean	Std. Deviation
6 - 15	1779	0	11	3.59	2.232
16 - 30	889	0	17	6.40	3.042
31 - 60	619	0	39	8.64	4.424
61 - 120	367	1	54	12.14	8.050
≥ 120	244	1	68	21.78	16.489

Figure 8. Co-location network in a medium-sized guild

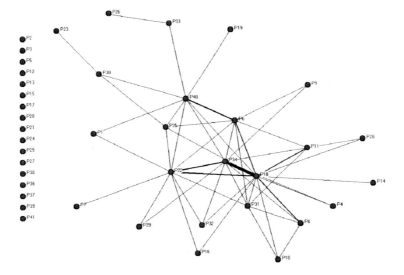

Grouping for Fun and for Profit: Effects of Social Networks on Group Dynamics

In the previous section, we described how social activities in WoW are less prevalent than we might have imagined. In particular, while the endgame is more intensely social, the early stages of the game tend to favor "solo play." This translates into fairly sparse social networks for the game's most central player associations, the guilds.

But while this paints an interesting overview of social life across the entire game population, it is also important to recognize that guilds are incredibly diverse. Some are small groups with pre-existing ties in the physical world and no interest in complex collaborative activities. Others are very large, made up mostly of strangers governed by a command-and-control structure reminiscent of the military. In previous work, we have explored the range of possibilities between these two extremes and documented the motivations that lead players to guilds of one type or the other (Williams et al., 2006). Across all types, one trend was particularly clear: guilds are fragile social groups, and many do not survive very long (see also Ducheneaut, Yee, Nickell, & Moore, 2006a).

This fragility is almost certainly due to a broad combination of factors. Leadership style, for instance, is often cited by players (Williams et al., 2006). Game design is another contributor: players "burn out" due to the intense "grind" required to advance in MMOGs (Yee, 2006b) and leave the game, abandoning their guild at the same time. "Drama" (public conflict between two or more guild members) and internal politics (e.g., arguments over who gets access to the most powerful "loot" dropped by monsters) have also been the demise of many guilds. But it could also be possible that a guild's social network influences the group's eventual fate. Indeed, it seems reasonable to hypothesize that some aspects of the structure of a guild contribute to its eventual success, just like the structure of any organization plays a role in its efficiency (Mintzberg, 1978). The data we gathered about the structure of social networks in guilds gives us an opportunity to answer this question and explore how social relationships formed online affect the eventual survival of a group.

Our data collection software gave us access to the following social network variables:

- **Size:** Number of characters bearing a given guild tag during the sampling period. We hypothesized that size could have a positive impact on a guild's evolution since "the rich get richer" on many WoW servers—that is, a few very large guilds tend to dominate and attract the most dedicated players as a server matures (Ducheneaut, Yee, Nickell, & Moore, 2007).

- **Density:** Connections between guild members can be mapped out as a matrix. The density of a guild is the percentage of matrix cells that are filled in. As we saw earlier and in Ducheneaut, Yee, Nickell, and Moore (2006a), guild social networks in WoW tend to be sparse. Density allows us to explore whether or not guilds benefit from higher social connectivity.
- **Maximum sub-graph size:** Largest interconnected cluster of members in a guild's social network. This measure gives a rough sense of how large sub-groups can get within a guild. Larger groups often experience more coordination issues and overhead, which could impact survivability and performance.
- **Mass count:** The number of sub-graphs larger than three in a guild's social network, that is, how many independent sub-units there are. Fragmentation of the membership might create more manageable and more successful groups within a guild, or it could impede information sharing and be detrimental.

We also had access to some simple game-specific metrics reflecting the role and performance of each player in a guild:

- **Level (average, median, and standard deviation) and number of level 60 characters:** Indicators of how experienced the guild members are. A large number of level 60 players knowing a lot about WoW could presumably help a guild in the long run. And overall guilds of higher level might fare better than lower ones.

- **Average time spent together:** A measure of schedule compatibility—the higher the value, the more members are online at the same time (we normalize this value using each guild's size to be able to compare them). Schedule incompatibilities are often mentioned by players as an important reason for leaving a guild (Williams et al., 2006).
- **Average time spent in "instances" (dungeons):** An indicator of the importance of planned group activities in a guild, as opposed to ad hoc quest parties and individual quests.
- **Class balance:** A good playgroup in WoW often has representatives of different classes, since they are highly complementary by design. We use a chi-square score to measure overall balance or imbalance. The chi-square score calculates the deviation of each class count from the expected count for a given size (e.g., there being eight classes for each faction, a perfectly balanced guild of 80 members would have ten members of each class). Bigger scores mean bigger imbalances (we normalize the result using each guild's size).

Having computed the above for each guild in our sample, we then tried to assess their impact on two success indicators for a guild: its survival, and the rate of advancement of its members.

To study guild survival, we took two month-long samples, one from July 2006 and the other from December 2006, and extracted all unique guilds in both. If a guild seen in the early sample was not observed in the later one, we marked it as "dead." Otherwise, we marked it as "survived." Using this method, we had 3,537 unique guilds in our July sample. Of those, 1,917 (or 54%) were not seen again in December and marked as "dead."

We then ran a logistic regression with survival as the dependent variable and all the metrics mentioned earlier as predictors. The Cox & Snell R-Square for the resulting model was .200 (Table

Table 3. Guild survival model summary

Step	-2 Log likelihood	Cox & Snell R Square	Nagelkerke R Square
1	4088.392	.200	.268

Table 4. Classification table for the survival model

			Predicted		
			12_Survival		Percentage
Observed			.00	1.00	Correct
Step 1	12_Survival	.00	1467	450	76.5
		1.00	570	1050	64.8
	Overall Percentage				71.2

Table 5. Regression coefficients for the survival model

	B	S.E.	Wald	df	Sig.	Exp(B)
@07_guildsize	.054	.011	24.481	1	.000	1.055
@07_max_subgraph_size	-.048	.012	15.845	1	.000	.953
@07_mass_count	.077	.109	.502	1	.479	1.081
@07_total_count	-.080	.072	1.237	1	.266	.923
@07_density	3.586	.916	15.339	1	.000	36.081
@07_centrality	-1.527	.889	2.948	1	.086	.217
@07_LvlAvg	.021	.006	13.935	1	.000	1.021
@07_LvlMedian	-.002	.003	.389	1	.533	.998
@07_LvlSD	.046	.010	23.283	1	.000	1.048
@07_Count60	-.022	.008	7.143	1	.008	.978
@07_AvgTogether	.090	.074	1.466	1	.226	1.094
@07TogetherRatio	-1.243	.377	10.887	1	.001	.288
@07_InstanceTimeRatio	7.011	1.782	15.481	1	.000	1109.076
@07_ClassBalance	.003	.005	.423	1	.515	1.003
@07_BalanceRatio	-.288	.054	28.135	1	.000	.750
Constant	-1.541	.195	62.413	1	.000	.214

3)—a number that may initially seem low but is in fact well within the accepted norms for similar social science research (Cohen, 1988)[3]. And again, we openly acknowledge that our model cannot be entirely accurate since we can only collect a limited number of variables.

Using a strict cut-off, the model provided by the logistic regression was accurate in 76.5% of the "death" cases and 64.8% of the "survival" cases (Table 4)—better than chance alone. The predictive values of each variable we used are listed in Table 5.

For a measure of player advancement, we computed a standardized character advancement score. A character's raw advancement is simply the number of levels the character has advanced over one month (for the analyses below, from July to August 2006). In this case, we subtracted the starting level from the ending level. Because a 10- level advancement by a level 1 character is

Table 6. Guild advancement model summary

Model	R	R Square	Adjusted R Square	Std. Error of the Estimate
1	.313[a]	.098	.094	1.31596

Table 7. Regression co-efficients for the advancement model

Model		Unstandardized Coefficients		Standardized Coefficients	t	Sig.
		B	Std. Error	Beta		
1	(Constant)	-.574	.101		-5.681	.000
	@08_guildsize	-.016	.005	-.505	-3.296	.001
	@08_max_subgraph_size	.018	.006	.470	3.043	.002
	@08_mass_count	.250	.065	.107	3.876	.000
	@08_total_count	.033	.039	.021	.839	.402
	@08_density	-.134	.431	-.010	-.312	.755
	@08_centrality	.898	.424	.078	2.117	.034
	@08_LvlAvg	.001	.003	.008	.328	.743
	@08_LvlMedian	.002	.002	.025	1.244	.213
	@08_LvlSD	.014	.005	.056	2.711	.007
	@08_AvgTogether	.139	.034	.226	4.044	.000
	@08TogetherRatio	.574	.186	.071	3.078	.002
	@08_InstanceTimeRatio	-2.092	1.069	-.035	-1.957	.050
	@08_ClassBalance	.007	.002	.056	2.890	.004
	@08_BalanceRatio	-.018	.024	-.019	-.762	.446

much less significant than a 10-level advancement by a level 50 character (the later stages of the game require much more time and effort to progress), we standardized character advancement by calculating the average (and standard deviation) of advancement for every starting level. In other words, we compared each character only with others who also started at the same level at the same time. This was done by calculating the z-score of advancement for every character. Characters who were already level 60 at the beginning of the sampling period were excluded.

We then computed a standardized guild advancement score—simply the average of the standardized advancement scores of every member in that guild. This guild score was thus a reflection of how much the guild as a whole advanced during the sampling period. Again, characters that were already level 60 at the beginning of the sampling period were excluded.

Using the same predictors as before, we ran a multiple regression with guild advancement as the dependent variable. The R-Square for the resulting model was .098 (Table 6)—smaller than before but still within acceptable limits. The predictors of character advancement are listed in Table 7.

Both models identified six significant predictors of survival and advancement (Table 5 and Table 7) that we discuss in more detail below. Before examining each of them, it is worth noting that four of these predictors are identical in each model (guild size, class balance, level standard deviation, and maximum sub-graph size), a good indication that these variables have an important impact on both the survival and efficiency of a group—but two of them also had opposite effects in each model, revealing an interesting tension between survival and efficiency.

Looking at the four predictors identified by both models in more detail we find:

- Class balance (co-efficient B for model 1 (M1): .003; standardized co-efficient for model 2 (M2): .056): more balanced guilds survive better than others, and they also allow their members to progress more quickly in the game. This seems logical when considering the game's design: classes have complementary skills and therefore, balanced groups are more enjoyable to play with and perform better.

The importance of class balance becomes more interesting when we consider that the distribution of classes over the entire population is very imbalanced (Ducheneaut, Yee, Nickell, & Moore, 2006a; 2006b)—priests (a crucial healing class), for instance, are in notoriously short supply. And therefore, their presence in one balanced guild means class imbalance (and probably limited longevity and performance) in another. The quest for a well-balanced roster leads to churn, as players from the needed classes are recruited away from one guild to another. Pro-active recruitment of needed classes is therefore important for the success of a guild: letting social networks form purely at random is not an efficient strategy.

- Guild size (M1: .054; M2: -.505): intuitively it is reasonable to believe that there is strength in numbers and therefore that large groups should have better odds of surviving—a hypothesis confirmed by our first model. But in an interesting contrast, model 2 reveals that a large guild size is actually an impediment to rapid progress in the game for its members. Perhaps the smaller groups offer a more "intimate" environment where players help each other move forward in the game, whereas larger groups have the strength

required to tackle the toughest dungeons and therefore constantly attract players in search of high-end items, which contributes to their long-term survival.

A pattern such as this illustrates that players look for different social networks over their tenure in the game. Small groups may be more appealing in the early stages, when progress is important, while bigger and more "anonymous" structures become necessary to access the endgame's content. This need for larger groups of very dedicated ("hardcore") players at the endgame is often cited as a major reason for quitting the game after level 60 has been reached (Williams et al., 2006): this kind of social experience is quite obviously not appealing to all players.

- Level standard deviation (M1: .046; M2: 0.056): a wider level spread contributes positively to both survival and advancement. Our hypothesis that a concentration of high-level characters would increase the guild's knowledge pool, and therefore its survival, does not seem to hold here. But an alternative explanation could be that a wide-level spread is indicative of fresh recruits joining the ranks, replacing natural attrition through burnout and transfers to competing guilds. A wider level spread is also advantageous for leveling: it ensures that there will always be someone in the guild with a level close enough to play with—and this is whether each player advances faster or slower than the guild's norm.

- Maximum sub-graph size (M1: -.048; M2: 0.470): in a fashion similar to size, this variable has opposite effects in each model. Controlling for guild size, guilds with smaller sub-groups are more likely to survive, perhaps because they avoid coordination issues, as we hypothesized. But the larger the sub-groups in a guild, the faster players advance. The issue here seems to revolve around forming groups that are large enough to be efficient but also small enough to be enjoyable to play with.

Other significant predictors not shared between the two models included:

- Time in instances (M1: 7.011): interestingly, guilds that focus on the most complex game areas survive better. Since these dungeons usually require more planning and coordination than simply "roaming the world," it could be a reflection of a more organized guild (as opposed to one limited to ad hoc quest groups).
- Density (M1: 3.586): better-connected guilds apparently survive more often than others. Anthropologists like Dunbar (1993) have proposed that a certain amount of "social grooming" is necessary to hold a group together. A larger number of ties might be indicative of higher cohesion and more peer pressure to participate in guild activities, increasing its odds of success.
- Schedule compatibility ("Together ratio") (M2: 0.186): perhaps unsurprisingly, guilds with members whose time online overlaps significantly have a positive impact on advancement—they make finding partners for joint play sessions easier.
- Mass count (M2: .107): a guild fragmented into many cohesive subunits is more beneficial to its members' advancement. This fits well with WoW's design: most "quests" are designed to be challenging enough for small groups of up to five players. Guilds where players can repeatedly team with up to four other members of approximately the same level should therefore facilitate advancement.

Taken as a whole, the metrics we just presented form a fairly coherent picture of the ingredients required for a group to survive in an online game, and it looks as if some forms of social networks are more beneficial than others. First, the data suggests that random associations between strangers should be avoided. Guilds that pro-actively recruit members to balance their roster fare better in the long run, a lesson many players learn during their first few months in the game. It is quite common for newcomers to join their first guild based on a "random invite" in the main cities, but this guild is rarely the one they will ultimately stay in. At the "endgame" (when players reach 60), a much more formal recruitment process is usually in place, with the guild leader and his officers vetting any addition to their group after careful consideration. In other words, you cannot be friends with anybody: social networks will stabilize around characters that "fit" together.

Second, managing growth and size appears to be another important set of issues. Small groups seem to be best in the early life of a guild, while larger entities perform and survive better as players gain in experience. And while groups must resist the urge to grow their network too quickly, they must also pay attention to renewing their ranks frequently enough: a wide range of member's experience, from newcomer to seasoned veteran, is beneficial to the performance and survival of the group. The issue of size is also important for the internal organization of the guild. Social networks broken down into fairly small and dense sub-units focused on well-defined tasks have higher odds of success than more amorphous and sprawling structures.

Many of the trends we identified above and in the previous section might sound "obvious" to long-term WoW players, and indeed, they fit our own intuition about successful strategies in the game fairly well. But our data allows us to substantiate such intuitions and focus on areas that could prove important for the design of future online communities, gaming-related or not. We now discuss the implications of our findings in more depth.

DISCUSSION

A "Looser" Form of Social Networks and Sociability

Computer games have often been reviled as the source of many social ills, in particular, a supposed (but not convincingly proven) link between gaming and violent behavior (Anderson & Bushman, 2001). The arrival of MMOGs provided a refreshing contrast: at last, gamers could point to an environment where collaboration between strangers was the norm and sociability the end goal. Convincing analyses have been written comparing MMOGs to a kind of "third place" (Steinkuehler & Williams, 2006) taking over the role of fast-disappearing social hangouts of the physical world, like the local corner pub or bowling alley (Putnam, 2000). In this context, how can we make sense of the data we presented showing that, on average, social networks in WoW tend to be fairly sparse? Does it mean that MMOGs have failed in promoting the sociability that so many thought was their main claim to fame?

We do not believe this to be the case. Instead, we would like to argue that the structure of social networks in WoW is illustrative of a broader set of changing expectations about sociability online, particularly from young Internet users. Indeed, the mention of sociability tends to evoke images of mythical old villages where everybody knows everybody (Bender, 1978). Idealized social networks are based on tight links, closest in spirit to the bonds seen in a family or kinship group. There is a tendency to associate "social" environments with such characteristics and dismiss anything less as "asocial" or "failed" social spaces. But this mythical conception has not kept pace with the changes introduced by technology in the past decade. The ubiquity of electronic communication means (from IM to cell phones, or even IM on cell phones) has enabled an entire generation of users to pay "continuous partial attention" (Friedman, 2001) to a larger and looser social circle than

was previously possible. For instance, teenagers using SMS are used to a form of constant, low involvement social connectivity with their friends (Palen, 2002). They exchange frequent but short SMS "pings" simply to check on each other's status and "keep their network alive," so to speak. Users of social networking sites collect friends like others do with coins (Boyd, 2006): there is satisfaction and pleasure in being surrounded by lots of acquaintances online. And even in the physical world, what we could call the "Starbucks phenomenon" also illustrates a similar trend: many customers go there to work on their laptop, an activity they could do perfectly well elsewhere if it were not for a crucial missing ingredient: being surrounded by other people. Again, the goal here is not to interact with the other patrons. It is simply to enjoy the feeling of being in a place populated by other human beings. In this it does not exactly fit Oldenburg's definition of a third place (Oldenburg, 1989), which emphasizes direct interactions between visitors as a key feature. It is perhaps closer in spirit to a European street café where people watching, not necessarily conversation, is the main activity.

The "collective solitude" (Malaby, 2003) we see in WoW now makes more sense in light of these parallel trends. During the early stages of their tenure in the game, players will log in and set off on a quest on their own. There is no request and often no need for a group: the objectives can be accomplished more quickly alone. And yet, this solitary activity is far from asocial. As players moves through the world they are in constant contact with their guild, monitoring the background chatter in the guild's chat channel. They see other player avatars engaged in various activities in the world. They have the feeling of being in an inhabited space where the presence of others is constantly visible. There can be satisfaction in this looser form of social connectivity and, as our data illustrates, this is apparently the right mix for a large fraction of WoW's 8 million players. Later on, as group tasks take center stage and progress depends much more on collective action, players will form tighter and more structured networks in the form of high-end "raiding guilds" (more on this in the next section below). Not all players, however, are willing to transition to his more "hardcore" social experience (Williams et al., 2006). Blizzard recognized this after the game was released: they progressively added more high-level content that can be accessed alone (e.g., quests where players earn "reputation" with one of the game's factions, allowing them to purchase gear equivalent to the one obtained from raiding instances). This trend is particularly visible in the "Burning Crusade" expansion they released early in 2007.

Social networks in WoW might therefore reflect a transition in the kind of sociability people are looking for online, with a movement towards interactions that are simultaneously looser and shorter, but also more frequent and more massive. In other words, people are very much looking for the company of others but they might not necessarily want to interact at length with them. WoW provides an ideal environment where this need can be satisfied, a point substantiated by evidence from other MMOGs that failed to attract as many players. In previous games, grouping was much more emphasized in the early phases of the game, leading to denser social networks (Jakobson & Taylor, 2003) but also obviously limiting these games' appeal (Everquest, WoW's closest competitor in the U.S., peaked at a population of 0.5 million). So while WoW might not be exactly the kind of third place envisioned by others (Steinkuehler & Williams, 2006), it still plays a valuable social role by offering the kind of "on-demand," non-constraining social environment sought after by most of the new media generation.

It is also interesting to note that social networking services (e.g., Friendster, Facebook) serve a similar purpose: while creating links to other individuals is easy and only requires a simple "invite," these links are not necessarily the source of extended social interactions. Boyd (in

press) has documented extensively the practices surrounding the use of these sites by teenagers and the parallels with the behaviors we observed in WoW are striking. In particular, Boyd shows how social networking sites let teenagers "write a digital body into being" through their carefully crafted profiles. WoW makes this metaphor more tangible by providing players with an actual body through their avatar. WoW players pay significant attention to the image projected by this avatar: wearing a rare and powerful set of armor, for instance, is a mark of accomplishment. In fact, it is frequent for players to leave avatars such as this standing in the middle of a crowded public space in the main cities, simply for other players to admire! As such, WoW is as much about constructing a digital identity as it is about killing monsters. But this game of identity construction only makes sense if there are "networked publics" and "invisible audiences" (Boyd, in press) to witness it. WoW therefore supports the same kind of "social voyeurism" (Boyd, in press) one sees on MySpace and elsewhere: it is often more about "hanging out" than active social interactions, more about observing and acting in a public space than forming tight relationships. This makes gaming communities look like a natural extension of other online social networking sites, a space where the same practices are at play instead of a separate domain protected by a "magic circle" (Huizinga, 1949) transforming social relationships between the players.

Organizing Successful Social Networks Online

While MMOGs appear from the outside to be entirely about fun and play, the reality of participating in the game can sometimes be surprisingly different. For instance, acquiring some powerful items requires hours of tedious "grinding," that is, repeatedly killing the same monsters again and again until they drop the requisite amount of material. And as players approach the endgame, entering the toughest dungeons requires the concerted efforts of "raids" of up to 40 players. These can be a real logistical nightmare: raid leaders have to coordinate the schedules of these 40 players (and have backup available in case of no-shows), assign responsibilities and form subgroups, define tactics, establish the rules for sharing the bounty from the event, make sure that all players come with the equipment required, and so forth. There is therefore a curious blurring of the boundaries between work and play in MMOGs (Yee, 2006b), and in fact some of the game's activities are so close to what would be required in a corporate environment that some suggested an experience as a guild leader would make a worthwhile addition to a resume (J. Brown & Thomas, 2006). Others have argued that the "video game generation" is acquiring valuable knowledge from games that will help them transform the workplace (Beck & Wade, 2004), and this even though MMOGs were not originally designed with the teaching of specific skills in mind.

But what exactly are players learning in these games that could be valuable in the workplace? Our data about the structure of social networks in successful guilds sheds some light on this question. Indeed, it looks as if very specific forms of organization ultimately prevail in WoW. A successful and long-lasting endgame guild must be both large and broken down into small, dense sub-units of about five players using characters with diverse skills (that is, diverse classes) and well-defined roles. To stay alive and perform well the group will also need to adopt a pro-active recruitment strategy, bringing in a constant influx of players at varying levels of expertise. The ideal-type (Weber, 1949) of a successful guild therefore looks like Figure 9 below.

The figure above looks surprisingly similar to the organic, team-based structures that are prevalent in many corporations nowadays. It therefore looks as if WoW familiarizes its players with organizational forms that they will have a high chance of encountering in the physical world

(if they are not already employed and part of a similar structure). Because of the game's design, players are also given clear roles (their class) that naturally steer them into specific positions in their guild's social network. This may later affect the way these players behave in the workplace (for instance, WoW players might prefer working in small teams with clearly defined individual responsibilities).

This similarity between workplace organization and guild structure blurs the distinction between play and work even further: after a long day at the office, a player joining his guild for a raid online will join a group that is in many ways similar to what he just left! The fact that he or she does the latter much more willingly than going to work in the morning is an interesting puzzle, indicating that modeling a workplace's organization after a game guild to make it more enjoyable might not be very successful: they are organized in basically the same way. The root of the pleasure offered by MMOGs must therefore be found in places other than the form of social networks they support—a question that game theorists have been grappling with for a long time (Huizinga, 1949; Koster, 2005) and that is beyond the scope of this chapter.

Figure 9. Ideal-type social network for a successful guild

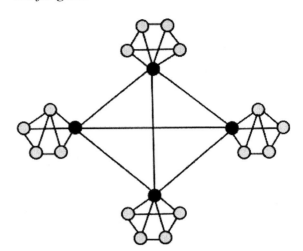

Beyond the perspective of individual participants, our data also has implications for the structuring and management of organizations, most clearly illustrated by Figure 9. In particular, it seems to indicate that diverse, organic structures stand a better chance of success than others. While a single organizational form is not always the best (Mintzberg, 1978), past research has argued that efficiency and survival depend in great part on the organization's environment (Hannan & Freeman, 1984; Winter, 1990), resulting in inertia and a pressure towards uniformity. However, these theories were difficult to test empirically due to the chaotic nature of business environment everywhere. But note that WoW offers an essentially uniform environment for organizations to emerge: by design guilds all have similar objectives (progressing through the game's toughest instances), players are equipped with a well-defined and limited set of skills (based on their class), the level of uncertainty is constant (encounters with "mobs" and "bosses" are scripted by a computer program and therefore predicable), and so forth. WoW is a structured environment that submits organizations to the same set of constraints. It is therefore interesting to see that under these controlled conditions, organizations with similar structures (schematized in Figure 9) will survive and thrive. This seems to give support to ecological theories of organizational change (Hannan & Freeman, 1984; Winter, 1990) emphasizing the role of the environment in an organization's success. The particular form achieved (team-based, organic) is not necessarily the best in all contexts but it clearly seems to be the most resilient in WoW's environment.

CONCLUSION

Online games can be fascinating laboratories to observe the dynamics of groups online. In particular, the ease of collecting large-scale interaction data makes them ideally suited to analyzing the formation and evolution of social networks in player groups. In this chapter, we have used such a data set to reach conclusions pointing at some important evolutions in the nature of sociability online, as well as the potential of online collaborative spaces to impact activities in the physical world.

Regarding the former, our observations show that while MMOGs are clearly social environments, the extent and nature of the players' social activities differ significantly from previous accounts. In particular, joint activities are not very prevalent, especially in the early stages of the game. WoW's subscribers, instead of playing with other people, rely on them as an audience for their in-game performances, as an entertaining spectacle, and as a diffuse and easily accessible source of information and chitchat. For most, playing the game is therefore like being "alone together"—surrounded by others, but not necessarily actively interacting with them. As we argued, this seems analogous to trends observed in other environments (electronic or otherwise) and points at a possible "loosening" of sociability. We do not mean to imply that this is in any way damaging (or improving) on the diverse ways humans have interacted in society over the ages. Indeed, there is no evidence from WoW that players feel their social experience is impoverished—it is in fact quite the opposite. We simply want to point out that, based on WoW's success, this suggests alternative design strategies for online games (and online spaces more generally) where encouraging and supporting direct interactions might be less important than designing for the "spectator experience" and a sense of social presence (Reeves, Benford, O'Malley, & Fraser, 2005).

We have also been able to show that social structures in WoW tend to crystallize around a common template. The design of the game certainly influences this pattern: for instance the emphasis on small quest parties with complementary, well-defined roles, translates directly into guild structures made of small sub-units loosely interconnected with each other. Our data also indicates that online social networks are more resilient when they are actively planned and managed. A constant influx of new blood coupled with a growth management plan will help a guild thrive without collapsing under its own weight. Overall, these interaction patterns steer players towards certain forms of teamwork that might transfer to group activities outside of games. Such data is particularly relevant in light of current debates about the educational value of MMOGs and their possible impact on the workplace.

Finally, WoW also illustrates how, under controlled conditions, organizations tend to converge on a similar form maximizing their efficiency and survivability. This gives credence to ecological theories of organizational change that, until now, had been difficult to test empirically for lack of a controlled experimental environment. Moreover, this more generally illustrates how online games could represent an ideal platform to empirically test social-scientific problems in a variety of domains where replicability and control over the environment are important (Castranova, 2006). We believe such use of games for research purposes is a promising avenue for future work.

REFERENCES

Anderson, C., & Bushman, B. (2001). Effects of violent video games on aggressive behavior, aggressive cognition, aggressive affect, physiological arousal, and pro-social behavior: A meta-analytic review of the scientific literature. *Psychological Science, 12,* 353-359.

Bartle, R. (1996). Players who suit MUDs. *Journal of MUD research, 1*(1).

Bartle, R. (2004). *Designing virtual worlds.* Indianapolis, IN: New Riders Publishing.

Beck, J., & Wade, M. (2004). *Got game: How the gamer generation is reshaping business forever.* Boston, MA: Harvard Business School Press.

Bender, T. (1978). *Community and social change in America.* Baltimore, MD: The John Hopkins University Press.

Bernheim Brush, A., Wang, X., Combs Turner, T., & Smith, M. (2005). Assessing differential usage of Usenet social accounting meta-data. *Proceedings of CHI 2005* (pp. 889-898). New York, NY: ACM.

Blizzard. (2007). January 11, 2007 press release. Retrieved from http://www.blizzard.com/press/070111.shtml.

Boyd, D. (2006). Friends, Friendsters, and Top 8: Writing community into being on social network sites. *FirstMonday, 11*(12).

Boyd, D. (in press). Why youth (heart) social network sites: The role of networked publics in teenage social life. In: D. Buckingham (Ed.), *McArthur Foundation series on digital learning.* Cambridge, MA: MIT Press

Brown, B., & Bell, M. (2004). CSCW at play: 'There' as a collaborative virtual environment. *Proceedings of CSCW'04* (pp. 350-359). New York, NY: ACM.

Brown, J., & Thomas, D. (2006). You play World of Warcraft? You're hired!. *Wired, 14*(4).

Castranova, E. (2003). On virtual economies. *Game Studies, 3*(2).

Castranova, E. (2006). On the research value of large games. *Games and Culture, 1*(2), 163-186.

Cohen, J. (1988). *Statistical power analysis for the behavioral sciences (2nd ed.).* Hillsdalle, NJ: Lawrence Erlbaum Associates.

Cuciz, D. (2001). The history of MUDs. Retrieved October 7, 2003, from http://www.gamespy.com/articles/january01/muds1/index4.shtm.

Curtis, P. (1992). Mudding: Social phenomena in text-based virtual realities. *Proceedings of Directions and Implications of Advanced Computing (DIAC'92) Symposium.* Berkeley, CA.

Ducheneaut, N., Yee, N., Nickell, E., & Moore, R. (2006a). "Alone together?" Exploring the social dynamics of massively multiplayer online games. *Proceedings of CHI 2006* (pp. 407-416). New York, NY: ACM.

Ducheneaut, N., Yee, N., Nickell, E., & Moore, R. (2006b). Building a MMO with mass appeal: A look at gameplay in World of Warcraft. *Games and Culture, 1*(4), 1-38.

Ducheneaut, N., Yee, N., Nickell, E., & Moore, R. (2007). The life and death of online gaming communities: A look at guilds in World of Warcraft. *Proceedings of CHI 2007* (pp. 839-848). New York, NY: ACM.

Dunbar, R. (1993). Co-evolution of neocortical size, group size and language in humans. *Behavioral and brain sciences, 16*(4), 681-735.

Fine, G. (1983). *Shared fantasy: Role-playing games as social worlds*. Chicago, IL: The University of Chicago Press.

Friedman, T. (2001). Cyber-Serfdom. *The New York Times.*

Granovetter, M. (1973). The strength of weak ties. *American Journal of Sociology, 78,* 1360-1380.

Hannan, M., & Freeman, J. (1984). Structural inertia and organizational change. *American Sociological Review, 49,* 149-164.

Huizinga, J. (1949). *Homo ludens, a study of the play element in culture*. London: Routledge and Kegan Paul.

Jakobson, M., & Taylor, T. (2003). The Sopranos meets EverQuest: Social networking in massively multiplayer online games. *Proceedings of DAC 2003* (pp. 81-90). Melbourne, Australia.

Koster, R. (2005). *A theory of fun for game design*. Scottsdale, AZ: Paraglyph Press.

Lazzaro, N. (2004). *Why we play games: Four keys to emotion without story*. Oakland, CA: Xeodesign.

Malaby, T. (2003). *Gambling life: Dealing in contingency in a Greek city*. Chicago, IL: University of Illinois press.

Mintzberg, H. (1978). *The structuring of organizations*. Englewood Cliffs, NJ: Prentice Hall.

Nardi, B., & Harris, J. (2006). Strangers and friends: Collaborative play in World of Warcraft. *Proceedings of CSCW 2006*. New York, NY: ACM.

Olausson, M. (2007). Games industry transformed as one-third of games software revenues will be generated online by 2011. http://www.strategyanalytics.net/default.aspx?mod=PressReleaseViewer&a0=3569.

Oldenburg, R. (1989). *The great good place*. New York, NY: Marlowe & Company.

Palen, L. (2002). Mobile telephony in a connected life. *Communication of the ACM, 45*(3), 78-82.

Putnam, R. (2000). *Bowling alone: The collapse and revival of American community*. New York, NY: Simon & Schuster.

Reeves, S., Benford, S., O'Malley, C., & Fraser, M. (2005). Designing the spectator experience. *Proceedings of the conference on human factors in computing systems (CHI 2005)*. New York, NY: ACM.

Seay, A., Jerome, W., Lee, K., & Kraut, R. (2004). Project massive: A study of online gaming communities. *Proceedings of CHI 2004* (pp. 1421-1424). New York, NY: ACM.

Steinkuehler, C., & Williams, D. (2006). Where everybody knows your (screen) name: Online games as "third places". *Journal of Computer-Mediated Communication, 11*(4).

Taylor, T. (2003). Power gamers just want to have fun?: Instrumental play in a MMOG. *Proceedings of the 1ˢᵗ Digra conference: Level up*. The University of Utrecht, The Netherlands.

Taylor, T. (2006). *Play between worlds.* Cambridge, MA: The MIT Press.

Wasserman, S., & Faust, K. (1994). *Social network analysis: Methods and applications.* Cambridge, UK: Cambridge University Press.

Weber, M. (1949). *The methodology of the social sciences* (E. Schills & H. Finch, Trans.). New York, NY: The Free Press.

Williams, D., Ducheneaut, N., Xiong, L., Zhang, Y., Yee, N., & Nickell, E. (2006). From treehouse to barracks: The social life of guilds in World of Warcraft. *Games and Culture, 1*(4), 338-361.

Winter, S. (1990). Survival, selection and inheritance in evolutionary theories of organization. In: J. Sing (Ed.), *Organizational evolution: new directions* (pp. 269-297). Thousand Oaks, CA: Sage Publications.

Woodcock, B. (2005). *An analysis of MMOG subscription growth – Version 21.0.* Retrieved July 12, 2005, from http://pw1.netcom.com/~sirbruce/Subscriptions.html.

Yee, N. (2001). The Norrathian scrolls: A study of EverQuest (Version 2.5). Retrieved October 7, 2003, from http://www.nickyee.com/eqt/report.html.

Yee, N. (2002). Ariadne - Understanding MMOR-PG addiction. http://www.nickyee.com/hub/addiction/home.html.

Yee, N. (2005). Facets: 5 motivation factors for why people play MMORPGs. Retrieved August 16, 2005, from http://www.nickyee.com/facets/home.html.

Yee, N. (2006a). The demographics, motivations and derived experiences of users of massively-multiuser online graphical environments. *PRESENCE: Teleoperators and Virtual Environments.* Cambridge, MA: MIT Press.

Yee, N. (2006b). The labor of fun: How video games blur the boundaries of work and play. *Games and Culture, 1,* 68-71.

ENDNOTES

[*] This work is based on two earlier publications: *Alone together? Exploring the social dynamics of massively multiplayer games,* in Proceedings of CHI 2006, © ACM, 2006. http://doi.acm.org/10.1145/1124772.1124834 *The life and death of online gaming communities: a look at guilds in World of Warcraft,* in Proceedings of CHI 2007, © ACM, 2007. http://doi.acm.org/10.1145/1240624.124075

[1] An expansion pack was released in early 2007, opening up new zones to explore and increasing the maximum level to 70.

[2] In order to break down the game's large subscriber base into more manageable units, players must choose a specific server to play on. Each server can host a community of about 20,000 players (there are more than 150 servers available in the U.S.). Three server types are available. The most common is PvE (player versus environment) where players cannot kill other players by default, unlike PvP (player-versus-player) servers. The third server type is RP (role-playing) for players who prefer to "stay in character" during the game. We observed behaviors in at least one exemplar of each to make sure play style did not affect our metrics.

[3] Cohen states that an R of .37 would be considered "large" (with a corresponding R-Square value of .14), for data collected during highly-controlled experimental conditions. Considering that our analysis was conducted on a large naturalistic sample with a great deal of extraneous noise, an R-Square of .200 is therefore quite high.

Chapter VI
Collaboration Challenges in Community Telecommunication Networks

Sylvie Albert
Laurentian University, Canada

Rolland LeBrasseur[1]
Laurentian University, Canada

ABSTRACT

This article reviews the literature on networks and, more specifically, on the development of community telecommunication networks. It strives to understand the collaboration needed for innovative projects such as intelligent networks. Guided by a change management framework, collaboration within a community network is explored in terms of the formation and performance phases of its development. The context, content, and process of each phase is analyzed, as well as the interaction of the two phases. User involvement and technology appropriation are discussed. Collaboration challenges are identified and linked to the sustainability of the community network. Policy makers are presented with a model that gives some insight into planning and managing a community network over time.

INTRODUCTION

Collaboration in networks and managing performance across organizations has gained the attention of researchers (Huxham & Vangen, 2000). Our comprehension of collaborative networks[2] has progressed substantially over a couple of decades (Oliver & Ebers, 1998), but it lacks integration (Ebers, 2002).

Collaborative networks cover a range of purposes such as innovation requiring heavy investment in R&D, international ventures, and the delivery of public services like health and education. This article is focused on telecommunication networks that operate within a physical and shared community space. The more ambitious community networks aim to become "intelligent" communities with broad participation and significant impact on the local social and economic development. To understand them as a dynamic phenomenon, a framework is needed that can accommodate and organize the conceptual pillars of organizational environment, structure, culture, leadership, and management. Pettigrew (1992, 1987) offers such a framework, and Ebers (2002) and LeBrasseur et al. (2002) demonstrate its effective application.

Organizations in all sectors have become more interested in inter-organizational collaboration to encourage synergy, innovation, and economic development. Although there are many pockets of successful collaborative efforts, there is a continuing need to identify the challenges and opportunities inherent to community networks. With this focus, this article is divided into four main sections. First, collaborative networks are defined and described, and community telecommunication networks and their potential for supporting intelligent communities are analyzed. Second, key collaboration challenges that impact on the development of a community network are introduced. Third, the literature is reviewed and organized according to the context, content, and process involved in these community networks during their two phases of development–formation and performance. The collaboration challenges present in each phase of development are explored, including challenges that the users experience. Fourth, the article concludes with policy implications for network planners.

TELECOMMUNICATION NETWORKS AS AN EXAMPLE OF COLLABORATION

Collaboration is the pooling of resources (e.g., information, money, labour), by two or more stakeholders or partners[3], to solve a set of problems, which neither can solve individually (Gray, 1985). It involves an interactive process whereby organizations, using shared rules, norms, and structures, act or decide on issues related to a problem domain (Wood & Wood, 1991). The intentional goal-oriented collaborative arrangement that emerges is that of a network (Poyhonen & Smedlund, 2004).

Networking represents a particular form of organizing or governing exchange relationships among organizations and is an alternative to markets and hierarchies (Ebers, 2002, p. 23). Network partners maintain their autonomy and retain residual property rights over their resources that have been pooled to achieve mutually agreed outcomes (Bailey & McNally-Koney, 1996; Brown et al., 1998; Gray & Hay, 1986; Huxham & Vangen, 2000; Oliver & Ebers, 1998). The principal coordination mechanisms for allocating resources are negotiation and concurrence. Informal social systems, rather than bureaucratic ones, coordinate complex products or services and reduce uncertainty (Jarillo, 1988; Jones et al., 1997).

Networks have gained in importance over the last two decades. For the private sector, globalization and the speed of change have encouraged collaborative efforts. For government, downloading[4] since the 1990s has forced new ways to view management of programs and services for resource maximization (Bradford, 2003; Bailey et al., 1996). Municipalities and regions have also demonstrated an increased interest in collaboration efforts and network development to attract new opportunities and maintain their competitive advantage. Collaborative networks typically increase the scale and visibility of program efforts, increase support for projects, and leverage capital to enhance feasibility, speed, and effectiveness (O'Toole, 1997). Synergy is achieved through improved resource management and intensive exchanges on specific projects.

To achieve synergistic gains and programming enhancements from sharing resources, risks, and rewards, stakeholders need to shift their focus toward collaborative rather than competitive advantage (Lowndes & Skelcher, 1998). Too often in the past, public sector organizations built independent silos and their private sector counterparts viewed potential partners as competitors rather than collaborators. Public policies dealing with ambitious or complex issues, like community sustainability, are likely to require networked structures that allow for the pooling and mobilization of resources from both private and public sectors within a government policy initiative (O'Toole, 1997).

Community telecommunication networks reflect the trend in western society away from bureaucratic government to network governance (Sorensen, 2002): the latter delivers more services efficiently with less risk and uncertainty (Considine & Lewis, 2003; Jones et al., 1997). Stakeholders and collaborators include municipalities, health, education, social services organizations, and private sector organizations. These networks are part of a wider agenda to increase the country's capability for the knowledge-based economy.

There are several kinds of community networks (Gurstein, 2000; Pigg 2001), ranging from those serving a restricted membership (usually called private networks) to those serving a broader segment of the community or region. A private network may, for example, link several schools and/or municipal sites, and members would include the students, administration, and staff of these organizations. In contrast, a community network is built on a platform that gives broad access to community citizens, businesses, and agencies; it encourages many stakeholders to become a user and service provider. These stakeholders may come together simply to upgrade

an aging infrastructure, especially when market forces cannot be relied upon to meet community needs or to co-build economic foundations. Leading communities strive to build partnerships and synergy to overcome barriers to access, job creation, and innovation (Agres et al.,1998; Eger, 2001; Tan, 1999; Industry Canada, 2002a, 2002b). Community networks facilitate information dissemination, discussion, and joint activity by connecting neighbours, creating new opportunities, and empowering residents, institutions, and regions (Carroll & Rosson, 2001; Igbaria et al., 1999; Canadian National Broadband Task Force, 2001).

A community network has four basic components: a telecommunication infrastructure with broadband capability, applications or content, devices (such as computers, cellular telephones, i-pods, and blackberries), and users. The development of a community telecommunication network typically occurs through a governing board representing the needs of users, which is supported by a small management structure (e.g., executive committee and network manager). The network relies on information and communication technologies (ICTs) and allows the community to import and export knowledge, encourage innovation, and overcome distance. The opportunities for economic and social development are contingent on attracting many users and creating a culture of "digital" use. The network must fulfill user needs and be attentive to their requirements, which may include a fair price, access to computers and the Internet, and training and education.

Infrastructure investment in the telecommunication network aims for the widest possible coverage of the community and region, with the constraint of reasonable cost. Investment also tries to ensure that users have access devices; some users have modest means, and schools and other organizations may have budget constraints. On the human resources front, technical training of local staff may be required to install the infrastructure and devices, and provide support to users. Organizations may need to re-design processes in order to meet the changing needs of their supplier and distribution partners, and to offer services online to end-users. The transformation effort may also require promotion campaigns to attract both individual and organizational users. These many resource challenges imposed on the community require a collaborative effort to pool resources and find innovative solutions.

A community network has users at the individual, organizational, and community levels of human activity and endeavours. Individuals or end-users use the network to communicate with friends, play games, access information, obtain training, and occasionally innovate. Organizations are often stakeholders and use the network for a wide variety of purposes (Waits, 2000), including providing information and services, and selling online. They are intermediate users (Williams et al., 2005) and are the drivers of the development of the network. These organizations are the channels through which collective innovation is exercised and community change takes place (de la Mothe, 2004; Rycroft, 2003). At the community level, these individuals and organizations create aggregate demand and use of the network, and determine the sustainability of the network. The challenge is to create a culture of "digital" use that is integrated into the broader culture that is shared by community members.

During the development of the network, user involvement can be traced through participation in articulating a "digital" vision for the community, in the purchase of access devices and services that will connect users to the network (e.g., telephone, cable, wireless, computers, and Internet), and in the utilization of applications being made available through these access devices. Users may also be involved in creating employment by innovating on the network configuration, and in helping to create a culture of use by providing additional attractive applications.

Good governance requires legitimacy with an appropriate range of stakeholders, and involves building cohesion and commitment. Relationships are voluntary, and network survival depends upon the collective will and commitment of the stakeholders. The intentionally-planned network takes on a collaborative structure composed of local residents, non-governmental organizations, private sector businesses, and government. The stakeholders create a product that reflects the concerns, priorities, and aspirations of the local population. If the infrastructure, devices, and applications meet the needs of the users, a culture of "digital" use emerges as an organic extension of existing community ways and practices. Without broad participation, the network is likely to reflect narrow interests and weaken the community's social sub-system, which in turn will limit the economic success of the network.

A sustainable community telecommunication network makes consistent and positive contributions to the economic and social development of the community (ITU, 2003), thereby enhancing the community's capital base. In large measure, these positive outcomes depend upon the collaboration of partners. They also reinforce the efforts invested in collaboration. Networking allows individuals, professionals, and entrepreneurs to access information and knowledge, learn about a wide range of issues, recognize opportunities, and achieve innovative products and services (Suire, 2004; Martin & Matlay, 2003; Corbett, 2002; Ardichvili & Cardozo, 2000; Kickul & Gundry, 2000). Whether a community network realizes its potential depends upon how well it is developed.

The above discussion portrays the formal structure of a community network as a fluid organization composed of volunteers with the purpose of facilitating the community's transition and participation in the information society. However tempting, this viewpoint is non-critical in nature; it ignores the community context and processes by which the network emerges (Pigg, 2001; Day 2002).

COLLABORATION CHALLENGES FOR COMMUNITY NETWORKS

Communities around the world have demonstrated that transformation is possible using network technology. For example, Sunderland (UK) reduced unemployment from 30% to 4% by moving from a shipbuilding and coal industrial base to a knowledge and technology economy. Similarly, Spokane Washington (USA), once a railroad town reliant on natural resources, dramatically improved the fortunes of its downtown by installing the highest density of broadband in the country. In Tianjin (China), a major push on broadband connectivity was accompanied by rapid user growth, from 20,000 to 2,700,000 in two years. Their stories make ample reference to the intensive collaboration of many actors, but the patterns of influence are not well articulated.[5] Bell (2001) compared six urban communities noted for their telecommunication achievements and identified two effective patterns of collaboration: (1) a comprehensive and formal plan, and (2) a coherent pattern of individual initiatives. Similarly, Williams et al. (2005) reviewed numerous ICT initiatives, both small and large, and emphasized the overlapping nature of the planning, implementation, and use stages of development. These patterns are explored under the phases of network development section of this article.

Individuals and organizations involved in the creation of a community network face four collaboration challenges:

1. Defining and agreeing on the transformation effort (includes vision, transformation, and planning)
2. Assembling and mobilizing resources (includes interdependence, tasks, and structure)
3. Assembling and mobilizing trust (includes prior experience, communication, and distribution of power among collaborators)
4. Balancing leadership and collaborative management (includes the broadening requirements of the network, user appropriation, and power).

These challenges are tied to the coherence and adaptability of the network, and specifically to the dynamic relationship between the formation and performance phases of its development. Collaboration is inter-woven in each of these challenges. Network sustainability is achieved by collaboration efforts that evolve during the network's development.

PHASES OF DEVELOPMENT OF A COMMUNITY NETWORK

We propose that network development takes place in two phases that are iterative in nature. Phase 1, the formation of the community network, is marked by the emergence of a leader and/or a board of directors, to respond to environmental pressures. These pressures may occur as a result of globalization and the need to remain competitive in the face of other communities or regions. It may occur as a result of downsizing or social development pressures (e.g., lack of medical practitioners, youth out-migration). The broad goals of the network are developed, including a representation of the future user. Phase 2, network performance, involves the concrete objectives and steps that the board takes to achieve the community goals that were agreed upon and the measures taken to attract and retain users. User involvement can and should take place in both phases of development.

Smaller communities need collaborators to solve a wide variety of challenges including infrastructure availability. Larger communities tend to have more resources and thus need collaboration to resolve economic and social pressures rather than infrastructure issues. In this second phase,

Table 1. Influencing factors at the formation phase

Context	Content	Process
• Economy • Social/cultural • Political • Urbanization • Funding • Technology • Globalization & competition • Cost Benefit/ Synergy	• Vision • Power • Board Membership • Concept of Sustainability • User representation	• Values • Expectations • Goals • Planning • Leadership (transformational, visionary)

the network can develop a culture and structure that gives meaning and coherence to a variety of projects. Some communities are more liberal and hands-off, allowing the private sector and citizens to develop content and opportunity. Others intentionally plan a vision of community transformation based on an improved telecommunication infrastructure. Phase 1 depends highly on leadership dynamics whereas Phase 2 is closer to managerial dynamics but with a distinctive collaborative flavor. These two phases are interdependent over time in that formation sets the stage for performance, and performance impacts on the board and leadership dynamics. Positive outcomes at the performance phase consolidate the dynamics of the formation phase; negative outcomes challenge the board and leadership and initiate a re-formation phase. This iterative process was demonstrated in the feedback loop identified by Arino and de la Torre (1998) and Thomas (1993).

Because networks are fluid in nature (pooling from existing resources, changing membership, and varied timelines) and focused on both results and relationships, two interactive phases are considered sufficient. The two phases are supported by case studies of strategic alliances (Doz, 1996) that found that successful partners actively exchanged information, re-evaluated the project (in terms of efficiency, equity and adaptability), and consequently readjusted the initial conditions of their cooperation. They are also consistent with the ICT social learning findings of Williams et al. (2005).

Formation Phase

The push and pull factors in the environment impact on the community members and prompt them to consider uniting their forces to address the issue or opportunity that has been identified. Under the leadership of a visionary, and through ample interpersonal communication, a group is assembled that represents the initial membership of a potential network. If a consensus on vision and goals is attained, the group becomes the founding board of a network and plans for the performance phase. The principal outcome is a collaborative base on which to build the network. Table 1 provides an overview of the critical factors present in the formation phase.

Context of Formation

The outer context or environment includes factors such as economic, political, culture, demographics, funding opportunities, pressures from government agencies, and technology innovation trends (Agres et al.,1998; Bailey & McNally-Koney, 1996; Igbaria et al., 1999; Keenan & Trotter, 1999; and Tan, 1999). Global competitiveness and turbulence are the underlying catalysts for creating networks for organizations, communities, and governments (Poyhonen & Smedlund, 2004; Scheel, 2002).

Interdependencies exist because organizations possess or control vital resources (material, human, political, structural, or symbolic) and thus are the source of environmental pressures for one another (Wood & Wood, 1991). Organizations seek to reduce these pressures and manage the interdependencies by gaining control over crucial resource supplies. The network form, as opposed to markets and hierarchies (e.g., vertical integration), provides a neutral space within which organizations can meet to explore solutions and synergies.

International bodies such as the World Bank (1999), the United Nations (1998), and OECD (1997) have adopted the paradigm of the information society as a guide to many of their development policies. According to Castells (1996, 1997, 1998), ICTs have produced a network society in which mobilizing knowledge and information have become more important than mobilizing physical resources. He argued that both organizations and individuals can benefit from electronic networks; they support the development and dissemination of knowledge and information, and facilitate innovation. Castells warns that these changes are accompanied by growing wealth disparities, social fragmentation, and dislocation. Governments are addressing these concerns, in part, by financially supporting the creation of community networks with broad accessibility. Locally, these new opportunities are often communicated through the chamber of commerce and other economic development agencies to mobilize or inspire stakeholders into action.

Communities come in all sizes and density, and all are influenced by the urbanization trend. Rural settings are witnessing the exodus of their youth and an erosion of their economic base as cities attract both talent and investment, including initiatives in telecommunications (OECD, 2004). Recent studies of Canadian rural communities concluded that ICTs can act as enablers of community building and development processes (New Economy Development Group Inc., 2001; Canadian Advisory Committee on Rural Issues, 2004). Given that the Internet is content-rich, offers online education, facilitates social networking, and offers a platform for the creation of new enterprises and the expansion of existing ones, the viability of the digital community network becomes crucial for the future of small communities.

When governments create generous programs to create community networks (e.g., Brown et al., 1998), communities are pressured to apply for capital funds even when they may not have the organizational and resource capacity to sustain the network. Smaller communities have relatively fewer and less diverse resources and a push-style policy may be the only way to spur action. Another example of a push factor is when a major telecom firm seeks a community partner for a demonstration project, or when the private sector chooses to make an investment to upgrade its infrastructure. The telecom supplies the ICTs, but the community stakeholders still need to demonstrate and plan on how the technology can be applied to personal and organizational purposes. Often, infrastructure is built and languishes until there are other pressures in the environment of the community, such as closure of a major employer or the arrival of a strong champion. At other times, communities struggle with the lack of open access that inhibits economic development and competition. Pushing for open access can discourage the involvement of incumbent carriers, at least at the onset. The key here is to evaluate how context issues can stimulate communities into action toward their transformation.

Content of Formation

Stakeholders need to find the community vision attractive and see a benefit for themselves and for their organization. When the problem is broad in scope and complex, such as economic development, it requires a larger variety of stakeholders with legitimate interest to devise solutions and bring sufficient resources to bear. Stakeholders must have the right and the capacity to participate, and include organizations with legitimate power as well as those who will be affected by the network.

Collaborative action necessarily involves interdependence between individuals and organizations (Ouchi, 1980) and can yield both intangible (e.g., image of citizenship) and tangible benefits (e.g., cost reductions and additional revenues). Interdependence is strongly linked to the vision of the network and the factors motivating stakeholders. It allows for an exchange among stakeholders that is built on trust, and an understanding of mutual benefit or advantage. According to Olk and Young (1997), the more ties an organization has to others in a network, the less likely is it to act opportunistically. Blois (1990) argued that collaborators should engage in bargaining on who will accept responsibility for certain elements of the transaction costs. They must come to the table understanding their role and develop a level of interdependence and mutual benefit in order to sustain the network effort.

The economic and social exchanges that take place are mediated by mutual trust. Ring (2002) distinguishes between "fragile" and "resilient" trust. The former is typical of opportunistic settings such as markets and involves the formal processes of negotiation, transaction, and administration. In contrast, the latter is the foundation of successful networks and is based on the informal processes of sense-making, understanding, and commitment. However, prescribing resilient trust does not ensure that is takes place. Ring proposed that it will emerge when the participants have a shared history of experience and when reputations for reliability are well established. On the other hand, Doz (1996) has documented the role of trusted intermediaries in helping other participants to shift gradually from fragile to resilient trust. We conclude that if a community has rich social relations, it can establish resilient trust early, but that parachuting in partners and stakeholders makes fragile trust more likely. However, if trusted intermediaries become involved, they can build the level of trust within the network.

There is a need for legitimate authority, credibility, and multiple memberships (Bailey & McNally-Koney, 1996; Gray & Hay, 1986) if a sustained transformation is to occur. Jones et al. (1997) have argued that networks need to restrict membership access and choose its members according to their reputation and status. Important stakeholders may choose to join a network or a project because of the presence of other members. A smaller number of leaders may allow the network to realize quick wins, reduce coordination costs, and improve interaction frequency. One could argue that success will breed success—trust will increase, motivation will increase, and faster output can be generated. This view is less applicable to community networks where innovation, legitimacy, and broad reach is critical and leads to a large membership and numerous exchanges. Therefore, a smaller, more restricted network may be mobilized quickly and act efficiently, but be less effective in producing varied output. The larger network may slow the pace of change, but may be important enough to attract accomplished leaders. Structure issues become important in managing a larger group of stakeholders and are discussed in the performance phase of the network.

Another content issue is sustainability. Stakeholders want to know, "How much will it cost," but few ask "How will the network become sustainable in the long-run?" Sustainability is a function of revenues (stemming from the use of the infrastructure and its applications), and the costs of the network (human resources, equipment, and materials). There are opportunities for synergistic gains when partners chose to purchase as a group, or share the operating costs. At the formation phase, the concept of sustainability is hazy, but becomes clearer as projects develop during the performance phase. Nevertheless, the board must carefully address the sustainability issue early to ensure that it becomes incorporated into their common frame of reference.

In the formation stage, the planning includes an explicit model of future users, their communication needs, and their likely use of the telecommunication network. Williams et al. (2005, p. 112,

Figure 5.2) identify ways for direct involvement of users, such as user panels, market research, and trials. They also identify sources of indirect evidence about users through information on demand and markets for similar products, and competitive offerings. With the additional input of board members who understand their community, a representation of the users is developed. This user-centered approach is helpful in guiding the design of the system and identifying training and promotion requirements. However, Williams et al., emphasize its limitations and the design fallacy that it breeds: "the presumption that the primary solution to meeting user needs is to build ever more extensive knowledge about the specific context and purposes of an increasing number and variety of users in the technology design" (p.102). The idea of perfect user representation ignores the reality that users are active agents and appropriate the technology later, primarily in the performance phase of network development.

Communities would be wise to involve users in all facets of their formation stage, but users are often thought of as passive participants that can be surveyed for the eventual purchase of devices or services at the performance stage. Yet, users have concerns over ownership, access and distribution of information, privacy, security, and copyrights (Agres et al., 1998), and most of these issues need consideration early on. However, the design fallacy mentioned above emphasizes the limitations of comprehensive user involvement in the formation phase.

Process of Formation

Leaders and champions can enhance or constrain the development of a community network (Industry Canada, 2002; Jones et al., 1997; Huxham & Vangen, 2000). Leaders tap into the collective awareness of the community stakeholders and mobilize the initial change efforts by supplying a vision and practical steps to realize it (Bailey & McNally-Koney, 1996; Roberts & Bradley,

1991). Sustaining collaboration depends on the emergence of a common view of the community and shared organizational values. Leaders and champions play a role in consolidating and expanding the collaborative initiatives, but a wider involvement is needed to foster innovation. It is important to have a community cross-section of members as well as individuals with sufficient power to rally other stakeholders. The parties must freely participate, knowing and agreeing on who is involved and in what capacity (Glatter, 2004; Roberts & Bradley, 1991); prior experience and trust facilitate the membership drive.

Network goals are created, implemented, evaluated, and modified through purposeful social construction among network stakeholders and partners (Van de Ven & Poole, 1995; Ring & Van de Ven, 1994). Network effectiveness may be defined as the harmonization, pursuit, and attainment of the goals sought by the various stakeholders and partners. With diverse stakeholders, it becomes difficult to satisfy all parties equally; therefore, managing expectations and potential conflicts help to maintain the social cohesion of the network. Members will likely persist so long as they can positively identify with the intermediate and long term outcomes, whether they are social or economic in nature.

According to Hardy and Phillips (1998), when individuals come to share a vision of the issues and the solutions, they become stakeholders and begin to create a collective identity with mutually agreed upon directions and boundaries that, in time, may become a permanent network. The catalyst is a transformational leader who encourages collaboration as a means to create synergy for innovation, growth, or to protect against future turbulence. Engaging the stakeholders in a planning exercise can address their many concerns; tasks and roles can be organized and assigned within the network to fit their expectations. Because work is complex and elaborate in networks, planning and coordinating task-specialized activities is required (Roberts & Bradley,

1991). However, planning follows the visioning that the leader has enacted.

Challenges in the Formation Phase

Defining and Agreeing on the Transformation Effort

It is argued that a multi-sectoral and multi-organizational network is needed for a transformation to an intelligent community. The wide variety of stakeholders impact the style of leadership and structure needed for joint initiatives. The leader (or leaders in the case of shared roles) shares a vision of a desirable future and initiates a flexible structure that can accommodate differences in orientation (profit versus not for profit), time horizons (short versus long term), and civic engagement (self versus community focus). Given the diversity of stakeholders, the visioning must be consistent and persuasive, but large enough in scope so that stakeholders can personalize the vision to suit their personal and organizational interests. Key activities include:

- Utilizing context issues to create a sense of urgency and sell the concept of the community network
- Identifying solutions to problems and synergistic opportunities
- Preparing a plan for producing meaningful and motivating outcomes

Agreeing on the vision depends on the availability and abilities of the local leader. Individuals with strong communication skills, an established reputation of trustworthiness, an ability to deliver on promises made, and conceptual skills to craft a vision are in short supply. While large communities have a greater pool of candidates, small communities may have to draw more on external talent and work hard on establishing trustworthiness.

Assembling and Mobilizing Resources

The community network depends upon its board to acquire the physical, financial, and organizational resources that make a broadband network functional. Collaboration among stakeholders and partners facilitates the pooling of their resources. Choosing board members should flow from resource requirements and the likelihood that the stakeholders recruited or volunteering are favorably disposed to sharing with other organizations. Community citizenship of board members channels the resources to create and enhance the network. Key activities include:

- Assembling the representatives of a variety of public and private sector organizations to form the board, including both small and large stakeholders;
- Mobilizing the resources controlled by board members and reaching out to obtain vital resources from the environment.

Too many resources may harm the development of the network if the board lacks the capability to make good use of them. Waste would damage the network's reputation and make future resource acquisitions more difficult. Likewise, too few resources can harm the network because the scope of activities would be narrow and appeal to only a small segment of the community's population. A narrow focus would appear self-serving and lack broad legitimacy.

Assembling and Mobilizing Trust

For the board to be effective in creating and enhancing the network's resource base, its members must trust each other so that extensive sharing becomes possible. When stakeholders engage in joint efforts and initiatives, they are putting the community first and themselves second, making them vulnerable to exploitation by less citizen-

Table 2. Influencing factors at the performance phase

Context	Content	Process
• Structure • Roles • Trust • Power of stakeholders • Interdependence & Culture	• Goals • Achievement/output • Innovation	• Team management • User appropriation • Communication

minded organizations. When trust exists on the board, stakeholders can tolerate some exposure. Therefore building and maintaining trust in a realistic manner is essential to the network's resource base and projects. Key activities include:

- Assembling the board membership on the basis of reputation, prior experience, and diversity of stakeholders;
- Creating a shared vision that reflects the underlying values of community spirit;
- Distinguishing between fragile and resilient trust, and building the latter.

Building and maintaining resilient trust is at the core of the inter-dependent culture that emerges in the network. When a transformational vision is complemented with solid resources and trust, the community network has met the challenges of the formation phase of its development and is ready to shift into the performance phase.

Performance Phase of Development

The performance phase of network development is centred on concrete projects that require the pooling of resources by its members. The resources may be tangible (finances, staff secondment, office space, and equipment) and intangible (time, information, influence, and reputation) in nature. Pooling is facilitated by both the culture and structure of the network in which horizontal interactions, exchanges among equals, are based on trust. These resources are organized and controlled to attain the project objectives, and the management style is collaborative and account-

able to the membership of the network. Pursuing these objectives gives collaborators opportunities to learn how they can make the network function effectively. In the short term, the level of attainment of the project's objectives dominates; small wins and their public recognition are important to confirm the value of the network (Bouwen & Taillieu, 2004). Effective project management is needed. In the long term, the board focuses on the level of attainment of the broad goals of the network. To ensure that the projects and the general management of the network are aligned with the original vision and goals, effective leadership is required. Table 2 provides an overview of the critical factors in the performance phase.

CONTEXT OF PERFORMANCE

The interdependence of members within a community network is reflected in both its structure (O'Toole, 1997) and culture. Structure requires careful attention because a poor structure—one that gives too much power to one partner or that does not embody the values of stakeholders—will affect the performance and longevity of the collaboration.

Poyhonen and Smedlund (2004) and Nooteboom (1999) identified three network structures: vertical, horizontal, and diagonal. The latter consists of firms and organizations from several different lines of business. A diagonal structure is appropriate for community networks because it includes as many collaborators as possible to create synergy and innovation within and between sectors; transformational, as opposed to incremental change, is facilitated. The success of collaborative networks is contingent on managing the ambiguity, complexity, and dynamics of the structure. It becomes more important in the performance phase because it must sustain an action plan and organize resources to carry it out. However, a telecommunication network is developed to resolve dynamic context issues and can only do so within a process of continuous improvement. A rigid structure that minimizes innovation diminishes the network's sustainability. Though difficult to assess, the effectiveness of the structure can be judged by its internal coherence and fit with the culture of the network. This puzzle, identified by Bailey & McNally-Koney (1996), needs a solution that retains the fluidity of communications and decision-making, while providing for a framework for productivity and sustainability.

Collaboration is associated with incremental innovation when partners share on several levels: a larger purpose, explicit and voluntary membership, an interactive process, and temporal property (Roberts & Bradley, 1991). Hardy and Phillips (1998) pointed out that more powerful stakeholders may force collaboration on weaker players to control them. Consequently, there is a lessening of the level of interdependence and common vision. Weaker stakeholders are bound to minimize their participation and find excuses to exit the network when they are being coerced. Though asymmetrical power is a likely reality, leaders that seek innovation must put less emphasis on control and more on incentives and opportunities.

Creating a culture of collaboration gives coherence to the stream of actions that builds the community network. Collaboration is described as a relational system of individuals within groups in which individuals share mutual aspirations and a common conceptual framework (Bailey & McNally-Koney, 1996). Individuals are guided by their sense of fairness and their motives toward others (caring and concern, and commitment to work together over time). Through communication and shared experiences, they create a system of shared assumptions and values, and accepted approaches and solutions to problems, including collective sanctions, to safeguard exchanges and reinforce acceptable behaviors (Jones et al., 1997). Sanctions may include exclusion from certain benefits (present or future) and opportunities (participation in projects), and as a last measure forced exit (temporary or permanent) from the network.

Collaborators often choose to stay in a poorly performing network based on the strength of their social ties. However, if they conclude that they can meet all of their needs outside of the network, they may view the network as superfluous (Brown et al., 1998). Linkages or interdependence must be solid and intentional (Bailey & McNally-Koney, 1996) and may be a strong indicator of sustainability (Olk & Young, 1997). Conversely, Brown et al. (1998) identified that greater resource interdependence makes successful partnerships more difficult to achieve. In order to find common ground and encourage persistence, the reasons for enhancing an interdependence need to be emphasized, and stakeholders must want to belong and believe in the vision.

Content of Performance (Specific Projects)

The content of performance includes a wide variety of projects that meet the goals of the network, including the needs of stakeholders and users. Among them are projects to launch or upgrade an infrastructure, acquire devices to deliver applications, develop content for the network, and promote the network to potential users. The outcomes include cost savings to deliver services, revenues from users, and additional capability for the social and economic development of the community.

Waits (2000) described collaborative networks in terms of their pursuits:

- **Co-inform:** Actions to identify members and impacts, promote a heightened awareness of the issues, and improve communication among the members;
- **Co-learn:** Educational and training programs sponsored by the network;
- **Co-market:** Collective activities that promote member products or services abroad or domestically;
- **Co-purchase:** Activities to strengthen buyer supplier linkages or to jointly buy expensive equipment;
- **Co-produce:** Alliances to make a product together or conduct R&D together;
- **Co-build economic foundations:** Activities to build stronger educational, financial, and governmental institutions that enable them to compete better.

Some of these pursuits appear easier to realize and only require fragile trust (co-inform and co-learn). They are more likely to give quick "small wins." Others may be challenging and require resilient trust (co-market, co-purchase, and co-produce); their success will take more time but are more highly valued. Co-building economic foundations appeals less to self-interest and more to a communal interest, and depends on a broad vision that will lead to a series of concrete actions and sustained effort. Waits' objectives are compatible with each other, but have different time horizons and commitments. The strength of the formation phase influences the commitment of stakeholders in the development phase. In particular, a strong collaborative climate encourages them to be patient and willing to invest additional time and resources to achieve long term goals.

PROCESS OF PERFORMANCE

Leaders require managerial sophistication to recognize appropriate circumstances and tools for collaboration (Glatter, 2004). In networks, collaboration depends upon an ongoing communicative process (Lawrence et al., 1999). Roles and responsibilities are negotiated in a context where no legitimate authority is necessarily recognized (Glatter, 2004; Lawrence et al., 1999; Lowndes & Skelcher, 1998). Like in partnerships, there is concern for trust, politics, emotions, and results. Furthermore, leaders require an understanding of user appropriation of the digital network to effectively channel the collaborative efforts.

Du Gay et al. (1997) describe the appropriation of technology as an active process in which users make choices around the selection and local deployment of the technological components, and create meaning and sense of the technology. Appropriation has both a technical and cultural side. In this spirit, Williams et al. (2005) have argued that user appropriation has two distinct but inter-related processes: innofusion (users adjust and innovate to improve the usefulness of the technology) and domestication (users adapt the use of the technology to integrate it meaningfully in their activities). When both processes are fully engaged, the community may be said to have a "digital" culture that sustains the network.

The pace of change within the network must be properly managed. Effective use of communication will allow collaborators to react and contribute. Because of large boards and membership and turnover in representation, some collaborators may not know everyone or their status. Indeed, some may be confused over the degree of autonomy they have in making decisions for their organization (Huxham & Vangen, 2000). Changes in government mandates and organizational priorities create uncertainty as collaborators plan and structure the network. Communication and recognition of accomplishments become important to keep everyone focused.

The board's effectiveness in tackling problems within their community as well as within their respective organizations will directly influence the achievement of the intelligent community objectives. Leaders need to guide the board and create bridges with important outside players. They must align the requirements of their own organization with the vision of the intelligent community initiative for success; they must create a high performance team environment (Albert, 2005; Wheelan, 1999; Smith, 1994). This standard is not easily achievable, especially for a volunteer board with diverse membership and affiliation.

Challenges in the Performance Phase

Continuing Challenges from the Formation Phase

The consensus on the community vision that was created in the formation phase needs to be reinforced. The leader can remind stakeholders of the urgency to capture opportunities, but must incorporate measures for sustaining collective efforts. Key transformation activities include:

- Expanding planning and monitoring projects and measures of performance;
- Marketing the network concept to mobilize and gain the support of the wider community and further engage the stakeholders.

In terms of resources, the community network continues to depend upon its board to acquire resources to develop, acquire, and develop applications to attract numerous users. Key activities include:

- Modifying board membership to improve the resource base of the network as projects change over time;
- Engaging both small and large partners for innovation to create new resources;
- Creating a small management structure for the performance phase of the network.

As for trust, the performance phase requires continuing sharing of resources in the face of uncertain outcomes. Key activities include:

- Applying different trust standards as the situation warrants;
- Encouraging the broad sharing of resources instead of specialized contributions.

Resilient trust can block new stakeholders and partners from joining the network; they may have key resources but be deemed untrustworthy. In such a case, the network requires the flexibility to resort to fragile trust with its emphasis on formal agreements and contracts. The reverse situation can also damage the network, when fragile trust dominates relationships. While formal contracts increase accountability of the parties, they are narrow in scope and participation is contingent on self-interests being satisfied. Community considerations remain secondary. In time and through active leadership, these new members may buy into community citizenship through association and success.

Balancing Leadership and Collaborative Management

Both the formation and performance phases of development have their champion. The leader dominates the formation (and re-formation) phase through visioning, planning, and attracting and retaining stakeholders with key resources and disposed to collaborate. The manager guides and maintains the performance phase, and ensures that both tangible and intangible benefits are created for the stakeholders and the community.

The "collaborative" manager is needed to reinforce the user appropriation by supporting the innofusion and domestication in which users engage. By encouraging the involvement of intermediaries (e.g., Chamber of Commerce, owner of a cybercafé, entrepreneur who wants to keep control), the network manager allows the network to evolve along lines that reflect the different groups and segments in the community's population (Williams et al., 2005).

Formal planning becomes less important, as a pattern of coherent projects becomes established.

At the same time, these intermediaries (or small groups of individuals in large networks) interact to keep the board informed and reinforce their individual efforts. By working together, they ensure that the vision of the network creates a coherent set of initiatives and projects, and opportunities and issues relevant to the board meetings are identified. Key activities include:

- Encouraging innovation and proper planning to achieve the transformation effort;
- Reaching out to intermediaries to broaden user involvement;
- Ensuring that the vision that binds the board members remains true to the community values as the network develops and expands;
- Confronting head-on the need to modify the board composition to respond to internal or external factors;
- Managing projects with a blend of fragile and resilient trust, the former with binding contracts and the latter with negotiation and concurrence;
- Choosing projects that are likely to succeed and that are valued by the stakeholders;
- Building and maintaining redundant communication systems, both formal and informal, to reflect the culture of inter-dependence that binds the stakeholders of the network.

The network can be damaged by a dominant leader or manager who insists on being involved at all times and on controlling the process, whether at the board or project level. This situation emerges when there is a failure to share multiple roles and to act as a team. The lack of experienced persons may push one individual to assume both the leadership and managerial role; this solution ensures positive momentum, but may block future sharing of roles as the incumbent becomes entrenched. Similarly, the abundance of strong and experienced personalities facilitates the sharing of roles, but may slow down momentum as too many persons insist on prominence. Developing a team spirit

among members of the board and management should be encouraged as early as possible in the network's development (Albert, 2005).

Collaboration Challenges for Users

At the formation stage, the infrastructure and applications are planned and guided by a vision. Stakeholder requirements are addressed in the planning of the network through the methods of user representation. At the performance stage, when the network is functional, the users actualize the network in both expected and emerging ways. A community network is validated by the applications it makes available to its users, and the extent to which the users actually use them. Furthermore, the design features of the telecommunication network influence the collaboration opportunities that the network creates. When the network design enhances collaboration, it has succeeded in creating effective socio-technical patterns (Huysman & Wulf, 2005; Evans & Brooks, 2005).

Challenges for Individual Users

IT and a community network challenge the individual because they put into question existing ideas and routines, and add knowledge and skill requirements. Being open to change means making efforts to understand and use the network. The younger generation makes more use of the internet than the established older generation for social contact and is likely to push for internet connection in the home (Bernier & Laflamme, 2005; Crowley, 2002). The older adults are more likely to be introduced to ICT changes in the workplace. Age aside, the Internet facilitates the local-global link through which knowledge and expertise from around the world can be channelled to community members (Stevenson, 2002). Creative individuals can interact to exchange expertise and create innovations (e.g., open source development), and are motivated by reputation and recognition built into the Web site (Fischer et al., 2004). To generate ideas, group support systems that ensure anonymity appear more effective (Pissarra & Jesuino, 2005). In general, the individual must learn to assess the trustworthiness of the Internet information sources (Franklin, 1999; May, 2002) and assume risks when making transactions online. Similarly, participating in virtual communities and discussion forums challenges the individual to change roles from spectator to contributor (Ginsberg, 2001) and activist.

Challenges for Organizational Users

Organizations that are stakeholders in the community network need to share their "network" vision with their board members, managers, employees, and organizational partners within their supply chains and customer/client networks. Key individuals likely were involved in the network formation stage to ensure that the design of the systems would support expected transactions and activities. At the performance stage, each organization is challenged to mobilize its ICTs, skill base and network use, and do so in dialogue and coordination with their organizational networks. Internally, this means empowering employees and lower levels of management through information systems and decision-making authority. Externally, this refers to the network of relations and the integration of the organizational and community networks. Failure to have extensive collaboration diminishes the benefits that the community network can deliver to stakeholders. Knowledge sharing (Van den Hooff et al., 2004) and knowledge management (Ackerman & Haverton, 2004) are useful frameworks for channelling this collaboration. In addition, involvement can include intra-preneurship (Von Oetinger, 2005) and joint ventures supported by collaborative groupware (McKnight & Bontis, 2002). The organization can also reach out to innovators and entrepreneurs in the community, who view the network as their

business platform, and initiate partnerships. The above array of activities pushes leaders and senior managers to adopt an organizational model that incorporates trust.

Challenges for the Community

As the community network is fully implemented, the stewardship vision (Block, 1993) incipient in the formation phase must be reinforced by extending inclusiveness to all segments of the local population, imagining a broad culture of use, and providing for economic development with a digital component. Community leaders should have concrete programs to diminish access barriers such as network connectivity at a reasonable cost (or at no cost for public terminals) and to training and education. Adoption of the network will vary across socio-economic dimensions, and programs are needed that are adapted to specific groups such as youth, seniors, and the non-profit and small business sectors. Developing and implementing these programs can take place with community stakeholders in collaborative projects. An innovation culture (Martins & Terblanche, 2003), linked to the network, can be encouraged.

A culture of "digital" use is emerging in many communities; the Internet and its many activities are being integrated into everyday routines of social communication, work, and play (Bernier & Laflamme, 2005; Crowley, 2002; Wellman et al., 2001). In contrast, civic participation has had less success. The evidence indicates that internet use reinforces civic participation and makes it more sophisticated, but does not increase the levels of activity (Shah, 2002; Uslaner, 2004; Warkentin & Mingst, 2000; Wellman et al., 2001). Pigg (2001) has argued that networks can be designed to enhance civic participation, but so far, these designs have failed to incorporate the nature of participation. The designs typically focus on customer services and support instead of sharing of information, ideas, and knowledge to influence civic decisions. With a customer focus, the civic authorities may increase the satisfaction of its citizenry, whereas a participation focus obliges the authorities to share decision-making powers and accept more uncertainty in the process and outcomes.

CONCLUSION

A community network faces four inter-related collaboration challenges during its development that are tied to transformation, resources, trust, and management. When these challenges are met, the network will have a solid culture and structure of interdependence, and the flexibility to change over time. The network will maintain a positive momentum that is constructive and manageable, and lead to medium and long-term sustainability. When these challenges are not met adequately, the pace of change will be either too slow or too fast, or blocked at some point in time. Sustainability of the network will be compromised unless the underlying issues are addressed.

These four challenges are anchored in the proposed network development model where formation and performance phases, and adaptation through reformation are critical for the sustainability of the community network. Policy makers and change agents among the stakeholders of community networks are well advised to shape their interventions with the aim of establishing and maintaining positive momentum, while paying continued attention to issues of visioning, resources, trust, leadership, and management. They would do well to expand their views of technology development to include user appropriation and the challenges that users face. They must accept the uncertainty that is inevitable with user involvement to support the goal of network sustainability.

REFERENCES

Ackerman, M., & Haverton, C. (2004). Sharing expertise: The next step for knowledge management. In M. Huysman & V. Wulf (Eds.) *Social capital and information technology* (Chapter 11). Cambridge, USA and London, England: The MIT Press.

Agres, C., Edberg, D., & Igbaria, M. (1998). Transformation to virtual societies: Forces and issues. *The Information Society, 14*(2), 71-82.

Albert, S. (2005). Smart community networks: Self-directed team effectiveness in action. *Team Performance Management, 1*(5), 144-156.

Ardichvili, A., & Cardozo, R. N. (2000). A model of the entrepreneurial opportunity recognition process. *Journal of Entreprising Culture, 8*(2), 103-119.

Arino, A., & de la Torre, J. (1998). Learning from failure: Towards an evolutionary model of collaborative ventures. *Organizational Science, 9*(3), 306-325.

Bailey, Darlyne, & McNally-Koney, K. (1996). Interorganizational community-based collaboratives: A strategic response to shape the social work agenda. *Social Work, 41*(6), 602-610.

Bell, R. (2001). *Benchmarking the intelligent community—a comparison study of regional communities.* The Intelligent Community Forum of World Teleport Association.

Bernier, C., & Laflamme, S. (2005). Uses of the Internet according to type and age: A double differentiation. [Usages d'Internet selon le genre et l'age: Une double differenciation] *The Canadian Review of Sociology and Anthropology/La Revue Canadienne De Sociologie Et d'Anthropologie, 42*(3), 301-323.

Block, P. (1993). *Stewardship—Choosing service over self-interest.* San Francisco: Berrett-Koehler Publishers.

Blois, K. (1990). Research notes and communications—transaction costs and networks. *Strategic Management Journal, 11,* 493-496.

Bouwen, R., & Taillieu, T. (2004). Multi-party collaboration as social learning for interdependence: Developing relational knowing for sustainable natural resource management. *Journal of Community & Applied Social Psychology, 14,* 137-153.

Bradford, R. (2003). Public-private partnerships? Shifting paradigms of economic governance in Ontario. *Canadian Journal of Political Sciences, 36*(5), 1005-1033.

Brown, M., O'Toole, L., & Brudney, J. (1998). Implementing information technology in government: An empirical assessment of the role of local partnerships. *Journal of Public Administration Research and Theory, 8*(4), 499-525.

Canadian National Broadband Taskforce. (2001). *Report of the national broadband taskforce: The new national dream: Networking the nation for broadband access.* Ottawa, Canada: Industry Canada.

Canadian Rural Partnership. (2004, October). *Report of the advisory committee on rural issues.* Paper presented at the Third National Rural Conference, Red Deer, Canada.

Carroll, J. M., & Rosson, M. (2001). Better home shopping or new democracy? Evaluating community network outcomes. *3*(1), 372-377.

Castells, M. (1996). *The rise of network society, vol. 1 of the information age: Economy, society and culture.* Oxford: Blackwell.

Castells, M. (1997). *The power of identity, vol. 2 of the information age: Economy, society and culture.* Oxford: Blackwell.

Castells, M. (1998). *End of millennium, vol. 3 of the information age: Economy, society and culture.* Oxford: Blackwell.

Caves, R. (2001). E-commerce and information technology: Information technologies, economic development, and smart communities: Is there a relationship? *Economic Development Review, 17*(3), 6-13.

Considine, M., & Lewis, J. (2003). Networks and interactivity: Making sense of front-line governance in the United Kingdom, the Netherlands and Australia. *Journal of European Public Policy, 10*(1), 46-58.

Corbett, A. (2002). Recognizing high-tech opportunities: A learning and cognitive approach. *Frontiers of Entrepreneurship Research* (pp. 49-60).Wellesley, MA: Babson College.

Crowley, D. (2002). Where are we now? Contours of the internet in Canada. *Canadian Journal of Communication, 27*(4), 469-508.

Day, C. (2002). *The information society—a sceptical view.* Malden, MA: Blackwell Publishers.

De la Mothe, J. (2004). The institutional governance of technology, society, and innovation. *Technology in Society, 26,* 523-536.

Doz,Y. (1996). The evolution of cooperation in strategic alliances: Initial conditions or learning processes? *Strategic Management Journal, 17,* 55-83.

Du Gay, P., Hall, S., Janes, L., Mackay, H., & Negus, K. (1997). *Doing cultural studies: The story of the Sony, Walkman,* London and New Delhi: Sage.

Ebers, M. (2002). *The formation of inter-organizational networks.* Oxford: Oxford University Press.

Eger, J. (2001, November). *The world foundation for smart communities.* Retrieved January 28, 2003 from www.smartcommunities.org

Evans, J., & Brooks, L. (2005). Understanding collaboration using new technologies: A structural perspective. *Information Society, 21*(3), 215-220.

Fischer, G., Scharff, E., & Ye, Y. (2004). In M. Huysman & V. Wulf (Eds.). *Social capital and information technology* (Chapter 14). Cambridge, MA and London: The MIT Press.

Franklin, U. (1999). *The real world of technology.* Toronto: House of Anansi Press.

Ginsburg, M. (2001, November). *Realizing a framework to create, support, and understand virtual communities.* Maastricht, Holland: Infonomics.

Glatter, R. (2004). Collaboration, collaboration, collaboration: The origins and implications of a policy. *MiE, 17*(5), 16-20.

Gray, B. (1985). Conditions facilitating interorganizational collaboration. *Human Relations, 38*(10), 911-936.

Gray, B., & Hay, T. (1986). Political limits to interorganizational consensus and change. *The Journal of Applied Behavioral Science, 22*(2), 95-112.

Gurstein, M. (2000). *Community informatics: Enabling communities with information and communications technologies* (Introduction, pp. 1-29). Hershey, PA: Idea Group Publishing.

Hardy, C., & Phillips, N. (1998). Strategies of engagement: Lessons from the critical examination of collaboration and conflict in interorganizational domain. *Organizational Science, 2*, 217-230.

Hock, D. (2000). Birth of the chaordic age, *Executive Excellence, 17*(6), 6-7.

Huxham, C., & Vangen, S. (2000). Ambiguity, complexity and dynamics in the membership of collaboration. *Human Relations, 53*(6), 771-805.

Huysman, M., & Wulf, V. (2004). *Social capital and information technology.* Cambridge, MA and London: The MIT Press.

Huysman, M., & Wulf, V. (2005). The role of information technology in building and sustaining the relational base of communities. *The Information Society, 21*(2), 81-89.

Igbaria, M., Shayo, C., & Olfman, L. (1999). *On becoming virtual: The driving forces and arrangements* (pp. 27-41). New Orleans, LA: ACM.

Industry Canada. (2002a, April 4). *Fostering innovation and use.* Retrieved July 30, 2002 from http://broadband.gc.ca/Broadband-document/english/chapter5.htm

Industry Canada. (2002b, April 4). *Smart communities broadband.* Retrieved July 12, 2002 from http://smartcommunities.ic.gc.ca/index_e.asp

ITU (International Telecommunications Union). (2003). *World summit on the information society* (pp. 1-9). Retrieved from www.itu.int

Jarillo, C. (1988). On strategic networks. *Strategic Management Journal, 9*(1), 31-41.

Jones, C., Herterly, W., & Borgatti, S. (1997). A general theory of network governance: Exchange conditions and social mechanisms. *Academy of Management Review, 22*(4), 911-945.

Keenan, T., & Trotter, D. (1999). The changing role of community networks in providing citizen access to the Internet. Internet Research. *Electronic Networking Applications and Policy, 9*(2), 100-108.

Kickul, J., & Gundry, L. (2000). Pursuing technological innovation: The role of entrepreneurial posture and opportunity recognition among internet firms. In *Frontiers of Entrepreneurship Research*, MA: Babson College.

Lawrence, T., Phillips, N., & Hardy, C. (1999). Watching whale watching. *The Journal of Applied Behavioral Science, 35*(4), 479-502.

LeBrasseur, R., Whissell, R., & Ojha, A. (2002). Organizational learning, transformational leadership and implementation of continuous quality improvement in Canadian hospitals. *Australian Journal of Management, 27*(2), 141-162.

Lowndes, V., & Skelcher, C. (1998). The dynamics of multi-organizational partnerships: An analysis of changing modes of governance. *Public Administration, 76*, 313-333.

Martin, L., & Matlay, H. (2003). Innovative use of the Internet in established small firms: The impact of knowledge management and organizational learning in accessing new opportunities. *Qualitative Market Research, 6*(1), 18-26.

Martins, E. & Terblanche, F. (2003). Building organisational culture that stimulates creativity and innovation. *European Journal of Innovation Management, 6*(1), 64-74.

May, C. (2002). *The information society—A sceptical view.* Cambridge, UK: Polity Press.

McKnight, B. & Bontis, N. (2002). E-improvisation: Collaborative groupware technology expands the reach and effectiveness of organizational improvisation. *Knowledge and Process Management, 9*(4), 219-227.

New Economy Development Group Inc. (2001). *Sustainability project on sustainable communities.* Paper presented at the Canadian Rural Partnership. Rural Research and Analysis, Government of Canada.

Nooteboom, B. (1999). Innovation and inter-firm linkages: New implications for policy. *Research Policy, 28*(8), 793.

OECD. (1997). Organisation for economic co-operation and development. *Towards a global information society.* Paris: OECD.

OECD. (2004). Organization for economic co-operation and development. *Information and communication technologies and rural development.* Paris, France: OECD Publication Service.

Oliver, A., & Ebers, M. (1998). Networking network studies: An analysis of conceptual configurations in the study of inter-organizational relationships, *Organization Studies, 19*, 549-83.

Olk, P., & Young, C. (1997). Why members stay in or leave an R&D consortium: Performance and conditions of membership as determinants of continuity. *Strategic Management Journal, 18*(11), 855-877.

O'Toole, L. (1997). Treating networks seriously: Practical and research-based agendas in public administration. *Public Administration Review, 57*(1), 45-52.

Ouchi, W. (1980). Markets, bureaucracies, and clans. *Administrative Science Quarterly, 1*, 129-141.

Pettigrew, A. (1992). The character and significance of strategy process research. *Strategic Management Journal, 13*, 5-16.

Pettigrew, A. (1987). Context and action in the transformation of the firm. *Journal of Management Studies, 24*(6), 649-670.

Pigg, K. (2001). Applications of community informatics for building community and enhancing civic society. *Information, Communication & Society, 4*(4), 507-527.

Pissarra, J., & Jesuino, J. (2005). Idea generation through computer-mediated communication: The effects of anonymity. *Journal of Management Psychology, 20*(3/4), 275-291.

Poyhonen, A., & Smedlund, A. (2004). Assessing intellectual capital creation in regional clusters. *Journal of Intellectual Capital, 5*(3), 351-365.

Ring, P. (2002). Processes facilitating reliance on trust in inter-organizational networks. In M. Ebers (Ed.), *The formation of inter-organizational networks* (pp. 113-45). Oxford, England: Oxford University Press

Ring, P., & Van de Ven, A. (1994). Developmental processes of cooperative interorganizational relationships. *Academy of Management Review, 19*, 90-118.

Roberts, N., & Bradley, R. (1991). Stakeholder collaboration and innovation: A study of public policy initiation at the state level. *Journal of Applied Behavioral Science, 27*(2), 209-227.

Rycroft, R. (2003). Technology-based globalization indicators: The creativity of innovation network data. *Technology in Society, 25*(3), 299-317.

Scheel, C. (2002). Knowledge clusters of technological innovation systems. *Journal of Knowledge Management, 6*(4), 356-367.

Shah, D. (2002). Nonrecursive models of internet use and community engagement: Questioning whether time spent online erodes social capital. *Journalism & Mass Communication Quarterly, 79*(4), 964-987.

Snow, C. & Thomas, J. (1993). Building networks: Broker roles and behaviours. In P. Lorange, B. Chakravarthy, J. Roos, & A. Van de Ven (Eds.), *Implementing strategic processes: Change, learning and co-operation* (pp. 217-38). Oxford: Blackwell.

Sorensen, E. (2002). Democratic theory and network governance. *Administrative Theory & Praxis, 24*(4), 693-720.

Stevenson, T. (2002). Communities of tomorrow. *Futures, 34*(8), 735-744.

Suire, R. (2004). Des réseaux de l'entrepreneur aux ressorts du créatif Quelles stratégies pour les territoires? *Revue Internationale PME, 17*(2), 123-143.

Tan, M. (1999). Creating the digital economy: Strategies and perspectives from Singapore.

International Journal of Electronic Commerce, 3(3), 105-22.

United Nations. (1998). *Knowledge societies: Information technology for sustainable development.* Report prepared by R. Mansell & U. Wehn. Oxford: United Nations Commission on Science and Technology for Development/Oxford University Press.

Uslaner, E. M. (2004). Trust, civic engagement, and the Internet. *Political Communication, 21*(2), 223-242.

Van de Ven, A. & Poole, M. (1995). Explaining development and change in organizations. *Academy of Management Review, 20*(3), 510-540.

Van den Hooff, B., de Ridder, J. & Aukema, E. (2004). Exploring the eagerness to share knowledge: The role of social capital and ICT in knowledge sharing. In M. Huysman, & V. Wulf (Eds.), *Social capital and information technology* (Chapter 7). Cambridge, USA and London, England: The MIT Press.

Von Oetinger, B. (2005). From idea to innovation: Making creativity real. *The Journal of Business Strategy, 25*(5), 35-41.

Waits, M. (2000). The added value of the industry cluster approach to economic analysis, strategy development, and service delivery. *Economic Development Quarterly, 14*(1), 35-50.

Warkentin, C., & Mingst, K. (2000). International institutions, the state, and global civil society in the age of the World Wide Web. *Global Governance, 6*(2), 237-257.

Wellman, B., Haase, A. Q., Witte, J., & Hampton, K. (2001). Does the internet increase, decrease, or supplement social capital? Social networks, participation, and community commitment. *American Behavioral Scientist, 45*(3), 436-455.

Wheelan, S. (1999). *Creating effective teams: A guide for members and leaders* (p. 154). Thousand Oaks, CA: Sage Publications.

Williams, R., Stewart, J., & Slack, R. (2005). *Social learning in technological innovation—Experimenting with information communication technologies.* Cheltenham, UK and Northampton, USA: Edward Elgar.

Wood, D., & Wood, G. (1991). Toward a comprehensive theory of collaboration. *Journal of Applied Behavioral Science, 27*(2), 139-162.

World Bank (1999). *World development report 1998/99: Knowledge for development.* New York: Oxford University Press.

Zollo, M., Reuer, J., & Singh, J. (2002). Interorganizational routines and performance in strategic alliances. *Organizational Science, 13*(6), 701-713.

ENDNOTES

[1] The authors acknowledge the helpful comments of the reviewers. By addressing their concerns and suggestions, this article found a better balance between organizational and involvement issues.

[2] Multi-organizational collaboration, partnerships, and networks are considered interchangeable terms and refer to a variety of organizations collaborating for a common purpose. "Collaborative network" is proposed as an inclusive alternative.

[3] A stakeholder is defined as an organization that contributes programs and services to the network. A partner is one that makes a financial contribution to the overall project.

[4] The term downloading has become a popular expression in Canada as a result of higher levels of government shifting responsibility for programs to lower levels of government. Municipalities have inherited a number of costs and responsibilities previously held by the province and the province has inherited responsibilities previously held by the federal government.

[5] These communities have been highlighted at the annual conference of ICF (Intelligent Communities Forum).

This work was previously published in International Journal of Technology and Human Interaction, Vol. 3, Issue 2, edited by B. C. Stahl, pp. 13-33, copyright 2007 by IGI Publishing, formerly known as Idea Group Publishing (an imprint of IGI Global).

Chapter VII
The Impact of the Internet on Political Activism:
Evidence from Europe

Pippa Norris
Harvard University, USA

ABSTRACT

The core issue for this study concerns less the social than the political consequences of the rise of knowledge societies; in particular, the capacity of the Internet for strengthening democratic participation and civic engagement linking citizens and government. To consider these issues, Part I summarizes debates about the impact of the Internet on the public sphere. The main influence of this development, as it is theorized in a market model, will be determined by the "supply" and "demand" for electronic information and communications about government and politics. Demand, in turn, is assumed to be heavily dependent upon the social characteristics of Internet users and their prior political orientations. Given this understanding, the study predicts that the primary impact of knowledge societies in democratic societies will be upon facilitating cause-oriented and civic forms of political activism, thereby strengthening social movements and interest groups, more than upon conventional channels of political participation exemplified by voting, parties, and election campaigning. Part II summarizes the sources of survey data and the key measures of political activism used in this study, drawing upon the 19-nation European Social Survey, 2002. Part III examines the evidence for the relationship between use of the Internet and indicators of civic engagement. The conclusion in Part IV summarizes the results and considers the broader implications for governance and democracy.

INTRODUCTION

The rise of knowledge societies represents one of the most profound transformations that has occurred in recent decades. The diffusion of information and communication technologies (ICTs) promises to have major social consequences by expanding access to education and training, broadening channels of expression and social networks, as well as revolutionizing the nature of work and the economy. The primary impact of this development has been evident in affluent societies, but the Internet has also been widely regarded as an important instrument for social change in poorer nations around the globe (Franda, 2002; UN, 2002).

PART I: THEORIES OF THE IMPACT OF KNOWLEDGE SOCIETIES ON DEMOCRACY

There are multiple theories about how the growth of knowledge societies could potentially influence civic engagement in contemporary democracies. Four main perspectives can be identified in the literature.

The Internet as a Virtual Agora

The most positive view is held by cyber-optimists who emphasize the Panglossian possibilities of the Internet for the involvement of ordinary citizens in direct, deliberative, or "strong" democracy. Digital technologies are thought to hold promise as a mechanism facilitating alternative channels of civic engagement exemplified by political chat rooms, remote electronic voting in elections, referenda, plebiscites, and the mobilization of virtual communities, thereby revitalizing levels of mass participation in public affairs (Barber, 1998; Budge, 1996). This view was certainly popular as

the Internet rapidly expanded in the United States during the mid-1990s and the radical potential of digital technologies for democracy continues to be expressed by enthusiasts today (Gilder, 2000; Rash, 1997; Rheingold, 1993; Schwartz, 1996).

Moreover, the general claim that the knowledge society will stimulate widespread citizen deliberation in affairs of state so that the Internet functions like a virtual Agora while attractive as a normative ideal, became less plausible once it was widely recognized by many observers that there are substantial disparities in who becomes involved in digital politics. Studies of politically-oriented discussion groups, bulletin boards, and online chat rooms have found that these largely fail as deliberative forums, instead serving as places to reinforce like-minded voices due to their "easy entrance, easy exit" characteristics (Davis, 1999; Davis & Owen, 1998; Wilhelm, 2001). The survey evidence from many countries indicates that those who take advantage of the opportunities for electronic civic engagement are often activists who were already most predisposed to participate via the traditional channels of political participation (Hill & Hughes, 1998; Selnow, 1998; Toulouse & Luke, 1998). The Internet is a medium of choice par excellence, so it seems improbable that political Web sites, chat rooms and online news will reach many citizens who are otherwise disengaged, apathetic, or uninterested, if they choose to spend their time and energies on multiple alternative sites devoted to everything from the stock market to games and music (Bonfadelli, 2002; Johnson & Kaye, 2003). In this regard, the Internet seems analogous to the segmented magazine market, where some subscribe to the *Atlantic Monthly* and the *Economist* and *Foreign Affairs*, but others pick *Golfing Weekly* or *Playboy*. Therefore, claims for the potential of the knowledge society to revitalize mass participation or strong democracies find little support from the available empirical studies.

The Knowledge Elite and Social Inequalities

As the Internet evolved during the last decade, a darker vision developed among cyber-pessimists who regard the knowledge society as a Pandora's Box reinforcing existing inequalities of power and wealth and generating deeper divisions between the information rich and poor. In this perspective, the global and social divides in Internet access mean that, far from encouraging mass participation, the knowledge society will disproportionately benefit the most affluent sectors in the developed world (Golding, 1996; Hayward, 1995; Murdock & Golding, 1989; Weber, Loumakis, & Bergman, 2003). For example, the first phase of the UN World Summit on the Information Society (WSIS) held in Geneva in December 2003 concluded that the Internet holds great prospect for development for billions of people around the globe, endorsing ambitious principles and action plans, and yet no agreement was reached about the transfer of financial and technological resources necessary to facilitate wider electronic access in poorer nations (ITU, 2003). Despite the great potential for technological innovations leading towards political change, observers suggest that in established democracies, traditional interest groups and governments have the capacity to reassert their control in the virtual political sphere, just as traditional multinational corporations have the ability to reestablish their predominance in the world of e-commerce (Hill & Hughes, 1998; McChesney, 1999; Selnow, 1998; Toulouse & Luke, 1998). In authoritarian regimes, as well, studies have found that access to publishing and disseminating information on the Internet, can be strictly restricted by governments, such as limitations imposed in Cuba, Saudi Arabia, and China (Boas, 2000; Drake, Kalathil, & Boas, 2000; Hill & Hughes, 1999; Kalathil & Boas, 2003).

Politics as Usual

The third perspective, which has become more commonly heard in recent years, is articulated by cyber-skeptics who argue that both of these visions are exaggerated. In this view, the potential of the knowledge society has failed so far to have a dramatic impact on the practical reality of "politics as usual," for good or ill, even in countries such as the United States at the forefront of digital technologies (Margolis & Resnick, 2000). This perspective stresses the embedded status quo and the difficulties of achieving radical change to political systems through technological mechanisms. For example, commentators suggest that during the 2000 American election campaign, George W. Bush and Al Gore used their Web pages essentially as glossy shop windows, fundraising tools, and campaign ads, rather than as interactive "bottom up" formats facilitating public comment and discussion (Foot & Schneider, 2002; Media Matrix, 2000). During the 2004 presidential election in the United States, the fundraising function also seems to have predominated in the campaign for Vermont Democratic Governor, Howard Dean, and the Kerry-Edwards Web site.

Elsewhere, content analysis of political party Web sites in countries as diverse as the United Kingdom, France, Mexico, and the Republic of Korea has found that the primary purpose of these Web sites has been the provision of standard information about party organizations and policies that were also widely available offline, providing more of the same rather than anything new, with still less interactive facilities.

Party presence on the Internet seems to represent largely an additional element to a party's repertoire of action along with more traditional communication forms rather than a transformation of the fundamental relationship between political

*parties and the public, as some earlier advocates
of cyber-democracy hoped.* (Gibson, Nixon, &
Ward, 2003, p. X)

Studies of the content of government department Web sites in many countries at the forefront
of the move towards e-governance (e.g., the
United States, Canada, and India) and surveys
of users of these Web sites have also found that
these Web sites are often primarily used for the
dissemination of information and the provision
of routine administrative services. The Internet
thereby serves as an aid to good governance by
increasing government transparency, efficiency,
and customer-oriented service delivery, but it
does not function as a radical medium facilitating
citizen consultation, policy discussion, or other
democratic inputs into the policymaking process
(Allen, Jullet, & Roy, 2001; Chadwick & May,
2003; Fountain, 2001; Haque, 2002; Stowers,
1999; Thomas & Streib, 2003). In the skeptical
view, technology is a plastic medium that flows
into and adapts to pre-existing social molds and
political functions.

The Political Market Model

The last theoretical perspective — the one developed in this study — can be characterized as
the political market model. In this account, the
impact of the knowledge society depends upon
the interaction between the "top-down supply" of
political information and communications made
available via the Internet, e-mail, and the World
Wide Web from political institutions, notably
government departments, parliaments, political
parties, the news media, interest groups, and social movements, and upon "demand" in the use of
information and communications about politics
among the online public.

This model suggests that, in turn, demand
depends upon the social characteristics of the
online population, especially the preponderance
of younger, well-educated citizens who are com-

monly among the heaviest users of the Internet, and
their prior political interests and propensities. The
theory suggests that, given these assumptions, use
of the Internet in the public sphere is most likely
to strengthen and reinforce cause-oriented and
civic-oriented dimensions of political activism,
which are more popular among the well-educated
younger generation, while having far less impact
upon traditional channels of participation through
voting, parties, and election campaigns (Norris
2001, 2002).

Therefore, rather than accepting that either
everything will change as radical forms of direct
democracy come to replace the traditional channels of representative governance (as optimists
hope), that the digital divide will reinforce socio-
economic disparities in politics (as pessimists
predict), or alternatively that nothing will change
as the digital world merely replicates "politics
as usual" (as the skeptics suggest), the political
market model suggests that it is more sensible to
identify what particular types of democratic practices will probably be strengthened by the rise of
the knowledge society, understanding that these
developments remain a work in process.

PART II: CONCEPTUAL
FRAMEWORK, EVIDENCE, & DATA

What evidence would allow us to examine these
propositions, particularly testing the impact of the
Internet upon political activism? To understand
these issues, we need to recognize that involvement in public affairs can take many different
forms, each associated with differing costs and
benefits. This study compares the impact of
frequency of use of the Internet on four main dimensions of activism: voting, campaign-oriented,
cause-oriented, and civic-oriented. These are
summarized into a 21-point "Political Activism
Index" combining all dimensions[1]. The basic items
used to develop this Index are listed in Table 1
and reported fully in Appendix A.

Table 1. Political Activism in Europe, ESS-2002

Percentage that have...	Regular internet user (%)	Not regular user (%)	Activism Gap (%)	Sig
VOTING				
Reported voting in the last national election	28	26	+2	***
CAMPAIGN-ORIENTED				
Contacted politician	22	13	+9	***
Worn campaign badge	12	6	+6	***
Donated money to party	11	7	+4	***
Worked for party	6	4	+2	***
Party member	6	5	+1	***
CAUSE-ORIENTED				
Bought product for political reason	41	17	+24	***
Signed petition	35	16	+19	***
Boycotted product	25	11	+14	***
Demonstrated legally	10	5	+5	***
Protested illegally	2	1	+1	***
CIVIC-ORIENTED				
Member sports club	35	14	+21	***
Member trade union	33	17	+16	***
Member consumer group	25	11	+14	***
Member hobby group	20	10	+10	***
Member educational group	12	4	+8	***
Member professional group	14	6	+8	***
Member environmental group	9	4	+5	***
Member humanitarian group	9	4	+5	***
Member church group	15	11	+4	***
Member social club	11	10	+1	***
TOTAL 21-POINT ACTIVISM INDEX				
Mean index score	4.43	2.56	+1.87	***

Voting in regular elections is one of the most ubiquitous forms of citizen-oriented participation, requiring some initiative and awareness for an informed choice but making fairly minimal demands of time, knowledge, and effort. Through the ballot box, voting exerts diffuse pressure over parties and elected officials, and the outcomes of elections affect all citizens. Participating at the ballot box is central to citizenship in representative democracy, but due to its relatively low costs, the act is atypical of other more demanding forms of participation. The Internet can be expected to encourage voting participation mainly by lowering some of the information hurdles to making an informed choice, although the provision of remote electronic voting through a variety of new technologies can be expected to have a more radical impact on turnout (Tolbert & McNeal, 2003).

Campaign-oriented forms of participation concern acts focused primarily on how people can influence parliament and government in representative democracy, mainly through political parties in British politics. Verba, Nie, and Kim (1978) focus on this aspect when they define political participation as "…those legal activities by private citizens that are more or less directly aimed at influencing the selection of governmental personnel and/or the actions they take." Work for parties or candidates, including party membership and volunteer work, election leafleting, financial donations to parties or candidates, attending local party meetings, and get-out-the-vote drives, typifies this category. Parties serve multiple functions in representative democracies, notably simplifying and structuring electoral choices, organizing and mobilizing campaigns, aggregating disparate interests, channeling political debate, selecting candidates, structuring parliamentary divisions, acting as policy think tanks, and organizing government. Not only are parties one of the main conduits of political participation, they also serve to boost and strengthen electoral turnout. If mass party membership is under threat, as many indicators suggest, this could have serious implications for representative democracy (Mair & Biezen, 2001; Scarrow, 2001).

Campaigning and party work typically generate collective rather than individual benefits, but require greater initiative, time, and effort (and sometimes expenditure) than merely casting a ballot. The Internet can be expected to provide new opportunities for activism in parties and election campaigns (e.g., through downloading information, joining parties or donating funds, and participation in discussion groups hosted on party or candidate Web sites) (Gibson, Nixon, & Ward, 2003; Hague & Loader, 1999; Norris, 2001;). Experience of campaign-oriented activism is gauged in this study by a five-battery item, including whether people are members of a party and whether they have donated money to a party, worked for a party, contacted a politician,

or worn a campaign badge during the previous 12 months.

Cause-oriented activities are focused primarily upon influencing specific issues and policies. These acts are exemplified by consumer politics (e.g., buying or boycotting certain products for political or ethical reasons), taking part in demonstrations and protests, and organizing or signing petitions. The distinction is not watertight; for example, political parties can organize mass demonstrations, and social movements often adopt mixed action strategies that combine traditional repertoires such as lobbying representatives, with a variety of alternative modes such as online networking, street protests, and consumer boycotts. Nevertheless, compared with campaign-oriented actions, the distinctive aspect of cause-oriented repertoires is that they are most commonly used to pursue specific issues and policy concerns among diverse targets, both within and also well beyond the electoral arena.

These acts seek to influence representative democracies within the nation-state through the conventional channels of contacting elected officials, ministers, civil servants, and government departments, but their target is often broader and more diffuse, possibly in the non-profit or private sectors, whether directed at shaping public opinion and lifestyles, publicizing certain issues through the news media, mobilizing a networked coalition with other groups or non-profit agencies, influencing the practices of international bodies such as the World Trade Organization or the United Nations, or impacting public policy in other countries. Experience of cause-oriented activism is measured in this study by a five-battery item, including whether people have signed a petition, bought or boycotted products for a political reason, demonstrated legally, or protested illegally during the previous 12 months.

Lastly and by contrast, **civic-oriented** activities involve membership and working together in voluntary associations, as well as collaborating with community groups to solve a local problem.

The core claim of Toquevillian theories of social capital is that typical face-to-face deliberative activities and horizontal collaboration within voluntary organizations far removed from the political sphere (exemplified by trade unions, social clubs, and philanthropic groups) promote interpersonal trust, social tolerance, and cooperative behavior. In turn, these norms are regarded as cementing the bonds of social life and creating the foundation for building local communities, civil society, and democratic governance. In a win-win situation, participation in associational life is thought to generate individual rewards, such as career opportunities and personal support networks, as well as facilitating community goods by fostering the capacity of people to work together on local problems. Putnam suggests that civic organizations such as unions, churches, and community groups play a vital role in the production of social capital where they succeed in bridging divisive social cleavages, integrating people from diverse backgrounds and values, promoting "habits of the heart" such as tolerance, cooperation, and reciprocity, thereby contributing towards a dense, rich, and vibrant social infrastructure (Pharr & Putnam, 2000; Putnam, 1993, 1996, 2000, 2002). This dimension involves direct action within local communities (e.g., raising funds for a local hospital or school) where the precise dividing line between the social and political breaks down.

Trade unions and churches, in particular, which have long been regarded as central pillars of civic society in Europe, have traditionally served the function of drawing citizens into public life. For a variety of reasons, including the way that voluntary associations can strengthen social networks, foster leadership skills, heighten political awareness, create party linkages, and facilitate campaign work, people affiliated with church-based or union organizations can be expected to participate more fully in public life (Cassel, 1999; Radcliff & Davis, 2000). Access to the knowledge society can be expected to expand social networks and information, facilitating membership in civic associations and social groups, although the evidence as to whether the Internet strengthens or weakens social capital remains under debate (Bimber, 1998; Horrigan, Rainie, & Fox, 2001). Experience of civic activism is measured here by a 10-point scale summarizing membership in a series of different types of voluntary organizations and associations, including traditional sectors such as trade unions, church groups, and social clubs, as well as "new" social movements exemplified by groups concerned about the environment and humanitarian issues.

The summary 21-point Political Activism Index, which provides an overview, is composed very simply by adding together experience of each of these different types of acts (each coded 0/1). It should be noted that in this conceptual framework, this study focuses upon political *activity*; we are concerned with *doing* politics rather than being attentive to public affairs or having psychological attitudes such as trust in parliament or political efficacy, which are thought to be conducive to civic engagement. The study, therefore, does not regard exposure or attention to mass communications, including following campaign events in newspapers or watching party political broadcasts during the election, as indicators of political activism per se. These factors may, indeed, plausibly contribute towards participation and thereby help explain this phenomenon as prior pre-conditions, but they are not, in themselves, channels that citizens can use for expressing political concerns or mobilizing group interests.

Survey Evidence & Data Sources

To establish the extent and significance of the role of the Internet on political activism, the primary source of evidence for this study is drawn from the 19-nation European Social Survey 2002 (ESS-19). This is a new, academically driven study designed to chart and explain the interaction between Europe's changing institutions and the attitudes, beliefs, and behavior patterns of its diverse populations[2]. The survey includes a wide range of items designed to monitor citizen involvement, including a battery of a dozen items that can be used to create a summary political activism scale, as well as multiple indicators of political interest, efficacy, trust, party allegiances, subjective well-being, family and friendship bonds, and a rich array of detailed socio-demographic data, including household composition, ethnicity, type of area, and occupational details. This survey provides recent evidence, and it also facilitates comparison among similar advanced industrialized European societies and democratic states. The size of the total pooled sample (with over 36,000 cases) also allows us to monitor differences among smaller European populations, such as ethnic minorities.

The survey currently includes four nations in Scandinavia (Norway, Sweden, Finland, and Denmark), six nations in Northern Europe (Britain, Germany, Luxembourg, Ireland, the Netherlands, and Switzerland), four from Mediterranean Europe (Greece, Spain, Italy, Portugal, and Israel), and four post-Communist societies in Central Europe (the Czech Republic, Hungary, Poland,

and Slovenia). All these countries were classified by Freedom House in 2001-02 as fully "free" in their political rights and civil liberties, using the Gastil Index. Most can also be categorized as affluent post-industrial economies, with an average per capita GDP in 2002 ranging from $16,000 (in Greece) to $30,000 (in Norway), although all of the post-Communist states except Slovenia fall below this level.

Internet Use

In some of these societies, the knowledge society has been widely diffused, with two-thirds or more of the public using the Internet at least occasionally. By contrast, in other societies, few of the public accesses the Internet. The survey monitored Internet use by the question in Example 1.

This is a limited measure that does not gauge what people do online or where they commonly seek information, nor does it distinguish among access to the Internet, email, or World Wide Web. These are only some forms of access to the knowledge society, and other electronic technologies may be equally important, such as

Example 1.

*"Now, using this card, how often do you use the internet, the World Wide Web or e-mail – whether at home or at work – for your **personal**[1] use?"*		
No access at home or work	00 (41%)	}
Never use	01 (17%)	}
Less than once a month	02 (3%)	} Regular use
Once a month	03 (2%)	}
Several times a month	04 (4%)	}
Once a week	05 (5%)	}
Several times a week	06 (11%)	}
Every day	07 (16%)	}
(Don't know/No answer)		

[1] *"Personal use"* is defined by the ESS-2002 as private or recreational use that does not have to do with a person's work or occupation.

text messaging; mobile or cell phones; or cable, satellite, and interactive television. In addition, people may also use the Internet at work, and the measure does not attempt to monitor the length of experience of using the Internet. Nevertheless, this item provides a standard measure of exposure to the Internet widely used in other studies, which gives a suitable benchmark for cross-national comparison.

The main cross-national contrasts that emerged on this item are illustrated in Figure 1, which compares a third of Europeans in the sample who report that they *regularly* use the Internet (defined here as personal use of the Internet at least weekly) in the ESS-19. The remaining two-thirds say they never used the Internet or used it far less regularly than weekly. As many other Eurobarometer surveys have regularly reported, sharp differences are evident in Internet access within Europe (Norris, 2001). In Scandinavia (notably Denmark, Sweden, and Norway), regular Internet use is widespread among the majority of the population. Many of the countries fall into the middle of the distribution where anywhere from one-fifth to one-half use the Internet at least weekly. By contrast, in some countries in Mediterranean and post-Communist Europe, less than a fifth of the public made regular use of this technology, notably in Greece, Hungary, Poland, and Spain, which were all at the bottom of the distribution.

PART III: ANALYSIS & RESULTS

How do those Europeans who are and are not regular users of the Internet compare across the different types of political activism? We can first compare the overall patterns using the pooled ESS-19 sample without using any prior social or attitudinal controls, and then go on to consider the results of the multivariate analysis and differences among European nations. One important qualification to note is that in the analysis, we cannot establish the direction of causality in these models; with a single cross-sectional survey, it is impossible to disentangle satisfactorily whether use of the Internet facilitates and encourages political activism, or whether prior habits of political engagement lead towards continuing activism via electronic channels. To establish causality in any media effects, we really need either to analyze repeated panel surveys among the same respondents over successive years, or to examine experimental research designs, neither of which are available on a cross-national basis (Kent, Jennings, & Zeitner, 2003; Norris, 2000; Norris & Sanders, 2003). In the model, based on standard theories of political socialization, we assume that the cultural values and norms of behavior are acquired from formative experiences with family, school, and community in early youth. We theorize that these processes are likely to shape long-term and enduring political orientations and habitual norms of behavior, such as patterns of partisan identification, ideological values, and forms of activism. We assume that use of the Internet is a relatively recent and, therefore, short-term influence that will facilitate and reinforce the cognitive and attitudinal factors associated with habitual political activism (e.g., expanding people's awareness of election issues or party policies) but will not necessarily alter or transform broader patterns of civic engagement.

Given these assumptions, Table 1 shows a clear and consistent pattern: regular Internet users are significantly more politically active across all 21 indicators. The overall score on the mean Political Activism Index, which summarizes this pattern, was 4.43 for regular Internet users compared with 2.56 for others, a substantial and significant difference. Yet the size of the activism gap does vary among different types of engagement; it is relatively modest in reported voting turnout as well as across most of the campaign-oriented forms of activism, such as party membership, party volunteer work, and party donations. By contrast, the gap is substantial (in double digits)

Figure 1. Proportion of Regular Internet Users in Europe, ESS-2002

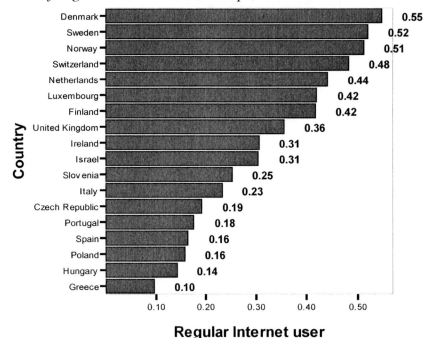

Regular Internet user

among many forms of cause-oriented activism, such as buying or boycotting products for political reasons and signing petitions, as well as in membership of certain types of civic organizations notably belonging to sports clubs, trade unions, consumer groups, and hobby groups.

To see whether this activism gap was an artifact of the way that regular Internet use was measured, Figure 2 illustrates the mean distribution of the political activism index across all categories of Internet use, ranging from no access at home or work to personal use of the Internet every day. The figure confirms that the overall scale of political activism rises sharply and steadily with each category of Internet use, more than doubling across the whole scale.

Moreover, if the patterns are analyzed by country, again similar results are evident in every society. As Figure 3 shows, political activism rises steadily with increasing Internet use in nearly all nations, and the only exceptions to this are Portugal and Poland where levels of technological diffusion remain very limited.

Despite this clear and important pattern, the theoretical framework in this study suggests that, given the characteristics of the online population, we should find systematic variations in engagement by the different types of political activism, and, indeed, this is confirmed by the data. Figure 4 illustrates the strong and significant linear relationship between use of the Internet and civic activism in a wide range of voluntary organizations and local associations (R=318***). The cause-oriented activism scale is also significantly associated with the frequency of using the Internet (R =.318***). Nevertheless, voting activism is relatively flat across levels of Internet use, and the correlation proves to be significant but negative in direction (R= -0.024**), while the campaign-oriented activism scale shows only a modest positive correlation (R=.136). The results suggest that any association between access to the Internet and political activism is heavily contingent upon the particular forms of participation that are under analysis.

Figure 2: Internet Use & Political Activism Index

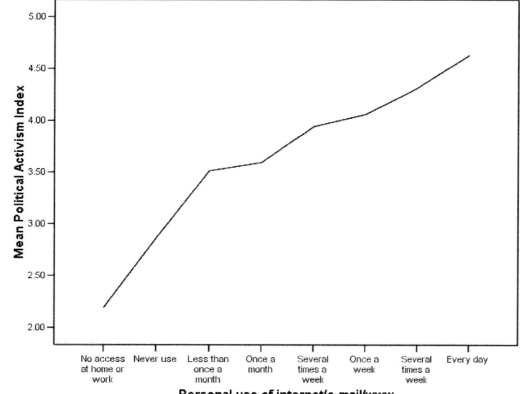

Nevertheless, many factors may be influencing this process, including the prior social characteristics and cultural attitudes of Internet users. To examine these issues we need multivariate regression models. The main explanations of political activism can be categorized into the following four groups:

1. **Structural** explanations emphasizing the resources that facilitate civic engagement; notably, time, education, and income, which are closely associated with demographic groups and social status;
2. **Cultural** accounts focusing upon the motivational attitudes that draw people into public affairs, such as a sense of political efficacy, institutional confidence, and citizenship duty;

3. **Agency** explanations prioritizing the role of mobilizing organizations such as churches and unions, as well as the role of the news media and informal social networks, which bring people into public affairs. The use of the Internet can best be conceptualized in this model as a mobilizing agency;
4   **Historical** accounts suggesting that there could be a regional effect generated by traditions in each area; notably, the length of time that representative democracy has operated in Scandinavia, Western Europe, and the "third-wave" democracies in the Mediterranean region and post-Communist societies that only experienced free and fair elections from the early 1990s onward.

Given this framework, Table 2 first includes the standard demographic and socioeconomic

Figure 3. Internet Use & Political Activism Index by Nation

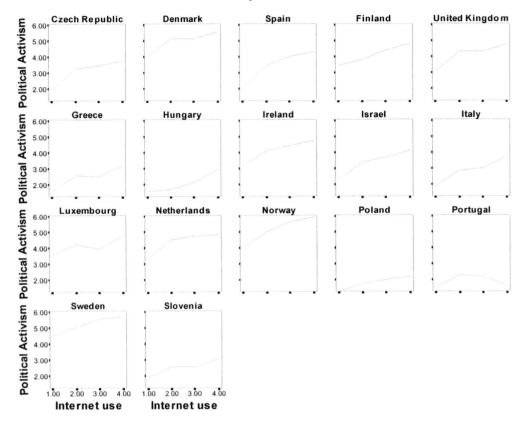

variables that many studies have commonly found to influence participation, including belonging to an ethnic minority, educational qualifications, household income, social class, work status, total hours normally worked per week, marital and family status, and religiosity. These were entered into the model in this order before adding the cultural attitudes of frequency of political discussion, the importance of politics, social and political trust, internal and external political efficacy, a sense of civic duty, and interest in politics. The mobilizing agency variables were then entered, including social networks and attention to politics on television, radio, and newspapers. The use of the Internet was entered at the end of this category to see whether there was any residual impact associated with this technology net of all other factors. Lastly, the major European regions

were added, coded as dummy variables, where the Nordic region was the default category for comparison.

The results in the pooled model confirm the significance of many of these factors upon the political activism scale. The only exceptions proved to belong to an ethnic minority, the amount of hours in the paid workforce, and the salience of politics, which all proved to be non-significantly related to participation, contrary to expectations. But after adding the complete battery of controls, use of the Internet continued to be significantly related to political activism, suggesting that this relationship is not simply explained away as a result of the prior social or attitudinal characteristics of those who are most prone to go online. The most important factors predicting activism (measured by the strength of the standardized

Figure 4. Internet Use & Types of Political Activism

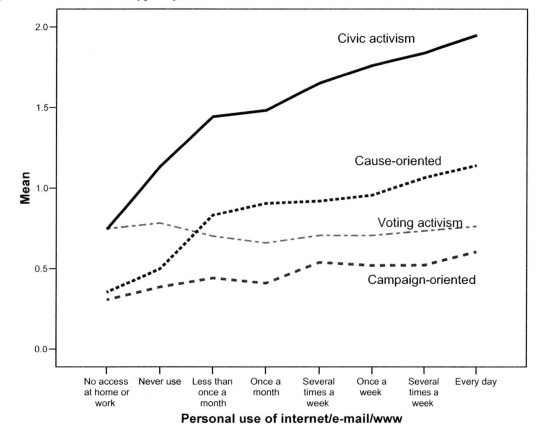

regression coefficients) concern internal political efficacy (a feeling that the person could influence the political process), age, education, region, and civic duty. After these factors, use of the Internet proved the next strongest predictor of activism, which was more important than other indicators such as social and political trust or use of any of the news media. The overall model explained more than one-third of the variance in activism (R^2=.37).

Similar regression models were then run with identical controls to predict the four types of political activism under comparison, using the pooled sample. Without showing all the coefficients, the summary of the results in Table 3 shows that use of the Internet was significantly associated with voting, cause- and civic-oriented forms of activism, but not with campaign-oriented forms of activism. This confirms that, rather than claims about the effect of the knowledge society on activism, we do need to distinguish among the types of participation that generate different effects. The reason for these differences most probably lies in the residual effect of the typical social background and the political values of Internet users, notably the propensity of well-educated younger generations to predominate online, as noted in many studies of the well-known "digital divide" (Norris, 2001).

Table 2. The impact of Internet use on political activism, with controls

	B	Std. Error	Beta	Sig.
(Constant)	-1.39	0.28		0.00
SOCIAL STRUCTURE				
Gender	-0.17	0.05	-0.03	0.00
Age (years)	0.02	0.00	0.13	0.00
Belong to ethnic minority	0.03	0.13	0.00	0.81
Educational qualifications	0.22	0.02	0.11	0.00
Income	0.07	0.01	0.06	0.00
Work status	0.38	0.06	0.06	0.00
Total hours per week in main job + O/T	0.00	0.00	0.00	0.88
Married	0.19	0.05	0.03	0.00
Have children at home	0.13	0.05	0.02	0.01
Importance of religion	0.12	0.05	0.02	0.01
CULTURAL ATTITUDES				
Discuss politics/current affairs, how often	-0.14	0.01	-0.09	0.00
Important in life: politics	0.01	0.01	0.01	0.54
Social trust	0.02	0.00	0.04	0.00
Trust in national political institutions	-0.02	0.01	-0.03	0.01
Trust in international institutions	-0.03	0.01	-0.04	0.00
Internal political efficacy	0.27	0.01	0.18	0.00
External political efficacy	0.12	0.01	0.08	0.00
Civic duty scale	0.04	0.00	0.11	0.00
How interested in politics	-0.34	0.04	-0.09	0.00
MOBILIZING AGENCIES				
How often socially meet with friends, relatives or colleagues	0.17	0.02	0.08	0.00
TV watching, news/ politics/current affairs on average weekday	-0.12	0.02	-0.05	0.00
Radio listening, news/ politics/current affairs on average weekday	0.03	0.01	0.02	0.06
Newspaper reading, politics/current affairs on average weekday	0.09	0.03	0.03	0.00
Personal use of internet/e-mail/www	0.10	0.01	0.10	0.00
REGION				
Northern Europe	-0.30	0.06	-0.05	0.00
Mediterranean Europe	-1.35	0.08	-0.16	0.00
Post-Communist Europe	-1.73	0.09	-0.23	0.00
Adjusted R^2	.373			

Source: European Social Survey, 2002 (ESS-19). Pooled sample N. 31741 in 18 ESS nations, excluding Germany (where Internet use was not monitored).

Note: The models represent the result of ordinary least squares regression analysis where the total political activism index is the dependent variable. The index counts participation in each form of activity as one and sums the 21-point scale. The figures represent the unstandardized beta coefficient (B), the standard error (s.e.), the standardized beta coefficient (Beta), and the significance (sig). The default dummy regional variable was the Nordic region. All variables were checked to be free of problems of multi-collinearity by tolerance statistics. See Table1 for the items in each scale.

Table 3. Impact of Internet use on types of political activism, with controls

Type of activism	B	Std. Error	Beta	Sig.	Adjusted R²
Voting	.005	.001	.034	.002	.145
Cause-oriented	.036	.004	.095	.000	.213
Campaign-oriented	.006	.004	.018	.102	.161
Civic-oriented	.042	.006	.073	.000	.308

Source: European Social Survey, 2002. Pooled sample N. 31741 in 18 ESS nations, excluding Germany (where Internet use was not monitored).

Note: The models represent the result of ordinary least squares regression analysis on each form of activism as the dependent variables. For the full range of prior controls in the models (not reported here), see Table 2. The figures represent the unstandardized beta coefficient (B), the standard error (s.e.), the standardized beta coefficient (Beta), and the significance (sig).

PART IV: CONCLUSIONS & DISCUSSION

The theory developed in this study considers the more pessimistic claims that the development of the Internet will serve to reinforce the voices of the powerful, the more skeptical arguments that it will merely reflect "politics as usual," and the more optimistic view that the knowledge society will transform governance as we know it and strengthen levels of mass political participation. The study hypothesizes that contemporary democracies are a market where the impact of the Internet depends in part upon the "supply" of political information and communications, primarily from political agencies, and also upon the "demand" for such information and communication from the mass public. In turn, the public's demand comes from the social and cultural profile of the online population reflecting long-standing patterns of civic engagement. As a result, use of the Internet is significantly related to overall patterns of political activism, even with multiple prior controls, but there are several distinct dimensions or channels of activism. The survey evidence analyzed in this study confirms that the rise of the knowledge society in Europe has indeed had the greatest positive consequences for politics by strengthening cause-oriented and civic-oriented activism, rather than by encouraging mass participation in campaigns and elections.

What are the broader implications of this pattern for democracy and for the future of electronic governance? We can speculate that the primary beneficiaries of this process will probably be political actors lacking traditional organizational resources that are useful in politics, such as those without a large-scale, fee-paying mass membership base, substantial financial assets, and paid full-time bureaucratic officials. This type of organization is exemplified by new social movements, transnational advocacy networks, alternative social movements, protest organizations, community activists and development workers, single-issue causes from all shades of the political spectrum, as well as minor parties. The knowledge society is not expected to drive these insurgent movements, but rather to facilitate their organization, mobilization, and expression (Keck & Sikkink, 1998). These organizations have the greatest incentives and the fewest constraints to using the knowledge society. If this perspective is correct, then the result of the rise of the Internet may be greater pressures on governments to respond to the demands of single-issue groups and more amorphous social networks. By contrast, established political parties and traditional interest groups can be expected to adapt far more slowly to the knowledge society, because they are capable of drawing upon alternative organizational and financial resources, including legal authority, full time paid officials, press officers, lobbyists, and grassroots fee-paying mass memberships. Yet these are the umbrella organizations, particularly parties, which are capable of aggregating diverse issues into broader programmatic platforms, encouraging compromise, deliberation, and bargaining among members and channeling demands on a more predictable basis into government. It remains to be seen how far these developments alter the channels of participation in representative democracy in Europe and elsewhere, but the consequences will probably provide government with greater opportunities to connect with citizens and to greater challenges in the inevitable pressures that arise from satisfying multiple fragmented zero-sum constituencies represented by single-issue politics.

REFERENCES

Allen, B.A., Juillet, L., Paquet, G., & Roy, J. (2001). E-governance & government on-line in Canada: Partnerships, people & prospects. *Government Information Quarterly, 18*(2), 93-104.

Barber, B. R. (1998). Three scenarios for the future of technology and strong democracy. *Political Science Quarterly,* I(4), 573-589.

Bimber, B. (1998). The Internet and political transformation: Populism, community and accelerated pluralism. *Polity XXXI,* (1), 133-160.

Bimber, B. (2001). Information and political engagement in America: The search for effects of information technology at the individual level. *Political Research Quarterly, 54*(1), 53-67.

Boas, T. C. (2000). The dictator's dilemma? The Internet and U.S. policy toward Cuba. *The Washington Quarterly, 23*(3), 57-67.

Bonfadelli, H. (2002). The Internet and knowledge gaps: A theoretical and empirical investigation. *European Journal of Communication, 17*(1), 65-84.

Budge, I. (1996). *The New Challenge of Direct Democracy.* Oxford: Polity Press.

Cassel, C.A. (1999). Voluntary associations, churches, and social participation theories of turnout. *Social Science Quarterly, 80*(3), 504-517.

Chadwick, A. & May, C. (2003). Interactions between states and citizens in the age of the Internet: "E-government" in the United States, Britain and the European Union. *Governance, 16*(2), 271-300.

David, R. (1999). *The Web of Politics.* Oxford: Oxford University Press.

Davis, R. & Owen, D. (1998). *New Media and American Politics.* New York: Oxford University Press.

Drake, W.J., Kalathil, S., & Boas, T. C. (2000, October). Dictatorships in the digital age: Some considerations on the Internet in China and Cuba. *iMP: The Magazine on Information Impacts.* Retrieved from: www.cisp.org/imp

Foot, K.A. & Schneider, S.M. (2002). Online action in campaign 2000: An exploratory analysis of the US political web sphere. *Journal of Broadcasting & Electronic Media, 46*(2), 222-244.

Fountain, J. E. (2001). *Building the Virtual State: Information Technology and Institutional Change.* Washington, DC: Brookings Institution Press.

Franda, M. (2002). *Launching Into Cyberspace: Internet Development and Politics in Five World Regions.* Boulder, CO: Lynne Rienner.

Gibson, R., Nixon, P., & Ward, S. (eds.). (2003). *Political Parties and the Internet: Net Gain?* London: Routledge.

Gilder, G. (2000). *Telecom: How Infinite Bandwidth Will Revolutionize Our World.* New York: Free Press.

Golding, P. (1996). World wide wedge: Division and contradiction in the global information infrastructure. *Monthly Review, 48*(3), 70-85.

Hague, B. N. & Loader, B. D. (eds.). (1999). *Digital Democracy: Discourse and Decision Making in the Information Age.* New York: Routledge.

Haque, M.S. (2002). E-governance in India: Its impacts on relations among citizens, politicians and public servants. *International Review of Administrative Sciences, 68*(2), 231-250.

Hayward, T. (1995). *Info-Rich, Info-Poor: Access and Exchange in the Global Information Society.* K.G. Saur.

Hill, K. A. & Hughes, J. E. (1998). *Cyberpolitics: Citizen Activism in the Age of the Internet.* Lanham, MD: Rowan & Littlefield.

Hill, K. & Hughes, J. E. (1999). Is the Internet an instrument of global democratization? *Democratization, 3,*29-43.

Horrigan, J., Rainie, L., & Fox, S. (2001). Online communities: Networks that nurture long-distance relationships and local ties. *Pew Internet & American Life Project.* Retrieved from: www. pew internet.org

ITU. (n.d.). Retrieved from: http://www.itu. int/wsis/

Johnson, T.J. & Kaye, B.K. (2003). Around the World Wide Web in 80 ways: How motives for going online are linked to Internet activities among politically interested Internet users. *Social Science Computer Review, 21,*(3), 304-325.

Kalathil, S. & Boas, T. C. (2003). *Open Networks Closed Regimes: The Impact of the Internet on Authoritarian Rule.* Washington, DC: Carnegie Endowment for International Peace.

Keck, M. E. & Sikkink, K. (1998). *Activists Beyond Borders: Advocacy Networks in International Politics.* Ithaca, NY: Cornell University Press.

Kent, J. M. & Zeitner, V. (2003). Internet use and civic engagement: A longitudinal analysis. *Public Opinion Quarterly, 67*(3), 311-334.

Mair, P. & van Biezen, I. (2001). Party membership in twenty European democracies 1980-2000. *Party Politics, 7*(1), 7-22.

Margolis, M. & Resnick, D. (2000). *Politics as Usual: The Cyberspace "Revolution."* Thousand Oaks, CA: Sage.

McChesney, R. W. (1999). *Rich Media, Poor Democracy.* IL: University of Illinois Press.

Media Matrix (2000, October). *Campaign 2000: Party politics on the World Wide Web.* Retrieved from: www.media metrix.com

Murdock, G. & Golding, P. (1989). Information poverty and political inequality: Citizenship in the age of privatised communications. *Journal of Communication, 39,* 180-195.

Norris, P. (2000). *A Virtuous Circle.* New York: Cambridge University Press.

Norris, P. (2001). *Digital Divide.* New York: Cambridge University Press.

Norris, P. (2002). *Democratic Phoenix: Reinventing Political Activism.* New York: Cambridge University Press.

Norris, P. (2003). The bridging and bonding role of online communities. In P. N. Howard & S. Jones (Eds.), *Society Online: The Internet in Context.* Thousand Oaks, CA: Sage.

Norris, P. & Sanders, D. (2003). Medium or message? *Political Communications.*

Pharr, S. & Putnam, R. (eds.). (2000). *Disaffected Democracies: What's Troubling the Trilateral Countries?* Princeton, NJ: Princeton University Press.

Putnam, R. D. (1993). *Making Democracy Work: Civic Traditions in Modern Italy.* Princeton, NJ: Princeton University Press.

Putnam, R. D. (1996). The strange disappearance of civic America. *The American prospect, 24.*

Putnam, R. D. (2000). *Bowling Alone: The Collapse and Revival of American Community.* New York: Simon and Schuster.

Putnam, R. D. (ed.). (2002). *Democracies in Flux.* Oxford: Oxford University Press.

Radcliff, B. & Davis, P. (2000). Labor organization and electoral participation in industrial democracies. *American Journal of Political Science, 44*(1), 132-141.

Rash, Jr., W. (1997). *Politics on the Net: Wiring the Political Process.* New York: W.H. Freeman.

Rheingold, H. (1993). *The Virtual Community: Homesteading on the Electronic Frontier.* Reading, MA: Addison Wesley.

Scarrow, S. (2001). Parties without members? In R. J. Dalton & M. Wattenberg (Eds.), *Parties Without Partisans.* New York: Oxford University Press.

Schwartz, E. (1996). *Netactivism: How Citizens Use the Internet.* Sebastapol, CA: Songline Studios.

Selnow, G.W. (1998). *Electronic Whistle-Stops: The Impact of the Internet on American Politics.* Westport, CT: Praeger.

Shah, D.V., Kwak, N., & Holbert, R.L. (2001). "Connecting" and "disconnecting" with civic life: Patterns of Internet use and the production of social capital. *Political Communication, 18*(2), 141-162.

Stowers, G.N.L. (1999). Becoming cyberactive: State and local governments on the World Wide Web. *Government Information Quarterly, 16*(2), 111-127.

Thomas, J.C. & Streib, G. (2003). The new face of government: Citizen-initiated contacts in the era of e-government. *Journal of Public Administration Research and Theory, 13*(1), 83-101.

Tolbert, C.J. & McNeal, R.S. (2003). Unraveling the effects of the Internet on political participation? *Political Research Quarterly, 56*(2), 175-185.

Toulouse, C. & Luke, T. W. (eds.). (1998). *The Politics of Cyberspace.* London: Routledge.

United Nations/American Society for Public Administration (2002). *Bench Marking e-Government: A Global Perspective.* New York: United Nations/DPEPA.

Verba, S., Nie, N., & Kim, J.-on (1978). *Participation and Political Equality: A Seven-Nation Comparison.* New York: Cambridge University Press.

Weber, L.M., Loumakis, A., & Bergman, J. (2003). Who participates and why? An analysis of citizens on the Internet and the mass public. *Social Science Computer Review, 21*(1), 26-42.

Wilhelm, A. (n.d.). *Democracy in the Digital Age: Challenges to Political Life in Cyberspace.* New York: Routledge.

ENDNOTES

[1] Since the dimensions are theoretically defined and constructed, based on understanding the role of different forms of participation in representative democracy, the study did not use factor analysis to generate the classification or measurement.

[2] For more details of the European Social Survey, including the questionnaire and methodology, see http://naticent02. uuhost. uk.uu.net/index.htm. Data for an initial nineteen countries, along with comprehensive documentation, is accessible at http://ess.

nsd.uib.no. The survey is funded via the European Commission's 5th Framework Program, with supplementary funds from the European Science Foundation which also sponsored the development of the study over a number of years. I am most grateful to the European Commission and the ESF for their support for this project and to the work of the ESS Central Coordinating Team, led by Roger Jowell, for making this survey data available.

3   *"Personal use"* is defined by the ESS-2002 as private or recreational use that does not have to do with a person's work or occupation.

Chapter VIII
Toward Improved Community–Supporting Systems Design:
A Study of Professional Community Activity

Malte Geib
University of St. Gallen, Switzerland

Christian Braun
University of St. Gallen, Switzerland

Lutz Kolbe
University of St. Gallen, Switzerland

Walter Brenner
University of St. Gallen, Switzerland

ABSTRACT

In this article, we analyze the design factors of community systems in two real-world professional communities — a learning network and an expert network — that employ a mix of communication modes, that is, face-to-face communication and computer-mediated communication. Our objectives are to determine which design factors influence community activity and therefore community output. We furthermore intend to make recommendations to improve the design of community systems that support professional communities using a mix of communication modes. Our study is exploratory and based on action research given the lack of studies on the design of community-supporting systems in professional communities that employ a mix of communication modes. To illustrate similarities and to enhance the generalizability of our findings, we analyzed two real-world professional communities in-depth, namely, a learning network and an interorganizational expert network. Our study shows that face-to-face communication is the primary mode of communication in these communities; the community systems that they employ only have a supporting function. This leads us to a few design guidelines for the systems that support such communities. Generally, community systems have to support professional communities' work processes and relationship development. Important functions for work-process support are those that support face-to-face meetings (for the preparation and wrap-up of meetings) and that explicitly support specific work processes. Important functions for relationship development are functions that enable or facilitate face-to-face meetings, for example, member profiles

INTRODUCTION

In recent years, it has become normal to support geographically dispersed communities with advanced forms of computer-mediated communication (CMC) systems, usually based on Internet technology. These community-supporting systems (in short, community systems), frequently termed *teamware* (Schulte, 1999) or *groupware* (Bach, Vogler, & Österle, 1999), support the interactive exchange and creation of documents, online discussions, chat rooms, and role-based personalization. Besides communities that rely solely on CMC (frequently termed *virtual communities*; Rheingold, 1998), the majority of professional communities employ a mix of CMC and other communication modes (i.e., telephone, fax, face to face). Much research has been devoted to the analysis of virtual communities (e.g., Bieber et al., 2002a; Bieber et al., 2002b; Godio, 2000; Rheingold) and to the comparison of CMC with other communication modes (e.g., Etzioni & Etzioni, 1999; Wiesenfeld, Raghuram, & Garud, 1999). However, there has been little research on the design of community-supporting systems in professional communities that employ a mix of communication modes.

To address this gap, the objective of our research was to analyze community system design factors in professional communities such as learning and expert networks that employ a mix of communication modes. We addressed the following research questions in detail:

1. Which community system design factors influence community activity and therefore community output?
2. How should community systems supporting professional communities be designed?

Because our research was exploratory, we used an action research (AR) approach (Checkland & Holwell, 1998). Action research is often used in the information-systems domain for the exploratory analysis of systems design in real-world settings (Davison, Martinsons, & Kock, 2004; Mansell, 1991).

Two real-world communities were the object of our in-depth study: a learning network of postgraduate students and an interorganizational expert network consisting of experts from different companies working in the areas of customer-relationship management (CRM) and knowledge management (KM).

In the following section, we describe the research model developed from the literature on computer-mediated communication and virtual communities that which presents the causal relationships discovered in previous research relevant to our research questions. Next, we describe our research methodology. Subsequently, we describe and discuss the results of our research to arrive at propositions for the design of community systems supporting professional communities. Finally, we summarize our findings and discuss further research opportunities.

Figure 1. Research model

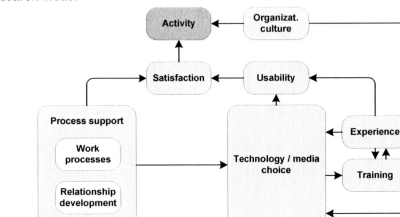

THEORETICAL BACKGROUND

Professional Communities

The notion of community is a socioscientific collective term for a specific type of social group (Poplin, 1979; Sutton & Munson, 1976). Although there is no generally accepted definition, a community can be defined as a group of socially interacting persons who are mutually tied to one another and regularly meet at a common place (Hillery, 1955). With the diffusion of electronic information and communication systems, communities have increasingly turned to computer-mediated communication.

In respect to their objectives and scope, communities using CMC can be classified into three major types (Markus, 2002). Socially oriented communities form to support the development of social relationships between individuals and have no economic goal. Commercially oriented communities form to directly support a profit-oriented economic goal (cp Hagel & Armstrong, 1997). Professionally oriented communities (in short, professional communities) consist of companies' employees who communicate and share

information to support their professional tasks (Godio, 2000). In this article, we focus on the analysis of professional communities.

Professional communities can be differentiated into expert networks and learning networks (Markus, 2002). Expert networks are formed by experts focused on a specific topic with the aim of acquiring and developing knowledge through their mutual interactions and discussions as members of the network. An expert network emerges through voluntary association and may be either intra- or interorganizational. A socioscientific explanation of the expert-network phenomenon is given by Wenger (1997), who calls this community type a "community of practice." Wenger, McDermott, and Snyder (2002) offer a pragmatic definition of expert networks as "groups of people who share a concern, a set of problems, or a passion about a topic, and who deepen their knowledge and expertise in this area by interacting on an ongoing basis." Learning networks are formed by professionals with the objective of joint education, training, or learning (Markus, 2002). Examples of these are virtual corporate universities (Kraemer & Müller, 1999).

Community Systems

With the propagation of the Internet, most CMC systems became based on Internet technology. We use the term community system to describe the Internet-based application system that enables community members to interact with one another.

To structure our analysis of community systems for professional communities, we use a research model that describes the relationships between community system design factors and community activity prevalent in the literature on CMC (see Figure 1).

In the following sections, we define the concepts used in the research model and explain the relationships between them.

Process Support

Communities use community systems to support their communication-based processes (Bieber et al., 2002a; Watson-Manheim & Belanger, 2002). These can be roughly divided into relationship-development processes and work processes (or task-oriented processes). In relationship-development processes, community members establish relational intimacy by exchanging social information (Chidambaram, 1996). In contrast, work processes are executed by community members to solve a problem or to work on a specific task. Examples of work processes are coordination, information gathering, knowledge sharing, conflict resolution, negotiation, and information dissemination (Watson-Manheim & Belanger).

Technology and Media Choice

In the design of community systems, the choice of technology and media depends on the work processes and relationship-development processes that they should support (Stanoevska-Slabeva & Schmid, 2000; Watson-Manheim & Belanger, 2002). Well-established technology is also often

chosen on the basis of previous experience with this technology. The choice of technology may therefore depend on the community members' previous technology experience if one assumes that they influence the design process (Chidambaram, 1996; Watson-Manheim & Belanger). The choice of technology may also depend on the organizational culture (Watson-Manheim & Belanger; Wiesenfeld et al., 1999). Subject to their previous experience and choice of technology, community members require training in using the community system to ensure that it is effectively used (Wiesenfeld et al.). A community system's usability determines whether people will find the system easy to use (Bieber et al., 2002a). This is primarily influenced by the choice of a suitable technology and users' experience with the chosen technology.

Satisfaction, Activity, and Performance

Community members' satisfaction with the community system is influenced by the degree of process support offered by the system (Chidambaram, 1996). The system's usability plays an important role in the degree of satisfaction experienced. The community members' activity is defined as the frequency with which community members use the system for communication with one another. Activity is furthermore primarily dependent on the community members' satisfaction with the system and also influenced by organizational culture. For example, Hiltz and Johnson's (1990) study showed that the best predictor of satisfaction with CMC was the (virtual) activity among group members. Experience's (indirect) effect on activity is acknowledged by Chidambaram, who says that "experience with the medium can affect the extent of use...of the medium."

According to McDermott (2002), activity—included in our research model (Figure 1) — is the most basic concept by which we can measure communities' performance. Performance can generally

Figure 2. Performance measurement framework for communities (McDermott, 2002)

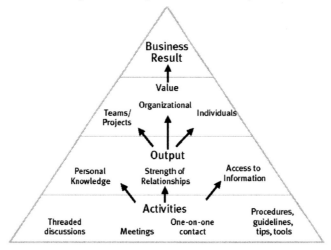

be measured on different levels, each with a different impact on business result (see Figure 2).

Activities comprise, for example, meetings, discussions, and one-to-one contacts. Measuring activities can be helpful in giving some indication of the communities' health. However, these measures do not demonstrate the communities' contribution to its members or organizations. To determine this contribution, it is necessary to measure communities' performance in terms of output and value (McDermott, 2002).

In focusing on the community systems' contribution to the overall performance of communities, we restrict performance measurement to the activity level. This is necessary because the community systems' goal is to facilitate the community members' activities and to make them independent of restrictions imposed by space and time (Bieber et al., 2002a). Community systems' impact is therefore restricted to the activity level as the systems only influence business results by facilitating activities.

METHODOLOGY

Given the lack of studies on the design of community-supporting systems in professional com-

munities that employ a mix of communication modes, our study is exploratory and the research sites are real-world communities. To illustrate the similarities and to enhance the generalizability of our findings, we made an in-depth analysis of two professional communities, namely, a learning network and an interorganizational expert network.

Action research (AR) is an appropriate methodology for the exploratory analysis of systems design in real-world settings (Davison et al., 2004; Mansell, 1991). AR focuses on solving organizational problems through intervention, while at the same time contributing to scholarly knowledge (Davison et al.). In the AR process, the researcher enters a real-world situation and becomes involved as both participant and researcher (Checkland & Holwell, 1998). AR's iterative characteristic implies a cyclic process of intervention, with one or several cycles of activities being conducted (Davison et al.).

Checkland and Holwell (1998) argue that in order for AR results to be valid, the research process has to be recoverable by interested outsiders. It is therefore essential to state the epistemology (the set of ideas and the process in which these ideas are used methodologically) through which outsiders make sense of the research, and thus define what they regard as acquired knowledge

Figure 3. AR process model (Checkland & Holwell, 1998; Davison et al., 2004; Susman & Evered, 1978)

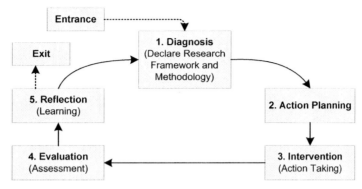

(Checkland & Holwell). Figure 3 shows the AR process that we followed for one cycle in respect to each of the two communities.

The organizational problem to be solved in respect to each professional community was improving the community's work and relationship-development processes through the design of a community-supporting system.

A detailed understanding of the surrounding environment is a prerequisite for the determination of an appropriate intervention, therefore the data-collection techniques employed before, during, and after the action-taking stages should ensure a rich pool of data for subsequent analysis (Davison et al., 2004). Furthermore, a thorough review of the existing literature is useful not only to inform the research's focus and process, but also to help position the research within scholarly knowledge (Davison et al.). We therefore developed a research model from the literature (see Figure 1).

In the diagnosis phase, we started our research with a thorough diagnosis of the community's current situation. This was done through an analysis of the community's documentation and interviews with community members regarding their requirements. Subsequently, we identified the community members, their roles, and their work and relationship-development processes. We also gained insights into the choice of appropriate tech-

nologies, media, and functions supporting these processes. Finally, we also acquired information on community members' experience and training, as well as on their general cultural context.

In AR, the diagnosis will directly inform the planning of actions, and planned actions will subsequently be implemented and evaluated. In the action-planning phase, we planned the design of the community system according to the users' requirements as based on their processes. In the intervention phase, we developed and implemented the community system.

In the evaluation phase, we compared the intervention outcomes with the project objectives and expectations. We therefore gathered performance data that were relevant within our research model's context to measure the community system's success. This was done by measuring the community members' activities when using the community system. The starting point of this data collection was the access logs generated by the Web server (Lotus Domino server) that handles the communication between the community members and community applications (Lotus Notes databases, Lotus Team Workplace, and Lotus Sametime). The analysis steps were as follows:

1. We collected the access logs, which recorded page views. A page view is the result of

Figure 4. BEC screenshot

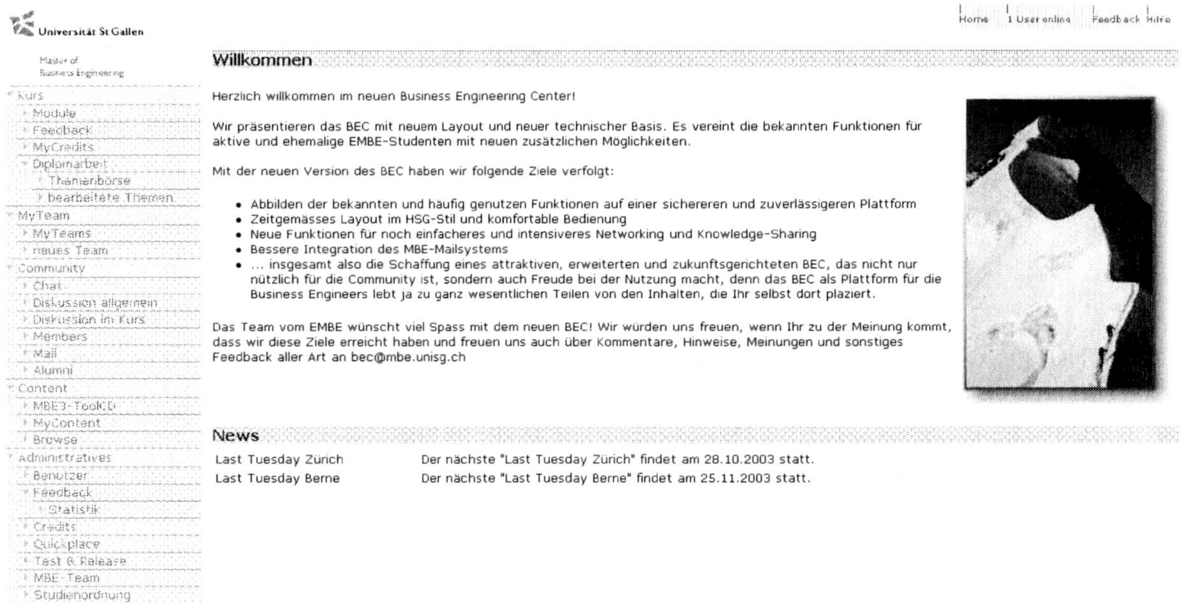

a request for a particular Web page and therefore denotes the requesting person's activity.

2. To eliminate the effects produced by a community system's administration (which also generates entries in the access logs), we filtered the entries containing system administrators' user names and Internet protocol (IP) addresses. Consequently, the results of the analysis only reflect the community members' activities.

3. To aggregate results, we grouped the Web pages and forms according to functional areas. We determined the number of page views (the sum of the related Web pages and forms' page views) for each functional area and the percentage of total page views. This percentage is an indicator of how important the specific functional area is for the community members.

To conduct this evaluation, we used the Web-log analysis tool WebTrends, which can cope with the specificities of access logs generated by Lotus application servers.

In the reflection (learning) phase, we analyzed deviations between project outcomes and expectations. The goal was to gather knowledge on the relationships between a community system's design factors and the community members' activity. We discussed the differences between the outcomes and expectations and developed hypotheses to explain them.

RESULTS

The BEC: A Learning Network

Overview

The University of St. Gallen's Executive MBA in business engineering (MBE) is a part-time postgraduate course for managers in leading positions. The program is intended to qualify professionals for all aspects of business transformation (Winter,

Figure 5. The process of study

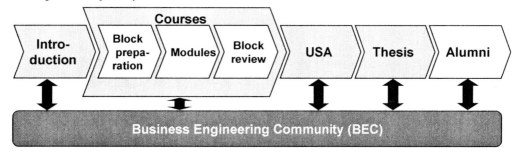

2002). At present, the MBE HSG has about 90 participants in two courses and approximately 270 alumni.

To support participants during the courses and afterward, the MBE organization decided to implement a community system called the Business Engineering Community (BEC) in 1998. By fostering interaction between participants, especially during practice weeks and after the study, the BEC contributes to and maintains community building. Because the system was designed to support interaction and relationship development among the current participants and alumni, we focus on these two groups of community members. The current release of the BEC system was first implemented in February 2002.

The Design of the BEC

The study of the system can be divided into several phases, which are shown in Figure 5. The BEC has to support all the phases from "Introduction" to "Alumni." Additionally, the BEC has to provide functions that support relationship development between participants. In the following section, each phase of the participants' work process is described.

In the introduction phase, the participants acquire information on the program, venues, organization, and contact persons. They edit their own profiles, view other participants' profiles, and get used to the BEC's functions. During courses, participants

obtain information on timetables, documents, their credits, and instructors. They have to do (preparatory) exercises in groups, communicate with one another, exchange related documents, and discuss related topics. They thereafter provide feedback on the modules and meetings. The program also contains a four-week stay at a North-American university. Apart from information on the stay and the local companies that they will visit, the work processes in the U.S. are identical to those in the previous phases. The thesis is written in groups of two to four persons. The participants therefore need to build teams, and search for and discuss possible topics. After the completion of the program, the alumni are primarily interested in maintaining the community and in networking. They organize events, search for experts, and exchange knowledge and experiences.

To support the study's different phases and the corresponding processes, the MBE organization decided to implement a community system. The MBE organization thus created the BEC's functional specifications based on experiences with an earlier release, user feedback, and the requirements mentioned above. The new BEC system was implemented by an external service provider and was launched in February 2003. It is currently operated and maintained by the MBE organization.

The BEC's functions, which support the community members' processes, can be divided into five areas, supplemented by a sixth category for "support functions":

- **Course support:** This area contains information on modules and meetings, with relevant documents available for download. Participants can also provide feedback on modules and individual meetings. In addition, participants can access statistics relating to their study credits. To support the participants in their endeavor to find a topic for their thesis, a discussion forum is available in which topics can be suggested and discussed.

- **Teamwork:** In order to support the participants' thesis work, their jointly done exercises, and the organization of joint events, this area enables the building of private and public teams. Within a team area, the system provides functions such as document exchange, collaborative document creation, application sharing, and a common calendar.

- **Communication:** The BEC offers both synchronous and asynchronous communication. Synchronous communication is supported by a chat function or instant messaging, video and audio conferencing, application sharing, and a whiteboard. Asynchronous communication is supported by discussion forums and an integrated e-mail system.

- **Member profiles:** This area contains a list of all member profiles grouped according to the courses the members attended. Each participant can edit his or her own profile and access other participants' profiles.

- **Content:** In this area, related content can be published and categorized. Possible content types are book recommendations, citations, links, attachments, and events.

- **Support functions:** In addition to the functions just mentioned, the BEC provides supporting functions such as user help, a feedback function, and search and news functions.

The MBE's cultural context in respect to technology use is primarily shaped by the different participants. The MBE program is attended by professionals from all disciplines and industries with different backgrounds and affinity for technology. Most participants have no experiences with the community system's technology even though the system's implementation is based on an established and widespread IBM Lotus technology. Consequently, the MBE organization offers a short explanation of the community system's functions during the introduction phase of the program. The functions are furthermore designed to be largely self-explanatory, although online user help is available.

The CKP-Net: An Expert Network

Overview

The Competence Center Customer> Knowledge>Performance (CC CKP) is a knowledge network between the University of St. Gallen's Institute of Information Management (IWI-HSG) and six major Swiss and German financial-services companies that finance the competence center. The aim of this network is the development of knowledge in the areas of customer-relationship management (CRM) and knowledge management with a focus on performance management.

Generally, the CC CKP consists of a core team — a project manager and researchers of the IWI-HSG — and several of the participating companies' employees (participants). The network has a steering committee on which each participating company is represented, and which meets biannually to discuss the network's research alignment.

The core team's task is to develop knowledge that the participants can use within their companies, while the knowledge network as such should support its participants' work and relationship-de-

Figure 6. CKP-Net screenshot

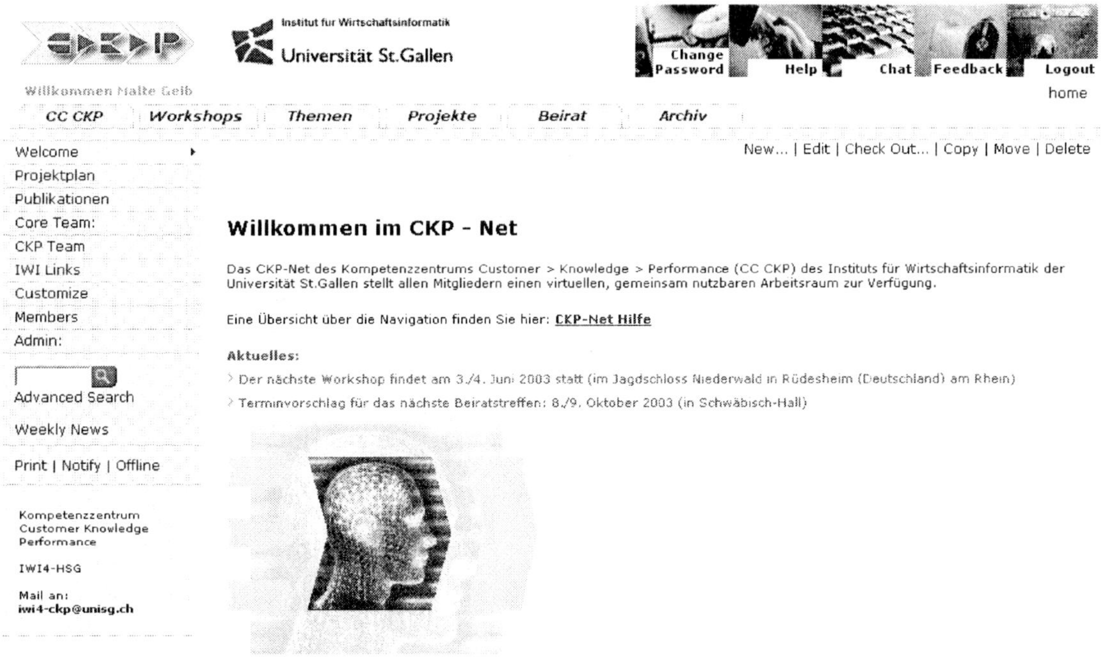

velopment processes. To support these processes, a community system, called CKP-Net, had to be established.

The Design of CKP-Net

The CC CKP has five different processes that have to be supported by CKP-Net: workshops, literature research, project work, steering-committee meetings, and relationship building.

Workshops are conducted four times a year and deal with varying topics. During a workshop, the core team members present state-of-the-art concepts and future trends, whereas the participants report on the status of related projects in their companies and the challenges that they currently face. The core team and participants also take part in group work to exchange knowledge on a new area of research. Both the steering-committee members and the participants are involved in the preparation of workshops. Each company's steering-committee member has to select par-

ticipants to attend such a workshop. The selected participants then have to prepare for the workshop by familiarizing themselves with the workshop's topics. After a workshop, many of the participants and steering-committee members need to access the presentations and results of group work for utilization in their individual work.

Apart from the workshop documents, the participants and steering-committee members often do literature research, for example, for projects that are not carried out in collaboration with the competence center. Consequently, CKP-Net has to support the publication of research documents and a topic-oriented structured search as well.

The core team members also support the participating companies' employees by means of projects within their respective companies. Project work that the participants and core team carry out requires an intensive exchange of documents, for example, documents explaining the enterprise environment, project plans, and concepts. CKP-Net therefore has to facilitate the exchange of documents and the collaborative creation of documents.

It must also be possible to publish agendas, presentations, and the results of discussions in steering-committee meetings on CKP-Net to allow the steering-committee members easy access to these.

In order to build relationships within the competence center, it is useful for the core team, participants, and steering committee to communicate with one another at times other than during the workshop meetings. All stakeholders' contact details should therefore be published within CKP-Net.

To support all these processes, the core team decided to implement a community system. Because previous competence centers had already worked with community systems for several years, CKP-Net was designed based on experiences with these systems and the above-mentioned requirements. In January 2003, it was launched and had an expected life span of two years. Its functions, which support the community members' processes, can be divided into the following areas:

- **General Information:** This tab contains documents on project plans, a list of publications, and important links.
- **Team Information:** Two documents provide the contact information of core team members, participants, and steering-committee members, as well as photos of the core team members.
- **Workshops:** This tab includes documents pertaining to planned and conducted workshops (information on location, agenda, workshop presentations, and photos of conducted workshops).
- **Research Topics:** Included under this tab are several academic papers and presentations dealing with research topics that are relevant to the participants and steering-committee members.

- **Project Rooms:** Each of the participating companies has its own collaborative work space that can be accessed via this tab. A work space includes support for the exchange and collaborative creation of documents, as well as discussion forums.
- **Steering Committee:** This tab contains documents about planned and conducted steering-committee meetings (information on location, agenda, presentations, and photos of conducted steering-committee meetings).
- **Archive:** Integrated under this tab are workshop documents and the documentation of previous competence centers' specific research topics.
- **Chat:** By clicking on this button, each CKP-Net user can activate an integrated Lotus Sametime client application for awareness and instant messaging (AIM). This client application also provides opportunities for audio and video meetings, as well as application sharing.
- **Support Functions:** Further support functions include integrated help, a feedback function, and search and news functions.

Summary of Results

Figure 7 summarizes the previous sections' results, as well as the activity analysis' results (rows labeled "Process-Supporting Functions & Use of Functions by Community Members"). The first column in this row contains the process-supporting functions and functional areas described in the previous section. The second column ("Page Views") indicates how often a document related to the specific function was viewed. For example, the figure 6,822 in the first row indicates that documents related to information about modules and meetings (e.g., timetables, statistics on own credits, course presentations) were accessed 6,822 times by the community members. The third col-

Figure 7. The process of study

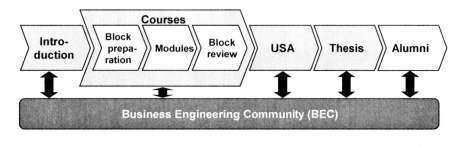

Figure. 8 CKP-Net screenshot

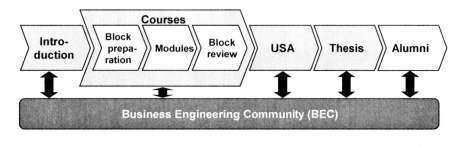

umn shows the percentage of page views in relation to the total number of page views (42,745).

Comparison of the Research Sites

To compare the research sites, we can use Figallo's (1998) classification criteria for communities, which is based on community members' behavior (e.g., degree of personal interactivity, subject scope, cohesion of members), complemented with the research model's criteria, except for usability and satisfaction (because these were not measured but approximated by means of activity measurement).

- **Degree of personal interactivity:** Both communities have a high degree of face-to-face interactivity during personal meetings (courses and workshops). Interaction by means of the community systems is therefore only moderate and confined to the absolutely necessary.

- **Subject scope:** The subject scope in both communities is relatively narrow as both of them deal with a specific subject area. In the BEC's case, this is business engineering, while in CKP-Net's case, this is CRM and KM.

Table 1. Summary of results

		BEC			CKP-Net		
Community	Objective	Qualify professionals for all aspects of business transformation			Inter-organizational knowledge development in the areas of CRM and KM		
	Members	• Current participants of the MBE HSG (ca. 90) • Alumni MBE HSG (ca. 270)			• Steering committee (ca. 7) • Participating companies' employees (ca. 50) • Core team members (ca. 7)		
	General cultural context regarding technology use	Professionals from all disciplines and industries with different backgrounds and technology affinity			Financial industry professionals from marketing, sales, service, and IT departments with different backgrounds and technology affinity		
	Work processes and relationship development	*Participants and alumni:* • access course information • communicate • work together • search for/edit profiles • exchange information/documents • organize events/meetings Participants: • access credits • prepare thesis • give feedback			Participants and steering committee: • project collaboration • workshop preparation • workshop document retrieval • document search • communication Steering committee: • steering committee meeting document retrieval		
Community System	**Goal of the community system**	Support work processes and relationship development among current participants and among alumni			Support work processes and relationship development among core team members and participants		
	Technology	Integrated Solution using Lotus Notes/Domino, Lotus Team Workplace, Lotus Sametime			Integrated Solution using Lotus Team Workplace and Lotus Sametime		
	Process-supporting functions & Use of functions by community members (activity) [February to May 2003]		**Page views**	**%**		**Page views**	**%**
		Course support			General information	36	3.62
		Information about modules and meetings	6822	15.96	Member profiles	154	15.48
		Feedback on modules	1453	3.40	Workshop information	620	62.31
		Feedback on meetings	150	0.35	Research documents	63	6.33
		View credits	22	0.05	Project collaboration rooms	40	4.02
		Thesis topic bourse	4231	9.90	Steering committee	36	3.62
		Finished thesis topics	4726	11.06	Archive	46	4.62
		Teamwork			Chat	0	0.00
		Teamwork area	5968	13.96	Support functions	0	0.00
		Communication					
		Chat	436	1.02			
		General discussion	1784	4.17			
		Course discussion	5909	13.82			
		Member Profiles					
		Member profiles	7022	16.43			
		Content Administration					
		Content	1317	3.08			
		Browse	2905	6.80			
		Σ	42745	100	Σ	995	100

continued on following page

Table 1. continued

	Experience	Most members had no experiences with the community system or its technology before using the system.	Most members had no experiences with the community system or its technology before using the system.
	Training	• Short explanation of functions during introductory phase of the program • Functions are widely self-explanatory • Online user help	• Short explanation of community system's functions during workshops (30 minutes) • Functions are widely self-explanatory • Online user help

- **Cohesion of members:** In respect to both research sites, the cohesion of members is sustained by a semiformal organization: in the BEC's case, the course organization, and in the CKP-Net's case, the organization of the competence center.

- **General cultural Context:** Both communities are interorganizational and therefore have members from organizations with different cultural contexts and affinities for technology. In the BEC's case, the members' cultural context is highly heterogeneous, whereas in CKP-Net's case, the cultural context is more homogeneous because members come from the same industry and business departments.

- **Work and relationship-development processes:** The two communities' work processes reveal similar characteristics. There are processes for the preparation and wrap-up of person-to-person meetings (courses and workshops), and collaborative processes to create documents or project outcomes (teamwork and project collaboration). Moreover, both communities demonstrate the need for relationship development. However, the MBE community has a greater need for the support of communication processes (discussions) than CC CKP.

- **Technology/media choice:** Both communities employ similar technology for their community systems.

- **Experience and training:** Because community members have no previous experience with the chosen technology, both communi-

ties offer their members a short explanation of the system functions in an introductory person-to-person meeting as well as online help within the systems. The systems' functions also have to be widely self-explanatory to avoid the need for extensive training.

In conclusion, both communities show very similar characteristics. This strengthens the generalizability of our findings.

DISCUSSION

In this section, we present the results of the action research process's reflection (learning) phase (Figure 3). We discuss the results of the previous section in order to deduce propositions for an improved design of community systems that support professional communities.

The functional areas of both community systems were designed in accordance with the community members' work and relationship-development processes. However, there are significant differences regarding the community members' activity in respect to the use of the functions. In the following sections, we discuss the implications for the support of work processes and relationship development.

Support of Work Processes

It is apparent that the most frequently visited functional area in CKP-Net was "Workshop Information," and in the BEC's case, this was

"Course Support." In contrast, the least visited area in the BEC was "Content Administration," and "Support Functions" and "Chat" in CKP-Net. Generally, we observe that functions related to face-to-face meetings — the preparation for or wrap-up of meetings — such as "Course Support," "Teamwork," and "Workshop Information" are used far more than other functions. This cannot be attributed to a difference in experience or training because these are roughly the same for the different functional areas. Our conclusion is that in these professional communities, interaction by means of face-to-face meetings plays a primary role, whereas interaction by means of the community systems plays a secondary role. These systems are therefore only regarded as supportive tools for face-to-face meetings and not as a primary means of communication as they are in virtual communities.

Moreover, we can see that functions that are directly connected to work processes, for example, information about modules and meetings and "Course Discussion" in the BEC, or "Workshop Information" in CKP-Net, are used much more frequently than general functions like "Archive," "Chat," or "General Information" in CKP-Net.

The functions of community systems supporting professional communities should therefore be designed so that they first support the community members' face-to-face meetings, and second, so that they are directly related to a specific work process. Community members need to know how they can directly benefit from a specific function in their work processes. If a function is not explicitly assigned to a work process, community members do not realize its usefulness.

Support of Relationship Development

An interesting observation was that in both community systems, the "Member Profiles" area was the second most frequently accessed area. Most of the community members meet on a regular

basis, either in workshops or in courses, and can therefore engage in relationship building during these events. While research has confirmed that face-to-face communication offers a better means for relationship building than CMC (Chidambaram, 1996), the "Member Profiles" areas are nevertheless extensively used. Relationship-development support therefore seems to be an integral functional part of community systems supporting professional communities.

In respect to the BEC, the "Member Profiles" activity can be partly explained by the fact that the majority of the community members are alumni who do not participate in courses, but are only interested in relationship development and maintenance. Moreover, participants in different courses — who do not regularly meet one another — may use the system to retrieve additional information about people whom they have met.

In CKP-Net, the "Member Profiles" area seems to complement regular face-to-face communication in workshops very well. Members may use it to retrieve additional information about people whom they have met in workshops, or to retrieve contact details so that they can make telephone contact.

On the other hand, functions that can potentially be used for relationship-development processes, such as discussion forums or chat, are not used very much. This leads us to the conclusion that the "Member Profiles" area is essentially being used by community members to obtain detailed personal information on other community members, for example, information on their companies, job descriptions, and work areas, to extend their knowledge on fellow community members in order to facilitate (or enable) non-computer-based communication.

Besides the functions that support work processes related to face-to-face meetings and relationship development, the others are seldom used. This is particularly true of most synchronous and asynchronous communication functions; for example, the "Chat" function in CKP-Net was

Table 2. Design guidelines for community-supporting systems in professional communities

		Important functions	**Unimportant functions**
Process support	Relationship Development	Functions that enable or facilitate face-to-face meetings, e.g.: • *Member Profiles*: to retrieve further information on company, job description, work areas, contact details etc. of community members	Functions for general computer-mediated communication, e.g.: • Chat • General Discussion
	Work Processes	Functions that • support face-to-face meetings (preparation, wrap-up) and • are directly assigned to work processes.	Functions that • do not support face-to-face meetings or • are not directly assigned to work processes (such as general computer-mediated communication).

never used and the project rooms were rarely used. In the BEC, "Chat" and "General Discussion," too, were rarely used, while "Teamwork Area" and "Course Discussion" were by contrast used quite frequently, mainly for the exchange of documents and the discussion of topics related to courses.

This supports our hypothesis that the primary means of communication between community members is face-to-face meetings. The community systems are only used for interaction among community members if the functions offer support for face-to-face meetings as in the case of "Teamwork Area" and "Course Discussion." Moreover, communication functions are not used for relationship development, but for the support of work processes. Therefore, communication functions that do not directly support work processes, like, for example, the "Chat" functions, are obviously dispensable.

CONCLUSION AND OUTLOOK

Our goal was to analyze which design factors of community systems influence community activity, and how community systems supporting professional communities should therefore be designed. Based on the findings of a study of two real-world professional communities — a learning network and an expert network — we drew a few conclusions (Figure 8) that are valid for the communities analyzed. These conclusions may help in the design of community systems for professional communities. However, a study with a statistically relevant sample must be performed before our conclusions can be assumed as generally valid for all professional communities.

In communities that employ a mix of communication modes of CMC, telephone, and face-to-face communication, the competition between the different media has to be considered in supporting community systems' design in addition to other factors relevant to the design of community systems (Figure 8). Our study shows that face-to-face communication is the primary mode of communication; community systems only have a supporting function. This leads us to deduce some design guidelines for systems supporting such communities.

Generally, community systems have to support professional communities' work processes and relationship-development processes. Important functions for work-process support are functions that support face-to-face meetings (for the preparation for and wrap-up of meetings) and that explicitly support specific work processes. In contrast, functions that do not support face-to-face meetings or are not explicitly assigned to work processes are dispensable and should not be implemented. Important functions for relationship development are functions that enable or facilitate face-to-face meetings, for example, member profiles that enable members to retrieve further information on other community members' companies, job descriptions, work areas, contact details, and so forth. On the other hand, functions for general computer-mediated communication, for example, chat or general discussion areas, are dispensable.

Critically reviewing our work, it was possible to draw conclusions for improved community-supporting systems design, but further empirical research, for example, by carrying out qualitative interviews with community members, is necessary to interpret our findings and to learn what motivates the community members' virtual activity.

One important question remaining to be answered is what influence the design of the functions in a community system has on a professional community's overall performance. To answer this question, we have to analyze and combine measurement results from different performance levels (activities, output, and value; see Figure 2). Currently, we are working on metrics to measure performance in terms of output and value in the analyzed communities. Our research objective is to show the link between the technology application and business results of a professional community.

REFERENCES

Bach, V., Vogler, P., & Österle, H. (Eds.). (1999). *Business Knowledge Management: Praxiserfahrungen mit Intranet-Basierten Lösungen*. Berlin, Germany: Springer.

Bieber, M. et al. (2002a). Toward virtual community knowledge evolution. *Journal of Management Information Systems, 18*(4), 11-35.

Bieber, M. et al. (2002b). Towards knowledge-sharing and learning in virtual professional communities. In *Paper presented at the 35th Annual Hawaii International Conference on System Sciences*, Hawaii.

Checkland, P., & Holwell, S. (1998). Action research: Its nature and validity. *Systemic Practice and Action Research, 11*(1), 9-21.

Chidambaram, L. (1996). Relational development in computer-supported groups. *MIS Quarterly*, 143-165.

Davison, R. M., Martinsons, M. G., & Kock, N. (2004). Principles of canonical action research. *Information Systems Journal, 14*(1), 65-86.

Etzioni, A., & Etzioni, O. (1999). Face-to-face and computer-mediated communities: A comparative analysis. *The Information Society, 15*, 241-248.

Figallo, C. (1998). *Hosting Web communities: Building relationships, increasing customer loyalty, and maintaining a competitive edge*. New York: John Wiley & Sons.

Godio, C. (2000). Building a virtual professional community: The case of Poolweb.it. In *Paper presented at the Third International Conference on Virtual Communities*, London.

Hagel, J., & Armstrong, A. G. (1997). *Net gain: Expanding markets through virtual communities*. Boston: Harvard Business School Press.

Hillery, G. A. (1955). Definitions of community: Areas of agreement. *Rural Sociology, 20*, 118-120.

Hiltz, S. R., & Johnson, K. (1990). User satisfaction with computer-mediated communication systems. *Management Science, 36*(6), 739-764.

Kraemer, W., & Müller, M. (1999). Virtual corporate university: Executive education architecture and knowledge management. In A.-W. Scheer (Ed.), *Electronic business and knowledge management*. Heidelberg, Germany: Physica.

Mansell, G. (1991). Action research in information systems development. *Journal of Information Systems, 1*, 29-40.

Markus, U. (2002). *Integration der Virtuellen Community in Das Customer Relationship Management*. Unpublished dissertation, University of Saarland, Saarbrücken.

McDermott, R. (2002). Measuring the impact of communities. *Knowledge Management Review, 5*(2), 26-29.

Poplin, D. E. (1979). *Communities: A survey of theories and methods of research* (2nd ed.). New York: McMillan.

Rheingold, H. (1998). Virtual communities. In F. Hesselbein (Ed.), *The community of the future*. San Francisco: Jossey-Bass.

Schulte, T. (1999). *Group computing workspace*. Unpublished dissertation, University of St. Gallen, St. Gallen.

Stanoevska-Slabeva, K., & Schmid, B. F. (2000). Requirements analysis for community supporting platforms based on the media reference model. *Electronic Markets, 10*(4), 250-257.

Susman, G. I., & Evered, R. D. (1978). An assessment of the scientific merits of action research. *Administrative Science Quarterly, 23*(14), 582-603.

Sutton, W. A., & Munson, T. (1976). *Definitions of community*. New York: American Sociological Association.

Watson-Manheim, M. B., & Belanger, F. (2002). Exploring communication-based work processes in virtual work environments. In *Paper presented at the 35th Annual Hawaii International Conference on System Sciences*, Hawaii.

Wenger, E. (1997). *Communities of practice: Learning, meaning, and identity*. Cambridge: Cambridge University Press.

Wenger, E., McDermott, R., & Snyder, W. M. (2002). *Cultivating communities of practice: A guide to managing knowledge*. Boston: Harvard Business School Press.

Wiesenfeld, B. M., Raghuram, S., & Garud, R. (1999). Communication patterns as determinants of organizational identification in a virtual organization. *Organization Science, 10*(6), 777-790.

Winter, R. (2002). An executive MBA program in business engineering: A curriculum focusing on change. *Journal of IT Education, 1*(4), 279-288.

This work was previously published in International Journal of Technology and Human Interaction, Vol. 1, No. 4, edited by B. C. Stahl, pp. 19-36, copyright 2005 by IGI Publishing, formerly known as Idea Group Publishing (an imprint of IGI Global).

Chapter IX
Teens and Social Networking Services:
An Overview

Maryann Mori
Evansville Vanderburgh Public Library, USA

ABSTRACT

This chapter provides an overview of the ways teens interact with social networking services. It acknowledges that teens are active users of social networking sites, and the implications of this usage affect and/or cross social, moral, educational and political lines. By reviewing current trends and statistics from various authors and sources, this chapter provides background information to understanding the growth and importance of online social networking among the Internet generation. Topics include demographics, ramifications on social behavior, adults' concerns, policies designed to restrict teens' Internet access, educational benefits and future directions of teens' use of social networking services. Realizing the importance and influence of online social networks among teens should provide readers with a better understanding of how these sites can not only be used for educational and marketing purposes, but also be integrated within work environments.

INTRODUCTION

Adults may refer to the online sites as social networking services or sites, online social networks, interactive Web applications, or variations on a theme of Web 2.0. But as adults create titles and descriptions for these sites, "teens are speeding ahead, making it up as they go, including the language and the tools and their uses. To them, these sites are just another tool for socializing"

(Magid & Collier, 2007, p. 2). Teens generally refrain from using any of the adult variations of titles and simply refer to the services and sites by function or commercial site name. By reviewing current trends, uses, effects and concerns of teens' use of social networking services, this chapter provides background information about the continued growth and importance of online social networking among teens.

In order to increase awareness and understanding of the various implications of social networking as they influence teens, this chapter will attempt to do the following:

- Review the way the Internet in general and social networking services specifically have influenced teen generations;
- Examine teens' online behavior and their use of social networking services;
- Discuss why social networking sites are so attractive to teens;
- Consider the ways social networking affects teens' interaction in online and real-life social situations;
- Address the concerns of parents, other adults and media reports of online dangers;
- Review information about various legislations and policies designed to restrict minors' use of social networks;
- Present successful and creative uses of social networking among teens;
- Show that social networking services are a major part of teens' lives and a viable aspect that will continue to increase in usage among teens and impact their adult lives.

While the exact age of teens varies among sources, the term usually describes students in middle school and high school. The American Library Association's division of Young Adult Library Services Association (YALSA) defines *teens* as students ages 12-18 (American Library Association [ALA]:Young Adult Library Services Association [YALSA], n.d.). It is the definition generally used for purposes of this chapter.

When Donald Tapscott wrote his book *Growing Up Digital: The Rise of the Net Generation* in 1998, he referred to teens as the Net generation (also Net Gen or N-Gen). Teens born after the rise of computer technology have been given an assortment of generational titles including the Internet generation, Generation M (for Media) (CBS, 2005), Gen Y and MySpace generation. The Pew Research Center for the People and the Press calls these teens "Generation Next" (2007). The assortment and interchangeability of titles seem appropriate for a generation that is used to constant change in technology. For purposes of this chapter either Net Generation or Next generation (or variances of those two titles) will be used to describe the generation. The titles describe a generation used to multi-tasking and instant information (Tapscott, 1998). This generation is willing to compromise privacy (Kelsey, 2007) in exchange for accessing the world 24/7 via the Internet. They are more literate in visual concepts than previous generations (D. Oblinger & J. Oblinger, 2005), yet equally comfortable with text that amply appears on the screens of computers, cell phones and video games. They are a generation that is inclusive and social (D. Oblinger & J. Oblinger, 2005), as well as interactive and investigative (Tapscott, 1998). Specifically, they are a generation born around 1980—after Generation X which comprises individuals born from 1966-1980 (Pew Research Center, 2007). Tapscott refers to the Net generation as those people "born between 1977 and 1996 inclusive" and declares that "internationally the Net Generation is huge, numbering over two billion people" (Tapscott & Williams, 2006, p. 46). Next generation teens are creative, and they have found an outlet for their creativity by using social networking services to express themselves, and to evaluate each other and their world.

INFLUENCES OF THE INTERNET AND SOCIAL NETWORKING SERVICES ON TEENS

Anastasia Goodstein (2007) wrote in her book *Totally Wired: What Teens and Tweens are Really Doing Online,* that while teen trends may have changed, the basic struggles of adolescent development have not changed much from previous generations. Goodstein believes these wired teens, like their predecessors, are still "trying out different identities, learning responsibility, being impulsive and idealistic, feeling invincible, dealing with physical changes, distancing from parents, and creating meaningful relationships with friends" (2007, p.2). One thing that does denote a change for the Net generation, however, is the fact that this generation is "the first cohort to grow up fully wired and technologically fluent" (Hempel & Lehman, 2005, p. 88), and that fact has had an obvious effect on teens.

Professors Diana G. Oblinger (2005) and James L. Oblinger (2005), editors of *Educating the Net Generation*, identify five characteristic differences in the way Next Gen students analyze and absorb information. Oblinger and Oblinger credit all of these characteristics directly to technology's influence on the generation. Among these differences are students' ability to understand more visual communication, to easily navigate between the virtual and physical worlds, to learn through self-discovery, to quickly retarget their attention (similar to multi-tasking), and to respond quickly and anticipate equally fast responses (D. Oblinger & J. Oblinger, 2005). Social networking services feature capabilities that cater to these types of characteristics by including ample visual stimulation through photographs, videos, virtual environments and vlogs; allowing students to have real-life types of communication, relationships and experiences in a virtual setting; giving teens the opportunity to explore topics, express their ideas and learn for themselves; and enabling instant messaging and rapid posting of constantly-changing

information. Another observation by Oblinger and Oblinger is the desire for socialization by Net generation learners, who prefer activities that encourage "social interaction" (2005, p. 2.6). In many online situations, this social interaction becomes mass collaboration or what Tapscott calls "peer production" (2006, p.11). Additionally, these teens have an "openness to diversity, differences, and sharing;" "are at ease meeting strangers on the Net;" are "emotionally open," and have "developed a mechanism of inclusiveness that does not necessarily involve personally knowing someone admitted to their group" (D. Oblinger & J. Oblinger, 2005, p 2.6).

USE OF THE INTERNET AND SOCIAL NETWORKING SERVICES AMONG TEENS

According to 2007 reports by the Pew Internet & American Life Project, 93% of American teens use the Internet (Lenhart & Madden, 2007b, p.3), and "more than half (55%) of all online American youths ages 12-17 use online social networking sites" (Lenhart & Madden, 2007a, p.1). Berkeley doctoral candidate Danah Boyd believes the latter figure is low. Boyd, who has become the oft-quoted and recognized leader in social networking research, particularly as it pertains to teens, says that in her experience with teens, 70-80% of them have an online profile (2007b, Methodological notes, para. 4). Boyd acknowledges that not all the teens she interviews are active on their profile accounts or may not have created the profiles themselves (rather, allowing friends to create profiles for them). She believes 50% indicates the percentage of teens who are active (as opposed to inactive) users of social networking services (2007b, Methodological notes, para. 4).

Globally, the number of people accessing the Internet and (often) social networking sites is increasing. In July 2007, comScore, which calls itself "a global leader in measuring the digital world" (Lipsman, 2007c), released global statistics regarding the use of social networking sites among Internet users over the age of fifteen. According to comScore's executive vice president of international markets, "social networking has really taken off globally" (Lipsman, 2007c). Observing an increase in the daily visits to social networking sites, comScore says "it would appear that social networking is not a fad but rather an activity that is being woven into the very fabric of the global Internet" (Lipsman, 2007c). In the United Kingdom, people aged15-25 are "25% more likely to be online than the general population" (Lipsman, 2007b). In Australia, nearly half of all children ages 6-17 are online daily (Woodhead, 2007). Australian teens ages 15-17 go online daily, often to access social networking sites (Woodhead, 2007). Canada boasts "the world's ninth-largest Internet population" with 80% of the population visiting social networking sites (Canada online overview, 2007). As of May 2007, Japan's Mixi, the nation's largest social networking service, had eight million registered users (McNicol, 2007). Half a million teens are part of Mixi's registered users (Katayama, 2006). CyWorld has 18 million Korean users (Schonfeld, 2006) with 90% of Korean teens and twenty-somethings having an account (Ihlwan, 2005). Orkut, Google's social networking site, has made major inroads in Latin America, particularly in Brazil (Kharif, 2007). 12.4 million unique users from Latin America visited Orkut in August 2007, twice the amount of visitors from that same region to MySpace and Facebook combined (Kharif, 2007).

Lenhart and Madden's study analyzes American teens' online behavior by demographics and shows that younger teens with online profiles are fairly divided between the genders until they get older (2007a, p.3). A larger gender division occurs when age becomes a factor. Seventy percent of online girls ages 15-17 have created a profile, while 57% of online boys this age have done likewise (Lenhart & Madden, 2007a, p.3).

An earlier Pew Internet report (Lenhart, Madden, & Hitlin, 2005) indicates a major increase in Internet use as teens advance in grade levels. These figures denote general online use and not necessarily use of social networking sites. While 60% of 6th grade students were shown to be online, by 7th grade the number rose to 82%, and by grade eleven 94% of teens indicated being online (Lenhart et al., 2005, p.1). Age is also a factor in the frequency of Internet use. American teens between the ages of 15-17 frequent the Internet more than younger students, with 59% of those older teens going online at least once a day (Lenhart et al., 2005, p.2).

The amount of time teens spend online continues to increase. Nielsen/NetRatings from October, 2006 showed the amount of time American teens spend online increased 27% within a three-year time period (Bausch & Han, 2006). The survey shows that American teens spent an average of nearly 27 hours per month online (Bausch & Han, 2006). A study with variances from the aforementioned comparison indicates the hours European visitors over age 15 spend on social networking sites and rates the United Kingdom with the highest time spent at an average of 5.8 hours per month, followed by Germany at 3.1 hours per month (Gavin, 2007). "Heavy users" in the U.K. spend an average of 22 hours on social networking sites (Gavin, 2007). According to Lenhart and Madden (2007b), daily use of the Internet by American teens has risen from 42% in a study conducted in 2000 up to 61% in a similar study conducted in 2006 (p.3). Teens are spending much of their online time visiting social networking sites. "[Forty-eight percent] of teens visit social networking Web sites daily or more often; 26% visit once a day, 22% visit several times a day" (Lenhart & Madden, 2007a, p.2).

Sites that are especially popular among this age group tend to be those that are social networking in nature (Lipsman, 2007b). Bob Ivins, executive vice president and managing director of comScore Europe, says the high Internet usage among younger people shows that the Internet is "integral" to this generation (Lipsman, 2007b). "Younger people use the Web for communications, content, community and commerce more than other age segments," says Ivins (Lipsman, 2007b). So many young Australians are using the Internet that statistics among youth ages 6-17 have now plateaued at 92% (Woodhead, 2007). Commenting on American students' use of social networking sites, Ken Cassar, chief analyst for Nielsen/Net Ratings says, "The Internet is as much a part of children's lives as TV, school and books. We can expect the time kids spend online to increase along with expanded offerings on the Web and the growing network of their friends and family who use the Web frequently" (Bausch & Han, 2006).

One of the ways teens use social networking services is by creating and maintaining a personal profile page on a site such as MySpace, Facebook, Orkut, Bebo or one of many other such commercial sites. These profiles usually include photographs, comments, surveys, likes and dislikes, and personal interests. Video clips, songs, and decorations often complement the profile. Online profiles may be compared to interactive scrapbooks or photo albums. Since keeping their profile pages interesting is an important aspect for teens, it is possible that many teens are spending their online time posting new information to their profile. The Nielsen/NetRatings survey shows that American teens' favorite Internet sites are those which offer tools or assistance in developing content or layouts for online profiles (Bausch & Han, 2006). However, according to Lenhart and Madden, the overwhelming reason American teens cite for visiting their social networking sites so often is to "stay in touch with friends" (2007a, p.2).

Social networking sites are often compared to the malls, soda shops and other assorted hangouts that appealed to previous generations of teens. "Social networking sites have become the vir-

tual commons where teens go to hang out with their friends" (Rapacki, 2007, p.29). In a *People* magazine article about MySpace, psychologist David Walsh said "Kids have always congregated with other kids. Two generations ago, it was at the corner candy store. Now, in this high-tech age, MySpace is the candy store on steroids" (Hewitt et al. 2006, pp. 116, 118). Teens do many of the same things online that previous generations did in school hallways, friends' rooms, locker rooms or local hangouts. They talk, laugh, gossip, share and flirt with each other. Just how many teens are on which sites is difficult to determine, primarily because the numbers keep increasing so rapidly, and as Boyd recently observed, "one of the biggest problems with studying youth culture is that it's a moving target, constantly shifting based on a variety of social and cultural forces" (2007b, Methodological notes, para. 3). Couple that moving target with rapidly evolving aspects of technology, and statistics often become difficult to track. In December 2005, *BusinessWeek* named three popular social networking sites and showed that the number of users ages 12 to 24 accounted for 45% of all users on MySpace, 50% of all users on Xanga, and 57% of all users on Facebook (Hempel & Lehman, pp.90, 92, 94). The January 2007 Pew Internet report also shows that MySpace, Facebook and Xanga are popular sites among American teens (Lenhart & Madden, 2007a, p.4).

ComScore released statistics on July 31, 2007, revealing the "expansion of social networking across the globe" among various users ages fifteen and over (Lipsman, 2007c). The study lists seven sites, all of which experienced significant growth from the previous year ranging from a 56% increase for Hi5 to 774% for Tagged (Lipsman, 2007c). ComScore notes that "specific social networks have a tendency to skew in popularity in different regions" (Lipsman, 2007c). MySpace and Facebook are the top contenders in North America, Bebo's audience appeal is in Europe, Orkut's following is in Latin America, and Asia-

Pacific regions prefer Friendster (Lipsman, 2007c). Hi5 and Tagged are identified as having "more balance in their respective visitor bases, drawing at least 8% from each of the five worldwide regions" (Lipsman, 2007c).

Boyd (2007) offers an interpretation of teens' preferences for specific sites as those preferences fall within social issues. On her blog, Boyd discusses recent trends of high school students transferring their online profiles to Facebook from MySpace, a change she believes reflects socio-economic factors rather than age or gender (2007b). Boyd calls this exodus a "fragmentation" (2007b, para. 1) rather than a shift, and her essay has been summarized as suggesting "MySpace users tilt toward the lower middle classes" (Atal, 2007). Although Boyd admits the essay she posted on her blog is not academic in nature, she writes that she has recently seen a clear division in the kinds of students using MySpace versus Facebook. Facebook, which was previously open only to college students, opened its membership in 2005 to include high school students. Boyd acknowledges that students who are from families where education is emphasized are the ones now using Facebook (2007b). She believes MySpace is the preferred social networking site for teens whose parents did not go to college, and who themselves will be expected to get a job rather than pursue higher education after high school (2007b). Boyd divides the two groups of teen users, those on Facebook versus those on MySpace, as hegemonic and sub-altern, respectively (2007b). She admits that the terms are not completely adequate for her descriptions but adds, "Sub-altern teens who go to more mixed-class schools see Facebook as 'what the good kids do' or 'what the preps do.' … [T]he hegemonic teens see MySpace as 'where the bad kids go'" (2007b, Socio-economic divisions, para. 9). Boyd summarizes her observations by saying that this "division around MySpace and Facebook is just another way in which technology is mirroring societal values" (2007b, Thoughts and meta thoughts, para. 2). Additional research is necessary regarding this division.

BusinessWeek notes that many of the same online users are utilizing both MySpace and Facebook and quotes comScore as reporting "a 64% overlap" of those people who use both sites (Atal, 2007). *BusinessWeek* does not indicate the ages of the people in their findings.

THE ATTRACTION OF SOCIAL NETWORKING TO TEENS

Regardless of which teen is using which social networking site, just what is the appeal of these sites to teens? Social networking sites are the commons or hangout for Next generation teens. Because this hangout is in a virtual world, it not only means that it is open any time, but also that it is, more often than not, clear of parental control. Parents are often not as tech-savvy as their online children and therefore do not always frequent the same online social networks as their teens. Candice M. Kelsey (2007), author of *Generation MySpace: Helping Your Teen Survive Online Adolescence*, compares MySpace to a kind of virtual "clubhouse" for teens—a clubhouse with access through the "doors" of every computer, PDA and some cell phones (2007, p. 2). Kelsey adds that MySpace is a "parent-free zone" where teens "can pretend to be anything or anyone they want" (2007, p. 2), both of which are additional appeal factors to teens. The same descriptions can be said of most social networking sites frequented by teens.

Boyd agrees that the absence of parental or adult authority is part of the appeal of social networking sites among teens. As quoted in Kelsey's book, Boyd says "MySpace is the product of youth creating space of their own. Teens are looking for a release from the control of their usually unstable homes. …It is a control issue at heart" (Kelsey, 2007, p. 13). Boyd also says that technology (namely social networking) is helping teens cope with their often stressful and fragmented lives by providing places to socialize and develop a sense of "community" with other teens (2007b, Thoughts and meta thoughts, para. 7).

Tapscott rightly predicted that the Internet would soon become a place that would "carry audio and full-motion, full-color video" and that "anyone…with a video camera and PC will soon be able to broadcast to the world" (1998, p. 50). He declared that "tens of millions of N-Geners around the world are taking over the steering wheel" (p. 26) of the media and added that this generation was unique in that it was the first group to take "control of critical elements of a communications revolution" (p. 26). Again, the issue of control becomes a factor when reviewing reasons social networking sites appeal to teens. Teens grabbed hold of the steering wheel, and as Magid and Collier declare in a subtitle, "Teens Are in the Driver's Seat" (2007, p. 172). Instead of being just spectators to information, stories, events and news (as previous generations had to be with television and print sources), teens are now content creators and contributors through the concepts and capabilities of social networking sites.

With little parental involvement or control, teens are very open in their online postings and express an attitude of independence—aspects which, for many adults, open issues of Internet ethics. Teens' postings often include "raw content" (Hewitt et al., 2006, p. 119) such as crude language and risqué photographs or videos, in addition to discussions of sex, alcohol and drugs (Simon & Majewski, 2007). As Tapscott (1998) noted, independence and openness, as well as free expression are some of Net generation's characteristics, although past generations of teens have also freely shared dirty pictures and discussed taboo topics among themselves when parents or caregivers were absent. Part of the way teens develop independence is by exploring their identities as they mature, and social networking sites can contribute to this self-identity process by allowing teens to experiment with different representations or identities of themselves online.

Tapscott addressed the topic of "vanity" (p. 113) in his book although he believed the opportunity for teens to post personal information online was a way for students to develop their self-esteem.

Some adults believe teens' social networking use goes beyond building self-esteem and use the word *narcissism* to assess teens' love affair with social networking. Psychologist Michael Brody boldly declares "digital technology is associated with self absorption, narcissism and isolation" (2006, p. 8). Boyd acknowledges teens' desires for fame, something akin to "peer validation" (2007a, para. 7) and admits that technology such as social networking allows for free distribution for teens and other "fame-seeking narcissists" to post themselves online "in the hopes of being seen and being validated" (2007a, para. 7). Boyd's comments echo Lenhart and Madden who show that a major attraction of social networks for teens is the feedback and sense of belonging to a group that they receive from the sites (2007b, p. 13). To some teens, having their image and ideas noticed by others on the Internet is the equivalent of fame.

When *University Business* wrote an article about social networking services (Sickler, 2007), research was conducted with college students about their use of Facebook and MySpace. Although slightly older than teenagers, these college students' comments echo many teens' views of social networking sites:

- "It is way too much fun to think that people are looking at me and paying attention to me in their free time"
- "It reminds me that I have friends"
- "I also like that it is an excellent way to get people to stare at pictures of me and basically worship me by writing things on my Facebook wall" (Sickler, 2007).

While Boyd does not believe social networking sites cause narcissism, she does believe sites such as MySpace serve as "a platform for people to seek attention" (2007a, para. 15). Mike Riera, author of several parenting books, says," I think the very nature of being a teen is very narcissistic. They're so in love with themselves that they think everyone else will love what they have to say, too" (Goodstein, 2007, p. 34).

SOCIAL NETWORKING SERVICES AND TEEN SOCIAL BEHAVIOR

Having their say on blogs is yet another way teens are socializing and promoting themselves online. According to Forrester Research, blogging—including publishing a blog— is "booming" among North American youth ages 13 to 17 (Charron & Florentino, 2006). Blogs, which may be compared to online diaries, allow teens to express themselves in an environment free from parents, to explore their own identities, to form virtual relationships, and to locate people with common interests (Goodstein, 2007, pp. 30-32). An interesting aspect of online socializing is the way anonymity affects teens' interaction with each other. Teens online find that they are not judged by physical characteristics such as race, clothing styles or age as they might be in real life (Goodstein, 2007, p. 66; Lenhart & Madden, 2007b, p. iii). Goodstein references a *San Jose Mercury News* article that discusses teens at a particular high school who socialize virtually with classmates they would never socialize with in person. "For some teens, the friends they meet on blogs remain online friends who don't interact at all offline, even if they pass each other in the hallways" (Goodstein, 2007, p. 32).

The New York Times published an article about the rise in popularity of self-portraits, especially among teens (Williams, 2006). Williams' article refers to the generation as one "raised on a mantra of self-esteem" who now is comfortable with taking pictures of themselves and posting them online for anyone to see. Williams quotes a developmental psychologist as saying young

adults have an idea known as "the imaginary audience"—that is, "the idea that adolescents think people are more interested in them than they actually are" (2006). Although the concept may not be new, today's teens seem "more comfortable with public self-exposure" (Williams, 2006).

Unfortunately, many teens are willing to do or post anything to gain exposure online, which causes actions that raise additional concerns about Internet ethics. According to a *USA Today* report, some children identified in Internet child pornography are actually photographs of older teens who have taken provocative photos of themselves and posted them online (Sher, 2007). Kelsey's research indicates this phenomenon is common and growing among American teens, especially girls. Kelsey writes, "girls are ferociously searching for boys' attention, and MySpace is the ideal platform for achieving this goal. The sexier the photos, the taglines, and the screen names are, the more male MySpace friends a girl will earn" (2007, p. 144). In a random search of high school students' profiles, a professor at Fresno State found photographs of sexual poses on 59% of the sites (Kelsey, 2007, p. 148). Detective James McLaughlin of the Keene, New Hampshire police department says, "I don't think a week goes by where we don't see two to three adolescents post nude photos of themselves" (Hewitt et al, 2006, p. 120).

A *Washington Post* article indicates peer pressure as one of the growing reasons teens exaggerate their online postings (Bahrampour, Aratani, & Stockwell, 2006). However, sometimes students are tricked into posting provocative photographs of themselves. Older men create fake profiles and disguise themselves as teen boys who then identify "lonely" girls (based upon information contained in the girls' profiles) and become a "boyfriend" to the girl (Sher, 2007). With a little coaxing, such at-risk young females end up being seduced online and convinced to send the so-called boyfriend a sexually graphic picture, a process sometimes called "sexual grooming." The United States Justice Department refers to these kinds of solicitations as "cyber enticement" (Sher, 2007). Emily Vacher is an FBI undercover agent who says this type of online behavior is "a trend, and it's scary" (Sher, 2007).

There are other forms of misrepresentation that take place on social networking sites. For example, MySpace has a minimum age requirement of fourteen to join, yet "the most common example of misrepresentation [online] is teens under age fourteen lying about their age to beat the minimum age requirement for using the service" writes teen services librarian Sean Rapacki (2007, p. 30). As already noted, teens can post profiles that reveal anything they want, including a totally different personality from what they display in real life. Kelsey describes her shock at viewing a social networking profile of one of her students—a student she described as polite, conservative and quiet. The student's MySpace page, however, reflected "an angry young woman in full gang attire" with numerous references to sex, derogatory slang, and assorted images and phrases that were completely contradictory to the image the student portrayed on a daily basis at school (Kelsey, 2007, p. xxii). Lenhart and Madden (2007b) show that over half (56%) of online American teens have posted some false information to their online profiles (p. 23). However, only 8% of online teens have created mostly or entirely fake profiles (Lenhart & Madden, 2007b, p. 23). Boys are more likely than girls to post false information to their profiles (Lenhart & Madden, 2007b, p. 24). When Kelsey asked a psychotherapist about which representation of a student is real—the online or real-life version—the psychotherapist responded that neither version correctly identifies a student since teens are still developing their identities (Kelsey, 2007, pp. 158-159).

Teens often falsify information on their social networking profiles in an attempt to get the most visits to a page, or to collect the most *friends* on their profiles (Kelsey, 2007). The concept of meeting people and collecting friends online describes *friending*, a word used to describe the

development of online relationships. Boyd writes that friending is "a key component of social network sites" (2006, abstract). "Friending" writes Kelsey, "is a newly coined verb direct from the MySpace lexicon, short for befriending. It simply means *the act of accepting or being accepted by a new contact with the mutual intent of labeling one another 'friend' [sic]*" (Kelsey, 2007, p. 81). "Friending supports pre-existing social norms, yet because the architecture of social network sites is fundamentally different than the architecture of unmediated social spaces, these sites introduce an environment that is quite unlike that with which we are accustomed" (Boyd, 2006, abstract). Just as past generations had cliques, and teens' social statuses were dependent upon their circle of friends, so do today's teens rely upon the circle of online friends with whom they keep company to establish their status. The difference, however, is that friends in the online world are often really strangers, a fact that raises concerns about online behavior and relationships.

Visitors to an online profile can ask for a "friend request" or to be "added" to the teen's profile page. Being included on another teen's profile (especially if that other teen is deemed socially cool) can elevate an individual to wider and often higher social circles. Likewise, a teen whose profile has numerous friends is showing that he or she is popular and worthy of having even more friends. Not only does the teen accumulate a higher number on his or her profile listing of friends, but that teen is then added to the profile page of the persons whom the teen accepts as friends. Since profile pages often list the number of friends the profiler has, friending thus becomes a numbers game as well as a vicious popularity competition. "As people navigate Profiles [sic], they build an image of who people are through their Friends [sic]" (Boyd, 2006, Friending as context creation, para. 2). Kelsey calls the friending process a "commodities-trading style of relating" where teens judge each other "merely by how many other people like him or her" (2007, p. 86). "Listing your buddies and your friends is a way of establishing yourself, of feeling connected and feeling like you're accepted" says adolescent psychologist Susan Lipkins (Kelsey, 2007, p. 83).

In addition to collecting numerous online friends (often numbering in the thousands), teens are also ranking those online relationships. MySpace initiated the concept of a *Top 8* friends list. Instead of listing friends in the order of the date of their acceptance to a profiler's page, the profilers themselves can put friends in a pecking order, so to speak. "By implementing a 'Top 8' feature, MySpace changed the social dynamics around the ordering of Friends [*sic*]" (Boyd, 2006, But am I, para. 2). Teens often admit that they do not really know many of the so-called friends on their lists, and they realize the damaging consequences of *friends lists*, especially among younger teens who may not be strong enough mentally or emotionally to understand why they may not be part of a Top 8 list. "MySpace is a psychological warfare" says one teen (Boyd, 2006, But am I, para. 4). Dr. Lipkins says "friending is not just a pastime, it's also an indication of social success or failure" (Kornblum, 2006). Teens can add, rearrange, and even delete friends with little more effort than clicking a computer key. "If someone seems interesting or you want to get to know them better, what's the loss in Friending [*sic*] them? As far as most participants are concerned, Friendship [*sic*] doesn't mean anything really, so why not?" (Boyd, 2006, To friend or not, para. 9). Quoted in a *USA Today* article, Michael Bugeja, author of *Interpersonal Divide: The Search for Community in a Technological Age,* makes the following distinction between the superficial online friending list and the real-life list of friendships: "Friending really appeals to the ego, where friendships appeal to the conscience" (Kornblum, 2006).

BusinessWeek's cover story titled "The MySpace Generation" (Hempel & Lehman, 2005) notes that social networks are "creating new forms of social behavior that blur the distinctions be-tween online and real-world interactions" (p. 89) and "today's young generation largely ignores the difference" (p. 89). Even some teens are beginning to worry about their generation's attitudes regarding friendship. "All those friendships aren't real" says one 17-year-old student (Kornblum, 2006). Another teen says, "MySpace cuts out real communication between people.… Since the communication is so meaningless, it makes relationships meaningless" (Kelsey, 2007, p. 85). Dr. Larry D. Rosen, professor at California State University, has spent over two decades examining what he calls "the psychology of technology" (Rosen, 2006, p. 1). In a 2006 study, Rosen researched pairs of teens and parents and found that teens had "about 200 friends" on their MySpace accounts with 75 of those friends being deemed "close friends," in spite of the fact that teens had never met them (p. 2).

ADULTS' CONCERTS

The amount of time teens spend online concerns some adults who wonder about the possibility of teens becoming addicted to computer use. Psychologists seem divided on the issue of Internet addiction, and the topic is still deemed relatively new in the field of psychology, although Dr. David Greenfield, a clinical psychologist in Connecticut, believes the concept is "getting more and more recognition" (Klimkiewicz, 2007). Concerns about teens' "Internet gaming addiction" has led the Chinese government to initiate a nationwide program to "promote civilized Internet use" and limit the amount of time students under age eighteen spend online gaming (M. Lee, 2007). The discussion of online or Internet addiction has been debated for only ten years, and the American Psychiatric Association has not yet recognized the description as a disorder (Klimkiewicz, 2007). However, a Stanford University study shows that "one in eight Americans exhibited at least one sign of problematic Internet use" (Klimkiewicz, 2007). Psychiatrists who disagree with the diagnosis of Internet addiction believe that people who spend large amounts of time online are often suffering from other problems such as depression or anxiety (Klimkiewicz, 2007). Dr. John Grohol, a psychiatrist who oversees PsychCentral.com, believes that previous generations have had similar experience of abuses of new communication modes and says, "When you introduce a new technology into society, it takes a generation or two before it becomes well integrated" (Klimkiewicz, 2007). Rosen's study reveals that 20% believe "MySpace has negatively affected school, job, family and friends" (2006, p. 3) and that depression and Internet addiction were attributed to more time spent on MySpace in spite of the fact that more online friends were a benefit of time spent there (p. 3).

Kelsey devotes an entire chapter in her book to the subject of teen addiction to MySpace. She observes that many of the effects from frequent MySpace use are similar to those of other compulsive behaviors or addictions, and she readily admits that she believes teens have become Internet addicted to MySpace (2007, p. 17). Kelsey writes that an addiction can be described as "an uncontrollable compulsion to repeat a behavior regardless of its negative consequences" (2007, p. 16). She quotes teens who admit that MySpace is "ruining" their lives, is "unhealthy," and "addicting" (2007, p. 16), yet those same teens will say they are unwilling to give up their MySpace profiles. One user of Japan's Mixi comments, "It's fun getting replies and comments to your diaries. Pretty soon, you get addicted" (Katayama, 2006). Dr. Michael Brody, professor of American Studies at the University of Maryland and CEO of the Psychiatric Center in Washington, D.C., says, "The words 'addicting' and 'obsessive' seem to describe much of the teen involvement in these electronic activities" (2006, p. 8). Kelsey's book includes the narrative of Rob Alderman, a graduate student who struggled to give up his MySpace profile. While Kelsey acknowledges that

Alderman is beyond the teen years, his struggle is still the same as that of many teens she has interviewed. Alderman tells of his staying awake late at night in order to be part of a social network, of typing so often that the letters faded from his keyboard, and of spending more time with his online friends than his real-life friends (Kelsey, 2007, p. 23). "You can be who you want, when you want, with whom you want. In fact, it's so perfect and so addictive that it's easy to spend all of our time there, pouring ourselves into our own little MySpace kingdoms," says Alderman (Kelsey, 2007, p. 23). Alderman compares his online interactions to "worshipping at the MySpace altar" (Kelsey, 2007, p. 23).

A 2005 study by the Stanford Institute for the Quantitative Study of Society, as reported in *The Standford Daily*, revealed results of "social isolation" among those individuals with high Internet usage (Hanson, 2005). "[T]ime spent on the Internet is time taken away from other activities. Every minute spent on the computer is a minute taken away from face-to-face relationships with family and friends" (Hanson, 2005). Authors of the study reported that "each hour spent on the Internet reduces face-to-face time by 23.5 minutes" (Hanson, 2005).

Lenhart et al. (2005), however, found different results in their studies of online teens. They found that teens between the ages of 12-17 actually spend more physical time rather than online time with their friends (Lenhart et al., 2005, p. 30). On average, teens spend "10.3 hours a week with friends doing social activities outside of school and about 7.8 hours talking with friends via technology like the telephone, email, IM or text messaging" (p. 30). Additionally, 83% of teens participate in at least one group activity such as a school club or youth organization (Lenhart et al., 2005, p. 12). The author of this chapter has observed groups of teens in a public library setting who use computers to access social networking sites. Often these teens are interacting online with people sitting at a neighboring computer, or several of the teens will congregate around one computer and view aspects of a social networking site together, making comments to each other in the process. Thus, while the teens may individually be on the Internet, they are simultaneously interacting with real-life friends and not isolating themselves from real-life socialization. As previously stated, researchers and psychologists are still divided on the issue of Internet addiction and its ramifications on real-life social interactions. Additional research is needed, especially where these topics concern adolescents. Whether or not a formal acknowledgement of online or Internet addiction disorder is made, "teens are affected by this electronic culture and in turn, are effecting further changes in it" (Brody, 2006, p. 8).

In addition to their concerns about addiction, many adults (especially parents) fear that young people are making themselves too vulnerable to contact from online predators. Headlines and assorted media reports of such predators help feed adults' fears. Police warn there are predators who purposely search social networking sites in order to find their next victim, and finding that next victim is not hard for these predators to do according to Detective Frank Dannahey, an officer with the Rocky Hill, Connecticut Police Department. Dannahey provided written testimony before the Committee on Energy and Commerce Subcommittee on Oversight and Investigations, United States House of Representatives, about his findings as an online undercover detective. Early in 2006, Dannahey went undercover as a teen and created a MySpace account. He called himself "Matt" and claimed to be nineteen years old. Dannahey testified, "I have seen technology change in a direction that both benefits and assists online predators in carrying out their criminal activity. With the majority of America's teens online, the pool of potential online victims is vast" (2006, para. 1). He highlights the following results of his undercover social networking scenario: Teens as young as 14 and 15 years old willingly allowed Matt (presumably an adult) as a friend on their private profiles; many teens allowed Matt as a friend with no questions asked; teens voluntarily shared personal information; teens posted inappropriate and provocative photos of themselves on their profiles; teens routinely discussed their social activities and included dates, times and locations of such activities, as well as phone numbers to contact them; online surveys that include detailed personal information about the teen were common aspects of teen profiles (2006).

Dannahey summarizes his findings by observing that "teens are very trusting of people they meet online and are very willing to share their personal thoughts and information with virtual strangers" (2006, para. 6). He adds that bulletins, which often post real-time information, and the aforementioned surveys are key components whereby predators can glean pertinent information to learn details about a teen's daily routine, personal interests, and contact information. Dannahey's undercover assignment was developed in conjunction with a Dateline NBC broadcast and in reaction to the sexual assaults of seven teenage girls within a one-month time period in Middletown, Connecticut—assaults that were all the result of MySpace encounters (Dannahey, 2006).

Although many teens seem to realize (at least to some extent) the fact that their social networking profiles can be public information, they are not overly concerned about this fact. One sixteen-year-old says, "We're willing to give up some of our privacy to connect with people easier. The realization that people can find you online isn't that threatening to this generation" (Kelsey, 2007, p. 272). In spite of being comfortable sharing personal information online, teens are becoming more cautious with what they post to their online profiles. Lenhart and Madden indicate that 66% of American teens' online social networking profiles have limited access (2007a, p. 5). Fifty-nine percent of teens limit their profiles to viewing only by their friends, and the actual percentage of teens who post ample personal information to a public access profile is only 3% (Lenhart & Madden, 2007a, p. 5). However, as Detective Dannahey's undercover profile revealed, teens sometimes accept friend requests from people who are adults and total strangers, often without question or thought. Teens may also fail to realize that although they may be careful in setting their own page to private, their personal information can end up on someone else's page, and that second person may not have private settings. Lenhart and Madden (2007b) note that "many, but not all, teens are aware of the risks of putting information online in a public and durable environment. Many, but certainly not all, teens make reasonable, informed choices about what to share in what context" (p. 30). Lenhart and Madden further observe that "the warnings and concern coming from parents and educators are not falling on deaf ears" (2007b, p. 36).

Some of those warnings have come from news reports which abound with details of adult sexual predators who pretended to be teens online and lured unsuspecting, vulnerable young people to personal meetings where the teens were subsequently assaulted. ABC News and Good Morning America aired a report titled "All Children Vulnerable to Online Predators" and included the following quote as a byline in its online version: "Authorities Say 1 in 5 Children Has Been Approached By Online Predators" (Muir, 2006). The report included the story of a teen who had been swept into the online world of self-promoted sex sites by an online predator. "My experience is not as isolated as you might hope," said the teen, who added that "there are hundreds of kids in the United States alone who are right now wrapped up in this horror" (Muir, 2006).

Stories such as the one published and aired by ABC News focus on extreme incidents and often utilize the numbers reported in the Youth Internet Safety Survey (YISS) (Wolak, Mitchel & Finkelhor, 2006), a national survey conducted in the United States by the Crimes Against Children Research Center. Two such surveys were conducted. YISS-1 statistics were gathered from August 1999 to February 2000, while YISS-2 surveys were conducted from March to June 2005 (Wolak et al., 2006, p. 1). The ABC News "1 in 5" quote about children being approached by online predators stems from YISS-1. YISS-2, the more recent survey, shows a decrease in this number with 1 in 7 youth receiving "unwanted sexual solicitations" (Wolak et al., 2006, p. 1). An interesting discovery of the YISS-2 study is the additional information noted about the "1 in 7" sexual solicitation. YISS-2 shows that "43% of all solicitations and 44% of aggressive solicitations" were made by individuals under the age of eighteen (Wolak et al., 2006, p. 17). In other words, in many cases it is teens themselves who are making the solicitations of each other. Additionally, 14% of solicitations came from people the teen knew in person prior to receiving the solicitation (Wolak et al., 2006, p. 17). In 2000, a Pew Internet report showed that 60% of teens had received online contact from a stranger (Lenhart & Madden, 2007b, p. 34). A 2006 study shows the number dropped to 32% of teens who have been contacted online by a complete stranger, and of those teens, 65% of them say they ignored or deleted such contacts (Lenhart & Madden, 2007b, p. 34). Additionally, only 7% of online teens say they have been contacted by a stranger to the point of "feeling scared or uncomfortable" (Lenhart & Madden, 2007b, p. 35). According to the National School Boards Association, only .08% of students between the ages of nine to seventeen have met someone in person (without parental consent) after an online introduction (NSBA, 2007).

Teens often face a more immediate threat than predators on social networking sites—bullies. "Cyberbullying" is defined as "willful and repeated harm inflicted through the medium of electronic text" (Patchin & Hinduja, 2007). Cyberbullying can include a variety of tactics, such as sending nasty or threatening messages, posting untrue or exaggerated stories about the victim, impersonating the victim, or intentionally excluding someone from an online group. "Cyber-bullying is nothing short of social terror by technology" (Kelsey, 2007, p. 108) and is "the most common 'risk' for middle-school-age social networkers" (Magid & Collier, 2007, pp. 114, 115). A comparison of the two YISS surveys (Wolak et al., 2006) show that online harassment increased 50% by youth ages 10 to 17 (p. 10). The YISS-2 survey also notes that the number of students who say they have harassed or embarrassed someone else online has increased to 9%—up from YISS-1's 1% statistics (Wolak et al., 2006, p. 11). "The Internet is apparently being used more and more for the bullying and harassment widespread among many youth peer groups" (Wolak et al., p. 11). Half of teens surveyed at Ireland's Young Scientists' Exhibition said they had "experienced or witnessed" cyberbullying, with 10% saying it had happened "lots of times" (Cullen, 2007). An Associated Press story about online bullying indicates that Internet bullying, which allows harassment and insults to be sent to victims anonymously "can be more damaging to victims than traditional bullying like fistfights and classroom taunts" (Norton, 2007).

The New York Times published an article titled "Teenagers Misbehaving, for All Online to Watch" (Norton, 2007) which discusses teens' seeming obsession with posting online pictures or videos of violent behavior, including the abuse and beating of other teens—an extreme form of cyberbullying. While adolescent bullying is nothing new, it has "taken on a new dimension as online cinema verite. Instead of being whispered about among friends and then fading away, such rites of ridiculousness are now routinely captured on video and posted on the Internet for worldwide perusal, and posterity" (Kilgannon, 2007). The article included comments by Nancy E. Willard, author of *Cyberbulling and Cyberthreats,* who observes that teens may not realize the seriousness of posting themselves (or others) committing crimes such as vandalism and abuse, "but a lot of teens have this idea that life is a game and it's all just entertainment" (Kilgannon, 2007).

LEGISLATION AND RESTRICTIONS

In an effort to combat cyberbullying, predators, and pornography, the United States Congress introduced legislation in 2006 known as the Deleting Online Predators Act (Fitzpatrick) or DOPA, as it was more commonly abbreviated. The bill targeted schools and libraries in an attempt to establish Internet policy that would "protect minors from commercial social networking Web sites and chat rooms" (Fitzpatrick, 2006). DOPA passed the House in July, 2006 but later died in Senate (American Library Association [ALA], 2007). At the beginning of 2007, Senator Ted Stevens of Arkansas introduced S. 49, the "Protecting Children in the 21st Century Act" which is also known as the Deleting Online Predators Act of 2007. S.49 includes three components or titles. It is the second title that most affects teens. Title II mimics DOPA but targets schools and libraries by requiring them to enforce Internet safety policies that prohibit cyberbullying and to prohibit access to commercial social networking sites and chat rooms without parental consent and/or educational purposes (Stevens, 2007). As of July, 2007, this bill had been referred to the Senate's Committee on Commerce, Science, and Transportation (GovTrack). Not trusting another defeat in Congress, at least six states have initiated their own versions of DOPA—bills designed to place more restrictions on social networking among minors (Medina, 2007).

Other countries are equally concerned about Internet predators and are developing ways to establish some sort of Internet policy or protection plan for children online. Australia's federal governmental program, NetAlert, has a task force created to "examine the potential use of networking sites by pedophiles to groom children for sexual abuse and exploitation" (Wilson, 2007). The Council of Europe, which comprises 46 countries (including the United States), is hoping to pass a treaty that "seeks to protect children by criminalizing online behavior like 'sexual grooming'" (Carvajal, 2007). Germany already has a public service commercial that has become a "cult classic" on YouTube—one that is designed to warn children about "potential hazards" they may face online (Carvajal, 2007). The European School-net hosts "Safer Internet Day" which involves schools in countries throughout Europe, as well as Australia, the United States and Canada (Richardson, 2007). The annual event has developed a "worldwide blogathon" which allows hundreds of schools throughout the world "to create internet safety awareness material" (Richardson, 2007). The Korean National Assembly is seeking ways to prevent "cyberviolence" (Katayama, 2006). In the United States, several states are seeking legislation to establish an age verification system (Medina, 2007). Such a system could require minors to prove they are old enough to meet minimum age requirements to establish social networking profiles and/or prevent older users from disguising themselves as teens.

Adam Thierer, director of The Progress & Freedom Foundation's Center for Digital Media Freedom, wrote a lengthy report titled "Social Networking and Age Verification: Many Hard Questions; No Easy Solutions," published in March, 2007. Thierer writes "Age verification is extremely complicated, and it would be even more complicated in this case because public officials are demanding the age verification of minors as well as adults, which presents a wide array of special challenges and concerns" (2007, p. 3). Thierer examines a variety of those challenges and summarizes his concerns with three generalizations about age verification, namely that such attempts would raise concerns of privacy issues as well as freedom of speech, it would not be foolproof, and finally that "education is absolutely necessary" (2007, p. 3) as the ultimate solution to preventing many of the problems that concern parents and politicians. Thierer also believes "that part of what is driving the push to regulate social networking sites is that many adults simply don't understand this new technology and have created

a sort of 'moral panic' around it" (2007, p. 10). This misunderstanding, says Thierer, is also fear-driven by "a handful of highly publicized cases of minors being contacted and later abducted or abused by child predators on social networking sites" (2007, p. 5).

Tapscott (1998) implied the same reasons for adults' concerns over the then-new Internet. He believed the Internet posed "a challenge to the existing order on many forms" (1998, p. 50) and that adults who were more comfortable with their pre-existing forms of media and communication were "being made uneasy by a new generation and a new communications media that is controlled by no one" (1998, p. 50). Tapscott, like Thierer, also believed that "kids and the new technology are often unfavorably portrayed publicly" (1998, p. 45), and he noted that denial of the Internet to minors was often an answer to adults' concerns rather than education about online safety.

Attempts to curb cyberbullying are also being made by many U.S. states and schools (Norton, 2007). Although educators acknowledge the need for "guidelines" that would effectively help punish cyberbullying, others warn that such guidelines and laws cannot prevent cyberbullying, "You can't legislate norms, you can only teach norms" says a Rhone Island educator (Norton, 2007). The American Civil Liberties Union also believes it will be difficult to create legislation that would effectively prevent cyberbullying without imposing upon "free-speech rights" (Norton, 2007).

Perhaps due to negative media exposure, MySpace, one of the most popular of the social networking sites for teens, has developed several ways to make its site safer for minors. Partnering with the National Center for Missing & Exploited Children, MySpace will now post Amber Alerts of missing children (Lehman, 2007). The site has also attempted various verification systems that will prevent contact of older users with younger ones and allow parents to monitor their children's profiles to verify ages of other users (Lehman, 2007). MySpace has also initiated a "full privacy setting" and deleted hundreds of thousands of under-age users (Lehman, 2007). More recently, MySpace deleted over 29,000 registered sex offenders' profiles from its site (Associated Press, 2007). MySpace received especially negative media coverage when several families filed lawsuits against the company, claiming the site did not do enough to protect the families' teenage daughters from predators (Lee, 2007). One such lawsuit was dismissed by a Texas judge who declared, "If anyone had a duty to protect Julie Doe, it was her parents, not MySpace" (E. Lee, 2007). The dismissed lawsuit involved a 13-year-old girl who misrepresented herself as an 18-year-old on her MySpace page and was sexually assaulted by a 19-year-old man whom she met in person after being introduced to him on MySpace (E. Lee, 2007). In January, 2008, MySpace was subpoenaed by a United States federal grand jury in connection with the 2006 incident of a teenage girl who committed suicide after the boy with whom she had been corresponding on the social networking site rejected her (Glover & Huffstutter, 2008). It was later revealed that the "boy" with whom the girl had been corresponding was actually an adult woman who knew the girl (Glover & Huffstutter, 2008). No criminal charges were filed against that adult woman since prosecutors were "unable to find a statute under which to pursue a criminal case" (Glover & Huffstutter, 2008). However, prosecutors in the U.S. attorney's office of Los Angles, California believe there are possibilities of filing charges against the woman based upon wire fraud and cyber fraud (Glover & Huffstutter, 2008). Although the original case transpired in Missouri, the California prosecutors are assuming jurisdiction since the headquarters of MySpace are located in that state (Glover & Huffstutter, 2008). Other attorneys and prosecutors worry that 1st Amendment free speech issues may be compromised if an indictment in such a case were to occur (Glover & Huffstutter, 2008). The story of the subpoena, which appeared in a *Los Angeles Times* article, states that "it could be difficult to draw the line between constitutionally protected free speech and conduct that is illegal" (Glover & Huffstutter, 2008). Facebook also faces challenges. The New York State attorney general subpoenaed Facebook after undercover investigators "were solicited by adult sexual predators and could access pornographic images and videos" (Adegoke, 2007b). The subpoena is a result of a 50-state joint investigation and accuses Facebook of "not keeping young users safe from sexual predators and not responding to user complaints" (Adegoke, 2007b).

Some schools and public libraries are imposing their own Internet policies by restricting minors' use of social networking sites. According to the National School Boards Association, 52% of all U.S. school districts "specifically prohibit any use of social networking sites in school" (NSBA, 2007). At the beginning of 2006, a school district in Washington prohibited students from registering on Facebook with school e-mail addresses (Bahrampour et al., 2006). One parochial school even banned the use of social networking sites at students' homes (Bahrampour et al., 2006). MySpace was banned from some Florida schools after parents complained about the site (CBS, 2006), and a high school in Vermont banned blogging sites after deeming them non-educational (McKenna, 2005). At least one public library has banned MySpace from its public access computers. Wake County Public Library in Raleigh, North Carolina imposed such a ban after its library saw too much gang activity—activity the library's director says stemmed from postings on MySpace (Oleck, 2007a). The American Library Association (ALA) does not promote banning social networking sites from school and library computers. The ALA Council has passed a Resolution in Support of Online Social Networks which clearly affirms "the importance of online social networks to library users of all ages for developing and using essential information literacy skills" (ALA, 2006).

SOCIAL NETWORKS AS EDUCATIONAL SITES

Adults who realize the prominence of social networking sites in the lives of teens are choosing to use the sites as educational tools rather than banning them. ALA's division of Young Adult Library Services Association (YALSA) believes "social networking technologies have many positive uses in schools and libraries" (ALA: YALSA, 2007). YALSA encourages the use of social networking technologies by school and public libraries in order to help teens receive the following educational benefits: learning and creating together, receiving feedback, developing a "sense of community," learning from adults about safe and smart uses of social networking (ALA:YALSA, 2007, p. 2).Teens are already incorporating for themselves those first three benefits as they interact with each other on social networking sites. Steven Johnson wrote in a *Time* magazine article, that technology is "sharpening the minds of Generation M, not dumbing them down.... They're learning to analyze complex systems with many interacting variables, to master new interfaces, to find and validate information in vast databases, to build and maintain extensive social networks crossing both virtual and real-world environments, to adapt existing technology to new uses. And they're learning all this in their spare time—for fun!" (2006, p. 56).

The kind of learning that can occur from social networking sites is what Marc Prensky calls "engaging" (2005, p. 60). Prensky says Net Gen students are used to "being empowered to choose what they want ... and to see what interests them ...and to create their own personalized identity" (2005, p. 62), yet schools typically choose to teach subjects with traditional, non-tech methods—methods Prensky describes as "stale," "bland" and "yesterday's education for tomorrow's kids" (2005, p. 62).

The National School Boards Association (NSBA) conducted a study of United States students between the ages of nine and seventeen and found that 96% of them are using social networking sites (NSBA, 2007). One of the most encouraging outcomes of this report is that nearly 60% of these students are using social networking sites for educational purposes, with 50% of the students using the sites to "talk specifically about schoolwork" (NSBA, 2007). Among the many uses of their preferred social networking sites, these teens and preteens are sharing music, videos and photos; creating content (including site building), and blogging (NSBA, 2007). "There is no doubt that these online teen hangouts are having a huge influence on how kids today are creatively thinking and behaving," says the executive director of NSBA, Anne Bryant (Hunter, 2007). Bryant believes the "challenge" for educators is to "keep pace with how students are using these tools in positive ways and consider how they might incorporate this technology into the school setting" (Hunter, 2007).

Stephen Abram, a librarian and vice-president, innovation, for SirsiDynix, has written much about educational uses of technology with teens. He offers tips for using social networking sites to teach students information fluency (2006). Abram suggests that educators teach a program for teens about *pimping* (decorating) MySpace pages and interject online safety components into the program (2006). "A few asides can offer a lot of cyberknowledge," says Abram (2006, para. 4). Abram also suggests that using virtual worlds to create an avatar "with a great back story" could help students learn more about characterization in novels (2006, para. 5). He says students are already researching information about the characters and avatars that are found on many video games and "this creative act demonstrates that kids actually will do research for fun" (2006, para. 5). Some teachers have successfully created interest in literature by assigning students the task of creating a MySpace profile page for a character from a book (Kelsey, 2007, p. 26). Teens have readily accepted the assignment, created impressive projects and learned about literary tools in the process (Kelsey, 2007, p. 26).

YALSA published a "toolkit" guide to using social networks as a means to facilitate learning in schools and libraries (ALA: YALSA, 2007). The organization cites several ways in which social networking services can be used to enhance learning among teens. For example, school newspapers can be published online as blogs, wikis can encourage student reading and writing, teen advisory groups can host and post to MySpace profiles on behalf of libraries or school clubs, and book and author discussion groups can occur through blogs and MySpace accounts (ALA:YALSA, 2007).

The *Chicago Tribune* featured an article about the use of blogs among educators as a means to allow "kids a chance to share what's important to them" (Black, 2007). A teacher who successfully uses blogs in the classroom chose this medium in order to allow otherwise quiet students a chance to participate in class discussions. "The student who may be quiet in class will sometimes be liberated by it," says the teacher (Black, 2007).

School Library Journal included an article that encouraged using MySpace to teach aspects of art, social studies and music (Harris, 2006, p. 30). Teens who were asked why technology is an important part of their education noted that they had observed struggling students become better students through the use of computers (D. Oblinger, & J. Oblinger, 2005, p. 2.3). Modesto City Schools (California) became one of the first school districts in the United States to use the virtual world Teen Second Life (Balassone, 2007). Modesto partnered with Kyoto Gakuen High School in Japan to conduct synchronous student exchanges in Teen Second Life (Balassone, 2007). The collaborating English teacher at the school in Kyoto believes Second Life's "interactive nature" and game-like elements can make his students more likely to want to study English (Balassone, 2007). Universities are beginning to see the benefits of virtual worlds. Hundreds of colleges and universities, including Harvard Law School and New York University, are already conducting classes in Second Life (Balassone, 2007). Eye4You Alliance created an entire island in Teen Second Life that is devoted to education (Hale, 2007). The first college fair held in Teen Second Life occurred on that island in October, 2007 and had approximately 150 teen avatars in attendance (Hale, 2007). The University of Kentucky (UK) was one college that participated in the fair. The school sponsored university representatives (in the form of avatars) at its display, featured video display, gave a synchronous presentation, and even passed out UK t-shirts to visiting avatars (Hale, 2007). "I personally talked with teens from the Netherlands, England, New York and Texas," said one of the school's representatives (Hale, 2007). Having a presence in Second Life gave the school an opportunity to expand its geographic boundaries in ways it might not have been able to do in the real world.

Some public libraries are utilizing social networking to create online book discussion sites. Such sites have proven effective in outreach to young adults. Message boards, blogs, MySpace profiles, and book review capabilities linked from library online catalogs are just some of the ways online social networks are being used to encourage reading among teens (Rettberg, 2006). As of July 2007, 55 American public libraries and one Canadian library have profiles on MySpace (Oleck, 2007b). Hennepin County's public library in Minnesota created a teen-friendly MySpace page in 2006 and has seen "more than 21,000 monthly MySpace page views...and 500 weekly pass-throughs" from the profile to its library Web page (Oleck, 2007b). Libraries have embedded their online catalogs into social networking sites such as MySpace and linked their databases from similar sites (Farkas, 2007). "Creating presence in social networking software makes the library more visible and more convenient to access" says Meredith Farkas, a distance learning librarian (2007). A message on a youth librarians' electronic mailing list included comments from librarians who have had positive experiences using social networking services as outreach to teens. Those librarians who had incorporated the use of online social networks into their teen services commented that teens deemed libraries "cool" for having a MySpace page; teen participation at libraries increased because of a presence on a social networking site; the sites proved to be a tremendous means of reaching teens and promoting reading and library programs to students (Neville, 2006).

Teens use social networking services to write poetry, create instructional videos, compose songs, develop interactive Web sites for activities and organizations that interest them, and counsel other teens online. In fact, the National Suicide Prevention Lifeline has reported that one of the reasons for an increase in calls to their hotline has been teens spotting distress signals on other teens' social networking profiles (Magid, & Collier, 2007, p. 174). As some teens openly express their suicidal thoughts on their profiles, other teens are paying attention to those signals and offering referral help. Australia's Inspire Foundation created a game-like virtual world known as Reach Out Central to promote mental health issues and management specifically among young people (Hoffman, 2007). It is the first such game created to assist with mental health issues (Hoffman, 2007).

Teens seek advice from each other online about issues pertaining to drugs and alcohol. They post messages to their social networking sites about the dangers of recreational drug use and where to go for help for loved ones suffering from substance abuse (Simon, & Majewski, 2007). They also use social networking services as places to grieve and mourn. Online social networks "have become as important to young people in death as they were in life" (Heher, 2007). Tom Anderson, president of MySpace, was recently quoted in a *Miami Herald* article as saying, "We often hear from families that a user's profile is a way for friends to celebrate the person's life, giving friends

a positive outlet to connect with one another and find comfort during the grieving process" (Beras, 2007). Teens are one of the generations most likely to use social networking services for bereavement purposes (Beras, 2007).

Chris DeWolfe, one of the creators of MySpace, thinks "the mainstream media have so far missed the boat on the extent to which MySpace serves as a platform for doing good" (2007, p. 74). He argues that the younger generation who frequents MySpace is not self-absorbed and disconnected from society; rather, he states that this generation cares "about community, and they're actively engaged in civic causes" (2007, p. 74). DeWolfe cites examples of his company's social networking site being used to further such causes as feeding the homeless and promoting democracy worldwide.

MOVING FORWARD WITH TEENS AND TECHNOLOGY

It is obvious that Next generation's use of social networking sites affects the way they interact with each other, the way they learn, and the way they access and assess information. These effects will transform the future workforce. In fact, such transformations and acceptance of technology in the workplace are already visible now that many Net generation students have graduated from college. For example, in October 2007, the United States National Center for Health Statistics released statistics about physicians who use electronic medical records (EMR) in their practices. The study showed a 60% increase in the use of EMR as compared to usage in 2001, with age of the physician being a definite factor in usage (Hing, Burt, & Woodwell, 2007). EMR are used more than twice as much among physicians under age 35 as compared to doctors between 55 to 64 years of age (Hing et al., 2007).

In their book *Wikinomics: How Mass Collaboration Changes Everything,* Tapscott and Williams (2006) describe seven Net generation "norms" in the workplace: speed, freedom, openness, innovation, mobility, authenticity, and playfulness (p. 54). These norms or expectations are the result of mass collaboration, peer production and the interactivity of Web 2.0 applications this generation has come to take for granted. Tapscott and Williams refer to mass collaboration as a "participation revolution" and believe that "new models of peer production can bring the prepared manager rich new possibilities to unlock innovative potential in a wide range of resources that thrive inside and outside the firm" (2006, p. 17). They call these models "wikinomics"—a "new art and science of collaboration" (2006, p. 18). When Facebook incorporated a wikinomics-type of business by releasing its code to outside developers, it saw a 28% increase in users within two months (Kharif, 2007). Yahoo has plans for opening its site to outside developers, and Google is also introducing software they call OpenSocial which allows music and video creations to be distributed on multiple sites (Google launches social-networking software, 2007). Openness, as noted by Tapscott and Williams, is what the Net generation desires. "Having been nourished on instant messaging, chat groups, playlists, peer-to-peer file sharing, and online multiplayer video games, [the Net Gen] will increasingly bring a new collaborative ethos into the workplace. Working together and sharing their knowledge across organizational boundaries—in much the same way as they swap songs and videos over the Internet—will be perfectly normal for tomorrow's workforce" (Tapscott & Williams, 2006, p. 247).

One source for collaborative sharing is virtual worlds or immersive worlds—3-D interactive sites where users engage within the site through use of an avatar. EMarketer estimates that 24% of under-age-eighteen people access virtual worlds monthly, and they predict usage will continue to increase (Williamson, 2007). Linden Labs' "Second Life" virtual world has a population that is "growing by 15 to 20 percent per month" (Tapscott & Williams, 2006, p. 126) and has

over eight million avatars or registered members (Jana, 2007). Second Life, an adult virtual world, has a counterpart known as Teen Second Life for people under age 18. Other popular virtual worlds include World of Warcraft and Vside, a music-oriented world that its creators hope "will become a destination for teens and young adults who want a next-generation entertainment experience" (Takahashi, 2007). Gaia, another popular teen virtual world, increased its number of unique users from .5 million to 2.5 million in less than a year's time (Liew, 2007). Many of the extremely successful virtual worlds are "targeted at kids and teens" (Liew, 2007), the generation most eager to adopt interactive technology, a fact not overlooked by businesses. When Active Worlds created a 3-D application for Facebook, it was noted as "a new milestone on 3-D Internet implementation" (Virtual Worlds Management, 2007). "The push is on for interoperability and a set of standards which will drive Virtual World technology into the future" said Active World's chairman, J.P. McCormick (Virtual Worlds Management, 2007). It is anticipated that businesses will turn more and more to virtual worlds as they seek to attract teen users. North American and European respondents to the Online Research Barometer survey predict increases in the use of "online respondent providers," and European researchers anticipate a decline in the use of telephone and face-to-face methodologies in favor of online research (Greenfield Online-Ciao, 2007).

A company in Finland is already using its virtual world, Habbo, to solicit marketing information from teens. Through Habbo, the company was able to "survey more than 42,000 [teens—via avatars] in 22 countries" (Jana, 2007). Habbo boasts 76 million avatars from 29 nations worldwide (Jana, 2007). Habbo's creator, the Sulake company, "realized it could tap its millions of avatars for information on real-life teen trends around the world" (Jana, 2007). Sulake found that 60% of its respondents were between ages 13-15 (Jana, 2007). Responses came from countries such as

Britain (which had the most respondents), United States, Norway, Venezuela, Portugal and Austria with gender responses being nearly evenly divided (51% female and 49% male) (Jana, 2007). Using virtual worlds to obtain teen-trend data is a current and future strategy (Jana, 2007). "The membrane between our real and our virtual worlds has become very thin, especially for teens today. For this generation, interacting in the virtual world isn't just a trend. It's their life," says Robyn Waters, head of a trend-watching firm (Jana, 2007).

Social networking sites are definitely big business. In 2005, News Corp. spent $580 million to purchase MySpace, and in 2006 Google purchased YouTube for $1.65 billion (Noguchi, 2006). Microsoft agreed to pay $240 million to Facebook for a mere "1.6 percent stake in the Web phenomenon" (Wakabayashi, 2007). Microsoft believes Facebook will become a "hub for all sorts of Web activity" and eventually attract 300 million users (Wakabayashi, 2007). Corporations realize that teen users of social networking sites, however, can be fickle. Nielsen-NetRatings' list of "most popular teen sites" often contains sites that are listed one year but are never mentioned the following year as teens' tastes change (Noguchi, 2006). "They're not loyal. Young audiences search for innovative and new features. They're constantly looking for new ways to communicate and share content they find or create, and because of that group mentality, friends shift from service to service in blocs [*sic*]," says Ben Bajarin, market analyst for Creative Strategies, Inc. (Noguchi, 2006). At the 2006 Piper Jaffray Global Internet Summit in California, there was debate over the future of social networks, with some skeptics wondering if such sites are merely fads (Olsen, 2006). Older teen attendees at the summit gave indication they are already growing out of their MySpace phase, although younger teens indicated they were still big users of the site (Olsen, 2006). By 2007, teens in the United Kingdom were already transferring loyalties from MySpace to Bebo and Facebook (Moulds, 2007). "You are getting a lot of younger people who are shunning MySpace because it is seen to be part of the establishment," says John Delaney, a technology analyst (Moulds, 2007). Other reasons for teens' abandonment of MySpace include the increasing numbers of parents and teachers reading teens' profiles, risks of predators, and new services from other sites (Noguchi, 2006). Sweden's Stardoll, a virtual world aimed at teen and preteen girls, acquired over seven million users from several countries within its first four years of existence, and the site's chief executive attributes part of its success to the fact that users of previous social networking sites "are maybe getting tired of having pages where they feel forced to look sexy or cool or write some outrageous stuff in order to stand out" (Adegoke, 2007a). Datamonitor released a report in 2007 by analyst Ri Pierce-Grove who said, "The extraordinary proliferation of online social networks is fueled by real innovation and is substantially changing the way we communicate. However, the hothouse atmosphere of easy capital, media attention and user curiosity which stimulates creativity will not be sustained" (Lomas, 2007). Pierce-Grove's report expects the number of registrants for social networking services to "plateau" by 2012" (Lomas, 2007).

Realizing the transience of social networking sites, MySpace has already begun to expand its services internationally in the hopes of maintaining it popularity. MySpace has communities in Europe, Latin America, North and South America, and Asia and plans to expand into additional countries (Dudeck & Akselrud, 2007). MySpace's managing director for international, Travis Katz, says the move to rewrite its code into non-Western languages "was the right thing to do; international growth is the key to our future" (Abboud, 2007). Internet companies based in America usually focus first on English-speaking markets before expanding to international non-English speaking possibilities (Abboud, 2007). European markets can provide a huge base of users, but the variety of languages spoken within those countries often pose "linguistic barriers" for start-up countries outside of North America (Abboud, 2007). Netlog is one company that has broken through those barriers and has created one of the largest social networking sites in Europe (Abboud, 2007). Using college exchange students to translate the site rather than the entire code, Netlog has attracted users between ages 14-24 as its typical market (Abboud, 2007).

Mobile markets are another area of increase in social networking services. Mobikade is "a free off portal social networking service" in Japan that acquired 500,000 members in its first six months (Inbabble, 2007). It already has plans to expand into the UK, Italy, Germany and the U.S. (Inbabble, 2007). Japanese teens are accustomed to using mobile Internet, and Mobikade predicts that European teens will become likewise. Mobikade's head of business, Atul Sasane says, "We have experienced the growth of the off portal market in Japan and this puts us in a very strong position to create strategies to capitalize on the opportunities unfolding in the UK market" (Inbabble, 2007). It is this high acceptance of mobility in Japan that led Transcosmos Inc. to create Meet-Me, a Japanese version of Second Life. Being deemed very American with its pioneering "ability to create something from nothing," Second Life has seen only 7% of its users come from Japan (Terada, 2007). Ken Aihara, who oversees Virtual Tokyo in Second Life, does not think Second Life will "take off among Japanese users until it becomes accessible from mobile phones" which are more popular than desktop computers among Japanese teens (Terada, 2007). Worldwide, Second Life has its largest audience in Europe, although America and Germany tie as countries with the highest number of in-world users (Lipsman, 2007a).

CONCLUSION

Having grown up with technology, Net generation teens have developed different habits and characteristics than their predecessors. But, according to Goodstein, "not much has really changed about being a teenager" (2007, p. 12). "Deep down most of us experienced the similar impulsiveness, invincibility, and highs and lows otherwise known as teen angst, puberty, or if you believe in modern psychology, a phase called adolescent development" (Goodstein, 2007, p. 12). What has changed, notes Goodstein, is that technology has "magnified and publicized" teen behavior (2007, p. 12) which raises "new issues for our society around privacy, safety, and parenting" (2007, p. 15).

Undoubtedly, much debate will continue to revolve around the issue of social networks and teens, with adults offering a variety of solutions. A decade ago, Tapscott offered viable advice to those who wondered "What is happening to our children?" (1998, p. 7). While he admitted there was "much to be learned" and that "many real dangers" would require "good management" by adults, he answered adults' fears with the following paragraph:

Everybody relax. The kids are all right. They are learning, developing, and thriving in the digital world. They need better tools, better access, more services, and more freedom to explore, not the opposite. Rather than hostility and mistrust on the part of adults, we need a change in thinking and in behavior on the part of parents, educators, lawmakers, and business leaders alike. (Tapscott, 1998, p. 7)

Thierer agrees. "There is simply no substitute for education" (2007, p. 25), he says. Thierer believes that if the government, media and schools want to improve and safeguard teens' use of social networking sites, those organizations need to actively promote programs that teach students about critical thinking skills and parents about parental controls (Thierer, 2007, p. 25). Says Thierer, "Lawmakers and educators need to focus on finding the 'teachable moments'" (2007, pp. 25,

26), and parents need to be more involved with their children (2007, p. 28).

Additionally, workplaces need to prepare for this generation's entry. "N-Gen's norms reflect a desire for creativity, social connectivity, fun, freedom, speed, and diversity in their workplaces. Attracting, engaging, and retaining these employees in an increasingly competitive environment will demand that companies understand the Net Generation and the individuals who will emerge as its leaders" (Tapscott & Williams, 2006, p. 248).

REFERENCES

Abboud, L. (2007, November 1). How Netlog leaps language barriers. *Wall Street Journal Online*. Retrieved November 3, 2007, from http://online.wsj.com/public/article_print/SB119387616952078433.html

Abram, S. (2006, November). Some tricks to build information fluency—part 2. *MultiMedia & Internet@Schools, 13*(6), 6-28.

Adegoke, Y. (2007a, June 1). Kids socialize in a virtual world as avatars. *Reuters.* Retrieved November 3, 2007, from http://www.reuters.com

Adegoke, Y. (2007b, September 24). NY subpoenas Facebook over safety from predators. *Reuters.* Retrieved November 4, 2007, from http://www.reuters.com

American Library Association. (2006). Resolution in support of online social networks. Retrieved July 5, 2007, from http://www.ala.org/ala/oif/ifissues/onlinesocialnetworks.pdf

American Library Association. (2007). Three states and feds pursue social networking controls. Retrieved February 26, 2007, from http://www.ala.org/ala/alonline/currentnews/newsarchive/2007/february2007/ ALA_print_layout_1_350364_350364.cfm

American Library Association: Young Adult Library Services Association (YALSA) (2007). Teens & social networking in school & public libraries: A toolkit for librarians & library workers. Retrieved July 21, 2007, from http://www.ala.org/ala/yalsa/profdev/SocialNetworkingToolkit_March07.pdf

American Library Association, Young Adult Library Services Association (YALSA) (n.d.). *Data & resources Web sites.* Retrieved July 21, 2007, from http://www.ala.org/ala/yalsa/teenreading/dataresources/dataresources.htm

Associated Press. (2007, July 24). MySpace deletes 29,000 sex offender profiles. *MSNBC.com.* Retrieved August 4, 2007, from http://www.msnbc.msn.com/id/19939181/print/1/displaymode/1098/

Atal, M. (2007, July 2). MySpace, Facebook: A tale of two cultures. *BusinessWeek.* Retrieved July 22, 2007, from Business Source Premier database.

Bahrampour, T., Arantani, L., & Stockwell, J. (2006, January 17). Teens' bold blogs alarm area schools. *The Washington Post.* Retrieved July 26, 2007, from Newspaper Source database.

Balassone, M. (2007, January 14). Virtual reality: Modesto and Japanese students will use Second Life to interact. *The Modesto Bee.* Retrieved November 4, 2007, from Newspaper Source database.

Bausch, S., & Han, L. (2006, October 11). U.S. teens graduate from choosing IM buddy icons to creating elaborate social networking profiles, according to Nielsen/Netratings. Retrieved March 26, 2007, from www.nielsen-netratings.com/pr/pr_061011.pdf

Beras, E. (2007, May 27). Loved ones mourned on Web sites: The memorializing on the personal pages of three South Florida men—whose killings remain unsolved—represents a growing trend:

online grieving. *The Miami Herald.* Retrieved July 23, 2007, from McClatchy-Tribune Collection database.

Black, L. (2007, January 24). Blogging clicks with educators: Online forums make assignments, ideas more accessible to students and parents. *The Chicago Tribune.* Retrieved March 23, 2007, from Newspaper Source database.

Boyd, D. (2006). Friends, friendsters, and top 8: Writing community into being on social network sites. *First Monday, 11*(2).

Boyd, D. (2007a). Fame, narcissism and MySpace. Many2Many: A group weblog on social software. Retrieved July 26, 2007, from http://many.corant. com/archives/2007/03/17/fame_narcissism_and_ myspace.php

Boyd, D. (2007b). Viewing American class divisions through Facebook and MySpace. *Apophenia blog essay.* Retrieved July 22, 2007, from http:// www.danah.org/papers/essays/ClassDivisions. html

Brody, M. (2006). Understanding teens in this age of digital technology. *Brown University child and adolescent behavior letter, 22*(12), 8-8.

Canada online overview. (2007). *E-Marketer.* Retrieved October 8, 2007, from http://www. emarketer.com

Carvajal, D. (2007, August 19). Fighting antisocial behavior on social networking sites. *International Herald Tribune.* Retrieved October 8, 2007, from http://www.iht.com/bin/print.php?id=7171219

CBS News. (2005, May 10). Generation M: Natural multitaskers. *CBSNews.com.* Retrieved July 29, 2007, from http://www.cbsnews.com/stories/2005/05/10/eveningnews/printable694344. shtml

CBS News. (2006, February 16). No place here for MySpace. *CBSNews.com.* Retrieved August 4, 2007, from http://www.cbsnews.com/sto-ries/2006/02/16/earlyshow/living/parenting/main1323212.shtml

Charron, C., & Florentino, R. (2006, March 24). Teens take the lead on social computing. *Forrester.* Retrieved July 30, 2007, from http:// www.forrester.com/Research/Document/Excerpt/0,7211,39157,00.html

Cullen, P. (2007, February 7). Teenagers' profiles accessible on social websites. *Irish Times.* Retrieved February 20, 2007, from Newspaper Source database.

Dannahey, F. (2006). Making the Internet safe for kids: The role of ISP's and social networking sites. Written testimony given before the Committee on Energy and

Commerce Subcommittee on Oversight and Investigations: United States House of Representatives. Retrieved July 23, 2007, from http://energycom-merce.house.gov/reparchives/108/Hearings/06282006hearing1955/ Dannahey.pdf

Dewolfe, C. (2007). The MySpace generation. *Forbes, 179*(10), 72-74.

Dudeck, D., & Akselrud, T. (2007, July 12). MySpace outperforms all other social networking sites. *News Corporation.* Retrieved October 8, 2007, from http://www.newscorp.com/news/news_345.html

Farkas, M. (2007). Going where patrons are: Outreach in MySpace and Facebook. *American Libraries, 38*(4), 27.

Fitzpatrick, M. (2006). H.R. 5319: Deleting online predators act of 2006. 109th

Congress. Retrieved from http://thomas.loc.gov/cgi-bin/query/D?c109:4/temp/~mdbs59VVUS

Gavin, J. (2007, October 10). UK social networking site usage highest in *Europe.comScore.* Retrieved October 21, 2007, from http://www.comscore. com/press/release.asp?press=1801

Glover, S., & Huffstutter, P. (2008, January 9). L.A. grand jury issues subpoenas in Web suicide case. *Los Angeles Times.* Retrieved January 30, 2008, from http://www.latimes.com/news/printedition/california/la-me-myspace9jan09,0,993796.story

Goodstein, A. (2007). *Totally wired: What teens and tweens are really doing online.* New York, NY: St. Martin's Press.

Google launches social-networking software. (2007, October 31). *Dallas News.com.* Retrieved November 4, 2007, from http://www.dallasnews.com

GovTrack.us. (n.d.). S. 49: A bill to amend the Communications Act of 1934 to prevent the carriage of child.... *GovTrack.us.* Retrieved July 24, 2007, from http://www.govtrack.us/congress/bill.xpd?bill=s110-49

Greenfield Online-Ciao Surveys. (2007, October 18). Use of online surveys for market research to increase. *MarketingVOX.* Retrieved October 21, 2007, from http://www.marketingvox.com

Hale, W. (2007, October 24). UK visits with teens at virtual college fair. *UK News.* Retrieved November 3, 2007, from http://news.uky.edu/news/display_article.php?artid=2812&mode=print

Hanson, K. (2005, February 28). Study links Internet, social contact. *The Stanford Daily.* Retrieved July 5, 2007, from http://daily.stanford.edu/article/2005/2/28/studyLinksInternetSocialContact

Harris, C. (2006). MySpace can be our space. *School Library Journal, 52*(5), 30.

Heher, A. (2007, February 16). Teens go online to grieve for friends. *The Courier & Press,* pp. A-1, A-12.

Hempel, J., & Lehman, P. (2005, December 12). The MySpace generation. *BusinessWeek, 3963,* pp. 86-96.

Hewitt, B., Dodd, J., York, M., Finan, E., Nelson, M., Fleming, A., et al. (2006). MySpace nation: The controversy. *People, 65*(22), 113-121.

Hing, E., Burt, C., & Woodwell, D. (2007). Advance Data, No. 393. U.S. Department of Health and Human Services, National Center for Health Statistics.

Hoffman. L. (2007, October 20). Virtual life delivers tools for a real life. *The Australian.* Retrieved November 4, 2007, from Newspaper Source database.

Hunter, B. (2007, August 14). New study explores the online behaviors of U.S. teens and 'tweens. Retrieved August 23, 2007, from http://www.nsba.org/site/doc.asp?TRACKID=&VID=2&CID=90K&DID=41336

Ihlwan, M. (2005, September 26). E-society: My world is Cyworld. *BusinessWeek.* Retrieved October 26, 2007, from http://www.businessweek.com/print/magazine/content/05_39/b3952405.htm?chan=gl

Inbabble. (2007). Interview: Atul Sasane, head of new business about Mobikade social networking, free games and free SMS. Retrieved October 8, 2007, from http://inbabble.com

Jana, R. (2007, August 14). Mining virtual worlds for market research. *Business Week Online.* Retrieved October 19, 2007, from Business Source Premier database.

Johnson, S. (2006). Don't fear the digital. *Time,167*(13), 56-56.

Katayama, L. (2006, September 11). Social networking sites catch on in Japan. *Japan Today.* Retrieved October 26, 2007 from, http://www.japantoday.com/jp/feature/1137

Kelsey, C. (2007). *Generation MySpace: Helping your teen survive online adolescence.* New York, NY: Marlowe.

Kharif, O. (2007, October 8). Google's Orkut: A world of ambition. *Business Week.* Retrieved October 26, 2007, from http://www.business-week.com/print/technology/content/oct2007/tc2007107_530965.htm

Kilgannon, C. (2007, February 13). Teenagers misbehaving, for all online to watch. *The New York Times.* Retrieved July 23, 2007, from News-Bank database.

Klimkiewicz, J. (2007, January 26). Internet junkies: Hooked online: One in eight Americans find it hard to log off. *The Hartford Courant.* Retrieved July 25, 2007, from Newspaper Source database.

Kornblum, J. (2006, September 20). Meet my 5,000 new best pals. *USA Today.* Retrieved March 3, 2007, from Academic Search Elite database.

Lee, E. (2007, February 15). MySpace suit dismissed by judge in Texas/Family said site didn't protect underage users. *San Francisco Chronicle.* Retrieved May 23, 2007, from Newspaper Source database.

Lee, M. (2007, July 17). China limits online game time for teens. *USA Today.* Retrieved July 25, 2007, from http://usatoday.com

Lehman, P. (2007, January 25). Building a safer MySpace. *BusinessWeek Online.* Retrieved August 4, 2007, from Academic Search Elite database.

Lenhart, A., Madden, M., & Hitlin, P. (2005). Teens and technology: Youth are leading the transition to a fully wired and mobile nation. Pew Internet & American Life Project. Retrieved March 16, 2007, from http://www.pewinternet.org/pdfs/PIP_Teens_Tech_July2005web.pdf

Lenhart, A., & Madden, M. (2007a). Pew Internet project data memo: Social networking Web sites and teens: An overview. Pew Internet & American Life Project. Retrieved January 8, 2007, from http://www.pewinternet.org/PPF/r/198/report_display.asp

Lenhart, A., & Madden, M. (2007b). Teens, privacy & online social networks: How teens manage their online identities and personal information in the age of MySpace. Pew Internet & American Life Project. Retrieved January 8, 2007, from http://www.pewinternet.org/pdfs/PIP_Teens_Privacy_SNS_Report_Final.pdf

Liew, J. (2007). Kids and teens have pushed at least 6 immersive online worlds to over 2m UU/mth in the U.S. Lightspeed Venture Partners blog. Retrieved November 3, 2007, from http://lsvp.wordpress.com/2007/04/23/

Lipsman, A. (2007a, May 4). comScore finds that "Second Life" has a rapidly growing and global base of active residents. *comScore.com.* Retrieved November 4, 2007, from http://www.comscore.com/press/release.asp?press=1425

Lipsman, A. (2007b). UK teens and young adults spend 24 percent more time online than the average internet user. *comScore.com.* Retrieved October 21, 2007, from http://www.comscore.com/press/release.asp?press=1469

Lipsman, A. (2007c, July 31). Social networking goes global. *comScore.com.* Retrieved October 21, 2007, from http://www.comscore.com/press/release.asp?press=1555

Lomas, N. (2007, October 19). Analyst: Social networking faces uncertain future. *Cnet Networks.* Retrieved November 4, 2007, from http://www.news.com

McKenna, B. (2005, March 29). High school bans blogging. *Rutland Herald.* Retrieved August 4, 2007, from http://www.rutlandherald.com/apps/pbcs.dll/article?AID=/20050329/NEWS/503290316/1027

McNicol, T. (2007, May 1). Mixi vs. MySpace—a fight for your bytes. *The Japan Times.* Retrieved October 26, 2007, from http://search.japantimes.co.jp/cgi-bin/fl20070501zg.html

Magid, L., & Collier, A. (2007). *MySpace unraveled: A parent's guide to teen social networking.* Berkley, CA: Peachpit Press.

Medina, J. (*2007, May 6*). States ponder laws to keep web predators from children. *The New York Times.* Retrieved July 25, 2007, from http://www.nytimes.com/2007/05/06/nyregion/06myspace.html?ei=5070&en=947320815b

Moulds, J. (2007, August 16). Young shun MySpace for Bebo and Facebook. *Telegraph Media Group.* Retrieved October 26, 2007, from http://www.telegraph.co.uk

Muir, D. (2006, April 6). All children vulnerable to online predators. *ABC news.* Retrieved July 21, 2007, http://abcnews.go.com/pring?id=1812054

National School Boards Association (NSBA). (2007). Creating & connecting/Research and guidelines on online social—and educational—networking. Retrieved August 23, 2007, from http://www.nsba.org/site/view.asp?CID=63&DID=41340

Neville, K. (2006). Compilation: Library Myspace Accounts. Message posted to Public Libraries serving Young Adults & Children [PUBYAC], 17:42:49, archived at http://www.pubyac.org/archives.htm

Noguchi, Y. (2006, October 29). In teens' Web world, MySpace is so last year. *The Washington Post.* Retrieved October 8, 2007, from http://www.washingtopost.com

Norton, J. (2007, February 21). Online bullying compels states to act: Critics question whether legislation can curb kids' bad behavior. *MSNBC.* Retrieved July 23, 2007, from MSNBC http://www.msnbc.msn.com/id/17265901/

Oblinger, D., & Oblinger, J. (2005). Is it age or IT: First steps toward understanding the net generation. In: D. Oblinger & J. Oblinger (Eds.), *Educating the net generation* (pp. 2.1-2.20). Boulder, CO: Educause.

Oleck, J. (2007a, June 8). Wake County (NC) public library defends MySpace ban. *School Library Journal.* Retrieved August 4, 2007, from http://www.schoollibraryjournal.com/article/CA6449925.html

Oleck, J. (2007b). Libraries use MySpace to attract teens. *School Library Journal, 53*(7), 16-16.

Olsen, S. (2006, December 19). Social networks—future portal or fad? *Cnet.* Retrieved November 4, 2007, from http://www.news.com/

Patchin, J., & Hinduja, S. (n.d.). News: What's new on cyberbullying.us. *Cyberbullying.us.* Retrieved July 22, 2007, from http://www.cyberbullying.us

Pew Research Center for the People and the Press. (2007). A portrait of "Generation Next": How young people view their lives, futures and politics. Retrieved November 3, 2007, from http://people-press.org/reports/display.php3?ReportID=300

Prensky, M. (2005, September/October). Engage me or enrage me: What today's learners demand. *EDUCAUSEreview.* Retrieved March 15, 2007, from http://www.educause.edu/ir/library/pdf/erm0553.pdf

Rapacki, S. (2007). Social networking sites: Why teens need places like MySpace. *YALS: Young Adult Library Services,* Winter, 28-30.

Rettberg, C. (2006). Teen book discussions go online. *YALS: Young Adult Library Services, Fall,* 35.

Richardson, J. (2007, January 25). Celebrating safer Internet Day across the world. *Insafe.* Retrieved November 3, 2007, from http://www.saferinternet.org/ww/en/pub/insafe/news/sid2007.htm

Rosen, L. (2006). Adolescents in MySpace: Identity formation, friendship and sexual predators. Retrieved July 5, 2007, from http://www.csudh.edu/psych/Adolescents%20in%20MySpace%20-%20Executive%20Summary.pdf

Schonfeld, E. (2006, July 27). Cyworld ready to attach MySpace. *Business 2.0 Magazine.* Retrieved October 26, 2007, from http://money.cnn.com/magazines/business2/business2_archive/2006/08/01/8382263/index.htm

Sher, J. (2007, May 1). The not-so-long arm of the law. *USA Today.* Retrieved May 24, 2007, from Academic Search Elite database.

Sickler, E. (2007, March) Students comment on Facebook. *University Business Daily.* Retrieved March 21, 2007, from http://www.universitybusiness.com/viewarticle.aspx?articleid=724&pf=1

Simon, E., & Majewski, E. (2007, April 20). A qualitative study of online discussions about teen alcohol & drug use. *Caron Treatment Centers.* Retrieved July 5, 2007, from http://www.caron.org/pdfs/Report%20on%20Teen%20Online%20Conversations.pdf

Stevens, T. (2007). S.49: Protecting children in the 21st century act. 110th Congress. Retrieved July 23, 2007, from http://thomas.loc.gov/cgi-bin/query/F?c110:1:./temp/~c110YE7UM4:e7495

Takahashi, D. (2007, August 21). Virtual world Vside hits right note. *San Jose Mercury News.* Retrieved October 19, 2007, from Newspaper Source database.

Tapscott, D. (1998). *Growing up digital: The rise of the Net Generation.* New York, NY: McGraw-Hill.

Tapscott, D., & Williams, A. (2006). *Wikinomics: How mass collaboration changes everything.* London: Penguin Books.

Terada, S. (2007, October 25). Japanese businesses setting up virtual shop in Second Life. *The Japan Times.* Retrieved November 4, 2007, from McClatchy-Tribune Collection database.

Thierer, A. (2007). Social networking and age verification: Many hard questions; no easy solutions. *Progress on point, 14.5,* 1-33.

Virtual Worlds Management. (2007, October 31). Active Worlds embeds 3-D worlds in Facebook. *Virtual Worlds News.* Retrieved November 4, 2007, from http://www.virtualworldsnews.com/2007/10/active-words-e.htm

Wakabayashi, D. (2007, October 25). Microsoft beats Google to Facebook stake. *Reuters.* Retrieved November 4, 2007, from http://www.reuters.com.

Williams, A. (2006, February 29). Here I am taking my own picture. *The New York Times,* p. 9.1. Retrieved August 4, 2007, from New York Times database.

Williamson, D. (2007, September). Kids and teens: Virtual worlds open new universe. *eMarketer.* Retrieved October 8, 2007, from http://www.emarketer.com/Report.aspx?code=emarketer_2000437&src=report_summary_reportsell

Wilson, L. (2007, September 14). Web stalkers targeted. *The Australian.* Retrieved October 19, 2007, from Newspaper Source database.

Wolak, J., Mitchell, K., & Finkelhor, D. (2006). Online victimization of youth: Five years later. *National Center for Missing & Exploited Children.* Retrieved July 15, 2007, from http://208.252.21.169/en_US/publications/NC167.pdf

Woodhead, B. (2007, October 16). Survey finds Aussie kids are the web's pro surfers. *The Australian.* Retrieved October 19, 2007, from Newspaper Source database.

Section II
Social Networking Sites for Teenagers and Young Adults

Chapter X
Student Use of Social Media:
University Policy and Response

Tamara L. Wandel
University of Evansville, USA

ABSTRACT

This chapter presents information on the usages and intent of social media by college students and administrators. Primary and secondary quantitative data is provided, as well as qualitative information obtained from interviews of multiple constituents. Researchers and postsecondary employees can more effectively examine technological trends in regard to online social networking for non-academic purposes after considering this data. Theories of self-esteem, interpersonal communication, decision making, and innovation diffusion are integrated throughout the chapter.

INTRODUCTION

Millions of American high school and college students have one thing in common: they log in daily to Web sites to view recently uploaded photographs, check out opinions on blogs, and see if friends have made any changes to their onscreen profiles. Individuals born between 1981 and 2000, coined *Millenials*, are growing up in a world in which participation in online social networking

is considered conventional behavior. Timothy Hawkes, the headmaster of The King's School in Sydney, Australia, perhaps summarized it best. As quoted in *The Sydney Morning Herald* (Goodman, 2007), Hawkes said, "…technology isn't part of students' lives these days. It is their lives."

Social networks refer to a collection of individuals linked together by a set of relations (Downes, 2005). Associated research tends to focus on social network analysis, a framework intended to enhance the sharing and interaction among groups and communities (Cho, Stefanone, & Gay, 2002). Online social networks possess a parallel purpose, with Web sites intended to assist users in meeting new people or staying connected with friends or associates. The Web sites allow for searches based on a multitude of factors including affiliations such as a college or high school. Some sites like Shelfari are designed around a common interest, in this case targeting book aficionados. Other online social networks are centered on a professional component, a quasi modern-day version of the now more traditional networking after-hours event. Two such examples include LinkedIn and MyRagan, designed for all professionals and professional communicators, respectively.

Online social networks are also termed virtual communities or profile sites, and the relationship-building capacity of these sites present more than simplistic social consequences. Network participants are exposed to groups centered on the advantages and/or disadvantages of specific colleges, clubs and professors. Higher education institutions are beginning to recognize that reputation, campus culture and even enrollment figures may be impacted by online social networking.

The objective of this chapter is to present the response of university administrators and students to the use of online social networking for non-academic purposes. Qualitative data from student and administrator interviews helps shape the chapter and allows for candid and relevant anecdotes surrounding the topic. The use of primary and secondary quantitative data offers insight and perspective to a compelling, complex and constantly evolving topic. Theories of self-esteem, interpersonal communication, decision making, and innovation diffusion are integrated throughout the chapter.

OSN REINING GIANT FOR COLLEGE STUDENTS

The interests of college students are as diverse as the myriad of online social networking (OSN) sites available to them. From Bebo to Classmates.com to Friends Reunied to Friendster, university students have numerous OSN options as they put their technologically savvy skills to use in finding their niche. One network in particular dominates the college scene with over 85% market share of four-year universities in the United States: Facebook.

Originally called *thefacebook,* and targeting college students, Facebook is now the second most trafficked online social networking site following MySpace. In hipper context, Facebook is "...the online hangout of just about every college student in the nation" (Levy, 2007). Mark Zuckerberg, the man credited with Facebook, dropped out of Harvard University to focus full-time on his creation. Like MySpace co-founders Tom Anderson and Chris DeWolfe, Zuckerberg had become frustrated at his own experience and felt he could develop something better than what existed. The story goes that he believed Harvard University was too slow in creating an online student directory, so he made sure his own version was both expedient and impressive. After 6,000 students at Harvard registered with thefacebook, within the first three weeks, Zuckerberg piloted the program at Stanford and Yale (Naposki, 2006). The online social networking site quickly became a sought-after commodity and officially became known as *Facebook* in August 2005.

Facebook initially required a college or university .edu domain extension, but the site has since expanded. High schools and companies now have access to the online social network within certain regions. The official site at www.facebook.com has a section detailing "How this expansion affects you," the Facebook member. It starts by explaining:

Now you can get all your friends on Facebook—people who couldn't get on before because their schools didn't offer e-mail addresses, because they went to work instead of colleges, because they graduated before Facebook even existed, or for any other reason.

Evidently people heeded the call. The site had 24 million members by June 2007 (Kirkpatrick, 2007) and more than 60 million active users as of January 2008, representing an average 3% weekly growth since January 2007. It is no wonder Facebook's originator understands the Millenial generation—Zuckerberg is 23 years old.

SOCIAL MEDIA AND CONNECTIVITY

Facebook has more than three million users aged 25 to 34, and even more users younger than that (Ronn, 2007). With so many online social networking users falling in what is considered the traditional college-age category, there is a need to understand the link between the communication taking place via social networks and how it fits into the larger picture of relationships and overall well-being. Wood's research on personal relationships (1995) determined investment, commitment, trust and comfort with relational dialectics as the four defining characteristics of a successful relationship. Westerners' emphasis on verbal disclosure as an important trust-building mechanism was further noted. This need for verbal acknowledgement and response has important implications for administrators in postsecondary institutions, particularly because many college students feel overwhelmed and lonely as they embark on their first real venture away from home for an extended time. As quoted in *Everyday Encounters* (Woods, 1996), a student stated:

The worst time in my whole life was my first semester here. I felt so lonely being away from my family and friends at home. Back there we were really close, and there was always somebody to be with and talk to, but I didn't know anybody on this campus. I felt all alone and like nobody cared about me. I became depressed and almost left school, but then I started seeing a guy and I made a couple of friends. Everything got better once I had some people to talk to and be with.

The mission statements of postsecondary institutions often center on themes of academic integrity, attaining in-depth knowledge of a particular discipline, well-roundedness and civic-mindedness. But educators and administrators recognize that if students are not content, if they are lonely and depressed and not focusing on their studies, then their self-esteem, sense of responsibility and ultimately their educational experience may be lost or at least substantially weakened.

Theories of self-esteem have established that human beings possess a universal desire to protect and enhance their self-esteem (Rosenberg, Schooler, & Schoenback, 1989). At no point in life are peer acceptance and feedback on one's self more important than in adolescence, and these are two distinct features of online social networking sites (Valkenburg, Peter, & Schouten, 2006). From the college recruitment stage to retaining students through graduation, a recurring theme is connectivity. Students should feel welcome, at ease and comfortable in their home away from home.

Academic Decision-Makers Response to Student Expectations

Academic decision makers must consider new ways of reaching students for recruiting purposes as well as connecting with students as part of retention efforts, and some of these efforts involve technological innovations. The use and need of technology by higher education administrators is altered as the expectations and usage of technology changes by students. In fact, computers, the

Internet and social media may be changing so fast that it is impossible to predict the impact. But what is recognized, according to Baase (2003), is that these technological changes in work processing methods have resulted in a loss of community. E-mail, Skype and other mediums are replacing traditional face-to-face conversations. So while technology is often lauded for bringing the global world together, it is simultaneously faulted for creating an unnatural barrier in community.

Many higher education administrators are in the unenviable situation of not having appropriate technology required to act as expert decision makers when it comes to increasingly evolving technology. This is closely aligned to the decision making theory called *incrementalism*, in which individuals may not be able to perform their job responsibilities at the highest level because they do not possess all the facts, information and technology required. In this case, decision makers enact former solutions to current problems and work within a bounded rationality in which they choose an "incremental alternative rather than a fundamentally newly designed approach" for solving problems (Hoy & Tarter, 1995).

But when it comes to constantly changing technology, is an incremental alternative enough to reach students who possess an entirely different set of communication and connection ideals? Typically, the initial decision to have a certain technology available for student use is made at the institutional level (Robinson, Jr., 2006), but in the case of OSN, it may be more an issue of student expectations and current usage driving technology decisions by administrators. Student demand is forcing administrators to play catchup and create novel ways and approaches for "informative provision and instruction" (Sellers, 2005). Administrators need to not only manage their own collegial community but find ways to encourage community for students.

Communicating with Prospective and Current College Students

Knowing of the growing popularity of Millenials to utilize online social networking sites, it is not surprising that higher education administrators are beginning to view these networks as valid mechanisms to reach student audiences, including prospective students. The broader communicative strategy in this case is referred to as e-recruitment, and the tactics focus on communication with prospects via instant messaging, e-mail and online social network profiles.

It appears prospective college students do not mind this encroachment on their virtual lives, especially if they can control initiating the communication. An E-Expectations Class of 2007 report by Noel-Levitz (2006) discussed the propensity for prospective college students to utilize technology or, in some cases, express a desire to utilize various Web-based applications. Excerpts from the published survey data show student responses to completing certain activities on college Web sites:

- 72% have or would like to exchange instant messages with an admissions counselor or student worker
- 72% have or would like to complete a form to RSVP for a campus event
- 70% have or would like to inquire online
- 64% have or would like to read profiles of faculty
- 64% have or would like to e-mail a faculty member
- 64% have or would like to read a blog written by a member of the faculty
- 63% have or would like to read a blog written by a current student
- 63% have or would like to view a virtual tour

- 62% have or would like to personalize a Web site (meaning they received a unique experience based on information supplied)
- 61% have or would like to e-mail current students from the site (Noel-Levitz, 2006)

These statistics indicate a majority of survey respondents desire activities in Web-based form. A chief benefit to higher education institutions using OSN and other Web-based activities is the relative ease in maintaining connectivity through the posting of information or by e-mailing others, and Millenials have come to expect instantaneous communication. According to Lenhart and Madden (2007), e-mail is the highest ranking Internet activity by teens, with 57% going online to retrieve information about colleges and universities. This underscores a need for colleges and universities to utilize Web-based applications in their recruiting plans. In today's competitive market where each prospective student is crucial to a college or university's full-time equivalent figures, Web sites must be interactive. The more opportunity a Web site has for personalization based on a user's interest, the more likely a Millenial will stay interested.

Once students are enrolled in a postsecondary institution, that interaction must continue. Tinto's predictive model of student integration (1982; 1993) discusses how interactions in both the academic and social realms play a significant role in the attrition process. Factors including peer-to-peer interaction and peer-to-faculty interaction are positively related to degree completion.

Online social networking may prove to be an invaluable tool in assisting students who are easing into college life. Roommates are often introduced to each other through Facebook or MySpace, learning about each other's interests, study habits or partying tendencies through online profiles. Students learn about residence hall life and which clubs might be of interest to them. Once enrolled in college, online social networks prove to be a constant source of information for students.

Profiles and groups encourage attendance at campus events, promote specific clubs, fraternities or sororities, and allow college students to view last-minute changes to an academic calendar through bulletin board announcements.

College student Donald Moore thinks it is smart business for organizations to participate in online social networking. "Almost everyone is on some type of social network, so why not communicate an upcoming event this way since so many people check them out constantly? If you send an invitation to 100 people and only one responds, it is still a success because that is one more response than you had before you started. Why not take advantage of free publicity?"

Connectivity in Times of Bereavement

Online social networking remains undeniably constructive as a means of connecting individuals regardless of geographic constraints. The aftermath of the April 16, 2007 massacre occurring on the campus of Virginia Tech University provides insight into a unique value that online social networking provides to college students. Students throughout the U.S. united after the Virginia Tech tragedy by creating online groups and posting comments expressing their concern and grief. The language was often candid, emotional and sentimental. One of the many group descriptors read, "In memory of those lost and those grieving at Virginia Tech. This is a group to honor those who have lost someone just know that you are not alone the world is watching and we are all praying. Today we are all hokies!!"

It was clear that many of the postings originated from those not directly impacted. College students blessed not to have been straightforwardly affected by the incident were nonetheless trying to make sense of the tragedy and working to find a way to reach out and show compassion. One student from Ontario, Canada is a member of a 1,625-member Facebook group titled *A Canadian Tribute To All*

Those Involved In The Virginia Tech Shooting. An excerpt from her posting reads, "I don't know any of the people who died in that horrible act, but my heart goes out to each student and all the families involved. You don't need to know anyone to be sad for them." For this individual and others, the Facebook group was a virtual memory wall offering a chance to emotionally embrace.

Until May 2007, Facebook's policy was to delete profiles of the deceased. That policy was altered after online protests and a letter campaign were initiated in response to friends and family of Virginia Tech victims learning that profiles of victims were to be removed (Hortobagyi, 2007). "…these pages are what's left of their voices, and the rest of their voices have been stolen from us," said Virginia Tech student John Woods (Hortobagyi, 2007).

As is the case with the Virginia Tech mourners, it is not just friends or family that are posting comments on online social network sites. Some students who have never interacted with the deceased reach out to find a shared connection in the confusion and despair that comes from the loss of life and the struggle to move on and find meaning from a tragic situation. In a posting for a Facebook group dedicated to remembering a young Midwestern college student who died of heart failure, an individual posted a comment, "He sounds like a great guy. I'm sorry I didn't know him." Others that did know him use everyday vernacular indicative of young people, "he had a heart attack, 26 and dying of a heart attack, that's soooo HORRIBLE! stephen and i worked together like 3 or 4 yrs ago. we would always butt heads but you never want to see this happen to anyone regardless of the relationship you have with them, he's way too young [sic]."

Bereaved college students are an extremely vulnerable cohort to issues of self-confidence and self-efficacy, often feeling a loss of control to external events and factors. These students find their identity formation challenged, and this formation is an important developmental milestone for those in their late teens and early 20s (Balk, 2001). Identity formation challenges mean bereaved students question their own competence and self-worth. Depression, generalized anger, and behaviors categorized as self-destructive are reported outcomes of bereaved students who do not progress through the grieving process in a healthy manner (Silverman, 1987; Tyson-Rawson, 1996).

This issue is critical to colleges and universities as it can influence a student's ability to successfully experience college life. "If for no other reason than a university's interest to increase student retention, graduation, and long-term alumni support, it makes sense for a university to engage systematically in efforts to assist bereaved students" (Balk, 2001).

It is not a mere handful of students impacted by bereavement. Studies indicate that 22-30% of college undergraduates are in the first 12 months of grieving the death of a family member or a friend, and 35-48% of college students are in the first 24 months of grieving the death of a family member or a friend (Balk, 1997; Wrenn, 1999). Colleges and universities have reason to pay attention to bereavement influences and processes as many students are touched by loss during their college years.

One bereavement framework in particular, attachment theory, appears applicable to online social networks. Attachment theory describes bereavement as the outcome of bonds, mainly emotional bonds, sundered by death (Bowlby, 1980). The theory depicts a bereaved's simultaneous process of letting go of emotional attachments to the deceased while striving to invest in other social sources. Peers are often a vital source of social support, yet often are unaware of the critical assistance they can provide. As Barnett (1982; 1987) describes, most college students are incapable of transforming their empathic understanding in a helping fashion because they lack the skills or understanding of what to do. College students untouched by bereavement typically demonstrate both ignorance and fear when in the presence of a grieving peer.

It is in this area that attachment theory and online social networking may prove to find an important association. Talking about grief provides a means to maintain interpersonal relationships and also to invest in attachments with others (Balk, 1997). Many college students are uncomfortable talking about grief or other emotive topics through face-to-face communication. However, over the Internet, they find it soothing and comforting to display sensitivities. For years, funeral homes have offered condolence opportunities via the Internet. Perhaps the posting of comments via online social networking sites is a natural progression.

As online social networking becomes a better researched and highly prevalent mechanism for peer support, higher education administrators will need to determine how to utilize online social networking sites as part of best-practice intervention programs to reach out to or assist bereaved students.

HIGHER EDUCATION ADMINISTRATOR USE OF OSN

From serious issues such as bereavement, to simply use social media as a means for promotion of campus events, administrators are trying to make sense of how best to utilize technological innovations. To confound the issue, much of the verbiage used by Millenials makes it clear that parents or other adults are the outsiders treading at times on unwelcome ground. Acronyms like PBM, PIR, P911 and POS may seem as innocuous as CUL (see you later), but they can have far more serious implications (PBM = Parent Behind Me; PIR = Parent In Room; P911 = Parent Alert; and POS = Parent Over Shoulder).

It is not surprising given this "keep out" emphasis that, while the larger sphere of online social networking use by higher education administrators is growing, many other administrators are still unsure of how best to approach or utilize social media. A survey of over 1,000 higher education administrators found that fewer than 40% of college or university administrators worked at institutions that had created groups on an online social network site (Wandel, 2007). Groups in this case refer to an element of online social net-

Table 1. Exhibit A (Wandel, 2007)

Exhibit A	
University Use of OSN sites	**Column N%**
Publicizing student organizations	83.3
Planning campus programs	56.5
Announcing upcoming events & deadlines/university calendar	51.6
Publicizing non-university events	19.0
Providing information to current students regarding academics	12.4
Recruitment of new students	9.9
Alumni relations	7.1
Retention efforts	6.3
Distributing information to faculty, administrators and staff	1.3
Fundraising	0.8

works, particularly Facebook, in which members can create and join a faction similar to a group or organization in the physical world. Administrators recognized Facebook as the dominant forum used by college students, and 97% of postsecondary officials also chose to access Facebook, while only 23% used MySpace.

For those college administrators participating in OSN, the majority use it as a vehicle to communicate with students about organizational or programming issues. Over 83% said they use Facebook and other sites as a way to publicize student organizations, and over 56%t said they use the forums as a way to help plan campus programs. In addition, over half of the respondents indicated they use online social network sites to announce upcoming events and deadlines as part of a university calendar system. Exhibit A offers a ranking of why university and college administrators stated they use online social network sites.

Rollins College serves as a successful example of using OSN as a tool to promote its orientation/welcome back session. "There wasn't a seat open, because the word went out on Facebook and people actually replied, 'Yeah, I'll be there.' By knowing that other people were going to be participating it started to build steam and build

community," said director of Rollins Explorations Doug Little (Santovec, 2006).

Online social networking sites can even be utilized when college or university administrators do not form official groups. Over half of surveyed college administrators report they casually or unofficially monitor student activities, trends and interests (Currie, 2007). Survey respondents reported 36.2% accessed an online social network site on a daily basis, and another 32% accessed a site at least once a week (Wandel, 2007). Higher education administrators are increasingly using online social networks as related to their work. For example, postsecondary institutions such as Utica College, SUNY New Paltz and Colorado State have Facebook groups dedicated to career matters.

CONCERNS AND CONSIDERATIONS GERMANE TO HIGHER EDUCATION

From a higher education perspective, a plethora of considerations exist when students, administrators and educators are involved with online social networks. At the top of the list are concerns of privacy and student safety. Katy Lowe

Table 2. Exhibit B (Wandel, 2007)

Exhibit B	
Perceived Concerns of OSN sites	**Column N%**
Privacy issues	84.6
Student safety	78.1
Liability issues concerning alcohol or drug use	69.5
Legal responsibility	54.4
Freedom of speech issues	43.0
Difficulty regulating the posting of information	41.1
Postings may create social disruptions on campus	35.2
Student access (or lack of) to computers	8.9

Schneider (personal communication, May 31, 2007), associate dean of students at Hanover College, said she and her staff try to emphasize not only the professional implications of having information posted online, but also the threat to safety that can ensue if students list private and personal information in a public forum. "One thing our director of security often says is if Ted Bundy had been alive today, his murder spree would have included hundreds because stalking would have been much easier. 'I'm blond, early 20s, 5'5" and live at 517 Chi Alpha in Room 3' listed in a student's profile can make her an easy target for crime."

While safety and issues related to cyber-stalking have garnered much attention in scholarly journals as well as mainstream media, other concerns exist. Legal, ethical and social implications abound regarding OSN practices. Exhibit B illustrates a ranking of concern as reported by higher education administrators.

Legal Issues

Jessica Binkerd may have been an online social networking participant to achieve a hedonic experience, but the photographs on her MySpace profile ultimately proved anything but pleasurable for her. The photographs were used against her as she was sentenced to more than five years in prison for driving under the influence and vehicular manslaughter. Photographs of the University of California, Santa Barbara student drinking alcoholic beverages with friends were posted after the date of the fatal accident (Wagstaff, 2007).

Photographs have proved as evidence in numerous other cases. Lowe Schneider describes an example of when a fraternity hosted a philanthropic event in which one participant became so intoxicated that he had to be rushed to the hospital for alcohol poisoning. The fraternity members claimed no alcohol was consumed at the event. "We searched Facebook with the title of the auction and within seconds came up with 20 pictures of students consuming alcohol at the event in plain sight," said Lowe Schneider. "We used these photos in judicial action. We try to be careful not to search Facebook looking for violations, but if information is contradictory, we will use it to assist us."

Cameron Walker became embroiled in a public controversy when he became the first person expelled from a college for Facebook-related activities. Walker, at the time president of Fisher College's Student Government Association, was also an "officer" of a Facebook group that criticized a campus police sergeant and created a petition to get him fired (Stone, 2006). According to Walker, the sergeant had harassed students in order to encourage situations where arrests could be made. Walker claimed the Facebook group he and another student created was a prank. To support this, he pointed to his Facebook group's officer title, which he selected, as "Duke of Propaganda." The administrators at Fisher College in Boston did not see the humor, and they cited Walker as being in violation of the Student Code of Conduct against "verbal, written, graphic, or electronic abuse, harassment, coercion, or intimidation of an individual."

Many college students feel it is unfair to use online social networking profiles or postings against an individual. "I know some universities use Facebook as a tool to bust underage drinkers as well as catch people doing thing they should not be doing," said college student Kathryn Piepho. "I just feel like universities are over-stepping their boundaries by viewing students' Web pages."

Of course, it is not only students that can bring about litigious or public controversy. Vetted by attorneys, Roger Williams University formally adopted a proactive social networking and blogging policy in summer 2007 for faculty and staff when using a university e-mail address (Roger Williams University, 2007). An excerpt from the policy states:

Roger Williams University provides access to the World Wide Web for all of its employees as a privilege and in many cases a necessity to meet the responsibilities of their job. This includes the use of social networking sites, and access to an array of blogs—and even permission to write a blog of one's own—as part of one's professional activities. The University defines "professional activities" as those that advance the University's mission of education, research and public service.

In light of that definition, each employee is reminded when he or she blogs or accesses a social networking site with a Roger Williams University e-mail address, the employee is a representative of the University and must act accordingly. That means an employee can access such sites as Facebook or MySpace to communicate with students, faculty, staff or other professional colleagues in matters related to their teaching and/or professional responsibilities at Roger Williams.

Employees who use a Roger Williams e-mail account must consult their supervisor and/or Dean in advance of their intention to use social networking sites. In addition, staff or faculty using either an RWU address or a personal address to create or post comments to blogs should include this disclaimer: The postings on this site are my own and don't necessarily reflect Roger Williams University's opinion, strategies or policies.

Some activities that would NOT be considered acceptable uses of the Internet from a Roger Williams account include but are not limited to:

- Posting items anonymously or under a pseudonym;
- Conducting personal social relationships unrelated to University activities;
- Using and creating an account with dating and/or matchmaking sites;
- Engaging in partisan political fundraising activity;
- Engaging in online gambling;

- Posting comments or writing blogs that are obscene or untrue;
- Using social networking sites or blog postings to harass others;
- Selling goods or services for personal financial profit.

The policy further details the use of personal e-mail accounts when participating in online social networking sites. It will be interesting to analyze over time how this policy is accepted by faculty and staff. Will it decimate the confidence of faculty by restricting their speech? Will staff appreciate the guidelines to help ensure abuses are limited? It will also be interesting to learn how many other institutions choose to adopt similar policies.

Impact of OSN on the Student-Athlete

In addition to explicitly stating the expectations and responsibilities for employees, many college and university administrators view OSN policies as an opportunity to assist and even benefit another cohort, that of high profile student-athletes. This group is subject to increased scrutiny for participation in online social networking sites. In response to this, the University of Michigan at Ann Arbor is one of many postsecondary institutions electing to take a proactive stance. As of 2007-08, it became mandatory for students to sign a pledge regarding good conduct on social networking sites as part of the student-athlete code of conduct.

Judy Van Horn (personal communication, May 9, 2007), associate athletic director/senior woman administrator at the University of Michigan, said the intent is to use the pledge to educate students. "It's better for us to find inappropriate material on an athlete's profile than for a news reporter to do so," she said. A university representative checks each online account once a semester to make sure all language and photographs are appropriate.

As Van Horn explained, it is what is considered appropriate that is often debated. "Using the f-word or having sexually explicit photographs may not be offensive to a student, but it is still shocking to others," she said. If anything inappropriate is found, Van Horn said a process is in place to have the offensive material taken down within 24 hours.

As social networking sites garner increased attention, Van Horn said students are getting smarter and taking advantage of closed groups. Closed groups define members and place restrictions on who can post and view comments within a group. In the past, the University of Michigan had student-athletes "clean up" their personal sites but they remained connected to other questionable groups. "You lose control any time you join a group," Van Horn explained. Identity theft is also a problem. Van Horn said six sites have misrepresented the University's star quarterback as his own, and two other sites misrepresented the head coach.

The University of Michigan's Department of Athletics created the Student-Athlete Conduct Policy as an educational tool, focusing on three areas: Internet Social Networking Community Sites, Athletic Department Policy, and Recommendations. The language from the policy includes:

Internet Social Networking Community Sites. *Internet sites such as Facebook.com, MySpace.com, Xanga.com, Friendster.com and others provides individuals with an opportunity to interact with an extraordinary expansive universe of new people and connect with current friends. Postings on personal profiles, groups and chat rooms are in the public domain and easily accessible by anyone including reporters, parents, coaches, groupies, predators, employers, and graduate school admissions officials. Once information is posted, it can be retrieved by computer savvy individuals even after it has been deleted.*

Athletic Department Policy. *Participation in intercollegiate athletics at the University of Michigan is a privilege, not a right. Athletic Department conduct policy currently states, "Student-athletes shall deport themselves with honesty and good sportsmanship. Their behavior shall AT ALL TIMES reflect the high standards of honor and dignity that characterize participation in competitive sports at the University of Michigan." While the Athletic Department does not prohibit student-athlete involvement with internet based social networking communities, this high standard of honor and dignity encompasses comments and postings made to internet sites. The Athletic Department reserves the right to take action against any currently enrolled student-athlete engaged in behavior that violates University, Department, or team rules, including such behavior that occurs in postings on the internet. This action may include education, counseling, team suspension, termination from the varsity team and reduction or non-renewal of any athletic scholarships.*

Recommendations. *Immediately review any internet websites you may have posted on the internet to ensure that the postings are consistent with University, Department, and team rules and that they present you in a way you want to be portrayed. For your safety and privacy, you should refrain from posting and should promptly remove any personally identifiable information such as telephone number, address, class schedule and places frequented as well as any photos you may have posted. Alert the Compliance Services Office of any sites that falsely appear to be yours as this constitutes identity theft, and the University will assist your efforts to have the offensive site removed. Be cautious about which chat groups you join to be sure you want to be publicly associated with that group. Once you become a member, you are linked to the discussion that takes place within that group. Only the group's administrator is able to delete your group membership or postings made to a group site.*

On a broader scale, the NCAA Student-Athlete Advisory committee has discussed the issue of athletes' profiles but, according to assistant director of member services Jess Rigler (personal communication, June 4, 2007), does not set forth policy on the topic. "We leave it up to the individual institutions to set policy on this," he said. While the NCAA Student-Athlete Advisory committee does not track the number of policies that exist, Rigler estimates that "...almost all of the Division I schools have some sort of policy regarding social networks and about half of the Division II schools have a policy in place." He explained the key, however, is in how well written and followed the policies are from one campus to another.

Coaches are striving to find ways to encourage dialogue of OSN usage with the aim that education and awareness of the topic will produce a kind of galvanization of student-athletes. If students are spurred to action and understand the importance of promoting positive images for themselves, their team and their universities, then monitoring sites becomes less of a burden for coaches and administrators. Courtney Felke, a senior playing NCAA Division I women's basketball, said, "Our head coach told us to modify the information that we had posted online because of how easily the information is accessible to other people and how information can be misconstrued. We haven't had any issues, but we're working to be proactive. More than once there have been discussions about this."

Other colleges are hosting guest speakers to introduce the topic of OSN, and still others choose to approach the issue through written correspondence. A letter from Bill Maher (Canisius, 2007), director of athletics at Canisius College, is sent to each student-athlete to educate them regarding online social networking and to remind them that unique responsibilities and expectations come with serving as a student-athlete.

Dear Canisius Student-Athlete:

Facebook.com and other similar websites have generated national concern about the safety and welfare of high school and college students. This concern has created intense discussions particularly on college campuses and more specifically, within athletic departments.

The focus of these discussions has been on the posting of student-athlete profiles and photographs on these websites. Many student-athletes have elected to post pictures of themselves and teammates engaging in inappropriate activity. Examples of this activity includes: underage drinking, hazing rituals, drug use, smoking, and even questionable sexual behavior. In some instances, these photos have led to disciplinary action against student-athletes and against teams including forfeitures of contests at institutions across the country.

The media has become aware of these sites and has gained access to some of this information posted. These outlets have been able to exploit student-athletes by simply copying what has been posted and allowing scrutiny of student-athlete behavior in a grander scheme. It also draws attention to the institution in a negative fashion. Opposing teams have even capitalized on the website by downloading pictures and using them as motivation for themselves or to taunt a specific student-athlete.

All of our athletic teams have policies on underage drinking, hazing and inappropriate behavior. Your decision to post items on facebook.com or similar websites is a personal one; however, the Athletic Department and your individual team policies should serve as a filter for what you decide to put on line. Any public pictures or comments determined to be contrary to these departmental policies and/or the Student-Athlete Code of Conduct will be treated as violations of said policies and handled accordingly.

Your coaching staff has explained the Department's expectations in this area, so please ensure that you take the appropriate steps to avoid additional consequences. If this behavior continues, your coach will be in a position to suspend you from competition and potentially recommend a dismissal from the program and a non-renewal of your athletic scholarship.

You must remember that you represent Canisius College at all times. Do not post pictures, comments or information on the websites that would/could embarrass you, your team, or Canisius College, or that are clearly contrary to the expectations for the student-athletes. It is a privilege to represent Canisius College in athletic competition, so your good personal judgment in this area is expected.

Our competitive goals are clear – to win Championships within the Metro Atlantic Athletic Conference. For us to reach these goals, it takes a level of personal commitment from each student-athlete in our program. The personal decisions you make on a daily basis will determine our overall success. Do your part to help us win MAAC Championships.

After controversial photographs of several student-athletes appeared publicly due to postings on online social networking sites, the athletic office determined it best to educate students and limit future problems. Some institutions, including Loyola University Chicago and Kent State, have moved in an even more aggressive manner, completely banning student-athlete membership in online social networks. These types of bans do have critics who question the First Amendment rights of students being violated by such blatant prohibition. To date, any violation appears to be dismissed as the expectations of student-athletes are significantly higher than that of other students. This is not only the case with online social networks, but also in other rights-restriction capacities such as drug testing. However, the issue of First Amendment concerns is far from clear-cut

and precedent-setting cases are likely to emerge in the next few years.

Employer Ethics and Expectations

"Have you checked your Facebook page lately? I have."

Imagine being 18 years old, seeking your first relevant work experience, and receiving that message. Through mock interviews with Hanover College's Center for Business Preparation, Lowe Schneider saw this very statement written by an employer on a student's evaluation.

Public access to what many feel is private information is causing concern and discussions on college campuses nationwide. Ethical questions abound as to whether it is fair for employers to look at online social networking sites to gain information about job candidates. To what degree students and prospective employees are protected under privacy laws and ethical boundaries when it comes to accessing these profiles is at the core of the debate. Is viewing an online profile considered the same as reading an article in a newspaper about a person and learning information about him or her? Is it a matter of being entitled to as much information about job candidates as possible, regardless of how the information is obtained?

"I hate the fact that universities are getting involved in online networks," said college student Lauren Deas. "I have so many great pictures that I can't even show in fear of losing a potential job or scholarship."

But despite such concerns, 40% of companies say that they would at least consider using Facebook profiles before making a hiring decision (Read, 2007). Thirty-two percent of students think it is unethical for companies to scan the Facebook profiles of job candidates, but only 17% of employers feel the same way. Chris Wiley and Mark Sisson, authors of the widely cited University of Dayton study, found that many students tend to draw sharp lines between their personal and professional lives and see Facebook as a tool to be used in a personal manner. One reason students may feel this way is that they often embellish on their online postings or profiles. Many college students acknowledge they purposefully misrepresent themselves. For example, 8% of students say they exaggerate their alcohol or drug use in Facebook postings. But should employers have to decipher reality from fantasy? Of businesses polled in the University of Dayton study, 326 said they were not convinced that students could make a clean break between their Facebook personas and their professional demeanor, so these employers see value in viewing online social networking sites to learn about job candidates.

Company officials do not appear apprehensive about Internet searches jeopardizing the law. Employment attorneys say it is not illegal for employers to search the Internet or publicly available Web sites created by applicants to see what information they can find. Moreover, the attorneys note the privacy issue is even ethically minimal if someone has put information about themselves on the Internet where millions of people have access to it (Pitfalls, 2006). Of course, employers could use Facebook to determine students' gender, race or sexual preference, but only 13% of the officials said they felt that scanning Facebook might violate equal opportunity employment laws.

The National Association of Colleges and Employers found that 27% of employers surveyed had reviewed job candidates' personal information on sites such as MySpace or Facebook or had conducted broader Internet searches on applicants (NACE, 2006). These non-comprehensive, unofficial background checks are easy to conduct. Most often, the reviews are conducted by interns or employees who are recent graduates since both groups have college e-mail addresses, enabling them to easily view online profiles (Finder, 2006).

As the senior associate director of the career center at Duke University, Kara Lombardi (personal communication, April 24, 2007) finds most human resource personnel "take an official stance that they do not formally use online social

networks, but we do know that many are unofficially using it. Many of the employers that recruit on campus will bring young alums to campus to help interview. These alums, who do not work in HR, will look up candidates on Facebook. We have heard back from alums about deciding not to interview students based on what is posted in their profile."

Similar to the experiences of many college administrators, Lombardi was first introduced to the world of online social networking not by colleagues but by students. Peer educators in her office first acquainted her with Facebook, and she quickly garnered interest after learning the exorbitant amount of time students spend on OSN. Since then, Duke University's career center has embraced an appreciation for the benefits of online social networking, while working to ensure students understand the potential consequences associated with them. The career center posts on its Web site a statement developed in summer 2006:

Considerations for Blogs and Social Networks like MySpace and Facebook

Duke University takes free expression seriously and goes to great lengths to protect that right. Social networks such as Facebook and MySpace have expanded opportunities to express yourself, connect with friends and to build your network. Still, there are several responsibilities to consider when you create your persona and post messages online.

- **What you post is public information.** You have a much larger audience than you might be aware.
- **What you post is going to be around for a while.** Because caching and other forms of technology can capture your postings, information is accessible even after you've removed it.

- **What you post can harm others.** You are free to express yourself on social networks in ways that you feel are appropriate for you. However, it is important that you respect the privacy and rights of others. Posting things about others can place both you and your subject in a contentious situation.

- **What you post may affect your future.** There is a growing trend for employers to check Google and social networks to gather information about potential candidates. The online persona you create today may be available when you begin your internship or full-time job search or when you apply to professional or graduate school—even if you think you've deleted it. Carefully consider how you want people to perceive you before you give them the chance to misinterpret your profile and pictures.

As Lombardi describes, the career center's approach is "...to warn students that what they post is available for everyone to see so they should make sure they are presenting themselves in a way that won't damage their image. We found that most students are posting pictures and using language that they probably won't want a potential employer to see." She also said that while Duke University does not offer student workshops solely on the topic of online social networking, the topic is integrated into other workshops associated with recruiting, orientation, résumé and cover letters, and interviewing. Or, as she put it, it's discussed "...anytime we have a captive audience."

Lombardi's legal and ethical concern over online social networking centers on the issue of privacy. She cites a NACE Spotlight Online June 2006 article posted on the Duke University career center's Web site, an article showcasing the ethical issues surrounding the privacy of profile pages. The article describes a young man searching for an internship and, wanting to showcase himself in the most positive light; he recognized that many of the photographs and much of the language on

his profile jeopardized this. He heeded advice to limit access to his profile. During an interview, he was surprised to be questioned about specific references to his Facebook account and the information posted on it. He did not think this information could be viewed to outsiders because he had limited his privacy settings. The interviewer explained that working for a state agency meant recruiters could access his Facebook account under the rules of the Patriot Act.

While some students vehemently oppose this seeming intrusion, others do not see their peers as victims in these circumstances. College student Lindsey Holder said, "People shouldn't be so naïve as to think that the Internet is private. I don't think people would see any problem with a job candidate not being hired because he has his own public access show that showcases his weekend binges, so why is it any different that he has devoted his own online profile to do the same? I understand that not everything that gets posted, photos in particular, can be controlled, but these businesses are putting their public faces on the line. I think they are entitled to feel confident that their new employees are representing them in the best light."

College student Sarah Powell agrees. "I think that it is a good idea to have employers look at student profiles. If I were an employer, I would not want to hire a student who parties and gets drunk all the time. That to me shows a lack of maturity. If a student does not want certain information seen or revealed to people, then it shouldn't be placed on the Web."

Rights and Responsibilities

Information gleaned from online profiles is not only used by off-campus employers, but extends to on-campus experiential education situations. Lowe Schneider of Hanover College said that she and her staff view Facebook pages when a student applies to be an orientation leader. "Particularly since these students are to be role models in our community, it's important to see what messages are out there," she said.

The ethical and legal issues associated with online social networking are a prevalent theme of discussion among the student life staff at Hanover College. There are First Amendment considerations to ensure students have the freedom to express themselves. But when that expression infringes on the rights and privacy of others, what are the results? Lowe Schneider offered a recent example of when a student posted pictures from a party on his Facebook page, and one of the pictures included a prominent female student leader violating the College's alcohol policy. The student asked her peer to take down the photograph and he refused. "So whose rights are more important here and how does the college judicial system intervene?" Lowe Schneider ponders.

Derek Morgan (personal communication, June 7, 2007) has served as a director of student activities for four years at the Colorado School of Mines. He works with all student organizations, Greek life, orientation programs, student government and campus programming. Several members of his student life staff have personal Facebook accounts and use the accounts to invite students to campus events. The accounts are also used as a vehicle to connect with students, view group pages, and share photographs from recent events. Morgan considers online social networking to be similar to cell phones and e-mail, all valuable mediums to communicate with others. "Online social networks are just another way to efficiently and effectively communicate with each other," he said. "They are an instant way to communicate."

Morgan said his school initially had a few Facebook groups such as the Intramural Sports office group and the Outdoor Recreation Center group that are no longer in existence. According to Morgan, a Facebook representative called the School to explain that offices and departments could not have accounts. To comply, the School now simply makes announcements about events

through the personal pages of directors and other administrators. A Facebook group that remains active is the Mines Activity Council programming board group for the school. The group administrators update the account weekly, making announcements about upcoming events and submitting pictures from previous events to the group's 162 members.

Morgan believes online social networking groups can be particularly helpful for first-year students, through the creation of orientation groups, residence hall groups, and other interest groups designed with the first-time student or transferring student in mind. He stated it would be hard to prove retention is positively impacted by online social networking, but noted, "Students that participate in the networks probably feel better about their experience and more involved with their campus community."

Like Lombardi at Duke University, Morgan sees privacy issues as a concern. "There is the debate whether pictures on Facebook or MySpace can and should be used in disciplinary cases," he said. "Student groups advertising illegal activities or things that violate school policy could be an issue, like fraternity pages showing pictures of hazing activities or underage drinking."

Ethically, he sees even more challenges facing student affairs professionals. He raises two important questions: 1) As an advisor of student organizations, how far do I go to make sure all students' Facebook pages are free of negative pictures and comments? 2) Does the school have an obligation to control content when a student has a page based on his or her enrollment in the school?

Linguistic Fantasy or Reality

Those higher education administrators interviewed for this chapter expressed concern over the issue of privacy and the type of personal information students are divulging on profile pages. After conducting interviews with students, an interesting commonality began to emerge. They too were concerned about privacy, but from a different vantage point. Students are concerned with privacy invasion, but mainly because they fear unseasoned online social networkers will not be able to distinguish between the real person behind the fantasy profile. With more than 100 million profiles on MySpace alone, students are working hard to be bold, unique and stand out in any way possible (Pospisil, 2006). Students see online social networking as their time for play, for fantasy. As college student Lauren Trisler said, "I'm not the same person on my profile as I am in real life."

College student Danny Pfrank echoed this sentiment and added that he sees online social networking as a stage-specific endeavor. "Facebook and other online social networks always seemed to me as something you do throughout high school and college and then you get rid of as soon as you are in the 'real world.'"

Perhaps his thinking stems from the fact that many elements of non-professional behavior can be found within the OSN realm. It is not only discussions of drunken debauchery or risqué photographs found within personal profiles. Facebook has a clipart gallery of "gifts" that can be purchased and sent to another member for $1 each. It is a clever concept, with many of the 160-plus gifts seemingly designed with sophomoric humor in mind. Imagine clipart gifts including jock straps, pacifiers, a screw, handcuffs, bikinis, a thong, and a roll of toilet paper.

There are also groups that could make a conservative college or university official cringe. An article in *The Boston Globe* in 2005 (Schweitzer) details students discussing on their Facebook sites their use of marijuana and a desire to have sex with certain university professors, with the group titled *my goal in College is to fuck a professor*. Group names are often created using edgy or offensive language. A ten-minute search of group sites around the nation in June 2007 brought up a unique sampling:

- I Hate When I Cheat off a smart person test and I still Flunk with 468 members
- Hey, President Brogan: WE WANT OUR $577,950 BACK! with 229 members
- B+?! F*ck you, Professor…Just give me the A- with 91 members
- Anti-America with 52 members
- Al Qaeda Terrorist and Anti Liberal Network with 44 members
- ANTI Hilary Clinton for president '08 with 59,873 members
- Actually Mr. Bush, you're an idiot with 3,456 members
- Petition against Professor Stephen Kaufman with 548 members

Whether these groups make a person squirm in discomfort, laugh, or simply be content knowing we live in a society of free expression, a challenge arises when a person is linked to an unintended group based on another affiliation or friend. It is common for students to realize all too late that they are associated with a group without having directly chosen to do so.

Tracy Mitrano, director of IT policy at Cornell University, has written several thoughtful pieces detailing how caution should be exercised when using online social networks. One of these, appropriately titled *Thoughts on Facebook* (Mitrano, 2006), discusses how what may seem appropriately funny as a teenager could be embarrassing or even disastrous as an individual gets older. Her example details a young man proud of his well-endowed anatomy, and how he boasted of this fact in an online chat room.

Years later, after being turned down from a job he really wanted, he found out the reason. The potential employer had found this information on the Internet, and the topic was deemed unprofessional enough to warrant a reason for not selecting the individual for the job. The young man requested the information be removed from the original site, but he was told that it was not possible since a commercial Internet Service Provider (ISP) was the domain of his posted information. It was an issue of caching, which in oversimplified terms is the storage of Web files for later use. Caching, as Mitrano explains, "…means that if you post something on Facebook, let's say for a day or two, just to be funny or to make a point, even if you take it down or change it, it remains accessible to the rest of the world on the Internet anyway (Mitrano, 2006)."

Implications for Administrators

How long all this information will be accessible is anyone's guess, but diffusion theory may help reveal the rate that OSN can be expected to continue its emergence as a critical influencer on students and administrators. This theory helps determine the rate of diffusion of a technological innovation, as well as assists in identifying the variables that may encourage or impede the acceptance or adoption of the technology by a community of people.

Diffusion theory is grounded in the idea that adopters make voluntary decisions to either accept or reject a technological innovation based on the expected benefits from independent use. In IT diffusion it should be noted that the adoption may be encouraged or required by management as opposed to being determined by independent use. This encouragement or mandate may influence whether adoption by a critical mass has been established (Katz & Shapiro, 1986). Achieving critical mass with a community of users is crucial. If critical mass is achieved, the innovation is likely to be universally adopted and, if not, the technology is typically abandoned (Markus, 1987).

Those higher education administrators surveyed for this chapter were in consensus that while they felt a critical mass of prospective students and current students use OSN, how the technology will ultimately be used for recruitment and retention purposes is still evolving. Online social networking may be considered an innovation that has progressed through the stages of diffusion in

what is considered an extremely short timeframe as compared to the time most technological innovations move through the process. The stages of diffusion according to the innovation decision process theory (Rogers, 1995) are knowledge, persuasion, decision, implementation, and confirmation, and the stages of IT implementation include initiation, adoption, adaptation, acceptance, routinization, and infusion (Kwon & Zmud, 1987). Online social networking has moved through knowledge to confirmation, and from initiation to infusion, for a critical mass in only a few years. Facebook helped ensure IT diffusion to a critical mass by offering its site to more than just students. Through open enrollment, a domino effect is created so that the site becomes increasingly compelling as more people, and more connections, are made.

Not only are these connections compelling from a social standpoint, but online social networking sites could be one of the most effective ways to engage today's students and to strengthen their bonds to the university in a way that improves enrollment, increases retention, and establishes the foundation for strong and committed alumni relations. With such a new forum, at least in comparison to enrollment and communication strategies that have been utilized for decades, it is important for administrators to consider the issues and implications of using online social networks to communicate. Specifically, college and university administrators should consider:

- Creating strategic plans to communicate with prospective students as well as ongoing correspondence upon admittance. High school students make decisions about what college to attend based on a myriad of factors, including Web sites, campus visits, discipline offerings, cost, location, and friends and family. College and university administrators should not underestimate the power of online social networking sites that promote and highlight campus features.

Even more, online social networks can help prospective students feel socially accepted even before participating in a campus visit. As part of a comprehensive e-recruiting campaign, online social networks are a relatively inexpensive and efficient way to communicate.

- Developing workshops on the topic of online social networking. While most everyone involved in academia is used to hearing and reading about safety issues related to OSN, many unexplored areas of this particular form of social media exist. Students can benefit from learning how best to utilize online social networking sites to gain a feel for campus culture. For example, a discussion could occur as to what OSN groups exist to promote weeknight or weekend happenings to help the student feel connected. Offering training or information-based workshops during orientation sessions may be useful, but incorporating them into discussions throughout the year is ideal. Some students have reported feeling overwhelmed by the amount of time they spend on OSN sites (Currie, 2007), almost as an addiction, and discussions of how to healthily and effectively enjoy OSN may prove valuable.
- Extending these workshops to faculty and administrators. Many faculty and administrators are intimidated by online social networking sites and are unsure of how, if at all, to access and utilize groups and sites. Most online technology discussions revolve around how to impact learning. But the critical examination of "extended learning" outside the classroom should be a topic as well. A panel of faculty and staff can help colleagues brainstorm the social media and academic link, offering definition to an often gray area of what is appropriate. Workshops can also help faculty and administrators gain an appreciation of OSN as a way to reach students about departmental clubs, research

or campus-related interests. OSN sites are not designed as educational tools, but they can be immensely effective in communicating to students about academic-related information.

- Writing an official policy. Official policies on online social networking practices are becoming more prevalent at colleges and universities. Cornell University offers an extensive policy, including information about *why* policies, safety measures, and self-responsibility are important. Roger Williams University has an online social networking and blogging policy dedicated to employees. The policy requires employees to consult with their dean for approval before accessing an online social network when using a university e-mail account (Roger Williams University, 2007). For those college and university administrators uncomfortable with an official policy or statement that may infringe or stifle First Amendment rights, it remains a helpful exercise to review other college or university policies. These discussions can be informative and useful as college administrators determine the level, if any, of involvement a campus has with social networks.
- Promoting organizational clubs, organizations, social gatherings or other events through online social networking sites. At Eastern Illinois University, peer educators are finding success in using Facebook to actively encourage the idea of a smoke-free campus (Currie, 2007). Groups at other colleges and universities show a strong online presence through Facebook groups touting minority tolerance and diversity acceptance, residence hall rules, science clubs, and pre-professional associations.
- Targeting special-interest groups such as student-athletes, transfer students or parents. Public relations efforts geared toward niche audiences can be effective but costly. Online

social networks make it feasible to reach targeted segments or publics with personalized information, something enrollment experts say is critical in today's highly technological and competitive environment (Noel-Levitz, 2006).

- Coordinating meetings with high school teachers, principals, guidance counselors, students, and university administrators on the subject of OSN. The majority of college attendees enter directly from high school. Collaborative efforts between high school and college administrators can only strengthen understanding of the use, benefits, and concerns of communicating with students in today's high-technology environment. Particularly when it comes to high school-college transition issues, college administrators may benefit greatly by hearing perspectives from others. To be locked away in the proverbial ivory tower implies administrators may be out of touch and unaware of the needs of Millenials. It behooves all educational administrators to gain a respect and understanding of social media.

CONCLUSION: CONNECTIVITY

This chapter details new findings regarding the use of online social networking sites by college and university administrators. It also presents a compilation of data and information in respect to many of the dominating issues surrounding online social networking, including legal issues, concerns over privacy, and how OSN may prove useful to bereaved college students. As with most topics, there are advantages and disadvantages. Online social networking is no exception. Groups and profiles exist that are fun, interesting, informative, entertaining, clever and repugnant.

Like it or not, communicating via online social networking sites is what millions of young people do each day. A market research study commissioned by MySpace, Isobar and Carat (Never Ending Friending, 2007) found a tie in the top two choices of what 15-34-year-olds would do if they had 15 minutes of time: they would either check out a social networking site or talk on their cell phone.

With approximately 90% participation among U.S. college undergraduate students, Facebook alone is transforming the way younger generations communicate (Ellison, Steinfeld, & Lampe, 2006). Institutions of higher education no longer have the luxury of serving as what Levitz and Noel (2000) refer to as "non-intrusive institutions," passively assuming students will value and be involved in their educational experience. University officials must analyze how best to use online social networks as proactive tools. As part of her College's Early Alert Team, Lowe Schneider views the Facebook pages of students struggling academically or socially. Oftentimes the profiles and postings can help her glean information about the source of the struggle or identify key support systems that might be effective to the individual student.

Most educators and university administrators agree that when student success is not left to chance, when institutions utilize all available tools to assist in encouraging and helping students, is when attrition rates are lowest. The earlier connectivity is established, the more likely a student will feel engaged to a particular college or university, and the more engaged or connected, the better chance the student has of successfully graduating. As Duke University administrator Lombardi said, students seek involvement as soon as they are accepted to a college or university, so participation in specialized online social networking groups helps them develop a community prior to arriving on campus.

Because of this connection, and the growing ethical and legal issues surrounding online social networking sites, many postsecondary institutions are electing to create and maintain their own online social networking architectural systems. Hanover College, Western Illinois University, Wilkes University, and others have campus online social networking systems available to users. The University of Alabama has further extended its networking initiatives to parents of first-year students with the development of *myBama Family Connection* (Santovec, 2006).

If nothing else, college administrators may find it imperative to take an active interest in online social networking sites for the time it is takes away from academic studies. Consider the online social networking group titled *When I Flunk Out of College, It's All Facebook's Fault*.

REFERENCES

Baase, S. (2003). *A gift of fire* (2nd ed.). Englewood Cliffs, NJ: Prentice Hall.

Balk, D. (1997). Death, bereavement and college students: A descriptive analysis. *Death Studies, 25*, 67-84.

Balk, D. (2001). College student bereavement, scholarship, and the university: A call for university engagement. *Brunner-Routledge, 67*-84.

Barnett, M. (1982). Empathy and pro-social behavior in children. In: T. Field, A. Huston, H. Quay, L. Troll, & G. Finley (Eds.), *Review of human development*. New York, NY: Wiley.

Barnett, M. (1987). Emphathy and related responses in children. In: N. Eisenberg & J. Strayer (Eds.), *Empathy and its development*. New York, NY: Cambridge University Press.

Bowlby, J. (1980). *Attachment and loss: Volume 3. Loss—sadness and depression*. New York, NY: Basic Books.

Canisius College. (n.d.). *Facebook letter*. Retrieved from http://209.85.165.104/search?q=cache:X0T-C7Y9qCtMJ:www.canisius.edu/images/userIm-ages/athletics/Page_2173/Facebook%2520letter.doc+dear+canisius+student-athlete&hl=en&ct=clnk&cd=1&gl=us on July 4, 2007.

Cho, H., Stefanone, M., & Gay, G. (2002). Social network analysis of information sharing networks in a CSCL community. *Proceedings of Computer Support for Collaborative Learning*, (pp. 43-50).

Currie, L. (2007). Using social network sites responsibly. *The Peer Educator, 29*, 5-8.

Downes, S. (2005). Semantic networks and social networks. *The Learning Organization, 12*, 411.

Ellison, N., Steinfeld, C., & Lampe, C. (2006). Spatially bounded online social networks and social capital: The role of Facebook. *Proceedings of the Annual Conference of the International Communication Association*.

Finder, A. (2006). For some, online persona undermines resume. *New York Times*, pp. 1-2.

Goodman, J. (2007). Click first, ask questions later: Understanding teen online behaviour. *Aplis, 20*, 84-86.

Hortobagyi, M. (2007, May 9). Slain students' pages to stay on Facebook. *USA Today*, Life Section, P9.

Katz, M., & Shapiro, C. (1986). Technology adoption in the presence of network externalities. *Journal of Political Economy, 94*, 822-841.

Kirkpatrick, D. (2007). Facebook's plan to hook up the world. *Fortune, 155*, 127-130.

Klaassen, A. (2007). Making friends with the social networks. *Advertising Age, 78*, 14.

Kwon, T., & Zmud, R. (1987). Unifying the fragmented models of information systems implementation. In: J. Boland & R. Hirshheim (Eds.), *Critical issues in information systems research* (pp. 227-251). New York, NY: John Wiley.

Levy, S. (2007, August 27). Facebook grows up. *Newsweek,* pp. 41-42.

Lenhart, A., & Madden, M. (2007). Social networking Web sites and teens: An overview. *Pew Internet & American Life Project.* Retrieved June 10, 2007, from http://www.pewinternet.org/PPF/r/198/report_display.asp.

Levitz, R., & Noel, L. (2000). Taking the initiative: Strategic moves for retention. USA Group. Noel-Levitz.

Markus, M. (1987). Toward a 'critical mass' theory of interactive media: Universal access, interdependence and diffusion. *Communications Research, 14,* 491-511.

Mitrano, T. (2006). Thoughts on Facebook. Retrieved June 7, 2007, from http://www.cit.cornell.edu/info/policy/memos/facebook.html.

National Association of Colleges and Employers (NACE). (2006). Spotlight Online for Career Services Professionals. Retrieved June 28, 2007, from http://www.lib.unipi.gr/files/nace/2006/Spotlight_Online_07_07_2006.pdf.

Naposki, K. (2006, January). Facebook: The craze that has crashed into college life may have other consequences. *The Pendulum Online.* Retrieved June 20, 2007, from http://www.elon.edu/e-web/pendulum/Issues/2006/01_19/features/special-feature.xhtml.

Never Ending Friending. (2007). Commissioned by MySpace, Isobar & Carat. Retrieved July 3, 2007, from http://www.tns-us.com/knowledge/docs/40161_Online_Book.pdf.

Noel-Levitz. (2006). E-expectations class of 2007 Report: Engaging the "social networking" generation. Retrieved June 15, 2007, from http://www.noellevitz.com.

Pitfalls of checking job applicants' personal Web pages. (2006). *Managing Accounts Payable,* 4-6.

Pospisil, J. (2006). *Hacking MySpace.* Indianapolis, IN: Wiley Publishing, Inc.

Read, B. (2007, January 12). U. of Dayton study examines professional risks of Facebook. *The Chronicle of Higher Education.* Retrieved June 1, 2007, from http://chronicle.com/weekly/v53/i19/19a03102.htm.

Roger Williams University. Policies: Social Networking/Blogging. Retrieved July 3, 2007, from http://www.rwu.edu/newsandevents/publicaffairs/policies/socialnetworking.htm.

Rogers, E. (1995). *Diffusion of innovations* (4th ed.). New York, NY: The Free Press.

Ronn, K. (2007, June 13). Social networking: Closer than you think. *Business Week Online,* 12.

Rosenberg, M., Schooler, C., & Schoenbach, C. (1989). Self-esteem and adolescent problems: Modeling reciprocal effects. *American Sociological Review, 54,* 1004-1018.

Santovec, M. (2006). Using online networking to engage and retain students. *Recruitment and retention in higher education, 20,* 1-5.

Schweitzer, S. (2005, September 26). When students open up—a little too much. *The Boston Globe.*

Sellers, M. (2005, October/December). Moogle, Google, and garbage cans: The impact of technology on decision making. *International Journal of Leadership in Education, 8,* 365-374.

Silverman, P. (1987). The impact of parental death on college-age women. *Psychiatric Clinics of North America, 10,* 387-404.

Stone, B. (2006, August 21-28). Web of risks. *Newsweek.*

Tinto, V. (1982). Limits of theory and practice in student attrition. *Journal of Higher Education, 53,* 687-700.

Tinto, V. (1993). *Leaving college: Rethinking the causes and cures of student attrition.* Chicago, IL: The University of Chicago Press.

Tyson-Rawson, K. (1996). Adolescent responses to the death of a parent. In: C. Corr & D. Balk (Eds.), *Handbook of adolescent death and bereavement,* (pp. 155-172). New York, NY: Springer.

Valkenburg, P., Peter, J., & Schouten, A. (2006). Friend networking sites and their relationship to adolescents' well-being and social self-esteem. *CyberPsychology & Review, 9,* 584-590.

Wagstaff, E. (2007, February 28). Court case decision reveals dangers of networking sites. *Daily Nexus.* University of California, Santa Barbara.

Retrieved June 28, 2007, from http://www.daily-nexus.com/article.php?a=13440.

Wandel, T. (2007, July). *Educational institution responses to online social networking.* Paper presented at the World Communication Association Conference. Brisbane, Australia.

Wood, J. (1995). *Relational communication.* Belmont, CA: Wadsworth.

Wood, J. (1996). *Everyday encounters: An introduction to interpersonal communication.* Belmont, CA: Wadsworth.

Wrenn, R. (1999). The grieving college student. In: J. Davidson & K. Doka (Eds.), *Living with grief: At work, at school, at worship,* (pp. 131-141). Levittown, PA: Brunner/Mazel.

Chapter XI
Facebook Follies:
Who Suffers the Most?

Katherine Karl
Marshall University, USA

Joy Peluchette
University of Southern Indiana, USA

ABSTRACT

This study examined the relative impact of "inappropriate" postings on job candidates' Facebook profiles on hiring decisions. Such postings included negative work-related attitudes, the use of profanity, and comments regarding alcohol abuse, use of drugs and sexual activities. Respondents indicated that all five types of information were relevant to such decisions and that they would be unlikely to pursue candidates who posted such information. However, such information was viewed as being more relevant for female candidates than male candidates. In addition, respondents were more likely to pursue male candidates than female candidates who posted such information. Thus, females were found to suffer the most. Although negative work-related attitudes and drug use were considered more relevant to hiring decisions than the other types of information, respondents were least likely to pursue candidates whose Facebook profiles contained comments regarding negative work-related attitudes and alcohol use. Implications and suggestions for future research are presented.

INTRODUCTION

Research has shown that communications on the Internet are less inhibited than public communications, that is, individuals will say or do things on the Internet that they would not ordinarily do in real life (Sproull & Kiesler, 1991; Kayany, 1998; Niemz, Griffiths, & Banyard, 2005). Countless examples of these uninhibited communications can be found on Facebook, one of the most popular social networking sites (Levy, 2007). For example, a recent study of 200 Facebook profiles found that 42% had comments regarding alcohol, 53% had photos involving alcohol use, 20% had comments regarding sexual activities, 25% had semi-nude or sexually provocative photos, and 50% included the use of profanity (Peluchette & Karl, 2007). These authors also examined wall comments, or "public" messages that individuals post on each others' profiles and found that about 50% involved issues of partying, 40% involved negative comments about other people, 25% involved derogatory comments about employers, 18% sexual activities, and 10% negative racial comments.

It has been suggested that these Facebook follies, or this reckless tendency to post anything and everything on one's profile, is in part due to students' perceptions that the likelihood of anyone other than other students or recent alumni seeing their posting is remote (Lupsa, 2006). Yet, recent evidence suggests that employers are looking. According to Taylor (2006), using Internet search engines such as Google, blogs (Web logs), and social networking Web sites (Facebook, MySpace) has become commonplace for screening potential job candidates. In support, a 2006 ExecuNet survey of 100 executive recruiters found that 77% use search engines as part of their recruitment process and that 35% have eliminated job candidates based on information they have found on the Internet (Jones, 2006). That is up from 26% reported in the 2005 survey (Forster, 2006). A study conducted at the University of Dayton revealed that 40% of employers would consider applicants' Facebook profiles as part of their hiring decision (Lupsa, 2006). Finally, a study by CareerBuilder.com revealed that 26% of the 1,150 hiring managers they surveyed said they used Internet search engines in their candidate screening process and 12% said they used social networking sites. Of those hiring managers that used social networking sites, 63%

said they did not hire the person based on what they found (Sullivan, 2006).

So, what kind of information are these hiring managers using to screen applicants? According to the aforementioned study by CareerBuilder.com (Sullivan, 2004), 19% said they eliminated candidates from further consideration because they had bad-mouthed their previous company or a fellow employee, 19% were eliminated because they had posted information about drinking or using drugs, and 11% were eliminated because they posted provocative or inappropriate photographs. The purpose of this study was to examine the relative impact of these Facebook follies on hiring decisions for male and female candidates. More specifically, we examine the following five types of information: (1) negative work-related attitudes, (2) comments regarding alcohol abuse, (3) comments regarding use of drugs, (4) comments regarding sexual activities, and (5) use of profanity.

Negative Work-related Attitudes

Based on the notion that it is much easier to train people to learn new skills than it is to change their inherent attitudes, many companies have adopted the "hire for attitude, train for skill" philosophy (O'Connor, 2000; Greengard & Byham, 2003). Perhaps the most well known example of this is Southwest Airlines who looks for people who can embrace change, keep promises, follow through, and bring a sense of humor and fun to their work (O'Connor, 2000). Empirical research also suggests that hiring managers consider attitude to be an important attribute in new recruits. For example, the results of a 1994 survey revealed that employers valued attitude more highly than ability when hiring an administrative employee (Flynn, 1994). Another survey of hiring managers conducted by the *New York Times* Job Market found that 85% considered personality to have great importance in hiring decisions (Milne, 2002). Other factors considered important were:

multi-tasking (84%), ability to learn new skills (84%), leadership (75%), and analytical ability (67%). In another study, practitioners rated the hirability of a series of hypothetical candidate profiles that varied on the Big Five personality traits and general mental ability (Dunn, Mount, Barrick, & Ones, 1995). Typically, managers viewed general mental ability and conscientiousness as the most important attributes related to an applicant's hirability. Conscientious individuals are generally hard working and reliable and possess traits including self-discipline, carefulness, thoroughness, and organization (Goldberg, 1990). Together, this research suggests that Facebook profile comments related to procrastination, dislike of work, or low self-discipline should be perceived negatively by hiring managers. Therefore, it is predicted:

H1: Hiring managers will consider Facebook comments indicating a negative work-related attitude to be relevant in making a hiring decision.
H2: Hiring managers will not continue to pursue candidates who have included comments on their Facebook profile indicating a negative work-related attitude.

Alcohol Abuse

It has been estimated that alcohol costs American businesses $134 billion in productivity losses, mostly due to missed work (Anderson & Goplerud, 2005). Alcohol abuse has also been associated with turnover, lower productivity and accidents (Kandel & Yamaguchi, 1987; Blum, Roman & Martin, 1993; Holcom, Lehman & Simpson, 1993). Moreover, workers with alcohol problems are almost three times more likely than workers without drinking problems to have injury-related absences (Webb, Hennrikus, Kelman, Gibberd, & Sanson-Fisher, 1994). Alcohol use on and off the job can also cause problems for nondrinking co-workers. One out of five employees report alcohol problems of people they work with cause them to fear injury, work harder, redo work or cover for the drinker (Mangione, Howland, & Lee, 1998).

Research also shows that even though alcoholism is a disease covered under the Americans with Disabilities Act, many Americans still have a bias against alcoholics in hiring decisions. For instance, a telephone survey of 1,500 adults across the U.S. found that if these respondents had to choose between two equally qualified job candidates—one a recovering alcoholic and one who has never needed treatment for alcoholism—47% would hire the candidate who never needed treatment, 34% said they had no preference, and only 14% would hire the recovering person (Survey reveals bias against recovering alcoholics and addicts, 1999). Given these findings, we predict that:

H3: Hiring managers will consider Facebook comments indicating alcohol abuse to be relevant in making a hiring decision.
H4: Hiring managers will not continue to pursue candidates if they find examples of alcohol abuse in the candidate's Facebook profile.

Use of Drugs

The U.S. Department of Labor estimates that substance abuse costs businesses more than 100 billion dollars every year (Ireland, 1991; Many good reasons, 2005). This is due to lost productivity, absenteeism, theft, accidents, and additional healthcare costs. Another report by the National Institute on Drug Abuse revealed that the typical drug-abusing worker uses three times the normal amount of sick benefits and is five times more likely than other employees to file a workers' compensation claim. He or she is involved in accidents 3.6 times more often, is late three times more often and has 2.5 times as many absences of eight days or more (Pouzer, 1991).

The aforementioned survey of 1,500 adults in the U.S. found that when responders were asked to choose between two job candidates—one a recovering drug addict and one who had never needed treatment—60% said they would hire the candidate who never needed treatment, 26% said they had no preference, and only 10% said they would hire the recovering addict (Survey reveals bias against recovering alcoholics and addicts, 1999). Another survey of several hundred human resource professionals revealed that many would not reject a candidate based on a conviction for marijuana possession if it had happened only once and occurred a long time ago. For example, some sample answers included "To me, a single marijuana conviction at age 18 would be in the same league as a speeding ticket," "Kids are kids," and "What someone did at age 18 is not necessarily a reflection of what he will do as an adult" (Fisher, 2002). Thus, we propose:

H5: Hiring managers will consider Facebook comments indicating illegal drug use to be relevant in making a hiring decision.
H6: Hiring managers will not continue to pursue candidates if they find examples of illegal drug use in the candidate's Facebook profile.

Profanity

In *Cursing in America*, Jay (1992) claims that cursing at inappropriate times can reduce a speaker's credibility, persuasiveness, and perceived professionalism. In support, Bostrom, Baseheart, and Rossiter (1973) examined reactions to people who swear and found that using profanity in a communication generally had a detrimental effect on the perceived credibility of the communicator. Another study conducted by Hamilton (1989) found that obscenity increased audience disgust with the message and negative perceptions of the source. Another study found that observers who heard a speaker who used profanity formed more negative impressions of the speaker than observers who heard a speaker who did not use

profanity (Cohen & Saine, 1977). Based on these findings, we predict:

H7: Hiring managers will consider Facebook comments including profanity to be relevant in making a hiring decision.
H8: Hiring managers will reject candidates from further consideration if they find examples of profanity in the candidate's Facebook profile.

Gender differences have also been found. In general, men use offensive language more than women (Foote & Woodward, 1973; Lakoff, 1973; Bailey & Timm, 1976; Staley, 1978; Rieber, Wiedemann, & D'Amato, 1979; Selnow, 1985; De Klerk, 1991; Jay, 1992; Bate & Bowker, 1997), women hold more negative attitudes toward the use of such language (Rieber et al., 1979; Selnow, 1985; Jay, 1992), and swearing is usually perceived as acceptable for men but inappropriate for women (Burgoon & Stewart, 1975; Mulac & Lundell, 1980; Burgoon, Dillard, & Doran, 1983; Mulac, Incontro, & James, 1985; De Klerk, 1991). Based on the reasoning that traditional female sex roles have discouraged the use of profanity, while norms associated with the male sex role often promote profanity in everyday speech, we predict that:

H9: Hiring managers will consider Facebook comments including profanity to be more relevant for female candidates than male candidates.
H10: Hiring managers will be less likely to pursue female candidates who use profanity than male candidates who use profanity.

Sexual Activity

Sexual behavior or conversations with sexual content are considered taboo in the workplace largely due to concerns about potential sexual harassment charges, office gossip, distraction, and lost productivity (Sills, 2007). Yet, office romance is on the rise, where more and more employees are seeking both dates and mates at work (Lever, Zellman, & Hirshfeld, 2006). Some surveys report that one in ten employees have actually admitted that they have "made love while at work" (Lever, Zellman, & Hirshfeld, 2006). Another concern for employers is online sexual activity (Cooper, Safir, & Rosenmann, 2006). For example, in a survey of 40,000 adults, 20% reported engaging in online sexual activity while at work (Cooper, Scherer, & Mathy, 2000). Workplace online sexual activity also results in lost productivity and could potentially result in sexual harassment claims if an employee were to see a coworker's computer screen with pornography or if he or she were to receive e-mails with sexual content (Stanton & Weiss, 2000). Thus, it is likely that if hiring managers were to find that an applicant has described his or her sexual activities on his or her Facebook profile, they would be concerned that this applicant may do the same in the workplace. Therefore, we predict:

H11: Hiring managers will consider Facebook comments describing one's sexual activities to be relevant in making a hiring decision.

H12: Hiring managers will not continue to pursue candidates if they find examples of sexual activities in the candidate's Facebook profile.

The term "double standard" is used to describe findings that show most people have less permissive attitudes toward female sexual behavior than male sexual behavior (Sprecher, McKinney, & Orbuch, 1987; Spears, Abrams, Sheeran, Abraham, & Marks, 1991). For example, the results of a meta-analysis suggest that men compared to women, have more permissive attitudes about sex; they are more accepting of premarital sex and less likely to feel guilty about it than women (Oliver & Hyde, 1993). They also found that women are more likely to endorse the double standard than

men. In their review of 30 studies published since 1980, Crawford and Popp (2003) also found evidence for the continued existence of sexual double standards. Evidence for double standards in the workplace has also been found. Anderson and Hunsaker (1985) found that women who are romantically involved with someone at work are more negatively evaluated regarding their competence and motivations than romantically involved men. Similarly, Devine and Markiewicz (1990) found that female managers who were involved in a workplace romance were expected to be more at risk of losing their jobs than their male partners. Other studies have shown gender-based double standards in the evaluation of the competence of men versus women, whereby women were held to higher standards than men or women were less likely to be rated as more competent than men even when having better credentials (Foschi, Lai, & Sigerson, 1994; Foschi, 1996). Given these findings, we predict that:

H13: Hiring managers will consider Facebook comments regarding sexual activities to be more relevant for female candidates than male candidates.

H14: Hiring managers will be less likely to pursue female candidates who discuss their sexual activities than male candidates who discuss their sexual activities.

Relative Impact of Type of Profile Information

As stated earlier, one purpose of this study was to examine the relative impact of five types of information (negative work-related attitudes, alcohol abuse, use of drugs, sexual activities, and use of profanity) on hiring decisions for male and female candidates. While the existing literature provides support for why hiring managers may find this type of information relevant in making hiring decisions, we could find no research to support why candidates with one type of information might be viewed more negatively than those with another type of information. Thus, we make no predictions regarding the relative impact of the five types of information.

METHOD

Sample

This study utilized a sample of 148 graduate students enrolled in human resource management and organizational behavior courses at two medium-sized universities, one located in the Midwest and the other located in the southeastern part of the United States. Participation was voluntary although participants were given some minimal course credit for doing so. All students in each class agreed to participate. About 42% of the respondents were male (N=62) and the mean age was 29.7 years. The average hours worked per week was 34.8, and the average number of years of work experience was 8.84.

Experimental Design

This study examined one within-subjects factor (type of Facebook information) and one between-subjects factor (gender of job candidate). Type of Facebook information consisted of five levels: (1) negative work-related attitudes, (2) alcohol abuse, (3) illegal drug use, (4) sexual activities, and (5) use of profanity. Gender of job candidate consisted of two levels: male versus female.

Survey Instrument

The survey instrument consisted of two sections: (1) demographic items including gender, age, hours worked per week, work experience; and (2) the five employee selection scenarios. Each of the five scenarios was followed by items measuring respondents' opinions regarding the relevance of Facebook information for hiring decisions, and their intent to pursue each candidate.

Employee Selection Scenarios. After completing the demographic information, respondents were given the following instructions. "Assume that you are a manager in charge of hiring an outside salesperson for your department. You have received several resumes and are currently in the process of screening out those who you feel do not meet the job requirements. The following five candidates are among those who applied for the position. They are all senior marketing majors at Midwestern University, with similar work experience and GPAs (ranging from 3.5 to 3.7). They are all females (or males, depending on the survey the respondent received) and are either 22 or 23 years old. To aid you in your decision making, the HR manager has provided you with information found on the students' Facebook profiles. Please read the information that follows and answer the questions at the end of each profile."

Following these instructions, each respondent read information about the five candidates from the following common Facebook profile categories: activities, interests, favorite quotes, about me, and groups. All of the information used in the profiles was taken from actual Facebook pages and was selected based on whether it fit one of the variables we examine in this study: alcohol use, drug use, profanity, sexual activity, and negative work-related attitudes. For example, the sexual activity profile for the female candidate included the following: "I'm a stripper on the weekends . . . college doesn't pay for itself ya know!!!" (activities), "Men are like tires you always need a spare!!" (favorite quotes), and "If homework were a hot guy I would do him every night" (groups). The profanity profile had the "F" word listed 450 times under favorite quotes and "People who love the F word" under groups. The negative work-related attitude profile included: "working at a job I hate, avoiding doing homework, being lazy" (activities), "I work at a Credit Union and I get paid to sit on my ass and stare at a computer screen all day!" (about me), and "I hate my job but need the money so I can't quit!!"

(groups). The drug use profile included: "Smoking, chillin, wasting time, wasting away" (activities), "PARTYING!!!! Smokin' the reefer, killing brain cells" (interests), "Legalize all drugs; Local pipe smokers union 420; Drinkers, smokers, & tokers" (groups). The alcohol profile included: "I really don't do much but drink beer and sit around" (activities); "Beer pong, drinking, partying, hanging out with friends" (interests); "Live it up and drink it down" and "A drunk man's words are a sober man's thoughts!!!" (favorite quotes); and "I need a drink," "Alcoholic anonymous droupouts," and "There is nothing absolute in life . . . except Vodka" (groups).

Relevance of Facebook information. Following each scenario, respondents were asked six items which measured their opinion regarding the relevance of Facebook information. Sample items include: "I believe the information above is useful," "The information above is irrelevant" (reverse scored), and "I don't believe the information above is indicative of this person's work behavior" (reverse scored). All items were rated on a five-point scale (*1=Strongly Disagree, 5=Strongly Agree*). Co-efficient alpha for this scale ranged between .75 and .85.

Intent to pursue candidate. Each scenario was also followed by three items which measured the respondent's intent to continue to pursue each job candidate. These items were as follows: "I would invite this candidate for an interview," "I would not pursue this candidate any further" (reverse scored), and "I would call the references listed on his/her resume." All items were rated on a five-point scale (*1=Strongly Disagree, 5=Strongly Agree*). Co-efficient alpha for this scale ranged between .86 and .88.

To prevent an order effect, the five scenarios contained in each survey were arranged in 12 different orders. The results of a mixed-model ANOVA with repeated measures revealed order did *not* have a significant effect on respondents' opinions regarding the relevance of the information [F (11, 133) = .93, *p* = .52] or their intent to pursue each candidate [F (11, 135) = .55, *p* = .86].

Table 1. Means and Standard deviations for the relevance of various types of Facebook information and intent to pursue the job candidate.

Facebook Profile Information	Relevance of Information						Intent to Pursue Job Candidate					
	Gender of Job Candidate				Total		Gender of Job Candidate				Total	
	Male		Female				Male		Female			
	Mean	SD	Mean	SD	Mean	SD	Mean	SD	Mean	SD	Mean	SD
Negative Work-related Attitude	3.45	1.02	3.78	0.89	3.59[b]	0.98	2.86	1.25	2.40	1.17	2.67[b]	1.23
Alcohol Abuse	3.27	0.95	3.67	0.97	3.44[a]	0.97	2.82	1.22	2.53	1.21	2.70[b]	1.22
Drug Use	3.46	1.01	3.73	0.95	3.57[b]	0.99	2.63	1.25	2.10	1.06	2.41[a]	1.20
Profanity	**3.31**	1.02	**3.64**	1.07	3.45[a]	1.05	**2.57**	1.25	**2.16**	1.08	2.40[a]	1.20
Sexual Activity	**3.14**	1.03	**3.81**	0.85	3.42[a]	1.01	2.62	1.28	2.24	1.07	2.46[a]	1.21
Estimated Marginal Mean	3.33		3.73				2.70		2.29			
Standard Error	.10		.11				.11		.13			

Note: Means with different superscripts are significantly different from one another at p < .05. Male and female means in boldface are significantly different from one another at p < .05.

RESULTS

Means and standard deviations for all five types of information by gender of job candidate are shown in Table 1. In general, respondents were in moderate agreement that all five types of information would be relevant in making hiring decisions (overall means ranged between 3.44 and 3.59) and they generally disagreed that they would continue to pursue the five job candidates (overall means ranged between 2.10 and 2.53). Thus, hypotheses one through eight and hypotheses 11 and 12 were supported.

To examine whether respondents held higher standards for women than they did men (i.e., a double standard), we conducted two ANOVAs with perceived relevance of the information as the dependent variable and two ANOVAs with intent to pursue the candidate as the dependent variable. As predicted in hypothesis 9 and 10, respondents perceived the information on profanity [$F (1, 147) = 4.05, p = .046$] and sexual activity [$F (1, 146) = 17.87, p = .000$] to be more relevant for female candidates than male candidates. Respondents were also less likely to pursue female candidates than male candidates who included profanity in their Facebook profile [$F (1, 147) = 4.54, p = .03$] or described their sexual activities, however, this difference was only marginally significant [$F (1,146) = 3.58, p = .06$]. Thus, hypothesis 13 was supported, but hypothesis 14 was only partially supported.

To examine the relative impact of the five types of information on respondents ratings of the relevance of the Facebook information, we conducted an ANOVA with repeated measures in which gender of the job candidate was entered as the between subjects variable and type of information was the within subjects variable. A significant main effect for both gender of the job candidate [$F (1, 143) = 7.22, p = .008$] and type of information [$F (4, 143) = 3.31, p = .011$] was found. The interaction between type of information and gender of the job candidate was only marginally

significant [$F (1, 143) = 3.77, p = .07$]. These results show that, in general, respondents were more likely to rate the information as being more relevant for female candidates than male candidates. To test for significant differences between means, we selected the pairwise comparison option in SPSS using the least significance difference test. These results show that Facebook profiles containing information related to sexual activities, alcohol use and profanity were considered less relevant than negative work-related attitudes or drug use.

To examine the relative impact of the five types of information on respondents' intent to pursue the five job candidates, we conducted another ANOVA with repeated measures in which gender of the job candidate was entered as the between subjects variable and type of information was the within subjects variable. A significant main effect for both gender of the job candidate [$F (1, 145) = 5.89, p = .016$] and type of information [$F (4, 145) = 6.11, p = .000$] was found. The interaction between gender and type of information was not significant [$F (4, 145) = .53, p = .71$]. In general, respondents were more likely to pursue male candidates than female candidates. Once again, to test for significant differences between means, we selected the pairwise comparison option in SPSS using the least significance difference test. These results show that respondents were least likely to pursue job candidates with Facebook profiles containing information related to sexual activities, drug use and profanity, and most likely to purse those who included comments regarding negative work-related attitudes and alcohol use.

Finally, we conducted some post hoc analyses to determine whether our male respondents rated the candidates any differently than our female respondents. Two additional ANOVAs with repeated measures were conducted in which gender of the job candidate and gender of the respondent were entered as the between subjects variables and type of information was the within subjects variable. When relevance of the information was entered as the dependent variable, we found a significant

Figure 1. Interaction between gender of job candidate and type of Facebook information on respondents ratings of information relevance

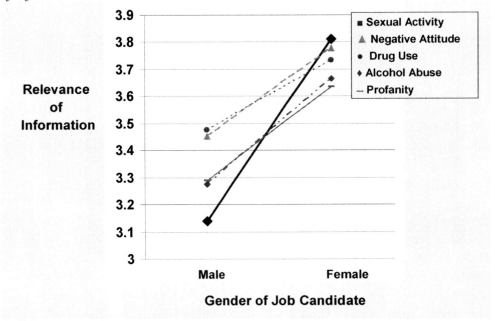

main effect for gender of the respondent [F (1, 141) = 5.89, p =.016], gender of the job candidate [F (1, 141) = 7.91, p =.016], and type of information [F (4, 141) = 3.20, p = .013]. The interaction between type of information and gender of the job candidate was also significant [F (4, 141) = 4.21, p = .002]. These results show that female respondents, compared to male respondents, gave higher ratings regarding the relevance of all Facebook profile information (the estimated marginal means were 3.68 and 3.32 respectively, the standard error for each was .11 and .10, respectively). The interaction between type of information and gender of the job candidate is shown in Figure 1. These results show that Facebook profile information regarding sexual activity is considered least relevant for male candidates but most relevant for female candidates. When intent to pursue the job candidate was entered as the dependent variable, we found a significant main effect for gender of the job candidate [F (1, 143) = 6.89, p =.01], and type of information [F (4, 143) = 5.91, p = .000]. The main effect for gender of respondent was only

marginally significant [F (1,143) = 2.77, p = .098] and there were no significant interactions.

DISCUSSION

In this study, we examined the impact of Facebook follies, or the posting of information regarding unacceptable work behaviors (i.e., negative work-related attitudes, alcohol abuse, drug use, profanity, and sexual activities) on respondents' hiring decisions for hypothetical job candidates. Our intent was to determine: who suffers the most from Facebook follies, men or women? We also wanted to determine whether one type of information was more detrimental to job candidates than another.

Our results showed that all five types of information are considered relevant by our respondents and they indicated they would be unlikely to pursue candidates who posted such information. We also found that women are more likely than men to suffer negative consequences from such profile content. Our respondents rated the Facebook information as being more relevant for female job candidates than male candidates and they were also more likely to pursue male candidates than female candidates who had posted such information. Regarding type of information, our results showed that negative work-related attitudes and drug use were considered more relevant to their decision than information related to sexual activities, alcohol use and profanity. However, our respondents indicated they would be less likely to pursue job candidates with Facebook profiles containing information related to sexual activities, drug use and profanity than candidates who posted comments regarding negative work-related attitudes and alcohol use. While our earlier research (Peluchette & Karl, 2007) found that men are more likely than women to post extreme or risqué information on their social network profiles, the results of this study suggest that women are more likely to suffer in the job market if they post such information.

Given the potentially negative consequences of social networking profile content, college and universities have a responsibility to be proactive in advising students as to the risks involved in how they create and use their profiles. In particular, students should be advised not to include information regarding inappropriate work-related behaviors such as drug use, alcohol use, profanity, sexual activities, or negative work-related attitudes. Such advice should also include the recommendation that students select privacy controls which will limit who can see their profile. Because many students participate in co-ops/internships during their college years, it is important that the risks associated with social networking activity and content be addressed in freshman orientation sessions and reinforced at various points during students' college careers. Fraternities and sororities should also be active in ensuring that their members are aware of the potentially harmful impact of such information. As social organizations, Greek life often has a reputation for excessive alcohol use which could have particularly negative consequences for females. Most importantly, career services centers on college campuses should be heavily involved in ensuring that students are aware of this issue as they prepare to transition into the workforce. In addition, faculty who teach courses focused on career preparedness should also address this as part of their curriculum.

While our study provided some valuable insight into the relationship between Facebook postings and hiring decisions, we recognize that there are limitations that provide opportunities for further research. One limitation is that this study utilized a convenience sample of graduate students some of which had little or no hiring experience. Thus, our results may not be representative of most managers who make hiring decisions. Future research should utilize a sample of hiring managers. Another limitation of this study is that we did not include a "normal" Facebook profile for comparison purposes. That, is we do not know whether respondents would be less likely to pursue job candidates who post information regarding drug use, alcohol use, sexual activity, profanity or negative work-related attitudes than someone who posted common socially acceptable and politically correct information (e.g., he or she likes sports, going to movies, hanging out with friends, shopping, etc.). A third limitation is that our hypothetical candidates' Facebook profiles were developed for maximum impact. That is, a very high quantity of information related to the variable of interest (e.g., profanity, drug use, etc.) was included in the job candidates' profiles. It is possible that a small amount of profanity, or one comment about one's sexual activities might not affect a hiring manager's intent to pursue a candidate. On the other hand, any mention of drug use may result in a candidate being rejected from further consideration. To address this limitation, future research should include profiles with both low and high levels of what we have referred to as Facebook follies.

While this study has provided useful findings regarding the impact of social networking profile content on the employment process, it is important that both the use and implications of social networking continue to receive research attention. Given the widespread popularity of this communication medium for young people, further research will allow insight into both the negative and positive implications of profile content and activity.

REFERENCES

Anderson, C., & Hunsaker, P. (1985). Why there's romancing at the office and why it's everyone's problem. *Personnel, 62,* 57-63.

Anderson, D., & Goplerud, E. (2005). Alcohol problems: Finding solutions to save lives and money. *Benefits & Compensation Digest, 42*(10), 34-39.

Bailey, L., & Timm, L. (1976). More on women's and men's expletives. *Anthropological Linguistics, 18,* 438-449.

Bate, B., & Bowker, J. (1997). *Communication and the sexes.* Prospect Heights, IL: Waveland.

Blum, T., Roman, P., & Martin, J. (1993). Alcohol consumption and work performance. *Journal of Studies on Alcohol, 54*(1), 61-70.

Bostrom, B., Baseheart, J., & Rossiter, C. (1973). The effects of three types of profane language in persuasive messages. *The Journal of Communication, 23*(4), 461-475.

Burgoon, M., Dillard, J., & Doran, N. (1983). Friendly or unfriendly persuasion. *Human Communication Research, 10,* 283-294.

Burgoon, M., & Stewart, D. (1975). Empirical investigations of language intensity: I. The effect of sex of source, receiver and language intensity on attitude change. *Human Communication Research, 1,* 244-248.

Cohen, M., & Saine, T. (1977). The role of profanity and sex variables in interpersonal impression formation. *Journal of Applied Communications Research, 5*(2), 45-51.

Cooper, A., Safir, M., & Rosenmann, A. (2006). Workplace worries: A preliminary look at online sexual activities at the office—emerging issues for clinicians and employers. *CyberPsychology & Behavior, 9*(1), 22-29.

Cooper, A., Scherer, C., & Mathy, R. (2000). Overcoming methodological concerns in the investigation of online sexual activities. *CyberPsychology & Behavior, 4*(4), 437-448.

Crawford, M., & Popp, D. (2003). Sexual double standards: A review and methodological critique of two decades of research. *Journal of Sex Research, 40*(1), 13-26.

De Klerk, V. (1991). Expletives: Men only?. *Communication Monographs, 58,* 156-169.

Devine, I., & Markiewicz, D. (1990). Cross-sex relationships at work and the impact of gender stereotypes. *Journal of Business Ethics, 9,* 333-338.

Dunn W., Mount, M., Barrick, M., & Ones, D. (1995). Relative importance of personality and general mental ability in managers' judgments of applicant qualifications. *Journal of Applied Psychology, 80*(4), 500-509.

Fisher, A. (2002). I got caught smoking pot. Who's going to hire me now?. *Fortune, 146*(5), 224.

Flynn, G. (1994). Attitude more valued than ability. *Personnel Journal, 73*(9), 16.

Foote, R., & Woodward, J. (1973). A preliminary investigation of obscene language. *Journal of Psychology, 83,* 263-275.

Forster, J. (2006) Job recruiters dig up dirt on candidates' Web pages. *Akron Beacon Journal,* May 1.

Foschi, M. (1996). Double standards in the evaluation of men and women. *Social Psychology Quarterly, 59*(3), 237-254.

Foschi, M., Lai, L., & Sigerson, K. (1994). Gender and double standards in the assessment of job candidates. *Social Psychology Quarterly, 57*(4), 326-339.

Goldberg, L. (1990). An alternative "description of personality": The Big-Five factor structure. *Journal of Personality and Social Psychology, 59,* 1216-1229.

Greengard, S., & Byham, B. (2003). Gimme attitude!. *Workforce, 82*(7), 56-59.

Hamilton, M. (1989). Reactions to obscene language. *Communication Research Reports, 6,* 67-69.

Holcum, M., Lehman, W., & Simpson, D. (1993). Employee accidents: Influences of personal characteristics, job characteristics, and substance use in jobs differing in accident potential. *Journal of Safety Research, 24,* 205-211.

Ireland, K. (1991). The $100 billion high. *Personnel Journal, 70*(2), 85.

Jay, T. (1992). *Cursing in America.* Philadelphia, PA: Benjamins.

Jones, K. (2006). 'Digital dirt' derailing job seekers. Retrieved August 26, 2007, from http://www.informationweek.com/story/showArticle.jhtml?articleID=190302836.

Kandel, D., & Yamaguchi, K. (1987). Job mobility and drug use: An event history analysis. *The American Journal of Sociology, 92*(4), 836-878.

Kayany, J. (1998). Contexts of uninhibited online behavior: Flaming in social newsgroups on Usenet. *Journal of the American Society for Information Science, 49*(12), 1135-1141.

Lakoff, R. (1973). Language and woman's place. *Language and Society, 2,* 45-80.

Lever, J., Zellman, G., & Hirschfeld, S. (2006). Office romance. *Across the Board, 42*(2), 32-41.

Levy, S. (2007). Are MySpace users now spacing out?. *Newsweek, 149*(22), 26.

Lupsa, C. (2006). Facebook: A campus fad becomes a campus fact. The social-networking Web site isn't growing like it once did, but only because almost every US student is already on it. *The Christian Science Monitor.* Retrieved July 2, 2007, from http://www.csmonitor.com/2006/1213/p13s01-legn.html.

Mangione, T., Howland, J., & Lee, M. (1998). *New perspectives for worksite alcohol strategies: Results from a corporate drinking study.* Boston, MA: JSI Research and Training Institute.

Many good reasons for providing a drug-free workplace. (2005). *Alcoholism & Drug Abuse Weekly, 17*(46), 5.

Milne, J. (2002). Hiring managers value personality, multi-tasking and the ability to learn. *Canadian Manager, 27*(1), 5.

Mulac, A., Incontro, C., & James, M. (1985). Comparison of the gender-linked language effect and sex-role stereotypes. *Journal of Personality and Social Psychology, 49,* 1098-1109.

Mulac, A., & Lundell, T. (1980). Differences in perceptions created by syntactic-semantic productions of male and female speakers. *Communication Monographs, 47,* 111-118.

Niemz, K., Griffiths, M., & Banyard, P. (2005). Prevalence of pathological Internet use among university students and correlations with self-esteem, the General Health Questionnaire (GHQ), and dis-inhibition. *CyberPsychology & Behavior, 8*(6), 562-570.

O'Connor, B. (2000). Make attitude your goal. *Works Management, 53*(2), 13.

Oliver, M., & Hyde, J. (1993). Gender differences in sexuality: A meta-analysis. *Psychological Bulletin, 114*(1), 29-51.

Peluchette, J., & Karl, K. (2007, October). *The prevalence of Facebook faux pas and students' "devil may care" attitudes.* Paper presented at the Midwest Academy of Management Meeting. Kansas City, MO.

Pouzar, E. (1991). Rehabilitating workers hooked on drugs. *Risk Management, 38*(3), 28-34.

Rieber, R., Wiedemann, C., & D'Amato, J. (1979). Obscenity: Its frequency and context of usage as compared in males, non-feminist females, and feminist females. *Journal of Psycholinguistic Research, 83,* 201-223.

Selnow, G. (1985). Sex differences in uses and perceptions of profanity. *Sex Roles, 12,* 303-312.

Sills, J. (2007). Love at work. *Psychology Today, 40*(2), 64-65.

Spears, R., Abrams, D., Sheeran, P., Abraham, C., & Marks, D. (1991). Social judgments of sex and blame in the context of AIDS: Gender and linguistic frame. *British Journal of Social Psychology, 30,* 37-48.

Sprecher, S., McKinney, K., & Orbuch, T. (1987). Has the double standard disappeared? An experimental test. *Social Psychology Quarterly, 50,* 24-31.

Sproull, L., & Kiesler, S. (1991). *Connections: New ways of working in the networked organization.* Cambridge, MA: The MIT Press.

Staley, C. (1978). Male-female use of expletives: A heck of a difference in expectations. *Anthropological Linguistics, 20,* 367-380.

Stanton, J., & Weiss, E. (2000). Electronic monitoring in their own words: An exploratory study of employee's experiences with new types of surveillance. *Computer in Human Behavior, 16,* 423-440.

Sullivan, S. (2006). One-in-four hiring managers have used Internet search engines to screen job candidates; One-in-ten have used social networking sites. *CareerBuilder.com Survey Finds.* Retrieved August 26, 2007, from http://www.careerbuilder.com/share/aboutus/pressreleasesdetail.aspx?id=pr331&ed=12%2F31%2F2006&sd=10%2F26%2F2006&cbRecursionCnt=1&cbsid=a5015667d80f4b599c46d2b08f406b67-241548812-RI-4&ns_siteid=ns_us_g_One%2din%2dFour_Hirin_.

Survey reveals bias against recovering alcoholics and addicts. (1999). *Alcoholism & Drug Abuse Weekly, 11*(48), 3.

Taylor, S. (2006). Seeking secrets in cyberspace. *Staffing Management, 2*(3).

Webb, G., Hennrikus, D., Kelman, G., Gibberd, R., & Sanson-Fisher, R. (1994). The relationships between high-risk and problem drinking and the occurrence of work injuries and related absences. *Journal of Studies on Alcohol, 55*(4), 434-446.

Chapter XII
Trust in Social Networking:
Definitions from a Global, Cultural Viewpoint

Max Kennedy
University of Kentucky, USA

Toru Sakaguchi
Northern Kentucky University, USA

ABSTRACT

This chapter attempts to understand the trust in social network services, where users post their personal information online to everyone with or without any specific relationships. Many definitions of trust were examined through a literature review in electronic commerce and virtual community areas, and it was found that most of them were based on a specific relationship, such as a buyer-seller relationship. However, one concept of trust—generalized trust, also known as dispositional trust—was found to best fit the situation of social networking. Generalized trust in social networking is further discussed from a cultural viewpoint. As an example, a Japanese SNS, Mixi, was analyzed in detail. Future research direction on trust in social networking is discussed as well.

INTRODUCTION

Trust has been conceptualized by previous research in a variety of ways ... and researchers have long acknowledged the confusion in the field. (Gefen, Karahanna, & Straub, 2003, p. 55)

There have been many studies done on the issues surrounding trust online. In a global environment, much of the recent research concerning trust has dealt with e-commerce and collaboration efforts occurring over the Internet (e.g., Ba & Pavlou, 2002; Dellarocas, 2003; Gefen et al.,

2003; Backhouse, Hsu, Tseng, & Baptista, 2005; Salam, Iyer, Palvia, & Singh, 2005; Chow & O, 2006). These studies tend to define trust in the context of reliability and the predictability of the business or person to perform as expected (Gefen et al., 2003). In these definitions, the object of trust is an interpersonal relationship with either a specific person or a specific business.

Social networking refers to a category of online applications, also known as social network services (SNSs), that help connect friends, business partners, or other individuals together (Alabaster, 2006). With the relatively recent rise in popularity of social network services, such as MySpace, which currently has over 100 million accounts, users of social networking are giving out personal information to the public at large with little, if any, expectation of the future performance or predictability of another person or business. Although users seem to trust something, the definitions of trust mentioned above do not seem to be applicable to SNSs.

This study will examine trust literature for the different types of trust mentioned and see whether the current studies are applicable for studying trust in social networking. Additionally, since what seems to be being trusted by someone who posts their own personal information online to a SNS is the public at large, this study will examine if there are some differences between cultures on how much and what type of information a person is willing to share in this type of situation.

This study is important because there is not enough research involving trust in social networking or research that takes into account cultural differences in social networking. With the rapid rise of SNSs, trust is of interest to: 1) users of such applications because they may want to know more about the issues of information disclosure to the public; 2) marketers who are preparing to mine SNSs for data, because they may want to know about cultural differences in the type and quality of the data they mine; 3) academic researchers

examining SNSs, because they may need a new perspective of trust.

BACKGROUND

Social Network Services

The term "social network" originates from Barnes' work in the 1950s in Sociology, and originally referred to an informal system of personal contacts that cut across organizational boundaries (Barnes, 1987). In recent times, the term is being used to refer to online applications that connect individuals with family members and friends. Using blogs, chat rooms, e-mail, or instant messaging, users of social network services (SNSs) can communicate, either within a limited community, or with the world at large (Alabaster, 2006). One of the most popular SNSs today, MySpace, had 2.4 million members in November 2004 and 26.7 million a year later (Kornblum, 2006). One and a half more years, as of May 2007, when this chapter was written, the number is 192 million (Wikipedia, 2007). This popularity, especially among teenagers, is also drawing the attention of parents and schools who are concerned about the nature of some of the pages on the site and the safety of young users who give too much information about themselves (Kornblum, 2006). MySpace prohibits users under 14, but kids sometimes lie about their ages. Still, they have probably learned a long list of important safety and privacy lessons already: buckle up; do not talk to strangers; hide your diary where your nosy brother cannot find it, and so forth, yet they have not probably learned another lesson: Do not post information about yourself online that you do not want the whole world to know (FTC, 2006).

There are certain degrees of trust involved in giving out information to the public, but as a review of the literature will show later in this study, the trust when applied to social networking is seemingly different from those types of trusts used for e-commerce and other traditional collaboration activities online. Like e-commerce sites, SNSs are a new phenomenon with limited bandwidth available for knowing or learning to trust the other party. However, unlike e-commerce sites, users of SNSs do not give out information to any specific entity, nor expect any future performance or predictability from a specific party in return. Since the core of SNSs is the fact that the contents of the sites are generated by the users, everybody in the network can view the user-generated contents; the user-generated content is the basis for the success of the sites like Wikipedia or YouTube (Brown, 2006). Therefore, it can be said that SNSs are broadcast networks broadcasting the information to the "perceived" members of the network, but unlike the broadcast medium of old, everyone can be broadcasters of the information and unlike Web pages of old, all the broadcasters are "perceivably" linked together in a network of users. Problems occur when those perceived network of close friends include agents who have less-than-friendly intentions (FTC, 2006). Knowing such, why do users of SNSs trust other users and broadcast their personal information?

Trust Online

Trust has been studied as a central aspect of e-commerce and other transactions online. There are many definitions of trust and expectations of trust available (Gefen et al., 2003). Gefen et al. (2003) have analyzed the various types of trust in creating their model for trust and TAM in online shopping. They consider that trust may be: at the heart of all relationships, or the defining attribute of relationships; a reducer of risk and social uncertainty; based on familiarity; raised by seals of approval and affiliations; and crucial in many economic activities that may have undesirable outcomes in which one party can take advantage of another party. They also provide a summary of the various types of trust studied dating from 1971 to 2002 in their article (Gefen et al., 2003).

There are many new studies of trust in e-commerce since their work (e.g., Gefen & Straub, 2003; Pavlou, 2003; Chow & O, 2006). The summary of these studies (in progress) are presented according to Gefen et al.'s (2003) categories in Appendix, Table 1. Besides e-shopping, other online issues related to trust have been studied including reputation and online buying on auction sites, word-of-mouth buying networks and feedback, privacy statements and expectations, certification services and many other things, tending to show a uniqueness of the online environment for such studies (Ba & Pavlou, 2002; Dellarocas, 2003; Salam, Iyer, Palvia, & Singh, 2005; Backhouse, Hsu, Tseng, & Baptista, 2005; Chow & O, 2006). The issue of limited bandwidth through which information can be known between the seller and the buyer and the newness of the phenomenon are often mentioned as the reasons for the interest in studying trust in e-commerce (Ba & Pavlou, 2002).

Paul and McDaniel (2004) consider how trust reduces complexity in a complex world and enable parties to collaborate on virtual collaboration teams. They consider trust as enabling complexity reduction, as aiding collaboration, and determining the effectiveness of relationships, reducing transaction costs, and facilitating learning and innovation. They further mention that trust is part of directing people that you do not see. These things come closer to the type of trust that is involved in posting on a SNS online, as they involve people you do not see.

The rest of their study focuses on interpersonal trust. Interpersonal trust includes: calculative trust, based on forming ideas about trust in an economic relationship; competence trust, whether the other party is capable of performing as said; relational trust, also called benevolence trust, or how much one party feels the other intends to do good regardless of economic incentive; and integrated trust, which is all of these forms of trust integrated and mixed together in various ways depending on the circumstance.

TRUST IN A VIRTUAL COMMUNITY

Another field of study, which deals with trust, is "virtual community." A virtual community is a group of people that primarily or initially communicates or interacts via the Internet. In a sense, a virtual community is a larger, generalized concept of social network services, which includes Usenet, IRC, chat rooms, and electronic mailing lists, among other things. A few recent studies on trust in virtual communities are summarized in Table 2 using the same format.

Some of the literature about virtual communities is still about buyer-seller relationships (Shubert & Ginsburg, 2000; Castelfranchi & Tan, 2002), since that is what businesses care about the most. "Leisure-Time Communities" like SNSs may not be as interesting yet for business researchers as "Virtual Communities of Transactions" (Shubert & Ginsburg, 2000) currently are. However, Leismeister, Ebner, and Krcmar (2005) suggest that the term "trust" can be classified into three types: interpersonal, system, and dispositional. Interpersonal trust is a type of trust in a specific person or organization on a personal level. System trust is not based on the trustee (the other party) but on the perceived property or reliance on a system or institution, such as a monetary system. Dispositional trust is the general attitude of a person seeking trustworthiness toward others. Radin (2006) refers to this generalized trust in people as "thin trust," and Mutz (2005) as "social trust." According to McKnight et al. (1998; cited in Leismeister et al., 2005), this type of trust has two assumptions: one presumes that others are normally trustworthy; and trusting others leads to better outcomes regardless of whether the others are really good or bad.

We will now examine the definitions of trust commonly used in these studies, and how these definitions may relate to that of the trust inherent in SNS actions such as posting personal information to the virtual community or sometimes literally to the world.

DISCUSSION

Definition of Trust in SNSs

There are many varied definitions of trust. Most of these definitions are based on a relationship that is implied in the trust. In the case of SNSs, users post personal information presumably to the members of the community, yet in most cases it is actually broadcast to everyone: friend and foe; neighbor and stranger; known and unknown. Therefore, the definition of trust dealing with a specific relationship, such as a buyer-seller relationship, is hard to use to explain the trust the users of SNSs have toward the group of people who visit their sites and read their postings. However, there are some studies dealing with more generalized trust.

Uslaner (2004) distinguishes between two categories of trust: a strategic trust based on our experience with people doing specific things, and a generalized trust that he further sub-defines as moralistic trust. The first type of trust, strategic trust, is widely found in business/economic literature since it occurs in buying and selling relationships. The second type of trust, generalized trust is also found in the literature (e.g., dispositional trust in McKnight et al. (2004a) and Leimeister et al. (2005); and thin trust in Radin (2006); and social trust in Mutz (2005)). Uslaner's (2004) moralistic definition of trust revolves around an optimistic viewpoint. According to him, "A handful of bad experiences should not withdraw us from social connections" (p. 29). In Uslaner's viewpoint, the future of the Internet may require faith in humanity, a moralistic trust. In general, Uslaner's view can be subsumed under generalized trust definitions.

The sources of trust Ba and Pavlou (2002) mention, that is, familiarity, calculativeness of costs and benefits, and values, and the types of trust, that is, benevolence and credibility, generally apply better to trust toward specific parties rather than toward the general public. Calculativeness, that is, the calculation of risk of revealing some information versus the chance of gaining other information or acquaintanceship, could explain some sources of trust on a SNS. For some users, a SNS is a place they may gain something. Carter (2005) reported at least two-thirds of the users of Cybercity she interviewed said meeting friends or creating new friends was their most important reason for joining the community. Those users may have provided their personal information to attract new people of interest to them, weighing the risks and benefits of doing so.

Paul and McDaniel's (2004) view of trust as a reducer of complexity and enabler of collaboration on virtual collaboration teams may be another aspect of trust in SNSs. Since it is almost impossible to examine all the participants of a given social network, users cannot help but trust them. According to Gefen et al. (2003), trust is the expectation that others will not behave opportunistically and take advantage of the situation, that they will be dependable, behave appropriately, and fulfill commitments, even in cases when they are dependent and vulnerable. According to Gefen et al. (2003):

(Trust is) a deep seated human need to understand the social surroundings... that people are by their nature free agents and as such their behavior is not necessarily rational or predictable... When a social environment cannot be regulated through rules and customs, people adopt trust as a central social complexity reduction strategy... By trusting, people reduce their perceived social complexity through a belief that may be irrational, but rules out needing to analyze future behaviors. (p. 55)

If trust is used to reduce uncertainty in action, the degree people try to reduce uncertainty is different from culture to culture.

Cultural Differences

There are cultural differences in how people interact with one another. Hofstede (1980; 1991; 1994) suggested that five dimensions of culture

were useful to measure differences between cultures: power distance, uncertainty avoidance, individualism (vs. collectivism), masculinity (vs. femininity), and long-term (vs. short-term) orientation.

According to Hofstede (1994), the effect of uncertainty avoidance, a desire for predictability, can affect trust, and suggests the possibility of research in how information is shared online between cultures. This has direct bearing on the nature of global communications and systems. With the growth of new technologies such as social networking or collaboration tools, the importance of global cultural differences may become more prominent. The following example illustrates the effect of difference in "uncertainty avoidance" on the design of SNSs.

Japan is rated as a country with a very high uncertainty-avoidance score (see Table 3) compared to the U.S. and other Anglo-nations (Hofstede, 1991). *Mixi*, the most popular SNS in Japan with over 10 million user accounts (as of August 5, 2007), is such an example to show the difference in culture between Japan and the U.S.

Case Study of Mixi

Mixi was launched in February 2004 (Cashmore, 2006). *Mixi* (the company name was e-Mercury then) was publishing Internet content on *Find-Job*, which provided recruiting information. One day, an international student-worker suggested Mr. Kasahara, then president of *e-Mercury*, use a SNS. He was using U.S.-based *Friendster* to contact other international students and exchange information. Mr. Kasahara tried *Friendster* and thought that it had the potential to be introduced in Japan. On the other hand, he also thought the *Friendster's* concept of "connecting unknown people for a career advantage," which is probably more typical in the U.S., might not be accepted well in the Japanese culture. He studied many existing SNSs and tried to evolve a new form of SNS in Japan (Sasaki, 2007).

At that time, there were already some SNSs in Japan, such as *Orcut* (Google) and *Gree* (Rakuten). While these SNSs were more business-oriented and geared toward extending business acquaintances, *Mixi* set its strategic position in the opposite direction. As there was a cultural background in which teenagers in Japan valued being connected with "known" friends through mails on portable phones (it is actually text messaging in the U.S., but that is what it is called there), *Mixi* tried to be an infrastructure by which they can connect with those friends easily. As a result, *Mixi* did not aim at "openness" in which users will develop new acquaintances, but its main focus is on a service by which a user will write a diary and his or her friends will put in a comment (Sasaki, 2007). To assure this "closed" characteristic, *Mixi* offers some distinct features when compared to most of the SNSs found in the U.S., like MySpace.

For example, the contents of the sites constructed by users, including the personal information posted by users, are visible only to members of *Mixi*. In a sense, the broadcasted information on *Mixi* is limited to the closed community. Also, the membership to *Mixi* is limited by invitation from the members. This limits the possibility of malicious users from participating in the community. Another distinctive feature is the fact that users can see who visited their pages. Even if you are searching for some information and stumble upon somebody's diary, you leave a footprint in his/her log. The owner of the diary will see who visited the site and find your name on it, and will trace it back to your pages and check to see if you are somebody he/she knows, or are just a visitor. If he/she thinks you are a malicious user, he/she can block your access to their diaries and other pages (Cashmore, 2006; Schellong, 2006). All these features give users a greater sense of security, and therefore, less "uncertainty." There are some SNSs, such as *Oskut*, which are in the U.S. and also "invite-only;" but by far, there are more SNSs for open access in the U.S. Cahsmore

(2006) thinks that the *Mixi* format will not succeed in the U.S.

It is not certain, however, if this is only related to Hofstede's "uncertainty-avoidance" dimension, or if it has something to do with the "individualism-collectivism" dimension. Japan is a collectivistic culture, as opposed to an individualistic culture like the U.S. (see Table 3). In a collectivistic culture, "we," as meaning the insiders of a group the person belongs to, means that they are all trustworthy, and "they," the outsiders, are not. In an individualistic culture, "I," including close family members and a few best friends, are the only ones you trust (Hofstede, 1991). People may be friendly to others, but they are not trusted. Therefore, for those from individualistic cultures, the disclosure of information on MySpace is surprisingly open. On the other hand, for a collectivistic culture, even though the level of personal information on *Mixi* could be more open than MySpace, *Mixi* user's openness of the information does not get as much attention because it is open to "us."

One example that shows *Mixi*'s success because of its cultural orientation is the fact that younger people started using *Mixi* more than *2-Channel*, the once top young online community. A study by Web Advertising Bureau of Japan, Advertising Association Inc., revealed that the users of *2-Channel* were getting older, with about 53% of users over 30 years old. On the other hand, 62% of *Mixi*'s users are in their 20s (Sasaki, 2007). *2-Channel* is a bulletin-board type site where people talk anonymously. The anonymity gives the users freedom of speech; therefore, the discussion often becomes harsh, sometimes to the extent of a flame war. On the other hand, *Mixi* is more closed and you know who made the comments. Naturally, the comments become warm and cozy. Also, if the user limits the level of accessibility only to direct friends (*My Mixi*, or *Maimiku* in Japanese), he/she can write on very sensitive matters and get some advice from friends. This comfortableness of being there is one of the reasons *Mixi* became the fastest growing SNS in Japan.

As stated in the review of literature, at the root of social networking is a type of general trust toward the group as a whole, and people use trust to reduce complexity and uncertainty and to enable collaboration and communication. This is belief in the nature of the culture, and is reflected in the views that a person has of the society at large. This should vary from culture to culture, and according to Hofstede (1994), is reflected in the culture's dimensions of uncertainty avoidance and possibly individualism-collectivism. Consequently, what people are willing to post online may vary from culture to culture. The *Mixi* example has illustrated the difference between Japanese culture, in which SNSs such as *Mixi* try to accommodate the desire to connect to "known" people, and U.S. culture, in which SNSs are geared toward connecting unknown people for a career advantage. The issues arise in the U.S. as individual information is open to the "not trusted" public, whereas in Japan, the information is provided only in a "closed" community. In either case, the definition of trust discussed in this chapter applies to the SNSs. Knowing the success of the Japanese SNSs will lead to future development, especially with the issues raised in the U.S.

FUTURE TRENDS

There are some problems current with the rise of social networking. For users, there is the problem of not being aware of all the information they may be giving away. This problem is more typical in the U.S. compared to Japan. Because the community is "closed" to known friends in Japanese SNSs, such as *Mixi*, users do not need to reveal their real names. *Mixi* encouraged users to use their real names at first. However, it has toned down its policy since an incident when it was found that an actress who admitted past illegal

activities was using *Mixi* with her real name, and her pages were flooded with harsh comments from other users (Harada, 2007). Still, some users are posting individual information without caution. Some ways to educate users to be aware of the dangers of revealing such information should be sought. In the case of U.S. SNSs, such as MySpace, the problem is more complex. As the main objectives of using SNSs are to make new friends, expand business contacts, and so forth, it is inevitable that some individual information to gain trust from other people is revealed. Some features used in Japanese SNSs may be applicable to the U.S. despite some previous thought that it might not be popular in the U.S. due to the cultural differences. For example, the "footprint" function by which the users are notified who visited their sites and in case of a malicious visitor, they are given an option of blocking the user from visiting and/or reading their blogs or diaries. An "invitation-only" function could be another possibility to limit the opportunity for malicious users to get into the community. Although it is not perfect, if combined with other methods, these features could enhance the security (Harada, 2007).

As for future research, opportunities in social networking and people's perception of trust will emerge. Such issues include:

- How much information is actually and accurately being given away/collected?
- To what extent do people trust the public and/or a specific party that requires them to give data?
- What benefits do people perceive to gain from giving away individual information?
- How aware are users of data being collected; what factors (e.g., ignorance/knowledge in cyber crimes) affect the behaviors of the users?
- What cultural differences exist in the act/behavior/attitude/perception of users?
- What effect do the reassurances from the service providers (i.e., it is not really open,

you are among friends only, etc.) have on what people post?

- What role does the advance in technology play in all this?

CONCLUSION

This chapter examined the trust in SNSs where users post personal information to everyone with or without specific relationships. Many definitions of trust were reviewed and it was found that most of them were based on a specific relationship such as a buyer-seller relationship. One concept of trust, generalized or dispositional trust, may be the best to fit the online situation. Also, from a global, cultural viewpoint, Hofstede's (1980; 1991; 1994) uncertainty-avoidance and individualism dimensions were illustrated as related to the behavior and trust given to the public at large by the users of the SNSs.

Social networking is growing at a phenomenal rate, adding new features and users along the way. This phenomenon gives tremendous new opportunities for academicians and practitioners. For example, marketers will seek new ways to mine this enormous pile of data for their own use. Yet, with people growing aware of these activities, less information may be available as they try to hide their activities. Techniques to preserve privacy and gain information will increase as both parties seek to achieve their purpose. In the end, the general global perception of what should be revealed and available online may be standardized. For example, witness the effect of spam on handing out e-mail addresses online.

REFERENCES

Alabaster, J. (2006, November 7). News Corp taking MySpace to Japan. *Smartmoney.com.* Retrieved January 31, 2007, from http://www. smartmoney.com/bn/ON/index.cfm?story=ON-20061107-000427-0906.

Anderson, D. (2005). What trust is in these times? Examining the foundation of online trust. *Emory Law Journal, 54*(3), 1441-1474.

Ba, S., & Pavlou, P. (2002). Evidence of the effect of trust building technology in electronic markets: Price premiums and buyer behavior. *MIS Quarterly, 26*(3), 243-268.

Backhouse, J., Hsu, C., Tseng, J., & Baptista, J. (2005). A question of trust. *Communications of the ACM, 48*(9), 87-91.

Barnes, J. (1987). Letter: This week's citation classic. *Current Contents, 1*(23), 18.

Brown, M. (2006, June 2). Social networking. *desitinationKM.com, viewpoints.* Retrieved November 11, 2006, from http://www.destinationkm.com/articles/default.asp?ArticleID=1171.

Carter, D. (2005). Living in virtual communities: An ethnography of human relationships in cyberspace. *Information, Communication and Society, 8*(2), 148-167.

Cashmore, P. (2006, July 8). Mixi, Japan's biggest social network. *Mashable!* Retrieved November 13, 2006, from http://mashable.com/2006/07/08/*Mixi*-japans-biggest-social-network/.

Casteifranchi, C., & Tan, Y. (2002). The role of trust and deception in virtual societies. *International Journal of Electronic Commerce, 6*(3), 55-70.

Cazier, J., Shao, B., & St. Louis, R. (2006). E-business differentiation through value-based trust. *Information & Management, 43*(6), 718-727.

Chow, W., & Angie N. (2006). A study of trust in e-shopping before and after first-hand experience is gained. *The Journal of Computer Information Systems, 46*(4), 125-130.

Dellarocas, C. (2003). The digitization of word of mouth: Promise and challenges of online feedback mechanisms. *Management Science, 49*(10), 1407-1424.

Everard, A., & Galletta, D. (2006). How presentation flaws affect perceived site quality, trust, and intention to purchase from an online store. *Journal of Management Information Systems, 22*(3), 56-95.

Federal Trade Commission (FTC). (2006, May). Social networking sites: Safety tips for tweens and teens. Retrieved November 11, 2006, from http://www.ftc.gov/bcp/edu/pubs/consumer/tech/tec14.htm.

Flavián, C., Guinalíu, M., & Gurrea, R. (2006). The role played by perceived usability, satisfaction and consumer trust on Web site loyalty. *Information & Management, 43*(1), 1-14.

Gefen, D., Rose, G., Warkentin, M., & Pavlou, P. (2005). Cultural diversity and trust in IT adoption: A comparison of potential e-voters in the USA and South Africa. *Journal of Global Information Management, 13*(1), 54-78.

Gefen, D., Karahanna, E., & Straub, D. (2003). Trust and TAM in online shopping: An integrated model. *MIS Quarterly, 27*(1), 51-90.

Geng, X., Whinston, A., & Zhang, H. (2004). Health of electronic communities: An evolutionary game approach. *Journal of Management Information Systems, 21*(3), 83-110.

Harada, K. (2007). Social networking of the world is rich and colorful (in Japanese). In: Shoeisha (Ed.), *A study of SNS*, (pp. 46-69). Tokyo, Japan: Shoeisha, Co. Ltd.

Ho, T., & Weigelt, K. (2005). Trust building among strangers. *Management Science, 51*(4), 519-530.

Hoffman, L., Lawson-Jenkins, K., & Blum, J. (2006). Trust beyond security: An expanded trust model. *Communications of the ACM, 49*(7), 94-101.

Hofstede, G. (1980). *Culture's consequences: International differences in work-related values.* Beverly Hills, CA: Sage Publications.

Hofstede, G. (1991). *Cultures and organizations: Software of the mind.* London: McGraw-Hill.

Hofstede, G. (1994). Management scientists are human. *Management Science, 40*(1), 4-13.

Huang, J., & Fox, M. (2006). An ontology of trust: Formal semantics and transitivity. *Proceedings of the 8th international conference on Electronic commerce: The new e-commerce: Innovations for conquering current barriers, obstacles and limitations to conducting successful business on the internet,* (pp. 259-270).

Jøsang, A., Keser, C., & Dimitrakos, T. (2005). Can we manage trust. *Proceedings of the 3rd International Conference on Trust Management (iTrust), 2477,* (pp. 93-107).

Jøsang, A., Ismail, R., & Boyd, C. (2007). A survey of trust and reputation systems for online service provision. *Decision Support Systems, 43*(2), 618-644.

Keat, T., & Mohan, A. (2004). Integration of TAM-based electronic commerce models for trust. *Journal of American Academy of Business, Cambridge, 5*(1-2), 404-410.

Kornblum, J. (2006, January 8). Adults question MySpace's safety. *USAToday, Tech.* Retrieved November 11, 2006, from http://www.usatoday.com/tech/news/2006-01-08-myspace-sidebar_x.htm.

Leimeister, J., Ebner, W., & Krcmar, H. (2005). Design, implementation, and evaluation of trust-supporting components in virtual communities for patients. *Journal of Management Information Systems, 21*(4), 101-131.

Lim, K., Sia, C., Lee, M., & Benbasat, I. (2006). Do I trust you online, and if so, will I buy? An empirical study of two trust-building strategies.

Journal of Management Information Systems, 23(2), 233-266.

Mainelli, M. (2003). Risk/reward in virtual financial communities. *Information Services and Use, 23*(1), 9-17.

McKnight, D., & Choudhury, V. (2006). Distrust and trust in B2C e-commerce: Do they differ?. *Proceedings of the 8ᵗʰ international conference on Electronic commerce: The new e-commerce: innovations for conquering current barriers, obstacles and limitations to conducting successful business on the internet,* (pp. 482-491).

McKnight, D., Kacmar, C., & Choudhury, V. (2004a). Dispositional trust and distrust distinctions in predicting high- and low-risk Internet expert advice site perceptions. *E-Service Journal, 3*(2), 85-109.

McKnight, D., Kacmar, C., & Choudhury, V. (2004b). Shifting factors and the ineffectiveness of third party assurance seals: A two-stage model of initial trust in a Web business. *Electronic Markets, 14*(3), 252-266.

Metzger, M. (2006). Effects of site, vendor, and consumer characteristics on Web site trust and disclosure. *Communication Research, 33*(3), 155-179.

Mutz, D. (2005). Social trust and e-commerce experimental evidence for the effects of social trust on individuals' economic behavior. *Public Opinion Quarterly, 69*(3), 393-416.

Patnasingam, P., Gefen, D., & Pavlou, P. (2005). The role of facilitating conditions and institutional trust in electronic marketplaces. *Journal of Electronic Commerce in Organizations, 3*(3), 69-82.

Paul, D., & McDaniel, R. (2004). A field study of the effect of interpersonal trust on virtual collaborative relationship performance. *MIS Quarterly, 28*(2), 183-227.

Pavlou, P., & Dimoka, A. (2006). The nature and role of feedback text comments in online marketplaces: Implications for trust building, price premiums, and seller differentiation. *Information Systems Research, 17*(4), 392-414.

Pavlou, P., & Gefen, D. (2004). Building effective online marketplaces with institution-based trust. *Information Systems Research, 15*(1), 37-59.

Radin, P. (2006). "To me, it's my life": Medical communication, trust, and activism in cyberspace. *Social Science & Medicine, 62*(3), 591-601.

Ratnasingam, P. (2005). E-commerce relationships: The impact of trust on relationship continuity. *International Journal of Commerce and Management, 15*(1), 1-17.

Ridings, C., Gefen, D., & Arinze, B. (2002). Some antecedents and effects of trust in virtual communities. *Journal of Strategic Information Systems, 11*(3-4), 271-295.

Salam, A., Iyer, L., Palvia, P., & Singh, R. (2005). Trust in e-commerce. *Communications of the ACM, 48(2),* 72-77.

Sasaki, T. (2007). Social networking changes the relationship between the net and the teal (in Japanese). In: Shoeisha (Ed.), *A study of SNS,* (pp. 6-41). Tokyo, Japan: Shoeisha, Co. Ltd.

Schellong, A. (2006, October 12). Social networking services and disaster management in Japan. *Complexity and Social Networks Blog of the Institute for Quantitative Social Science and the Program on Networked Governance, Harvard University.* Retrieved November 13, 2006, from http://www.iq.harvard.edu/blog/netgov/networked_governance/.

Schubert, P., & Ginsburg, M. (2000). Virtual communities of transaction: The role of personalization in electronic commerce. *Electronic Markets, 10*(1), 45-55.

Stewart, K. (2006). How hypertext links influence consumer perceptions to build and degrade trust online. *Journal of Management Information Systems, 23*(1), 183-210.

Uslaner, E. (2004). Trust online, trust off-line. *Communications of the ACM, 47*(4), 28-29.

Wikipedia. (2007). Social network service. Retrieved July 11, 2007, from http://en.wikipedia.org/wiki/Social_network_service.

APPENDIX

Table 1. Newer conceptualization of trust

Study	Trust Conceptualization	Trust Object	Measures
Anderson (2005)	Transactional Trust: A unilateral trust in the system governing the transaction, not the other party (bilateral trust). Similar to trusted computing initiatives.	System governing transaction	Conceptual
Caziera, Shaob, and St. Louis (2006)	Willingness to be vulnerable and characteristic-based trust	Buyer-seller relationship. E-business differentiation through trust	Adopted from Zucker et al. (1986)
Chow and O (2006)	Ability, benevolence, and integrity	Buyer-seller relationship before and after first-hand experience of e-shopping	Adopted from Jarvenpaa et al. (1998)
Everard and Galletta (2006)	How presentation flaws affect perceived site quality, trust, and intention to purchase from an online store	Buyer-seller relationship on Web site	Adopted from McKnight et al.(1998)
Flavián, Guinalíu, and Gurrea (2006)	Construct of honesty, benevolence and competence	Buyer-seller relationship on Web site	Perceived Web site honesty, benevolence and competence
Gefen and Straub (2003)	Willingness to depend Display honesty and willingly fulfill its commitments	Buyer-seller relationship in e-services	Adopted from Gefen (2000)
Gefen, Rose, Warkentin, and Pavlou (2005)	Trust in adoption of new IT system (eVoting)	Trust in seller/administra-tor of e-voting system, cultural diversity	Adopted from Gefen et al. (2003)
Geng, Whinston, and Zhang (2004)	The sustained competitive advantages of honest members over cheaters throughout the evolution of a community.	E-communities (trust-health in whole community)	Mathematical model: Trust is a function of punishment and time
Hung and Fox (2006)	Expectancy, belief in expectancy, and willingness to be vulnerable	Trust in transitiveness from a social network	Adopted from Mayer et al. (1995)
Ho and Weigelt (2005)	Personal relationships, embeddedness	Trust building game (trust creation between strangers—i.e., anonymous eBay relations with specific others	Adopted from Granovetter et al. (1985)
Jøsang, Keser, and Dimitrakos (2005)	"Reliability trust and decision trust"	Directional relationship between trustor and trustee in trust management	Reliability trust: Adopted from Gambetta et al. (1998; 1990); Decision-trust: McKnight et al. (1996; 1998)
Jøsanga, Ismailb, and Boydb (2006)	"Reliability trust and decision trust"	Buyer-seller relationship and reputations online	Reliability trust: Adopted from Gambetta et al. (1998; 1990); Decision trust: McKnight et al. (1996; 1998)
Stewart (2006)	Trusting beliefs (similar to portal affiliation, with both sides of link examined)	Relationship between hyperlinks/Web sites as viewed by user (p. 3)	Adopted from McKnight et al.(1998)
Keat, and Mohan (2004)	Degree to which person perceives trust	E-commerce: perception that technology is trustworthy; and disposition to trust other party.	Conceptual model development

continued on following page

Table 1. continued

Study	Trust Conceptualization	Trust Object	Measures
Kim, Xu, and Koh (2004)	Trust: other party will behave in a dependable manner	Buyer-seller relationship.	McKnight et al. (1998)
Lim, Sia, Lee, and Benbasat (2006)	Cognitive-based trust	Buyer-seller relationship online	Adopted from Mayer et al.(1995) McKnight et al.(1998) Jarvenpaa et al. (2000)
McKnight, Kacmar, and Choudhury (2004a)	Dispositional trust: tendency to believe in the positive attributes of others in general Alt: willing to depend or become vulnerable to general other people	General others (advice giving Web sites in this case) as opposed to specific others in interpersonal trust.	Operationalized as 1. Faith in humanity-general 2. Faith in humanity-professionals 3.Trusting stance
Mcknight, Kacmar, and Choudhury (2004b)	Dispositional trust (propensity to trust)	A specific Web business.	Adopted from McKnight et al. (2002)
McKnight and Choudhury (2006)	Trusting beliefs and trusting intention	Buyer-seller Relationship	Adopted from Mayer et al. (1995), McKnight (1998)
Metzger (2006)	Trust: the expectation that an exchange partner will not engage in opportunistic behavior	Relationships between buyer/seller.	Adopted from Jarvenpaa et al. (2000)
Mutz (2005)	Social trust: generalized trust in people	Buyer-seller economic behavior	Social trust is manipulated in experimental design and manipulation check questionnaire
Paul and McDaniel (2004)	Interpersonal trust, including: calculative trust, competence trust, relational trust, and integrated trust	Virtual collaborative relationship	Comparative case studies: Trust was operationalized as self-interest, ability, empathy, and integrated interpersonal trust
Pavlou (2003)	The belief that the other party will behave in a socially responsible manner, and , by so doing, will fulfill the trusting party's expectations without taking advantage of its vulnerabilities	Traditional (in a specific party), and in integrity of transaction medium (infrastructure)	Adopted from Jarvenpaa et al. (1999)
Pavlou, and Dimoka (2006)	Benevolence (goodwill trust) and credibility	Buyer-seller relationship in online marketplaces	Adopted from Doney et al. (1997)
Ratnasingam (2005)	Technology trust: derived from the security mechanisms and standardized routine business processes embedded in the e-commerce technologies Relationship trust: the subjective probability with which organizational members collectively assess that a particular transaction will occur according to their confident expectations	Relationships buyer-seller in e-commerce, technology trust in e-commerce	Conceptual
Ratnasingam, Gefen, and Pavlou (2005)	Institutional trust in electronic marketplaces	Trust of institution in buyer-seller relationships in online market	Situational normality, structural assurances, facilitating conditions Adopted from Pavlou et al. (2003)
Uslaner (2004)	Strategic trust: based on our experience with people doing specific things, Moralistic trust: a generalized humanity trust	Buyer-seller relationship	Conceptual

Table 2. Conceptualization of trust in virtual community

Study	Trust Conceptualization	Trust Object	Measures
Castelfranchi and Tan (2002)	Willingness to rely on the other party's internal (ability, knowledge, motivation, commitment, morality, social disposition) and external environment and circumstances	1. Environment and infrastructure 2. Agent and mediating agent 3. Potential partners 4. The authorities	Conceptual
Leismeister, Ebner, and Krcmar (2005)	Adopted from Gambetta (1990), and Abdul-Rahman et al. (2000): 1. Interpersonal trust 2. System trust 3. Dispositional trust	1. Another agent 2. System or Institution 3. General 'others'	Empirical: 1. Perceived Competence 2. Perceived Goodwill/ benevolence
Mainelli (2003)	Trusting information given, trusting others to understand information provided, trusting individuals to act as expected, trusting others to make decisions on your behalf, entrusting others with your assets	"Financial" community	Conceptual
Radin (2006)	Derived from Putnam (2000), Thick trust: deep trust, including the assurance that the other side will not give away critical information Thin trust: a thinner trust in the generalized other	Thick trust: within dense networks of business associates, relatives, friends and neighbors Thin trust: Generalized other	"laboratory" case study
Ridings, Gefen, and Arinze (2002)	Derived from Gefen (2002): an implicit set of beliefs that the other party will refrain from opportunistic behavior and will not take advantage of the situation	The collective entity of others (generalize)	Adapted from Jarvenpaa et al. (1998): the scales reflect the multiple interdependencies that exist in a group
Shubert and Ginsburg (2000)	(Trust itself is not defined)	Buyer-seller relationship	Conceptual

Table 3. Cultural dimensions with selected countries

Country	UAI	PDI	IDV	MAS	LTO
U.S.	46	40	91	62	29
UK	35	35	89	66	25
Australia	51	36	90	61	31
China	40	80	15	55	118
Hong Kong	29	68	25	57	96
Japan	92	54	46	95	80

Note: UAI: uncertainty-avoidance index; PDI: power-distance index; IDV: individualism; MAS: masculinity; LTO: long-term orientation (source: based on information from Hofstede (1991))

Chapter XIII
Virtuality and Reality:
What Happens When the Two Collide?

Celia Romm-Livermore
Wayne State University, USA

Gail Livermore
Spin Master Ltd., Canada

ABSTRACT

This conceptual chapter explores the distinction between virtual and real environments, the situations when they might clash and the implications from this clash. We start by categorizing virtual environments. Next, we present a framework for comparing the rules that govern behavior in different virtual and real environments. We list a number of situations where virtual and real environments can collide and explore the characteristics of such situations. Finally, we discuss the implications from clashes between virtual and real environments and what society can or should do about such potential and actual clashes.

INTRODUCTION

In mid July 2007, the bizarre story of John Mackey, co-founder and CEO of Whole Foods, was published in the *Wall Street Journal* (Banjo, 2007). As reported by this source, John Mackay founded Whole Foods in 1980. Within the next decade and as a result of the acquisition of a number of other health food stores, the company grew exponentially, leading it to go public in January, 1992.

Within a few more years, Whole Foods became the major health food chain in the U.S. The only competition to its market dominance was Wild Oats Markets Inc.

At about the same time that Whole Foods opened its 100th store in 1999, its founder and CEO, John Mackey, started posting anonymous messages on a Yahoo finance message board, identifying himself as "Rahodeb." In his messages, "Rahodeb" shared flattering information about Whole Foods and disparaging remarks about Whole Foods major competitor, Wild Oats Markets Inc.

The messages on the Yahoo finance message board continued for a number of years while the value of the shares of Whole Foods went up and the value of the shares of Wild Oats Markets Inc. went down.

In February 2007, Whole Foods announced plans to acquire Wild Oats Markets Inc. for $565 million. Following this announcement, the Federal Trade Commission filed a suit against Whole Foods, attempting to block the purchase of Wild Oats Inc. on anti-trust grounds. As part of its submission, which eventually was leaked to the media, the Federal Trade Commission made public the e-mail messages posted by Whole Foods' CEO, John Mackay.

The publication of the e-mail messages resulted in a media debate between Mr. Mackay's detractors and defenders. While some anti-trust experts claimed that Mr. Mackey's messages may have resulted in his company reaching the market dominance that it has attained at the expense of its competitor, Wild Oats Markets Inc., Mr. Mackey's defenders said that his anonymous comments, though boastful, provocative and possibly impulsive, were no different from his public ones and were never intended to disclose insider information about his company or move stock prices. In any case, the fact that he made these comments anonymously meant that they did not have the "weight" that they would have had, had it been known that they were written by the founder and CEO of Whole Foods.

As for Mr. Mackay, he told visitors to his Whole Foods Web site that he had made the online comments because he "had fun doing it," alluding to the fact that "having fun" is the major motivation for many members in online communities to participate in discussions in this environment.

The Whole Foods deal was eventually finalized when a three-judge panel rejected the Federal Trade Commission's request for a delay of the lower court judge's ruling in favor of the acquisition. As a result, Whole Foods and Wild Oats were free to complete their deal as planned (Kesmodel, 2007).

The story of John Mackay, the CEO of Whole Foods and his adventures online, raises a series of interesting questions that this chapter focuses on. In particular, it raises the following three questions:

1. What happens when the virtual world (where making anonymous comments about various issues is totally legitimate) and the real world (where CEO's are not supposed to spread information about their company and its relationships with its competitors without taking full responsibility for this disclosure) collide?
2. What happens when the collision between the virtual and real worlds leads to tangible results such as the thriving of one company and the demise of another?
3. Should the rules of behavior in the virtual world be the same as the rules of behavior in the real world, particularly when one world (environment) impacts the other?

In the following sections of this chapter, we will start by categorizing virtual environments. Next, we will develop a framework for comparing the rules that govern behavior in virtual and real environments. We will list a number of situations where virtual and real environments can collide and explore the characteristics of such events. Finally, we will discuss the implications from clashes between virtual and real environments and what society can or should do about such potential and actual clashes.

Note that this is a preliminary glimpse into a phenomenon that is emerging at the time of the writing of this chapter. Consequently, much of the data on which this chapter is based is derived from media sources rather than from scholarly articles. Also, as the topic of our chapter is in the process of change, it is possible that some of the clashes that we discuss in the following sections may not have manifested yet. Still, the differences between the rules of behavior in virtual and real environments are already evident and one can at least start to discuss them.

Our hope is that the conceptual framework that we present here will be the basis for future empirical and theoretical research into the rules that govern behavior in virtual and real environments, the manner in which they shape transactions between their members, and the actions that society may need to take in future to prevent undesirable clashes between the virtual and the real worlds.

However, before we consider the different rules that govern behavior in virtual and real environments, it is important to define and categorize virtual environments. For the purpose of this chapter, we define a "virtual environment" as "an environment where individuals interact with each other via electronic means." By implication, a "real environment" is defined as "an environment where individuals interact with each other face-to-face."

It is important to note that our definitions for the two environments do NOT specify the *purpose* of the interactions between participants. Indeed, we define both virtual and real environments as ones that encompass both social and commercial transactions between members. We also include in the range of transactions under each type of environment those that involve single individuals (one-to-one) and many individuals (one-to-many or many-to-many).

We consider many types of activities as possible in a real environment. Thus, communication (for any purpose), socializing (with any number of people), and transacting (with any number of people or organizations) will all fit the category of possible activities in a real environment. Similarly, the activities within virtual environments may include the establishment of a presence on a Web site (blogging), communicating with other members of a virtual environment (participating in chat rooms, news groups, discussion groups or virtual worlds), and transacting online, which may include simply buying goods and services online or participating as both a buyer and a seller in an online market or auction site.

CATEGORIZING VIRTUAL AND REAL ENVIRONMENTS

Following Romm, Setzekorn and Rippa, (2007), we categorize environments (virtual or real) based on the nature of the relationship between participants. In the original paper by these authors, the discussion was restricted to categorizing social networking services and the central relationship that defines each category was between participants in the virtual environment and the commercial provider of the service. Here, we expand this categorization to include both commercial and social environments and we also include both virtual and real environments. However, the essence of the categorization is similar, as we, like Romm, Setezkorn and Rippa, also base our categorization on the *nature* of the relationship between the participants in each environment and the *scope* of the relationship.

Following Romm, Setzekorn and Rippa (2007), we categorize virtual and real environments based on two dimensions:

1. The Nature of the relationships in the environment—which refers to whether the relationships between participants in a given environment are primarily "social" or primarily "commercial;" and

2. The Scope of the relationships in the environment—which refers to whether the relationships between participants in a given environment are based primarily on a "one-to-one" basis or on "one-to-many" (or many-to-many) basis.

As for the "nature of the relationship" dimension, we consider it as having two dimensions: "commercial" and "social." We define "commercial" relationships within an environment as relationships that involve an exchange of money between participants. We define "social" relationships as relationships that do not involve an exchange of money between participants.

It should be noted, however, that we are aware that the distinction between the two is not necessarily that clear, as many commercial relationships (such as signing a contract between two companies) may involve lengthy social interactions between participants before the commercial relationship is cemented. Similarly, many so-called social relationships (such as a marriage) might involve complex commercial transactions between the participants in the relationship (such as during the negotiations on a pre-nuptial agreement).

As for the second dimension in our model, "the scope of the relationship," even though we make a distinction between "one-to-one" and "one-to-many" relationships and even though we assume that both types of relationships exist both in the virtual and the real world, we are aware that the distinction between these categories might be blurred in some cases.

Thus, one-to-one commercial relationships might involve individuals buying from a company (that obviously involves more than one individual) while the one-to-many relationships, might involve individuals transacting with a number of companies, each with its own group of employees. This blurring might also occur in non-commercial relationships where individuals might interact with representatives of organizations on a one-to-one basis. Still, as long as the individual who is interacting with a commercial or social entity is doing so primarily through one individual, we consider it a one-to-one relationship.

The combining of the above dimensions, produces a typology of four distinct environments that might exist in either the virtual or the real world. Each environment is referred to in terms

Figure 1.

Categorizing Real and Virtual Environments

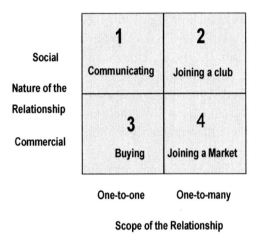

of the major activity that defines the relationships between its members. Figure 1 shows the 2 X 2 model that is produced once we combine the two dimensions.

As indicated in Figure 1, our model differentiates between the following four types (categories) of environments:

1. **Communicating:** This category results from the interaction of "social' (on the "nature of the relationship" dimension) and "one-on-one" (on the "scope of the relationship" dimension). This category defines environments where the major thrust of the relationships between participants is on communication. In the real environment, this would relate to face-to-face relationships where friends (or colleagues, or family members) interact with each other on a one to one basis. In the virtual world, platforms that enable similar relationships are social networking or blogging services, such as MySpace, or Facebook. These environments provide a space for individuals to set up a virtual presence on the Web site. YouTube is another example of this type of environ-

ment. Here, the communication between members extends to members' ability to display and share home videos. A similar concept is demonstrated by SecondLife, a virtual reality Web site that offers members the opportunity to create a virtual "home" and interact socially (through avatars) with other members.

2. **Joining a club:** This category results from the interaction of "social" (on the "nature of the relationship" dimension) and "one-to-many" (on the "scope of the relationship" dimension). This category defines environments where the major thrust of the relationships between participants is on joining a pre-existing group or a club. In the real environment this would relate to face-to-face encounters with groups of people such as in a bar, a club, an interest group or a political party. In the virtual world, platforms that enable similar relationships are online chatrooms, newsgroups, bulletin boards or group hosting services such as YahooGroups. These services enable members to establish or join a pre-existing virtual environment, providing them with a range of tools for managing the group environment.

3. **Buying:** This category results from the interaction of "commercial" (on the "nature of the relationship" dimension) and "one-to-one" (on the "scope of the relationship" dimension). This category defines environments where participants pay money to purchase goods and services. In the real world, this category would relate to face-to-face transactions between individuals (or commercial entities) that involve an exchange of funds. In the virtual world, this category will include the whole gamut of e-commerce business-to-consumer, business-to-business and business-to-government transactions where individuals purchase goods and services. It is important to note that some companies use the "joining a club" model to engage their customers in social-like relationships. For example, both Amazon.com and Dell.com built their business model around the concept of virtual communities of customers who advise each other on how to use the company's products or who "sell" the company's products to each other. Still, since these companies are in the business of making money, they would fit under this category and not the previous one.

4. **Joining a market:** This category results from the interaction of "commercial" (on the "nature of the relationship" dimension) and "one-to-many" (on the "scope of the relationship" dimension). This category defines environments where different sellers compete between each other for an individual's business. In the real world, this category would relate to face-to-face situations where individual buyers choose between different vendors in a mall or a market situation, as well as, to an auction event where different potential buyers compete for a good or a service. In the virtual world, this model would apply to online auction sites such as eBay, as well as to the whole industry of e-dating, where customers compete with each other in an auction-like manner to establish romantic relationships with each other. Obviously, the difference between the "buying" and the "market" categories is the element of competition (between either buyers or sellers).

It should be noted that even though our model suggests that the four categories are distinct, there are many instances when these environments converge both in the real and the virtual world. Thus, in the real world, there are many examples where social and commercial transactions are conducted simultaneously. In the virtual world, several services already combine aspects from several of the above categories. One interesting

Table 1. Comparing expectations and rules of behavior in Virtual and Real Environments

Environment	Real	Virtual
Communicating	Personal identity is known	Personal identity not known
	Truthfulness is expected	Truthfulness not expected
	Continuation of relationship expected	No expectation of on-going relationships
	Politeness expected	Politeness not expected or considered desirable
Joining a club	Personal identity is known	Personal identity not known
	Truthfulness is expected	Truthfulness not expected
	Long term expected	On-going relationships not expected
	Social attributes expected to fit	Social attributes not known
Buying	Identity of buyer is known	Buyer needs to prove identity
	Identity of seller is known	Seller needs to prove identity
	Truthfulness (in cash transactions) assumed	Truthfulness results from third party "guaranteeing" transactions
	Service available at limited times and places	Service available any time, any place, and for less
	Ability to compare prices limited	Comparing prices unlimited
	Customers receive on-site pre- and post-purchase service from company	Customers expected to serve themselves by using Web site features
	Taxes are paid on all transactions when applicable	Many transactions tax exempt
Joining a Market	Identity of seller is known	Seller not known but might be ranked
	Identity of buyer not necessarily known	Buyer not known but might be ranked
	Truthfulness (in cash transactions) assumed	Truthfulness results from third party "guaranteeing" transactions
	Service available at limited times and places	Service available any time, any place and for less (or at limited times as per transactions)
	Ability to compare prices limited only by size of market	Comparing prices unlimited
	Customers receive on-site pre service from vendors—post service may not be available	Customers expected to serve themselves by using features of Web site—may receive additional service from individual vendors
	Taxes are paid on all transactions when applicable	Many online transactions are tax exempt

example would be, SecondLife, a social networking platform that offers members an opportunity to create a virtual home (category 1), establish or join chatrooms (category 2), buy and sell virtual goods and services (category 3), and bid for goods and services in virtual auctions (category 4). There is evidence that other major social networks Web sites such as MySpace and Facebook are following suit but offering their members a growing number of services that combine the various categories in our model.

COMPARING THE RULES OF BEHAVIOR IN VIRTUAL AND REAL ENVIRONMENTS

Based on the discussion in the previous sections, we will now consider the differences between the expectations and rules of behavior in each type of environment. As the discussion will demonstrate, for each type of environment, the differences between the virtual and the real are many. Consequently, the potential for conflict when one moves from one environment to the other is great. For a summary of the major points in the following discussion, please refer to Table 1.

1. **Communicating:** As indicated in Table 1, the major features of this environment in its real (versus virtual) manifestation, as far as members' behaviors are concerned, is that members know each other face-to-face. As a result, members expect each other to be truthful, authentic, and open. They expect the relationship between them to continue beyond the present and appreciate and expect members to be kind and polite to each other.

Contrast this with the virtual environment, such as on e-mail or in social networking services, where members do not necessarily know each other and do not expect others to be truthful, authentic or open with them. Contrast it also with the style of communication that is typical to the Internet, where acronyms and emoticons replace words and sentences and where bluntness replaces politeness (Baker, 2005). Paradoxically, some authors note that when members in virtual "communicating" environments do engage in open communication, such as in dating communities, they tend to go overboard, resulting in much more intense and passionate relationships that are common in face-to-face relationships of the same duration (Ben-Ze'ev, 2004).

2. **Joining a club:** As indicated in Table 1, the major features of this environment, in its real (versus virtual) manifestation, as far as members' behaviors are concerned, is again, that members meet each other face-to-face. As a result of the face-to-face interactions, the expectation of truthfulness, authenticity and openness in this environment is just as strong as in the previous one and so are the expectations for continuation of the relationships into the future. The only difference between this environment and the

previous one is in its selectivity. In order to join a club, a member needs to meet some demographic or other membership criteria that the group defines and that the member (unless he or she is the founder of the club) does not have much control over.

Comparing these expectations and rules of behavior to the virtual environment, shows that, again, virtual clubs do not expect (nor practice) truthfulness, authenticity or openness. Indeed, there is a lot of research that shows that members of virtual groups welcome anonymous membership and are tolerant of anonymous contributions from their members (Ben-Ze'ev, 2004; Baker, 2005). However, the major difference between the real and virtual social clubs is the issue of selectivity. While in the real world, social clubs can see whether a potential member fits their criteria, in the virtual world, members can and do "invent" themselves, with the other members of the groups not knowing or caring about their true identity.

3. **Buying:** As indicated in Table 1, the major features of this environment, in its real (versus virtual) manifestation, as far as members' behaviors are concerned, is that the identities of both buyers and sellers are known because the transaction between them is conducted face-to-face. If the buying transaction fee involves cash, truthfulness is evident. If the transaction is conducted through other means (checks, credit card), its integrity is guaranteed by the currency. In any case, in real buying environments, customers expect and receive pre- and post-purchase service. However, the service is restricted by time and place and customers' ability to compare prices across stores is limited too.

Compare this with the e-commerce environment where both buyers and sellers need to prove their identity (through a third party) before a transaction can take place and where "truthfulness" is a result of a third party always guaranteeing the transaction. Compare it also with the enormous flexibility that is available to e-commerce customers through unlimited price comparisons, and the availability of service any time, any place and for less than the equivalent face-to-face transaction (Meuter & Ostrom, 2000). Compare it also with the fact that many transactions online are tax (state tax) exempt, making them more lucrative to both buyers and sellers. Again, paradoxically, the flexibility that e-commerce transactions provide may come with a price in that customers are expected in many cases to "serve themselves." Taken to the extreme, this can mean that customers are provided with a lower quality service than in the face-to-face environment (Romm, Farag, & Oliver, 2005).

4.   **Joining a market:** As indicated in Table 1, the major features of this environment, in its real (versus virtual) manifestation, as far as members' behaviors are concerned, is that the identities of both buyers and sellers are usually unknown to each other. Consequently, the expectation of truthfulness is limited and transactions have to be conducted by using cash. There is also no expectation of a long-term relationship between buyer and seller and post-transaction service is expected to be limited or not available at all. On the positive side, markets, in their real world manifestation, offer a relatively enhanced ability to compare prices and consequently obtain more attractive deals from vendors.

When we compare the real and virtual manifestations of this environment, we find that the virtual manifestation is quite similar to the real. Here again, sellers and buyers are unknown. However, many virtual services (such as eBay) provide ranking or buyers and sellers, making

choices among them much easier, indeed, even easier than in the real world. Truthfulness in the virtual world results from third parties guaranteeing the transaction, which again, does not differ much from the real market situation, where transactions almost invariably are conducted in cash. The most important distinction between the virtual and the real is in the flexibility that the virtual market provides versus the real market. While both offer easy comparative pricing, only the virtual market is available any time and any place and only the virtual market offers many transactions that are tax (state tax) exempt.

WHEN ARE CLASHES BETWEEN THE VIRTUAL AND THE REAL LIKELY TO OCCUR?

The discussion in the previous sections is helpful in predicting when and where clashes between the virtual and the real are likely to occur. When we compare the two sides of Table 1, several phenomena seem to be evident:

1.   Expectations of truthfulness are the most important feature that differentiates the "real" from the "virtual" environments.
2.   The differences in expectations of truthfulness seem to be more pronounced in the social environments ("communication" and "joining a club") than in the commercial environments ("buying" and "joining a market").
3.   The differences in expectations of truthfulness seem to be pronounced in one-to-one environments ("communication" and "buying") than in one-to-many environments (joining a club and joining a market).

Thus, our analysis suggest a continuum of expectation of truthfulness that corresponds to the likelihood of clashes between the virtual and the real, with some environments more likely to

Figure 2.

Continuum of Environments and the Probability of
Clashes between the Virtual and the Real

1	2	3	4
Communicating	Joining a club	Buying	Joining a market
High probability For Clash	Medium high Probability For clash	Medium low Probability For clash	Low probability For clash

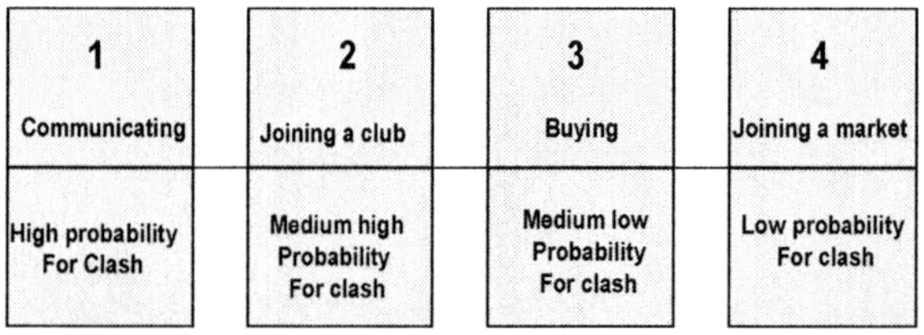

experience clashes than others. Figure 2 presents a pictorial depiction of this continuum.

As indicated in Figure 2, on one extreme end of the continuum, we find environments where truthfulness will be *most* expected (and the difference between the real and the virtual will be most pronounced because of lack of trust), such as the "communicating" type environments. In these environments, where relationships are both "social" and "one-on-one," the expectations for truthfulness are highest and the difference between the virtual and the real on the issue of truthfulness are likely to be most pronounced. For this reason, we would expect transitions from the virtual to the real within these environments to be most likely to lead to clashes, for example, conflicts between the virtual and the real will most likely occur when people move between the virtual and real in the communicating environments.

The opposite would apply in environments where truthfulness is least expected (and the difference between the real and the virtual the least pronounced because of lack of trust), such as the "joining a market" type environments. In these environments, where relationships are both "commercial" and "one-to-many" the expectations of truthfulness are lowest and the difference between the virtual and the real on the issue of truthfulness is the least pronounced. For this reason, we would expect transitions from the virtual to the

real within these environments to be the least likely to lead to clashes.

Since truthfulness seems to be a much stronger expectation in the social arena ("communication" and "joining a club" environments) than it is in the commercial arena ("buying" and "joining a market"), we would expect environments that are "social" (irrespective of scope) to be more likely to produce clashes than environments that are "commercial." Hence, in the continuum in Figure 2, "joining a club" is ranked higher on potential to produce clashes between the virtual and the real than "buying."

It is important to remember, however, that the only transitions that are likely to produce clashes are *within* a category of environments. Thus, when a person moves within a "communicating" environment (from the real to the virtual or the other way around), we would expect a high probability of clash, as opposed to a situation where a person moves from the real to the virtual within a "joining a market" environment. The first case is expected to contain a high probability of conflict because of the big emphasis on trust in the real environment versus the virtual one, while the second case is expected to contain a low probability of conflict because of the lesser emphasis on trust in the real versus the virtual environment.

Bearing this in mind, let us consider some specific examples of clashes between the virtual and real and how our model can help explain them:

1. **Communicating:** Recent articles in the popular media (insert references) mention a growing phenomenon, employers who use information that prospective employees posted on their private social networking sites as sources of information about the prospective employees. Based on the reports in the media, a growing number of employers are hiring social networking experts to conduct background searches on prospective employees. The information from the searchers is then used to make decisions on

whether an individual is going to be offered a job and the level of job offered (White, 2007). Furthermore, some employers continue to use information gleaned from social networking Web sites as a basis for decisions about promoting their employees or even terminating employment (White, 2007). Given that some of the data that is available on social networking Web sites is old (the individual may have posted it when he or she were teenagers), some job searchers are hiring experts to "clean" their image online (Lavallee, 2007).

The use of information posted by individuals on their blogs for selection, promotion and termination of employees is a good example of a clash between the virtual and the real in the "communicating" environment. The arena for this clash is the communicating arena because the data that employers use is posted by individuals for sharing with their friends and family (interaction of the "social" and "one-to-one" dimensions in our model). It is not intended to be used by individuals outside the immediate social circle of the person who posts it. Once it is captured and used by employers for purposes that could be discriminatory, there is a potential for clash between the expectations of the virtual arena, where such information is exchanged for "fun" and those of the real world, where such information can and is used for life-changing decisions.

2. **Joining a club:** The story of Mr. Mackay and his use of the Yahoo finance group to promote his company and denigrate the competition (which we discussed at the very beginning of this chapter) is a good example of a conflict between the virtual and the real in the "joining the club" environment. The arena for this clash is the "joining the club" arena because Mr. Mackay was engaged in a "social" interaction on a "one-to-many" basis. The manner in which he shared the

information (anonymously) was acceptable within the confines of the virtual environment. Indeed, all the other members in that environment communicated anonymously as well. The intention of all participants was to keep the information that was shared within the club. The conflict or clash occurred when the behavior that Mr. Mackay engaged in (for several years!) became known and the rules that apply to the same behavior in the real world were imposed on it. Thus, if Mr. Mackay was interacting with his buddies in a real-world financial club, the members of the club would be aware of his identity and any attempt on his part to influence them toward investing in his company or not investing in the competition would not be seen as inappropriate.

3. **Buying:** The popular literature in recent years is replete with stories of online identity theft. In many cases, the criminals obtain confidential information from Internet users by posing as legitimate businesses (sometimes very well-known businesses) who are trying to "confirm" the social security number, address, of other information of their customers. Individuals who fall prey to these schemes do so because they believe the e-mail message that is supposedly sent to them by their bank. Once they do, the information is used by the criminals to gain control of their bank account or use their details to open accounts in the name of the victim.

Identity theft schemes are a good example of a clash of the virtual and the real in the "buying" environment because they represent an interaction between the "commercial" and "one-to-one" dimensions in our model. The conflict here is a result of the differences in expected trust between the two environments. While "buying" in the real environment is associated with a relatively high level of trust because customers and vendors know each other, the same environment, when it manifests as virtual, is associated with a much lower level of trust. When naïve customers who are used to transact in the real environment (where they know their vendor face-to-face and trust him or her) are faced with requests to share their personal information in the virtual environment, they apply the same rules with the same expectation of truthfulness as they would in the real environment. Since the rules in the virtual environment are different and their trust is misguided, it results in them becoming victims of fraud.

4.   **Joining a market:** A recent development in the e-dating industry is drawing interest in the popular media. This development is the use of ranking by e-dating Web sites. The concept is not new. It has been used for years by auction Web sites, most notably, eBay. Indeed, the eBay business model is based on the fact that buyers and sellers are not completely unknown to each other as is the case in a real face-to-face market but are somewhat known because they are constantly and continuously being ranked by each other. The trouble is that while this principle works perfectly for eBay, when it comes to e-dating Web sites, ranking a person by other daters could result in that person becoming completely "undatable." Indeed, taken to the extreme, a low ranking of a person on an e-dating Web site can result in a total destruction of a person's reputation to the point where he or she might never be able to find a marriage partner. This could lead some injured parties to consider a defamation suit against the individuals who have defamed them and/or the e-dating service that made the destruction of their reputation possible.

The ranking of e-daters is a good example of a clash between the virtual and the real in the "joining a market" environment because it meets the criteria of "commercial" and "one-to-many" in our model. The clash in this case is a result of the different expectations and behaviors in real and virtual markets. While in real markets, buyers and sellers are not ranked by each other, in virtual markets, they are. E-dating is an example of a situation where the encounters start in the virtual environment but then, once the daters meet face-to-face, "migrate" to the real world. When ranking of daters take place in the virtual environment, it is acceptable to all. However, when it migrates to the real environment, and particularly when the ranking does not apply to a piece of merchandise but to the whole person, participants in the transaction can and do get hurt. The conflict in this case is a result of both the uniqueness of the e-dating industry, which is not exactly the same of other markets and the result of the migration back and forth, which is typical of this industry, between the virtual and real environment.

IMPLICATIONS AND DIRECTIONS FOR FUTURE RESEARCH

The purpose of this chapter was to explore the differences between real and virtual environments of different types and the clashes that can result from movement between them. As we demonstrated in the previous sections, the behaviors that are exhibited in different real and virtual environments and the expectations that underlie these behaviors determine the extent to which clashes between the virtual and the real are likely to occur. To conclude this chapter, we would like to consider some of the implications and directions for future research that emanate from the discussion in this chapter.

The first implication from this research is that while some behaviors in the virtual environment are prescribed by commercial services, other behaviors are based on participants' expectations, and, as such are subjective and open-ended. Future research may address this issue by exploring the expectations that participants have about different types of virtual environments, the extent that these expectations differ from the equivalent real environments and the extent to which these expectations are met or dashed by the participants' experiences.

Since, expectations are subjective and might be affected by demographic variables; it would be interesting to explore the extent to which expectations are affected by demographic, cultural or other variables. For example, some preliminary research shows that men and women experience e-dating Web sites differently because men tend to be more numerous on these Web sites than women are (Hitsch, Hortacsu, & Ariely, 2005). Future research may address this issue empirically by measuring men and women's expectations of the e-dating environment and studying changes in their respective expectations over time. Research might also address the extent to which specific attributes of the service (such as the introduction of ranking) affect men's and women's experience and the impact of other demographic variables (age, ethnicity, level of education, etc.) on the likelihood that a man or woman would use a service that employs ranking.

Another important implication of the discussion in this chapter has to do with education. If indeed a major aspect of life in the twenty first century has to do with knowing the rules of behavior in real and virtual worlds and being able to migrate "smoothly" from one environment to the other, then maybe the educational system should dedicate resources to teaching young people about it? Obviously, the ability of employers to use information that young people posted on their blogs for selection and promotion is predicated on the young person not being aware of this reality (Lavallee, 2007). Perhaps it is time to teach young people before they even venture into the virtual environment the rules of behavior there so that they will not become victims of their naiveté later in life.

Finally, the discussion in this chapter has many legal implications. The story of John Mackay raises the question of whether in some areas, for example, online investment discussion groups, participants need to identify themselves just as the behavior of insiders in other parts of the financial industry is regulated to prevent abuse of power. Also, perhaps the stipulations that regulate "inside" information should apply not only to information that is true and whose source is known but also to information that is untrue and whose source is anonymous?

In a similar vain, the story of the use of information from social networking Web sites on the job, by either employers or co-workers, raises some additional issues with legal implications. For example, one can wonder about the legality of using information that an individual shared with friends when he or she was under age to make decisions about this individual when he or she is an adult. If discrimination on the basis of race, ethnicity and gender is illegal, should not discrimination on the basis of one's behavior many years prior to being a candidate for a job (or while being a minor) be considered discriminatory too? Also, if employers or co-workers use information that was gleaned from an e-dating Web site to discredit a co-worker, should not this behavior be seen as discriminatory and prohibit by the same laws that currently prohibit discrimination for other reasons?

And, finally, the potential for defamation and destruction of individuals' reputation as a result of clashes between the virtual and the real deserves a closer look by researchers and policy making. If indeed millions of people become victims of crime (Loviglio, 2007) as a result of being uneducated about the distinctions between the rules of behavior in the virtual and real world, is it not time for society to take a more active role in trying to prevent these crimes? Is it not time for the credit bureaus to do more than warn people about illegal activity in their accounts *after* they have become victims of identity theft? Is it not time for the government to legislate warning before identity theft happens? Is it time for the government to demand that other services with potential for abuse such as e-dating Web sites should be regulated too?

Only the future will tell how many of these issues will be addressed by researchers and/or by society as a whole and how this will lead to an evolution of the social networking and e-dating industry as we know it today.

REFERENCES

Baker, A. (2005). *Double click: Romance and commitment among online couples.* Cresskill, NJ: Hampton Press.

Banjo, S. (2007, July 10). For Whole Foods CEO, brash style takes an unhealthy turn. *Wall Street Journal,* p. A10.

Ben-Ze'ev, A. (2004). *Love online: Emotions on the Internet.* Cambridge: Cambridge University Press.

Hitsch, J., Hortacsu, A., & Ariely, D. (2005). *What makes you click.* Paper presented at the AEA Meeting, Choice Symposium, Northwestern University. Estes Park.

Kesmodel, D. (2007, August 24). Court clears Whole Foods deal, FTC loses appeal to delay acquisition of Wild Oats, but other options remain. *Wall Street Journal,* p. A2.

Lavallee, A. (2007, June 13). Firms tidy up clients' bad online reputations. *Wall Street Journal,* p. B1.

Loviglio, J. (2007, June 16). Two sex convictions in online dating case. *Wall Street Journal,* p. B5.

Meuter, M., & Ostrom, A. (2000). Self-service technologies: Understanding customer satisfaction with technology-based service encounters. *Journal of Marketing, 64*(3), 50-64.

Romm-Livermore, C., Farag, N., & Oliver, D. (2005). *Turning customers into employees- research in progress.* Paper presented at the Sixth Annual Global Information Technology Management Conference. Anchorage, Alaska.

Romm, C., Setzekorn, K., & Rippa, P. (2007). *Categorizing and measuring social networking and e-dating Web sites.* Paper presented at the Seventh Annual Global Information Technology Management World Conference (GITM). Naples, Italy.

White, E. (2007, January, 1). Employers reach out to recruit with Facebook. *Wall Street Journal,* p. D3.

Section III
E–Dating Services

Chapter XIV
Segmentation Practices of e–Dating

Linda Jane Coleman
Salem State College, USA

Nisreen Bahnan
Salem State College, USA

ABSTRACT

This chapter investigates the current practices and strategies used by marketers of electronic dating services. This chapter does not develop or test a model, but rather is centered round an analysis of secondary data sources. Specific focus is placed on documenting the various demographic and psychographic segmentation basis and niche targeting strategies utilized by providers. An enormous ground swell is occurring of consumers participating in meeting a "significant other" through e-dating Web sites. People are increasingly relying on such services to meet people via the Internet: older, younger, black, white, pet lovers, religious, spiritual, and gay or straight individuals seeking partners for fun, companionship, commitment or conversation. This trend continues to grow. This chapter will cite a variety of networks that have blossomed over the years indicative of the interest and ideas related to this phenomenon. It also provides details of the nuances in the marketing and consumption of electronic-based personal relationships.

MARKETING EXHANGES FOCUSING ON PERSONAL RELATIONSHIPS

Marketing is prospering in the personal relationship service industry. Many strategies are being implemented to bring people together ranging from individual matchmakers to personal ads in newspapers, magazines, and video interviews where clients view each other's tapes. One of the latest trends that is growing in popularity and marketing success is electronic-based dating, made possible by the prevalence of technology.

Numerous Internet e-dating service start-ups have cropped up over the last 20 years. Of note also is the increase in people turning to e-personal relating services since September 11, 2001. The Internet now offers customers a convenient, affordable, and practical alternative to the past more traditional ways of dating and matchmaking. "E-personal relating" encompasses all forms of personal relating behavior involving individuals seeking friendship, love, and short- or long-term mates. This chapter identifies a wide variety of segmentation strategies used by e-dating marketers in an effort to differentiate and customize appeals in this highly competitive industry, as evidenced by the number of firms and approaches out there.

BACKGROUND

The notion of marketing as exchange has proven to be conceptually robust since its introduction in the mid 1970s. The marketing exchange concept was incorporated formally in the definition of marketing developed by the American Marketing Association (Brown, 1985). The concept of a marketing exchange involving a person as the product is not novel. Hirschman (1987) examined male- and female-placed personal ads as complex and heterogeneous marketing exchange.

Marketing exchanges may assume both a traditional (e.g., money in exchange for goods and services) and nontraditional nature (e.g., a vote and volunteered time in exchange for a candidate's promise to promote a particular ideology). Heterogeneous resources are exchanged and the primary research focus has been on the pattern of cross-category resource exchange. Diverse resources are being offered, in return for other resources, which are being sought by parties in the exchange. Foa (1976) proposes a social interaction theory to address multiple, heterogeneous resource exchanges. Foa describes social interaction in terms largely analogous to marketers' conceptions of exchange.

"Social experiences are interpersonal encounters in which resources are given and/or taken away . . . Whether or not an exchange will take place depends on [two types of] conditions . . . One pertains to the motivational state of the potential exchangers, their need to receive and capacity to give; the other set refers to the appropriateness of the environment for an exchange of a particular type" (Foa & Foa, 1974).

Foa's theory uses six categories of heterogeneous resources exchanged in a social interaction: goods, services, love, status, information, and money. They are defined as follows (Donnenworth & Foa, 1974, p. 786).

1. Love: An expression of affectionate regard, warmth, or comfort
2. Status: An evaluative judgment conveying high or low prestige, regard, or esteem
3. Information: Any advice, opinions or instructions
3. Money: Any coin or token that has some standard of exchange value
4. Goods: Any products or objects
5. Services: Activities on the body or belonging to the individual

The perceived similarity/proximity of resource categories in terms of particularism and concreteness do not necessarily translate into greater *likelihood of exchange* among nearby resources. Foa speculates that a complex set of social norms and customs exists that encourages exchange across certain resource categories (as being "socially appropriate") and discourage exchange across other resource categories (as being "socially inappropriate"). Because of social norms, some resources are more acceptable/unacceptable in exchange for other resources (Brinberg & Wood, 1983).

Among the most important status characteristics and resources possessed by men and women are physical attractiveness, intelligence, education, occupational prestige, and income. These features constitute resources in both the Foa sense and the marketing exchange sense, because consumers in Western cultures positively evaluate larger quantities of each and consequently they are exchanged actively for one another (Berger et al., 1977; Webster & Driskell, 1983; Buss, 1985).

Referring to human dating situations, Buss (1985) states that, "those who do possess the valued traits [i.e., resources] typically marry others with the same or with equally sought-after characteristics" (p. 49). In America, romantic love and personal compatibility are widely assumed to be the primary components of dating transactions (Buss, 1985; Buss & Barnes, 1986) and in the past single men and women were left to their own devices in finding one another. Commercial institutional facilitators sprung up to help enhance the exchange process. Among the most widespread of these commercial facilitating institutions were personal advertisements placed by consumers desiring to meet an appropriate individual for forming a couple (Harrison & Saeed, 1977; Lynn & Shurgot, 1984), now often done over the Internet (e-dating).

Personal advertisements, for which men and women pay to communicate their availability and marketable assets to others, serve as a unique and constructive context from which to examine complex marketing exchanges. First, they are clearly a form of marketing exchange, even in the most traditional economic sense. People must pay to place the advertisements, just as breakfast cereal companies and automobile manufacturers do. Second, like advertisements in a traditional marketing context, personal ads list a set of (presumed) desirable properties (viewed as resources) that are put forward to attract potential buyers. Third, a price is also stated in the advertisement, which consists of the set of properties/resources sought in return. Thus, in essence, personal advertisements represent the offering of people as products, as a set of marketable resources in search of an appropriate buyer (Hirschman, 1987). This chapter describes this industry as it evolves far beyond the initial stage of personal advertisements

in the 1970s. The e-personal relating services phenomenon has become the latest success story of the Internet revolution (Smith, 2005).

CHANGING TIMES

People are reconsidering the modern remedy to the single life. Since the September 11th terrorist attacks, dating service growth is increasing 10% plus annually in memberships. University of Wisconsin-Madison sociology professor John DeLamater reports that the demand for dating services in today's society is credible, "Dating services help people who have difficulty meeting potential partners in their normal day-to-day activities…. They assist people in finding others with their same interests." In the last 100 years, DeLamater reports, American social practices have changed a great deal. People no longer spend their entire lives in one town, and as a result they find themselves surrounded by strangers when it comes time to find a partner and settle down. Dating services have eased this challenge for many, but the impersonal connection can cause people to be tricked and misled. Dave Garde, regional manager of The Right One dating service, reports that his service is based on old-fashioned compatibility, "The Right One does extensive interviewing and profiling in an attempt to gather every possible bit of information in order to match people up." According to Garde, e-personal communicating is a very safe way to meet people, since providers go thorough criminal background checks. The success rates of dating services vary across the board. Garde claims that The Right One is 70%-80% successful in introducing couples that eventually develop long-term relationships. According to the Christian Science Monitor, two jointly owned dating services—Together and The Right One—were up 22% over the previous year, during the two weeks after the September 11th attacks on America. At around that same time, a survey of more than 7,500 eharmony.com customers found that 44% of respondents feel an increased desire to be in a long-term relationship. In times of national discomfort, people tend to seek companionship (Nesper, 2002).

Additionally, dating (correspondence) through the Internet allows people to connect on a level beyond simple physical attraction. A Colorado Springs secretary and a middle school band director from Illinois, who wed after meeting and dating on eHarmony.com, agree: "If we'd met each other on the street, we probably wouldn't have been together, because, as humans, we're all superficial and we go by appearances. Through the Internet, I got to know him from the inside out." EHarmony's service forces the couple to get right down to their values and beliefs before they even meet. Furthermore, unlike traditional off-line personal ads or video dating services, the Internet provides instant gratification. You can connect directly with potential mates all around the world with the click of a button.

It takes more than vital statistics to make an online love connection these days as dating services hone their matchmaking queries to include intangible "lifestyle" questions. Moving beyond age, size and eye color, online dating services are expanding their user profiles to pinpoint more specific traits and interests.

With the number of visitors growing steadily at online dating services, sites such as Match.com and Yahoo's ClubConnect are stepping up efforts to meet the needs and interests of diverse subscribers. "We've added more lifestyle questions to round out the glimpse of people online," said Trish McDermott, vice president of Romance at Match.com. "Dating is part science, art and emotional negotiation." Founded in 1995, Match.com has more than 3 million monthly visitors and about 380,000 subscribers. "Our success is a combination of subscriber growth and people wanting more meaningful relationships post September 11th," reports Match.com president. "It had an effect on people's attitude about dating and finding the right match."

"Online dating is proving to be a service that people are willing to pay for on the Internet," said Kathleen Roldan, spokeswoman for Match.com. The Dallas-based company reports around $7 million in profits and $25 million in revenues during each fiscal quarter. Up until recently, the only e-personal online relating services that made money were pornographic Web sites.

Dozens of companies are finding that people are willing to pay $20 to $25 a month to find their next relationship online. Success stories are driving that demand. Roldan said that Match.com receives more than 50 notifications of weddings or engagements each month. "It's the hip thing to do," said Stacey Herron, an analyst with industry research firm Jupiter Research. "It's more smiled upon."

Such acceptance was not always the case. In 1997, online dating was not even considered an industry because most people did not see it as legitimate, said Neil Warren, psychologist and co-founder of eHarmony.com. The stigma is diminishing. The top three dating services, Match.com, Yahoo Personals and Dreammates.com attract about 12.1 million visitors annually, according to Jupiter. Herron reports that dozens of newcomers have appeared on the scene, offering to match up niche audiences. PlanetOut.com, for instance, is becoming a well-known brand in the gay community, and Nerve.com caters to the young, urban, well-read "Sex in the City" types. Warren reports that marriage has been the least successful enterprise in North America, yet it is an institution that is at the very central part of peoples' lives. EHarmony relies on extensive personality surveys that take about an hour to complete. Couples are then matched based on the results of those surveys and compatible key characteristics, be it interests, values or spirituality. Warren's 17-person company bases its matching software on interviews of happily married couples. The site automatically turns away some users if its programmed heuristics concludes that the person is not ready for a serious relationship.

Technology also allows users to choose to keep their e-mail private until they learn more about people online demographically or through chats before meeting. Customers and firms alike must rely on information they both believe is safe and reliable. This brings up significant ramifications for this relatively new industry business model. Customers expect the online sites keep their information confidential while the firm must verify that the information their customers provide is giving value for their investment (Smith, 2005). .

New surveys of single people across the country indicate a noticeable shift in dating and relationship priorities, according to online dating site Match.com (http://www.match.com). In a survey of more than 2,200 singles, more than half of those surveyed indicate that finding a romantic relationship is more important to them today than it was a year ago. When asked to characterize the romantic relationship they are seeking today, 59% of women surveyed and 55% of men indicate that they are seeking a committed relationship or marriage, a shift from the year prior, where 40% of women and 37% of men indicated that a committed relationship or marriage is the type of relationship they were seeking.

In addition to a shift in relationship goals, the qualities singles find attractive in their dates may be changing. "In a recent Match.com poll, single women selected teachers as more eligible dates than CEOs, politicians or stockbrokers, suggesting that the attributes singles are seeking in a potential romantic mate may have shifted," reports Trish McDermott, vice president of Romance for Match. com. "Rather than power or personal wealth, single women may find men who are deeply committed to contributing to their community, and making a difference in the day-to-day lives of others, to be today's great catches."

Although the desire to find and form a committed romantic relationship may be felt more strongly, Match.com research suggests some of the basics of dating, including age-old gender-based misunderstandings and uncertainty regarding gift giving is still with us. Two recent polls of nearly 15,000 singles reveal a differing opinion regarding Valentine's Day gift giving. Sixty-three percent of single men surveyed indicate that "time alone," and not a gift, would be the best Valentine's Day present they could offer their mate this year, while 50% of single women surveyed indicate that receiving "nothing" for Valentine's Day could be cause for a break up.

Match.com, a wholly owned subsidiary of Ticketmaster and a part of USA Networks Interactive Group, is a leading subscription-based online dating site. The company's personals businesses claim more than 382,000 paying subscribers. With more than 2.5 million members with profiles posted, Match.com offers adults worldwide a fun, private and secure environment for meeting other singles. Match.com estimates that the firm is responsible for arranging hundreds of thousands of relationships for its members and has confirmed more than 1,475 marriages.

Hitwise Lifestyle in the UK notes that many e-dating Web sites report an imbalance in number of male and female visitors. "Gender differences are evident everywhere online," said LeeAnn Prescott, director of Research at Hitwise. "While the larger dating Web sites have more equal male/female visitor ratios, this data prove that online dating sites must work harder to provide a critical mass and balance of members in order to attract additional singles." An examination of the top 100 Web sites by gender reveals that the Web site with the largest percentage of female visitors for the week ending February 10, 2007 was Love Access (www.loveaccess.com), which comprised 87.4% of female visitors, followed by SeniorPeopleMeet.com, proving that older women are adopting online dating faster than older men and CatholicMatch.com, a Web site for connecting Catholics. The e-dating Web sites with the largest portion of male visitors for the week ending February 10, 2007 were Gay online dating Web sites (including ManHunt.com, Adam4Adam.com, and Gay.com), as well as Web sites focused on matching American men with foreign brides, such as AnastasiaWeb.com and Globaladies.com.

INTERNET DATING PRACTICES

When Mark Nesbitt told his friends more than four years ago he was dating a woman he had met on the Internet, some thought it was a bit zany. "Certainly back then, people felt Internet dating was shading on the oddball," says Nesbitt, president, CEO and co-owner of Vertex Consultants Inc., which advises companies (from Petro-Canada to Bank of Montreal) on consumer marketing.

Fast forward to today. The 49-year-old Nesbitt has been married for 18 months to Judy Farrant, the woman he met in January 1998 through a Web personals service run by Toronto-based Interactive Media Group (IMG), which re-launched itself last fall as Lavalife Inc. And many of the couple's friends are now converts. In fact, two of Farrant's friends have subsequently married or become engaged to people they met on the Internet. Another is set to marry a man Farrant had actually met first on a Web-arranged date. "After her own date with him, Judy decided that he was a great guy and figured her friend was the exact person for him," Nesbitt says. "When your friends see that you're with a person that's so much better for you than the others you've met through traditional means, it breaks down their inhibitions about Internet dating."

That's the type of testimonial the Lavalife CEO Peter Housley loves. A poster boy like Nesbitt, after all, legitimizes his claim that the Web is as good a way as any to find that nice, successful person who just might be the one. "I'd go so far as to say that if you are without a love interest and you are in your 30s or older, you should have your head examined if you aren't using the Internet," says Lavalife's CEO Peter Housley, "because if not, what are you doing to take control of your life?"

Housley admits there is some stiff competition, however, especially from Match.com Inc., About 7,000 men and women sign on as new customers each day. The service now has a total client base of about two million. As well, a study conducted by Nielson/Net Ratings last year ranked lavalife.com eighth in a list of the top 20 sites in the world with the most loyal customer following. No other Internet dating industry site was mentioned.

No wonder daters and mate seekers are falling in love with the Internet. Lavalife's research indicates that the percentage of North American singles that have tried Internet dating has grown from about two to three percent in 1999 to ten percent in 2002. The potential for arranging thousands of successful matches has barely been tapped, and Housley estimates that matchmaking services bring in about $1 billion annually in North America. "But it's mainly still based on bricks and mortar, and while these can be very profitable, it's only a tiny fraction of the market's potential."

Unlike the vast majority of Internet dating services, lavalife.com does not charge a monthly subscription fee, but charges per transaction. "It's free for anyone to look once you've registered, and you pay only when you want to make contact," says Housley.

SEGMENTATION STRATEGIES FOR MARKETING E-PERSONAL RELATING SERVICES

For many, online dating sites have become the new singles scene compared to more traditional places like clubs and bars. These sites attract a variety of people looking for romantic relationships, from receptionists to executives and long-time singles to widowers. Online matchmaking services can even accommodate specialized dating requirements for singles over 50, African-American singles, Jewish singles, gay and lesbian singles and singles in the same professions.

"It's a way for me to cut through wasted time of people who aren't what I'm looking for," said John Heinlein, 31, of Sunnyvale, California. He is an executive manager and a subscriber at Match. com. "The enhanced profiles give people a sense of who you are."

Internet dating services have become global as well. Online dating services now include custom brides-to-order from the Far East, Middle East, and the Soviet countries. The wide variety of offerings includes Web sites that offer one-night stands and others that allow individuals to communicate instantaneously with their new match.

In studying Internet dating service providers, strategy issues are difficult to separate from customer or end user concepts. Some Internet dating services, such as those offered by companies such as eHarmony.com and Match.com, are one of the fastest growing and popular online industries. The successful online dating companies are discovering how lucrative this market is, and by specializing in single-target markets, have come up with improvements to customer relationship marketing concepts (Smith, 2005), used by companies to manage their relationships with customers, including the capture, storage and analysis of customer information.

The online dating industry is utilizing specialized or niche market segmentation.

EHarmony.com specifically targets Christians who are looking for a relationship with someone with shared spiritual beliefs. Matching singles that are like–minded individuals, eHarmony.com extensively advertises their use of a scientific approach to matching individuals based on 29 physical and emotional dimensions that measure compatibility. They claim that these character traits: adaptability, curiosity, and intellect, family background and values, spirituality, and feelings about children, emotional temperament and skills (such as conflict resolution) are their key roles to achieving a higher success rate than their

competitors. EHarmony.com has the narrowest market segment, and is considered financially successful. Profitability appears to be directly correlated with the ability to customize market segment, and apply basic CRM principles, while still taking advantage of the convenient broadcasting aspects of the Internet. (Smith, 2005)

Other online dating service companies such as Seek4Love.com are not as well-known because they have not developed a specific target market. An inspection of their Web site reveals that they offer international dating services, pen pals, marriage, and matchmaking services. In most cases, consumers are very specific in their quest for a match.

Christine Ferris is searching online for that special someone. "I would like to meet a man who can relax and enjoy the woods, the fog, the sea, the mountains," says her profile on dating site True.com. "Someone who can feel the wonder of nature. I am a romantic and you are too." Also, her ideal man should "have health insurance and use it." Health insurance is expensive, complex and bureaucratic. These days, it's also sexy. Right up there with washboard abs, a steady job and a fun-loving personality, health coverage is emerging as a hot selling point among online daters. It's especially the case among suitors of a certain age who need, and prize, good benefits the most. Those who have it sometimes flaunt it as an asset, a sign to potential mates that they are serious, professional and grounded. Others troll for partners with blue-chip policies because they need coverage themselves, or want evidence—short of asking for a credit report—that a prospect isn't a slacker "I don't have time to waste," explains Ms. Ferris, a 45-year-old teacher from Sebastien, Fla. "If you care about yourself, then you're going to tend to care about other people as well." (Rubenstein, 2006)

CONSUMER DIVERSITY AND NICHE SEGMENTATION

Established in 1997, Jdate.com has about 350,000 members—including about 5,000 in Atlanta—and a virtual lock on Jewish dating online. "It's also part of a growing number of niche online dating sites that are the meeting places of the future," says Lisa Daily, an online dating columnist for singlestop.com and allthatwomenwant.com. From "advanceddegreesingles.com" to "largeandlovely. com" to "doggiedating.com," pet lovers, heavy people and those with master's degrees and above are just a click away from a plethora of people with common interests.

According to Jupiter Media Metrix, niche sites are luring singles away from general online dating sites, such as Match.com. It is unclear how big the online dating industry is or how many niche sites exist, because many of the companies are not public. But indications point to a lucrative and ballooning industry. With a total of eight online dating services, including gay11.com, MatchNet, the parent company of Jdate, is seeing its profits grow.

"I thought online dating would be a good business, and we decided to do niches," said Joe Shapira, MatchNet's chief executive officer. Despite the company's considerable revenues (close to $5 million per quarter), the bigger online dating sites are striking back. Match.com has affiliated itself with several niche sites, including one for older people—sassyseniors.com. Michael Brown, CEO of blacksingles.com, said niche sites streamline the search for a mate.

There's "saltandpeppersingles.com," for singles who want to date outside their race, and John Jablonski of largeandlovely.com said his site puts overweight singles at ease.

Esther Gwinnell, a professor of psychiatry at Oregon Health Sciences University, said niche sites are practical because singles can instantly move beyond a powerful issue in their life, whether it is weight, color or religion. She said niche sites also increase the odds of finding a match. "If you are a pet lover, you need to wade through folks who wouldn't identify with you," she explained. "This cuts out time because it's a whole lot more specific." But Gwinnell, author of *Online seductions: Falling in love with strangers on the Internet,* warned that niche sites often give singles a false sense of security. "There's already this sense that you belong to a group," she said. "In general rooms, there is a grain of suspicion. But in niche groups, there's this sense that it's safer, and people let their guard down" (Oliviero, 2002).

Online dating site Match.com and BET Interactive, LLC, the premier African-American portal and online urban music destination, have established a strategic partnership in which Match. com will be the exclusive provider of online dating on BET.com. This partnership gives BET.com users access to the more than 3 million members with profiles posted on the Match.com site. Voted "Best African American Community Site 2001 and 2002" by Yahoo! Internet Life magazine, BET.com (http://www.bet.com/) is tailored to the unique interests and issues of African Americans. BET.com provides original and licensed content, integrated community applications and convergent programming across a broad array of topics, including news, music, entertainment, style, health, money, romance, food and more (PR Newswire, 2002).

According to the American Social Health Association, more than 65 million Americans live with a viral sexually transmitted disease such as herpes, human papillomavirus (HPV), hepatitis B and HIV (Booth, 2005). This has prompted the emergence of a handful of niche dating sites with names like Positive Personals (for consumers diagnosed with HIV) and After H (for consumers living with herpes and HPV).

RELIGIOUS E-PERSONAL RELATING SERVICES

Many singles want dating services that cater to their religious preferences. Christians, Jews, Muslims and other religious groups have tailor-made dating services that are just a phone call or mouse click away. Equally Yoked is a Christian-based singles organization located in Bedford, a Fort Worth, Texas suburb.

Equally Yoked (www.equallyyoked.com) began in California in 1986 and has more than 20 offices nationwide. It takes its name from II Corinthians 6:14, a passage that warns believers not to unite with unbelievers, thus becoming "unequally yoked"—similar to oxen of different sizes pulling a single wagon.

It does not consider itself a dating service, but rather an extended family for Christian singles. The organization offers about 30 alcohol-free activities a month. To surf the site's profiles requires payments of $25.50 a month.

On JDate.com, an e-dating service targeting the Jewish community, initial communication is anonymous, and members can then decide whether they want to exchange contact information.

For the Muslim consumers, Soulmates (www.verypersonal.com), a $5.00 fee is charged for data sheets. Subsequently, a woman's "wakil," or guardian, arranges a meeting between interested parties.

GLOBAL INTERFACE

Ticketmaster, the world's leading ticketing and access company, and parent company of Match.com, signed an agreement to acquire Soulmates Technology, a global online personals group providing dating and matchmaking services in nearly 30 countries worldwide. The move accelerates Match.com's international expansion strategy and secures its position as a leading global provider of online dating services.

Based in Sydney, Australia, Soulmates Technology provides online dating services to more than 2 million registered users. Soulmates Technology delivers a private-label solution for portals seeking a customized personals interface that takes on the look and feel of their site. Through a relationship with MSN, Soulmates Technology is currently utilizing their technology to power MSN's personals in approximately 25 countries. With the capability to deliver online personals in more than 18 languages, and 32 global currencies, the acquisition of Soulmates Technology has given Match.com an immediate worldwide footprint.

"This transaction significantly accelerates Match.com's international growth by aligning us with several new international partners and providing a platform to deploy our brand worldwide" said John Pleasants, president and chief executive officer. "This transaction helps to secure Match.com as a category leader and further propel its future growth opportunities" (PR Newswire, 2002).

Several recent publications document the prevalence of online dating services in other countries of the world. For instance, a study was done in Australia surrounding the two stereotypes that older adults do not do computers—and certainly not the Internet, and older adults do not do sex—they are asexual. The results clearly indicated these stereotypes to be flawed. For the most part, the relationships described were meaningful, intimate and long-lasting. Further, the study concluded that given the anticipated future size of the older adult population and their increasing use of the Internet, it can only be expected that finding a partner online will quickly become the "norm" for much of this generation, as it has for countless others (Malta, 2007).

A report on digital dating in Canada reports that over a million Canadians have visited an online dating site, and the potential for online dating services in Canada is an additional 2-3 million adults. The report also came up with the findings that there are four main social forces driving the rapid growth of online dating:

- A growing proportion of the population is composed of singles, the main pool for online dating
- Career and time pressures are increasing, so people are looking for more efficient ways of meeting others for intimate relationships
- Single people are more mobile due to the demands of the job market, so it is more difficult for them to meet people for dating
- Workplace romance is on the decline due to growing sensitivity about sexual harassment.

Further findings include the following:

Online daters are sociable off-line. Twenty-four percent belong to a religious organization, 41% belong to clubs, 82% visit family or relatives at least once a month, and 53% go out with others for social or leisure activities more than once a week. Most people use online dating services mainly to find dates and establish a long-term relationship, not to flirt online, find a marriage partner or find a sexual partner. People use online dating services mainly because they create the opportunity to meet people one would otherwise never meet, they offer privacy and confidentiality, and they are more convenient than other ways of trying to meet people (Brym & Lenton, 2001).

Revenues of the leading European dating Web sites are expected to more than double over the next five years, from $200 million to $450 million, predicts Paris-based analyst Olivier Beauvillain of consultancy Jupiter Research. While sales in the U.S. are still higher than in Europe, they are expected to grow only 9% this year, to $515 million. "The European market is the most exciting right now" Beauvillain says.

The region's biggest online dating service is Meetic.com, a private company launched three years ago by Web entrepreneur Marc Simoncini. The site is set to hit 10 million members around St. Single's Day and has booked around $55 million in sales this year. In France, a country inextricably linked with romance, one adult in 15 is a Meetic member. In Italy and Spain, it is one in fewer than 50. In these and Meetic's eight other country sites—Austria, Belgium, Denmark, Germany, the Netherlands, Sweden, Switzerland, and Britain—membership is soaring by as much as 20,000 a day. More country sites have been added—Poland, Portugal, Greece, and Ireland. "As business models go, online dating sites approach perfection" says Simoncini. "All we needed was two months of free services, and then word of mouth took over. Now our customers are our products, and they deliver themselves to each other" (Tiplady, 2005).

COMMUNICATIONS RESEARCH AND PROMOTIONAL STRATEGIES OF E-PERSONAL-RELATING

Gibbs, Ellison and Heino (2006) investigate self-disclosure in the novel context of online dating relationships. They report that perceived online dating success is predicted by four dimensions of self-disclosure (honesty, amount, intent, and valence), although honesty has a negative effect. Moreover, online dating experience is a strong predictor of perceived success in online dating.

Unique and numerous opportunities occur for people to find a romantic partner. What happens when the online relationship goes off-line? Biever (2007) reports that a study was completed in 2006 by the non-profit Pew Internet Se American Life Project based in Washington D.C. She finds that 74% of single Internet users in the U.S. have taken part in at least one online dating-related activity, including sites specifically devoted to finding a match, while 15% of American adults (30 million people) say they know someone who has been in a long-term relationship with a partner they met online.

The Internet has some clear advantages over the real world as a place to meet people, says Dan Ariely, who studies online dating at the Massachusetts Institute of Technology's Media

Lab. "The problem of meeting people in modern life is very real. Online relationships are a way to experiment cheaply and in a non-dangerous way with romantic life." Ariely goes on to say that you can meet far more people online than you could ever hope to in a bar or in the office. And because online games and chat rooms often have a theme, they allow users to find people that share the same interests. Match.com and eHarmony.com, as well as other online dating sites, utilize algorithms that the originators say can select couples most likely to be a successful match.

Internet dating site, DatingDirect, has launched its first TV campaign, claiming to be the first site of its kind to do so. The ads will be shown on terrestrial, satellite and cable channels including Channel Four, UK Living and Paramount. The campaign broke January 2002. It was designed by OWN+P and produced and directed by Maverick Media, with Mediacom responsible for buying the media. The ad adopts the popular "Bridget Jones singleton theme," by using a series of sketches to encourage single women to click on DatingDirect's first major off-line marketing activity for over a year and its intent is to boost its database (New Media Age, 2002).

In July 2002, Ticketmaster's online dating service Match.com launched a $6.5 million, six-month-long TV campaign featuring individuals who met their mates on the site. Today, the service has an estimated $25 million advertising budget.

FUTURE TRENDS

The ways to expand this phenomenon do not appear to be exhausted. For example, mobile dating, also referred to as "mobile romance," is one of the more recent entries into online dating. So how does mobile dating work? Hopeful singles begin by signing up with companies like Zogo and MeetMoi along with Match.com, which will also be added to the list. Once members are registered,

singles then text message their current location via a zip code or street address. This provides instantaneous profiles of members within the area who meet the user's criteria. Currently, various services are being offered throughout the mobile dating market. One such service is browsing lists of members who fit the user's criteria. Members have the option of requesting a phone conversation with an individual of interest. A text message is then sent to the individual, if and when both parties consent, a call goes out to both mobile devices while concealing each members phone number (Vascellaro, 2007).

The economic future of online dating seems prominent. New technology is enabling singles to maintain their prospects while on the go. Mobile dating (Wong, 2006) is quickly becoming the hippest trend on the single scene. One customer of MeetMoi, Jeff Blum, expressed the convenience of mobile dating by saying, "I like the fact that we were talking right then and not waiting for e-mails to go back and forth. It all happened right away" (Vascellaro, 2007). This type of convenience has become the focal point for mobile dating, allowing the service of the Internet as an updated instant version on a customer's mobile devices.

Socialight is a company in the market who allows its members to use "virtual sticky notes" to post their current locations. When other members approach that location of the user, they are notified via text message of the users' location. Jumbuck Entertainment is a company that offers speed dating on the go. The service charges its members $3 a month which enables customers to log onto "virtual lobbies" where they choose flirting partners (Vascellaro, 2007). Users can have up to ten-minute conversations with the flirting partner; each partner has personal descriptive criteria such as their age and location that is available for members to view.

Mobile dating is beginning to take shape but appears to be more appealing to a younger segment of mobile users. This phenomenon of mobile romance relies heavily on the use of text messaging which has grown rapidly among younger mobile users. Of the younger mobile users, more than three in four use text. This compares to one in four adult mobile users who do not make use of text messaging features (CNN, 2006). The mobile dating market is growing at a strong and steady pace with about 3.6 million U.S. mobile users taking advantage of the newest convenience of mobile dating (Wall Street Journal, 2007).

It is clear that marketing to singles has a wide variety of avenues to which organizations have not yet explored. For example, Sox Appeal has been developed as a means of providing opportunities for Red Sox fans to connect. Scout Productions along with New England Sports Network has teamed up to present a reality television show that mixes singles, speed dating and Red Sox games. The show features a single Red Sox fan and three blind dates that last a total of two innings per date. It is during the seventh inning stretch that the Sox fan chooses which date he or she would like to spend the rest of the game with. The reality show may even expand to include same sex dates. Producer Eric Korsh said the show was "open to anything" when asked about the possibility of same sex dates appearing on the show (Boston Herald, 2007). This new trend of reality blind dates during sporting events adds new dimension to the possibility of new markets for which companies may begin to target singles. The trends mentioned throughout continue to grow along with new angles to the same idea as in Sox Appeal. There is no reason to think that this would not expand to other types of sports and sports teams and grow more in-depth and breadth in the offerings. One example could include the addition of a singles lounge within a ballpark, possibly even offering speed dating during innings and or prior to the game.

CONCLUSION

An enormous ground swell is occurring of people wanting to meet people. This chapter describes the many options and opportunities for people of all walks of life to meet one another. One need only select the vehicle that suits him/her best in pursuing e-personal relating possibilities. Now, much of this research can be done in the comfort and privacy of one's home. Much of the support can come from organizations and services set up specifically for the purpose of helping people meet people.

This chapter focuses on the diversity that exists among e-dating consumers—older, younger, black, white, pet lovers, religious, spiritual, and gay or straight individuals seeking partners for fun, companionship, commitment or conversation—and documents various demographic and psychographic segmentation basis currently being used by online dating services, in an attempt to attract a specialized target market.

REFERENCES

Brym, R., & Lenton, R. (2001, March 25). Love online: A report on digital dating in Canada. *MSN*. Retrieved December 2, 2007, from http://www.msn.ca.

Dvorak, J. (2006, December 26). Unreal life? Get a life. *PC Magazine*. Retrieved December 2, 2007, from Business Search Premier database.

Epstein, R. (2007). The truth about online dating. *Scientific American Mind*. Retrieved November 5, 2007, from Psychology and Behavioral Sciences Collection database.

Gangemi, J. (2006, September 21). A Myspace that speaks your language. *Business Week*. Retrieved November 5, 2007, from Business Source Premier database.

Goff, C. (2004, September 9). Contact has been made. *New Media Age*. Retrieved November 5, 2007, from Business Source Premier database.

Green, E. (2005, November 14). The web of social networking. *U.S. News & World Report*. Retrieved

November 5, 2007, from Business Source Premier database.

Han, W. (2004, September 6). Campus connection. *Time Inc.* Retrieved November 5, 2007, from Business Source Premier database.

Malta, S. (2007). Love actually! Older adults and their romantic Internet relationships [Electronic version]. *Australian Journal of Emerging Technologies and Society, 5,* 84-102.

McCall, M. (2006, April 15). Hooking up in the information age. *Wireless Week.* Retrieved December 2, 2007, from http://www.wirelessweek.com.

Patterson, A., & Hodgson, J. (2006). A speed-dating story: The lovers guide to marketing excellence. *Journal of Marketing Management, 22,* 455-471.

Stanley, T. (2006, April 17). Online-Dating sites get stood up by consumers. *Advertising Age.* Retrieved November 5, 2007, from Business Source Premier database.

Tiplady, R. (2005, February 8). Eye on Europe. *Business Week.* Retrieved December 2, 2007, from http://www.businessweek.com.

Chapter XV
Understanding and Facilitating the Development of Social Networks in Online Dating Communities:
A Case Study and Model

Jonathan Bishop
Glamorgan Blended Learning Ltd. & The GTi Suite & Valleys Innovation Centre & Navigation Park & Abercynon, UK

ABSTRACT

Online dating is a big business, allowing people from the comfort of their own home to view and read about potential mates all around the world. Different dating sites offer different services. However, it is not yet commonplace for Web sites dedicated to dating to use the social networking tools used by popular online communities, such as those that use the personal homepage and message board genres. The ecological cognition framework (ECF) provides a theoretical model regarding online dating communities' behavior and relationship development. A model based on the ECF is proposed and provides a basis for developing online dating services that effectively support relationship development. Two investigations are presented in this chapter, one that uses a case study approach to identify and describe online dating services from the perspective of a specific case and another that assess the effectiveness of existing online dating services based on the guidelines developed from the case study. The case study provides a useful insight into the nature of social networking from the perspective of a specific case, which led to guidelines for developing e-dating systems that when evaluated showed that the most popular social networking services also score well against the criteria proposed in those guidelines.

INTRODUCTION

According to Dvorak et al. (2003), people have always found ways to meet on the Internet, with online dating being a big business, allowing people from the comfort of their own home to view and read about potential mates all around the world. Through *virtual worlds* such as multi-user-dungeons (MUDs), they can interact, talk and compete against others in an online environment. According to Quansah (2004), different dating sites offer different services, though it is not yet commonplace for Web sites dedicated to dating to use the social networking tools offered by popular online communities. Liebowitz (2003) argues that social networking is a powerful way to bring people closer together suggesting social networking tools are ideally placed to enhance dating Web sites. According to Kuriansky there are a number of advantages to dating online, including the immediacy, the cost, access, practicing social skills, learning verbal expression, developing relationships, accessibility and control. Immediacy is beneficial because opportunities are just a click away, as the user can be writing a document or surfing the Net then switch to e-mail or instant messaging. The computer can cost less than phone calls, and with some services the dating is free. Access to the services is efficient whether wireless broadband or simple dial-up. Online dating allows the practicing of social skills as the user can make mistakes knowing they will never see that person again. It allows for the learning of verbal expression, as when the user types on their profile or in messages they practice expressing themselves in they way they want to. Computer contact can also help foster the friendship that is the basis for a long-lasting love by allowing the time and safety for a relationship to grow. Those who cannot get out of their locality due to accessibility restrictions can also benefit from online dating as they can keep in touch with others at a distance. The user is also in total control of where, where and with whom they connect, especially if the service uses the Circle of Friends.

The Circle of Friends method of social networking, developed as part of the VECC Project (see Bishop, 2002) has been embedded into several social networking sites. The benefit of the Circle of Friends over earlier technologies is that it puts the user in control. The first Web site to use it for dating was *Friendster* in 2002 when there were only a handful of sites using the technology, including A Guide to Robin Hood and Northern England and *Llantrisant Online*, although according to Kim and Aldrich (2005) there were at least 30 social networking sites based on the Circle of Friends in 2005.

Social networking tools often form part of online communities and it has been argued that these communities have the potential to radically transform social interaction and community formation (Lutters & Ackerman, 2003). There have been definitions of online communities based on the forms they take from Web sites that provide facilities to discuss particular subjects or interests to groups of people communicating using instant messaging tools (Bishop, 2003). Hunter (2002) defines an online community as a group of people who interact with each other, learn from each other's work and provide knowledge and information resources to the group related to certain agreed-upon topics of shared interest. There exists a possible technical definition, which could be that an information system is an online community if those that use it have to go through the Membership Lifecycle identified by Kim (2000).

Understanding how people develop relationships and the role of social networking technology such as the *Circle of Friends* in enhancing the dating experience requires a deeper understanding of human behavior.

UNDERSTANDING THE BEHAVIOUR OF ACTORS IN ONLINE DATING COMMUNITIES

It has long been argued that there should be a framework for understanding actors based on ecological perceptual psychology (Kyttä, 2003). Wilson and Keil (2001) indicate that early work into ecological psychology focused on movement-produced information, which had been largely neglected in other approaches. It is quite clear that any model to explain the behavior of actors that ignores the possibly of direct perception cannot fully explain the behavior or actors in an environment. To fully understand the actor's role in online communities, we must treat the virtual environment on par with the physical environment. Virtual environments contain other actors, structures and artifacts, such as mediating artifacts (Bishop, 2005). Both virtual and physical environments can provide stimuli that create impetuses in actors, and these actors will be driven to participate in both environments as a result of experiencing them.

The *ecological cognition framework* (Bishop, 2007a; 2007c) presented in Figure 1 suggests that there are five binary opposition forces that have impact on an actor that are activated when a change occurs in the actor's environment, which are social-antisocial, creative-destructive, order-chaos, vengeance-forgiveness, and existential-thanatotic. Examples of each segment of these binary opposition forces can be seen in online communities. Social forces are very common in driving actors to take part in human-computer systems, which are often social spaces. Rhiengold (2000) describes 'the social Web' in which people like him participate as a result of being driven by their longings to participate. Actors in these virtual environments often experience creative forces and will solve problems and create content. The existence of order forces is also apparent in information systems, where actors will carry out actions such as organizing bookmarks, rearrang-

ing pages and some actors may take control of a situation, such as when members are flaming each other in a chat session, and others will attempt to create order when a bulletin board goes off topic and will carry out actions to bring it back to the original topic, despite the fact that allowing a bulletin board to go off topic can increase sociability in the community (Bishop, 2002). Actions driven by vengeance forces are very apparent in human-computer systems, as actors in virtual environments are known to be very aggressive (Kiesler & Sproull, 1992; Wallace, 2001), carrying out actions such as flaming, and posting negative feedback on other community members. Existential forces, such as eating, while not obvious in virtual environments, have an impact on the actions of an action that is part of them. Actions resulting from anti-social forces are easily discovered in virtual environments, as actors will often flame others. Destructive forces are also apparent in information systems that can be edited, as some actors will 'blank' pages of content. Chaos forces can be seen in some functional systems that form part of virtual environments as people with attempt to provoke others. The result of forgiveness forces can be seen in some information systems, where actors will apologize to actors that they have had a disagreement with, often what has resulted from order forces.

The second level of the framework presented in Figure 1 is an actor's cognitions, which are goals, plans, values, beliefs and interests. The arrow in the ECF between Level 3 and the Environment is the response. The response changes the environment, either intrinsically through modifying the actor, or extrinsically through them modifying their environment.

A CASE STUDY OF SOCIAL NETWORKING AND DATING ONLINE

Selecting from different e-dating services can be a challenging process for individuals in their search for potential friends and partners. There is a plethora of social networking services available on the Web that individuals have to navigate their way through in order to achieve their goals. A number of questions can be asked, including what do people look to get out of social networking services, what makes a good social networking service and can current psychological frameworks be used to understand these applications. Some of the most widely used methods for researching online are interviewing, observation and document analysis (Mann & Stewart, 2000). Interviewing is the most widely applied technique for conducting systematic social inquiry in academic, clinical, business, political and media life with qualitative research being well established in this area (*ibid.*). According to Thyer (2001), interviewing participants is one way of accessing information beyond what has been observed, and that is related to the meaning of the experience. According to Barton (2006), there is no correct or incorrect way of interviewing participants, though Stables and Goodwyn (2004) recommend using follow-up interviews when conducting a study. Interviewing can form a core part of a case study. The basic case study entails the detailed and intensive analysis of a single case with some of the best known studies in business and management research being based on this method, which can be an investigation of a single organization, a single location, a person, or an event (Bryman & Bell, 2003). Some case studies investigating an organization have provided insights into the types of problems usability studies are likely to encounter, as well as some valuable lessons learned along the way in the organization (Rowley, 1994) and others looking at the development of online learning communities over a number of years have managed to refine design methodologies (Bishop, 2007d).

This first study in this chapter seeks to develop an understanding of online dating communities by evaluating the case of someone seeking to benefit from these services.

The Case

The case in question was of a young male in his early 20s who was educated to university level who took part in university social activities such as debating, book club and political activities, suggesting he had reasonable social skills and capabilities. The case over a period of a year used various online communities that could be used as online dating services and engaged with them to develop relationships with others. Utilizing the ecological cognition framework (Bishop, 2007a; 2007c) and the ecological cognitive learning theory model (Bishop, 2007b), an interviewing model was developed to assist the author in asking questions that would allow him to discover how the case used online dating services and how they interacted with others in them. The model suggests an interviewer should look at the intelligences used by the case, investigate the stages they go through when learning, investigate the process by which they perceive and respond to a stimulus, and investigate the cognitions they hold and develop and how this relates to the way they perceive the worlds around them.

Results

The interview explored the cognitions held by the case, including his goals for using social networking sites. While initially he did not claim to have any goals, it soon became clear that he selected people he would interact with based on whether they were looking for a relationship. The case indicated that he would not interact with another person without first finding out about them on their profile, suggesting that the learning cycle proposed by Bishop (2007b) is equally relevant to relationship building in that there needs to be some encoding of beliefs, values and interests before an actor will develop goals and plans to interact with someone, suggesting that there needs to be a degree of intimacy and liking before a relationship can progress. Also clear from the interview was that this particular case was concerned whether the people on the sites masked some malicious intention, such as to send them SPAM messages. The case claimed that along with photographs he assessed how much the individual used the service as an indication of whether they were genuine, suggesting that online dating communities could be more effective if the profile pages show that the individual has participated in community life, such as through taking or setting up quizzes, posting messages or leaving comments on others' pages. A feature that seemed important to the case was that the dating services should offer recommendation systems that suggest specific individuals that they might be interested in, and he suggested that he is more likely to be encouraged to interact with someone if the site recommends it suggesting that online dating services need to be persuasive in their approach to helping people find their match.

TOWARDS A MODEL FOR UNDERSTANDING RELATIONSHIPS AND DEVELOPING ONLINE DATING COMMUNITIES

The study demonstrated the relevance of the ecological cognition framework in understanding the behavior of actions in virtual environments, and the relevance of ecological cognitive learning theory to understanding relationships. The framework could also be used to understand the particular character traits of those using online dating communities. Bishop (2007b) proposes that for an actor to learn or be persuaded they have to experience five psychological effects: the belonging effect, the demonstration effect, the inspiration effect, the mobilization effect and the confirmation effect. Their respective processes of the bonding process, the sub-conscious encoding

Figure 1. A model for understanding relationships and developing online dating communities

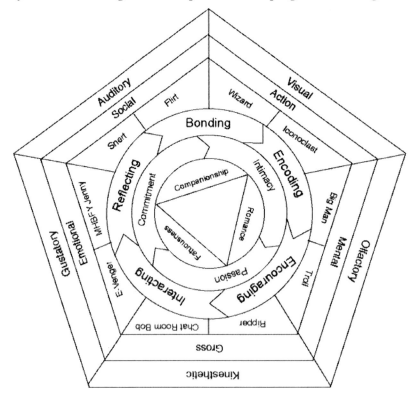

process, the encouragement process, the interaction process and the reflection process can create these effects. Some authors have suggested that seduction is a form of persuasion (e.g., Mbakwe & Cunliffe, 2003) and others have suggested that seduction is an important technique for increasing the chances of a successful dating outcome (e.g., MacKinney, 1991). In light of the study earlier in this chapter, Bishop's (2007b) lifecycle can be seen to be appropriate for understanding the development and maintenance of relationships. Also apparent is that this lifecycle can be mapped onto the *Triangular theory of love* (Sternberg, 1986), as it can be seen that the bonding stage, the encoding stage and part of the encouragement stage form part of what Sternberg calls intimacy; what Sternberg calls passion can be seen to fall into the encouragement and interaction stage of Bishop's lifecycle, and the reflection stage that leads back onto the bonding stage can be seen to occur when those in a relationship experience what Sternberg calls commitment.

- Recommendation 1: Utilize various genres of online community

Many authors of guidelines to building online communities have indirectly recommended using multiple models of online communities (e.g., Figallo, 1998; Kim, 2000; Preece, 2000). A Web site meeting the definition of an online community based on Kim's (2000) lifecycle could utilize more than one genre. As identified in the study above, a Web site is more able to assist with social networking and relationship building if it uses a variety of different models of discussion and networking at the different stages of the lifecycle presented in the model in Figure 2.

- Recommendation 2: Utilize the Circle of Friends social networking tool, or at minimum allow people to keep lists of actual or potential friends.

The ECF clearly places the actor in the environment, and the relationship between actors is clearly important. Many social network service providers have used the *Circle of Friends* to allow their actors using their service to manage their relationships with others effectively. The Circle of Friends, which was popularized by *Friendster* (Teten & Allen, 2005), allows actors to see not only their own friends as they could with instant messaging tools, but also allow them to see who their friends' friends are. As a social networking technology, the Circle of Friends fits into a long history of using the Internet as an environment for developing relationships and increasing sociability (Weng, 2007). The first social networking service on the Web was Classmates.com, which launched in 1995 and used the *Old School Tie* social networking method, which is defined as a method for building networks of users using the schools and universities they graduated from. This was followed in 1997 with the launch of *SixDegrees.com,* which utilized the *Web of Contacts* model, which is defined as a technique for displaying social networks using social networking analysis that the user does not manage it. The advantage of the Circle of Friends, which was developed in 1999 as part of the Virtual Environments for Community and Commerce (VECC) Project (see Bishop, 2002; 2007d), is that it allows the user to manage their network and decide who they want to be friends with. The 2001 implementation of the Circle of Friends as part of Llantrisant.com allowed users to classify their friends according to whether they trusted them or not, combining it with the Circle of Trust that was also developed in 1999. The Circle of Friends flourished in 2002 with the launch of Friendster, and is now part of many other communities including the popular *MySpace* and Facebook services.

- Recommendation 3: Utilize a recommendation or search system that encourages people to interact with others with similar cognitions to them

As the ecological cognition framework clearly suggests, a stimulus, such as a thought to do something or a request from another actor can only be turned into a response after an actor's cognitions, that is, their goals, plans, values, beliefs and interests have been activated and evaluated. Social networking sites can help in this process by removing the obstacles to actors interacting with others. One method for doing this is to use recommender systems, which have been used in e-commerce to reduce the number of products from the whole catalogue to ones that the customer would be interested in (Wang, 2004). Online dating services could utilize such systems to narrow down the number of individuals available to an actor in line with what they are looking for. This could be done using personality-based questionnaires as is done with OkCupid, personal characteristics, as is done with Match.com or keyword searches as Match.com and MySpace use.

Such systems may allow actors to be engaged in a state of *'flow'* so much so that they experience 'deference'. Csikszentmihalyi (1977; 1990) refers to a state of flow as being the state of mind where an actor will act with total involvement narrowing their attention focus and experiencing a loss of self-consciousness. Bishop (2007a; 2007c) suggests that if a virtual community does not create discomfort in the actor's mind, or *'dissonance'*, then the actor is more likely to become engaged in a state of flow and act out their desires, thus experiencing deference. Deference in this context is where an actor will receive a request to do something, such as someone asking them how they are and will respond immediately without any discomfort, in the example immediately saying they are 'fine' as if it is a reflex. However, Bishop (2007c) also points out that while engaging an actor in a state of flow might mean that they are more likely to experience deference and act out their desires to be social, there is also the possibility that they will act out their vengeance desires as well. This may be true as some studies have indicated that in virtual environments where

actors are likely to experience deference they are more likely to flame others (Orengo Castellá et Al., 2000).

THE FUTURE OF ONLINE DATING COMMUNITIES

A study was carried out with major dating services being identified through the earlier study in this chapter and through an Internet search. The services were scored based on how well they adhered to the recommendations. A dating service was given one point per online community genre it utilized, one point if it used the Circle of Friends or half a point if it used a friend list and one point if it complied with recommendation 3. The mean of number of points across the recommendations was calculated and this was the score given to the dating service.

The findings of the study reveal that the online dating services driven by subscriptions offer the least amount of social networking opportunities, as they often only utilize the personal homepage genre of online community, which only makes them effective for the bonding and encoding stage of the relationship. The dating services modeled on the free-at-the-point-of-use model scored much higher as many of them utilized the Circle of Friends social networking method and a wider number of online community genres. The highest scoring dating service was *Facebook*, which uses the personal homepage genre, the message board genre, the weblog and directory genre, as well as utilizing the Circle of Friends. The second highest scoring, Second Life utilizes virtual worlds, message boards, chat groups and profile pages to allow people to contact in a three-dimensional environment. The popularity of Facebook with its widespread use and its high score based on these guidelines suggest that the guidelines may be appropriate for evaluating the appropriateness of a social networking service for dating. According to Easton (1982), being able to predict outcomes

Table 1. Scores of major dating services

Dating Service	Score
Facebook	2.00
Second Life	1.83
Badoo	1.67
MySpace	1.67
Friendster	1.67
OkCupid	1.50
Plenty of Fish	1.17
FreeDating.co.uk	1.17
Bebo	1.00
Meetic	0.83
Match.com	0.83
LoopyLove	0.83

is one of the possible uses of a case study like the one in this chapter, and the above model and guidelines appear to be indicative of what will make a good e-dating service.

Implications for the Future of E-Dating Services

Goel (2005) argues that e-dating services are becoming a mainstream business with vendors keen to protect their reputation. Traditional online dating Web sites that follow the directory structure of e-commerce sites like Amazon such as *Match. com* and *Meetic* were the lowest scoring in the study, and these sites seem not to follow the model in Figure 2 as they treat participants as products to view rather than individuals to network with as MySpace and Facebook allow.

DISCUSSION

People have always found ways to meet on the Internet, with online dating being a big business, allowing people from the comfort of their own home to view and read about potential mates all around the world and through using virtual worlds

they can interact, talk and compete against others in an online environment. Different dating sites offer different services, though it is not yet commonplace for Web sites dedicated to dating to use the social networking tools used by popular online communities, which are a powerful way to bring people closer together, suggesting social networking tools are ideally placed to enhance dating Web sites. The Circle of Friends method of social networking has been embedded into several social networking sites, including MySpace and Facebook, which are services that host collections of online communities based on the personal homepage genre that also act as dating sites. The benefit of the Circle of Friends over earlier technologies was that it put the user in control. Social networking tools often form part of online communities and it has been argued that these communities have the potential to radically transform social interaction and community formation; and while there have been definitions of online communities based on the forms they take from Web sites that provide facilities to discuss particular subjects or interests to groups of people communicating using instant messaging tools, there exists a possible social definition, which could be that an information system is an online community if those that use it have to go through the Membership Lifecycle identified by Kim (2000).

It has long been argued that there should be a framework for understanding actors based on ecological perceptual psychology, with investigations attempting to prove that perception can be explained without resorting to assumptions about inner representations, or at least be explained so that the existence of inner representations is not necessary or essential in every situation. The study found that e-dating service providers should utilize various genres of online community, utilize the Circle of Friends social networking tool, or at minimum allow people to keep lists of actual or potential friends and utilize a recommendation or search system that encourages people to interact with others with similar cognitions to them.

ACKNOWLEDGMENT

The author would like to acknowledge the anonymous reviewers who provided comments and suggestions on earlier drafts of this chapter as well as acknowledge the contribution of those who took part in the study, in particular Mark Beech for his detailed answers to questions. The Centre for Research into Online Communities and e-Learning Systems is part of Glamorgan Blended Learning Ltd., which is a Knowledge Transfer Initiative, supported by the University of Glamorgan through the GTi Business Network of which it is a member.

REFERENCES

Adamic, L., & Adar, E. (2003). Friends and neighbors on the Web. *Social Networks, 25*(3), 211-230.

Aiken, L. (1998). *Human development in adulthood.* London: Springer.

Alonzo, M., & Aiken, M. (2004). Flaming in electronic communication. *Decision Support Systems, 36*(2004), 205-213.

Anon. (2003). Net grief for online 'suicide'. http://news.bbc.co.uk/1/hi/technology/2724819.stm.

Barton, K. (2006). *Research methods in social studies education: Contemporary issues and perspectives.* Charlotte, NC: Information Age Publishing.

Bishop, J. (2002). Development and evaluation of a virtual community. BSc(Hons) dissertation. http://www.jonathanbishop.com/ publications/display.aspx?Item=1.

Bishop, J. (2003). Factors shaping the form of and participation in online communities. *Digital Matrix Magazine, 85*(2003), 22-24.

Bishop, J. (2005). The role of mediating artefacts in the design of persuasive e-learning systems. *Proceedings of the Internet Technology & Applications 2005 Conference.* Wrexham: North East Wales Institute of Higher Education.

Bishop, J. (2006). *Social change in organic and virtual communities: An exploratory study of Bishop Desires.* Paper presented to the Faith, Spirituality and Social Change Conference. University of Winchester.

Bishop, J. (2007a). Increasing participation in online communities: A framework for human-computer interaction. *Computers in Human Behavior, 23*(2007), 1881-1893.

Bishop, J. (2007b). *The psychology of how Christ created faith and social change: Implications for the design of e-learning systems.* Paper presented to the Faith, Spirituality, and Social Change Conference. University of Winchester.

Bishop, J. (2007c). Ecological cognition: A new dynamic for human-computer interaction. In: B. Wallace, A. Ross, J. Davies, & T. Anderson (Eds.), *The mind, the body and the world: Psychology after cognitivism?* (pp. 327-345). Exeter: Imprint Academic.

Bishop, J. (2007d). Evaluation-centred design of e-learning communities: A case study and review. *Proceedings of the Second International Conference on Internet Technologies and Applications, ITA07,* (pp. 1-9). University of Wales.

Bryman, A., & Bell, E. (2003). *Business research methods.* Oxford: Oxford University Press.

Csikszentmihalyi, M. (1977). *Beyond boredom and anxiety.* San Francisco, CA: Jossey-Bass.

Csikszentmihalyi, M. (1990). *Flow: The psychology of optimal experience.* New York, NY: Harper & Row.

DeLamater, J. (2003). *Handbook of social psychology.* London: Springer.

Dvorak, J., Pirillo, C., & Taylor, W. (2003). *Online!: The book.* Upper Saddle River, NJ: Prentice Hall.

Feller, J. (2005). *Perspectives on free and open source software.* Cambridge, MA: The MIT Press

Figallo, C. (1998). *Hosting Web communities: Building relationships, increasing customer loyalty and maintaining a competitive edge.* Chichester: John Wiley & Sons.

Goel, N. (2005). Getting more personal. *PC Magazine,* January.

Harvey, L., & Myers, M. (1995). Scholarship and practice: The contribution of ethnographic research methods to bridging the gap. *Information Technology and People, 8*(3), 13-27.

Hinde, R. (1997). *Relationships: A dialectical perspective.* London: Psychology Press.

Hunter, B. (2002). Learning in the virtual community depends upon changes in local communities. In: K. Renninger & W. Shumar (Eds.), *Building virtual communities: Learning and change in cyberspace* (pp. 96-128). Cambridge: Cambridge University Press.

Huriansky, J. (2003). *The complete idiot's guide to dating.* London: Penguin Group.

Jamali, M., & Abolhassani, H. (2006). Different aspects of social network analysis. *Proceedings of the IEEE International Conference on Web Intelligence 2006,* (pp. 66-72).

Jansen, E. (2002). Netlingo: *The Internet dictionary.* Ojai, CA: Independent Publishers Group.

Jones, Q., & Grandhi, S. (2005). P3 systems: Putting the place back into social networks. *IEEE Internet Computing, September-October*(2005), 38-46.

Kiesler, S., & Sproull, L. (1992). Group decision making and communication technology. *Organizational Behavior and Human Decision Processes, 52*(1), 96-123.

Kim, P., & Aldrich, H. (2005). *Social capital and entrepreneurship.* Hanover, MA: Now Publishers Inc.

Kollock, P. (1999). The economies of online co-operation: Gifts and public goods in cyberspace. In: M. Smith & P. Kollock (Eds.), *Communities in cyberspace.* London: Routledge.

Kollock, P., & Smith, M. (1996). Managing the online commons: Cooperation and conflict in computer communities. In: S. Herring (Ed.), *Computer mediated communication; linguistic, social, and cross-cultural perspectives* (pp. 109-128).

Kyttä, M. (2003). *Children in outdoor contexts: Affordances and independent mobility in the assessment of environmental child friendliness.* Doctoral dissertation presented at Helsinki University of Technology. Espoo, Finland.

Levine-Young, M., & Levine, J. (2000). *Poor Richard's building online communities.* Lakewood, CO: Top Floor Publishing.

Lievowitz, J. (2003). *Addressing the human capital crisis in federal government: A knowledge management perspective.* London: Elsevier.

Lindahl, C., & Blount, E. (2003). Weblogs: Simplifying Web publishing. *IEEE Computer, 36*(11), 114-116.

Litvinoff, M. (1990). *The Earthscan action handbook: For people and planet.* London: Earthscan Publishers.

Lutters, W., & Ackerman, M. (2003). Joining the backstage: Locality and centrality in an online community. *Information Technology & People, 16*(2), 157-182.

MacKinney, K. (1991). *Sexuality in close relationships.* London: Lawrence Erlbaum Associates.

Mann, C., & Stewart, F. (2000). *Internet communication and qualitative research: A handbook for research online.* London: Sage Publications.

Mbakwe, C., & Cunliffe, D. (2003). Conceptualising the process of hypermedia seduction. *Proceedings of the 1st International Meeting of Science and Technology Design: Senses and Sensibility—Linking Tradition to Innovation Through Design,* (pp. 25-26). Lisbon, Portugal.

Mena, J. (1999). *Data mining your Web site.* Oxford: Digital Press.

Morahan-Martin, J., & Schumacher, P. (2003). Loneliness and social uses of the Internet. *Computers in Human Behavior, 19*(2003), 659-671.

Nielsen, J. (2006, October 9). Participation inequality: Encouraging more users to contribute. *Useit.com.* http://www.useit.com/alertbox/participation_inequality.html.

Orengo Castellá, V., Zornoza Abad, A., Prieto Alonso, F., & Peiró Silla, J. (2000). The influence of familiarity among group members, group atmosphere and assertiveness on uninhibited behavior through three different communication media. *Computers in Human Behavior, 16*(2000), 141-159.

Pantazis, C., Gordon, D., & Levitas, R. (2006). *Poverty and social exclusion in Britain: The millennium survey.* London: The Policy Press.

Preece, J. (2000). *Online communities: Designing usability, supporting sociability.* Chichester: John Wiley & Sons.

Quansah, E. (2004). *How to identify your soulmate.* Oxford: Trafford Publishing.

Reinin, B., Briggs, R., & Nunamaker, J. (1998). Flaming in the electronic classroom. *Journal of Management Information Systems, 14*(3), 45-59.

Rheingold, H. (1999). A slice of life in my virtual community. In: P. Ludlow (Ed.), *High noon on the electronic frontier: Conceptual issues in cyberspace.* Cambridge, MA: MIT Press.

Rhiengold, H. (2000). *The virtual community: Homesteading on the electronic frontier.* London: The MIT Press.

Rokach, A., & Neto, F. (2005). Age, culture, and the antecedents of loneliness. *Social Behavior and Personality, 33*(5), 477-494.

Rowley, D. (1994). Usability testing in the field; bringing the laboratory to the user. *Proceedings of the SIGCHI conference on human factors in computing systems; celebrating interdependence.* Boston, Massachusetts.

Shumar, W., & Tenninger, K. (2002). Introducing: On conceptualizing community. In: K. Renninger & W. Shumar (Eds.), *Building online communities: Learning and change in cyberspace* (pp. 1-20). Cambridge: Cambridge University Press.

Siddiquee, A., & Kagan, C. (2006). The Internet, empowerment, and identity: An exploration of participation by refugee women in a community Internet project (CIP) in the United Kingdom (UK). *Journal of Community & Applied Social Psychology, 16*(3), 189-206.

Smith, A. (2001). Problems of conflict management in virtual communities. In: M. Smith & P. Kollock (Eds.), *Communities in cyberspace.* London: Routledge.

Smith, C. (2000). Content analysis and narrative analysis. In: H. Reis & C. Judd (Eds.), *Handbook of research methods in social and personal psychology.* Cambridge: Cambridge University Press.

Stables, A., & Goodwyn, A. (2004). *Learning to read critically in language and literacy.* London: Sage Publications.

Sternberg, R. (1986). A triangular theory of love. *Psychological Review, 93*(2), 119-135.

Stockman, F., & Doreian, P. (1997). Evolution of social networks: Processes and principles. In: P.

Doreian & F. Stockman (Eds.), *Evolution of social networks.* London: Routledge.

Teten, D., & Allen, S. (2005). *The virtual handshake: Opening doors and close deals online.* New York, NY: American Management Association.

Thyer, B. (2001). *The handbook of social world research methods.* London: Sage Publications.

Wallace, P. (2001). *The psychology of the Internet.* Cambridge: Cambridge University Press

Wang, P. (2004). Recommendation based on personal preference. In: Y-Q. Zhang, A. Kandel, T. Lin, & Y. Yao (Eds.), *Computational Web intelligence: Intelligent technology for Web applications.* London: World Scientific Publishing (UK) Ltd.

Waston, G. (1982). *Learning from case studies.* London: Prentice-hall International.

Weng, M. (2007). *A multimedia social-networking community for mobile devices.* Unpublished thesis. Interactive Telecommunications Program, Tisch School of the Arts/ New York University.

Wilson, R., & Keil, F. (2001). *MIT encyclopedia of the cognitive sciences.* Cambridge: MIT Press.

Chapter XVI
E–Dating:
The Five Phases on Online Dating

Monica T. Whitty
Nottingham Trent University, UK

ABSTRACT

Online dating continues to grow in popularity as a way for individuals to locate a potential romantic partner. Researchers have examined how people present themselves on these sites, which presentations are more likely to lead to success, the effectiveness of the matchmaking tools that some companies employ, the stigma attached to using these sites and the types of people who are drawn to online dating. However, there is an absence of scholarly work on how these relationships progress compared to traditional models of courtship. This chapter sets out a model for the phases of online dating and compares this model with Givens' (1979) work on a traditional model of courtship. It is argued here the phases of online dating are very different to other courtship models. These differences pose new challenges and create new benefits to those who elect to find a partner via one of these sites.

WHERE CAN ONE FIND A ROMANTIC PARTNER ON THE NET?

Before moving on to consider online dating sites, it is important to understand that these sites emerged because it became obvious that there was a need and a market for such sites. As is well-known, the Internet was not originally set up as a social space, but rather as a space to transfer data. However, not long after (even in its most primitive textual form), friendships and romances began to blossom. People were meeting each other in all sorts of places, MUDs and MOOs (multi-users dungeons or domains, which are essentially role-playing sites), bulletin boards, chat rooms, newsgroups and gaming sites.

Bulletin board systems (BBs) were possibly the first place where romances initiated on the Internet. DeVoss (2007) has succinctly described how these relationships initiated in these sites and quite rightly points out that one could not escape gender roles in these spaces (even when people swapped gender). There are many anecdotal stories about how people played with self-narratives in these sites, one of which DeVoss describes is the story of a woman who called herself Princess:

Her registry claimed that she as 5'1", a 'curvaceous' 102 pounds, had deep brown eyes, and waist-length black hair. She flirted online, and male users would virtually flirt to enter her private chat room. As online time passed, the men...wanted to meet her...Over and over again, she resisted their efforts to entice her off the BBS and into physical public space. She wrapped herself in an elaborate story—that she was hiding from a violent ex-husband who was involved in organised crime...she wasn't allowed to give out her real name, phone number, address...
Somehow, however, one of the more aggressive male users...found out where she lived...only to find her the exact opposite of her online identity... They reported her to be phenomenally hefty, incredibly ugly, partially toothless, and surrounded by a gaggle of children. (p. 21-22)

Of course, just as with many face-to-face encounters, not everyone online is looking for a traditional heterosexual relationship. BBs were also a meeting place for people with more deviant sexual tastes. Wysocki (1998) reported her examination of "how and why individuals participate in sexually explicit computer boards; and to see if sex on-line is a way of *replacing* face-to-face relationships or a way of *enhancing* them" (p. 426). She found that participants enjoyed the anonymity the Internet affords. Moreover, given their lack of time in their personal life it allowed them to find individuals with similar sexual interests and to share sexual fantasies within the confines of their

own homes. Many of the people she surveyed were in fact happy to keep these sexual relationships online. More recently, Wysocki and Thalken (2007) examined adult Web sites to find that, in particular, older individuals (a mean age of 40 years), were more likely to use S & M adult Web sites. Most people using the sites included photographs; however, what took these researchers by surprise was that many of the photos included face shots (indicating no attempt to ensure complete anonymity). The mix of people using these sites did so to either engage in online sexual fantasies or to find partners who shared their fantasies and were prepared to enact them off-line.

Romances and friendships have also been known to develop in MUDS and MOOs, chat rooms and newsgroups. For example, in the mid-90s, Parks and Floyd (1996) found that two-thirds (60.7%) of their newsgroup sample had formed a personal relationship with someone they had met for the first time online. Of these, 7.9% stated that this was a romantic relationship. Utz (2000) found that 76.7% of the MUD users she surveyed reported forming a relationship online that developed off-line, of which, 24.5 % stated this was a romantic relationship. Whitty and Gavin (2001) found that individuals form real friendships in chat rooms and that some of these participants preferred that these relationships remain online.

THE CONSTRUCTION OF ONLINE DATING SITES

Given the numbers of people seeking others online for love and sex, it is little wonder that companies have tried to formalize this process as well as to make money from people who are prepared to seek out romance on the net. Online dating sites continue to abound online and increase in popularity. Yahoo.com claims almost 380 million visitors per month to their online dating site (Pasha, 2005), and FriendFinder.com say they have over 3.5 million active members (Dating Sites Reviews.com, 2006).

During the early days of the Internet, given the restricted technology capabilities and bandwidth, online dating sites looked more like newspaper personal ads. Individuals would read a profile and contact the person on the site to learn more about them and to gauge whether the other was also interested. Men were much more likely to subscribe to these sites than women and companies allowed women onto these sites for free to ensure men had an adequate selection.

These days, the sites are still typically set up to have their users construct a personal ad for themselves. The amount of information and detail people can add is obviously less restrictive due to increased bandwidth. Clients can, and generally do, show at least one photograph of themselves, and can also add video and voice to their profiles. Online daters can present information about themselves in a number of ways. They can rate themselves or check boxes indicating attributes such as their age, gender, location, job and physique (e.g., a choice ranging from slim to overweight). Some of these questions, such as age and gender are often a compulsory requirement. In addition, clients are usually given an opportunity to add to and expand upon this information. For example, they may elaborate on their hobbies and musical interests, or the type of person they are attempting to attract.

Not all online dating sites expect their clients to do all the matching work themselves. Some sites do the matching for the client. For example, some online dating sites will ask the client to fill out descriptive details and sometimes a personality scale. These sites claim to be able to 'scientifically' match individuals. The assumption is that there is a formula to matching appropriate people. This view, however, is somewhat contentious. Houran, Lange, Rentfrow, and Brukner (2004), for instance, have argued that such compatibility tests have provided little psychometric support. Nevertheless, it is argued here that even if these test lack scientific rigor they still assume some of the laborious work from the site users. In con-

trast, other sites provide a more flexible approach, whereby clients can opt to fill out such tests and be presented with profiles of clients deduced to be suitable matches or instead the client can wade through the sea of possibilities and select for themselves.

In addition to the general online dating sites such as, eHarmony, True.com, Match.com and so forth, there are also more specialized online dating sites which gather like-minded individuals together. For example, there are sites designed specifically for Christians, Jews, vegans, Goths or spiritual people. Such sites are similar to social groups which one might join in the hope of finding others that share the same values or interests. Moreover, it potentially cuts out some of the work associated with the search for the perfect other. These sites are discussed in more detail later in the chapter. For now, this chapter turns to examine how relationship development on an online dating site compares with traditional dating. It does so by firstly examining the traditional off-line courting process.

THE FIVE PHASES OF OFF-LINE DATING

Givens' (1979) developed a five-stage model to explain the traditional courting process. In his model the first phase is the 'attention phase'. During this phase an individual (typically a woman) will try to attract a person of the opposite sex by displaying non-verbal signs of attraction, such as primping, object caressing and using quick glances towards and away from the target. The second phase is the 'recognition phase', where flirting behavior consists of head cocking, pouting, primping, eyebrow flashes and smiles. Givens suggests that 'interaction' does not occur until the third phase. This is when conversation is initiated. During this stage, participants appear highly animated, displaying laughing or giggling. Interestingly, Givens notes that men are generally hesitant to approach women without some initial indication of interest from the woman. The fourth phase in his model is 'sexual arousal', which is finally followed by 'resolution'. As Whitty (2003) has argued, Givens' work not only demonstrates that women make the first move, but also highlights the importance of non-verbal cues in the signaling of sexual attraction. These signals are crucial in the game of flirting. Given that flirtatious behavior features heavily when one is trying to initiate contact with a potential romantic mate off-line, this chapter now turns to examine flirtation in a little more detail.

Flirtation

Flirtatious behavior is evident throughout the early phases that Givens has delineated. Success in finding a potential partner off-line might be in some ways attributed to how skilled an individual is at flirting. Moore (1985) observed individuals in bars and identified 52 facial expressions and gestures that women display when they flirt. Although these actions might be subtle, they can be enough to indicate attraction. Moreover, it is important to note that one gesture in isolation is typically not enough to indicate attraction. *Sometimes a smile is just a smile.* While flirting is not necessarily a prelude to sexual interaction, researchers, such as Moore (1985; 1998), have found that women who display them are more likely to be approached by a man who shares the same sentiment.

In order for flirtation to work, it needs to be ambiguous. This is why it typically involves a number of carefully orchestrated body gestures rather than a frank statement, such as 'I really fancy you'. As will be examined in more detail later on in this chapter, this poses an obvious problem online where the body is typically not physically present (note: Webcams, videos, and photos can make the body more present). Moreover, the 'dance' can be so subtle that it is not always conscious to the flirtee. First, however, I move to develop a model that delineates the phases involved in online dating.

THE FIVE PHASES OF ONLINE DATING

Theorists have devised models to explain formal matchmaking services, such as personal ads, video dating and computer matchmaking. Ahuvia and Adelman (1992), for example, have devised the SMI model (searching, matching, and interacting model). They parallel matchmaking services with basic market functions. For instance, in the market place initially 'searching' is required, that is, gaining information essential for exchange (in regards to matchmaking this means searching for information about a potential other). Second, 'matching' is required to bring together compatible exchange partners (in regards to matchmaking this would mean bringing together two singles that seem well matched). Ahuvia and Adelman swap the term 'transacting' for 'interacting'. They do so because transacting requires a negation of implementing an exchange and to do so with matchmaking an interaction needs to take place.

Internet dating does seem to include the three phases highlighted by Abuvia and Adelman. However, these phases do not necessarily neatly fit into the sequential order they propose. Matching, for instance can happen at two points. First, the site might suggest matches from a specific formula devised to 'scientifically' match individuals and then the client might search through the site's choices to decide who they believe is an appropriate match. Alternatively, the client might begin by searching through the sea of profiles until they find profiles that are suitable matches. Next, contact is made on the site initially to indicate interest in another and the other has to reciprocate mutual interest. From there the two potentials begin to interact and decide whether they wish to progress the relationship further.

There is some utility in drawing from Abuvia and Adelman's model to explain the process of online dating; however, I argue here for a more sophisticated model that also draws from Givens model of the traditional off-line courting process.

As outlined below, these phases include 'the attention phase', 'the recognition phase', 'the interaction phase', 'the face-to-face meeting', and finally 'resolution'. These phases have been derived from previous empirical work I have conducted on online dating (see Whitty, in press; 2007; Whitty & Carr, 2006). As is explained below, the phases do involve many of the processes Givens refers to; however, the phases are not necessarily ordered in the same way and each phase arguably requires additional skills.

Phase 1: The Attention Phase

During the 'attention phase', off-line a person (usually the woman) will try to attract a person of the opposite sex by displaying subtle non-verbal signals. With online dating, one does not have an immediate target to display subtle interest in. Instead, the person displays signs of attraction by selecting an attractive photograph to represent themselves. In the main, profiles that do not show a photograph are overlooked (Whitty & Carr, 2006). Moreover, women typically take more time and care selecting an attractive photograph of themselves. Overkill with a photograph, that is, a photograph professionally taken or looking too sexual, is treated skeptically. This might parallel with a woman showing too much interest in the first phase off-line—such a woman might be deemed a little too desperate.

During this attention phase, another unique way online daters might go about attracting others to their profile is via the name they use to represent themselves (what is commonly referred to as a screen name). Some use very flirtatious names (e.g., Imcute or Bubbly), while others select names that reflect their personal identity (e.g., mountainclimber). Others might select a non-flirtatious name (e.g., Jt28 or Smith48). Interestingly, in a recent study by Whitty and Buchanan (2007), it was found that certain screen names are deemed more attractive than others, and that men and women are more motivated to make contact

with individuals with different types of screen names. It was found that men more than women are attracted to and motivated to contact screen names which indicate physical attractiveness (e.g., 'Hottie' and 'Greatbody') and that women more than men are attracted to screen names which demonstrate intelligence ('Wellread' or 'Welleducated'). Overall, less flirtatious names were perceived by the majority of people as less attractive names.

The photograph and the person's screen name is usually the first bit of information others encounter on the site. If they like what they see, they might move to the next phase or they might (and typically do) seek out more information about the person. Therefore, continuing to hold another's attention prior to any interaction can be quite an arduous task for an online dater, and arguably they need to be quite skillful at crafting a profile (see Whitty, 2007).

As research has found, online daters tend to give much thought to their profiles. Sometimes a dater will trial a certain profile to see what types of people they attract or if indeed they attract anyone. Whitty (2007, p. 64) presents an extract from an interview where Lynne (named changed for confidentiality) explained what a painstaking task this was for her:

I: *O.K., looking at your own profile, how did you decide what information to include about yourself?*

L: *After many hours and trial and error, I changed it a few times ... I did want to describe myself in a way that would give a bit of a cross section of me and depending on what sort of results that I got ... with each profile I would then sort of go and revise that. Having said that, I have only revised it I think three times.*

I: *But you feel like you got different responses accordingly to different profiles?*

L: *Yeah a little bit.*

As Whitty (in press) reports, online daters often make great efforts to construct an attractive profile. In addition to a photo, the types of information daters said were important included their interests and hobbies (53%) and a description of their personality (35%). Furthermore, a number of the people she interviewed stated that it was important to inject humor into their profile (17%), state their occupation (13%), how intelligent they are (12%) and make their profile appear unique and different (12%).

It has been argued that a successful profile is not just a profile that stands out in a crowd by one which also appears 'real' or genuine and trustworthy (Whitty, 2007). Whitty (2007) suggests that online daters should ascribe to the BAR (balance between and attractive and real self) approach. Presenting an ideal presentation of the self does not work on online dating sites—as we see in the fourth phase, if people do not live up to their profiles they typically do not earn a second date. Presenting a real profile also means avoiding writing anything that appears too clichéd. For example, describing one's most romantic date as going for a stroll on the beach or sipping wine by log fires are seen by many as either naïve, untrustworthy or unoriginal. Ironically, by sounding too romantic, an online dater appears less real or authentic and hence a less appealing candidate. One participant in Whitty's (2007, pp. 64-65) research aptly described why he/she would avoid such profiles:

T: *I tend to stay away from those people with sort of cliché stuff. I think it appears in a lot of profiles ...*

I: *What would be some of the clichés that you would be turned off by?*

T: *With some, on some profiles it has a very sexual overtone, which puts me off totally. Sometimes it is like a passage of clichés, walks on the beach, romantic evenings, romantic getaways, a bottle of wine, and nice crackling fire. It just doesn't ring true,*

it just sounds like a, it doesn't seem very real.

Phase 2: The Recognition Phase

As with off-line courting, the second phase of online dating requires more flirtation and some recognition. Online dating sites have attempted to mimic this step in the construction of their Web sites. Rather than immediately e-mailing a member of the site that the client finds attractive, instead, online daters are often given the option to virtually flirt. That is, many sites give the option to send a 'form' note via the site, often referred to as a 'wink' or a 'kiss'. Akin to flirting off-line, this can appear less intrusive and more subtle than a more detailed e-mail introducing oneself and asking for the person to, in turn, self-disclose to them. Although this is probably an important and necessary step, it is argued later in this chapter that online dating sites' attempts to incorporate flirtation is still fairly clunky and this could well be a problem that some companies might want to address.

Phase 3: The Interaction Phase

Similar to off-line, the next phase in the online dating courting process involves interaction. This of course takes place online. It might initially take place through: an exchange of e-mails via the site; a site's instant messaging program; personal e-mail accounts; or an instant messaging program found off the site. It might then move on to phone (usually mobile phone) or SMS texting. As with courting off-line, this stage can also be very flirtatious. Although the traditional physical off-line cues are not present, substitutes can be found for these non-verbal cues (Whitty, 2003; 2004). One can describe in more detail how they look or the types of physical actions they would like to enact. Individuals also flirt by using emoticons, such as smiley faces and winks, and acronyms (e.g., LNK which represents love and kisses or QT which represents cutie).

As Whitty (2003; 2004) has found, individuals can indeed flirt online, despite the absence of traditional cues. Moreover, sometimes they can feel freer to flirt and express their sexuality than they might in face-to-face encounters. Similarly, Alapack, Blichfeldt, and Elden (2005) state that online the "living flesh is being transformed into a 'legible' body" (p. 52). They also state that a special online flirting language has evolved. In line with previous work (e.g., Whitty, 2003; Ben-Ze've, 2004) they also state that cyber-flirting can trigger physical and sexual reactions.

Empirical research has found that not only do individuals flirt online, but they do so in gender-defined ways (Whitty, 2004). Her survey of 5,697 participants found that women were more likely than men to flirt by using online substitutes for non-verbal cues. For example, they admitted to using more emoticons and acronyms to flirt online and described themselves as physically attractive. Men, in contrast, were more likely to initiate contact.

Typically this third phase is relatively short. While, some flirtation and self-disclosure takes place for online daters during the interaction, this phase is more about verifying information and setting up the face-to-face meeting (or one or both of the pair decide to drop out of the process). Given that profiles already provide a curriculum vitae about the individual, additional information about the person does not need to be disclosed. Hence, during this phase if the pair feels comfortable enough they move to setting up a face-to-face date. Conducting a face-to-face date rather than spending more time conversing and getting to know one another is preferable, as most online daters would agree that one cannot test out real 'chemistry' in an online environment. Spending too much time conversing without agreeing to a date is frowned upon by many—as such a person is often deemed a tease or insincere.

Phase 4: The Face-to-Face Meeting

The fourth phase is roughly equivalent to Givens' fourth stage titled the 'sexual arousal' stage. For online daters, the first date very much determines if there will be any further dates. This meeting is different to a 'traditional' first date where sexual attraction has already been established and the couple plan to spend a romantic evening together. Instead it is a meeting where the pair test out physical chemistry and see how well the person matches up with the profile. For safety reasons the meeting usually takes place in a public space (e.g., cafe shop, bar) and is most likely scheduled for a restricted amount of time (so that individuals can make a quick escape if the interaction does not run smoothly). Some devise contingency plans that if the meeting works out well it will continue onto a proper date—(e.g., dinner). Given the fears that individuals will not live out to their profiles, some online daters are savvy enough to check out their date from a vantage point and if they do not turn out looking exactly how they had hoped (e.g., if the photo is a few years out of date or they look somewhat larger than described), the person might not go through with the date (sometimes politely calling on the other's mobile with an excuse as to why they could not make it).

It has been found that 68% of participants believe that the first face-to-face meeting is a screening out process (Whitty, in press). If there is much discrepancy between the person and the profile, the person is usually judged as untrustworthy and not worthwhile pursuing. Common lies told on these sites tend to be about physical appearance. For example, it has been found that men are more likely to lie about their height and status, while women are more likely to lie about their weight (Whitty, in press; Whitty, & Carr, 2006; Hancock, Toma, Ellison, 2007).

A person might have written a profile that they can live up to in the flesh. However, during this first meeting, if one of both parties does not believe there is any physical chemistry or 'sexual arousal' (as Givens refers to), then the two might remain friends or discontinue any further contact.

Phase 5: Resolution

As with Givens' five stages of courting, resolution is the final stage of the online dating courting process. After the first meeting, individuals know whether they are sexually attracted to and whether they want to learn more about their date. If they are still uncertain, they might set up a couple more dates; however, they will generally do so while checking out other options on the site. If they are confident they are interested in moving forward they will typically take themselves off the site. Problems arise between couples if expectations are not meet and one is discovered to be still actively using the site when the other has taken themselves off.

STRENGTHS AND WEAKNESSES OF ONLINE DATING

This chapter now turns to the pros and cons of finding a romantic partner via an online dating site. It does so by paying particular attention to the five phases outlined above.

Flirting on the Net

As explained earlier, off-line flirting consists of a gamut of non-verbal behaviors. Moving through Givens' phases partly requires an ability to carefully orchestrate these gestures (e.g., amount and timing). Despite the absence of the physical body in cyberspace, individuals are able to cyberflirt (Whitty, 2003). As demonstrated, flirtation is evident in a number of the online dating phases.

In the first phase, people need to be quite strategic in their self-presentation. The advantage here (especially for the socially awkward and shy)

is that this is achieved asynchronously—giving individuals ample time to consider how they might best present themselves (e.g., photos developed in photoshop, choice of screen name, and details about themselves). The disadvantage is that different skills are required to the one's traditionally used off-line. Some may be oblivious as to which presentation of self will lead to the best result. Cyberspace arguably provides a safer and more playful space for self-presentations (Whitty, 2003). While this has its advantages in other places online, if people are too creative with their online dating profiles (e.g., making themselves appear more physically attractive, younger, wealthier, more interesting), then although this might attract others in the first instance, it is far less likely that they will sustain interest. Having to deal with numerous rejections in the end can have a negative effort on the individuals' self-esteem.

Flirtation continues in the second phase where individuals can send a flirtatious 'form note' through the site, often referred to as 'winks' or 'kisses'. As described earlier, when people flirt face-to-face, they usually display an array of non-verbal behaviors that may or may not be interpreted as attraction. Figuring out whether the other person is mutually attracted and trying to capture another's attention is part of the fun. Moreover, the end goal of flirting is not necessarily an attempt to form a relationship or even a sexual encounter. Online dating sites have obviously added the 'virtual flirt form note' into their design as a way to mimic off-line flirtation. Sending a virtual kiss or a wink appears less intrusive than an e-mail. However, it is not as ambiguous as a display of non-verbal gestures in an off-line setting. Moreover, if people contact others on a dating site they do so in order that they can meet others to form a relationship with. The intentions are far less ambiguous compared to flirting in other places. Sending a virtual note is a clear message that the person is interested in another and holds some hope that a relationship might develop. Therefore, it is argued here that online dating sites' attempts to mimic off-line flirting is still a little clunky and theoretically is not as effective as flirting in other situations (online or off-line).

One way around this problem might be to incorporate flirtatious applications similar to those used by social networking sites. For instance, many of Facebook's applications both enable and encourage flirtation—in a way that does not have to be construed as such. One can send friends virtual gifts (even virtual drinks). Gifts sent online do not have to signal attraction; however, if you were to give someone a physical gift off-line, such as flowers, a teddy bear or handcuffs, the intent would become more obvious. One can dedicate a song to someone online. A more obvious, but still playful application is comparing friends online. For example, this application asks which of two friends you would prefer to date—while this remains equivocal, it does present a flirtatious cue to another. An individual can also send a friend a nomination for a virtual prize. Sending them a nomination for 'the most likely to worship spongebob' would not perhaps be perceived as flirtatious as 'best looking male', or 'most likely to appear in playboy'.

The First Date: Safer but More Clinical

As explained earlier, for online daters the first date is usually set up in a public space for a restricted amount of time. People using these sites do so as they are aware that they are meeting strangers and they are cautious of the type of people they might be meeting. They are also unlikely to give away too much information that might reveal where they live or work. This is potentially safer than meeting potential romantic partners in a bar after a few drinks. However, the disadvantage of the first meeting is that it is much less a date and more like a job interview. Having to live up to the other person's expectations can be a challenge. Moreover, in normal courting situations each

person does not typically know as much about the person whom they are considering dating.

Self-Disclosures: Too Much Too Soon?

One of the most popular theories to explain relationship development is *social penetration theory* (Altman & Taylor, 1973). Social penetration theory is an incremental theory which argues that relationships move to greater levels of intimacy over time. According to this theory, how greater intimacy is achieved is typically through depth and breadth of self-disclosure. Breadth of self-disclosure refers to discussing a range of topics, such as information about one's family, career, and so forth. Depth refers to the more central core of one's personality; that is, the more unique aspects of one's self. The timing of how much one self-discloses is crucial to determining whether a relationship will continue to proceed. Rushing self-disclosure in the early stages of a relationship can seem unnatural and desperate and can lead to an abrupt end. According to social penetration theory, in the early phases of relationship development, one moves with caution, discussing less intimate topics and checking in the conversations for signs of reciprocity. Gradually, one feels safer to reveal aspects of themselves.

As can be seen in the five stages of online dating, there is far less opportunity for relationships to develop in the way proposed by the social penetration theory. On an online dating site the profiles are set up in such as way to reveal both depth and breadth. For instance, within the profiles, individuals typically have to provide information about surface levels aspects of themselves, such as eye color, drinking and smoking habits, relationship status, number and types of pets and occupation. In addition, they are given space to write more in depth about themselves, where they are asked to describe their personality, interests (what they read, music they listen to and so forth), their ideal date, and their political persuasion. They are encouraged on these sites to open up about all aspects of themselves. The sites argue that by doing so that they will attract the most appropriate person. Given the amount of information individuals are presented with it is no surprise the conversations that take place via e-mail, telephone and so forth prior to the first meeting are more to clarify information about the person as well as to arrange the meeting. Therefore, as Whitty (in press) suggests, online dating is arguably even more removed from what people are accustomed to when it comes to developing a relationship. There is less opportunity to test the waters gradually and check for reciprocity, instead, reciprocity is determined prior to communication with the individual. The advantage this gives online daters is that they are granted more control over their self-presentations. However, in turn, because the profile compiles all the information about the person in one chunk, it is easier to check. Hence, others are less forgiving when there is a mismatch between the person they meet face-to-face and the person they were presented with in the profile.

Sexual Attraction: Takes a While to Get There

As pointed out in the online dating model, determining 'physical chemistry' or 'sexual attraction' does not usually take place until the couple meet face-to-face. Off-line flirting usually takes places because one or both individuals find the other physically attractive. Individuals probably do not make it to the interaction phase if there is not at least some physical chemistry there. Of course knowing for sure if there is a desire to take the attraction further does not take place usually until phase 4 in Givens' model.

In comparison to face-to-face, online daters can only guess and hope that they find the person they have meet online to be someone they are physically attracted to and in turn if that person reciprocates that attraction. Judging from a couple

of photographs (which may well be out of date or developed in photoshop) is a tricky process and individuals can only hope that they will find the person physically attractive when they meet in the flesh. Moreover, research has also found that judgments are often skewed because people increase their expectations about the type of person who might be attracted to them (Whitty & Carr, 2006). So unlike off-line, where individuals initially find the other attractive and then move to get to know the person, for online daters it is more about knowing the person and then determining if there is any physical attraction. Spending the time interacting and then meeting can seem like a waste of time for individuals if they find there is not any physical chemistry when the pair meet face-to-face. Some online dating sites are encouraging users to also place videos of themselves on the site— this might go some way towards reducing the problem of delayed determination of physical attraction.

Spoiled for Choice

A unique aspect of online dating is that the site presents the client with a sea of possibilities—far more apparent choices than they are ever going to be presented with in most other situations. Every other person is there for the same reason: to find a romantic and/or sexual partner (typically a long-term romantic partner). The goal is not ambiguous, which as stated above has certain advantages and disadvantages. Being presented with so many options has been compared to being in a sweet shop (Whitty & Carr, 2006). However, the problem with this set up is that not all persons on the site are real potentials. The same type of person with the same type of physical attributes that one normally attracts off-line is realistically the only type of person who is going to reciprocate attraction. What online daters tend to do is to raise their expectations as to what they can realistically attract (Whitty & Carr, 2006).

The other problem with being presented with so many choices is that the online dater feels they can be hyper-critical of a person when they meet them face-to-face. Given they have a record of that person's claims if their date does not match up with their profile they can easily be discarded given that 'there are plenty more fish in the sea'.

Stigmatized Activity

A final problem worthy of note is that online dating has been found to be a stigmatized activity (Wildermuth, 2004). Peris et al. (2002), for instance, have argued that "it is generally assumed that people who enter cyberspace to form interpersonal relationships generally show greater difficulties in social face-to-face situations" (p. 44). Donn and Sherman (2002) found that undergraduate students were more likely than postgraduate students to believe that people who form relationships online were desperate. Wildermuth (cited in Wildermuth, 2004) found that even friends and family members of online daters expressed strong disapproval of their online activities. Not surprisingly, their views negatively impacted online daters' perceptions of the self. In the interviews carried out by Whitty (see Whitty & Carr, 2006; Whitty, 2007; in press), this stigmatization was also reported by online daters. To deal with this stigma, the online daters made friends on the dating site and created what they called a community. This community helped normalize their online dating activities.

This stigmatization also seems to be evident across some cultures. Malchow-Møller (2003), for instance, found that the French men she interviewed in a focus group stated that online dating is akin to personal ads and so like people who use personal ads, online daters must be desperate. She argues that Danes, in contrast, are more likely to perceive online daters as ordinary people. The problem with this study, however, is that the researcher only included two focus groups in her study and it would not be valid to assume that one focus group could represent Danes and

the other French, so further research is essential to test these claims. What does seem evident is that in the main, participants talked about online daters as a separate social group (even if some perceive them to be 'normal' people).

A stigmatized person's social identity is devalued in a particular social context (Crocker, Major, & Steele, 1998). Goffman (1963) contended that a stigma discredits a person and reduces them "from a whole and usual person to a tainted, discounted one." Online dating is obviously not the typical way individuals find a mate, but then not all atypical behaviors are stigmatized. So what researchers need to consider is why has online dating been perceived as a stigma? Why are these individuals, akin to those who write personal ads (Ahuvia & Adelman, 1992), perceived by many as desperate? I suggest here that it is not because online dating is a fairly new activity (especially given its similarity with personal ads which have been around for decades) but rather because of the process—as demonstrated in the online dating model proposed in this chapter the courting process follows different steps to the model of dating that individuals are more accustomed to.

CONCLUSION

To conclude, by drawing upon Givens' model of the traditional courtship process, this chapter was able to develop a model to explain the online dating process. This model argued for five phases including: 'the attention phase', 'the recognition phase', 'the interaction phase', 'the face-to-face meeting' and finally 'resolution'. Here it was noted that flirting is not as natural or ambiguous as it can be in other types of courtship (both online and off-line). Moreover, unlike face-to-face attraction, physical chemistry is not determined until much later down the line. The differences in the courtship process provide users of these sites with certain advantages and disadvantages. It is suggested here that online dating companies might want to re-dress some of the problems with the design and usage of their sites in order to enhance their clients' online dating experience.

REFERENCES

Ahuvia, A., & Adelman, M. (1992). Formal intermediaries in the marriage market: A typology and review. *Journal of Marriage and the Family, 54*(2), 452-463.

Alapack, R., Blichfeldt, M., & Elden, A. (2005). Flirting on the Internet and the hickey: A hermeneutic. *Cyberpsychology & Behavior, 8*(1), 52-61.

Bargh, J., McKenna, K., & Fitzsimons, G. (2002). Can you see the real me? Activation and expression of the "true self" on the Internet. *Journal of Social Issues, 58,* 33-48.

Ben-Ze'ev, A. (2004). *Love online: Emotions and the Internet.* Cambridge, UK: Cambridge University.

Cooper, A., & Sportolari, L. (1997). Romance in cyberspace: Understanding online attraction. *Journal of Sex Education and Therapy, 22*(1), 7-14.

Crocker, J., Major, B., & Steele, C. (1998). Social stigma. In: S. Fiske, D. Gilbert, & G. Lindzey (Eds.), *Handbook of social psychology, 2,* 504-553. Boston, MA: McGraw-Hill.

Dating Sites Reviews.com. (2006). Retrieved November, 21, 2007, from http://www.datingsitesreviews.com/staticpages/index.php?page=2010000100-FriendFinder

DeVoss, D. (2007). From the BBS to the Web: Tracing the spaces of online romance. In: M. Whitty, A. Baker, & J. Inman (Eds.), *Online matchmaking* (pp. 17-30). Houndmills: Palgrave Macmillan.

Donn, J., & Sherman, R. (2002). Attitudes and practices regarding the formation of romantic relationships on the Internet. *CyberPsychology & Behavior, 5*(2), 107-123.

Ellis, B., & Symons, D. (1990). Sex differences in sexual fantasy. *Journal of Sex Research, 27*(4), 527-555.

Givens, D. (1978). The non-verbal basis of attraction: Flirtation, courtship, and seduction. *Psychiatry, 41,* 346-359.

Goffman, E. (1963). *Stigma: Notes on the management of spoiled identity.* New York, NY: Prentice Hall.

Gwinnell, E. (1998). *Online seductions: Falling in love with strangers on the Internet.* New York, NY: Kodansha International.

Hancock, J., Toma, C., & Ellison, N. (2007). The truth about lying in online dating profiles. *Proceedings of the ACM Conference on Human Factors in Computing Systems (CHI 2007),* (pp. 449-452).

Higgins, E. (1987). Self-discrepancy theory. *Psychological Review, 94,* 1120-1134.

Houran, J., Lange, R., Rentfrow, P., & Bruckner, K. (2004). Do online matchmaking tests work? An Assessment of preliminary evidence for a publicized 'predictive model of marital success'. *North American Journal of Psychology, 6,* 507-526.

Kenrick, D., Sadalla, E., Groth, G., & Trost, M. (1990). Evolution, traits, and the stages of human courtship: Qualifying the parental investment model. *Journal of Personality, 58,* 97-116.

Lenhart, A., & Madden, M. (2007). Social networking Web sites and teens: An overview. *Pew Internet & American Life Project.* Retrieved August 28, 2007, from http://www.pewInternet.org/pdfs/PIP_SNS_Data_Memo_Jan_2007.pdf.

Malchow-Møller, A. (2003). Internet dating: A focus group investigation of young Danes' and

Frenchmen's attitudes towards the phenomenon. *Kontur, 7,* 11-20.

McKenna, K., Green, A., & Gleason, M. (2002). Relationship formation on the Internet: What's the big attraction?. *Journal of Social Issues, 58,* 9-31.

Moore, M. (1985). Non-verbal courtship patterns in women: Context and consequences. *Ethology and Sociobiology, 6,* 237-247.

Moore, M. (1998). Non-verbal courtship patterns in women: Rejection signalling: An empirical investigation. *Semiotica, 118,* 201-214.

Pasha, S. (2005, August 18). Online dating feeling less attractive. *CNN/Money.* Retrieved April 13, 2006, from http://money.cnn.com/2005/08/18/technology/online_dating/index.htm.

Parks, M., & Floyd, K. (1996). Making friends in cyberspace. *Journal of Communication, 46,* 80-97.

Peris, R., Gimeno, M., Pinazo, D., Ortet, G., Carrero, V., Sanchiz, M., & Ibanez, I. (2002). Online chat rooms: Virtual spaces of interaction for socially-oriented people. *CyberPsychology & Behavior, 5*(1), 43-51.

Rogers, C. (1951). *Client-centered therapy.* Boston, MA: Houghton-Mifflin.

Scharlott, B., & Christ, W. (1995). Overcoming relationship-initiation barriers: The impact of a computer-dating system on sex role, shyness, and appearance inhibitions. *Computers in Human Behavior, 11,* 191-204.

Townsend, J. (1993). Sexuality and partner selection: Sex differences among college students. *Ethology and Sociobiology, 14,* 305-330.

Townsend, J., & Wasserman, T. (1997). The perception of sexual attractiveness: Sex differences in variability. *Achieves of Sexual Behavior, 26,* 243-268.

Walther, J. (1996). Computer-mediated communication: Impersonal, interpersonal and hyperpersonal interaction. *Communication Research, 23,* 3-43.

Walther, J., Slovacek, C., & Tidwell, L. (2001). Is a picture worth a thousand words? Photographic images in long-term and short-term computer-mediated communication. *Communication Research, 28,* 105-134.

Whitty, M. (2002). Liar, Liar! An examination of how open, supportive and honest people are in chat rooms. *Computers in Human Behavior, 18*(4), 343-352.

Whitty, M. (2003). Cyber-flirting: Playing at love on the Internet. *Theory and Psychology, 13*(3), 339-357.

Whitty, M. (2004). Cyber-flirting: An examination of men's and women's flirting behaviour both off-line and on the Internet. *Behaviour Change, 21*(2), 115-126.

Whitty, M. (2007). The art of selling one's self on an online dating site: The BAR Approach. In: M. Whitty, A. Baker, & J. Inman (Eds.), *Online matchmaking* (pp. 57-69). Houndmills: Palgrave Macmillan.

Whitty, M. (in press). Revealing the 'real' me, searching for the 'actual' you: Presentations of self on an Internet dating site. *Computers in Human Behavior.*

Whitty, M., & Buchanan, T. (2007, manuscript under preparation). What's in a 'screen' name? The types of screen names online daters find attractive.

Whitty, M., & Carr, A. (2006). *Cyberspace romance: The psychology of online relationships.* Basingstoke: Palgrave Macmillan.

Whitty, M., & Gavin, J. (2001). Age/sex/location: Uncovering the social cues in the development of online relationships. *CyberPsychology & Behaviour, 4,* 623-630.

Wildermuth, S. (2004). The effects of stigmatizing discourse on the quality of online relationships. *CyberPsychology & Behavior, 7*(1), 73-84.

Wysocki, D. (1998). Let your fingers to do the talking: Sex on an adult chat line. *Sexualities, 1*, 425-452.

Wysocki, D., & Thalken, J. (2007). Whips and chains? Fact or fiction? Content analysis of sado-masochism in Internet personal advertisements. In: M. Whitty, A. Baker, & J. Inman (Eds.), *Online matchmaking* (pp. 178-196). Houndmills: Palgrave Macmillan.

Chapter XVII
How E–Daters Behave Online:
Theory And Empirical Observations

Celia Romm-Livermore
Wayne State University, USA

Toni Somers
Wayne State University, USA

Kristina Setzekorn
Smith Barney, Inc., USA

Ashley Lynn-Grace King
Wayne State University, USA

ABSTRACT

Following a review of the literature on e-dating, this chapter introduces the e-dating development model and discusses a number of hypotheses that can be derived from it. Also presented in the chapter are some findings from a preliminary empirical research that explored the hypotheses. The findings supported all the hypotheses, indicating that: (1) male and female e-daters follow different stages in their e-dating evolvement; (2) the behaviors that males and females exhibit as e-daters are different; and (3) the feedback that male and female e-daters receive from the environment is different too. The chapter is concluded with a discussion of the implications from this research to e-dating theory development and empirical research.

INTRODUCTION

We define e-dating as a process that takes place online and that results in the establishment of a personal relationship between two individuals. E-dating can be enabled by an e-dating service, for example, an online company that matches individuals to each other (such as Match.com,

YahooPersonals, eHarmony, etc.) or it can take place in other online environments, such as chatrooms, newsgroups, and so forth.

As for the goal of the relationship, we prefer not to use terms such as "romance," "flirting," or "courtship" because we acknowledge that the range of relationships that can be categorized as e-dating is wide and can encompass anything between cybersex and marriage.

The focus of this chapter is on the "e-dating career" which we define as the sum-total of all the behaviors and experiences that e-daters undergo while being e-daters. Just like a vocational career, the e-dating career may involve not just the behaviors initiated by the e-dater but also the responses that the e-dater receives from the environment. These may include positive, negative or no responses at all.

We prefer to use the term "career" to describe the e-dating process because this term denotes a long-term experience that can last months and even years. It also implies a series of discrete experiences (just like "jobs") that the individual can consider in retrospect as parts of the whole experience. The term "career" also implies overcoming hurdles, adjusting goals, and modifying strategies to fit new realities, for example, it implies, change, growth, and the development of new perceptions about the self—all of which we consider to be part and parcel of the e-dating experience.

Even though our emphasis in this chapter is on the subjective aspects of e-dating, it is important to consider some of the objective realities of this burgeoning new industry.

Online dating has been around for over two decades. It began in the early 1980s and has exploded into an extremely lucrative form of consumer-to-consumer sector of e-commerce. According to a study conducted by the Online Publishers Association (OPA) and comScore Networks, "U.S. residents spent $469.5 million on online dating and personals in 2004, the largest segment of 'paid content' on the web" (Consumer Search, 2005).

The e-dating industry is dominated by several large companies including Match.com, Yahoo Personals, and American Singles. They are followed by a multitude of other sites offering services for all aspects and preferences for dating, for example, JDate.com (which advertises itself as "the larges Jewish singles network"), ChristianSingles.com, BlackSinglesConnection.com, Gay.com., and so forth. According to TrueDating.com (TrueDating, 2006), Match.com is the world's leading online dating Web site, while Yahoo Personals is a close second, both boasting over 9 million members. The main factors contributing to the success of this industry include the relatively low start-up costs associated with running an online dating service and people's willingness to buy love online.

Even though e-dating is a dominant sector in e-commerce, very limited empirical research is available about it in the scientific literature. Our goal in this chapter is to propose a theory of e-dating development and to present the results of an empirical investigation that explored our theory.

The underlying assumption of our e-dating theory is that e-dating is a stage process in which individuals move through a number of steps or stages. Each stage is characterized by a different set of behaviors, with individuals moving from one stage to another as their e-dating "career" unfolds.

While the steps in the e-dating theory are assumed to be essentially the same for males and females, the two genders are assumed to follow a different sequence of these stages. Thus, the model assumes that because of cultural and environmental reasons, males tend to initiate contact earlier in the e-dating process than females do. Also, the theory assumes that relative to females, males are more active in behaviors that are associated with establishment and maintenance of contact.

In the following sections, we discuss the major theories and empirical research that relate to e-dating and how our theory fits in with the existing research. We proceed to present the e-dating theory, the hypotheses that we developed, and the empirical research that we conducted to explore the hypotheses. We conclude with a discussion of the implications from this research for future exploration of the theory and practice of e-dating.

LITERATURE ON DATING

Dating, or "adult romantic attachment" as this phenomenon is often termed in the scientific literature, is an interdisciplinary area of research. Some of the major contributions to the development of the body of theory in this area came from biology, sociology, economics, communication, and psychology.

In the following sections, we present the major questions that each of these disciplines raised in relation to the meaning of adult romantic attachment and some of the answers that it provided to these questions.

The major contribution of biology is in addressing the question of *why* people are attracted to one another and the reasons for the *strength* of this attraction. Thus, the biological literature on monogamy (Gubernick, 1994) suggests that people (and other animal species) are attracted to monogamous relationships because they solve the problem of paternity certainty. Since ovulation is concealed in women, men reduce the risk that their offspring may not be theirs by establishing and maintaining monogamous (romantic) relationships with women. Another explanation that follows this line of reasoning is that monogamous relationships offer protection for immature offspring, particularly given the relatively long time that it takes humans to mature sexually relative to other primates.

Applied to our research, the major contribution of the biological literature is in confirming the importance of adult romantic attraction because of its relationship to our survival as a species.

The major contribution of sociology is in addressing the question of *who* people tend to be romantically attached to. As indicated by Rosenfeld (2005), the literature on mate selection in sociology since the 1940s has been characterized by an interesting paradox. On one hand, the major theorists Merton (1941) and Davis (1941) promoted the "status-caste exchange" arguments, which perceived marriage as an exchange between unequals (men with money marry women of beauty), but on the other hand, there was little empirical evidence to promote these arguments.

Thus, contrary to this theory, the bulk of the research in the sociological literature in the past 70 years has actually demonstrated that people find mates who are similar to themselves in status, class, and education (Mare, 1991; Kalmijn, 1998); religion (Kennedy, 1952; Johnson, 1980; Kalmijn, 1991); and race (Heer, 1974; Lieberson & Waters, 1988; Kalmijn, 1993; Qian, 1997). In other words, married partners tend to be the same on every dimension except gender.

Applied to our research, the major contribution of the sociological literature is in establishing the principle that romantic attachment is rational and that even when men and women are convinced that they simply "fell in love" their actions seem to follow very predicable and rational patterns that suggest a process of rational decision making rather than pure emotion.

The major contribution of economics is in addressing the question of *what* considerations affect people's choice of specific partners. The central concept in the economic treatment of this issue is the concept of "marriage market," where men and women (agents) are assumed to behave strategically to maximize their outcomes from a relationship. The seminal work in this area by Becker (1974) focused on analyzing the manner in which men and women "sort" each other along characteristics such as income, education, and so forth. The underlying assumption of Becker's work was that each partner's "value" is based on the sum of his or her attributes. In order for an equilibrium or a "match" to take place, the two parties have to be convinced that the sum of their attributes or their "value" is the same (or similar) as that of their partner.

Applied to our research, the major contribution of the economic literature is in reiterating the principle that romantic attachment is a rational process of weighting alternatives and considering choices. Obviously, if this is indeed the case, then it stands to reason that this process would entail strategy, growth and change, which are central to our e-dating model.

The major contribution of psychology is in addressing the question of *how* people establish romantic attachments. One of the major frameworks for the study of romantic relationships in psychology is the adult attachment theory that was originally proposed by Hazan and Shaver in the 1980s (Hazan & Shaver, 1987). The theory is based on an earlier theory designed to explain the emotional bond between infants and their caregivers (Bowlby, 1980). According to Fraley and Shaver, (2000, pp. 134-135) the Hazan and Shaver adult romantic attachment theory is based on the following four propositions:

1. The emotional and behavioral dynamics of infant caregiver relationships and adult romantic relationships are governed by the same biological system. In both cases the motivation for attachment is to promote safety, comfort, and survival. Thus, adults typically feel safer when their partner is nearby, accessible and responsive.

2. The kind of individual differences observed in infant-caregiver relationships are similar to the ones observed in romantic relationships. Following this principle, Hazan and Shaver described three styles of adult romantic attachment: (a) secure, (b) anxious/ambivalent, and (c) avoidant.

3. Individual differences in adult attachment behavior are reflections of the expectations and beliefs people have formed about

themselves and their close relationships on the basis of their attachment histories; these "working models" are relatively stable, and, as such, may be reflections of care giving experiences.

4. Romantic love, involves the interplay of attachment, care giving and sex. These three separate systems serve different functions but together they reflect the same early experiences and attachment relationships that the individual had as an infant.

The Hazan and Shaver (1987) adult romantic attachment theory generated a stream of empirical studies, including research on the impact of working models on people's perceptions of their partners' intentions (Collins, 1996), the effect of working models on partner choice (Pietromonaco & Carnelley, 1994), relationship stability (Kirkpatrick & Davis, 1994), and relationship dissolution (Pistole, 1995).

Over the years, a number of criticisms of the theory led to a re-thinking and modification of some of its assumptions, including (1) the suggestion that not all romantic or couple relationships are attachment relationships and that some pair bonding relationships are actually not romantic in nature; (2) the original *three* "working models" that people can apply to relationships, can be better conceptualized as *four* "working models" (secure, preoccupied, fearful-avoidant, and dismissing-avoidant); and (3) the stability of the "working models" may not always apply, as some people seem to "overwrite" their early attachment models with new ones that are based on later attachment experiences (Farley & Shaver, 2000).

The Hazan and Shaver theory (1987) is the major basis on which our e-dating development model is based. Specifically, we accept the principle that "working models" (possibly ones originating from early childhood) affect the manner in which adults establish romantic attachments. Also, given that these "working models" are likely to be different for males and females because of their different socialization, it stands to reason that the behavior of adult male and female e-daters will be different too. Secondly, we accept the principle, proposed by the later versions of the theory (Farley & Shaver, 2000) that "working models" are subject to learning and change and that adult males and females are likely to overwrite them in response to changes in their external environment. Indeed, our conceptualization of e-dating as a change process in which coping mechanisms are adopted to deal with new conditions and circumstances can be seen as an example of the "re-writing" of "working models," as it denotes the constant evolvement of coping mechanisms throughout the e-dating career.

Building on the early literature on attachment and dating, a number of authors have attempted to explain the e-dating process. In the following sections, we consider some of the emerging research in this area and its implications to our e-dating model.

Prescriptive Literature on E-Dating

Much of the early literature on e-dating (Rose, 1999; Edgar, Jr., & Edgar, II, 2003; Greenwald, 2003; Silverstein & Lasky, 2004; Orr, 2004; Berry, 2005; Culbreth, 2005, and so forth) can be described as "prescriptive" because of its focus on instructing readers on how to conduct their e-dating careers effectively.

Still, given that not much formal research is available in the area of e-dating, these works can be credited for a number of important contributions, including: describing the various tasks that need to be undertaken by e-daters (Rose, 1999), offering advice on the technological features of the e-dating services (Silverstein & Lasky, 2004), highlighting the potential dangers of e-dating and explaining how one can protect one-self from the dangers that e-dating entails (Orr, 2004; Berry, 2005). Furthermore, the prescriptive literature can be credited with explaining the strategies that work best for certain "specialized" segments of

the e-dating population, such as men (Edgar, Jr., & Edgar, II, 2003), women (Rose, 1999; Greenwald, 2003), or baby boomers (Culbreth, 2005).

Even though these publications have not followed formal research methodology, the insights that can be derived from them, particularly on the behaviors that e-daters typically adopt, are important and have influenced our initial formulation of the stages in our e-dating theory.

Thus, without exception the prescriptive publications agree that e-daters (irrespective of gender) start their e-dating career by creating an online profile. They also agree that this is followed by "search" activities that involve consideration of other e-daters' profiles, and that eventually, e-daters initiate or respond to contacts from other e-daters. The above sources are also in agreement that while all e-dating contacts start in the online environment, eventually some e-dating relationships evolve to telephone and/or face-to-face contact. All of these assumptions are central to our e-dating theory.

Descriptive and Predictive Literature on E-Dating

More recent publications have attempted to go beyond the prescriptive by offering a more scientific methodology for data collection and analysis of e-dating research, with some attempts to offer theoretical models that describe, explain, interpret, and predict e-dating behaviors. The following discussion presents three of the most important approaches to the scientific study of e-dating,

Psychological/Philosophical: One of the most interesting attempts to interpret the nature of e-dating has been proposed by Aaron Ben-Ze'ev (2004). Based on interviews with cyberspace daters, this pioneering study explored the differences between "virtual" and "real" relationships. Some of the features that are listed by Ben-Ze'ev as distinguishing the virtual from the real spaces are:

1. The virtual space has a "seductive" nature to it that makes virtual relationships sometimes more intense and emotionally satisfying than real relationships.

2. The virtual space is more egalitarian in that it allows people to interact with each other irrespective of their demographic, physical or emotional attributes. Indeed, the virtual space is unique in that it offers its inhabitants the opportunity of "inventing" themselves.

3. Because of its limitless possibilities for self-presentation, the virtual space enables more deceit. Indeed, a very high percentage of Internet "lovers," according to this research, mis-represent (lie) about their attributes, feelings and behavior.

4. The virtual space is addictive and because of this (and other reasons) can be dangerous. Online daters may develop strong emotions toward partners in this environment that can eventually affect their real relationships.

5. Online relationships are incomplete and for this reason, to be complete, they need to migrate from the online to the face-to-face environment or from the virtual to the real space.

The Ben-Ze'ev research focuses on cyber-sex rather than on cyber-love. As such, the applicability of its findings to our e-dating theory is limited. Still, its emphasis on the differences between the two spaces and the need to migrate from one to the other in order for a relationship to become real are important assumptions on which our theory of e-dating development is based.

Economics: One of the very first investigations of e-dating from an economic perspective is the article "What makes you click: An empirical analysis of online dating (Hitsch, Hortacsu, & Ariely, 2005). The data set for this research recorded the activities of 23,000 users in the Boston and San Diego area during a 3 ½-month period in 2003.

The data set included self-reported information about users' age, income, education level, ethnicity, political inclinations, marital status, and so forth. The users also posted pictures of themselves on the site, which the researchers rated and ranked (using objective judges) for "attractiveness." The attractiveness rankings together with self-reported information about users' height, weight, and other physical characteristics enabled the researchers to create a measure of physical attractiveness that went beyond just the picture.

The most important aspect of this research was that the researchers were provided with information about the activities of the e-daters. Thus, as the authors note (Hitsch, Hortacsu, & Ariely, 2005), "At each moment in time, we know which profile they browse, whether they view a specific photograph, and whether they send or reply to a letter from another user. We also have some limited information on the contents of the e-mails exchanged: in particular, we know whether the users exchanged phone numbers or e-mail addresses" (p. 3).

The researchers based their model on exchange theory, with the objective being to assess the impact of some variables (notably, physical attractiveness, but also level of education, income, etc.) on e-daters "success," as measured by the likelihood of their e-mails being responded to and/or by other e-daters agreeing to exchange e-mail address and telephone number with them.

The findings from this research confirmed a number of assumptions that are central to our e-dating model:

1. The percentage of males in the e-dating site (55.5%) was higher than in the general population in both locations (49%) and also higher than the percentage of males among Internet users (also 49%). Other than this demographic difference, all other characteristics of the male and female population of daters were similar to those of the general population and of Internet users in the two

cities. Compared to the general population in the two cities, the authors reported that the e-dating users were somewhat younger (25-35), more educated and of higher income than the general population.

2. As a rule, the stated preferences of both males and females seemed to confirm the findings from the sociological literature reported on in the previous sections that people prefer to date others who are similar to them on all demographic variables. The authors report that this was true for education, income and race, particularly for women.

3. The percentages of people who state that their appearance is "above average" (very high) and those reporting that their appearance is below average (very low) suggests that users "inflate" their reports. This same phenomenon is also evident in regards to weight (much lower than the average for women in the general population) and height (much taller than the average for men in the general population), suggesting that men tend to inflate their height and women tend to deflate their weight in their e-dating profiles.

4. Males and females behaved differently online. Men were more likely to browse women's profiles than women were (searching behavior). Men were also more likely to send e-mail messages to women than women were, particularly when the men stated that they were interested in a serious relationship. Indeed, this category of men sent more e-mail messages than any other category of e-daters.

5. Males and females were different in the extent to which their actions produced results. Thus, the likelihood of a male to receive a response to an e-mail message was 40%, while the likelihood of a female (irrespective of looks or any other personal attributes) to receive a response to her e-mail message was 70%. The researchers found that attractive-

ness makes a difference here, with the least attractive women being 2-4 times more likely to send a first contact e-mail message to a man than the most attractive women. The same difference in selectiveness was also evident in the response rate.

6. The final outcomes for daters were that overall, women were browsed more often, received more first contact e-mails and e-mail containing a phone number and/or e-mail address than men. Thus, while men received on average 2.6 first contact e-mails, women received on average 12.6 e-mails; 54% of all men in the sample NEVER received a first contact e-mail at all, whereas only 19% of all women were never approached by e-mail.

7. As for the impact of self-reported attributes on the likelihood of receiving e-mail messages, it was most pronounced for underweight women (they received 77% more e-mail messages than women who reported that they were overweight) and "blondes." For men, the "penalty" for overweight was less severe. In contrast, stated income and "shortness" had a strong impact on men's e-dating "success" while they had a marginal impact on women's "success."

- **Sociology:** One of the most seminal sociological investigations of e-dating resulted in the book, "Double click: Romance and commitment among online couples" by Andrea Baker (2005). The uniqueness of this publication is that it is not just empirical (based on a scientifically designed survey of 89 couples that met online) but also predictive. The major goal of this research was to use survey and interview data to discover the keys for success in e-dating. Based on this research, the author outlined the POST model, a four factor model that purports to predict success in e-dating. The four factors include:

1. **Place** (where the e-daters met on- and off-line) - This research defined quite a number of different "places" for e-daters to meet. The findings indicated that the more specifically related to relationship building the meeting place was (such as a chat room dedicated to a topic that is of interest to both parties or an e-dating service) the more successful the relationship that resulted from meeting there was likely to be.

2. **Obstacles** (the number and types of obstacles that the e-daters faced and had to overcome) - The researcher defined two types of obstacles. Those that resulted from pre-existing relationships (marriage, cohabitation of one or more of the parties) and those that resulted from geographical distance. The findings indicated that more such obstacles existed at the beginning of the relationship the less likely was the relationship to be stable and long-term.

3. **Self-presentation** (self disclosure versus secrecy, deception versus truth, and appearances versus truth) - The findings from the above research indicated that self-disclosure, honesty and appearance that was congruent with the other party's expectations were associated with the relationship's positive outcome. Holding back information about one's self, particularly once the online relationship moves on the face-to-face stage, pretending to be someone other than who one really is and providing information about one's appearance that proved to be untrue once the e-daters met face-to-face were all predictors of failure of the e-dating relationship.

4. **Timing:** The findings from this research were that the longer the e-daters waited to meet each other face-to-face and the longer they waited to initiate a sexual relationship, the more likely they were to establish a successful relationship. Indeed, cybersex was one of the best predictors of an e-dating

relationship's failure. These authors interpret this finding to suggest that starting a sexual relationship too early on- or off-line hinders the development of other areas of shared interest and could potentially subdue other areas of potential conflict a couple encounters, resulting in the couple not knowing if they are truly compatible with each other.

The above study has a number of direct implications to our research. First, it confirms the fact that daters engage in different types of behavior throughout their e-dating career. It proposes the idea that some e-dating strategies are more successful than others and that successful male and female e-daters tend to use different strategies. This research also suggests through its in-depth interviewing with e-daters that strategies are not constant—they may change throughout the e-dating career, as e-daters become more aware of the constraints of the e-dating environment.

The strength of the Baker (2005) study is that unlike most of its predecessors, it was based on primary sources—the reports of e-daters in response to an open-ended questionnaire administered to them. However, as noted by the author, this methodology also had its weaknesses. E-daters who participated in this study reported on events that happened weeks and sometimes months before the survey was administered to them. This introspective methodology could have introduced distortions into the data that a more "real-time" approach, like the one employed in our study, does not have. Also, because the e-daters reports were made after the fact, it was difficult to use the data to describe the actual developmental process of e-dating, which is the main focus of our research.

TOWARD A THEORY OF E-DATING DEVELOPMENT

As indicated in the previous sections and based on the literature that we reviewed, our theory of e-dating development is based on the following premises:

1. The typical e-dating career consists of six stages or steps: (a) *Construction* of a profile; (b) *Searching* for appropriate matches; (c) *Sending* winks, e-mail messages, text messages, and so forth; (d) *Responding* to winks, e-mail messages, text messages, and so forth; (e) *Setting* up face-to-face dates; (f) *Conducting* face-to-face dates; and (g) *Concluding* the process by either starting a new cycle of the e-dating process, establishing a relationship with one date, or quitting the process all together without finding a desirable match.

2. Because of primarily cultural reasons, even though the steps in the e-dating process are identical for males and females, the *sequence* of these stages and the amount of time and energy that each gender spends on some of the stages differs. Thus, because males are expected to be the initiators in the dating game, they tend to start "searching" activities earlier and spend more time and energy on these activities than females do. Similarly, males also tend to engage in contact initiation activities (sending winks and e-mails) earlier in the e-dating process and they invest more time and energy in these activities throughout their e-dating career than females do.

3. Because males are more numerous on e-dating services than females are (and possibly because females are less inclined to initiate contact with males), the males' attempts to establish contact with females are less likely to be successful than the females' attempts to establish contact with males.

4. This reality, results in males *increasing* their investment of time and effort in initiating contact over time more than females do. Thus, while the two genders might start the e-dating process with similar behaviors and expectations, as the process unfolds and as a result of input from the environment (lack of response from females), males increase their contact initiation activities, while females decrease their engagement in such activities.

5. The end result from this process is that males are less successful (and possibly less satisfied) with their e-dating experiences relative to females.

Table 1 shows the typical e-dating development stages for each gender. Please note that the six stages can conclude after one "round" or repeat for a longer period of time, with new rounds initiated repeatedly. Also, the theory assumes that while some males might behave initially "like females" (initiating few contacts with females and expecting females to contact them) and some females might initially behave "like males" (initiating contact

Table 1. The typical female and male e-dating career

Females	Males
A. Constructing or revising a profile	**A. Constructing** or revising a profile
B. Searching for appropriate matches	**B. Searching** for appropriate matches
D. Receiving winks, e-mail messages or instant messages	**C. Sending** (and eventually receiving) winks, e-mail messages, or instant messaging
E. Setting up face-to-face dates (usually by telephone)	**E. Setting** up face-to-face dates (usually by telephone)
F. Conducting dates	**F. Conducting** dates
G. Concluding the process by either starting a new cycle, establishing a committed relationship or quitting all together	**G. Concluding** the process by either starting a new cycle, establishing a committed relationship or quitting all together

with males), as the e-dating process unfolds and because of the different input from the environment that males and females get, both genders "converge" into the "typical" sequence proposed by our theory.

Based on the above assumptions, we have outlined below a number of research questions that we explored empirically. For our initial investigation, we decided to restrict our research to the very first three assumptions in the model, namely, (1) the e-dating process consists of stages and that these differ for males and females; (2) the behavior of males and females throughout the e-dating process is different, and (3) the input that male and female e-daters receive from the environment (namely, from other e-daters) is different.

RESEARCH QUESTIONS

First Research Question

- **Does the e-dating process consist of distinct steps that are characterized by different behaviors?**

As indicated in the previous sections, the steps or stages in the e-dating process include: (1) constructing a profile, (2) searching, (3) initiating communication, (4) receiving communication, (5) setting face-to-face dates, (6) conducting dates, and (7) concluding the e-dating process.

- **Do males and females follow a different sequence of steps in the e-dating process?**

As mentioned in the previous sections, our model expects males to start the searching behaviors earlier and engage in more activities that involve establishment of contact with others than females do. Females, on the other hand, are expected to start the search behavior later and engage in it less frequently. Females are also expected to initiate less contact and respond to more contact from males.

Second Research Question

- **Do male and female e-daters behave differently throughout the e-dating process?**

In this preliminary research, we analyzed differences between male and female e-daters in a number of areas including: the intensity of search behavior, including the number of profiles searched, the establishment of a favorites list and the number of profiles included in it. We also explored the number of "winks," e-mail messages and text messages sent, the number of rejection messages sent, and the number of individuals barred from having contact with our respondents.

Our expectations were that while males will engage in more search and contact initiation behaviors (such as sending "winks," e-mail messages and text messages), females were expected to engage in more contact-limiting-behaviors such as sending rejection messages and barring other e-daters from having access to their profile. As for the setting and holding of dates, which are also active e-dating behaviors, our expectation was that since these require the cooperation of two parties, females will engage in more of these activities than males.

Third Research Question

- **Do male and female e-daters receive different inputs from the environment to their e-dating behavior?**

Our expectations were that male and female e-daters do indeed receive different input from the environment, with males getting fewer "winks," e-mail messages and text messages than female do. Also, as indicated in relation to the previous research question, because setting and holding dates is an activity that depends on the behavior of the other party (who needs to agree to the date), we expected males to have fewer dates than females.

EMPIRICAL INVESTIGATION

Sample and Instrument

Based on the literature in the previous sections, we constructed an inventory of e-dating activities that followed the six stages in our e-dating development theory (see Appendix 1 for the research inventory). We administered the inventory to a group of 22 volunteers from two undergraduate classes in a private Midwestern university in the U.S. during the first semester of the 2006-2007 academic year. The average age of the participants was 20.4 and the number of males and females was about equal (12 females and 10 males). All participants were white and the majority were of upper middle class background.

Data Collection Process

The participants in the study were not paid for their participation. Instead, they received a free three-month subscription to Match.com (paid by the researchers), the largest e-dating service in the industry. In addition, they received credit for one assignment in the two courses that they were doing with one of the investigators. Participants were informed that participation was not compulsory and if they chose not to participate they were provided with an alternative assignment to do for the course.

Participants were also informed that because of the small sample and the need to keep participants as "similar to each other as possible," only heterosexual students that were not in a committed relationship were invited to participate. Also, even though we did not require participants to be e-dating novices, all participants indicated that they had no previous e-dating experience prior to joining the study.

The participants were assured by the researchers that the data that they volunteered was only going to be analyzed in aggregate. No personal data about participants was to be made public. They did not receive information about our e-dating theory, but they were told that our major focus was their behavior, thoughts and feelings throughout the e-dating experience.

To establish a baseline of knowledge on e-dating for all participants, the researchers subscribed the participants to Match.com. This was followed with a two-hour lab tutorial on the various features of the Match.com service, including detailed information on how to create a profile, conduct and save searches, initiate contact and respond to contacts from others, and how to manage a personal Match.com account.

The management features of the account, which included a tally of: messages sent, messages received, winks sent, winks received, members rejected, members barred, members entered into favorites list, and so forth, were particularly important for our study because the participants were expected to report this information throughout the study.

Participants received 12 copies of the inventory and were asked to fill up and submit one copy per week, starting the third week of the semester. The majority of the participants submitted between 8 and 12 completed inventories. Even though participants were told that they could exit the study at any time and without an explanation, not one of the participants did so.

Findings

To address the above research questions, we conducted a number of analyses.

First research question

To address the first research question which addressed the issue of whether stages could be discerned in the activities of e-daters and whether

Table 2. Type of activity engaged in by gender.

Males (n= 10)	Week 1	Week 2	Week 3	Week 4	Week 5
	Constructing or revising a profile (70%)	Conducting a search for matches (50%)	Conducting a search for matches (50%)	Initiating contact with matches (57%)	Responding to contact from others (57%)
	Conducting a search for matches (20%)		Constructing or revising a profile and	Conducting a search for matches (28%)	
	Initiating contact with matches (10%)		Responding to contact from others (40%)		

Week 6	Week 7	Week 8	Week 9	Week 10	Week 11
Initiating contact with matches (43%)	Responding to contact from others (33%)	Initiating contact with matches (33%)	Initiating contact with matches (33%)	Setting up dates (100%)	Responding to contact from others (100%)
Responding to contact from others (43%)	Initiating contact with matches (33%)	Meeting dates (25%)	Setting up a dates (33%)		
	Setting up dates (33%)	Setting up dates (33%)	Meeting dates (25%)		

Females (n= 12)	Week 1	Week 2	Week 3	Week 4	Week 5
	Constructing or revising a profile (100%)	Constructing or revising a profile (50%)	Constructing or revising a profile (50%)	Conducting a search for matches (45%)	Responding to contact from others (82%)
			Responding to contact from others (25%)	Responding to contact from others (36%)	

Week 6	Week 7	Week 8	Week 9	Week 10	Week 11
Conducting a search for matches (36%)	Responding to contact from others (80%)	Responding to contact from others (63%)	Responding to contact from others (67%)	Responding to contact from others (60%)	Setting up dates (50%)
Responding to contact from others (27%)	Conducting a search for matches (20%)	Conducting a search for matches (25%)	Setting up dates (16%)	Setting up dates (20%)	Meeting dates (25%)
			Meeting dates (16%)	Meeting dates (20%)	Responding to contact from others (25%)

these stages were different for males and females, descriptive statistics was used to tabulate the activities of the respondents each week. Only activities that the respondents referred to as their "main" activity for the week were tabulated.

Table 1 shows the distribution of the respondents' main activity each week by gender. As demonstrated in the table, there were observable differences in the activities that males and females engaged in each week during the test period.

Thus, for week 1 the main activity engaged in by the majority of males (70%) and females (100%) was to construct or revise their Match. com profile. In week 2 and 3, half (50%) of the females were still constructing or revising their profile while half (50%) of the males had moved on and were conducting a search for matches.

Interestingly, in week 4, 57% of the males were initiating contact with others, an activity that a

few of the females (19%) started at the ninth week, and by the eleventh week only half (50%) of the females were initiating contact.

During week 5, most men (and women) were back to responding to contacts. In weeks 6 through 9, men were continuing to initiate contact with matches, an activity that women never engaged in over the eleven week period. Indeed, most women in weeks 7 through 10 were engaged in responding to contact from others.

To complete our analysis for the first research question, we used a chi square to explore whether gender (male vs. female) was related to the main activity e-daters engaged in each week. Even though differences were observed in the percentages, only weeks 3 and 8 were significant at the 0.05 level, and weeks 4, 9, and 10 were significant at the 0.10 level.

Second Research Question

To address the second research question which focused on e-daters' initiating contact with other e-daters, we examined e-daters' "active behaviors" such as the number of winks sent, e-mails sent, instant messages sent, rejection messages sent, and barring of other e-daters from communicating with the e-dater.

Using a t-test for independent samples analysis, we compared the active behaviors of males and females across all twelve weeks of the study period.

The results of this analysis are presented in Table 3. As indicated in the table, the differences between male and female e-daters were significant for all active behaviors. Thus, females were sending significantly fewer winks, e-mails, instant messages, and rejection messages. However, females barred more people from accessing their profile than did males. Paradoxically (but in line with the e-dating theory), the last "active" behavior shown in Table 3, the number of dates held over the twelve week study period, was significantly higher for females than males. This is a paradoxical finding because females were less active on every one of the behaviors in this category.

Third Research Question

To address the third research question which focused on the input that e-daters received from the environment, we examined the input that the e-daters received from others, such as the number of "hits" on their Match.com profile, the number of winks made to them, the number of e-mail messages sent to them, and the number of instant messages sent to them.

Using a t-test for independent samples analysis, we compared the behaviors of males and females. Table 4 shows these differences. As indicated in Table 4, the male and female e-daters differed significantly ($p < 0.05$) on three of the four behaviors in the table. Thus, females received significantly more hits, winks and e-mail messages. Also, although no significant difference was found between male and female receiving text messages, females still received instant messages more frequently than males.

DISCUSSION AND CONCLUSION

As indicated in the previous sections, our goal was to describe a theory of e-dating development

Table 3. Differences in e-daters active behaviors

Active Behaviors	Averages for Males and Females Over The Study Duration (12 Weeks)	T-test statistics (P-value) (Equal variances not assumed)
The number of winks sent	Females = 0.208 Males = 9.57	T= -11.42 (p=0.000)
The number of e-mails sent	Females = 0.207 Males = 9.56	T= -11.41 (p=0.000)
The number of instant messages (IMs) sent	Females = 1.43 Males = 7.87	T= -7.96 (p=0.000)
The number of rejection messages sent	Females = 0.495 Males = 1.59	T= -4.89 (p=0.000)
The number of people barred from accessing one's profile	Females = 2.89 Males = 0.000	T= 6.429 (p=0.000)
The number of dates held	Females = 1.16 Males = 0.101	T= 8.92 (p=0.000)

Table 4. Differences in responses from the environment to d-daters' behaviors.

Input from the Environment	Averages for Males and Females Over The Study Duration (12 Weeks)	T-test statistics (P-value) (Equal variances not assumed)
The number of visits ("hits") received to their profile	Females = 157.03 Males = 15.98	T= 7.43 (p=0.000)
The number of winks sent to them	Females = 71.44 Males = 6.63	T= 7.93 (p=0.000)
The number of e-mails sent to them	Females = 23.43 Males = 5.43	T= 7.07 (p=0.000)
The number of instant messages (IMs) sent to them	Females =0.376 Males = 0.130	T= 1.89 (p=0.061)

and to explore it empirically. The findings from our preliminary research suggest that:

1. Six distinct stages can be identified empirically in the e-dating career of male and female e-daters. These, as our theory predicted, include: (a) constructing a profile, (b) searching, (c) initiating communication, (d) receiving communication, (e) setting face to face dates, (f) conducting dates, and (g) concluding the e-dating process.

2. The sequence of stages for males and females is not the same, with males initiating contact with females earlier and investing more time and energy in initiating contact activities throughout the e-dating process than females do.

3. Even though some males and females exhibit behaviors that are typical of the other gender (some males establish a profile and wait for females to contact them and some females start contacting males right away instead of waiting for males to contact them), both genders tend to exhibit the behavior pattern outlined in our theory; namely, males tend to initiate more contact and females tend to initiate less.

4. The inputs that each gender receives from the environment are different and can pos-

sibly explain the differences in their behavior initially and over time. Thus, males tend to get fewer approaches from females across all "passive" behavioral categories (e.g., they receive fewer hits on their profile, winks, e-mail messages and text messages).

Obviously, this exploratory research can be extended in a number of different directions:

First, our e-dating theory proposed a number of hypotheses that we did not test in the preliminary investigation that we are reporting on in this chapter. Future investigations may extend the scope of this research to include questions like: Do the differences between male and female behavior increase over time? Does the input that the two genders receive from the environment change over time? Can the changes in behavior exhibited by e-daters be explained by changes in expectations? Obviously, answering each of the above questions in the affirmative would lend more support to the model that we proposed here. Thus, if the differences between the behavior of male and female e-daters increase over time, it would strengthen our contention that e-dating is, indeed, a developmental process in which behaviors change in response to changes in perceptions.

Second, our sample of undergraduate, white, upper middle class, heterosexual students can be extended to include participants of different ages, races, socio-economic classes, and social orientations. Furthermore, the number of participants in each of the above categories can be increased to allow for more generalizable conclusions.

Third, in this exploratory study, we used an open-ended questionnaire to elicit as much information about a range of topics related to e-dating. Future research might triangulate the research methodology by employing, on one hand, more quantitative measures of some of the variables that we identified here, and on the other, in-depth interviewing to identify additional variables that our inventory did not fully account for.

Fourth, if indeed e-dating services can be seen as different environments for male and female daters, this may have far-reaching implications. Thus, future research might explore the extent to which different e-dating services cater to the unique dating needs of males and females, by categorizing e-dating services as male or female "friendly."

Following this line of reasoning, male friendly services can be expected to create an environment that is friendlier to males by establishing rewards for females for responding to male contacts. An e-dating service that is already doing it is eHarmony. One of the unique features of the eHarmony service is that it correlates the number of "good matches" that an e-dater receives from the service with whether the e-dater responded to contacts from previously provided matches. This system is applied equally to males and females. Since females are less inclined to initiate contact and/or to respond to male contact than males are, this principle of rewarding e-daters for responding to contacts helps males more than it helps females.

Similarly, a female friendly service would establish an environment that is even friendlier to females than current services are by providing females with additional input on prospective male matches, such as through a ranking of all e-daters. Again, even though ranking would be applied equally to both males and females, since females are more often in a position to screen a large number of prospective matches, they would benefit more from ranking than males will. If a service offers this feature to its customers, the result would be a more attractive environment for females than for males.

Another implication from our research has to do with perceptions. If indeed the reality of e-dating for males and females is so different, are both genders aware of it? Does this awareness affect male and female inclination to use e-dating services? Is this awareness affected by age, social status, marital status or culture? Future research into e-daters perceptions might explore whether they can be modified. For example, if older females were aware that in their age group the ratio of males to females is even greater than in the younger age groups, would they be more inclined to become e-daters than they currently are? Will this awareness remove the stigma that is currently associated with e-dating, particularly in the older age groups?

Another related issue has to do with the strategies that e-daters employ to become successful in this process. Our study indicated that males and females tend to use different strategies. An interesting set of questions that relates to this finding is whether the strategies that each gender uses are affected by individual differences. For example, can a male who is particularly attractive (physically or thanks to a higher level of education or income) use more feminine strategies (initiate less contact) and still be successful? Are e-daters aware of how their individual attributes affect their strategies and their success rate? Do they modify their strategies based on this awareness?

Another related issue has to do with education. Given that e-dating is becoming ubiquitous, should the educational system invest resources in training young people to be efficient e-daters? Should males and females get *different* training on how to conduct themselves on an e-dating Web site given that the environment in which they operate is not the same? Should the educational system consider e-dating skills as important for young adults as driving, cooking, and other "survival skills"?

Another set of questions that the discussion in the previous section raises is related to the exposure that e-dating may involve and the risks that are associated with this exposure. Recent popular publications discuss the fact that the exposure of e-daters might lead (particularly in the case of female e-daters) to risks of violence (Loviglio, 2007; Moraski, 2007). The popular literature is replete with prescriptions on how to conduct "safe" e-dating.

Some e-dating services (e.g., True.com) have based their business model on providing their customers with background checks on other e-daters' criminal records and matrimonial status, lobbying for such searches to be enforced by law on all services or for services that do not conduct such searchers to acknowledge it on their Web sites (Heydary, 2006). Following this line of reasoning, an interesting direction for future research would be to explore the extent to which different e-dating business models are perceived by e-daters as more or less secure, the extent to which service providers can enhance the sense of security of their customers and the degree to which security enhancing features result in higher revenues for e-dating services.

Privacy concerns and the possible invasion of privacy that some e-dating services involve is another important direction for future research. Thus, ranking or categorizing e-dating services on how "invasive" they are could be an interesting future line of research on e-dating. Such categorization may reveal that some services provide more information to e-daters about other e-daters than is desirable. Indeed, some users of e-dating services (particularly, females) might experience the real-time features of e-dating services (e.g., provision of information to other daters on whether an e-dater is active in real time) as surveillance.

Given the variance in exposure between different e-dating services, it would be interesting to empirically explore how e-daters feel about the invasion of privacy that the various e-dating business models entail. Are males more comfortable with high levels of exposure than females? Are younger e-daters more comfortable with high levels of exposure than older e-daters are? Do demographic variables (such as level of education, ethnicity or income) impact the degree to which e-daters are willing to tolerate different levels of self-exposure or invasion of their privacy?

Another possible direction for future research is to explore how different "types" of e-dating services utilize different business models and how this impacts users. The e-dating arena consists of services that cater to marriage-oriented, friendship-oriented, or sex-oriented users (as well as to users who combine these orientations). Future research might explore the features that differentiate these types of e-dating services from each other, the degree of exposure of daters to each other is involved in each type, the extent to which e-daters are aware of the differences between the "types" and the degree to which the combination of features that each type represents affects the success of the business model used by the service.

Given that this chapter does not focus only on the behavior of e-daters, there are other, wider societal implications that follow from the discussion in the previous sections.

One such implication is the possible scope for abuse of information that e-daters make public. There are references in the popular literature to the use of information in social networking services by employers to spy on their employees (Lavallee, 2007; White, 2007). These reports suggest that many employers use information that individuals have posted on social networking and e-dating services (possibly a long time before the individual joined the labor force) as a basis for selection of candidates for jobs, promotion of employees, and even for harassment of employees on the job. Future research might explore the extent to which employers do indeed engage in spying on their employees by using data from social networking and e-dating services and the impact that this may have on employees' life at work.

The potential for abuse of social networking and e-dating services raises a set of other issues that involve the political and legal system. If indeed the social networking and e-dating sector poses potential dangers, should society regulate the industry to make sure that customers are more protected than they currently are? Should e-dating services be required to check their customers' criminal record or marital status? Should they be required to acknowledge on their Web site, in a manner similar to pharmaceutical companies, if they do *not* conduct such searches? Should e-dating services that involve "ranking" of e-daters by other e-daters in a manner similar to eBay's rating of buyers and sellers be outlawed because this practice involve the potential for defamation of customers? Should e-dating services be barred from discriminating against groups of e-daters that they do not wish to serve (e.g., gays)?

Only the future will tell how many of these issues will be addressed by researchers and/or by society as a whole and how this will lead to a transformation of e-dating as we know it today.

REFERENCES

Baker, A. (2005). *Double click: Romance and commitment among online couples*. Cresskill, NJ: Hampton Press.

Ben-Ze'ev, A. (2004). *Love online: Emotions on the Internet*. Cambridge: Cambridge University Press.

Berry, D. (2005). *Romancing the Web: A therapist's guide to the finer points of online dating*. Manitowoc, WI: Blue Waters Publications.

Bowlby, J. (1980). *Attachment and loss: Vol. 3, Loss, sadness and depression*. New York, NY: Basic Books.

Collins, N. (1980). Working models of attachment: Implications for explanation, emotion and behavior. *Journal of Personality and Social Psychology, 71,* 810-832.

Consumer Search. (2005). Online dating sites best rated dating sites, services. Retrieved May 26, 2006, from http://www.consumersearch.com/www/Internet/online-dating/fullstory.html.

Culbreth, J. (2005). *The boomers' guide to online dating*. U.S.: Rodale Inc.

Davis, K. (1941). Intermarriage in caste societies. *American Anthropologist, 43,* 376-395.

Edgar, H., Jr., & Edgar, H., II. (2003). *The ultimate man's guide to Internet dating: The premier men's resource for finding, attracting, meeting and dating women online*. Aliso Viejo, CA: Purple Bus Publishing.

Fraley, R., & Shaver, P. (2000). Adult romantic attachment: Theoretical developments, emerging controversies, and unanswered questions. *Review of General Psychology, 2*(2), 132-154.

Greenwald, R. (2003). *Find a husband after 35: Using what I learned at Harvard Business School*. Random House Publishing Book.

Gubernick, D. (1994). Bi-parental care and male female relations in mammals. In: S. Parmigiani & F. Vom Saal (Eds.), *Infanticide and parental care* (pp. 427-463). Chur, Switzerland: Harwood.

Hazan, C., & Shaver, P. (1987). Romantic love conceptualized as an attachment process. *Journal of Personality and Social Psychology, 52,* 511-524.

Heer, D. (1974). The prevalence of black-white marriage in the United States, 1960 and 1970. *Journal of Marriage and the Family, 36,* 246-258.

Heydary, J. (2006, September, 26). Regulation of online dating services sparks controversy. *Wall Street Journal*, p. A5.

Hitsch, J., Hortacsu, A., & Ariely, D. (2005). *What makes you click*. Paper presented at the AEA Meeting, Choice Symposium, Northwestern University. Estes Park.

Johnson, R. (1980). *Religious assortative marriage in the United States*. New York, NY: Academic Press.

Kalmijn, M. (1991). Shifting boundaries: Trends in religious and educational homogamy. *American Sociological Review, 56,* 786-800.

Kalmijn, M. (1993). Trends in black/white intermarriage. *Social Forces, 72,* 119-146.

Kalmijn, M. (1998). Intermarriage and homogamy: Causes, patterns, trends. *Annual Review of Sociology, 24,* 395-421.

Kennedy, R. (1952) Single or triple melting pot? Intermarriage in New Haven, 1870-1950. *American Journal of Sociology, 58,* 56-59.

Kirkpatrick, L., & Davis, K. (1994). Attachment style, gender and relationship stability: A longitudinal analysis. *Journal of Personality and Social Psychology, 66,* 502-512.

Lavallee, A. (2007, June 13). Firms tidy up clients' bad online reputations. *Wall Street Journal*, p. B1.

Lieberson, S., & Waters, M. (1988). *From many strands: Ethnic and racial groups in contemporary America.* New York, NY: Russell Sage.

Loviglio, J. (2007, June 16). Two sex convictions in online dating case. *Wall Street Journal*, p. B5.

Mare, R. (1991). Five decades of educational assortative mating. *American Sociological Review, 56,* 15-32.

Merton, R. (1941). Intermarriage and the social structure: Fact and theory. *Psychiatry, 4,* 361-374.

Moraski, M. (2007, June 16). Beware of digital Don Juans. *Wall Street Journal*, p. A5.

Orr, A. (2004). *Meeting, mating and cheating: Sex, love, and the new world of online dating.* New Jersey: Reuters.

Pietromonaco, P., & Carnelley, K. (1994).Gender and working models of attachment: Consequences for perceptions of self and romantic relationships. *Personal Relationships, 1,* 63-82.

Pistole, C. (1995). College students ended love relationships: Attachment style and emotion. *Jouranl of College Student Development, 1,* 53-60.

Qian, Z. (1997). Breaking racial barriers: Variations in interracial marriage between 1980 and 1990. *Demography, 34,* 263-276.

Rose, D. (1999). *Internet soul mates: Finding the love of your life through the Internet.* Phoenix, AZ: Productiones Deanna, LLC.

Rosenfeld, M. (2005). A critique of exchange theory in mate selection. *The American Journal of Sociology, 110*(5), 1284-2027.

Silverstein, J., & Lasky, M. (2004). *Online dating for dummies.* Hoboken, NJ: Wiley Publishing Inc.

TruDating. (2006). Online dating service directory. Retrieved May 25, 2006, from the http://www.trudating.com/.

White, E. (2007, January, 1). Employers reach out to recruit with Facebook. *Wall Street Journal*, p. D3.

APPENDIX I

E-Dating Research Inventory

Demographic Information:

Gender: M   F   **Age:_____ Major:_____**

This study is about e-dating. In particular, its purpose is to discover the decision and learning process through which students evolve during their e-dating experience using Match.com.

In order to participate in this study, you must meet the following criteria:

1. You have to be new to the e-dating experience. If you have extensive experience in e-dating, you should exclude yourself from participating in this study.

2. You should not be in a committed relationship. If you are in such a relationship, you should exclude yourself, too.

3. You are interested in establishing a committed relationship and willing to invest the time and energy that it will take to do so, as well as to invest the time and energy that it will take to document the process through this research.

If you are participating for extra credit, your responses will not be anonymous, as we will need your identity to add the extra credit to your grade.

Your responses may be kept anonymous if you do not request extra credit for your course.

You may drop out of the study at any time, but will forfeit the extra credit.

If you meet these criteria and accept these conditions, please sign below:

_____
Name

_____
Student Signature   Date

Date _____

ID Number _____

Questions for Students' Weekly Journals

Please fill in the answers to the following questions and submit every Friday.

Referencing your Match.com Web site activities this week, please answer the following questions:

    1. In which major activity did you engage in this week?

    a.   Constructing or revising a profile
    b.   Conducting a search for matches
    c.   Initiating contact with matches
    d.   Responding to contacts from others
    e.   Setting up dates
    f.   Meeting dates
    g.   Concluding the process

    Please circle the letter that corresponds to this week's major activity.

    If there was a close second, what was it?

Please describe in detail what you did this week in relation to each of the following activities:

Activity A - Constructing or Revising a Profile

    2. If you created or revised a profile this week, please print and attach it.
- Did you consult (i.e., show your profile and ask for feedback, or otherwise seek advice) anyone on the process? Please list those with whom (e.g., parent, sibling, roommate, friend, etc.) you consulted.
- What other resources did you use (e.g., books or online references) in constructing your profile?
- Did you find this difficult?
- Did you exaggerate, minimize or knowingly omit any aspect of your profile?
- If so, which aspects did you exaggerate, minimize or omit?
- If you revised your profile, what did you change? Why did you change it?

Activity B - Searching

    3. If you conducted searches this week, please tell us:
- Did you create your own customized search?
- If so, what attributes did you add/change beyond the basic attributes provided by the service?

- Did you save your search for future reference?
- Did you receive a list of "matches" from the service?
- If so, did you follow up on it?
- Did you follow up on one single match that you received from the service (Is it fate?)?
- Did you search the profiles of matches who approached you?
- Please estimate how many profiles you visited this week as part of your search process?
- Did you keep any profiles that you found in a "favorites" list?
- If so, how many did you place in "favorites" this week?

Activity C - Initiating Contact

5. If you initiated any contact with others this week, please tell us:
- How many winks did you send this week?
- How many e-mail messages did you send this week?
- How many instant messages did you send this week?
- How many rejection messages did you send this week?
- How many matches did you decide to "bar" from contacting you this week?
- How many of the people that you contacted this week do you think will respond?
- How many of the people that you contacted this week do you think you will meet?

Activity D - Receiving and Responding to Contact from Others

4. If you received any communication from others this week, please tell us:
- How many "hits" did your profile get this week? (report the current number of hits)
- How many winks did you get this week?
- How many e-mail messages did you get this week?
- How many instant messages did you get this week?
- Of those contacting you this week, with how many will you communicate in the future?
- How many of the people that contacted you this week do you think you will meet?

Activity E - Setting up Dates

6. If you scheduled any face-to-face dates this week, please tell us:
- How did you set the date(s) (telephone, e-mail, instant messaging, text-messaging, etc)?
- In each case, how many messages did you exchange with each match before scheduling the date(s)?
- In each case, did you initiate (ask the other person for) a date(s)?
- If any of the date(s) that you set were cancelled, why?
- How many people with whom you have scheduled dates this week do you think you will actually meet?
- With how many people that you scheduled dates this week do you think you will have a long-term relationship?

Activity F - Conducting Dates

7. If you conducted any face-to-face dates, please tell us:
- How many dates (list only those from Match.com) did you have this week?
- Did all your Match.com dates show up as planned?
- If they didn't show up, please tell us why they didn't (if you know):

Activity G - Concluding the dating process

8. If you concluded the e-dating process this week, please tell us:
- Do you intend to turn off your profile?
- If so, why?

Chapter XVIII
A Trination Analysis of Social Exchange Relationships in E–Dating

Sudhir H. Kale
Bond University, Australia

Mark T. Spence
Bond University, Australia

ABSTRACT

More than half a billion users across the globe have availed themselves of e-dating services. This chapter looks at the marketing and cross-cultural aspects of mate-seeking behavior in e-dating. We content analyzed 238 advertisements from online matrimonial sites in three countries: India (n=79), Hong Kong (n=80), and Australia (n=79). Frequencies of mention of the following ten attribute categories in the advertiser's self-description were established using post hoc quantitative analysis: love, physical status, educational status, intellectual status, occupational status, entertainment services, money, demographic information, ethnic information, and personality traits. Past research on mate selection using personal ads and the three countries' positions on Hofstede's dimensions of culture were used in hypotheses generation. The results support several culture-based differences in people's self-description in online personal ads; however, some anticipated differences were not realized, suggesting that some cultural differences may not be as strong as Hofstede (2001) suggests.

INTRODUCTION

Family researchers and psychologists have investigated the attributes people desire in their life partners for almost 70 years (cf. Neely, 1940; Smith & Monane, 1953). However, cross-cultural differences in attribute preferences did not receive much attention until about 15 years ago (Buss, 1989). While several researchers have used personal ads to identify the qualities heterosexual males and females are looking for in a potential mate (Harrison & Saeed, 1977; Hirschman, 1987; Goode, 1996), transporting this discourse to the domain of online personals is a somewhat recent development.

Arvidsson (2006) observes that Internet dating is an aspect of a more general trend to construct a common social world through communicative interaction. The "common social world" constructed through Internet personals will be impacted by the culture permeating the advertiser and the target audience (Barnlund, 1989; Kale, 1991). The core ideas and norms of a culture contribute toward an individual's internal representation of the self, and how that self is related to important others (Fiske, Kitayama, Markus, & Nisbett, 1998). Perceptions of the internal self will impact what the individual advertiser says about one's self when seeking a potential mate. Since individual cultures across the globe show considerable differences along several important dimensions (e.g., Hofstede, 1991), these differences should be reflected in search behavior and interpretations of romantic love and intimacy across cultures (Dion & Dion, 1996). In a recent investigation of online ads, Ye (2006) observed that significant cultural differences can be observed in mate selection between Chinese and Americans.

The present study focuses on how cultural differences impact people's external self-representation in e-dating. E-dating is of interest for two reasons: to gain insights into its explosive, widespread adoption throughout the World; and—what would seem to be a source of *resistance*

to adopting this communication channel—is that it is an "impoverished" medium (Walther, 1996): it is devoid of face-to-face interaction, which prompts unanswered questions concerning how individuals present themselves in a "faceless" situation.

According to social exchange theory, the sustainability of a relationship is determined by satisfaction with the rewards vis-à-vis the costs in that relationship as compared to available alternatives (Bagozzi, 1975; Hirschman, 1987). To enhance the odds of initiating and maintaining a viable intimate relationship, advertisers in personals ads are likely to offer and emphasize those aspects of self they believe a potential date or partner would find rewarding (Gonzales & Meyers, 1993). Which characteristics are deemed rewarding would be impacted by the culture of the target audience for e-dating (Hall & Hall, 1990; Kale, 1991).

This chapter explores differences in e-dating ads across three culturally diverse countries—India, Hong Kong, and Australia. The choice of countries was based on two considerations: first, to facilitate the content analysis, we wanted to choose countries where the use of English was widespread, and we wanted three countries which exhibited considerable across-country cultural diversity. Using Hofstede's (1991) dimensions of national culture, we have generated a series of hypotheses on how cultural differences will impact self-presentation in online personal ads. The hypotheses are then tested through a post hoc quantitative analysis of ads on e-dating sites in these countries. The results suggest important cultural differences in self-presentation as well as some significant interactions between sex and country in accounting for variance in self-presentation.

STUDY BACKGROUND

[O]nline dating systems have begun to influence not only individual lives but also cultural notions

of love and attraction ... But despite the incredible number of people using these services, we know little about how users perceive each other… It's possible, too, that different subpopulations of users within the site are seeking entirely different things and using different evaluative techniques. (Fiore, 2007)

Research on people's dating preferences is not new. Previous studies have explored differences in preferences with regard to an ideal partner between men and women (see Rajecki, Bledsoe & Rasmussen, 1991), reasons for placing personal ads (see Jason, Moritsugu, & De Palma, 1992), evidence of evolutionary influences in dating preferences (see Symons, 1979; Sadalla, Kenrick, & Venshure, 1987), motivations for interracial dating (see Yancey & Yancey, 1998), effects of forewarnings on evaluation of target profiles (see Leon, Rotunda, Sutton, & Schlossman, 2002), applications of the marketing exchange theory to lonely hearts ads (see Hirschman, 1977), and cross-cultural differences in desired mate attributes (see Buss, 1989; Parekh & Beresin, 2001; Ye, 2006).

The two research streams of male-female differences in partner expectations and applying evolutionary perspective to explain these differences are closely related. Several studies on personal ads and dating behavior have found that behaviors of men and women in the dating context are consistent with traditional sex-role stereotypes (Nevid 1984; Urberg, 1979; Davis, 1990). For instance, Davis (1990) looked at 328 personal advertisements sampled from a major Canadian newspaper. His findings suggest that the men were more likely to desire a particular physical attribute than women, and the women were more likely to stipulate that their companion be employed, possess intelligence, have a profession, and be financially well-off. In their study of 800 "lonely hearts" advertisements, Harrison and Saeed (1977) concluded that women were more likely than men to advertise their attractiveness,

seek financial security, and look for someone older than them. Men, more than women, were in search of attractiveness and youth, and in return offered financial security and professed their interest in marriage.

Cosmides and Tooby (1987) and Buss (1987) have been largely credited for spearheading the evolutionary psychology paradigm in mate selection. Cosmides, Tooby, and Barkow (1992, p. 3) define evolutionary psychology as "simply psychology that is informed by the additional knowledge that evolutionary biology has to offer, in the expectation that understanding the process that designed the human mind will advance the discovery of its architecture." The evolutionary perspective suggests that the ideal mate for a male is a female possessing high reproductive capacity, which mostly equates with a young female (Thornhill & Thornhill, 1983; Buss, 1987). Males, therefore, find females with relatively youthful facial characteristics attractive (Symons, 1979). For a female, the ideal male is someone who will successfully compete for resources and can provide for their offspring (Sadalla, Kenrick, & Venshure, 1987). Attributes such as robust health, clear skin, and strong muscles in a male are likely to be more attractive to females than average health, skin, and muscles (Alley & Cunningham, 1991). Consistent with the evolutionary perspective, men place more emphasis on physical attractiveness when choosing partners for sex or marriage, and women place relatively more emphasis on socio-economic status, earnings potential, and college education in choosing their mates (Barscheid & Walster, 1974; Townsend &Wasserman, 1997).

Leon et al. (2003) suggest that as the computer age has progressed, people's lives have become increasingly busy and the ability to meet potential mates is reduced. Personal ad dating, they write, is ubiquitous because it fulfills a social need and a niche. In their study of individuals who had placed newspaper personal ads, Jason, Moritsugu, and DePalma (1992) concluded that those placing ads were well educated and financially successful. Their reasons for seeking the newspaper as a channel for mate seeking were high mobility and lack of access to traditional modes of meeting others (i.e., friends, family, and work). Around 85% said they were new to the area, 69% reported difficulty in meeting people through social activities, 61% felt uncomfortable in meeting people in singles bars, and 59% reported lack of familial contacts for introduction to potential mates. In conclusion, the authors state that the self-advertisers either did not have other ways to explore potential relationships, or that they may have tired of the more conventional channels and means of introduction.

CONCEPTUAL FRAMEWORK

People hold a certain view of themselves on the basis of what is perceived as culturally appropriate by others in the culture or within the in group (Usunier, 1996). Building on Foa and Foa's (1974) social exchange theory and the status characteristics theory (see Berger, Cohen, & Zelditch, 1966; Bereger & Fisek, 1974; Humphreys & Berger, 1981), Hirschman (1987) identified ten resource categories that comprehensively encapsulate the resources offered and sought in exchange between men and women using personal advertisements. These categories are: love, physical status, educational status, intellectual status, occupational status, entertainment services, money, demographic information, ethnic information, and personality trait information.

Love comprises emotional commitment, companionship, warmth, and emotional/affective personality traits. *Physical status* involves those physical characteristics that are valued within a society. *Educational status* refers to formal education and college degrees. *Intellectual status* relates to characteristics typically associated with high intelligence. *Occupational status* refers to those occupations that are held in high regard within a society. *Entertainment services* refer to non-

sexual activities to be done with another person. *Money* is an expression of wealth, affluence, or financial well-being. *Demographic information* comprises general descriptive characteristics such as age, marital status, and place of residence. *Ethnic information* concerns specifics such as race, religion, nationality, and caste. *Personality trait* information refers to statements about one's personality but "does not include traits related to sexual or emotional characteristics" (Hirschman, 1987; p. 101).

We posit that the frequency of mentions of characteristics belonging to each of the ten categories described above would be associated with culture of the advertiser and the target audience (Kale, 1991). Operationalizing and explaining differences arising out of culture requires a suitable cultural framework (Kale & Barnes, 1992). Previous literature presents several frameworks with which to operationalize culture. Key among these are the classification schemata proposed by Kluckhohn and Strodtbeck (1961), Hall and Hall (1990), Inkeles and Levinson (1969), Trompenaars and Hampden-Turner (1998), Schwartz (1994), and Hofstede (1991; 2001). While there exists some disagreement among researchers as to which cultural framework is most appropriate, for the purposes of this study, we chose the one proposed by Geert Hofstede (1991). Of all the frameworks, Hofstede's (1991) seems to have the most overall acceptance, an intuitive appeal, and the advantage of quantification. Hofstede proposes five dimensions of culture: power distance, individualism, masculinity, uncertainty avoidance, and long-term orientation.

Power distance (PDI) is the extent to which the less powerful members of organizations and institutions (like the family) accept and expect that power is distributed unequally. This dimension represents the amount of inequality in the distribution of power, status, and wealth. It suggests that a society's level of inequality is endorsed by the followers as much as by the leaders. Power and inequality across humans are extremely fundamental facts of any society. All societies are unequal, but some are more unequal than others.

Countries are scored on the power distance dimension, receiving a number between 1 and 100. For this dimension, higher numbers means there is greater distance (inequality) in the distribution of power.

Individualism (IDV) assesses the bond between an individual and his or her fellow individuals. Individualist societies are characterized by loose ties across people; thus, in a country receiving a higher score everyone is expected to look after him/herself and his/her immediate family. On the collectivist side, we find societies in which people are integrated into strong, cohesive in groups, often extended families (with uncles, aunts and grandparents), clans, or tribes which continue protecting them in exchange for unquestioning loyalty.

Masculinity (MAS) versus femininity refers to the stereotypical sex-role differences across societies. In masculine cultures sex roles are sharply differentiated and traditional masculine values such as achievement, assertiveness, and competition are relatively more valued. In feminine cultures sex roles are less sharply distinguished and attributes such as nurturing and caring are relatively more valued. Masculine societies tend to be hero worshippers whereas feminine societies tend to sympathize with the underdog. The women in feminine countries have the same modest, caring values as the men. In masculine countries (those with high scores), women tend to be somewhat assertive and competitive, but not as much as men; masculine countries, therefore, show a considerable gap between men's values and women's values.

Uncertainty avoidance (UAI) reflects a society's level of tolerance for uncertainty and ambiguity. This dimension indicates to what extent a culture programs its members to feel either uncomfortable or comfortable in unstructured situations. Unstructured situations are novel,

unknown, surprising, and ambiguous. Strong uncertainty-avoiding cultures try to minimize the possibility of such situations by enacting strict laws and rules, safety and security measures, and through their belief in an absolute truth. People in strong UAI countries are also more emotional, and motivated by inner nervous energy. The opposite type, uncertainty accepting cultures (those with *low* UAI scores), are more tolerant of opinions different from what they are used to; they try to have as few rules as possible, and allow multiple truths to exist.

Long-term orientation (LTO) versus short-term orientation: Also called "Confucian Dynamism," this dimension assesses a society's capacity for patience and delayed gratification. Long-term oriented cultures—reflected in high LTO scores—tend to save more money and exhibit more patience in reaping the results of their actions. Short-term-oriented societies want to maximize the present rewards and are relatively less prone to saving or anticipating long-term rewards. Hofstede (2001, p. 359) writes, "Long Term Orientation stands for the fostering of virtues oriented towards future rewards, in particular perseverance and thrift. Its opposite pole, Short Term Orientation, stands for the fostering of virtues related to the past and present, in particular, respect for tradition, preservation of 'face' and fulfilling social obligations."

Scores for the three countries chosen for this research along the five cultural dimensions are shown in Table 1. Our starting position was to select Australia, our country of citizenship for

Table 1. Scores of India, Hong Kong, and Australia on Hofstede's cultural dimensions (Hofstede, 2001)

	PDI	IDV	MAS	UAI	LTO
India	77	48	56	40	61
Hong Kong	68	25	57	29	96
Australia	36	90	61	51	31
World Average	56.5	43	51	65	48

further analysis. We then endeavored to select two other countries that exhibited considerable differences in scores along the dimensions of PDI, IDV, UAI, and LTO; although as can be seen, there is little variance on masculinity, with all three countries scoring slightly above the world average.

Research Hypotheses

Based on earlier research on male-female representation of the self (Hirschman, 1987; Feingold, 1990; Gonzales & Meyers, 1993) and on the three countries' scores on Hofstede's cultural dimensions, we advance the following hypotheses, starting with gender effects.

H1: Women, relative to men, are:
    a.   More likely to make love-related references
    b.   More likely to mention physical characteristics
    c.   More likely to mention entertainment services
    d.   Less likely to mention money
    e.   Less likely to mention educational status
    f.   Less likely to make intellect-related references
    g.   Less likely to mention occupational status

H2: Relative to Australia, India and Hong Kong are:
    a.   Less likely to make love-related references
    b.   Less likely to mention physical characteristics
    c.   Less likely to mention entertainment services
    d.   Less likely to mention personality traits
    e.   More likely to mention money
    f.   More likely to mention educational status

    g.   More likely to make intellect-related references
    h.   More likely to mention occupational status
    i.   More likely to provide ethnic information
    j.   More likely to provide demographic information

THE STUDY

The present study is based on a sample of Australian, Indian, and Hong Kong online personal advertisements. By creating a personal profile on dating Web sites, the partner seeker is packaging an offering, a product if you will, as well as specifying to whom this offering should ideally appeal. Hirschman (1987) investigated male- and female-placed personal advertisements in magazines as examples of complex, heterogeneous marketing exchanges and stated "personal advertisements represent the offering of people as products, as a set of marketable resources in search of an appropriate buyer" (p. 101).

Dowd and Pallotta (2000) propose that people approach mate selection by looking at partners who share interests, beliefs, and economic potential and other areas of similarity. According to them, people think of love as an investment in their future well-being that must be approached carefully and rationally, much as consumers do when purchasing products and services.

The current study content analyzed Australian, Indian, and Hong Kong personal advertisement posted on dating Web sites in each respective country. A terse perusal of personal ads on the Hong Kong Web site revealed that many were from ex-pats who may not share that culture's dominant values and norms, thus Hong Kong specific hypotheses are guardedly advanced. A priori we anticipate seeing the biggest differences between Australia and India.

RESEARCH METHODOLOGY

Sample

A sample of 238 personal online advertisements (121 females and 117 males) were downloaded and printed from three dating Web sites: 79 personal ads were from the Australian Web site, www.rsvp. com, 79 from the Indian Web site, www.shaadi. com, and 80 from Hong Kong (www.singlesof-hongkong.com). To select individual ads, after logging on to each Web site the third personal ad posted was printed and every third ad thereafter. There is no reason to believe that this sample selection method would result in response bias; for example, personal ads are not organized by age, surname or religious affiliation. We limited our sample to heterosexuals that fell into the age range of 21-35.

Coding Scheme

All three of the Web sites had two sections. The first portion was pre-formatted with fill-in-the-blank headers such as education, occupation, hobbies, desired level of commitment and religion/ethnicity. This section was not analyzed for two reasons: (1) The headers were not consistent across the Web sites, and more importantly; (2) Our interest was in the self-presentation section. It is in this unstructured section that participants can draw attention to any aspects about themselves they desire to project—in other words, to engage in impression management. In many cases these narratives included repeating and/or elaborating upon information from the first section. As would be expected, in most cases these narratives also provided additional insights into the person's activities, interests and lifestyle. It was this section that was coded and content analyzed.

For our purposes, we counted words within the narratives that mapped onto 10 pre-determined categories, for example, love, personality traits, entertainment and physical characteristics (see

hypotheses H2a-j above for the complete list of categories). We acknowledge that words interpreted as signaling each of the 10 categories of interest can be debated. For our purposes, words categorized as 'love' had to have nurturing or bonding connotations, examples of which would include *family* or *caring*; personality trait descriptors would include comments like *up for a challenge* and *likes sports*; entertainment services referred to capabilities they had with which they could indulge a partner, such as *play the guitar* and *accomplished dancer*; physical characteristics was in reference to words that served to signal one's beauty or health, such as *not that good looking*, *I have all my own teeth*, and *charming smile*, and so forth.

Four students enrolled in a consumer behavior course who were not informed as to the purpose of the study categorized the narratives. A practice coding test run took place during which students sat separately and then compared their categorizations. The inter-rater reliability was unacceptably low. The source of the low inter-rater reliability was twofold. The first source of discrepancy that was quickly resolved was to limit the analysis to self-descriptions. Thus, coders were informed to not count any portion of a narrative that was directed at someone other than the person writing the narrative. Comments not directed at their self were typically about desired qualities in a mate, but on occasion included comments about family members or friends. The second source of disagreement stemmed from the fact that often narratives had seemingly redundant references, making it difficult to agree on the appropriate number of times to count a comment. Consider, for example, the following verbatim extract from an Australian male:

I have quite a hectic lifestyle ... busy most nights of the week ... and getting busier. ... I love having a good time as well as love going nuts and having fun ... I love having a good time...

Arguably this could be counted as just two personality traits, those comments related to a 'hectic lifestyle' and those that referred to 'having a good time'. However, it was decided that the person writing this narrative wanted to emphasize these points and therefore that the redundancies should be counted—in other words, we endeavored to be as liberal in our interpretation of word meaning as was feasible. This narrative was therefore counted as seven personality traits (three of which relate to their hectic lifestyle and four to having fun).

In light of the frequency with which redundancies like the aforementioned appeared, it was decided that the appropriate way to categorize words was by having two research assistants sit together to code each narrative and resolve any differences concerning how to categorize a word at that time. Given that each narrative is an independent sample it is reasonable to assume that should the narratives be categorized by different individuals there would be disparities, but these differences should approximate a normal distribution about the true mean.

For illustrative purposes, two verbatim narratives are presented complete with spelling and grammar errors along with the resultant coding counts for four of the categories of interest: love, personality trait, entertainment and physical characteristics.

Australian Male

"OK i know im **not that good looking** but maybe ive got more to offer than looks. I'm generally a *quiet* sort of person when I meet new people but as I get to know them I come out of my shell. I'm caring, *honest*, have a *good sense of humour* maybe even a bit warped sometimes, value friends and family. I think i'm pretty *easy going* and *like to get out* and *have a bit of fun* every now and then. Not much into clubbing more a pub with a few friends or backyard and a few drinks with friends person. All in all im just hoping to find that someone special.

Indian Female

"I am a *well mannered, happy* and *easy going* type of girl. I am very *hard working* and i love to support my partner. I am *very kind* and i love to be treated with kindness and love. *Down to earth* and i love to be with a big family and relations."

DATA ANALYSIS AND FINDINGS

For each of the ten categories of interest a 3 x 2 ANOVA was run, the dependent variables being country and gender. In all but two cases (money and ethnic information), the overall model's F-

Box 1. Australian male coding counts

Love:	3	(appropriate words underlined for illustrative purposes)
Personality trait:	6	(in *italics*)
Entertainment:	4	(including its obverse, 'Not much into clubbing')
Physical characteristic:	1	(in **bold**)

Box 2. Indian female coding counts

Love:	4	(underlined)
Personality trait:	6	(in italics)
Entertainment:	0	
Physical characteristic:	0	

statistic was significant at p = .05, hence only the significance of the main and two-way interaction effects are reported. In the case of money and ethnic information, the number of subjects reporting zero counts (i.e., made no reference to these issues) were n=232 and n=210, respectively, hence these categories were excluded from further analysis. Therefore, H1d, H2e and H2i are reported as having insufficient data, an interesting insight in itself.

We fully elucidate the analysis pertaining to love-related references, the first category of interest. Analyses for the other categories were similar, but the findings are presented more succinctly. Based on the 3 x 2 ANOVA with love-related references the dependent variable, there was a main effect due to country (p < .001) as well as a significant two-way interaction between country and gender (p<.001); however, there was no main effect due to gender (p=.865). Cell means appear in the figure below. Australians were significantly more likely to make love-related references (x = 1.92) than were either individuals from Hong Kong (x = 1.09) or India (x = .71). Pairwise comparisons revealed that the main effect of country was due to a significant difference between India and Australia (p < .001), as well as a significant difference between Hong Kong and Australia (p = .009); however, there was no significant difference between India and Hong Kong (p = .123). Findings related to country are therefore consistent with H2a.

To examine the two-way interaction, t-tests by gender within each country were conducted. Within India there was no significant difference in the number of love-related references between men and women (p = .133), whereas there was a significant difference between genders in both Hong Kong and Australia (p < .001). Surprisingly, men were more likely to make love-related references than were women in Hong Kong (means equal 1.73 and 0.45, respectively), whereas the reverse was true in Australia (mean equals 1.12 versus 2.79). We therefore cannot support H1a.

MEAN VALUES FOR LOVE-RELATED REFERENCES

There is a significant difference in the number of references to physical characteristics by country (p = 0.029) and sex (p < 0.001); there is no two-way interaction (p = 0.163). Gender differences are as predicted (H1b); however, H2b receives only partial support. Australians were more prone to mention physical characteristics than were Indians, but those from Hong Kong had the greatest proclivity overall.

With respect to entertainment services mentioned, there is a significant difference due to country (p < 0.001); and the predicted gender effect only approaches significance (p = 0.058). There is, however, a significant gender by country interaction (p = 0.029). Overall, and consistent with H2c, Australians are more likely to mention entertainment services than are individuals from India or Hong Kong. However, an interesting pattern emerges with respect to gender: India and Hong Kong males make more entertainment-related comments than do women, whereas the reverse is true in Australia. H1c is therefore not supported.

Concerning comments about personality traits, there was a main effect due to country (p < 0.001), but no significant difference due to

Figure 1.

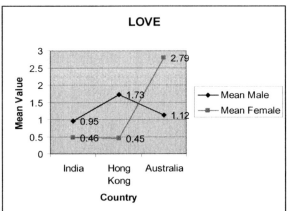

Figure 2.

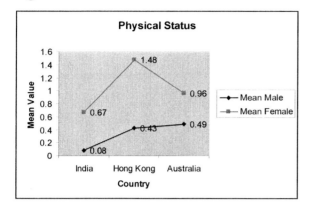

Figure 4.

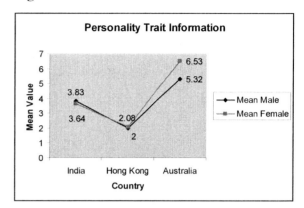

gender (p = 0.392) or the two-way interaction (p =0.367). These data support H2d: Australians are more prone to mention personality traits than are individuals from India or Hong Kong (and, as it turns out, Indians are more prone than are those from Hong Kong).

There is a significant difference in the number of references made about educational status by country (p<0.001); however, there is no significant gender effect (p = 0.358) nor two-way interaction (p = 0.778); H1e is therefore not supported. Indians made more education-related references than did individuals from Hong Kong or Australia, although there was no significant difference between the latter two; H2f therefore receives only partial support.

With respect to comments about one's intellect, there was as a significant effect due to country (p

= 0.011), but not a significant effect due to gender (p = 0.384) or the two-way interaction (p= 0.384), H1f is therefore not supported. Furthermore, contrary to expectations the main effect of country was opposite to the expected pattern: Australians were more likely to make intellect-related references than were individuals from either India or Hong Kong; H2g is therefore not supported.

There is a significant difference in references to occupational status by country (p = 0.004); but no significant difference due to sex (p = 0.662) or the sex by country interaction (p = 0.054); H1g is therefore not supported. Contrary to expectations, Australians were more prone to make occupation-related references than were individuals from India or Hong Kong; H2h is therefore not supported.

Figure 3.

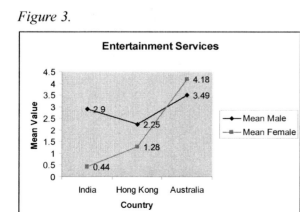

Figure 4.

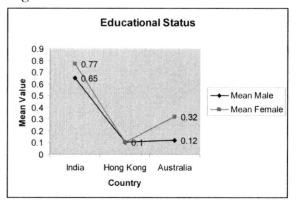

Figure 5.

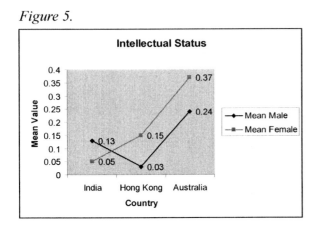

Figure 6.

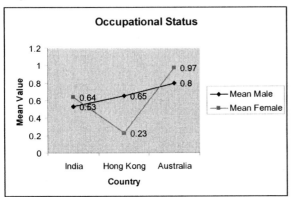

Figure 7.

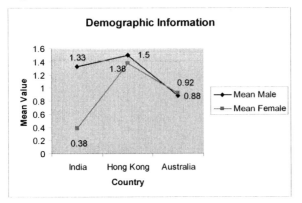

With respect to references to demographic information, there is a significant main effect due to country (p = 0.006) as well as gender (p = 0.041); there is also a significant two-way interaction (p = 0.036), the latter driven by India. While individuals from Hong Kong were more likely to mention demographic information than were individuals from Australia, the same cannot be said about individuals from India; thus, H2j receives partial support.

DISCUSSION

Findings of this study are interesting in that they reinforce some of the earlier findings and fail to support others. For example, it was expected that women will make more love-related offerings in their ads than would men. In this study, the support for sex-related differences between men and women in their self-descriptions related to love was not statistically significant, which is contrary to studies by Hirschman (1977), Gonzales and Myers (1993), and Koestner and Wheeler (1988). On the other hand, significant differences were reported in references to physical characteristics across both gender as well as country. Hong Kong residents made the most number of comments related to physical characteristics, possibly a reflection of the racial and ethnic diversity of advertisers from this region. (Recall that a perusal of Hong Kong ads suggested that many were posted by ex-pats.)

In keeping with evolutionary psychology, it was postulated that women would be more attracted to someone with a higher education, occupational status and intelligence. Consequently, men, to enhance the odds of initiating and maintaining a viable relationship were expected to stress their educational attributes, occupational status, and intellect more than women (see Gonzales & Myers, 1993). The current study did not support this evolutionary paradigm. This is a counter-intuitive finding that deserves more research.

We hypothesized that Australians would make more love-related references than Indians or Hong Kong residents. This was supported by our data analysis. In individualistic countries, people rank love as an important ingredient in a marriage whereas in collective societies, marriage is typically an arrangement that includes two families, not just individuals. It was also expected that individuals from individualistic societies would value novelty, variety, and pleasure (Hofstede, 1991). Consequently, individualistic Australians would mention entertainment services more than would the collectively oriented advertisers from India and Hong Kong. This was supported by our content analysis. Also supported was the expectation that Australians were more likely to mention their personality traits than Indians or Hong Kong residents.

An intriguing finding to emerge from this study was the insufficient mentions of money and financial status across all advertisers. It was anticipated that large power distance societies such as India would overtly mention financial status compared to small power distance societies such as Australia—this was not the case. For all intents and purposes, no one mentioned money.

Finally, two counter-intuitive findings deserve mention. In keeping with the large difference in power distance between Australia on the one hand, and India and Hong Kong on the other, it was expected that Australians were relatively less likely to make overt references to their intellect and occupational status. Content analysis of the ads suggested the exact opposite. Advertisers from India and Hong Kong made significantly less references to their intelligence and occupation as compared to the partner seekers from Australia. Other contributing factors such as the relatively low-context culture in Australia may have been responsible for these findings (see Hall & Hall, 1990).

CONCLUSION AND MANAGERIAL IMPLICATIONS

The Internet serves as a new and massive laboratory for sociological and psychological research. Leon et al. (2003) observe that the Internet can be utilized to conduct research efficiently due to the ease of implementation and the relatively few resources that are required. They further contend that the methodologies inherent in administering studies on the Internet or using samples from the Web appear as valid as those produced in lab settings. We consider this post hoc quantitative analysis of e-dating narratives a successful means of revealing cross-cultural differences.

Meeting others or dating through personals is very similar to Internet dating because in both cases the advertisers describe themselves in writing before any face-to-face encounter occurs. In order to get what they desire, advertisers typically project an image that would be deemed as attractive by the target audience. Underlying cultural values as well as gender differences are therefore expected to influence the self-presentation of lonely hearts advertisers. This study embraced Hofstede's (2001) widely used framework for classifying countries. Based on differences in each country's scores on Hofstede's five dimensions, we posited and subsequently confirmed differences in how potential mates present themselves, in particular in the number of references they made about love, physical status, entertainment services, personality traits, educational status and intellectual status. However, and importantly, support was lacking for several other characteristics, most notably references to 'money' and 'ethnicity', which were rare and non-significantly different across both genders and countries. The lack of money-related references seems particularly odd, given the myriad of studies suggesting that women seek men who can provide financial security (e.g.,

Barscheid & Walster, 1974; Harrison & Saeed, 1977; Davis 1990; Townsend & Wasserman, 1997). Apparently, commenting about one's money is not an opening gambit for men, a finding that is reflected in a casual perusal of women's sites, many of which do not include a photo or photos, a means of reflecting one's physical attractiveness, a characteristic widely acknowledged as sought after by men. We can only speculate, but protecting one's privacy is a plausible explanation for both gender's behaviors.

Despite instances of non-significant differences due to gender or country, the general trend is that there *are* differences across countries; thus, we should anticipate a proliferation of country specific Web sites as well as sub-culture-specific Web sites within a country. Consider the latter. In reference to targeting niche audiences, in the USA there is Jdate.com that caters to Jewish singles, largeandlovely.com, a site wherein those overweight can feel at ease, and for those with advanced degrees—a proxy for income—there are BrainDates.com and DocDates.com. In these cases, e-dating sites are "qualifying" participants on one attribute, presumably one that is non-compensatory to those seeking partners. Like any number of .com growth areas, we should first witness a proliferation in e-dating Web sites—a trend well underway—followed by a consolidation in Web sites. A rule of thumb is that the value of a social network—whether a mobile phone service provider, an auction site, a multiplayer online role playing game (MORG) or a dating service—is proportional to the square of the number of participants. In the e-dating realm, it will therefore behoove the less popular sites to consolidate: if you are an individual wanting to advertise, ceteris paribus, advertise in the medium that appeals to the largest, *appropriate* audience.

This study is not a definitive treatise that confirms or disproves cultural differences. Further studies should consider using more culturally diverse populations and perhaps a tighter taxonomy of the (ten) attributes comprising the advertisers'

self-descriptions advanced by Hirschman (1987). What we can say is that this study does qualify as one of the many successful applications of 'netology'—using the Internet to study social behaviors.

REFERENCES

Alley, T., & Cunningham, M. (1991). Average faces are attractive, but very attractive faces are not average. *Psychological Science, 2,* 123-125.

Arvidsson, A. (2006). Quality singles: Internet dating and the work of fantasy. *New Media & Society, 8*(4), 671-690.

Bagozzi, R. (1975). Marketing as exchange. *Journal of Marketing, 39*(October), 32-39.

Barnlund, D. (1989). *Communicative styles of Japanese and Americans.* Belmont, CA: Wadsworth.

Barscheid, E., & Walster, E. (1974). Physical attractiveness. In: L. Berkowitz (Ed.), *Advances in experimental psychology* (pp. 157-215). New York, NY: Academic Press.

Berger, J., Cohen, B., & Zelditch, M., Jr. (1966). Status characteristics and expectation states. In: J. Berger, M. Zelditch, Jr., & B. Anderson (Eds.), *Sociological theories in progress* (vol. 1, pp. 29-46). Boston, MA: Houghton Mifflin.

Berger, J., & Fisek, H. (1974). A generalization of the theory of status characteristics and expectation states. In: J. Berger, T. Conner, & M. Fisek (Eds.), *Expectation states theory* (pp. 163-205). Englewood Cliffs, NJ: Winthrop.

Buss, D. (1987). Sex differences in human mate selection criteria: An evolutionary perspective. In: C. Crawford, D. Crebs, & M. Smith (Eds.), *Sociobiology and psychology: Ideas, issues, and applications* (pp. 335-352). Hillsdale, NJ: Erlbaum.

Buss, D. (1989). Sex differences in human mate preferences: Evolutionary hypotheses in 37 cultures. *Behavioural and Brain Sciences, 12,* 1-49.

Cosmides, L., & Tooby, J. (1987). From evolution to behavior: Evolutionary psychology as the missing link. In: J. Dupre (Ed.). *The latest and the best: Essays on evolution and optimality* (pp. 227-306). Cambridge, MA: MIT Press.

Cosmides, L., Tooby, J., & Barkow, J. (1992). Introduction: Evolutionary psychology and conceptual integration. In: J. Barlow, L. Cosmides, & J. Tooby (Eds.), *The adapted mind: Evolutionary psychology and the generation of culture* (pp. 3-15). New York, NY: Oxford University Press.

Davis, S. (1990). Men as success objects and women as sex objects: A study of personal advertisements. *Sex Roles, 23,* 43-50.

Dion, K., & Dion, K. (1996). Cultural perspectives on romantic love. *Personal Relationships, 3*(1), 5-17.

Dowd, J., & Pallotta, N. (2000). The end of romance: The demystification of love in the postmodern age. *Sociological Perspectives, 43,* 549-581.

Fiore, A. (2007). Online dating research at Berkley. http://people.ischool.berkeley.edu/~atf/dating.

Fiske, A., Kitayama, S., Markus, H., & Nisbett, D. (1998). The cultural matrix of social psychology. In: D. Gilbert, S. Fiske, & G. Lindzey (Eds.), *Handbook of social psychology* (4th ed., pp. 915-981). New York, NY: McGraw Hill.

Foa, U., & Foa E. (1974). *Societal structures of the mind.* Springfield, IL: Charles C. Thomas.

Goode, W. (1996). Gender and courtship entitlement: Responses to personal ads. *Sex Roles: A Journal of Research, 34,* 141-170.

Gonzales, M., & Meyers, S. (1993). "Your mother would like me": Self-presentation in the personal ads of heterosexual and homosexual men and women. *Personality and Social Psychology Bulletin, 19,* 131-142.

Hall, E., & Hall, M. (1990), *Understanding cultural differences.* Yarmouth, ME: Intercultural Press.

Harrison, A., & Saeed, L. (1977). Let's make a deal: An analysis of revelations and stipulations in lonely hearts advertisements. *Journal of Personality and Social Psychology, 35*(4), 257-264.

Hirschman, E. (1987). People as products: Analysis of a complex marketing exchange. *Journal of Marketing, 51*(January), 98-108.

Hofstede, G. (1991). *Culture and organizations: Software of the mind.* London: McGraw Hill.

Hofstede, G. (2001).*Culture's consequences: Comparing values, behaviors, institutions, and organizations across nations.* Thousand Oaks, CA: Sage.

Humphreys, P., & Berger, J. (1981). Theoretical consequences of the status characteristics formulation. *American Journal of Sociology, 86*(5), 953-983.

Inkeles, A., & Levinson, D. (1969). National character: The study of modal personality and sociocultural systems. In: L. Gardner & E. Aronson (Eds.), *The handbook of social psychology* (vol. 4, pp. 418-516). Reading, MA: Addison Wesley.

Jason, L., Moritsugu, J., & DePalma D. (1992). Advertisements as a strategy for meeting people. *Psychological Reports, 71,* 1311-1314.

Kale, S. (1991). Culture-specific marketing communications: An analytical approach. *International Marketing Review, 8*(2), 18-30.

Kale, S., & Barnes, J. (1992). Understanding the domain of cross-national buyer-seller interactions. *Journal of International Business Studies, 23*(1), 101-132.

Kluckhohn, F., & Strodtbeck, F. (1961). *Variations in value orientations.* Westport, CT: Greenwood Press.

Koestner, R., & Wheeler, L. (1988). Self-presentation in personal advertisements: The influence of implicit notions of attraction and role expectations. *Journal of Social and Personal Relationships, 5,* 149-160.

Leon, D., Rotunda, R., Sutton, M., & Schlossman, C. (2003). Internet forewarning effects on ratings of attraction. *Computers in Human Behavior, 19,* 39-57.

Neely, W. (1940). Family attitudes of denominational college and university students, 1929 and 1936. *American Sociological Review, 4,* 512-522.

Nevid, J. (1984). Sex differences in factors of romantic attraction. *Sex Roles, 11,* 401-411.

Parekh, R., & Beresin, E. (2001). Looking for love? Take a cross-cultural walk through the personals. *Academic Psychiatry, 25,* 223-233.

Rajecki, D., Bledsoe, S., & Rasmussen, J. (1991). Successful personal ads: Gender differences and similarities in offers, stipulations, and outcomes. *Basic and Applied Psychology, 12,* 457-469.

Sadalla, E., Kenrick, D., & Venshure, B. (1987). Dominance and heterosexual attraction. *Journal of Personality and Social Psychology, 52,* 730-738.

Schwartz, S. (1994). Beyond individualism/collectivism: new cultural dimensions of value. In: U. Kim, H. Triandis, C. Kagitcibasi, S. Choi, & G. Yoon (Eds.), *Individualism and collectivism: Theory, method and applications* (pp. 85-119). Thousand Oaks, CA: Sage.

Symons, D. (1979). *The evolution of human sexuality.* New York, NY: Oxford University Press.

Thornhill, R., & Thornhill, N. (1983). Human rape: An evolutionary analysis. *Ethology and Sociobiology, 4,* 137-173.

Townsend, J., & Wasserman, T. (1997). The perception of sexual attractiveness: Sex differences in variability. *Archives of Sexual Behavior, 26,* 243-268.

Trompenaars, F., & Hampden-Turner, C. (1998). *Riding the waves of culture: Understanding cultural diversity in global business* (2nd ed.). New York, NY: McGraw-Hill.

Urberg, K. (1979). Sex role conceptualization in adolescents and adults. *Developmental Psychology, 15,* 90-92.

Usunier, J. (1996). *Marketing across cultures* (2nd ed.). Hertfordshire, UK: Prentice Hall.

Yancey, G., & Yancey, S. (1998). Interracial dating: Evidence from personal advertisements. *Journal of Family Issues, 19*(3), 334-348.

Walther, J. (1996). Computer-mediated communication: Impersonal, interpersonal, and hyperpersonal interaction. *Communication Research, 23,* 3-43.

Ye, J. (2006). Seeking love online: A cross-cultural examination of personal advertisements on American and Chinese dating Web sites. *Global Media Journal, 5*(8).

Chapter XIX
Online Matrimonial Sites and the Transformation of Arranged Marriage in India

Nainika Seth
University of Alabama in Huntsville, USA

Ravi Patnayakuni
University of Alabama in Huntsville, USA

ABSTRACT

Online personals have been a remarkably successful in the Western World and have been emulated in other cultural contexts. The introduction of the Internet can have vastly different implications on traditional societies and practices such as arranged marriages in India. This chapter seeks to investigate using an ethnographic approach the role of matrimonial Web sites in the process of arranging marriages in India. It seeks to explore how these Web sites have been appropriated by key stakeholders in arranging marriage and how such appropriation is changing the process and traditions associated with arranged marriage. The key contributions of this study are in that it is an investigation of complex social processes in a societal context different from traditional western research contexts and an exploration of how modern technologies confront societal traditions and long standing ways of doing things. Our investigation suggests that the use of matrimonial Web sites have implications for family disintermediation, cultural convergence, continuous information flows, ease of disengagement, virtual dating and reduced stigma in arranged marriages in India.

INTRODUCTION

Online personals have been a remarkable success story in the United States, attracting as many as 40 million unique visitors at their peak in 2003 (Mulrine, 2003). At a time when e-commerce ventures were being viewed with suspicion by investors and as the stock market hit new lows subsequent to its run up in 1999-2000, this was a significant phenomenon. Online personals typically cater to singles, providing them an opportunity to find mates or dates beyond their traditional social networks of friends, school, work, neighborhood or place of worship. Adapting to a different societal context, one that is more conservative and traditional, Web sites that assist in brokering marriages have emerged in India. In 2006, some 7.5 million users used their services, increasing from 4 million in 2004 (Lakshman, 2006). As in the case of online personals in U.S., which have the potential to affect how we arrange our social selves, online matrimonial sites can influence the process of arranging marriages with wider implications for family structure and relationships.

Marriage is viewed differently in India as compared to the West where it is largely a matter of individual choice. In India, marriage is viewed not so much as a union between two individuals as the beginning of an enduring relationship between two families. Weddings are usually protracted events that mark the end of lengthy negotiations between two extended families including aunts, uncles, and even cousins once step removed (Seymour, 1999). Referred to as 'arranged marriage', they are rarely based purely on individual preference, choice or love. Marriage symbolizes and affirms the collective nature of family and larger kinship units in which the families are embedded. In contrast, the western notion of marriage labeled as 'love marriage' is frowned upon by the more traditional family elders (Dion & Dion, 1996).

Globalization of the economy, urbanization and the increased influence of western popular culture from books to movies and television shows, have brought about changes in the society. 'From joint family to nuclear family' is an oft repeated phrase that is used to summarize changes in the family in India during modern times. The decline in the influence of extended and joint family ties has resulted in structural holes in family networks, making it difficult for families to find suitable life-partners for their children. This led to the emergence of matchmaking services and classified advertisements (referred to as matrimonials) in newspapers. With the advent of the Internet, a new channel in the form of matrimonial Web sites has emerged as an alternative way to find partners for marriageable members of the family. The introduction of technology in the form of matrimonial Web sites in an otherwise socially-enabled process provides the setting for a fascinating exploration of changing social mores and the interaction of technology and society.

Research on electronic dating, online personals, matchmaking and social networks is limited (Close & Zinkhan, 2003; Fiore & Donath, 2004), more so in the type of societal context provided by India. This chapter investigates the impact of matrimonial Web sites on the process and practices associated with arranged marriage in India. Specifically, it seeks to answer the research questions: (1) how are the affordances provided by matrimonial Web sites appropriated by stakeholders in the process of arranging marriage; (2) what is the impact of such appropriation on the process; and (3) how does the use of such technologies shape traditions and norms associated with marriage. The investigation is informed by the theory of social construction of technology where the central premise is that technology as designed provides users with a range of possibilities which shape usage and are in turn shaped by users. The intent of the study is not to propose and validate hypotheses but to gain a deeper insight into the phenomena and an understanding of the how technology is shaping and in turn shaped by users in such complex social processes. An ethnographic approach to data collection and analysis is deployed for this purpose in this investigation. The purpose of an ethnographic approach is not so much to show that technology is used but to show how it is socially appropriated. The key contributions of this study thus are an investigation of complex social processes in a societal context different from traditional western research contexts and the introduction of modern technologies where technology confronts with traditions and long standing ways of doing things. It will provide the platform for a wider exploration of the impact of modern computing and communication technologies on traditional societies.

THEORETICAL FOUNDATION

Early research in the adoption and use of IT approached the phenomenon from a technology deterministic perspective (Markus & Robey, 1988) that focused on the impact of IT, treating it as an exogenous, invariant and monolithic artifact. Researchers then argued that IT innovations are not necessarily adopted passively as standard templates of an idea, rather it undergoes a "developmental process in adoption" involving the redefinition of specific sub-components of the new technology and their interaction with local user context (Rice & Rogers, 1980).

Introduction of new technologies invariably exerts pressure on individuals, organizations and society to change, adjust, or adapt to the new technology. However, the effects of new IT are more a function of how they are used by people rather than a function of the technology itself. Actual behavior in the context of new technologies may often differ from intended use (Markus & Robey, 1988). People adapt systems to their particular work needs, or they may resist them or not use them at all.

Structuration theory has been proposed as a theoretical lens for developing a better understanding of the interaction between organizations, technology, and people (Orlikowski & Robey, 1991; Orlikowski, 1992b). Central to structuration theory is the concept of "duality of structure" which is used to theorize that structures that are inherent in new technologies are different from the structures that emerge in human action as people interact with these technologies. Further, theoretical extension of this approach has been put forth in the form of adaptive structuration theory that has been used for studying organizational change that accompanies usage of new technologies (DeSanctis & Poole, 1994). Drawing upon structuration (Giddens, 1984) and appropriation (Bijker & Law, 1992), Desanctis and Poole (1994) propose adaptive structuration theory for explaining the process of incorporating new technologies into work practices. Appropriation holds that people actively select how functionality and social structures embedded in the technology are used, and that a given feature may be deployed in different ways depending on how it is appropriated. Thus a key concept that emerges from organizational research in adoption and implementation is that structures, rules and resources provided by technologies and institutions are subject to appropriation by users.

Underlying the notion of social construction of technological systems (Bijker, Hughes, & Pinch, 1987) is a similar set of premises, albeit embedded in a larger sociological context. Social constructionist theory argues that just as technology is shaped by political, economic, social and technical factors, its use will be shaped by individual and societal influences (Bijker et al., 1987; Bijker & Law, 1992). Technology-as-designed provides a range of possibilities for appropriation by users. When technology is deployed by users, they appropriate technology in different ways so that technology-in-use is different from technology-in-design (Carroll, Howard, Vetere, Peck, & Murphy, 2002). As a result technology is shaped and reshaped over time and may eventually reach a state of equilibrium where it becomes embedded in users' lives. Its continued use will depend on recurring reproduction and reinforcement of appropriated use, failing which the technology may be disappropriated by users. Thus, according to social constructionist theory, the way in which a technology is used cannot be understood without understanding the context in which the technology is embedded. Rather than use that is faithful to design, instrumental uses and dominant attitudes influence the incorporation of new technologies by users. Moreover, the manner in which technology is appropriated further influences the design of technology which in turn shapes use and users indicating that there is no linear path between technology adoption, its use and its impact on society.

The advent of matrimonial Web sites represents the introduction of a new technology into the complex social process of arranged marriage. Their design, largely modeled upon the design of online personals in U.S., is likely to have features that mirror the more western societal context of finding dates and partners. The Web sites offer a number of affordances to users such as content rich personal profiles, more choice, ability to search and filter, many-to-many communication, direct communication and disintermediation among others. However, the adoption of such online services would not depend simply on the characteristics and availability of technology, but on how users appropriate and repurpose the technology artifact for their use. In addition, societal factors such as the image of these Web sites, testimonials and references from the close circle of family friends that bear influence in such matters will also play a critical role in the use of matrimonial Web sites. Context-specific technical characteristics associated with arranged marriages in India such as caste, sub-caste and 'dowry' will play a role in determining if these services are used and how they are used to accommodate such considerations. The social con-

struction of technology perspective allows us to investigate the adoption and use of matrimonial Web sites for arranging marriages to provide a rich and deep insight into the interplay between technology and complex socially embedded roles, relationships and rituals.

ARRANGED MARRIAGE IN INDIA

A nation of over one billion people, India is a country of many contrasts and contradictions. A visitor may witness signs of a progressive economy in its infrastructure, media and use of mobile communication devices. At the same time, institutions such as marriage and the role of women continue to be dominated by traditions. Sociologists categorize the Indian family structure as 'patrifocal' in nature (Seymour, 1999). Prevalent norms and values emphasize the interdependent nature of family relationships in contrast to independence and personal autonomy. From a very young age, children are socialized to identify with the family as a whole and discouraged from developing an autonomous self. They are conditioned to place the interests of the family ahead of their own. Alienating and confronting parents and family is still an anathema to most young people, especially in important decisions such as career selection and marriage. Furthermore, cultural mores frown upon the socialization among men and women in the form of dating and relationships. As a result, arranged marriage is still the dominant way for families and individuals to find partners for marriage. Once married, norms dictate that as a wife, a woman should put the needs of her husband and his extended family above her own needs. In a majority of instances, the newly married couple takes up residence at the bridegroom's parents' home.

The typical western view of arranged marriages tends to be biased by its own traditions and values which emphasize individual choice and responsibility. For many in the West, an arranged marriage represents women being treated as property. Their wishes subordinated to patriarchy's desire for property and power. They find it difficult to comprehend that women (or even men) could be pushed into marriage, sight unseen. Although some of these views are well-justified for sections of the society that are socially and economically handicapped and vulnerable. For many others, arranged marriages represent a lifetime of commitment to family and mutual goals. Arranged marriages can provide a degree of emotional security and economic stability that most people in the West would not expect from marriage. Even when raised in a western culture, Indians prefer arranged marriages. The practice has left Indians with the lowest rate of intermarriage of any major immigrant group in the United States with fewer than 10% marrying outside their ethnic group (Bellafante, 2005).

The process of arranging marriage can be a long and elaborate process involving the extended family and friends that culminates in elaborate wedding ceremonies that extend over several days. Traditionally, parents start the process when their children are considered to be of marriageable age, which in the case of women tends to be 22 or 23 years of age and for men around 26 years. The process may be put on hold if they are pursuing higher education or hastened when they start drawing a regular paycheck. The need for suitable alliances is broadcast to the extended family as well as friends. Biographic information about potential matches is exchanged using formal (résumé) and/or informal (oral description) communication. The process of selection is layered and nuanced involving many different considerations. Traditionally, the caste of a prospective match would be a major consideration. More recently, anecdotal evidence suggests that even though caste and sub-caste play a role, primacy is often awarded to level of education, profession, economic background (and potential) and the family of the prospective match. Informal background checks are performed to assess na-

ture, character, prior relationships, habits (such as smoking and drinking which are frowned upon) and reputation of the family. These checks are usually conducted through the informal network of friends and relatives. The screening process also involves astrologers (who may also perform the role of a priest for the family) who evaluate the horoscope of the prospective bride or groom for compatibility.

Once suitable matches are screened, the prospective groom and his family visit the prospective bride's family for a face-to-face meeting to assess compatibility of both the families and the prospective partners. Usually, the prospective partners are allowed to spend a brief amount of time to talk to each other. At this stage the process has progressed closer to a likely successful arrangement and has greater stakes for the families involved. Too many rejections (especially of the prospective bride) can create tension in the family and are considered to be a stigma on the family. More likely, one of a few of the handpicked matches results in satisfactory agreement among the families. What follows the agreement of marriage are complex negotiations about the logistics of marriage—where, when (at an auspicious time determined by astrologers), who will attend, number of guests, dowry if applicable, involvement of priests and rituals to be performed, among other myriad details. In most instances these negotiations exclude the bride and groom. The agreement is formalized with an engagement ceremony which can be relatively simple ceremony marked by an exchange of rings or in other instances as ceremonial as the wedding itself.

The brief description here summarizes the traditional arranged marriage, one that is still largely prevalent in the Indian society. However, over the past several decades, social and geographical mobility have weakened the extended family structure and increasingly replaced it with a more nuclear family structure. As a consequence, social networks provided by the extended family structure are no longer available to parents for finding suitable partners for their marriageable offspring. The absence of such social networks is felt even more by the large, growing, mobile and educated middle class of India. This led to the emergence of matchmaking services, classified advertisements, and more recently online matrimonial services. Rao and Rao (1982) indicate that such anonymous channels of matchmaking as matrimonial ads are more prevalent in urban India where a majority of the middle class reside. As the nuclear family structure becomes more prevalent, the trend in arranged marriage is to allow greater participation of the prospective bride and groom. Some argue that this is changing arranged marriage to one that is more of an 'assisted marriage' (Bellafante, 2005). Perhaps the most important change is the granting of 'veto' power by parents to their offspring on any marriage proposal introduced by them. Prospective partners often go on 'arranged' dates, which may be supervised under the watchful eyes of an elder relative. Sometimes there is an extended period of dating prior to a formal agreement to the marriage.

Earlier studies of arranged marriages in India have looked at role of dowry (Anderson, 2003), status of women (Rao & Rao, 1982) and application of Markov decision making models to the marriage decision making process (Batabyal, 1998). The advent of online matrimonial services introduces a technological artifact into the process of arranged marriages bringing technology to the forefront, amidst changing social practices. At the very least, the technology provides a number of affordances to families seeking partners for marriageable family members. In an otherwise information-sparse environment that consists of either the limited and cryptic information of a newspaper classified or the filtered and often embellished information provided by a brokerage service, online services allows their users to post extensive information about potential partners. No longer dependent on the social network, users have access to a significantly larger pool of prospective partners. The richer information in each profile enables users to perform more complex searches and use a variety of criteria to filter and screen potential partners. Depending on the online service, further communication may be facilitated with online chat and/or e-mail allowing for further exchange of information and interest. Finally, since the technology does not distinguish between parents or prospective partners, it has the potential to completely disintermediate the role of family members and emulate the more western model of individuals finding their own partners for marriage. Thus, the use of matrimonial Web sites in India provides a fascinating setting for examining how these affordances provided by the technology are appropriated. It provides an opportunity to examine changes in power and control structures and the relationship between technology and social institutions.

RESEARCH METHOD

The objective of this research is to examine the adoption and use of technology in situ in a complex social process involving numerous stakeholders in order to develop a grounded understanding of the phenomena. Our aim here is to observe what people actually do rather than what they say they do or what they say they should be doing. We rely on ethnography to observe, document and interpret the appropriation of technology in arranged marriages in India.

Ethnography as a research method was developed by social and cultural anthropologists where the researcher spends a considerable amount of time in the field observing the phenomenon within its social and cultural context (Myers, 1999). In recent years, an increasing emphasis has been placed by researchers on the social and organizational contexts of information systems and ethnographic research has emerged as an important tool for studying these contexts (Myers, 1999; Schultze & Leidner, 2002). Early IS research that used the ethnographic approach focused on human-computer communications (Suchman, 1987) and was the basis for the widely known *In the Age of the Smart Machine* by Zuboff (1988). More recently, ethnography has been used to study management of information systems (Davies & Nielsen, 1992), development of information systems (Orlikowski, 1991; Myers & Young, 1997), their implementation (Orlikowski, 1992a), knowledge work (Schultze & Leidner, 2002), and their impact (Randall et al., 1999).

With its emphasis on participant observation over extended periods of time, ethnography is considered to be one of the most in-depth research methods possible (Myers, 1999). The method places primacy over first-hand observations made by researchers who are immersed in the social and work lives of their subjects (Atkinson & Hammersley, 1994; Myers, 1999). By focusing on socially-situated observations, we develop rich descriptions of the how participants in arranged marriage engage with each other, adopt and appropriate technology and analyze the role of technology in shaping the social context to generate theoretical insights. As ethnographers we adopt a sense-making and learning role as compared to the more conventional scientific approach of formulating and testing hypotheses. The approach deploys a flexible and somewhat unstructured research design where the actual progression of the phenomenon (e.g., an arranged marriage) and study participants drive the data collection process.

As ethnographers, researchers act as their own research instrument; as a result they are driven by their unique identity, knowledge, experience and subjectivity. The researcher has to rely on his/her personal experience in engaging with the research phenomenon to develop an understanding and generate theoretical insights. The ethnographic narrative arising from the study then become experiences of shared subjectivity. In writing ethnography, researchers often engage in writing and rewriting their own identities (Chawla, 2006). Given that ethnography is often associated with observing cultural context as an outsider (Atkinson & Hammersley, 1994), we as natives[1] of the culture are in some ways 'insiders' to social setting in which we perform our investigation. However, it offers the advantage of being readily accepted, having a shared history, understanding of the context and related experiences. Moreover, participants are less likely to view us as outside observers because we look native, speak the language, and are to some degree (albeit loosely) embedded in the social fabric of their daily lives. Chawla (2006) argues that as an ethnographer, native or otherwise, researchers enter the field entrenched with degrees of outsiderness that instills a certain amount of objectivity and distance into their observation and analysis. Moreover, just like other research that adopts a more scientific approach, ethnographic research is expected to meet standards of objectivity (Schultze & Leidner, 2002). As scientists, ethnographic researchers have to balance subjectivity and objectivity in a manner that convinces the academic community of the generalizability and reliability of their inferences.

DATA COLLECTION AND ANALYSIS

Data for the study was collected over a span of fifteen months which included two visits, 63 days in 2006 and 49 days in 2007, studying Web sites and follow-up conversations over telephone. During the first visit, the authors spent time talking to people and collecting secondary data about matrimonial Web sites, investigating the sites and the success stories posted on these sites. In the second visit, secondary data was used as a basis for identifying broad issues and research questions for primary data collection. A majority of the time on both visits was spent in Mumbai, and supplemented by data collected from other major metropolitan cities over brief visits. As in studies of this nature, the emphasis is not as much on using a representative sample as it is to develop a deep understanding of the phenomenon. At the same time, we did wish to get a sampling of different families and the roles played by different members of the family in using online matrimonial services. The data collection process involved conversations with prospective partners, parents, siblings and close relatives which ranged from informal interviews to just observing conversations as they took place in households.

Since the focus of our investigation was online matrimonial services, a considerable amount of time was spent in understanding the technology itself. This involved two aspects; the first was to understand the nature and type of services provided by different Web sites[2]. We document these using the search, matching, and interaction framework (SMI) proposed by Ahuvia and Adelman (1992) in Table 1. The SMI framework is based on the primary roles performed by any market intermediaries namely, searching, matching and transacting. Ahuvia and Adelman (1992) developed the SMI framework to categorize the processes that are involved in the marriage market and proceeded to describe the marriage market intermediaries in terms of how they performed these processes. As marriages do not happen in a vacuum, the search-matching-interaction framework integrates the context in which the relationships dyads are embedded with the interpersonal processes involved in the formation of the relationship. The second aspect involved observing the ongoing appropriation of the online service by users as reflected in the profiles and success stories documented on these Web sites. These success stories are obviously intended as testimonials by other users for the service, but they provide an additional source of information and details on how the partners decided to adopt the service, how they used the service, and the role of other family members. While these secondary sources of data are not central to this investigation, they helped us in understanding of the context and develop a more complete understanding of the phenomenon.

During our visits, we spent a considerable amount of time talking to different families that were actively engaged in the process of finding a suitable partner for a family member. They were in different stages of the process; while some had just begun to test the waters, others were actively evaluating candidates. In one instance, we were able to follow the process right up to the actual wedding ceremony itself, which was attended by one of the authors. Our time in the field was spent initially in identifying families that would be suitable candidates for collecting data from the social network of our relatives in India and introductions made through this network. Conversations about arranged marriage took place in a variety of settings. A considerable amount of time was spent in participating in day-to-day activities of the participants, many of which involved shopping, eating out, or simply sharing a ride with them as they commuted either for work or social engagements. When a search is active, it was not too difficult to get a family talking as it would invariably be at the top of their minds. While families were observed as such, discussions took place over afternoon tea or a meal; there were many opportunities where there were one-to-one conversations. Apart from group settings, the cultural context and topic are such that women are more apt to discuss and share their feelings, emotions and thoughts on the subject in depth in a one on one conversation.

Ethnographic research suffers from unique issues of validity and reliability (LeCompte & Goetz, 1982); replication of these studies pose problems of variation in context. Collectively, we spoke to about 39 individuals during our stay and during subsequent follow-up telephone calls. Of these, 23 were women and 16 were men. Of the men, six were fathers of the women, four were brothers of the women, twq were uncles of the men and four were the men in the marriage market. Of the women, 12 were the women who were candidates for marriage, six were mothers of the women, four were sisters of the women, and one was the mother of a man in the marriage market. About three-fourths of the respondents were from the northern part of India and the remaining were from the southern part of India. All of our study participants were from metropolitan cities and because of the nature of our sampling process, we did not have access to people in small towns and rural India. The average household income of the participants likely ranged from 25,000 rupees per month (about 600 dollars) to about more than 100,000 rupees a month (2,400 dollars). We did not ask direct questions about income because such questions were not appropriate in the social milieu in which we were interacting with the participants. Thus the participants constituted members of the Indian middle and upper middle class. It is also our assumption that many lower-middle class families do not use the Internet for matrimonial matchmaking. Almost all of our participants belonged to the upper three castes in the Indian caste system, and our social network limited our access to lower castes. The first few of the participants were members of the authors' extended family, friends and larger circle of acquaintances who then directed us to others who were participating in matrimonial Web site-based matchmaking. This limitation in our sampling

limits the generalizability of our study. Our study is limited in scope to urban middle class families participating in the Web-based matchmaking and is influenced by the authors' perceptions of traditional arranged marriages in India, as well as what our study participants, especially the fathers and mothers, recounted about how arranged marriages used to take place in their time.

The nature of our conversations focused on information included in the profiles, how the process of arranged marriage was conducted using the Web sites, the role of the family versus the partners themselves and interactions between families and partners before and during the decision making process. The questions were woven into the conversation, sometimes requiring repeat interactions and were transcribed at the end of the day. Due to the nature of immersion in the field, it is not possible to precisely draw a boundary on how many hours of actual conversation form the pool of field experience. In order to keep track of our conversations, we kept a daily log individually that included both field notes and our own reflections. Once every week during our visits, both authors would spend a couple of hours going over their own and each other's logs to fill gaps and discuss progress.

Table 1. SMI services offered by matrimonial Web sites in India

Search (Information Gathering)	Matching (Decision Making)	Interaction (Relationship Formation)
• Religious • Social background (caste, sub-caste, Gotra[3], Manglik) • astrological information (horoscopes and sin signs) • lifestyle(smoking, alcohol consumption, vegetarian), • culture (languages spoken and values-liberal, traditional, modern, etc.) • complexion (fair or 'wheatish' rarely dark) • body type (slim or average never heavy • living conditions (income, living with parents, nationality, citizenship and work status in different countries such as U.S.	• Horoscope based matching • Push (results delivered in the mailbox) and pull matching (filtering based on user criteria) • Can pursue multiple matches simultaneously	• Contact through the service • Phone and e-mail addresses • Built-in chat services

Data coding and categorization was done manually by the each of the authors at the end of the study. The next step was discussion and synthesis of the variations in coding and categorization schemes used by the authors. At this step, where needed, further data was collected through follow-up phone conversations. Or coding and categorization schemes centered around our key research questions, the role of the family in initiation and the decision making process, the degree and length of courtships, the sequence of courtship in the matchmaking process, and the preferences of the participants and family members about the chosen characteristics of the potential partner.

CHANGING ROLES, SHIFTING TRADITIONS AND CULTURAL CONVERGENCE: ONLINE MATRIMONIAL SERVICES AND ARRANGED MARRIAGE

There are a growing number of Web sites that are dedicated to providing matrimonial services in India. Major players from U.S. in Internet-related businesses view this as a potential market and have tied up with Indian firms, for example, Yahoo! along with a venture capital firm has taken up a stake in BharatMatrimony.com. Microsoft has ties with Shaadi.com, another popular Web site. The number of users of these services has grown from about 4 million in 2004 to 7.5 million in 2006 according to estimates provided by Internet & Mobile Association of India (Lakshman, 2006). Although the online market in these services is only about 4% of the estimated $500 million spent on off-line matrimonial services, it is expected to continue to grow at the rate of 40%-50% every year. As the bulk of the off-line market consists of print classifieds, if trends in the U.S. newspaper industry are anything to go by, online matrimonial services could soon overtake print media. A growing educated middle-class

and sustained economic growth is only likely to further fuel the growth in these services.

Popular beliefs, especially in urban India, indicate that the popularity of these sites reflects the changing face of India. Traditionally, the family plays a very important role in arranged marriages in India. It begins with announcing the entry of the prospective bride or groom into the marriage market. The family influences the matching and selection process to preserve traditional notions of compatibility in terms of age, family culture, caste, community and horoscopes. Like most cultures, the bride is usually given away by the father, but unlike western culture not to the groom but to the groom's family. Once married, the bride becomes a member of the groom's family and is expected to have only weak ties to her own family. The fact that most grooms stay in their parents' homes, which is the norm, further reinforces the symbolic nature of this transition from one family to another for the bride. For this reason, the compatibility of the bride with the groom's family and not just the groom is considered to be of greater importance than the relationship between the groom and bride's family. To understand how families are using online matrimonial services for arranging marriages, we look at the matchmaking process in terms of search, matching and interaction. As we look at how technology is appropriated, we address the research questions: how do features presented by matrimonial Web sites used for arranging marriage, how are they changing the nature of the marriage process, and the norms and traditions associated with arranged marriage. We primarily focus on the role of family in the process against the backdrop of social and cultural changes permeating the Indian Diaspora.

SEARCH

The decision that a son or daughter should enter the marriage market is usually made by the parents and as a consequence the process is initiated by parents or a trusted family elder. For somebody to raise the matter of their own marriage would be considered bold and indicate that they are self-absorbed rather than thinking in terms of the interests of the family. Many young people in fact choose to avoid or postpone discussion of marriage using education or career as excuses because they believe they will be heading off confrontation between their expectations of a partner in marriage with those of the family. Some view it as a battle they will eventually 'loose' as the family will eventually 'force' them to compromise and make a choice. Others view it just the opposite, using delay as a tactic to wear down their parents as they start worrying about the window of marriageable age slipping away and are then ready to allow the son or daughter to have an upper hand in the selection process. All this suggests the absence of open communication within the family as individual members try to conform to their expected roles while engaging in signaling and power play.

Traditionally, the parents and family elders would start the process by raising the matter when they meet relatives and friends that they have started 'looking' for a match for their son or daughter. With the changing family structure and weakening social networks, this increasingly poses a challenge for families. For expatriates, who have been disconnected from these networks in India, the challenges are only greater. Choices may be few, not match the desired profile and the family also opens itself to pressure from the extended family. Before online matrimonial services, families would rely on third-party matchmaking services and classified advertisements. Finding the right matchmaking service presented its own challenge as most would not disclose the demographic nature of their pool of prospects. They might be skewed towards a particular community that the family was not interested in or avoid a community altogether thereby reducing the efficacy of that brokerage service. Family elders

indicate that until recently using matrimonial ads in newspapers was stigmatized and considered to be the last resort. Research in different national contexts indicates that till recently the users of matchmaking services were stigmatized (Darden & Koski, 1988). Classifieds were resorted to when families had problems finding matches the traditional way. Anonymous and charged by the word, parents would craft cryptic classifieds in attempt to compress all their myriad criteria in addition to posting basic biographic information into 50 words or less.

On the Web the restrictions posed by classifieds on the amount of information disappears. Whereas photographs would generally be exchanged only after the initial responses to classified were filtered, on the Web, most users post photographs along with the profile. This suggests that the stigma associated with using impersonal and anonymous methods has eroded in most cases. Many families view this as the preferred method because they feel that they have a better chance of finding suitable matches in view of the more detailed information and larger pool of prospects. By browsing the Web site, users can make a quick judgment about the demographics of the pool and its suitability to their selection criteria.

As it is customary in Hindu families for parents to search for their children's life partner, my parents were doing the same by speaking with relatives and also circulating our 'bio-data' via various electronic resources[4].[1]

Even with online services, parents continue to perform the role of initiating, searching and filtering potential partners. Gender stereotypes persist in the new medium. This is consistent with research on dating ads in other countries which suggest that gender and role stereotypes and expectations likely persist and change very gradually over time (Peres & Meivar, 1986; Koestner & Wheeler, 1988). Women indicate that in the Indian societal context even if they were actively involved in the process or actually posted their own profile, they wanted to maintain the appearance that the process was being initiated and managed by their parents. In all of our conversations, we seldom found the roles reversed or even an attempt to convey the appearance that they had been reversed. Women, in most cases, did not post their own profiles because they were afraid of being considered as 'fast and easy'. They would recount the experience of their friends who posted their own profiles had ended up in situations where the men were exchanging messages with them without any interest in marriage and were just looking to have a good time. Parents also perceived a greater responsibility in having their daughter married at the right time with the right match because they perceived that they were custodians of their daughters until they joined their 'true' family. This put greater pressure on parents to initiate and start the search for a suitable partner. Parents also believe they can pre-empt their daughters finding their own partners or avoid the issue especially in the case of career-oriented and ambitious women who were not interested in getting married in their twenties. One 28-year-old woman who is a consultant in a multinational firm explained:

I have to agree to put up with the ad because my parents keep pressurizing me…. at least this way it appears to them that I am interested in getting married and at the same time I can keep rejecting the matches they get for me.[2]

Her parents said:

the girls today want a very specific kind of husband .. he should be liberal and modern[5] in his thinking .. she does not like anyone we find in our community .. by posting this ad perhaps we

can find such a person in our specific caste and subcaste somewhere else.[3]

Another woman stated:

My profile was created by my elder brother and every day he checked for a partner for me.[4]

While parents conceded to their daughters' desire for a like-minded partner, they also sought to preserve traditional notions of the primacy of caste and community.

Interestingly, a greater proportion of the profiles of grooms were posted by prospective grooms themselves. Traditional gender stereotypes hold that men should be allowed greater independence (as long as they stayed or had their parents live with them). The perception that men are more technologically savvy created the circumstances for unmarried men to play a bigger role in online matchmaking. Parents felt they could deal with the low-tech nature of classifieds, but often felt ill equipped to deal with computers and the World Wide Web.

The shift from classified to online services has created increased opportunity for communication that was otherwise absent or predicated on non-verbal gestures and behavior. Once a classified is published, the action is followed with responses that come in batches and decline rapidly with time. The batched nature resulted in periods of waiting followed by some uncomfortable discussions among parents and their children. With online services, the profile has a greater shelf life yielding a steadier stream of responses. Moreover, there was the opportunity to engage in a more continuous as opposed to episodic search for potential partners. This created increased opportunity for communication within the family and more importantly for a tacit convergence of expectations.

Caste and sub-caste continue to be major considerations in search. In each of the online matrimonial services, a user could select bride or groom by caste, sub-caste, religion, language, state and age among other criteria. Almost everyone we talked to were very specific about religion and caste as filtering criteria. This was also reflected in the profiles that were posted on the Web sites. For example, a Hindu (religion), Brahmin (caste) female would want a Hindu, Brahmin male for a husband. In another posting, a 24-year-old woman from Mumbai sought a Hindu from the same caste speaking a specific language (Malayalam), but having moderate and liberal attitudes.

The profiles also reflected social taboos associated with suitable partners. Many users specifically mentioned smoking and drinking. Partners who did not smoke or drink are preferred. Social taboos associated with smoking and drinking persisted in the new medium. In talking to women, drinking alcohol was not preferred for men and absolutely taboo for women. Other criteria for search that persist in online profiles are horoscope and skin color. Most men sought partners who had a fair or 'wheatish' complexion demonstrating the continued belief in India that fair skin is associated with beauty.

MATCHING

Traditionally, arranged marriages have been brokered by family and friends, an elaborate process laced with social nuances that involves matching candidates on the basis of caste, community, religion and horoscopes. The family plays two important gate-keeping roles; the first is that of controlling the entry of new members into the family, especially the bride, and ensuring that they are compatible with the family's values and traditions. In its second role, the family perpetuates the caste, community and religious divisions in the society. These societal divisions are viewed as surrogates for compatibility and for ensuring that

traditions are carried on from one generation to the next. Our conversations with families showed that parents continued to perform this important gate-keeping role. In most cases, members of the family first screened the responses and made the first contact before allowing the prospective partners to meet each other.

We met in coffee day after our parents talked to each other.[5]

Our parents then arranged a meeting for us.[6]
My father showed an interested in his profile and give him contact no. and e-mail ID. He accepted and forward my profile to his parents .... then he talked to my father and said he want to come to my parent's home in Dehradun. Within a week he came and finalized the matter. Then my sister and Jijaji (Brother-in-law) went to his home at NOIDA and found suitable and said ok from our side. His parents and my parents talked to each other on the phone and after that the marriage was fixed.[7]

After reading my profile and showing it to her father, her second cousin phoned my father (who was the contact listed with my profile) requesting more information about me.[8]

Firstly, both my parents and my partner's parents contacted each other to make sure that all necessary requirements were suitable in order for the marriage proposal to materialize.[9]

I approached to her and received a response from her father.[10]

With online services, there is potential for disintermediation of the role played by parents and their status as gatekeepers starts to diminish. The process of screening and matching is no longer solely dependent on parents. Family could control information as either they went and met intermediaries or received the responses to classifieds. Now the information is always there, only a few clicks away. It is not surprising that sometimes the initiative towards matchmaking is now being taken by the prospective partners themselves. Even if they found their own partner, given the dominant role of parents and the strong bond with family, they would still seek the approval of their families. Whether it was the family that acted as a gatekeeper or a final consenting authority, the family is ever present in the matchmaking process.

My thanks to ... for bringing the two families together[11]

We interacted about our family details and the kind of partner being sought. We both were satisfied with each others' families, culture, background etc.[12]

*With the **consent** and blessings of our families.[13]*

It is interesting that even if partners took initiative, they would mimic the very criteria that would be applied by their families, such as caste, community and religion. It did not matter whether the profiles were posted by family elders or the candidates themselves; religion, language, community, caste and sub-caste were always a consideration. Almost all profiles mentioned their own religion and caste as well as their preferred religion and caste of the partner.

marrying a Muslim is out of question. [14]
our daughter-in-law is a Hindu ... we still wish our son would have chosen a Muslim girl.[15]

If I marry a Bengali (language) .. it will be easier for her to interact with my grandparents and extended family.[16]

Brahmins (caste group) are very particular about who they marry.[17]

The use of online matrimonial services in fact seems to make it easier to find someone within the sub-caste of your choice. In the absence of these matrimonial services, the ability to find someone within one's caste group depended on the reach of your extended family and the resources available. Families in the past would often compromise by marrying in the community outside the caste group because of limitations in the pool of applicants available. However, with geographical barriers removed by online services, it has become possible to find someone belonging to the exact same caste or sub-caste as that being sought by the family. This same someone (invariably the bride) is also willing to move halfway across the world to live with her newly wedded partner. Thus online services not only perpetuate traditional notions of an acceptable partner, but also provided increased choice. Sometimes, this would also create decision delay, as there was always hope that someone more perfectly matching the filtering criteria could come along in the future.

This is great! The girl of my dreams could be on the other side of the world.[18]

I can't believe that I can find someone who matches my exact profile needs thousands of miles away.[19]

Matching the horoscopes was also an important concern for many families. Some online services even provided this as an additional feature of their services.

the gotras should not be common. We would also ask for your details for purpose of horoscope matching[20]

Our families met and even the horoscopes matched well[21]

Sticking with our family tradition, we matched horoscopes and got elders consent.[22]

A cursory analysis would suggest that online matrimonial services simply replicate the off-line process of arranging marriages. It is evident that the criteria used for matching partners are largely carried over online. At the same time these services provide greater transparency and access that is loosening the grip of the family over information and eroding their role as gatekeepers. At times, the role is completely disintermediated by the presence of online services. Using online services increases the pool of potential partners and provides greater choice by breaking down geographical barriers and filling the gap created by weakening social networks. The increased choice does come at a cost—that of information overload.

INTERACTION

Perhaps the biggest change that online matrimonial services have introduced to arranged marriage is opportunity for interaction. In the traditional off-line mode, once a potential match was identified, the next step would be for the prospective groom's family (with or without the groom) to visit the prospective brides family at home. In more traditional families this may even be preceded by several visits by other relatives and/or meetings of both families at another relative's home. Setting up the visit was often a complex negotiation. The prospective partners are usually allowed to spend a brief amount of time alone to talk to each other. Other than that, it was rare for them to get an opportunity to get to know their future partner in marriage better. The bride and groom would also not have much say in any of the decisions about the wedding negotiations and arrangements.

With online services, many of these restrictions are being lifted. Prospective partners are often allowed to interview each other online without parental supervision. This represents an interesting shift in the role of the family in determining the compatibility of both partners. By allowing such communication, the responsibility of assessing compatibility and selection are gradually moving away from the family elders to the prospective candidates. Since the joint family structure is slowly disappearing, the parents often seem content to apply the broad criteria of religion, caste, age, economic background, and so forth, on the choice of a partner and leave the rest (personality, likes, dislikes, etc.) to their children. With the help of online services, a period of online courtship has emerged. Potential partners are allowed to get to know each other by exchanging e-mails, talking to each other over the phone or chatting online. In almost all instances, this was long-distance without any face-to-face meetings. Although most families still do not allow the prospective partners to meet alone or go out on a date, they did not seem to have a problem with electronic interaction. This step of getting to know a potential partner better seems to have emerged with modern communication technologies and precedes any formal meeting between the two families.

we chatted for 3 months[23]

she sent me an e-mail .. and the next day everything was finalized.[24]

We dated ....(electronically) .. for six months.[25]

We chatted and spoke on the phone for hours and found that we are a perfect match for each other.[26]

We chatted on (name of Web site) and thereafter we decided we r going to marry even before our families could meet.[27]

Earlier her family was not at all interested in me but slowly with our persistence they were forced to get us married.[28]

The norms of matchmaking in India have traditionally been different. After a meeting of the families, the bride's family would patiently wait for a response from the groom's family. If the days stretched into weeks and there was no response from the family, it indicated that they are not interested in pursuing the match further. The implicit rejection when a marriage proposal is turned down could also carry a social stigma. There are no such unspoken rules on online interaction. Chatting and dating can go on for a long time before there is any discussion of marriage. Online interaction allows users to disengage easily without any stigma associated with such rejection. This can at times create problems and emotional issues for some users who are not used to having such extended relationships.

we chatted for many months but he never wanted to take it forward..[29]

The traditional way of finding marriage partners through family and friends provides a certain amount of accountability; there is tacit trust which when violated can have social implications. With the search for partners going online, the process is taken out of a social context. While the search can cut across traditional social networks to find potential partners they are otherwise unlikely to reach, it makes judging the credibility of the information online even harder. Many families indicated that conducting a background check was very difficult with online matrimonial services. In some cases, the whole thing seemed to fall apart, after the families met as they did not approve of each other, or the family was different from what they had expected based on the descriptions provided online.

the girl was educated and pretty but she turned out to be crazy..[30]

the family did not seem as reputable as they claimed to be..[31]

In many instances, it was still possible to get some background checks done through family and friends. While the Web sites themselves did not provide any easy methods to facilitate a background check, some families went out of their way to do a background check by trying to find mutual contacts in the community who could help them with more information about the family. Also used in lieu of the background check was applying the traditional filters of religion, language, community, caste, and so forth, with the implicit assumption that users similar in background also bore a level of trustworthiness. The inability to validate the information from traditional networks is another reason why families found it useful to allow the potential partners to communicate. Families acquiesced to online and long-distance interaction so that prospective partners could sort out values, norms and beliefs. As long as the potential partner fit the traditional filters, families let the partners do further selection themselves.

In my profile, I had mentioned ... who happens to be my dad's uncle and his neighbor in (city name), and a common link between the two families. At that point of time he was in UK and I was in Bangalore. He called me and we had a conversation ... We exchanged all the details about us and both the families through .. uncle[32]

I received an e-mail stating that she was interested in speaking with me. Soon after ... we began to chat on the Internet via Yahoo! Messenger. As soon as we started to communicate ... our sessions lasted well into the wee hours of morning.[33]

Then we started chatting over msn. Which was on for 3 months[34]

It is evident that online matrimonial services have introduced new elements into the process of arranging marriage that are made possible by technology. The perception of relative anonymity and informal nature of the medium along with the absence of context provided by traditional social networks has allowed potential partners to play a greater role in the process. With the process shielded from the view of the immediate social network of the family and therefore any possibility of social sanction or stigma, new forms of interactions and steps in the process are emerging. Families do not have to engage in elaborate orchestration of the interaction between families prior to settling on a choice for partner. The informal nature of interaction and absence of face-to-face communication make it easier to engage and disengage and as an interesting consequence obviate the need for signaling and the ambiguity associated with signaling (are they interested or not?).

DISCUSSION

Our analysis of the use of online matrimonial services for arranged marriages reveals the possibilities created by technology and how they are appropriated by users. To many, the change may appear to be glacial in pace, but against the backdrop of a society that has a history and traditions dating back several millennia, they show shifting roles, changing traditions and convergence with the more modern view of marriage and family held by western culture. Information technology in the form of matrimonial Web sites creates both online and off-line possibilities for users as they go about the traditional process of finding life partners and new members for their families.

Families seeking partners for their marriageable son or daughter typically operate in an information-sparse environment. Reliance on the friends and family network meant that much of the information was subjective, by word of mouth but embedded in the social context. The cryptic nature of information from classifieds and the commercial nature of third-party services created many challenges for families. The digital world, where space is not at a premium, creates a more *information rich environment* in which the search can be conducted. The relative *anonymity* and *privacy* provided by using the service at home or an Internet café reduces concerns about any social stigma that may be associated with having to rely on such services rather than social networks. Moreover, our data suggests that as the institution of joint family recedes from family life, any negative association about the use of such services is disappearing.

With online services, the role of immediate social network, classifieds and third-party brokerage services is *disintermediated.* Technology allows users to *cut across boundaries* created by distance and social networks allowing creating a larger pool of potential candidates. To ease the process of selection, all Web sites provide *search tools* for users to specify their criteria. All Web sites capture and allow search across traditional criteria of religion, caste, community, language in addition to age and economic background. This reflects the influence of social context on the design of Web sites. At the same time, the technology is reducing the need for this information. In an information-sparse environment, the application of these criteria as filters served as surrogate indicators of compatibility, ensuring that the families of the bride and groom had similar values and traditions. In an information-rich environment where all kinds of information about habits, likes and dislikes is available, the need for surrogate indicators diminishes. This allows families and potential partners to express their subjective preferences that are more direct and reflect more rational criteria. As many of the Web sites are modeled after online personals popular in western cultures, these design elements in the form of such content and ability to communicate directly using e-mail and chat appear to engender a *cultural convergence* between western and Indian notions of partner selection. Some of the Web sites, as an indicator of such cultural convergence, provide dating services in addition to matchmaking services. Video profiles are also becoming an option that is used by some users on these sites.

The roles played by different family members in the process are also adjusting with the use of technology. Parents and/or other family act as gatekeepers to control the information flow from various sources as well as information about prospective matches. In the digital world, the information is (persistent) always available online and easily *accessible* to all members of the family. This weakens the role of parents as gatekeepers. It also changes the nature of the flow, which is more continuous as compared to the more episodic flow of classified advertisements and meeting with relatives or brokerage services. The *continuous flow* of information

creates more opportunities for interaction among family members over casual conversations. The increased communication surfaces concerns of different family members, bridges role boundaries and generation gap, and helps creates a greater consensus within the family.

Perhaps one of the more significant changes made possible with online services is the ability to have *direct* communication with potential partners and their family. Online communication does not bear the same credence as face-to-face meeting in formal social settings. The relatively anonymous and informal nature of interaction reduces the perceived risk of adverse social consequences of allowing prospective partners to communicate directly. Furthermore, devoid of the context provided by traditional social networks, families feel the need to allow more extensive communication between prospective partners to assess compatibility. This also allows the prospective partners to play a greater role in assessing compatibility

Figure 1. Change in SMI processes with the use of matrimonial Web sites

Search	Matching	Interaction
Information rich environment	Matchmaking based on traditional criteria	Email, chat and phone interaction
Provided anonymity and privacy		Extended courtship
Distance and geography no bar in finding the perfect match	Information access reduced Family role as gatekeeper to merely specifiers of criteria	Virtual dating may precede matchmaking
		Limited parental supervision
Gender, role and cultural stereotypes persist in matrimonial ads		Interaction brings to the fore credibility issues in online information
		Background checks may still be performed offline
		Family interaction reduced
		Easier to disengage if match does not work out
		Reduced stigma in disengaging

- Disintermediation of Family
- Cultural Convergence
- Information Persistence and Accessibility
- Continuous rather than episodic information flow and communication
- Ease of engagement and disengagement
- Reduced Stigma
- Virtual Dating

and making choices further disintermediating the role of other family members in matching and selection. Figure 1 graphically presents the results of our study.

LIMITATIONS AND DIRECTIONS FOR FUTURE RESEARCH

Our study investigates the influence of technology and its use on arranged marriage in India with the use of online matrimonial services. The study has several limitations in its present form. The nature of the research method creates limitations on replicability and generalizability of the study. As natives of the culture we were studying, we carried with us a tacit understanding of the social backdrop of our study. While the additional insight allows us to see subtle differences and changes and a more nuanced understanding of the phenomenon, at the same time, it creates the potential for subjectivity and bias.

Study subjects were Indians residing in India and did not include Indians residing in other countries who represented a significant proportion of users of online matrimonial services. The immersive nature of field study in ethnography made it difficult to study this segment as they visited India only for short periods of time and it was difficult to talk to them and observe them in a natural setting. However, among the families we studied, several had considered potential partners who were non-resident Indians.

Our study was conducted primarily in Mumbai and Delhi, which are large metropolitan cities. Culture, social mores and traditions differ significantly across urban and rural India. As a result, the narrative cannot be considered as reflective of India in general but primarily urban families. However, it should be noted that a majority of users of online matrimonial services reside in larger cities.

In our attempt to focus on the use of online matrimonial services, we did not study families that arranged marriages using more traditional methods. A more insightful comparison and contrast of the two different routes to arranged marriage would have helped to isolate the underlying changes driving the two processes.

CONCLUDING REMARKS

Online personals, e-dating and matrimonial Web sites are changing the rules of how relationships are formed and maintained in communities all over the world. In societies where dating itself is taboo according to social and religious norms, online matrimonial services are filling the gap left by the absence of social networks in societies transitioning to urban and modern culture. Since there are no established mores about using online media, the online matrimonial services mirror existing social practices. As the technology is used and appropriated by users, both social practices and the technology evolve. The use of online matrimonial services provides an interesting illustration of the social construction of technology.

The use of technology demonstrates a tension created by the affordances provided by technology and entrenched social traditions and practices. The use of online services has diluted the societal norms about socializing among opposite sexes but at the same time preserved traditional notions of compatibility by providing easy access to information about religion, caste and community. Although it is still not acceptable to go out on dates, online relationships are considered acceptable and allowed to continue over extended periods of time without parental supervision. Men and women who are seeking life partners are playing bigger roles in arranged marriage but still consider parents to be the final arbiters. Gender stereotypes continue to persist as women do not wish to give the appearance of driving the process but feel comfortable using the technology to actively participate in the process.

Online matrimonial services are not adopted as an instrument to bring about social change. To be accepted by families, they need to reflect and perpetuate societal and religious traditions and values. As they are recurrently used, the possibilities created by technology and its appropriation by users, creates a new equilibrium that reflects the new social reality created by technology and users. In the case of online matrimonial services, the subtle influence of technology cannot be overlooked as the use of online content, instant messaging and e-mail is expanding the influence of the younger generation over their elders in arranged marriage to create a new social norm that bears closer resemblance to western notions of marriage.

This has implications for the social construction of similar technologies in different societal and cultural contexts. When introducing new technologies with social implications such as cell phones and wireless services, the initial adoption of these technologies is only likely to succeed if on the surface these technologies mirror the traditional norms of behavior and social interaction. However, the appropriation of these technologies by users over a period of time brings about changes in social relationships and interactions. These changes, in their own way, change the structure and features of the technology, further driving social change. For example, India is one of the largest growth markets for the use of mobile phones and the phones were first used in India by affluent families and for business uses; over a period of time as prices came down, they found their way to the lower middle class, the rural areas and the self-employed such as street vendors and maids. In line with the new social classes that have adopted mobile phones, the technologies themselves changed to encourage usage, such as the predominance of pre-paid phone plans, long battery life and the use of am/fm radio as a standard feature, as these phones are used as music players by a majority of the population. This has further fueled the growth in the market of these phones in India.

REFERENCES

Ahuvia, A., & Adelman, M. (1992). Formal intermediaries in the marriage market: A typology and review. *Journal of Marriage and the Family, 54*(2), 452-463.

Anderson, S. (2003). Why dowry payments declined with modernization in Europe but are rising in India. *Journal of Political Economy, 111*(2), 269-310.

Atkinson, P., & Hammersley, M. (1994). Ethnography and participant observation. In: N. Denzin & Y. Lincoln (Eds.), *Handbook of Qualitative Research* (pp. 248-261). Thousand Oaks, CA: Sage.

Batabyal, A. (1998). Aspects of arranged marriages and the theory of Markov decision processes. *Theory and Decision, 45*(3), 241-253.

Bellafante, G. (2005, August 23). Courtship ideas of South Asians get a U.S. touch. *The New York Times.*

Bijker, W., Hughes, T., & Pinch, T. (1987). *The social construction of technological systems: New directions in sociology and history of technology.* Cambridge, MA: MIT Press.

Bijker, W., & Law, J. (1992). General introduction. In: W. Bijker & J. Law (Eds.), *Shaping technology/building society: Studies in socio-technical change.* Cambridge, MA: MIT Press.

Carroll, J., Howard, S., Vetere, F., Peck, J., & Murphy, J. (2002). *Just what do the youth of today want?*

Technology appropriation by young people. Paper presented at the The 35th Hawaii International Conference on System Sciences. Hawaii.

Chawla, D. (2006). Subjectivity and the "Native" ethnographer: Researcher eligibility in an ethnographic study of urban Indian women in Hindu arranged marriages. *International Journal of Qualitative Methods, 5*(4), 1-13.

Close, A., & Zinkhan, G. (2003). Romance and the Internet: The emergence of e-dating. In: B. Kahn & M. Luce (Eds.), *Advances in consumer research* (vol. 31, pp. 153-157). Valdosta, GA: Association for Consumer Research.

Darden, D., & Koski, P. (1988). Using personal ads: A deviant activity?. *Deviant Behavior, 9*(3), 383-400.

Davies, L., & Nielsen, S. (1992). An ethnographic study of configuration management and documentation practices in an information technology centre. In: K. Kendall, K. Lyytinen, & J. De Gross (Eds.), *The impact of computer supported technology on information systems development.* Amsterdam: Elsevier/North Holland.

DeSanctis, G., & Poole, M. (1994). Capturing the complexity in advanced technology use: Adaptive structuration theory. *Organization Science, 5*(1), 121-147.

Dion, K., & Dion, K. (1996). Cultural perspectives on romantic love. *Personal Relationships, 3*(1), 5-17.

Fiore, A., & Donath, J. S. (2004). *Online personals: An overview.* Paper presented at the CHI. Vienna, Austria.

Giddens, A. (1984). *The constitution of society: Outline of the theory of structuration.* Cambridge: Polity press.

Koestner, R., & Wheeler, L. (1988). Self-presentation in personal advertisements: The influence of implicit notions of attraction and role expectations. *Journal of Social and Personal Relationships, 5*(1), 149-160.

Lakshman, N. (2006). Here come the bride sites. *Business Week,* 42.

LeCompte, M., & Goetz, J. (1982). Problems of reliability and validity in ethnographic research. *Review of Educational Research, 52*(1), 31-60.

Markus, M., & Robey, D. (1988). Information technology and organizational change. *Management Science, 34*(5), 583-598.

Mulrine, A. (2003, September 29). Love.com: For better or for worse, the Internet is radically changing the dating scene in America. *U.S. News and World Report.*

Myers, M. (1999). Investigating information systems with ethnographic research. *Communications of the Association of Information Systems, 2*(23), 1-20.

Myers, M., & Young, L. (1997). Hidden agendas, power, and managerial assumptions in information systems development: An ethnographic study. *Information Technology and People, 10*(3), 224-240.

Orlikowski, W. (1991). Integrated information environment or matrix of

control? The contradictory implications of information technology. *Accounting, Management and Information Technologies, 1*(1), 9-42.

Orlikowski, W. (1992a). CASE tools as organizational change: Investigating incremental and radical changes in systems development. *MIS Quarterly, 17*(3), 309-340.

Orlikowski, W. (1992b). The duality of technology: Rethinking the concept of technology in organizations. *Organization Science, 3*(3), 398-427.

Orlikowski, W., & Robey, D. (1991). Information technology and the structuring of organizations. *Information Systems Research, 2*(2), 143-169.

Peres, Y., & Meivar, H. (1986). Self-presentation during courtship: A content analysis of classified advertisements in Israel. *Journal of Comparative Family Studies, 17*(1), 19-31.

Randall, D., Hughes, J., O'Brien, J., Rodden, T., Rouncefield, M., Sommerville, I., et al. (1999). Banking on the old technology: Understanding the organizational context of 'Legacy' issues. *Communications of the Association of Information Systems, 2*(8), 1-27.

Rao, V., & Rao, V. (1982). *Marriage, the family and women in Indi.* Delhi, India: Heritage Publications.

Rice, R., & Rogers, E. (1980). Reinvention in the innovation process. *Science Communication, 1*(4), 499-514.

Schultze, U., & Leidner, D. (2002). Studying knowledge management in information systems research: Discourses and theoretical assumptions. *MIS Quarterly, 26*(3), 213-242.

Seymour, S. (1999). *Women, family and child care in India: A world in transition.* Cambridge: Cambridge University Press.

Suchman, L. (1987). *Plans and situated actions: The problem of human-machine communication.* Cambridge: Cambridge University Press.

Zuboff, S. (1988). *In the age of the smart machine.* New York, NY: Basic Books.

ENDNOTES

[1] Both authors were born and raised in India and have resided in the U.S. for the past 15 years.

[2] A list of Web sites is listed in Appendix A

[3] A gotra is the lineage or clan assigned to a Hindu at birth based on an astrological condition.

[4] Each quote is replicated in Appendix B to translate the colloquial intent in conventional English. The quotes are identified by the number in subscript at the end of the quote.

[5] Being liberal and modern for most women in India means that the men do not subscribe to traditional stereotypes of women as homemakers and are subservient to the husband and his family. It has implications for everything from how they can dress to their careers.

APPENDIX A

List of Matrimonial Web sites:

1.	BharatMatrimony.com	www.bharatmatrtimony.com
2.	Hindumatrimony.com	www.hindumatrimony.com
3.	PunjabiMatrimony.com	www.punjabimatrimony.com
4.	iMilap.com	www.imilap.com
5.	Jeevansathi.com	www.jeevansathi.com
6.	A1 Indian Matrimonials	www.a1im.com
7.	Shaadi.com	www.shaadi.com
8.	eMatrimonials	www.geocities.com/ematrimonials
9.	Godbless Matrimonials	www.godblessmatrimonials.com/india/
10.	Matrisearch.com	matrisearch.com
11.	Falguni Mehta's Marriage Bureaus	www.falgunimehta.com/.

APPENDIX B

1. *As is customary in Hindu families, parents search for their children's life partner. My parents are doing the same by speaking to relatives and circulating my 'bio-data' using various electronic resources.*

2. *I have to agree to put up with the ad because my parents keep putting pressure me…. at least this way it appears to them that I am interested in getting married while at the same time I can keep rejecting the matches they propose.*

3. *The girls today want a very specific kind of person as a husband .. he should be liberal and modern in his thinking .. she does not like anyone we find from our community .. by posting this ad perhaps we can find such a person from our specific caste and subcaste.*

4. *My elder sister created my profile and every day she searched for a life partner for me.*

5. *We met for coffee the day after our parents felt positive about taking the next step.*

6. *Our parents then arranged for us to meet.*

7. *My father showed an interest in his profile and give him (prospective groom) our contact no. and e-mail ID. He accepted and forwarded my profile (prospective bride) to his parents …. He (prospective groom) then talked to my father and said he wanted to visit my parents at their home in Dehradun. He (prospective groom) visited my parents within a week and expressed his desire to marry me (prospective bride). Then my sister and Jijaji (Brother-in-law) visited his home at NOIDA and found the family acceptable and gave their consent for the proposal. His parents and my parents talked to each other over the phone and finalized the marriage."*

8. *After reading my bio-data and showing it to her father, she contacted her cousin, who then phoned my uncle (who happened to be the contact listed with my bio-data) to request more information about me.*

9. *First, both my parents and my partner's parents contacted each other to make sure that all necessary requirements were met in order for the marriage proposal to proceed further.*

10. *I approached to her and received a response from her father.*

11. *My thanks to ... for bringing the two families together*

12. *We talked about the details of our families and the kind of partner we sought. Both of us were satisfied with each others' families, culture, background etc.*

13. *With the consent (emphasis mine) and blessings of both our families.*

14. *marrying a Muslim is out of question*

15. *our daughter-in-law is a Hindu ... we still wish our son had chosen a Muslim girl (in marriage).*

16. *If I marry a Bengali (one who speaks Bengali and by implication from the state of West Bengal) .. it will be easier for her to interact with my grandparents and the extended family.*

17. *Brahmins (caste group) are very particular about who they marry.*

18. *This is great! The girl of my dreams could be on the other side of the world.*

19. *I can't believe that I can find someone who matches my exact needs, who may be thousands of miles away.*

20. *The gotras should not be the same. We would also ask for your horoscope for the purpose of matching it with ours.*

21. *Our families met and even our horoscopes matched well.*

22. *In keeping with our family tradition, we exchanged horoscopes and obtained parental consent.*

23. *we chatted for 3 months*

24. *She sent me an e-mail .. and the next day everything was finalized.*

25. *We dated ....(electronically) .. for six months.*

26. *We chatted (online) and spoke over the phone for hours. We found that we are a perfect match for each other.*

27. *We chatted on (name of Web site) and then decided that we are going to get married even before our families met.*

28. *Earlier her family was not at all interested in m,e but slowly with our persistence they were forced to let us get married.*

29. *We chatted for many months but he never wanted to take it forward..*

30. *The girl was educated and pretty but she turned out to be crazy*

31. *The family did not seem as reputable as they claimed to be..*

32. *In my profile, I had mentioned ... who happens to be my dad's uncle and their neighbor in (city name), and a common link between the two families. At that point in time he was in UK and I was in Bangalore. He called me and we had a conversation ... We exchanged all the information about us and both the families through .. uncle*

33. *I received an e-mail stating that she was interested in speaking to me. Soon after ... we began to chat on the Internet via Yahoo! Messenger. As soon as we started to communicate ... our sessions lasted well into the wee hours of morning.*

34. *Then we started chatting over msn. Which went on for 3 months.*

Compilation of References

Abboud, L. (2007, November 1). How Netlog leaps language barriers. *Wall Street Journal Online*. Retrieved November 3, 2007, from http://online.wsj.com/public/article_print/SB119387616952078433.html

Aberer K., et al. (2004). Emergent semantics. *Proc. of 9th International Conference on Database Systems for Advanced Applications (DASFAA 2004)*, LNCS 2973 (pp. 25-38). Heidelberg.

Abram, S. (2006, November). Some tricks to build information fluency—part 2. *MultiMedia & Internet@ Schools, 13*(6), 6-28.

Ackerman, M., & Haverton, C. (2004). Sharing expertise: The next step for knowledge management. In M. Huysman & V. Wulf (Eds.) *Social capital and information technology* (Chapter 11). Cambridge, USA and London, England: The MIT Press.

Adamic, L., & Adar, E. (2003). Friends and neighbors on the Web. *Social Networks, 25*(3), 211-230.

Adegoke, Y. (2007a, June 1). Kids socialize in a virtual world as avatars. *Reuters*. Retrieved November 3, 2007, from http://www.reuters.com

Adegoke, Y. (2007b, September 24). NY subpoenas Facebook over safety from predators. *Reuters*. Retrieved November 4, 2007, from http://www.reuters.com

Advertising Age. (2007). *Digital Marketing and Media Fast Pack*. Retrieved October 22, 2007, from http://www.adage.com/images/random/digitalfactpack2007.pdf

Agarwal, R., & Prasad, J. (1999). Are Individual Differences Germane to the Acceptance of New Information Technologies? *Decision Sciences, 30*(2), 361-391.

Agres, C., Edberg, D., & Igbaria, M. (1998). Transformation to virtual societies: Forces and issues. *The Information Society, 14*(2), 71-82.

Ahuvia, A., & Adelman, M. (1992). Formal intermediaries in the marriage market: A typology and review. *Journal of Marriage and the Family, 54*(2), 452-463.

Ahuvia, A., & Adelman, M. (1992). Formal intermediaries in the marriage market: A typology and review. *Journal of Marriage and the Family, 54*(2), 452-463.

Aiken, L. (1998). *Human development in adulthood*. London: Springer.

Aizpurua, I., Ortix, A., Oyarzum, D., Arizkuren, I., Ansrés, A., Posada, J., & Iurgel, I. (2004). Adaption of mesh morphing techniques for avatars used in Web applications. In: F. Perales & B. Draper (Eds.), *Articulated motion and deformable objects: Third international workshop*. London: Springer.

Ajzen, I., & Fishbein, M. (1980). *Understanding Attitudes and Predicting Social Behavior*. Englewood Cliffs, NJ: Prentice-Hall, Inc.

Ajzen, I., & Sexton, J. (1999). Depth of Processing, Belief congruence, and Attitude-Behavior Correspondence. In Chaiken, S. & Trope, Y. (Eds.), *Dual-Process Theories in Social Psychology*. New York, NY: The Guilford Press, 117-138.

Alabaster, J. (2006, November 7). News Corp taking MySpace to Japan. *Smartmoney.com*. Retrieved January 31, 2007, from http://www.smartmoney.com/bn/ON/index.cfm?story=ON-20061107-000427-0906.

Alapack, R., Blichfeldt, M., & Elden, A. (2005). Flirting on the Internet and the hickey: A hermeneutic. *Cyberpsychology & Behavior, 8*(1), 52-61.

Albert, S. (2005). Smart community networks: Self-directed team effectiveness in action. *Team Performance Management, 1*(5), 144-156.

Allen, B.A., Juillet, L., Paquet, G., & Roy, J. (2001). E-governance & government on-line in Canada: Partnerships, people & prospects. *Government Information Quarterly, 18*(2), 93-104.

Alleven, M. (2007, May 15). Help wanted: Community managers. *Wireless Week.*

Alley, T., & Cunningham, M. (1991). Average faces are attractive, but very attractive faces are not average. *Psychological Science, 2,* 123-125.

Alonzo, M., & Aiken, M. (2004). Flaming in electronic communication. *Decision Support Systems, 36*(2004), 205-213.

American Library Association, Young Adult Library Services Association (YALSA) (n.d.). *Data & resources Web sites.* Retrieved July 21, 2007, from http://www.ala.org/ala/yalsa/teenreading/dataresources/dataresources.htm

American Library Association. (2006). Resolution in support of online social networks. Retrieved July 5, 2007, from http://www.ala.org/ala/oif/ifissues/online-socialnetworks.pdf

American Library Association. (2007). Three states and feds pursue social networking controls. Retrieved February 26, 2007, from http://www.ala.org/ala/alonline/currentnews/newsarchive/2007/february2007/ALA_print_layout_1_350364_350364.cfm

American Library Association: Young Adult Library Services Association (YALSA) (2007). Teens & social networking in school & public libraries: A toolkit for librarians & library workers. Retrieved July 21, 2007, from http://www.ala.org/ala/yalsa/profdev/SocialNetworkingToolkit_March07.pdf

Andal-Ancion, A.., Cartwright, P., & Yip, G. (2003). The digital transformation of traditional businesses. *MIT Sloan Management Review, 44*(4).

Anderson, C., & Hunsaker, P. (1985). Why there's romancing at the office and why it's everyone's problem. *Personnel, 62,* 57-63.

Anderson, D. (2005). What trust is in these times? Examining the foundation of online trust. *Emory Law Journal, 54*(3), 1441-1474.

Anderson, D., & Goplerud, E. (2005). Alcohol problems: Finding solutions to save lives and money. *Benefits & Compensation Digest, 42*(10), 34-39.

Anderson, S. (2003). Why dowry payments declined with modernization in Europe but are rising in India. *Journal of Political Economy, 111*(2), 269-310.

Anon. (2003). Net grief for online 'suicide'. http://news.bbc.co.uk/1/hi/technology/2724819.stm.

Anon. (2003). *Net grief for online 'suicide'.* Retrieved from http://news.bbc.co.uk/1/hi/technology/2724819.stm

Ardichvili, A., & Cardozo, R. N. (2000). A model of the entrepreneurial opportunity recognition process. *Journal of Entreprising Culture, 8*(2), 103-119.

Arino, A., & de la Torre, J. (1998). Learning from failure: Towards an evolutionary model of collaborative ventures. *Organizational Science, 9*(3), 306-325.

Aristotle. (350 BCE). *Nichomachean Ethics.*

Armstrong, A., & Hagel, J. (1997). *Net gain: Expanding markets through virtual communities.* Boston, MA: Harvard Business School Press.

Arvidsson, A. (2006). Quality singles: Internet dating and the work of fantasy. *New Media & Society, 8*(4), 671-690.

Associated Press. (2007, July 24). MySpace deletes 29,000 sex offender profiles. *MSNBC.com.* Retrieved August 4, 2007, from http://www.msnbc.msn.com/id/19939181/print/1/displaymode/1098/

Atal, M. (2007, July 2). MySpace, Facebook: A tale of two cultures. *BusinessWeek.* Retrieved July 22, 2007, from Business Source Premier database.

Atkinson, P., & Hammersley, M. (1994). Ethnography and participant observation. In: N. Denzin & Y. Lincoln (Eds.), *Handbook of Qualitative Research* (pp. 248-261). Thousand Oaks, CA: Sage.

Ba, S., & Pavlou, P. (2002). Evidence of the effect of trust building technology in electronic markets: Price premiums and buyer behavior. *MIS Quarterly, 26*(3), 243-268.

Baase, S. (2003). *A gift of fire* (2nd ed.). Englewood Cliffs, NJ: Prentice Hall.

Bach, V., Vogler, P., & Österle, H. (Eds.). (1999). *Business Knowledge Management: Praxiserfahrungen mit Intranet-Basierten Lösungen.* Berlin, Germany: Springer.

Backhouse, J., Hsu, C., Tseng, J., & Baptista, J. (2005). A question of trust. *Communications of the ACM, 48*(9), 87-91.

Bagozzi, R. (1975). Marketing as exchange. *Journal of Marketing, 39*(October), 32-39.

Bahrampour, T., Arantani, L., & Stockwell, J. (2006, January 17). Teens' bold blogs alarm area schools. *The Washington Post.* Retrieved July 26, 2007, from Newspaper Source database.

Bailey, Darlyne, & McNally-Koney, K. (1996). Interorganizational community-based collaboratives: A strategic response to shape the social work agenda. *Social Work, 41*(6), 602-610.

Bailey, L., & Timm, L. (1976). More on women's and men's expletives. *Anthropological Linguistics, 18,* 438-449.

Baker, A. (2005). *Double click: Romance and commitment among online couples.* Cresskill, NJ: Hampton Press.

Baker, A. (2005). *Double click: Romance and commitment among online couples.* Cresskill, NJ: Hampton Press.

Balassone, M. (2007, January 14). Virtual reality: Modesto and Japanese students will use Second Life to interact. *The Modesto Bee.* Retrieved November 4, 2007, from Newspaper Source database.

Balk, D. (1997). Death, bereavement and college students: A descriptive analysis. *Death Studies, 25,* 67-84.

Balk, D. (2001). College student bereavement, scholarship, and the university: A call for university engagement. *Brunner-Routledge, 67*-84.

Banjo, S. (2007, July 10). For Whole Foods CEO, brash style takes an unhealthy turn. *Wall Street Journal,* p. A10.

Barbalet, J. M. (1998). *Emotions, Social Theory, and Social Structure: A Macrosociological Approach.* Cambridge: Cambridge University Press.

Barber, B. R. (1998). Three scenarios for the future of technology and strong democracy. *Political Science Quarterly, 1*(4), 573-589.

Bargh, J., McKenna, K., & Fitzsimons, G. (2002). Can you see the real me? Activation and expression of the "true self" on the Internet. *Journal of Social Issues, 58,* 33-48.

Barnes, J. (1987). Letter: This week's citation classic. *Current Contents, 1*(23), 18.

Barnett, M. (1982). Empathy and pro-social behavior in children. In: T. Field, A. Huston, H. Quay, L. Troll, & G. Finley (Eds.), *Review of human development.* New York, NY: Wiley.

Barnett, M. (1987). Emphathy and related responses in children. In: N. Eisenberg & J. Strayer (Eds.), *Empathy and its development.* New York, NY: Cambridge University Press.

Barnlund, D. (1989). *Communicative styles of Japanese and Americans.* Belmont, CA: Wadsworth.

Barscheid, E., & Walster, E. (1974). Physical attractiveness. In: L. Berkowitz (Ed.), *Advances in experimental psychology* (pp. 157-215). New York, NY: Academic Press.

Barton, K. (2006). *Research methods in social studies education: Contemporary issues and perspectives.* Charlotte, NC: Information Age Publishing.

Batabyal, A. (1998). Aspects of arranged marriages and the theory of Markov decision processes. *Theory and Decision, 45*(3), 241-253.

Bate, B., & Bowker, J. (1997). *Communication and the sexes.* Prospect Heights, IL: Waveland.

Baumeister, R. F., & Leary, M. R. (1995). The need to belong: Desire for interpersonal attachments as a fundamental human motivation. *Psychological Bulletin, 117,* 497-529.

Bausch, S., & Han, L. (2006, October 11). U.S. teens graduate from choosing IM buddy icons to creating elaborate social networking profiles, according to Nielsen/Netratings. Retrieved March 26, 2007, from www.nielsen-netratings.com/pr/ pr_061011.pdf

BBC. (2005). *ITV buys Friends Reunited Web site.* London: BBC Online. Retrieved from http://news.bbc.co.uk/1/hi/business/4502550.stm.

Bearden, W.O., Hardesty, D.M., & Rose, R.L. (2001). Consumer Self-Confidence: Refinements in Conceptualization and Measurement. *Journal of Consumer Research, 28*(June), 121-134.

Beaty, J., Hunter, P., & Bain, C. (1998). *The Norton introduction to literature.* New York, NY: W.W. Norton & Company.

Bell, R. (2001). *Benchmarking the intelligent community—a comparison study of regional communities.* The Intelligent Community Forum of World Teleport Association.

Bellafante, G. (2005, August 23). Courtship ideas of South Asians get a U.S. touch. *The New York Times.*

Benkler, Y. (2006). *The wealth of networks: How social production transforms markets and freedom.* Retrieved on July 14, 2007, from http://www.benkler.org/wealth_of_networks/index.php.

Ben-Ze'ev, A. (2004). *Love online: Emotions and the Internet.* Cambridge, UK: Cambridge University.

Ben-Ze'ev, A. (2004). *Love online: Emotions on the Internet.* Cambridge: Cambridge University Press.

Ben-Ze'ev, A. (2004). *Love online: Emotions on the Internet.* Cambridge: Cambridge University Press.

Beras, E. (2007, May 27). Loved ones mourned on Web sites: The memorializing on the personal pages of three South Florida men—whose killings remain unsolved—represents a growing trend: online grieving. *The Miami Herald.* Retrieved July 23, 2007, from McClatchy-Tribune Collection database.

Berger, J., & Fisek, H. (1974). A generalization of the theory of status characteristics and expectation states. In: J. Berger, T. Conner, & M. Fisek (Eds.), *Expectation states theory* (pp. 163-205). Englewood Cliffs, NJ: Winthrop.

Berger, J., Cohen, B., & Zelditch, M., Jr. (1966). Status characteristics and expectation states. In: J. Berger, M. Zelditch, Jr., & B. Anderson (Eds.), *Sociological theories in progress*

Berne, E. (1961). *Transactional analysis in psychotherapy.* New York, NY: Evergreen.

Berne, E. (1964). *Games people play: The psychology of human relationships.* New York, NY: Deutsch.

Bernier, C., & Laflamme, S. (2005). Uses of the Internet according to type and age: A double differentiation. [Usages d'Internet selon le genre et l'age: Une double differenciation] *The Canadian Review of Sociology and Anthropology/La Revue Canadienne De Sociologie Et d'Anthropologie, 42*(3), 301-323.

Bernstein, T., & Wagner, J. (1976). *Reverse dictionary.* London: Routledge.

Berry, D. (2005). *Romancing the Web: A therapist's guide to the finer points of online dating.* Manitowoc, WI: Blue Waters Publications.

Bettman, J.R., Johnson, E., & Payne, J.W. (1991). Consumer Decision-Making. In Robertson Thomas S., & Kasssarjian Harold H. (Ed.), *Handbook of Consumer Behavior.* Englewood Cliffs, NJ: Prentice Hall, 54-80.

Bieber, M. et al. (2002a). Toward virtual community knowledge evolution. *Journal of Management Information Systems, 18*(4), 11-35.

Bieber, M. et al. (2002b). Towards knowledge-sharing and learning in virtual professional communities. In *Paper presented at the 35th Annual Hawaii International Conference on System Sciences*, Hawaii.

Bijker, W., & Law, J. (1992). General introduction. In: W. Bijker & J. Law (Eds.), *Shaping technology/building society: Studies in socio-technical change.* Cambridge, MA: MIT Press.

Bijker, W., Hughes, T., & Pinch, T. (1987). *The social construction of technological systems: New directions in sociology and history of technology.* Cambridge, MA: MIT Press.

Bimber, B. (1998). The Internet and political transformation: Populism, community and accelerated pluralism. *Polity XXXI*, (1), 133-160.

Bimber, B. (2001). Information and political engagement in America: The search for effects of information technology at the individual level. *Political Research Quarterly, 54*(1), 53-67.

Bishop, J. (2002). *Development and evaluation of a virtual community.* Unpublished dissertation. http://www.jonathanbishop.com/ publications/display.aspx?Item=1.

Bishop, J. (2002). Development and evaluation of a virtual community. BSc(Hons) dissertation. http://www.jonathanbishop.com/ publications/display.aspx?Item=1.

Bishop, J. (2003). Factors shaping the form of and participation in online communities. *Digital Matrix, 85,* 22-24.

Bishop, J. (2003). Factors shaping the form of and participation in online communities. *Digital Matrix Magazine, 85*(2003), 22-24.

Bishop, J. (2005). The role of mediating artefacts in the design of persuasive e-learning systems. In: *Proceedings of the Internet Technology & Applications 2005 Conference.* Wrexham: North East Wales Institute of Higher Education.

Bishop, J. (2005). The role of mediating artefacts in the design of persuasive e-learning systems. *Proceedings of the Internet Technology & Applications 2005*

Conference. Wrexham: North East Wales Institute of Higher Education.

Bishop, J. (2006). Social change in organic and virtual communities: An exploratory study of bishop desires. *Paper presented to the Faith, Spirituality and Social Change Conference.* University of Winchester.

Bishop, J. (2006). *Social change in organic and virtual communities: An exploratory study of Bishop Desires.* Paper presented to the Faith, Spirituality and Social Change Conference. University of Winchester.

Bishop, J. (2007a). Increasing participation in online communities: A framework for human-computer interaction. *Computers in Human Behavior, 23*(2007), 1881-1893.

Bishop, J. (2007a). The psychology of how Christ created faith and social change: Implications for the design of e-learning systems. *Paper presented to the 2nd International Conference on Faith, Spirituality, and Social Change.* University of Winchester.

Bishop, J. (2007b). Increasing participation in online communities: A framework for human-computer interaction. *Computers in Human Behavior, 23,* 1881-1893.

Bishop, J. (2007b). *The psychology of how Christ created faith and social change: Implications for the design of e-learning systems.* Paper presented to the Faith, Spirituality, and Social Change Conference. University of Winchester.

Bishop, J. (2007c). Ecological cognition: A new dynamic for human computer interaction. In: B. Wallace, A. Ross, J. Davies, & T. Anderson (Eds.), *The mind, the body and the world* (pp. 327-345). Exeter: Imprint Academic.

Bishop, J. (2007c). Ecological cognition: A new dynamic for human-computer interaction. In: B. Wallace, A. Ross, J. Davies, & T. Anderson (Eds.), *The mind, the body and the world: Psychology after cognitivism?* (pp. 327-345). Exeter: Imprint Academic.

Bishop, J. (2007d). Evaluation-centred design of e-learning communities: A case study and review. *Proceedings of the Second International Conference on Internet Technologies and Applications, ITA07,* (pp. 1-9). University of Wales.

Black, L. (2007, January 24). Blogging clicks with educators: Online forums make assignments, ideas more accessible to students and parents. *The Chicago Tribune*. Retrieved March 23, 2007, from Newspaper Source database.

Block, P. (1993). *Stewardship—Choosing service over self-interest*. San Francisco: Berrett-Koehler Publishers.

Blois, K. (1990). Research notes and communications—transaction costs and networks. *Strategic Management Journal, 11*, 493-496.

Blum, T., Roman, P., & Martin, J. (1993). Alcohol consumption and work performance. *Journal of Studies on Alcohol, 54*(1), 61-70.

Boas, T. C. (2000). The dictator's dilemma? The Internet and U.S. policy toward Cuba. *The Washington Quarterly, 23*(3), 57-67.

Bonfadelli, H. (2002). The Internet and knowledge gaps: A theoretical and empirical investigation. *European Journal of Communication, 17*(1), 65-84.

Bostrom, B., Baseheart, J., & Rossiter, C. (1973). The effects of three types of profane language in persuasive messages. *The Journal of Communication, 23*(4), 461-475.

Bouwen, R., & Taillieu, T. (2004). Multi-party collaboration as social learning for interdependence: Developing relational knowing for sustainable natural resource management. *Journal of Community & Applied Social Psychology, 14*, 137-153.

Bowlby, J. (1980). *Attachment and loss: Vol. 3, Loss, sadness and depression*. New York, NY: Basic Books.

Boyd, D. (2004). Friendster and publicly articulated social networks. *Conference on Human Factors and Computing Systems (CHI 2004)*. ACM Press.

Boyd, D. (2006). Friends, friendsters, and top 8: Writing community into being on social network sites. *First Monday, 11*(2).

Boyd, D. (2007a). Fame, narcissism and MySpace. Many2Many: A group weblog on social software. Retrieved July 26, 2007, from http://many.corant.com/archives/2007/03/17/fame_narcissism_and_myspace.php

Boyd, D. (2007b). Viewing American class divisions through Facebook and MySpace. *Apophenia blog essay*. Retrieved July 22, 2007, from http://www.danah.org/papers/essays/ClassDivisions.html

Bradford, R. (2003). Public-private partnerships? Shifting paradigms of economic governance in Ontario. *Canadian Journal of Political Sciences, 36*(5), 1005-1033.

Braidotti, R. (2003). Cyberteratologies: Female monsters negotiate the other's participation in humanity's far future. In: M. Barr (Ed.), *Envisioning the future: Science fiction and the next millennium*. Middletown, CT: Wesleyan University Press.

Bressler, S., & Grantham, C. (2000). *Communities of commerce*. New York, NY: McGraw-Hill.

Brin, S., & Page, L. (1998). The anatomy of a large-scale hypertextual Web search engine. *Computer Networks and ISDN Systems, 30*(1-7), 107-117.

Brody, M. (2006). Understanding teens in this age of digital technology. *Brown University child and adolescent behavior letter, 22*(12), 8-8.

Brown, M. (2006, June 2). Social networking. *desitinationKM.com, viewpoints*. Retrieved November 11, 2006, from http://www.destinationkm.com/articles/default.asp?ArticleID=1171.

Brown, M., O'Toole, L., & Brudney, J. (1998). Implementing information technology in government: An empirical assessment of the role of local partnerships. *Journal of Public Administration Research and Theory, 8*(4), 499-525.

Bruner II, G. C., James, K. E., & Hensel, P. J. (2001). *Marketing Scales Handbook, Vol. III*, Chicago: American Marketing Association.

Brym, R., & Lenton, R. (2001, March 25). Love online: A report on digital dating in Canada. *MSN*. Retrieved December 2, 2007, from http://www.msn.ca.

Bryman, A., & Bell, E. (2003). *Business research methods*. Oxford: Oxford University Press.

Budge, I. (1996). *The New Challenge of Direct Democracy*. Oxford: Polity Press.

Burgoon, M., & Stewart, D. (1975). Empirical investigations of language intensity: I. The effect of sex of source, receiver and language intensity on attitude change. *Human Communication Research, 1,* 244-248.

Burgoon, M., Dillard, J., & Doran, N. (1983). Friendly or unfriendly persuasion. *Human Communication Research, 10,* 283-294.

Buss, D. (1987). Sex differences in human mate selection criteria: An evolutionary perspective. In: C. Crawford, D. Crebs, & M. Smith (Eds.), *Sociobiology and psychology: Ideas, issues, and applications* (pp. 335-352). Hillsdale, NJ: Erlbaum.

Buss, D. (1989). Sex differences in human mate preferences: Evolutionary hypotheses in 37 cultures. *Behavioural and Brain Sciences, 12,* 1-49.

Cacioppo, J. T., & Petty, R. E. (1982). The need for cognition. *Journal of Personality and Social Psychology, 42,* 116–131.

Cacioppo, J. T., Petty, R. E., & Kao, C. F. (1984). The Efficient Assessment of Need for Cognition. *Journal of Personality Assessment, 48* (3), 306-307.

Campbell, J., Fletcher, G., & Greenhil, A. (2002). Tribalism, conflict and shape-shifting identities in online communities. *Proceedings of the 13ᵗʰ Australasia Conference on Information Systems*. Melbourne, Australia.

Canada online overview. (2007). *E-Marketer.* Retrieved October 8, 2007, from http://www.emarketer.com

Canadian National Broadband Taskforce. (2001). *Report of the national broadband taskforce: The new national dream: Networking the nation for broadband access.* Ottawa, Canada: Industry Canada.

Canadian Rural Partnership. (2004, October). *Report of the advisory committee on rural issues.* Paper presented at the Third National Rural Conference, Red Deer, Canada.

Canisius College. (n.d.). *Facebook letter.* Retrieved from http://209.85.165.104/search?q=cache:X0TC7Y9qCtMJ:www.canisius.edu/images/userImages/athletics/Page_2173/Facebook%2520letter.doc+dear+canisius+student-athlete&hl=en&ct=clnk&cd=1&gl=us on July 4, 2007.

Carroll, J. M., & Rosson, M. (2001). Better home shopping or new democracy? Evaluating community network outcomes. *3*(1), 372-377.

Carroll, J., Howard, S., Vetere, F., Peck, J., & Murphy, J. (2002). *Just what do the youth of today want?*

Carter, D. (2005). Living in virtual communities: An ethnography of human relationships in cyberspace. *Information, Communication and Society, 8*(2), 148-167.

Carvajal, D. (2007, August 19). Fighting antisocial behavior on social networking sites. *International Herald Tribune*. Retrieved October 8, 2007, from http://www.iht.com/bin/print.php?id=7171219

Cashmore, P. (2006, July 8). Mixi, Japan's biggest social network. *Mashable!* Retrieved November 13, 2006, from http://mashable.com/2006/07/08/*Mixi*-japans-biggest-social-network/.

Cashmore, P. (2007). *MySpace makes $25 Million a month in ads*. Retrieved August 29, 2007, from http://mashable.com/2007/02/09/myspace-makes-25-million-a-month-in-ads/

Cassel, C.A. (1999). Voluntary associations, churches, and social participation theories of turnout. *Social Science Quarterly, 80*(3), 504-517.

Casteifranchi, C., & Tan, Y. (2002). The role of trust and deception in virtual societies. *International Journal of Electronic Commerce, 6*(3), 55-70.

Castells, M. (1996). *The rise of network society, vol. 1 of the information age: Economy, society and culture*. Oxford: Blackwell.

Castells, M. (1997). *The power of identity, vol. 2 of the information age: Economy, society and culture*. Oxford: Blackwell.

Castells, M. (1998). *End of millennium, vol. 3 of the information age: Economy, society and culture*. Oxford: Blackwell.

Caves, R. (2001). E-commerce and information technology: Information technologies, economic development, and smart communities: Is there a relationship? *Economic Development Review, 17*(3), 6-13.

Cazier, J., Shao, B., & St. Louis, R. (2006). E-business differentiation through value-based trust. *Information & Management, 43*(6), 718-727.

CBS News. (2005, May 10). Generation M: Natural multitaskers. *CBSNews.com.* Retrieved July 29, 2007, from http://www.cbsnews.com/stories/2005/05/10/eveningnews/printable694344.shtml

CBS News. (2006, February 16). No place here for MySpace. *CBSNews.com.* Retrieved August 4, 2007, from http://www.cbsnews.com/stories/2006/02/16/earlyshow/living/parenting/main1323212.shtml

Chadwick, A. & May, C. (2003). Interactions between states and citizens in the age of the Internet: "E-government" in the United States, Britain and the European Union. *Governance, 16*(2), 271-300.

Chak, A. (2003). *Submit now: Designing persuasive Web sites.* London: New Riders Publishing.

Chan, T-S. (1999). *Consumer behavior in Asia.* New York, NY: Haworth Press.

Charron, C., & Florentino, R. (2006, March 24). Teens take the lead on social computing. *Forrester.* Retrieved July 30, 2007, from http://www.forrester.com/Research/Document/Excerpt/0,7211,39157,00.html

Chawla, D. (2006). Subjectivity and the "Native" ethnographer: Researcher eligibility in an ethnographic study of urban Indian women in Hindu arranged marriages. *International Journal of Qualitative Methods, 5*(4), 1-13.

Checkland, P., & Holwell, S. (1998). Action research: Its nature and validity. *Systemic Practice and Action Research, 11*(1), 9-21.

Chidambaram, L. (1996). Relational development in computer-supported groups. *MIS Quarterly*, 143-165.

Cho, H., Stefanone, M., & Gay, G. (2002). Social network analysis of information sharing networks in a CSCL community. *Proceedings of Computer Support for Collaborative Learning,* (pp. 43-50).

Chow, W., & Angie N. (2006). A study of trust in e-shopping before and after first-hand experience is gained. *The Journal of Computer Information Systems, 46*(4), 125-130.

Church, K.W., & Hanks, P. (1990). Word association norms, mutual information, and lexicography. *Computational Linguistics, 16*(1), 22-29.

Close, A., & Zinkhan, G. (2003). Romance and the Internet: The emergence of e-dating. In: B. Kahn & M. Luce (Eds.), *Advances in consumer research* (vol. 31, pp. 153-157). Valdosta, GA: Association for Consumer Research.

Cohen, M., & Saine, T. (1977). The role of profanity and sex variables in interpersonal impression formation. *Journal of Applied Communications Research, 5*(2), 45-51.

Collins, A.M., & Loftus, E.F. (1975). A spreading-activation theory of semantic processing. *Psychological Review, 82*, 407-428.

Collins, N. (1980). Working models of attachment: Implications for explanation, emotion and behavior. *Journal of Personality and Social Psychology, 71*, 810-832.

Commerce Subcommittee on Oversight and Investigations: United States House of Representatives. Retrieved July 23, 2007, from http://energycommerce.house.gov/reparchives/108/Hearings/06282006hearing1955/Dannahey.pdf

Compeau, D. R., & Higgins, C. A. (1995). Application of social cognitive theory to training for computer skills. *Information Systems Research, 6*(2), 118-143.

Congress. Retrieved from http://thomas.loc.gov/cgi-bin/query/D?c109:4/temp/~mdbs59VVUS

Considine, M., & Lewis, J. (2003). Networks and inter-activity: Making sense of front-line governance in the United Kingdom, the Netherlands and Australia. *Journal of European Public Policy, 10*(1), 46-58.

Consumer Search. (2005). Online dating sites best rated dating sites, services. Retrieved May 26, 2006, from http://www.consumersearch.com/www/Internet/online-dating/fullstory.html.

Cook, T., & Gosh, A. (2001). The wireless data industry and the birth of m-commerce. *European Case Clearing House Case #2-101-039.*

Cooper, A., & Sportolari, L. (1997). Romance in cyber-space: Understanding online attraction. *Journal of Sex Education and Therapy, 22*(1), 7-14.

Cooper, A., Safir, M., & Rosenmann, A. (2006). Work-place worries: A preliminary look at online sexual ac-tivities at the office—emerging issues for clinicians and employers. *CyberPsychology & Behavior, 9*(1), 22-29.

Cooper, A., Scherer, C., & Mathy, R. (2000). Overcom-ing methodological concerns in the investigation of online sexual activities. *CyberPsychology & Behavior, 4*(4), 437-448.

Corbett, A. (2002). Recognizing high-tech opportuni-ties: A learning and cognitive approach. *Frontiers of Entrepreneurship Research* (pp. 49-60). Wellesley, MA: Babson College.

Cosmides, L., & Tooby, J. (1987). From evolution to behavior: Evolutionary psychology as the missing link. In: J. Dupre (Ed.). *The latest and the best: Essays on evolution and optimality* (pp. 227-306). Cambridge, MA: MIT Press.

Cosmides, L., Tooby, J., & Barkow, J. (1992). Introduction: Evolutionary psychology and conceptual integration. In: J. Barlow, L. Cosmides, & J. Tooby (Eds.), *The adapted mind: Evolutionary psychology and the generation of culture* (pp. 3-15). New York, NY: Oxford University Press.

Crawford, M., & Popp, D. (2003). Sexual double stan-dards: A review and methodological critique of two decades of research. *Journal of Sex Research, 40*(1), 13-26.

Crocker, J., Major, B., & Steele, C. (1998). Social stigma. In: S. Fiske, D. Gilbert, & G. Lindzey (Eds.), *Handbook of social psychology, 2,* 504-553. Boston, MA: McGraw-Hill.

Croughton, P. (2007). *Arena: The original men's style magazine.* London: Arena International.

Crowley, D. (2002). Where are we now? Contours of the internet in Canada. *Canadian Journal of Communica-tion, 27*(4), 469-508.

Csicsery-Ronay, I. (2003). Marxist theory and science fiction. In: E. James & F. Mendlesohn (Eds.), *The Cambridge companion to science fiction.* Cambridge: Cambridge University Press.

Csikszentmihalyi, M. (1977). *Beyond boredom and anxiety.* San Francisco, CA: Jossey-Bass.

Csikszentmihalyi, M. (1990). *Flow: The psychology of optimal experience.* New York, NY: Harper & Row.

Csikszentmihalyi, M., & Rochberg-Halton, E. (1981). *The meaning of things: Domestic symbols and the self.* Cambridge, UK: Cambridge University Press.

Culbreth, J. (2005). *The boomers' guide to online dating.* U.S.: Rodale Inc.

Cullen, P. (2007, February 7). Teenagers' profiles acces-sible on social websites. *Irish Times.* Retrieved February 20, 2007, from Newspaper Source database.

Currie, L. (2007). Using social network sites responsibly. *The Peer Educator, 29,* 5-8.

Dannahey, F. (2006). Making the Internet safe for kids: The role of ISP's and social networking sites. Written testimony given before the Committee on Energy and

Darden, D., & Koski, P. (1988). Using personal ads: A deviant activity?. *Deviant Behavior, 9*(3), 383-400.

Dating Sites Reviews.com. (2006). Retrieved November, 21, 2007, from http://www.datingsitesreviews.com/stat-icpages/index.php?page=2010000100-FriendFinder

Daugherty, T., Matthew S. E., & Gangadharbatla, H. (2005). e-CRM: Understanding Internet Confidence and Implications for Customer Relationship Management. In Clarke III & Flaherty (Eds.), *Advances in Electronic Marketing*. James Madison University: Idea Group Publishing, Inc.

David, R. (1999). *The Web of Politics*. Oxford: Oxford University Press.

Davies, L., & Nielsen, S. (1992). An ethnographic study of configuration management and documentation practices in an information technology centre. In: K. Kendall, K. Lyytinen, & J. De Gross (Eds.), *The impact of computer supported technology on information systems development*. Amsterdam: Elsevier/North Holland.

Davis, F.D., Bagozzi, R.P., & Warshaw, P.R. (1989). User Acceptance of Computer Technology: A Comparison of Two Theoretical Models. *Management Science, 35*(8), 982-1003.

Davis, K. (1941). Intermarriage in caste societies. *American Anthropologist, 43*, 376-395.

Davis, R. & Owen, D. (1998). *New Media and American Politics*. New York: Oxford University Press.

Davis, S. (1990). Men as success objects and women as sex objects: A study of personal advertisements. *Sex Roles, 23*, 43-50.

Davison, R. M., Martinsons, M. G., & Kock, N. (2004). Principles of canonical action research. *Information Systems Journal, 14*(1), 65-86.

Day, C. (2002). *The information society—a sceptical view*. Malden, MA: Blackwell Publishers.

De Klerk, V. (1991). Expletives: Men only?. *Communication Monographs, 58*, 156-169.

De la Mothe, J. (2004). The institutional governance of technology, society, and innovation. *Technology in Society, 26*, 523-536.

Deane, P. (2005). A nonparametric method for extraction of candidate phrasal terms. *Proceedings of ACL2005*.

DeLamater, J. (2003). *Handbook of social psychology*. London: Springer.

Dellarocas, C. (2003). The digitization of word of mouth: Promise and challenges of online feedback mechanisms. *Management Science, 49*(10), 1407-1424.

DeLone, W.H. and McLean, E.R. (2003). The DeLone and McLean Model of Information Systems Success: A Ten-Year Review. *Journal of Management Information Systems, 19*(4), 9-30.

DeSanctis, G., & Poole, M. (1994). Capturing the complexity in advanced technology use: Adaptive structuration theory. *Organization Science, 5*(1), 121-147.

Devine, I., & Markiewicz, D. (1990). Cross-sex relationships at work and the impact of gender stereotypes. *Journal of Business Ethics, 9*, 333-338.

DeVoss, D. (2007). From the BBS to the Web: Tracing the spaces of online romance. In: M. Whitty, A. Baker, & J. Inman (Eds.), *Online matchmaking* (pp. 17-30). Houndmills: Palgrave Macmillan.

Dewolfe, C. (2007). The MySpace generation. *Forbes, 179*(10), 72-74.

Dion, K., & Dion, K. (1996). Cultural perspectives on romantic love. *Personal Relationships, 3*(1), 5-17.

Donn, J., & Sherman, R. (2002). Attitudes and practices regarding the formation of romantic relationships on the Internet. *CyberPsychology & Behavior, 5*(2), 107-123.

Dowd, J., & Pallotta, N. (2000). The end of romance: The demystification of love in the postmodern age. *Sociological Perspectives, 43*, 549-581.

Downes, S. (2005). Semantic networks and social networks. *The Learning Organization, 12*, 411.

Doz, Y. (1996). The evolution of cooperation in strategic alliances: Initial conditions or learning processes? *Strategic Management Journal, 17*, 55-83.

Drake, W.J., Kalathil, S., & Boas, T. C. (2000, October). Dictatorships in the digital age: Some considerations on the Internet in China and Cuba. *iMP: The Magazine on Information Impacts.* Retrieved from: www.cisp.org/imp

Du Gay, P., Hall, S., Janes, L., Mackay, H., & Negus, K. (1997). *Doing cultural studies: The story of the Sony, Walkman,* London and New Delhi: Sage.

Dudeck, D., & Akselrud, T. (2007, July 12). MySpace outperforms all other social networking sites. *News Corporation.* Retrieved October 8, 2007, from http://www.newscorp.com/news/news_345.html

Dunn W., Mount, M., Barrick, M., & Ones, D. (1995). Relative importance of personality and general mental ability in managers' judgments of applicant qualifications. *Journal of Applied Psychology, 80*(4), 500-509.

Dvorak, J. (2006, December 26). Unreal life? Get a life. *PC Magazine.* Retrieved December 2, 2007, from Business Search Premier database.

Dvorak, J., Pirillo, C., & Taylor, W. (2003). *Online!: The book.* Upper Saddle River, NJ: Prentice Hall.

Eagly, A., Ashmore, R., Makhijani, M., & Longo, L. (1991). What is beautiful is good, but…: A meta-analytic review of research on the physical attractiveness stereotype. *Psychological Bulletin, 110*(1), 109-128.

Eastin, M. S. (2002). Diffusion of E-commerce: An Analysis of the Adoption of Four e-commerce Activities. *Telematics and Informatics, 19*(3), 251-67.

Eastin, M.S., & LaRose, R. L. (2000). Internet Self-Efficacy and the Psychology of the Digital Divide. *Journal of Computer-Mediated Communication. 6.* Retrieved August 27, 2007 from, http://www.ascusc.org/jcmc/vol6/

Ebers, M. (2002). *The formation of inter-organizational networks.* Oxford: Oxford University Press.

Edgar, H., Jr., & Edgar, H., II. (2003). *The ultimate man's guide to Internet dating: The premier men's resource for finding, attracting, meeting and dating women online.* Aliso Viejo, CA: Purple Bus Publishing.

Eger, J. (2001, November). *The world foundation for smart communities.* Retrieved January 28, 2003 from www.smartcommunities.org

Ellen, P., Bearden, W., & Sharma, S. (1991). Resistance to technological innovations: An examination of the role of self-efficacy and performance satisfaction. *Journal of the Academy of Marketing Science, 19,* 297-307.

Elliott, S. (2007, February 28). A CBS take on the YouTube madness. *The New York Times.*

Ellis, B., & Symons, D. (1990). Sex differences in sexual fantasy. *Journal of Sex Research, 27*(4), 527-555.

Ellison, N., Steinfeld, C., & Lampe, C. (2006). Spatially bounded online social networks and social capital: The role of Facebook. *Proceedings of the Annual Conference of the International Communication Association.*

eMarketer. (2006a). *Brands to Spend $1.8 Billion on Social Networking Sites by 2010.* Retrieved August 29, 2007, from http://www.emarketer.com/Article.aspx?id=1004085

eMarketer. (2006b). *Social Networking Online Boosts Bottom Line.* Retrieved August 29, 2007, from http://www.emarketer.com

Epstein, R. (2007). The truth about online dating. *Scientific American Mind.* Retrieved November 5, 2007, from Psychology and Behavioral Sciences Collection database.

Etzioni, A., & Etzioni, O. (1999). Face-to-face and computer-mediated communities: A comparative analysis. *The Information Society, 15,* 241-248.

Evans, J., & Brooks, L. (2005). Understanding collaboration using new technologies: A structural perspective. *Information Society, 21*(3), 215-220.

Everard, A., & Galletta, D. (2006). How presentation flaws affect perceived site quality, trust, and intention to purchase from an online store. *Journal of Management Information Systems, 22*(3), 56-95.

Farkas, M. (2007). Going where patrons are: Outreach in MySpace and Facebook. *American Libraries, 38*(4), 27.

Farris, G., Hartz, C., Krishnamurthy, K., McIlvaine, B., Postle, S., Taylor, R., Whitwell, G. (2003, November/December). Web-enabled innovation in new product development. *Research Technology Management Journal*, 24-35.

Federal Trade Commission (FTC). (2006, May). Social networking sites: Safety tips for tweens and teens. Retrieved November 11, 2006, from http://www.ftc.gov/bcp/edu/pubs/consumer/tech/tec14.htm.

Fellbaum, C. (Ed.). (1998). *WordNet: An electronic lexical database*. MIT Press.

Feller, J. (2005). *Perspectives on free and open source software*. Cambridge, MA: The MIT Press.

Feller, J. (2005). *Perspectives on free and open source software*. Cambridge, MA: The MIT Press

Figallo, C. (1998). *Hosting Web communities: Building relationships, increasing customer loyalty and maintaining a competitive edge*. Chichester: John Wiley & Sons.

Figallo, C. (1998). *Hosting Web communities: Building relationships, increasing customer loyalty, and maintaining a competitive edge*. New York: John Wiley & Sons.

Figallo, C. (1998). *Hosting Web communities: Building relationships, increasing customer loyalty and maintaining a competitive edge*. Chichester: John Wiley & Sons.

Finder, A. (2006). For some, online persona undermines resume. *New York Times*, pp. 1-2.

Finin, T., Ding, L., Zhou, L., & Anupam J. (2005) Social networking on the Semantic Web. *The Learning Organization: An International Journal, 12*(5), 418-435.

Fiore, A. (2007). Online dating research at Berkley. http://people.ischool.berkeley.edu/~atf/dating.

Fiore, A., & Donath, J. S. (2004). *Online personals: An overview*. Paper presented at the CHI. Vienna, Austria.

Fischer, G., Scharff, E., & Ye, Y. (2004). In M. Huysman & V. Wulf (Eds.). *Social capital and information technology* (Chapter 14). Cambridge, MA and London: The MIT Press.

Fishbein, M., & Ajzen, I. (1975). *Belief, Attitude, Intention and Behavior: An Introduction to Theory and Research*. Reading, MA: Addison-Wesley.

Fisher, A. (2002). I got caught smoking pot. Who's going to hire me now?. *Fortune, 146*(5), 224.

Fiske, A., Kitayama, S., Markus, H., & Nisbett, D. (1998). The cultural matrix of social psychology. In: D. Gilbert, S. Fiske, & G. Lindzey (Eds.), *Handbook of social psychology* (4th ed., pp. 915-981). New York, NY: McGraw Hill.

Fitzpatrick, M. (2006). H.R. 5319: Deleting online predators act of 2006. 109th

Flavián, C., Guinalíu, M., & Gurrea, R. (2006). The role played by perceived usability, satisfaction and consumer trust on Web site loyalty. *Information & Management, 43*(1), 1-14.

Fleming, J., & Courtney, B.E. (1984). The Dimensionality of Self-Esteem II: Hierarchical Facet Model for Revised Measurement Scales. *Journal of Personality and Social Psychology. 46*(February), 404-421.

Flynn, G. (1994). Attitude more valued than ability. *Personnel Journal, 73*(9), 16.

Foa, U., & Foa E. (1974). *Societal structures of the mind*. Springfield, IL: Charles C. Thomas.

Foot, K.A. & Schneider, S.M. (2002). Online action in campaign 2000: An exploratory analysis of the US political web sphere. *Journal of Broadcasting & Electronic Media, 46*(2), 222-244.

Foote, R., & Woodward, J. (1973). A preliminary investigation of obscene language. *Journal of Psychology, 83*, 263-275.

Forrester Research. (2006). *North American Consumer Technographics (NACTAS) 2006 Benchmark Survey*, Retrieved August 30, 2007, from http://www.forrester.com

Forster, J. (2006) Job recruiters dig up dirt on candidates' Web pages. *Akron Beacon Journal*, May 1.

Foschi, M. (1996). Double standards in the evaluation of men and women. *Social Psychology Quarterly, 59*(3), 237-254.

Foschi, M., Lai, L., & Sigerson, K. (1994). Gender and double standards in the assessment of job candidates. *Social Psychology Quarterly, 57*(4), 326-339.

Fountain, J. E. (2001). *Building the Virtual State: Information Technology and Institutional Change.* Washington, DC: Brookings Institution Press.

Fraley, R., & Shaver, P. (2000). Adult romantic attachment: Theoretical developments, emerging controversies, and unanswered questions. *Review of General Psychology, 2*(2), 132-154.

Franda, M. (2002). *Launching Into Cyberspace: Internet Development and Politics in Five World Regions.* Boulder, CO: Lynne Rienner.

Franklin, U. (1999). *The real world of technology.* Toronto: House of Anansi Press.

Franz, R., & Wolkinger, T. (2003). Customer Integration with Virtual Communities. *Case Study: The online community of the largest regional newspaper in Austria.* Proceedings of the Hawaii International Conference on System Sciences, January 6-9, 2003, Big Island, Hawaii.

Freeman, C., & Soete, L. (1999). *The economics of industrial innovation.* Cambridge, MA: MIT Press.

Freud, S. (1933). *New introductory lectures on psychoanalysis.* New York, NY: W.W. Norton & Company, Inc.

Fried, I. (2003). *Apple limits tunes file sharing.* Retrieved May 10, 2007, from CNET News.com.

Furlong, M. S. (1989). An electronic community for older adults: The Senior Network. *Journal of Communication, 39*(3), 145-153.

Gangemi, J. (2006, September 21). A Myspace that speaks your language. *Business Week.* Retrieved November 5, 2007, from Business Source Premier database.

Gavin, J. (2007, October 10). UK social networking site usage highest in *Europe.comScore.* Retrieved October 21, 2007, from http://www.comscore.com/press/release.asp?press=1801

Gefen, D., & Straub, D.W. (1997). Gender Differences in Perception and Adoption of E-Mail: An Extension to the Technology Acceptance Model. *MIS Quarterly, 21*(4), 389-400.

Gefen, D., Karahanna, E., & Straub, D. (2003). Trust and TAM in online shopping: An integrated model. *MIS Quarterly, 27*(1), 51-90.

Gefen, D., Rose, G., Warkentin, M., & Pavlou, P. (2005). Cultural diversity and trust in IT adoption: A comparison of potential e-voters in the USA and South Africa. *Journal of Global Information Management, 13*(1), 54-78.

Geier, J. (2004). *Location-based services realize benefits.* Retrieved May 10, 2006, from Mobilizedsoftware.com.

Gemunden, H., Ritter, T., & Heydebreck, P. (1996). Network configuration and innovation success: An empirical analysis in German high-tech industries. *International Journal of Research in Marketing, 5*(13), 449-462.

Geng, X., Whinston, A., & Zhang, H. (2004). Health of electronic communities: An evolutionary game approach. *Journal of Management Information Systems, 21*(3), 83-110.

Gibson, R., Nixon, P., & Ward, S. (eds.). (2003). *Political Parties and the Internet: Net Gain?* London: Routledge.

Giddens, A. (1984). *The constitution of society: Outline of the theory of structuration.* Cambridge: Polity press.

Gilder, G. (2000). *Telecom: How Infinite Bandwidth Will Revolutionize Our World.* New York: Free Press.

Ginsburg, M. (2001, November). *Realizing a framework to create, support, and understand virtual communities.* Maastricht, Holland: Infonomics.

Givens, D. (1978). The non-verbal basis of attraction: Flirtation, courtship, and seduction. *Psychiatry, 41,* 346-359.

Glatter, R. (2004). Collaboration, collaboration, collaboration: The origins and implications of a policy. *MiE, 17*(5), 16-20.

Glover, S., & Huffstutter, P. (2008, January 9). L.A. grand jury issues subpoenas in Web suicide case. *Los Angeles Times.* Retrieved January 30, 2008, from http://www.latimes.com/news/printedition/california/la-me-myspace9jan09,0,993796.story

Godio, C. (2000). Building a virtual professional community: The case of Poolweb.it. In *Paper presented at the Third International Conference on Virtual Communities*, London.

Goel, N. (2005). Getting more personal. *PC Magazine,* January.

Goff, C. (2004, September 9). Contact has been made. *New Media Age.* Retrieved November 5, 2007, from Business Source Premier database.

Goffman, E. (1959). *The presentation of self in everyday life.* Garden City, NY: Doubleday.

Goffman, E. (1963). *Stigma: Notes on the management of spoiled identity.* New York, NY: Prentice Hall.

Goldberg, L. (1990). An alternative "description of personality": The Big-Five factor structure. *Journal of Personality and Social Psychology, 59,* 1216-1229.

Golding, P. (1996). World wide wedge: Division and contradiction in the global information infrastructure. *Monthly Review, 48*(3), 70-85.

Goldstein, M. (1964). Perceptual reactions to threat under varying conditions of measurement. *Journal of Abnormal and Social Psychology, 69*(5), 563-567.

Gonzales, M., & Meyers, S. (1993). "Your mother would like me": Self-presentation in the personal ads of heterosexual and homosexual men and women. *Personality and Social Psychology Bulletin, 19,* 131-142.

Goode, W. (1996). Gender and courtship entitlement: Responses to personal ads. *Sex Roles: A Journal of Research, 34,* 141-170.

Goodman, J. (2007). Click first, ask questions later: Understanding teen online behaviour. *Aplis, 20,* 84-86.

Goodstein, A. (2007). *Totally wired: What teens and tweens are really doing online.* New York, NY: St. Martin's Press.

Google launches social-networking software. (2007, October 31). *Dallas News.com.* Retrieved November 4, 2007, from http://www.dallasnews.com

GovTrack.us. (n.d.). S. 49: A bill to amend the Communications Act of 1934 to prevent the carriage of child.... *GovTrack.us.* Retrieved July 24, 2007, from http://www.govtrack.us/congress/bill.xpd?bill=s110-49

Gray, B. (1985). Conditions facilitating interorganizational collaboration. *Human Relations, 38*(10), 911-936.

Gray, B., & Hay, T. (1986). Political limits to interorganizational consensus and change. *The Journal of Applied Behavioral Science, 22*(2), 95-112.

Green, E. (2005, November 14). The web of social networking. *U.S. News & World Report.* Retrieved November 5, 2007, from Business Source Premier database.

Greenfield Online-Ciao Surveys. (2007, October 18). Use of online surveys for market research to increase. *MarketingVOX.* Retrieved October 21, 2007, from http://www.marketingvox.com

Greengard, S., & Byham, B. (2003). Gimme attitude!. *Workforce, 82*(7), 56-59.

Greenwald, R. (2003). *Find a husband after 35: Using what I learned at Harvard Business School.* Random House Publishing Book.

Gross, R., Acquisti, A., & Heinz, A. (2005). *Information Revelation and Privacy in Online Social Networks.* Proceedings of the 2005 ACM workshop on Privacy in electronic society, 71-80.

Gubernick, D. (1994). Bi-parental care and male female relations in mammals. In: S. Parmigiani & F. Vom Saal (Eds.), *Infanticide and parental care* (pp. 427-463). Chur, Switzerland: Harwood.

Gurstein, M. (2000). *Community informatics: Enabling communities with information and communications technologies* (Introduction, pp. 1-29). Hershey, PA: Idea Group Publishing.

Gwinnell, E. (1998). *Online seductions: Falling in love with strangers on the Internet.* New York, NY: Kodansha International.

Hagel, J., & Armstrong, A. G. (1997). *Net gain: Expanding markets through virtual communities.* Boston: Harvard Business School Press.

Hagel, J., & Armstrong, A. G. (1997). *Net gain: Expanding markets through virtual communities.* Boston: Harvard Business School Press.

Hague, B. N. & Loader, B. D. (eds.). (1999). *Digital Democracy: Discourse and Decision Making in the Information Age.* New York: Routledge.

Hair, J. F., Anderson, R. E., Tatham, R. L., & Black, W. C. (1998). *Multivariate data analysis (5th ed.).* New Jersey: Upper Saddle River: Prentice Hall.

Hale, W. (2007, October 24). UK visits with teens at virtual college fair. *UK News.* Retrieved November 3, 2007, from http://news.uky.edu/news/display_ article.php?artid=2812&mode=print

Hall, E., & Hall, M. (1990), *Understanding cultural differences.* Yarmouth, ME: Intercultural Press.

Hamilton, M. (1989). Reactions to obscene language. *Communication Research Reports, 6,* 67-69.

Hamman, R. (2001). Granada broadband. *Presentation given at the 4th International Conference on Virtual Communities.* London.

Han, W. (2004, September 6). Campus connection. *Time Inc.* Retrieved November 5, 2007, from Business Source Premier database.

Hancock, J., Toma, C., & Ellison, N. (2007). The truth about lying in online dating profiles. *Proceedings of the ACM Conference on Human Factors in Computing Systems (CHI 2007),* (pp. 449-452).

Hanson, K. (2005, February 28). Study links Internet, social contact. *The Stanford Daily.* Retrieved July 5, 2007, from http://daily.stanford.edu/article/2005/2/28/studyLinksInternetSocialContact

Haque, M.S. (2002). E-governance in India: Its impacts on relations among citizens, politicians and public servants. *International Review of Administrative Sciences, 68*(2), 231-250.

Harada, K. (2007). Social networking of the world is rich and colorful (in Japanese). In: Shoeisha (Ed.), *A study of SNS,* (pp. 46-69). Tokyo, Japan: Shoeisha, Co. Ltd.

Haralick, R.M., Sternberg, S.R., & Zhuang, X. (1987). Image analysis using mathematical morphology. *IEEE Transactions on Pattern Analysis and Machine Intelligence, 9*(4), 532-550.

Hardy, C., & Phillips, N. (1998). Strategies of engagement: Lessons from the critical examination of collaboration and conflict in interorganizational domain. *Organizational Science, 2,* 217-230.

Harris, C. (2006). MySpace can be our space. *School Library Journal, 52*(5), 30.

Harrison, A., & Saeed, L. (1977). Let's make a deal: An analysis of revelations and stipulations in lonely hearts advertisements. *Journal of Personality and Social Psychology, 35*(4), 257-264.

Harvey, L., & Myers, M. (1995). Scholarship and practice: The contribution of ethnographic research methods to bridging the gap. *Information Technology and People, 8*(3), 13-27.

Hawkins, J. 1987. Computers and girls, rethinking the issues. *Sex Roles,13*(¾), 165-179.

Hayward, T. (1995). *Info-Rich, Info-Poor: Access and Exchange in the Global Information Society.* K.G. Saur.

Hazan, C., & Shaver, P. (1987). Romantic love conceptualized as an attachment process. *Journal of Personality and Social Psychology, 52,* 511-524.

Heer, D. (1974). The prevalence of black-white marriage in the United States, 1960 and 1970. *Journal of Marriage and the Family, 36,* 246-258.

Heher, A. (2007, February 16). Teens go online to grieve for friends. *The Courier & Press,* pp. A-1, A-12.

Hempel, J., & Lehman, P. (2005, December 12). The MySpace generation. *BusinessWeek, 3963,* pp. 86-96.

Herlocker, J., Konstan J., & Riedl, J. (2000). Explaining collaborative filtering recommendations. *Conference on Computer Supported Cooperative Work* (pp. 241-250).

Herring, S. C. (1996). Two variants of an electronic message schema. In S. C. Herring (Ed.), *Computer-mediated communication: Linguistic, social and cross-cultural perspectives* (pp. 81-106). Philadelphia: John Benjamins.

Heskell, P. *Flirt Coach: Communication tips for friendship, love and professional success.* London: Harper Collins Publishers Limited.

Hewitt, B., Dodd, J., York, M., Finan, E., Nelson, M., Fleming, A., et al. (2006). MySpace nation: The controversy. *People, 65*(22), 113-121.

Heydary, J. (2006, September, 26). Regulation of online dating services sparks controversy. *Wall Street Journal,* p. A5.

Higgins, E. (1987). Self-discrepancy theory. *Psychological Review, 94,* 1120-1134.

Hill, K. & Hughes, J. E. (1999). Is the Internet an instrument of global democratization? *Democratization, 3,* 29-43.

Hill, K. A. & Hughes, J. E. (1998). *Cyberpolitics: Citizen Activism in the Age of the Internet.* Lanham, MD: Rowan & Littlefield.

Hillery, G. A. (1955). Definitions of community: Areas of agreement. *Rural Sociology, 20,* 118-120.

Hiltz, S. R., & Johnson, K. (1990). User satisfaction with computer-mediated communication systems. *Management Science, 36*(6), 739-764.

Hinde, R. (1997). *Relationships: A dialectical perspective.* London: Psychology Press.

Hing, E., Burt, C., & Woodwell, D. (2007). Advance Data, No. 393. U.S. Department of Health and Human Services, National Center for Health Statistics.

Hirschman, E. (1987). People as products: Analysis of a complex marketing exchange. *Journal of Marketing, 51*(January), 98-108.

Hitsch, J., Hortacsu, A., & Ariely, D. (2005). *What makes you click.* Paper presented at the AEA Meeting, Choice Symposium, Northwestern University. Estes Park.

Ho, T., & Weigelt, K. (2005). Trust building among strangers. *Management Science, 51*(4), 519-530.

Hock, D. (2000). Birth of the chaordic age, *Executive Excellence, 17*(6), 6-7.

Hoffman, L., Lawson-Jenkins, K., & Blum, J. (2006). Trust beyond security: An expanded trust model. *Communications of the ACM, 49*(7), 94-101.

Hoffman. L. (2007, October 20). Virtual life delivers tools for a real life. *The Australian.* Retrieved November 4, 2007, from Newspaper Source database.

Hofstede, G. (1980). *Culture's consequences: International differences in work-related values.* Beverly Hills, CA: Sage Publications.

Hofstede, G. (1991). *Culture and organizations: Software of the mind.* London: McGraw Hill.

Hofstede, G. (1991). *Cultures and organizations: Software of the mind.* London: McGraw-Hill.

Hofstede, G. (1994). Management scientists are human. *Management Science, 40*(1), 4-13.

Hofstede, G. (2001). *Culture's consequences: Comparing values, behaviors, institutions, and organizations across nations.* Thousand Oaks, CA: Sage.

Holcum, M., Lehman, W., & Simpson, D. (1993). Employee accidents: Influences of personal characteristics, job characteristics, and substance use in jobs differing in accident potential. *Journal of Safety Research, 24,* 205-211.

Horrigan, J., Rainie, L., & Fox, S. (2001). Online communities: Networks that nurture long-distance relationships and local ties. *Pew Internet & American Life Project.* Retrieved from: www.pew internet.org

Hortobagyi, M. (2007, May 9). Slain students' pages to stay on Facebook. *USA Today,* Life Section, P9.

Houran, J., Lange, R., Rentfrow, P., & Bruckner, K. (2004). Do online matchmaking tests work? An Assessment of preliminary evidence for a publicized 'predictive model of marital success'. *North American Journal of Psychology, 6,* 507-526.

Huang, J., & Fox, M. (2006). An ontology of trust: Formal semantics and transitivity. *Proceedings of the 8ᵗʰ international conference on Electronic commerce: The new e-commerce: Innovations for conquering current barriers, obstacles and limitations to conducting successful business on the internet,* (pp. 259-270).

Huber, G. (1984). The nature and design of post-industrial organizations. *Management Science, 30*(8), 928-951.

Humphreys, P., & Berger, J. (1981). Theoretical consequences of the status characteristics formulation. *American Journal of Sociology, 86*(5), 953-983.

Hunter, B. (2002). Learning in the virtual community depends upon changes in local communities. In: K. Renninger & W. Shumar (Eds.), *Building virtual communities: Learning and change in cyberspace* (pp. 96-128). Cambridge: Cambridge University Press.

Hunter, B. (2007, August 14). New study explores the online behaviors of U.S. teens and 'tweens. Retrieved August 23, 2007, from http://www.nsba.org/site/doc.asp?TRACKID=&VID=2&CID=90K&DID=41336

Huriansky, J. (2003). *The complete idiot's guide to dating.* London: Penguin Group.

Huxham, C., & Vangen, S. (2000). Ambiguity, complexity and dynamics in the membership of collaboration. *Human Relations, 53*(6), 771-805.

Huysman, M., & Wulf, V. (2004). *Social capital and information technology.* Cambridge, MA and London: The MIT Press.

Huysman, M., & Wulf, V. (2005). The role of information technology in building and sustaining the relational base of communities. *The Information Society, 21*(2), 81-89.

Igbaria, M., Shayo, C., & Olfman, L. (1999). *On becoming virtual: The driving forces and arrangements* (pp. 27-41). New Orleans, LA: ACM.

Ihlwan, M. (2005, September 26). E-society: My world is Cyworld. *BusinessWeek.* Retrieved October 26, 2007, from http://www.businessweek.com/print/magazine/content/05_39/b3952405.htm?chan=gl

Inbabble. (2007). Interview: Atul Sasane, head of new business about Mobikade social networking, free games and free SMS. Retrieved October 8, 2007, from http://inbabble.com

Industry Canada. (2002, April 4). *Fostering innovation and use.* Retrieved July 30, 2002 from http://broadband.gc.ca/Broadband-document/english/chapter5.htm

Industry Canada. (2002, April 4). *Smart communities broadband.* Retrieved July 12, 2002 from http://smart-communities.ic.gc.ca/index_e.asp

Ingham, J., & Feldman, L. (1994). *African-American business leaders: A biographical dictionary.* Westport, CT: Greenwood Press.

Inkeles, A., & Levinson, D. (1969). National character: The study of modal personality and socio-cultural systems. In: L. Gardner & E. Aronson (Eds.), *The handbook of social psychology* (vol. 4, pp. 418-516). Reading, MA: Addison Wesley.

Ireland, K. (1991). The $100 billion high. *Personnel Journal, 70*(2), 85.

ITU (International Telecommunications Union). (2003). *World summit on the information society* (pp. 1-9). Retrieved from www.itu.int

ITU. (n.d.). Retrieved from: http://www.itu.int/wsis/

Jamali, M., & Abolhassani, H. (2006). Different aspects of social network analysis. *Proceedings of the IEEE International Conference on Web Intelligence 2006,* (pp. 66-72).

Jana, R. (2007, August 14). Mining virtual worlds for market research. *Business Week Online*. Retrieved October 19, 2007, from Business Source Premier database.

Jansen, E. (2002). *Netlingo: The Internet dictionary*. Ojai, CA: Independent Publishers Group.

Jansen, E. (2002). Netlingo: *The Internet dictionary*. Ojai, CA: Independent Publishers Group.

Jarillo, C. (1988). On strategic networks. *Strategic Management Journal, 9*(1), 31-41.

Jason, L., Moritsugu, J., & DePalma D. (1992). Advertisements as a strategy for meeting people. *Psychological Reports, 71,* 1311-1314.

Jay, T. (1992). *Cursing in America*. Philadelphia, PA: Benjamins.

Jensen, D., & Neville, J. (2002). Data mining in social networks. *National Academy of Sciences Symposium on Dynamic Social Network Analysis.*

John, O.P. (1990). The "Big Five" factor taxonomy: Dimensions of personality in the natural language and in questionnaires. In L. A. Pervin (Ed.), *Handbook of personality: Theory and research* (pp. 66-100). New York: Guilford.

Johnson, R. (1980). *Religious assortative marriage in the United States*. New York, NY: Academic Press.

Johnson, S. (2006). Don't fear the digital. *Time, 167*(13), 56-56.

Johnson, T.J. & Kaye, B.K. (2003). Around the World Wide Web in 80 ways: How motives for going online are linked to Internet activities among politically interested Internet users. *Social Science Computer Review, 21,*(3), 304-325.

Jones, C., Herterly, W., & Borgatti, S. (1997). A general theory of network governance: Exchange conditions and social mechanisms. *Academy of Management Review, 22*(4), 911-945.

Jones, K. (2006). 'Digital dirt' derailing job seekers. Retrieved August 26, 2007, from http://www.informationweek.com/story/showArticle.jhtml?articleID=190302836.

Jones, Q., & Grandhi, S. (2005). P3 systems: Putting the place back into social networks. *IEEE Internet Computing, September-October*(2005), 38-46.

Jones, Q., & Grandhi, S. (2005, September/October). A. P3 systems: Putting the place back into social networks. *IEEE Internet Computing,* 38-46.

Jordan, T. (1999). *Cyberpower: An introduction to the politics of cyberspace*. London: Routledge.

Jøsang, A., Ismail, R., & Boyd, C. (2007). A survey of trust and reputation systems for online service provision. *Decision Support Systems, 43*(2), 618-644.

Jøsang, A., Keser, C., & Dimitrakos, T. (2005). Can we manage trust. *Proceedings of the 3rd International Conference on Trust Management (iTrust), 2477,* (pp. 93-107).

Kalathil, S. & Boas, T. C. (2003). *Open Networks Closed Regimes: The Impact of the Internet on Authoritarian Rule*. Washington, DC: Carnegie Endowment for International Peace.

Kale, S. (1991). Culture-specific marketing communications: An analytical approach. *International Marketing Review, 8*(2), 18-30.

Kale, S., & Barnes, J. (1992). Understanding the domain of cross-national buyer-seller interactions. *Journal of International Business Studies, 23*(1), 101-132.

Kalmijn, M. (1991). Shifting boundaries: Trends in religious and educational homogamy. *American Sociological Review, 56,* 786-800.

Kalmijn, M. (1993). Trends in black/white intermarriage. *Social Forces, 72,* 119-146.

Kalmijn, M. (1998). Intermarriage and homogamy: Causes, patterns, trends. *Annual Review of Sociology, 24,* 395-421.

Kandel, D., & Yamaguchi, K. (1987). Job mobility and drug use: An event history analysis. *The American Journal of Sociology, 92*(4), 836-878.

Katayama, L. (2006, September 11). Social networking sites catch on in Japan. *Japan Today.* Retrieved

October 26, 2007 from, http://www.japantoday.com/jp/feature/1137

Katz, M., & Shapiro, C. (1986). Technology adoption in the presence of network externalities. *Journal of Political Economy, 94,* 822-841.

Kayany, J. (1998). Contexts of uninhibited online behavior: Flaming in social newsgroups on Usenet. *Journal of the American Society for Information Science, 49*(12), 1135-1141.

Keat, T., & Mohan, A. (2004). Integration of TAM-based electronic commerce models for trust. *Journal of American Academy of Business, Cambridge, 5*(1-2), 404-410.

Keck, M. E. & Sikkink, K. (1998). *Activists Beyond Borders: Advocacy Networks in International Politics.* Ithaca, NY: Cornell University Press.

Keenan, T., & Trotter, D. (1999). The changing role of community networks in providing citizen access to the Internet. Internet Research. *Electronic Networking Applications and Policy, 9*(2), 100-108.

Kelsey, C. (2007). *Generation MySpace: Helping your teen survive online adolescence.* New York, NY: Marlowe.

Kennedy, R. (1952) Single or triple melting pot? Intermarriage in New Haven, 1870-1950. *American Journal of Sociology, 58,* 56-59.

Kenrick, D., Sadalla, E., Groth, G., & Trost, M. (1990). Evolution, traits, and the stages of human courtship: Qualifying the parental investment model. *Journal of Personality, 58,* 97-116.

Kent, J. M. & Zeitner, V. (2003). Internet use and civic engagement: A longitudinal analysis. *Public Opinion Quarterly, 67*(3), 311-334.

Kesmodel, D. (2007, August 24). Court clears Whole Foods deal, FTC loses appeal to delay acquisition of Wild Oats, but other options remain. *Wall Street Journal,* p. A2.

Kharif, O. (2007, October 8). Google's Orkut: A world of ambition. *Business Week.* Retrieved October 26, 2007, from http://www.businessweek.com/print/technology/content/oct2007/tc2007107_530965.htm

Kickul, J., & Gundry, L. (2000). Pursuing technological innovation: The role of entrepreneurial posture and opportunity recognition among internet firms. In *Frontiers of Entrepreneurship Research,* MA: Babson College.

Kiesler, S., & Sproull, L. (1992). Group decision making and communication technology. *Organizational Behavior and Human Decision Processes, 52*(1), 96-123.

Kiesler, S., & Sproull, L. (1992). Group decision making and communication technology. *Organizational Behavior and Human Decision Processes, 52*(1), 96-123.

Kilgannon, C. (2007, February 13). Teenagers misbehaving, for all online to watch. *The New York Times.* Retrieved July 23, 2007, from NewsBank database.

Kim, A. (2000). *Community building on the Web: Secret strategies for successful online communities.* Berkeley, CA: Peachpit Press.

Kim, P., & Aldrich, H. (2005). *Social capital and entrepreneurship.* Hanover, MA: Now Publishers Inc.

Kirkpatrick, D. (2007). Facebook's plan to hook up the world. *Fortune, 155,* 127-130.

Kirkpatrick, L., & Davis, K. (1994). Attachment style, gender and relationship stability: A longitudinal analysis. *Journal of Personality and Social Psychology, 66,* 502-512.

Klaassen, A. (2007). Making friends with the social networks. *Advertising Age, 78,* 14.

Klimkiewicz, J. (2007, January 26). Internet junkies: Hooked online: One in eight Americans find it hard to log off. *The Hartford Courant.* Retrieved July 25, 2007, from Newspaper Source database.

Kluckhohn, F., & Strodtbeck, F. (1961). *Variations in value orientations.* Westport, CT: Greenwood Press.

Kodama, M. (in press). Innovation and knowledge creation through leadership-based strategic community: Case study on high-tech company in Japan. *Journal of Technovation.*

Koestner, R., & Wheeler, L. (1988). Self-presentation in personal advertisements: The influence of implicit notions of attraction and role expectations. *Journal of Social and Personal Relationships, 5,* 149-160.

Koestner, R., & Wheeler, L. (1988). Self-presentation in personal advertisements: The influence of implicit notions of attraction and role expectations. *Journal of Social and Personal Relationships, 5*(1), 149-160.

Kollock, P. (1999). The economies of online cooperation: Gifts and public goods in cyberspace. In: M. Smith & P. Kollock (Eds.), *Communities in cyberspace.* London: Routledge.

Kollock, P., & Smith, M. (1996). Managing the online commons: Cooperation and conflict in computer communities. In: S. Herring (Ed.), *Computer mediated communication; linguistic, social, and cross-cultural perspectives* (pp. 109-128).

Kornblum, J. (2006, January 8). Adults question MySpace's safety. *USAToday, Tech.* Retrieved November 11, 2006, from http://www.usatoday.com/tech/news/2006-01-08-myspace-sidebar_x.htm.

Kornblum, J. (2006, September 20). Meet my 5,000 new best pals. *USA Today.* Retrieved March 3, 2007, from Academic Search Elite database.

Kraemer, W., & Müller, M. (1999). Virtual corporate university: Executive education architecture and knowledge management. In A.-W. Scheer (Ed.), *Electronic business and knowledge management.* Heidelberg, Germany: Physica.

Kress, N. (2004). *Dynamic characters: How to create personalities that keep readers captivated.* Cincinnati, OH: Writer's Digest Books.

Kwon, T., & Zmud, R. (1987). Unifying the fragmented models of information systems implementation. In: J. Boland & R. Hirshheim (Eds.), *Critical issues in information systems research* (pp. 227-251). New York, NY: John Wiley.

Kyttä, M. (2003). *Children in outdoor contexts: Affordances and independent mobility in the assessment of environmental child friendliness.* Doctoral dissertation presented at Helsinki University of Technology, Espoo, Finland.

Kyttä, M. (2003). *Children in outdoor contexts: Affordances and independent mobility in the assessment of environmental child friendliness.* Doctoral dissertation presented at Helsinki University of Technology. Espoo, Finland.

Lakoff, R. (1973). Language and woman's place. *Language and Society, 2,* 45-80.

Lakshman, N. (2006). Here come the bride sites. *Business Week,* 42.

Landauer, T.K., Foltz, P.W., & Laham, D. (1998). An introduction to latent semantic analysis. *Discourse Processes, 25,* 259-284.

Lavallee, A. (2007, June 13). Firms tidy up clients' bad online reputations. *Wall Street Journal,* p. B1.

Lavallee, A. (2007, June 13). Firms tidy up clients' bad online reputations. *Wall Street Journal,* p. B1.

Lawrence, T., Phillips, N., & Hardy, C. (1999). Watching whale watching. *The Journal of Applied Behavioral Science, 35*(4), 479-502.

Leary, M.R., Kelly, K.M., & Schreindorfer, L.S. (2001). *Individual differences in the need to belong.* Unpublished manuscript, Wake Forest University, Winston-Salem, NC.

Leary, T. (1957). *Interpersonal diagnosis of personality.* New York: Ronald Press.

LeBrasseur, R., Whissell, R., & Ojha, A. (2002). Organizational learning, transformational leadership and implementation of continuous quality improvement in Canadian hospitals. *Australian Journal of Management, 27*(2), 141-162.

LeCompte, M., & Goetz, J. (1982). Problems of reliability and validity in ethnographic research. *Review of Educational Research, 52*(1), 31-60.

Lee, E. (2007, February 15). MySpace suit dismissed by judge in Texas/Family said site didn't protect underage users. *San Francisco Chronicle.* Retrieved May 23, 2007, from Newspaper Source database.

Lee, M. (2007, July 17). China limits online game time for teens. *USA Today.* Retrieved July 25, 2007, from http://usatoday.com

Lehman, P. (2007, January 25). Building a safer MySpace. *BusinessWeek Online.* Retrieved August 4, 2007, from Academic Search Elite database.

Leimeister, J., Ebner, W., & Krcmar, H. (2005). Design, implementation, and evaluation of trust-supporting components in virtual communities for patients. *Journal of Management Information Systems, 21*(4), 101-131.

Lenhart, A., & Madden, M. (2007). Social networking Web sites and teens: An overview. *Pew Internet & American Life Project.* Retrieved June 10, 2007, from http://www.pewinternet.org/PPF/r/198/report_display.asp.

Lenhart, A., & Madden, M. (2007). *Social Networking Websites and Teens: An Overview.* Pew Internet & American Life Project. Retrieved August 27, 2007 from, http://www.pewinternet.org/PPF/r/198/report_display.asp

Lenhart, A., & Madden, M. (2007). Pew Internet project data memo: Social networking Web sites and teens: An overview. Pew Internet & American Life Project. Retrieved January 8, 2007, from http://www.pewinternet.org/PPF/r/198/report_display.asp

Lenhart, A., & Madden, M. (2007). Teens, privacy & online social networks: How teens manage their online identities and personal information in the age of MySpace. Pew Internet & American Life Project. Retrieved January 8, 2007, from http://www.pewinternet.org/pdfs/PIP_Teens_Privacy_SNS_Report_Final.pdf

Lenhart, A., Madden, M., & Hitlin, P. (2005). Teens and technology: Youth are leading the transition to a fully wired and mobile nation. Pew Internet & American

Leon, D., Rotunda, R., Sutton, M., & Schlossman, C. (2003). Internet forewarning effects on ratings of attraction. *Computers in Human Behavior, 19,* 39-57.

Leung, L. (2001). College Student Motives for Chatting on ICQ. *New Media and Society, 3*(4), 483-500.

Levenshtein, V. (1965/1966). Binary codes capable of correcting deletions, insertions, and reversals, *Doklady Akademii Nauk SSSR, 163*(4), 845-848, 1965 (Russian). English translation in *Soviet Physics Doklady, 10*(8), 707-710.

Lever, J., Zellman, G., & Hirschfeld, S. (2006). Office romance. *Across the Board, 42*(2), 32-41.

Levine, R. (2006, August 7). The many voices of Wikipedia, heard in one place. *The New York Times.*

Levine-Young, M., & Levine, J. (2000). *Poor Richard's building online communities.* Lakewood, CO: Top Floor Publishing.

Levitz, R., & Noel, L. (2000). Taking the initiative: Strategic moves for retention. USA Group. Noel-Levitz.

Levy, S. (2007). Are MySpace users now spacing out?. *Newsweek, 149*(22), 26.

Levy, S. (2007, August 27). Facebook grows up. *Newsweek,* pp. 41-42.

Lewis, J. (2007). *Social Networking: Examining User Behavior.* Retrieved August 29, 2007, from http://www.webpronews.com/topnews/2007/04/10/social-networking-examining-user-behavior

Li, D., Li, J., & Lin, Z. (2007). Online consumer-to-consumer market in China—a comparative study of Taobao and eBay. *Electronic Commerce Research and Applications,* doi:10.1016/j.elerap.2007.02.010.

Lieberson, S., & Waters, M. (1988). *From many strands: Ethnic and racial groups in contemporary America.* New York, NY: Russell Sage.

Lievowitz, J. (2003). *Addressing the human capital crisis in federal government: A knowledge management perspective.* London: Elsevier.

Liew, J. (2007). Kids and teens have pushed at least 6 immersive online worlds to over 2m UU/mth in the U.S. Lightspeed Venture Partners blog. Retrieved November 3, 2007, from http://lsvp.wordpress.com/2007/04/23/

Life Project. Retrieved March 16, 2007, from http://www.pewinternet.org/pdfs/PIP_Teens_Tech_July2005web.pdf

Lim, K., Sia, C., Lee, M., & Benbasat, I. (2006). Do I trust you online, and if so, will I buy? An empirical study of two trust-building strategies. *Journal of Management Information Systems, 23*(2), 233-266.

Lindahl, C., & Blount, E. (2003). Weblogs: Simplifying Web publishing. *IEEE Computer, 36*(11), 114-116.

Lipsman, A. (2007a, May 4). comScore finds that "Second Life" has a rapidly growing and global base of active residents. *comScore.com.* Retrieved November 4, 2007, from http://www.comscore.com/press/release.asp?press=1425

Lipsman, A. (2007b). UK teens and young adults spend 24 percent more time online than the average internet user. *comScore.com.* Retrieved October 21, 2007, from http://www.comscore.com/press/release.asp?press=1469

Lipsman, A. (2007c, July 31). Social networking goes global. *comScore.com.* Retrieved October 21, 2007, from http://www.comscore.com/press/release.asp?press=1555

Litvinoff, M. (1990). *The Earthscan action handbook: For people and planet.* London: Earthscan Publishers.

Liu, H. (2003). Unpacking meaning from words: A context-centered approach to computational lexicon design. In Blackburn et al. (Eds.), *Modeling and Using Context, The 4th International and Interdisciplinary Conference, CONTEXT 2003,* LNCS 2680 (pp. 218-232). Springer.

Liu, H., & Maes, P. (2005a, Jan 9). InterestMap: Harvesting social network profiles for recommendations. *Proceedings of IUI Beyond Personalization 2005: A Workshop on the Next Stage of Recommender Systems Research,* San Diego, CA (pp. 54-59).

Liu, H., & Singh, P. (2004). ConceptNet: A practical commonsense reasoning toolkit. *BT Technology Journal, 22*(4), 211-226.

Livingstone, S., & Bober, M. (2006). *Children go online, 2003-2005.* Colchester, Essex: UK Data Archive.

Lomas, N. (2007, October 19). Analyst: Social networking faces uncertain future. *Cnet Networks.* Retrieved November 4, 2007, from http://www.news.com

Loviglio, J. (2007, June 16). Two sex convictions in online dating case. *Wall Street Journal,* p. B5.

Lowe, G. S. & Krahn, H. (1989). Computer skills and use among high school and university graduates. *Canadian Public Policy 15*(2). 175-88.

Lowndes, V., & Skelcher, C. (1998). The dynamics of multi-organizational partnerships: An analysis of changing modes of governance. *Public Administration, 76,* 313-333.

Lupsa, C. (2006). Facebook: A campus fad becomes a campus fact. The social-networking Web site isn't growing like it once did, but only because almost every US student is already on it. *The Christian Science Monitor.* Retrieved July 2, 2007, from http://www.csmonitor.com/2006/1213/p13s01-legn.html.

Lutters, W., & Ackerman, M. (2003). Joining the backstage: Locality and centrality in an online community. *Information Technology & People, 16*(2), 157-182.

MacKenzie, S., & Richard A. S. (1992). How Does Motivation Moderate the Impact of Central Processing on Brand Attitudes and Intentions? *Journal of Consumer Research 18* (March 1992), 519-529.

MacKinney, K. (1991). *Sexuality in close relationships.* London: Lawrence Erlbaum Associates.

Madden, M. (2006). *Internet Penetration and Impact.* Pew Internet & American Life Project, April 2006. Retrieved August 27, 2007, from http://www.pewinternet.org/PPF/r/182/report_display.asp

Maes, P., et al. (2005). Ambient semantics and reach media. *IEEE Pervasive Computing Magazine.* Submitted.

Magid, L., & Collier, A. (2007). *MySpace unraveled: A parent's guide to teen social networking.* Berkley, CA: Peachpit Press.

Mainelli, M. (2003). Risk/reward in virtual financial communities. *Information Services and Use, 23*(1), 9-17.

Mair, P. & van Biezen, I. (2001). Party membership in twenty European democracies 1980-2000. *Party Politics, 7*(1), 7-22.

Malchow-Møller, A. (2003). Internet dating: A focus group investigation of young Danes' and Frenchmen's attitudes towards the phenomenon. *Kontur, 7,* 11-20.

Malik, S. (2002). *Representing black Britain: A history of black and Asian images on British television.* London: Sage Publications.

Malta, S. (2007). Love actually! Older adults and their romantic Internet relationships [Electronic version]. *Australian Journal of Emerging Technologies and Society, 5,* 84-102.

Mangione, T., Howland, J., & Lee, M. (1998*). New perspectives for worksite alcohol strategies: Results from a corporate drinking study.* Boston, MA: JSI Research and Training Institute.

Mann, C., & Stewart, F. (2000). *Internet communication and qualitative research: A handbook for Research Online.* London: Sage Publications.

Mann, C., & Stewart, F. (2000). *Internet communication and qualitative research: A handbook for research online.* London: Sage Publications.

Mansell, G. (1991). Action research in information systems development. *Journal of Information Systems, 1,* 29-40.

Mantovani, F. (2001). Networked seduction: A test-bed for the study of strategic communication on the Internet. *CyberPsychology & Behavior, 4*(1), 147-154.

Many good reasons for providing a drug-free workplace. (2005). *Alcoholism & Drug Abuse Weekly, 17*(46), 5.

Mare, R. (1991). Five decades of educational assortative mating. *American Sociological Review, 56,* 15-32.

Margolis, M. & Resnick, D. (2000). *Politics as Usual: The Cyberspace "Revolution."* Thousand Oaks, CA: Sage.

Markus, M. (1987). Toward a 'critical mass' theory of interactive media: Universal access, interdependence and diffusion. *Communications Research, 14,* 491-511.

Markus, M., & Robey, D. (1988). Information technology and organizational change. *Management Science, 34*(5), 583-598.

Markus, U. (2002). *Integration der Virtuellen Community in Das Customer Relationship Management.* Unpublished dissertation, University of Saarland, Saarbrücken.

Martin, L., & Matlay, H. (2003). Innovative use of the Internet in established small firms: The impact of knowledge management and organizational learning in accessing new opportunities. *Qualitative Market Research, 6*(1), 18-26.

Martins, E. & Terblanche, F. (2003). Building organisational culture that stimulates creativity and innovation. *European Journal of Innovation Management, 6*(1), 64-74.

May, C. (2002). *The information society—A sceptical view.* Cambridge, UK: Polity Press.

Mbakwe, C., & Cunliffe, D. (2003). Conceptualising the process of hypermedia seduction. *Proceedings of the 1ˢᵗ International Meeting of Science and Technology Design: Senses and Sensibility—Linking Tradition to Innovation Through Design,* (pp. 25-26). Lisbon, Portugal.

McCall, M. (2006, April 15). Hooking up in the information age. *Wireless Week.* Retrieved December 2, 2007, from http://www.wirelessweek.com.

McCallum, A., Corrada-Emmanuel, A., & Wang, X. (2005). Topic and role discovery in social networks. *Proceedings of 19th International Joint Conference on Artificial Intelligence* (pp. 786-791).

McChesney, R. W. (1999). *Rich Media, Poor Democracy.* IL: University of Illinois Press.

McCracken, G. (1991). *Culture and consumption: New approaches to the symbolic character of consumer goods and activities.* Indiana University Press.

McCracken, G. (1997). *Plenitude.* Toronto: Periph: Fluide.

McDermott, R. (2002). Measuring the impact of communities. *Knowledge Management Review, 5*(2), 26-29.

McDonald, R. P., & Marsh, H. W. (1990). Choosing a multivariate model: Noncentrality and goodness of fit. *Psychological Bulletin, 707*(2), 247-255.

McKenna, B. (2005, March 29). High school bans blogging. *Rutland Herald.* Retrieved August 4, 2007, from http://www.rutlandherald.com/apps/pbcs.dll/article?AID=/20050329/NEWS/503290316/1027

McKenna, K., Green, A., & Gleason, M. (2002). Relationship formation on the Internet: What's the big attraction?. *Journal of Social Issues, 58,* 9-31.

McKnight, B. & Bontis, N. (2002). E-improvisation: Collaborative groupware technology expands the reach and effectiveness of organizational improvisation. *Knowledge and Process Management, 9*(4), 219-227.

McKnight, D., & Choudhury, V. (2006). Distrust and trust in B2C e-commerce: Do they differ?. *Proceedings of the 8th international conference on Electronic commerce: The new e-commerce: innovations for conquering current barriers, obstacles and limitations to conducting successful business on the internet,* (pp. 482-491).

McKnight, D., Kacmar, C., & Choudhury, V. (2004a). Dispositional trust and distrust distinctions in predicting high- and low-risk Internet expert advice site perceptions. *E-Service Journal, 3*(2), 85-109.

McKnight, D., Kacmar, C., & Choudhury, V. (2004b). Shifting factors and the ineffectiveness of third party assurance seals: A two-stage model of initial trust in a Web business. *Electronic Markets, 14*(3), 252-266.

McNicol, T. (2007, May 1). Mixi vs. MySpace—a fight for your bytes. *The Japan Times.* Retrieved October 26, 2007, from http://search.japantimes.co.jp/cgi-bin/fl20070501zg.html

Media Matrix (2000, October). *Campaign 2000: Party politics on the World Wide Web.* Retrieved from: www.media metrix.com

Medina, J. (*2007, May 6).* States ponder laws to keep web predators from children. *The New York Times.* Retrieved July 25, 2007, from http://www.nytimes.com/2007/05/06/nyregion/06myspace.html?ei=5070&en=947320815b

Mena, J. (1999). *Data mining your Web site.* Oxford: Digital Press.

Mena, J. (1999). *Data mining your Web site.* Oxford: Digital Press.

Menn, J. (2003). *All the rave: The rise and fall of Shawn Fanning's Napster.* New York, NY: Crown Business.

Merton, R. (1941). Intermarriage and the social structure: Fact and theory. *Psychiatry, 4,* 361-374.

Metzger, M. (2006). Effects of site, vendor, and consumer characteristics on Web site trust and disclosure. *Communication Research, 33*(3), 155-179.

Meuter, M., & Ostrom, A. (2000). Self-service technologies: Understanding customer satisfaction with technology-based service encounters. *Journal of Marketing, 64*(3), 50-64.

Milne, J. (2002). Hiring managers value personality, multi-tasking and the ability to learn. *Canadian Manager, 27*(1), 5.

Mitchell, W. (2005). *What do pictures want?: The lives and loves of images.* Chicago, IL: University of Chicago Press.

Mitrano, T. (2006). Thoughts on Facebook. Retrieved June 7, 2007, from http://www.cit.cornell.edu/info/policy/memos/facebook.html.

Mobile content and applications: Monetizing popular interactive services. (2000). *Jupiter Research Vision Report on Broadband and Wireless, 8.*

Moitra, D., & Krishnamoorthy, M. (2004, July/August). Global innovation exchange. *Research Technology Management Journal,* 32-38.

Mol, J., Wijnberg, N., & Carroll, C. (2005). Value chain envy: Explaining new entry and vertical integration in popular music. *Journal of Management Studies, 42*(2), 251-282.

Moore, M. (1985). Non-verbal courtship patterns in women: Context and consequences. *Ethology and Sociobiology, 6,* 237-247.

Moore, M. (1998). Non-verbal courtship patterns in women: Rejection signalling: An empirical investigation. *Semiotica, 118,* 201-214.

Morahan-Martin, J., & Schumacher, P. (2003). Loneliness and social uses of the Internet. *Computers in Human Behavior, 19*(2003), 659-671.

Moraski, M. (2007, June 16). Beware of digital Don Juans. *Wall Street Journal,* p. A5.

Morrison, E. (2002). Newcomers' relationships: The role of social network ties during socialization. *Academy of Management Journal, 45*(6), 1149.

Moulds, J. (2007, August 16). Young shun MySpace for Bebo and Facebook. *Telegraph Media Group.* Retrieved October 26, 2007, from http://www.telegraph.co.uk

Muir, D. (2006, April 6). All children vulnerable to online predators. *ABC news.* Retrieved July 21, 2007, http://abcnews.go.com/pring?id=1812054

Mulac, A., & Lundell, T. (1980). Differences in perceptions created by syntactic-semantic productions of male and female speakers. *Communication Monographs, 47,* 111-118.

Mulac, A., Incontro, C., & James, M. (1985). Comparison of the gender-linked language effect and sex-role stereotypes. *Journal of Personality and Social Psychology, 49,* 1098-1109.

Mulrine, A. (2003, September 29). Love.com: For better or for worse, the Internet is radically changing the dating scene in America. *U.S. News and World Report.*

Murchu, I.O., Breslin, J.G., & Decker, S. (2004). *Online Social and Business Networking Communities.* DERI Technical Report, August 2004.

Murdock, G. & Golding, P. (1989). Information poverty and political inequality: Citizenship in the age of privatised communications. *Journal of Communication, 39,* 180-195.

Murray, S., & Mobasser, A. (2007). Is the Internet killing everything?. In: P. Croughton (Ed.), *Arena: The original men's style magazine.* London: Arena International.

Mutz, D. (2005). Social trust and e-commerce experimental evidence for the effects of social trust on individuals' economic behavior. *Public Opinion Quarterly, 69*(3), 393-416.

Myers, M. (1999). Investigating information systems with ethnographic research. *Communications of the Association of Information Systems, 2*(23), 1-20.

Myers, M., & Young, L. (1997). Hidden agendas, power, and managerial assumptions in information systems development: An ethnographic study. *Information Technology and People, 10*(3), 224-240.

Naposki, K. (2006, January). Facebook: The craze that has crashed into college life may have other consequences. *The Pendulum Online.* Retrieved June 20, 2007, from http://www.elon.edu/e-web/pendulum/Issues/2006/01_19/features/specialfeature.xhtml.

National Association of Colleges and Employers (NACE). (2006). Spotlight Online for Career Services Professionals. Retrieved June 28, 2007, from http://www.lib.unipi.gr/files/nace/2006/Spotlight_Online_07_07_2006.pdf.

National School Boards Association (NSBA). (2007). Creating & connecting/Research and guidelines on online social—and educational—networking. Retrieved August 23, 2007, from http://www.nsba.org/site/view.asp?CID=63&DID=41340

Neely, W. (1940). Family attitudes of denominational college and university students, 1929 and 1936. *American Sociological Review, 4,* 512-522.

Never Ending Friending. (2007). Commissioned by MySpace, Isobar & Carat. Retrieved July 3, 2007, from http://www.tns-us.com/knowledge/docs/40161_Online_Book.pdf.

Nevid, J. (1984). Sex differences in factors of romantic attraction. *Sex Roles, 11,* 401-411.

Neville, K. (2006). Compilation: Library Myspace Accounts. Message posted to Public Libraries serving Young Adults & Children [PUBYAC], 17:42:49, archived at http://www.pubyac.org/archives.htm

New Economy Development Group Inc. (2001). *Sustainability project on sustainable communities.* Paper presented at the Canadian Rural Partnership. Rural Research and Analysis, Government of Canada.

Newman, M. (2001). Who is the best connected scientist? A study of scientific coauthorship networks. *Phys. Rev., E 64.*

Nielsen, J. (2006, October 9). Participation inequality: Encouraging more users to contribute. *Useit.com.* http://www.useit.com/alertbox/participation_inequality.html.

Niemz, K., Griffiths, M., & Banyard, P. (2005). Prevalence of pathological Internet use among university students and correlations with self-esteem, the General Health Questionnaire (GHQ), and dis-inhibition. *CyberPsychology & Behavior, 8*(6), 562-570.

Noel-Levitz. (2006). E-expectations class of 2007 Report: Engaging the "social networking" generation. Retrieved June 15, 2007, from http://www.noellevitz.com.

Noguchi, Y. (2006, October 29). In teens' Web world, MySpace is so last year. *The Washington Post.* Retrieved October 8, 2007, from http://www.washingtopost.com

Nooteboom, B. (1999). Innovation and inter-firm linkages: New implications for policy. *Research Policy, 28*(8), 793.

Norris, P. & Sanders, D. (2003). Medium or message? *Political Communications.*

Norris, P. (2000). *A Virtuous Circle.* New York: Cambridge University Press.

Norris, P. (2001). *Digital Divide.* New York: Cambridge University Press.

Norris, P. (2002). *Democratic Phoenix: Reinventing Political Activism.* New York: Cambridge University Press.

Norris, P. (2003). The bridging and bonding role of online communities. In P. N. Howard & S. Jones (Eds.), *Society Online: The Internet in Context.* Thousand Oaks, CA: Sage.

Norton, J. (2007, February 21). Online bullying compels states to act: Critics question whether legislation can curb kids' bad behavior. *MSNBC.* Retrieved July 23, 2007, from MSNBC http://www.msnbc.msn.com/id/17265901/

O'Connor, B. (2000). Make attitude your goal. *Works Management, 53*(2), 13.

O'Toole, L. (1997). Treating networks seriously: Practical and research-based agendas in public administration. *Public Administration Review, 57*(1), 45-52.

Oblinger, D., & Oblinger, J. (2005). Is it age or IT: First steps toward understanding the net generation. In: D. Oblinger & J. Oblinger (Eds.), *Educating the net generation* (pp. 2.1-2.20). Boulder, CO: Educause.

OECD. (1997). Organisation for economic co-operation and development. *Towards a global information society.* Paris: OECD.

OECD. (2004). Organization for economic co-operation and development. *Information and communication technologies and rural development.* Paris, France: OECD Publication Service.

Oleck, J. (2007a, June 8). Wake County (NC) public library defends MySpace ban. *School Library Journal.* Retrieved August 4, 2007, from http://www.schoollibraryjournal.com/article/CA6449925.html

Oleck, J. (2007b). Libraries use MySpace to attract teens. *School Library Journal, 53*(7), 16-16.

Oliver, A., & Ebers, M. (1998). Networking network studies: An analysis of conceptual configurations in the study of inter-organizational relationships, *Organization Studies, 19,* 549-83.

Oliver, M., & Hyde, J. (1993). Gender differences in sexuality: A meta-analysis. *Psychological Bulletin, 114*(1), 29-51.

Olk, P., & Young, C. (1997). Why members stay in or leave an R&D consortium: Performance and conditions of membership as determinants of continuity. *Strategic Management Journal, 18*(11), 855-877.

Olsen, S. (2006, December 19). Social networks—future portal or fad? *Cnet*. Retrieved November 4, 2007, from http://www.news.com/

Orczy, E. (1905). *The scarlet pimpernel*. Binding Unknown.

Orengo Castellá, V., Zornoza Abad, A., Prieto Alonso, F., & Peiró Silla, J. (2000). The influence of familiarity among group members, group atmosphere and assertiveness on uninhibited behavior through three different communication media. *Computers in Human Behavior, 16,* 141-159.

Orengo Castellá, V., Zornoza Abad, A., Prieto Alonso, F., & Peiró Silla, J. (2000). The influence of familiarity among group members, group atmosphere and assertiveness on uninhibited behavior through three different communication media. *Computers in Human Behavior, 16*(2000), 141-159.

Orlikowski, W. (1991). Integrated information environment or matrix of

Orlikowski, W. (1992). CASE tools as organizational change: Investigating incremental and radical changes in systems development. *MIS Quarterly, 17*(3), 309-340.

Orlikowski, W. (1992). The duality of technology: Rethinking the concept of technology in organizations. *Organization Science, 3*(3), 398-427.

Orlikowski, W., & Robey, D. (1991). Information technology and the structuring of organizations. *Information Systems Research, 2*(2), 143-169.

Orr, A. (2004). *Meeting, mating and cheating: Sex, love, and the new world of online dating*. New Jersey: Reuters.

Ouchi, W. (1980). Markets, bureaucracies, and clans. *Administrative Science Quarterly, 1,* 129-141.

Pantazis, C., Gordon, D., & Levitas, R. (2006). *Poverty and social exclusion in Britain: The millennium survey*. London: The Policy Press.

Parekh, R., & Beresin, E. (2001). Looking for love? Take a cross-cultural walk through the personals. *Academic Psychiatry, 25,* 223-233.

Parks, M., & Floyd, K. (1996). Making friends in cyberspace. *Journal of Communication, 46,* 80-97.

Pasha, S. (2005, August 18). Online dating feeling less attractive. *CNN/Money*. Retrieved April 13, 2006, from http://money.cnn.com/2005/08/18/technology/online_dating/index.htm.

Patchin, J., & Hinduja, S. (n.d.). News: What's new on cyberbullying.us. *Cyberbullying.us*. Retrieved July 22, 2007, from http://www.cyberbullying.us

Patnasingam, P., Gefen, D., & Pavlou, P. (2005). The role of facilitating conditions and institutional trust in electronic marketplaces. *Journal of Electronic Commerce in Organizations, 3*(3), 69-82.

Patterson, A., & Hodgson, J. (2006). A speed-dating story: The lovers guide to marketing excellence. *Journal of Marketing Management, 22,* 455-471.

Paul, D., & McDaniel, R. (2004). A field study of the effect of interpersonal trust on virtual collaborative relationship performance. *MIS Quarterly, 28*(2), 183-227.

Pavlou, P., & Dimoka, A. (2006). The nature and role of feedback text comments in online marketplaces: Implications for trust building, price premiums, and seller differentiation. *Information Systems Research, 17*(4), 392-414.

Pavlou, P., & Gefen, D. (2004). Building effective online marketplaces with institution-based trust. *Information Systems Research, 15*(1), 37-59.

Peluchette, J., & Karl, K. (2007, October). *The prevalence of Facebook faux pas and students' "devil may care" attitudes*. Paper presented at the Midwest Academy of Management Meeting. Kansas City, MO.

Penrose, E. (1959). *The theory of the growth of the firm*. New York, NY: Oxford University Press.

Peres, Y., & Meivar, H. (1986). Self-presentation during courtship: A content analysis of classified advertisements in Israel. *Journal of Comparative Family Studies, 17*(1), 19-31.

Peris, R., Gimeno, M., Pinazo, D., Ortet, G., Carrero, V., Sanchiz, M., & Ibanez, I. (2002). Online chat rooms: Virtual spaces of interaction for socially-oriented people. *CyberPsychology & Behavior, 5*(1), 43-51.

Pettigrew, A. (1987). Context and action in the transformation of the firm. *Journal of Management Studies, 24*(6), 649-670.

Pettigrew, A. (1992). The character and significance of strategy process research. *Strategic Management Journal, 13*, 5-16.

Pew Research Center for the People and the Press. (2007). A portrait of "Generation Next": How young people view their lives, futures and politics. Retrieved November 3, 2007, from http://people-press.org/reports/display.php3?ReportID=300

Pharr, S. & Putnam, R. (eds.). (2000). *Disaffected Democracies: What's Troubling the Trilateral Countries?* Princeton, NJ: Princeton University Press.

Pietromonaco, P., & Carnelley, K. (1994).Gender and working models of attachment: Consequences for perceptions of self and romantic relationships. *Personal Relationships, 1*, 63-82.

Pigg, K. (2001). Applications of community informatics for building community and enhancing civic society. *Information, Communication & Society, 4*(4), 507-527.

Pissarra, J., & Jesuino, J. (2005). Idea generation through computer-mediated communication: The effects of anonymity. *Journal of Management Psychology, 20*(3/4), 275-291.

Pistole, C. (1995). College students ended love relationships: Attachment style and emotion. *Jouranl of College Student Development, 1*, 53-60.

Pitfalls of checking job applicants' personal Web pages. (2006). *Managing Accounts Payable*, 4-6.

Poplin, D. E. (1979). *Communities: A survey of theories and methods of research* (2nd ed.). New York: McMillan.

Porter, M. (1998, November/December). Clusters and the new economics of competition. *Harvard Business Review*.

Pospisil, J. (2006). *Hacking MySpace*. Indianapolis, IN: Wiley Publishing, Inc.

Pouzar, E. (1991). Rehabilitating workers hooked on drugs. *Risk Management, 38*(3), 28-34.

Poyhonen, A., & Smedlund, A. (2004). Assessing intellectual capital creation in regional clusters. *Journal of Intellectual Capital, 5*(3), 351-365.

Prahalad, C. (1997). The role of core competencies in the corporation. In: M. Tushman & P. Anderson (Eds.), *Managing strategic innovation and change* (pp. 172-182). New York, NY: Oxford University Press.

Preece, J. (2000). *Online communities: Designing usability, supporting sociability*. Chichester: John Wiley & Sons.

Preece, J., Nonnecke, B., & Andrews, D. (2004). The top five reasons for lurking: improving community experiences for everyone. *Computers in Human Behavior, 20*(2), 201-223.

Prensky, M. (2005, September/October). Engage me or enrage me: What today's learners demand. *EDUCAUSEreview*. Retrieved March 15, 2007, from http://www.educause.edu/ir/library/pdf/erm0553.pdf

Propp, V. (1969). *Morphology of the folk tale*. Austin, TX: University of Texas Press.

Puccinelli, N. (2006). Putting your best face forward: The impact of customer mood on salesperson evaluation. *Journal of Consumer Psychology, 16*(2), 156-162.

Putnam, R. D. (1993). *Making Democracy Work: Civic Traditions in Modern Italy*. Princeton, NJ: Princeton University Press.

Putnam, R. D. (1996). The strange disappearance of civic America. *The American prospect, 24*.

Putnam, R. D. (2000). *Bowling Alone: The Collapse and Revival of American Community*. New York: Simon and Schuster.

Putnam, R. D. (ed.). (2002). *Democracies in Flux*. Oxford: Oxford University Press.

Qian, Z. (1997). Breaking racial barriers: Variations in interracial marriage between 1980 and 1990. *Demography, 34*, 263-276.

Quansah, E. (2004). *How to identify your soulmate.* Oxford: Trafford Publishing.

Radcliff, B. & Davis, P. (2000). Labor organization and electoral participation in industrial democracies. *American Journal of Political Science, 44*(1), 132-141.

Radin, P. (2006). "To me, it's my life": Medical communication, trust, and activism in cyberspace. *Social Science & Medicine, 62*(3), 591-601.

Rajecki, D., Bledsoe, S., & Rasmussen, J. (1991). Successful personal ads: Gender differences and similarities in offers, stipulations, and outcomes. *Basic and Applied Psychology, 12*, 457-469.

Randall, D., Hughes, J., O'Brien, J., Rodden, T., Rouncefield, M., Sommerville, I., et al. (1999). Banking on the old technology: Understanding the organizational context of 'Legacy' issues. *Communications of the Association of Information Systems, 2*(8), 1-27.

Rao, V., & Rao, V. (1982). *Marriage, the family and women in Indi.* Delhi, India: Heritage Publications.

Rapacki, S. (2007). Social Networking Sites: Why Teens Need Places like MySpace. *Young Adult Library Services, 5*(2), 28-30.

Rapacki, S. (2007). Social networking sites: Why teens need places like MySpace. *YALS: Young Adult Library Services,* Winter, 28-30.

Rash, Jr., W. (1997). *Politics on the Net: Wiring the Political Process.* New York: W.H. Freeman.

Ratnasingam, P. (2005). E-commerce relationships: The impact of trust on relationship continuity. *International Journal of Commerce and Management, 15*(1), 1-17.

Read, B. (2007, January 12). U. of Dayton study examines professional risks of Facebook. *The Chronicle of Higher Education.* Retrieved June 1, 2007, from http://chronicle.com/weekly/v53/i19/19a03102.htm.

Reinin, B., Briggs, R., & Nunamaker, J. (1998). Flaming in the electronic classroom. *Journal of Management Information Systems, 14*(3), 45-59.

Rettberg, C. (2006). Teen book discussions go online. *YALS: Young Adult Library Services, Fall,* 35.

Rheingold, H. (1993). A slice of life in my virtual community. In L. M. Harasim (Ed.), *Global networks: Computers and international communication* (pp. 57-80). Cambridge, MA: The MIT Press.

Rheingold, H. (1993). *The Virtual Community: Homesteading on the Electronic Frontier.* Reading, MA: Addison Wesley.

Rheingold, H. (1994). *The virtual community: Surfing the Internet.* London: Minerva.

Rheingold, H. (1998). Virtual communities. In F. Hesselbein (Ed.), *The community of the future.* San Francisco: Jossey-Bass.

Rheingold, H. (1999). A slice of life in my virtual community. In: P. Ludlow (Ed.), *High noon on the electronic frontier: Conceptual issues in cyberspace.* Cambridge, MA: MIT Press.

Rheingold, H. (2002). *Smart mobs: The next social revolution.* Cambridge, MA: Perseus Books.

Rhiengold, H. (2000). *The virtual community: Homesteading on the electronic frontier.* London: The MIT Press.

Rhiengold, H. (2000). *The virtual community: Homesteading on the electronic frontier.* London: The MIT Press.

Rice, R., & Rogers, E. (1980). Reinvention in the innovation process. *Science Communication, 1*(4), 499-514.

Richardson, J. (2007, January 25). Celebrating safer Internet Day across the world. *Insafe.* Retrieved November 3, 2007, from http://www.saferinternet.org/ww/en/pub/insafe/news/sid2007.htm

Ridings, C., Gefen, D., & Arinze, B. (2002). Some antecedents and effects of trust in virtual communities. *Journal of Strategic Information Systems, 11*(3-4), 271-295.

Ridings, C.M., & Gefen, D. (2004). Virtual Community Attraction: Why People Hang Out Online. *Journal of Computer-Mediated Communication, 10*(1).

Rieber, R., Wiedemann, C., & D'Amato, J. (1979). Obscenity: Its frequency and context of usage as compared in males, non-feminist females, and feminist females. *Journal of Psycholinguistic Research, 83,* 201-223.

Ring, P. (2002). Processes facilitating reliance on trust in inter-organizational networks. In M. Ebers (Ed.), *The formation of inter-organizational networks* (pp. 113-45). Oxford, England: Oxford University Press

Ring, P., & Van de Ven, A. (1994). Developmental processes of cooperative interorganizational relationships. *Academy of Management Review, 19,* 90-118.

Ritter, T. (1999). The networking company. *Industrial Marketing Management, 28,* 467-479.

Roberts, N., & Bradley, R. (1991). Stakeholder collaboration and innovation: A study of public policy initiation at the state level. *Journal of Applied Behavioral Science, 27*(2), 209-227.

Roger Williams University. Policies: Social Networking/Blogging. Retrieved July 3, 2007, from http://www.rwu.edu/newsandevents/publicaffairs/policies/social-networking.htm.

Rogers, C. (1951). *Client-centered therapy.* Boston, MA: Houghton-Mifflin.

Rogers, E. (1995). *Diffusion of innovations* (4th ed.). New York, NY: The Free Press.

Rokach, A., & Neto, F. (2005). Age, culture, and the antecedents of loneliness. *Social Behavior and Personality, 33*(5), 477-494.

Romm, C., Setzekorn, K., & Rippa, P. (2007). *Categorizing and measuring social networking and e-dating Web sites.* Paper presented at the Seventh Annual Global Information Technology Management World Conference (GITM). Naples, Italy.

Romm-Livermore, C., Farag, N., & Oliver, D. (2005). *Turning customers into employees-research in progress.* Paper presented at the Sixth Annual Global Information Technology Management Conference. Anchorage, Alaska.

Ronn, K. (2007, June 13). Social networking: Closer than you think. *Business Week Online,* 12.

Rose, D. (1999). *Internet soul mates: Finding the love of your life through the Internet.* Phoenix, AZ: Productiones Deanna, LLC.

Rosen, L. (2006). Adolescents in MySpace: Identity formation, friendship and sexual predators. Retrieved July 5, 2007, from http://www.csudh.edu/psych/Adolescents%20in%20MySpace%20-%20Executive%20Summary.pdf

Rosenberg, M. (1965). *Society and the adolescent self-image.* Princeton, NJ: Princeton University Press.

Rosenberg, M., Schooler, C., & Schoenbach, C. (1989). Self-esteem and adolescent problems: Modeling reciprocal effects. *American Sociological Review, 54,* 1004-1018.

Rosenbush, S. (2005). News Corp.'s Place in MySpace, *BusinessWeek,* July 19. Retrieved August 22, 2007, from http://www.businessweek.com/technology/content/jul2005/tc20050719_5427_tc119.htm

Rosenfeld, M. (2005). A critique of exchange theory in mate selection. *The American Journal of Sociology, 110*(5), 1284-2027.

Rothschild, L., & Darr, A. (2005). Technological incubators and the social construction of innovation networks: An Israeli case study. *Technovation, 25,* 59-67.

Rowley, D. (1994). *Usability testing in the field: Bridging the laboratory to the user.* Boston, MA.

Rycroft, R. (2003). Technology-based globalization indicators: The creativity of innovation network data. *Technology in Society, 25*(3), 299-317.

Sadalla, E., Kenrick, D., & Venshure, B. (1987). Dominance and heterosexual attraction. *Journal of Personality and Social Psychology, 52,* 730-738.

Salam, A., Iyer, L., Palvia, P., & Singh, R. (2005). Trust in e-commerce. *Communications of the ACM, 48(2),* 72-77.

Santovec, M. (2006). Using online networking to engage and retain students. *Recruitment and retention in higher education, 20,* 1-5.

Sarwar, B.M., et al. (2001). Item-based collaborative filtering recommendation algorithms. *The 10th Int'l World Wide Web Conference* (pp. 285-295). ACM Press.

Sasaki, T. (2007). Social networking changes the relationship between the net and the teal (in Japanese). In: Shoeisha (Ed.), *A study of SNS,* (pp. 6-41). Tokyo, Japan: Shoeisha, Co. Ltd.

Saussure, Ferdinand de (1915/1959). *Course in general linguistics* (W. Baskin, Trans.). New York: McGraw-Hill.

Saxenian, A. (1994). *Regional advantage: Culture and competition in Silicon Valley and Route 128.* Cambridge, MA: Harvard University Press.

Scarrow, S. (2001). Parties without members? In R. J. Dalton & M. Wattenberg (Eds.), *Parties Without Partisans.* New York: Oxford University Press.

Scharlott, B., & Christ, W. (1995). Overcoming relationship-initiation barriers: The impact of a computer-dating system on sex role, shyness, and appearance inhibitions. *Computers in Human Behavior, 11,* 191-204.

Scheel, C. (2002). Knowledge clusters of technological innovation systems. *Journal of Knowledge Management, 6*(4), 356-367.

Schellong, A. (2006, October 12). Social networking services and disaster management in Japan. *Complexity and Social Networks Blog of the Institute for Quantitative Social Science and the Program on Networked Governance, Harvard University.* Retrieved November 13, 2006, from http://www.iq.harvard.edu/blog/netgov/networked_governance/.

Schleiermacher, F. (1809/1998). General hermeneutics. In A. Bowie (Ed.), *Schleiermacher: Hermeneutics and criticism* (pp. 227-268). Cambridge University Press.

Schonfeld, E. (2006, July 27). Cyworld ready to attach MySpace. *Business 2.0 Magazine.* Retrieved October 26, 2007, from http://money.cnn.com/magazines/business2/business2_archive/2006/08/01/8382263/index.htm

Schoonhoven, C., & Jelinek, M. (1997). Dynamic tension in innovative, high-technology firms: Managing rapid technological change through organizational structure. In: M. Tushman & P. Anderson (Eds.), *Managing strategic innovation and change* (pp. 233-254) New York, NY: Oxford University Press.

Schubert, P., & Ginsburg, M. (2000). Virtual communities of transaction: The role of personalization in electronic commerce. *Electronic Markets, 10*(1), 45-55.

Schulte, T. (1999). *Group computing workspace.* Unpublished dissertation, University of St. Gallen, St. Gallen.

Schultze, U., & Leidner, D. (2002). Studying knowledge management in information systems research: Discourses and theoretical assumptions. *MIS Quarterly, 26*(3), 213-242.

Schwartz, E. (1996). *Netactivism: How Citizens Use the Internet.* Sebastapol, CA: Songline Studios.

Schwartz, S. (1994). Beyond individualism/collectivism: new cultural dimensions of value. In: U. Kim, H. Triandis, C. Kagitcibasi, S. Choi, & G. Yoon (Eds.), *Individualism and collectivism: Theory, method and applications* (pp. 85-119). Thousand Oaks, CA: Sage.

Schweitzer, S. (2005, September 26). When students open up—a little too much. *The Boston Globe.*

Scott-Joynt, J. (2005). *What Myspace means to Murdoch.* London: BBC Online. Retrieved from http://news.bbc.co.uk/1/hi/business/4697671.stm.

Seelye, K. (2006, August 23). Microsoft to provide and sell ads on Facebook, the Web site. *The New York Times.*

Sellers, M. (2005, October/December). Moogle, Google, and garbage cans: The impact of technology on decision making. *International Journal of Leadership in Education, 8,* 365-374.

Selnow, G. (1985). Sex differences in uses and perceptions of profanity. *Sex Roles, 12,* 303-312.

Selnow, G.W. (1998). *Electronic Whistle-Stops: The Impact of the Internet on American Politics.* Westport, CT: Praeger.

Serra, J. (1982). *Image analysis and mathematical morphology.* London: Academic Press.

Seymour, S. (1999). *Women, family and child care in India: A world in transition.* Cambridge: Cambridge University Press.

Shah, D. (2002). Nonrecursive models of internet use and community engagement: Questioning whether time spent online erodes social capital. *Journalism & Mass Communication Quarterly, 79*(4), 964-987.

Shah, D.V., Kwak, N., & Holbert, R.L. (2001). "Connecting" and "disconnecting" with civic life: Patterns of Internet use and the production of social capital. *Political Communication, 18*(2), 141-162.

Shardanand, U., & Maes, P. (1995). Social information filtering: Algorithms for automating 'word of mouth'. *Proceedings of the ACM SIGCHI Conference on Human Factors in Computing Systems* (pp. 210-217).

Shen, X., Radakrishnan, T., & Georganas, N. (2002). vCOM: Electronic commerce in a collaborative virtual worlds. *Electronic Commerce Research and Applications, 1,* 281-300.

Sher, J. (2007, May 1). The not-so-long arm of the law. *USA Today.* Retrieved May 24, 2007, from Academic Search Elite database.

Sheth, A., Ramakrishnan, C., & Thomas, C. (2005). Semantics for the Semantic Web: The implicit, the formal and the powerful. *International Journal on Semantic Web and Information Systems, 1*(1), 1-18.

Shumar, W., & Tenninger, K. (2002). Introducing: On conceptualizing community. In: K. Renninger & W. Shumar (Eds.), *Building online communities: Learning and change in cyberspace* (pp. 1-20). Cambridge: Cambridge University Press.

Sickler, E. (2007, March) Students comment on Facebook. *University Business Daily.* Retrieved March 21, 2007, from http://www.universitybusiness.com/viewarticle. aspx?articleid=724&pf=1

Siddiquee, A., & Kagan, C. (2006). The Internet, empowerment, and identity: An exploration of participation by refugee women in a community Internet project (CIP) in the United Kingdom (UK). *Journal of Community & Applied Social Psychology, 16*(3), 189-206.

Siklos, R. (2007, January 21). Big media's crush on social networking. *The New York Times.*

Sills, J. (2007). Love at work. *Psychology Today, 40*(2), 64-65.

Silverman, P. (1987). The impact of parental death on college-age women. *Psychiatric Clinics of North America, 10,* 387-404.

Silverstein, J., & Lasky, M. (2004). *Online dating for dummies.* Hoboken, NJ: Wiley Publishing Inc.

Simmel, G. (1908/1971). How is society possible? In D. N. Levine (Ed.), *On individuality and social forms: Selected writings.* University of Chicago Press.

Simon, E., & Majewski, E. (2007, April 20). A qualitative study of online discussions about teen alcohol & drug use. *Caron Treatment Centers.* Retrieved July 5, 2007, from http://www.caron.org/pdfs/Report%20on%20Teen%20Online%20Conversations.pdf

Smith, A. (2001). Problems of conflict management in virtual communities. In: M. Smith & P. Kollock (Eds.), *Communities in cyberspace.* London: Routledge.

Smith, C. (2000). Content analysis and narrative analysis. In: H. Reis & C. Judd (Eds.), *Handbook of research methods in social and personal psychology.* Cambridge: Cambridge University Press.

Smith, C. (2000). Content analysis and narrative analysis. In: H. Reis & C. Judd (Eds.), *Handbook of research methods in social and personal psychology.* Cambridge: Cambridge University Press.

Smith, J. (2006). *Becoming a part of the community.* WARC Report, October 2006.

Snow, C. & Thomas, J. (1993). Building networks: Broker roles and behaviours. In P. Lorange, B. Chakravarthy, J. Roos, & A. Van de Ven (Eds.), *Implementing strategic processes: Change, learning and co-operation* (pp. 217-38). Oxford: Blackwell.

Sorensen, E. (2002). Democratic theory and network governance. *Administrative Theory & Praxis, 24*(4), 693-720.

Spears, R., Abrams, D., Sheeran, P., Abraham, C., & Marks, D. (1991). Social judgments of sex and blame in the context of AIDS: Gender and linguistic frame. *British Journal of Social Psychology, 30,* 37-48.

Sprecher, S., McKinney, K., & Orbuch, T. (1987). Has the double standard disappeared? An experimental test. *Social Psychology Quarterly, 50,* 24-31.

Sproull, L., & Kiesler, S. (1991). *Connections: New ways of working in the networked organization.* Cambridge, MA: The MIT Press.

Staab, S., Santini, S., Nack, F., Steels, L., & Maedche, A. (2002). Emergent semantics. *IEEE Intelligent Systems, 17*(1), 78-86.

Stables, A., & Goodwyn, A. (2004). *Learning to read critically in language and literacy.* London: Sage Publications.

Staley, C. (1978). Male-female use of expletives: A heck of a difference in expectations. *Anthropological Linguistics, 20,* 367-380.

Stanley, T. (2006, April 17). Online-Dating sites get stood up by consumers. *Advertising Age.* Retrieved November 5, 2007, from Business Source Premier database.

Stanoevska-Slabeva, K., & Schmid, B. F. (2000). Requirements analysis for community supporting platforms based on the media reference model. *Electronic Markets, 10*(4), 250-257.

Stanton, J., & Weiss, E. (2000). Electronic monitoring in their own words: An exploratory study of employee's experiences with new types of surveillance. *Computer in Human Behavior, 16,* 423-440.

Sternberg, R. (1986). A triangular theory of love. *Psychological Review, 93*(2), 119-135.

Sternberg, R. (1986). A triangular theory of love. *Psychological Review, 93*(2), 119-135.

Stevens, T. (2007). S.49: Protecting children in the 21st century act. 110th Congress. Retrieved July 23, 2007, from http://thomas.loc.gov/cgi-bin/query/F?c110:1:./temp/~c110YE7UM4:e7495

Stevens, V. (2004). Webhead communities: Writing tasks interleaved with synchronous online communication and Web page development. In: J. Willis & B. Leaver (Eds.), *Task-based instruction in foreign language education: Practices and programs.* Georgetown, VA: Georgetown University Press.

Stevenson, T. (2002). Communities of tomorrow. *Futures, 34*(8), 735-744.

Stewart, K. (2006). How hypertext links influence consumer perceptions to build and degrade trust online. *Journal of Management Information Systems, 23*(1), 183-210.

Stockman, F., & Doreian, P. (1997). Evolution of social networks: Processes and principles. In: P. Doreian & F. Stockman (Eds.), *Evolution of social networks.* London: Routledge.

Stoehr, T. (2002). *Managing e-business projects: 99 key success factors.* London: Springer.

Stone, B. (2006, August 21-28). Web of risks. *Newsweek.*

Stone, B. (2007, March 3). Social networking's next phase. *The New York Times.*

Stowers, G.N.L. (1999). Becoming cyberactive: State and local governments on the World Wide Web. *Government Information Quarterly, 16*(2), 111-127.

Suchman, L. (1987). *Plans and situated actions: The problem of human-machine communication.* Cambridge: Cambridge University Press.

Suire, R. (2004). Des réseaux de l'entrepreneur aux ressorts du créatif Quelles stratégies pour les territoires? *Revue Internationale PME, 17*(2), 123-143.

Sullivan, S. (2006). One-in-four hiring managers have used Internet search engines to screen job candidates; One-in-ten have used social networking sites. *CareerBuilder.com Survey Finds.* Retrieved August 26, 2007, from http://www.careerbuilder.com/share/aboutus/pressreleasesdetail.aspx?id=pr331&ed=12%2F31%2F2006&sd=10%2F26%2F2006&cbRecursionCnt=1&cbsid=a5015667d80f4b599c46d2b08f406b67-241548812-RI-4&ns_siteid=ns_us_g_One%2din%2dFour_Hirin_.

Survey reveals bias against recovering alcoholics and addicts. (1999). *Alcoholism & Drug Abuse Weekly, 11*(48), 3.

Susman, G. I., & Evered, R. D. (1978). An assessment of the scientific merits of action research. *Administrative Science Quarterly, 23*(14), 582-603.

Sutton, W. A., & Munson, T. (1976). *Definitions of community.* New York: American Sociological Association.

Swanson, E.B. (1988). *Information System Implementation: Bridging the Gap between Design and Utilization.* Irwin, Homewood, IL.

Symons, D. (1979). *The evolution of human sexuality.* New York, NY: Oxford University Press.

Takahashi, D. (2007, August 21). Virtual world Vside hits right note. *San Jose Mercury News.* Retrieved October 19, 2007, from Newspaper Source database.

Tan, M. (1999). Creating the digital economy: Strategies and perspectives from Singapore. *International Journal of Electronic Commerce, 3*(3), 105-22.

Tanaka, J.S., & Huba, G.J. (1985). A fit index for covariance structure model under arbitrary GLS estimation. *British Journal of Mathematical and Statistical Psychology, 38*(2), 197-201.

Tapscott, D. (1998). *Growing up digital: The rise of the Net Generation.* New York, NY: McGraw-Hill.

Tapscott, D., & Williams, A. (2006). *Wikinomics: How mass collaboration changes everything.* London: Penguin Books.

Taylor, S. (2006). Seeking secrets in cyberspace. *Staffing Management, 2*(3).

Technology appropriation by young people. Paper presented at the The 35th Hawaii International Conference on System Sciences. Hawaii.

Teece, D. (1998). Design issues for innovative firms: Bureaucracy, incentives and industrial structure. In: A. Chandler Jr., P. Hagstrom, & O. Solvell (Eds.), *The dynamic firm: The role of technology, strategy, organization and regions* (pp. 134-165). New York, NY: Oxford University Press.

Terada, S. (2007, October 25). Japanese businesses setting up virtual shop in Second Life. *The Japan Times.* Retrieved November 4, 2007, from McClatchy-Tribune Collection database.

Terdiman, D. (2004, July 22). Open arms for open source news. *Wired News.*

Teten, D., & Allen, S. (2005). *The virtual handshake: Opening doors and close deals online.* New York, NY: American Management Association.

The Well website. www.well.com/aboutwell.html.

Thierer, A. (2007). Social networking and age verification: Many hard questions; no easy solutions. *Progress on point, 14.5,* 1-33.

Thomas, J.C. & Streib, G. (2003). The new face of government: Citizen-initiated contacts in the era of e-government. *Journal of Public Administration Research and Theory, 13*(1), 83-101.

Thornhill, R., & Thornhill, N. (1983). Human rape: An evolutionary analysis. *Ethology and Sociobiology, 4,* 137-173.

Thyer, B. (2001). *The handbook of social world research methods.* London: Sage Publications.

Tinto, V. (1982). Limits of theory and practice in student attrition. *Journal of Higher Education, 53,* 687-700.

Tinto, V. (1993). *Leaving college: Rethinking the causes and cures of student attrition.* Chicago, IL: The University of Chicago Press.

Tiplady, R. (2005, February 8). Eye on Europe. *Business Week.* Retrieved December 2, 2007, from http://www.businessweek.com.

Tolbert, C.J. & McNeal, R.S. (2003). Unraveling the effects of the Internet on political participation? *Political Research Quarterly, 56*(2), 175-185.

Toulouse, C. & Luke, T. W. (eds.). (1998). *The Politics of Cyberspace.* London: Routledge.

Townsend, J. (1993). Sexuality and partner selection: Sex differences among college students. *Ethology and Sociobiology, 14,* 305-330.

Townsend, J., & Wasserman, T. (1997). The perception of sexual attractiveness: Sex differences in variability. *Achieves of Sexual Behavior, 26,* 243-268.

Townsend, J., & Wasserman, T. (1997). The perception of sexual attractiveness: Sex differences in variability. *Archives of Sexual Behavior, 26,* 243-268.

Trompenaars, F., & Hampden-Turner, C. (1998). *Riding the waves of culture: Understanding cultural diversity in global business* (2nd ed.). New York, NY: McGraw-Hill.

TruDating. (2006). Online dating service directory. Retrieved May 25, 2006, from the http://www.trudating.com/.

Turkle. (1997). *Life on the screen: Identity in the age of the Internet.* New York, NY: Touchstone.

Tyson-Rawson, K. (1996). Adolescent responses to the death of a parent. In: C. Corr & D. Balk (Eds.), *Handbook of adolescent death and bereavement,* (pp. 155-172). New York, NY: Springer.

United Nations. (1998). *Knowledge societies: Information technology for sustainable development.* Report prepared by R. Mansell & U. Wehn. Oxford: United

Nations Commission on Science and Technology for Development/Oxford University Press.

United Nations/American Society for Public Administration (2002). *Bench Marking e-Government: A Global Perspective.* New York: United Nations/DPEPA.

Upoc Networks Website. www.upocnetworks.com.

Urberg, K. (1979). Sex role conceptualization in adolescents and adults. *Developmental Psychology, 15,* 90-92.

Uslaner, E. (2004). Trust online, trust off-line. *Communications of the ACM, 47*(4), 28-29.

Uslaner, E. M. (2004). Trust, civic engagement, and the Internet. *Political Communication, 21*(2), 223-242.

Usunier, J. (1996). *Marketing across cultures* (2nd ed.). Hertfordshire, UK: Prentice Hall.

Valkenburg, P., Peter, J., & Schouten, A. (2006). Friend networking sites and their relationship to adolescents' well-being and social self-esteem. *CyberPsychology & Review, 9,* 584-590.

Valkenburg, P.M., Peter, J., & Schouten, A.P. (2006). Friend Networking Sites and Their Relationship to Adolescents' Well-Being and Social Self-Esteem. *CyberPsychology & Behavior, 9* (5), 584- 590.

Van de Ven, A. & Poole, M. (1995). Explaining development and change in organizations. *Academy of Management Review, 20*(3), 510-540.

Van den Hooff, B., de Ridder, J. & Aukema, E. (2004). Exploring the eagerness to share knowledge: The role of social capital and ICT in knowledge sharing. In M. Huysman, & V. Wulf (Eds.), *Social capital and information technology* (Chapter 7). Cambridge, USA and London, England: The MIT Press.

Venkatesh, V., & Morris, M. (2000). Why Don't Men Ever Stop to Ask for Directions? Gender, Social Influence, and Their Role in Technology Acceptance and Usage Behavior. *MIS Quarterly, 24*(1), 115-139.

Verba, S., Nie, N., & Kim, J.-on (1978). *Participation and Political Equality: A Seven-Nation Comparison.* New York: Cambridge University Press.

Virtual Worlds Management. (2007, October 31). Active Worlds embeds 3-D worlds in Facebook. *Virtual Worlds News*. Retrieved November 4, 2007, from http://www.virtualworldsnews.com/2007/10/active-words-e.htm

Vogel, D. (1999). *Financial investigations: A financial approach to detecting and resolving crimes*. London: DIANE Publishing.

von Hippel, E. (1988). *The sources of innovation*. New York, NY: Oxford University Press.

von Hippel, E. (2001). Innovation by user communities: Learning from open-source software. *MIT Sloan Management Review, 42*(4) 82-86.

von Hippel, E. (2005). *Democratizing innovation*. Cambridge, MA: MIT Press.

von Oetinger, B. (2005). From idea to innovation: Making creativity real. *The Journal of Business Strategy, 25*(5), 35-41.

Vranica, S. (2007, January 8). P&G boosts social-networking phenomenon. *The Wall Street Journal.*

Wagstaff, E. (2007, February 28). Court case decision reveals dangers of networking sites. *Daily Nexus*. University of California, Santa Barbara. Retrieved June 28, 2007, from http://www.dailynexus.com/article.php?a=13440.

Waits, M. (2000). The added value of the industry cluster approach to economic analysis, strategy development, and service delivery. *Economic Development Quarterly, 14*(1), 35-50.

Wakabayashi, D. (2007, October 25). Microsoft beats Google to Facebook stake. *Reuters*. Retrieved November 4, 2007, from http://www.reuters.com.

Wallace, P. (2001). *The psychology of the Internet*. Cambridge: Cambridge University Press.

Wallace, P. (2001). *The psychology of the Internet*. Cambridge: Cambridge University Press

Walther, J. (1996). Computer-mediated communication: Impersonal, interpersonal and hyperpersonal interaction. *Communication Research, 23*, 3-43.

Walther, J. (1996). Computer-mediated communication: Impersonal, interpersonal, and hyperpersonal interaction. *Communication Research, 23,* 3-43.

Walther, J., Slovacek, C., & Tidwell, L. (2001). Is a picture worth a thousand words? Photographic images in long-term and short-term computer-mediated communication. *Communication Research, 28,* 105-134.

Wandel, T. (2007, July). *Educational institution responses to online social networking*. Paper presented at the World Communication Association Conference. Brisbane, Australia.

Wang, P. (2004). Recommendation based on personal preference. In: Y-Q. Zhang, A. Kandel, T. Lin, & Y. Yao (Eds.), *Computational Web intelligence: Intelligent technology for Web applications*. London: World Scientific Publishing (UK) Ltd.

Warkentin, C., & Mingst, K. (2000). International institutions, the state, and global civil society in the age of the World Wide Web. *Global Governance, 6*(2), 237-257.

Wasserman, S. (1994). *Social network analysis: Methods and applications*. Cambridge University Press.

Waston, G. (1982). *Learning from case studies*. London: Prentice-hall International.

Watson, G., & Johnson, D. (1972). *Social psychology: Issues and insights*. Philadelphia: J. B. Lippincott.

Watson-Manheim, M. B., & Belanger, F. (2002). Exploring communication-based work processes in virtual work environments. In *Paper presented at the 35th Annual Hawaii International Conference on System Sciences*, Hawaii.

Watts, D.J., Dodds, P., & Newman, M. (2002). Identity and Search in Social Networks. *Science, 296* (5571) 1302-1306.

Webb, G., Hennrikus, D., Kelman, G., Gibberd, R., & Sanson-Fisher, R. (1994). The relationships between high-risk and problem drinking and the occurrence of work injuries and related absences. *Journal of Studies on Alcohol, 55*(4), 434-446.

Weber, L.M., Loumakis, A., & Bergman, J. (2003). Who participates and why? An analysis of citizens on the Internet and the mass public. *Social Science Computer Review, 21*(1), 26-42.

Wellman, B., & Gulia, M. (1999). The network basis of social support: A network is more than the sum of its ties. In B. Wellman (Ed.), *Networks in the global village: Life in contemporary communities* (pp. 83-118). Boulder, CO: Westview Press.

Wellman, B., Haase, A. Q., Witte, J., & Hampton, K. (2001). Does the internet increase, decrease, or supplement social capital? Social networks, participation, and community commitment. *American Behavioral Scientist, 45*(3), 436-455.

Weng, M. (2007). *A multimedia social-networking community for mobile devices.* Unpublished thesis. Interactive Telecommunications Program, Tisch School of the Arts/ New York University.

Wenger, E. (1997). *Communities of practice: Learning, meaning, and identity.* Cambridge: Cambridge University Press.

Wenger, E., McDermott, R., & Snyder, W. M. (2002). *Cultivating communities of practice: A guide to managing knowledge.* Boston: Harvard Business School Press.

Werry, C. (2001). Imagined electronic community: Representations of online community in business texts. In: C. Werry & M. Mowbray (Eds.), *Online communities: Commerce, community action and the virtual university.* Upper Saddle River, NJ: Prentice Hall.

Wheelan, S. (1999). *Creating effective teams: A guide for members and leaders* (p. 154). Thousand Oaks, CA: Sage Publications.

Wheeless, L., & Grotz, J. (1977). The measurement of trust and its relationship to self-disclosure. *Communication Research, 3*(3), 250-257.

White, E. (2007, January, 1). Employers reach out to recruit with Facebook. *Wall Street Journal,* p. D3.

White, E. (2007, January, 1). Employers reach out to recruit with Facebook. *Wall Street Journal,* p. D3.

Whitman, B., & Lawrence, S. (2002). Inferring descriptions and similarity for music from community metadata. In *"Voices of Nature," Proceedings of the 2002 International Computer Music Conference* (pp. 591-598).

Whitman, B., & Smaragdis, P. (2002). Combining musical and cultural features for intelligent style detection. *Proceedings of the 3rd International Conference on Music Information Retrieval.*

Whitty, M. (2002). Liar, Liar! An examination of how open, supportive and honest people are in chat rooms. *Computers in Human Behavior, 18*(4), 343-352.

Whitty, M. (2003). Cyber-flirting: Playing at love on the Internet. *Theory and Psychology, 13*(3), 339-357.

Whitty, M. (2004). Cyber-flirting: An examination of men's and women's flirting behaviour both off-line and on the Internet. *Behaviour Change, 21*(2), 115-126.

Whitty, M. (2007). The art of selling one's self on an online dating site: The BAR Approach. In: M. Whitty, A. Baker, & J. Inman (Eds.), *Online matchmaking* (pp. 57-69). Houndmills: Palgrave Macmillan.

Whitty, M. (in press). Revealing the 'real' me, searching for the 'actual' you: Presentations of self on an Internet dating site. *Computers in Human Behavior.*

Whitty, M., & Buchanan, T. (2007, manuscript under preparation). What's in a 'screen' name? The types of screen names online daters find attractive.

Whitty, M., & Carr, A. (2006). *Cyberspace romance: The psychology of online relationships.* Basingstoke: Palgrave Macmillan.

Whitty, M., & Gavin, J. (2001). Age/sex/location: Uncovering the social cues in the development of online relationships. *CyberPsychology & Behaviour, 4,* 623-630.

Wiesenfeld, B. M., Raghuram, S., & Garud, R. (1999). Communication patterns as determinants of organizational identification in a virtual organization. *Organization Science, 10*(6), 777-790.

Wikipedia. (2007). Social network service. Retrieved July 11, 2007, from http://en.wikipedia.org/wiki/Social_network_service.

Wildermuth, S. (2004). The effects of stigmatizing discourse on the quality of online relationships. *Cyber-Psychology & Behavior, 7*(1), 73-84.

Wilhelm, A. (n.d.). *Democracy in the Digital Age: Challenges to Political Life in Cyberspace.* New York: Routledge.

Williams, A. (2006, February 29). Here I am taking my own picture. *The New York Times,* p. 9.1. Retrieved August 4, 2007, from New York Times database.

Williams, R., Stewart, J., & Slack, R. (2005). *Social learning in technological innovation—Experimenting with information communication technologies.* Cheltenham, UK and Northampton, USA: Edward Elgar.

Williamson, D. (2007, September). Kids and teens: Virtual worlds open new universe. *eMarketer.* Retrieved October 8, 2007, from http://www.emarketer.com/Report. aspx?code=emarketer_2000437&src=report_summary_reportsell

Wilson, L. (2007, September 14). Web stalkers targeted. *The Australian.* Retrieved October 19, 2007, from Newspaper Source database.

Wilson, R., & Keil, F. (2001). *MIT encyclopedia of the cognitive sciences.* Cambridge: MIT Press.

Winter, R. (2002). An executive MBA program in business engineering: A curriculum focusing on change. *Journal of IT Education, 1*(4), 279-288.

Wolak, J., Mitchell, K., & Finkelhor, D. (2006). Online victimization of youth: Five years later. *National Center for Missing & Exploited Children.* Retrieved July 15, 2007, from http://208.252.21.169/en_US/publications/NC167.pdf

Wood, D., & Wood, G. (1991). Toward a comprehensive theory of collaboration. *Journal of Applied Behavioral Science, 27*(2), 139-162.

Wood, J. (1995). *Relational communication.* Belmont, CA: Wadsworth.

Wood, J. (1996). *Everyday encounters: An introduction to interpersonal communication.* Belmont, CA: Wadsworth.

Woodhead, B. (2007, October 16). Survey finds Aussie kids are the web's pro surfers. *The Australian.* Retrieved October 19, 2007, from Newspaper Source database.

World Bank (1999). *World development report 1998/99: Knowledge for development.* New York: Oxford University Press.

Wrenn, R. (1999). The grieving college student. In: J. Davidson & K. Doka (Eds.), *Living with grief: At work, at school, at worship,* (pp. 131-141). Levittown, PA: Brunner/Mazel.

Wysocki, D. (1998). Let your fingers to do the talking: Sex on an adult chat line. *Sexualities, 1,* 425-452.

Wysocki, D., & Thalken, J. (2007). Whips and chains? Fact or fiction? Content analysis of sadomasochism in Internet personal advertisements. In: M. Whitty, A. Baker, & J. Inman (Eds.), *Online matchmaking* (pp. 178-196). Houndmills: Palgrave Macmillan.

Yancey, G., & Yancey, S. (1998). Interracial dating: Evidence from personal advertisements. *Journal of Family Issues, 19*(3), 334-348.

Yang, G. (2003). The Internet and the rise of a transnational Chinese cultural sphere. *Media, Culture & Society, 25,* 469-490.

Ye, J. (2006). Seeking love online: A cross-cultural examination of personal advertisements on American and Chinese dating Web sites. *Global Media Journal, 5*(8).

Zadeh, L.A. (2004, Fall). Precisiated natural language. *AI Magazine.*

Zajonc, R. (1962). Response suppression in perceptual defense. *Journal of Experimental Psychology, 64,* 206-214.

Ziv, N. (2005). Toward a new paradigm of innovation on the mobile platform: Redefining the roles of content providers, technology companies, and users. *Proceedings of the Mobile Business Conference.* Sydney, Australia.

Ziv, N. (2008). Interview with Steve Spencer, CEO of Upoc on January 15, 2008 in New York City.

Ziv, N., & Mulloth, B. (2006). An exploration on mobile social networking: Dodgeball as a case in point. *Proceedings of the Mobile Business Conference.* Copenhagen, Demark.

Ziv, N., & Mulloth, B. (2007). The evolution of a mobile services provider in a global context: Upoc as a case in point. *Proceedings of the Mobile Business Conference.* Toronto, Ontario.

Zmud, R.W. (1979). Individual differences and MIS success: A review of the empirical literature. *Management Science, 25*(10), 966-79.

Zollo, M., Reuer, J., & Singh, J. (2002). Interorganizational routines and performance in strategic alliances. *Organizational Science, 13*(6), 701-713.

Zuboff, S. (1988). *In the age of the smart machine.* New York, NY: Basic Books.

About the Contributors

Celia Romm-Livermore is full professor at Wayne State University, Detroit. She published three books: *Virtual Politicking* (1999), *Electronic commerce: A global perspective* (1998), and *Doing business on the Internet* (1999). She also published over a 150 journal articles, chapters in collective volumes, and conference papers. Her research was published in such journals as: *The Harvard Business Review, Communications of the ACM, Information & Management,* and *Transactions on Information Systems.*

Kristina Setzekorn is a financial advisor with Smith Barney, Inc. in Evansville, IN. She earned her PhD at Southern Illinois University-Carbondale, where she majored in MIS and minored in operations management. Her MBA is from Southern Illinois University-Edwardsville and her BS is from Iowa State University. In her previous academic career, Dr. Setzekorn taught MIS, global IT strategy, telecommunications, microeconomics and operations. Her research dealt with performance impacts of information and coordination, at individual, organizational and supply chain levels.

* * *

Nisreen Bahnan is assistant professor at Salem State College Bertolon School of Business in Salem, Massachusetts. She has earned her PhD in business studies from Temple University in Philadelphia, Pennsylvania. She is presently teaching principles of marketing, marketing management and consumer behavior. She has presented at conferences and published articles in the fields of services marketing and consumer behavior.

Jonathan Bishop, a chartered IT professional, is a director of Glamorgan Blended Learning Ltd and chair of its Centre for Research into Online Communities and e-Learning Systems. He has developed and researched online communities since the 1990s and is noted for inventing the Circle of Friends social networking technology and the PARLE e-learning system for which he was a finalist in the Innovation category of the New Statesman New Media Awards in 2004. He holds a BSc(Hons) in multimedia studies, specializing in online communities for the Web and TV, an MSc in e-Learning, specializing in persuasive technology and an LLM in European union law, specializing in the e-learning industry. In his spare time he enjoys taking part in debating competitions, swimming, listening to music, watching films, and playing video games.

Linda Jane Coleman is a former bank officer, production manager, cash control manager, and board of director's member. She has published many articles and consults with businesses and universities in the areas of human resources, and marketing. Currently, Ms. Coleman is chairperson of the Marketing and Decision Sciences committee and a professor of marketing at Salem State College Bertolon School of Business in Salem, Massachusetts. She is presently teaching international marketing and special topics in marketing.

Nicolas Ducheneaut is a senior member of the research staff in the Computing Science Lab at the Palo Alto Research Center. Prior to joining PARC, he obtained his PhD from the University of California, Berkeley. His research focuses on understanding how people interact in online social spaces, and what technology could be built to support these interactions better. Recently, he co-founded the PlayOn project and conducted the largest study of player behavior in massively multiplayer games to date, collecting data about the social networks created by more than 300,000 characters over two years in World of Warcraft. More information about his research can be found in his publications at http://www.parc.com/nicolas.

Harsha Gangadharbatla, PhD (The University of Texas at Austin) is an assistant professor in the Department of Advertising at Texas Tech University. His research interests include, but are not limited to, interactive advertising, social and economic effects of advertising, and alternative media strategies. His work has appeared in the *Journal of Interactive Advertising, the International Journal of Advertising,* and *the Journal of Computer Mediated Communication* among others.

Sudhir H. Kale, PhD is professor of marketing and co-director of the Globalization and Development Center at Bond University in Australia. With over 100 publications to his credit, Dr. Kalé's research has been published in top scholarly journals including *Journal of Marketing, Journal of Marketing Research, Journal of Applied Psychology, Journal of International Business Studies,* and *Journal of International Marketing.* Of late, he has shifted his research focus to the study of customer relationship management (CRM), spirituality in marketing, and the marketing aspects of casino management. Dr. Kalé serves on the editorial review board of several journals in gaming, management and marketing. He has conducted over 200 executive development seminars and workshops across four continents on a range of topics such as the Enneagram, applications of the Myers-Briggs type indicator in management, corporate culture, and psychological aspects of selling.

Katherine A. Karl is a professor in the graduate school of management at Marshall University. She received her MBA and PhD in business administration from Michigan State University with a major in organizational behavior and human resource management. Her research publications have focused on the topics of job values, performance feedback, the use of videotaped feedback in management education and development, social networking Web sites, and human resource policies and practices regarding employment terminations, workplace attire, workplace romance, and workplace fun.

Max Kennedy is a PhD student in decision science and information systems and teaches classes at the University of Kentucky. His research interests include trust, privacy, e-commerce, social networks, and the emerging Web 2.0. He is a member of AIS, ACM, Pinnacle Honor Society and the Project Management Institute (SWOPMI)—where he received an award for leading a project team in a sponsored contest. He also owns an online business called *Only the Best*, and has worked as a software engineer in industry. He has a B.S. in anthropology and a M.S. IS from Northern Kentucky University, and a forthcoming MBA.

Ashley King is currently undertaking a bachelor's degree in business, specializing in finance, at Wayne State University, Michigan. She expects to graduate in May 2008. In addition to her studies, she plays Division I ice hockey at Wayne State University. Her future plans include moving back to her hometown of Winnipeg, Manitoba, where she intends to pursue a career in finance.

Gail Livermore heads the research department at Spin Master Ltd., an international Canadian children's entertainment company. Gail's bachelor's degree in marketing and human resources management is from Central Queensland University in Australia. She earned her MBA at Wilfred Laurier University, Canada.

Maryann Mori is currently teen specialist librarian for the Evansville Vanderburgh Public Library in Evansville, Indiana, where she also supervises the Popular Materials Center at EVPL's Central Library. She has also worked in children's services and adult reference. Mori received her MLIS from the University of Illinois with a special focus on youth services. She completed her undergraduate work in liberal studies from the University of Evansville. She has created a successful teen program at EVPL with an emphasis on current teen trends, including gaming, and anime/manga. She has presented at the Internet Librarian conference in Monterey, California and is scheduled to present at the American Library Association conference in Anaheim. She resides in Evansville, Indiana with her husband Akira.

Ravi Patnayakuni is an associate professor of information systems in the Department of Economics and Information Systems at the University of Alabama in Huntsville. His research focuses on supply chain partnerships, information technology business value and knowledge management. His research has been published in *MIS Quarterly, Journal of Management Information Systems, IEEE Transactions on Engineering Management, Communication of the ACM, Journal of the Association of Information Systems, Omega, Communications of the AIS* and *Information Systems Journal*. He received his PhD from Southern Illinois University at Carbondale in 1997.

Joy Van Eck Peluchette is a professor of management in the College of Business at the University of Southern Indiana. She received her DBA from Southern Illinois University at Carbondale with a major in organizational behavior and her MSIR and BBA from West Virginia University. She teaches primarily in the areas of organizational behavior and leadership. Her research publications are in the areas of workplace fun, impression management, workplace attire, social networking, and leadership behavior.

Toru Sakaguchi is an associate professor of business informatics at Northern Kentucky University. He completed his PhD in management information systems at the University of Memphis. His research interests are in global information technology management and online privacy issues. His publications appear in *Information Resource Management Journal, Journal of Global Information Technology Management, Information Systems Management*, and other journals.

Nainika Seth is an assistant professor of information systems in the Department of Economics and Information Systems at the University of Alabama in Huntsville. She received her PhD from Southern Illinois University at Carbondale in 2002. Her research interests include IT infrastructure, IT value and the role of IT in supply chains. Her research has been published in *MIS Quarterly, Journal of Management Information Systems, Communications of the ACM, Omega, Information Resources Management Journal* and presented at the *ICIS conference*.

Toni M. Somers is professor of information systems management in the School of Business Administration at Wayne State University. She received her PhD from the University of Toledo and an MBA degree from Bowling Green State University. Her research interests focus on information technology adoption and implementation. She has published in *Information Systems Research, Decision Sciences, Journal of Management Information Systems, Information and Management,* and *Production and Operations Management Journal,* among other journals. She is on the editorial board of *Journal of Information Technology Case and Application Research.*

Mark T. Spence, PhD, joined Bond University, Australia, in 2002, where he is associate professor of marketing. He has taught a variety of marketing courses to undergraduates, postgraduates and executives, including consumer behavior, marketing strategy, market research and entrepreneurship. He has presented executive development workshops in the United States, Macau and in Europe. He has published in top academic journals including the *Journal of Marketing Research, Journal of Consumer Research, the European Journal of Marketing, Organizational Behavior and Human Decision Processes, Business Horizons,* and *Psychology and Marketing.*

Tamara L. Wandel is an assistant professor of communication at the University of Evansville. She teaches media writing, strategic public relations, and integrated communication campaigns. She is a former director of public relations in the State University of New York education system. Dr. Wandel's current research interests include studies on communication practices and global connectivity via social media. In 2007, she presented original data regarding online social networks at the World Communication Association conference in Brisbane, Australia.

Monica Whitty is lecturer in the Division of Psychology at Nottingham Trent University in the UK. She is the first author of *Cyberspace Romance: The Psychology of Online Relationships* (2006, Palgrave), and *Trust, Lies and Truth on the Internet* (2008, Routledge). In recent years, her work has focused on online dating, cyber-relationships, Internet infidelity, misrepresentation of self online, cyberstalking, cyberethics, and Internet and e-mail surveillance in the workplace.

Nick Yee is a research scientist in the Computing Science Laboratory at the Palo Alto Research Center. He obtained his PhD in 2007 from Stanford University where he studied social interaction and self-representation in virtual environments using a wide variety of methods, including experimental designs, surveys, field studies, and data-mining.

Nina D. Ziv is a professor in the Department of Management at Polytechnic University in New York City and serves as co-director of the Executive Master's Management Degree Programs at Polytechnic. Professor Ziv is also the academic director of the Institute for Technology and Enterprise [ITE], based at 55 Broad Street, where she is leading the strategic initiative on content innovation. Professor Ziv's major research interests are in the areas of content innovation and wireless innovation where she has focused on the challenges managers face when integrating digital-based and wireless innovations into their firms and sectors. Most recently, she has been conducting research on the social networking arena as a platform for innovation and on the increasing importance of users as a source of innovation in the Web 2.0 business environment. Professor Ziv is also interested in the restructuring of industries as a result of digital-based innovations and the impact of this restructuring on the development of urban centers of creativity and innovation such as New York City. Before joining Polytechnic University, Professor Ziv spent 15 years in the technology industry. She was a vice president of technology strategy and planning at Merrill Lynch in New York City where she spearheaded many innovative leading-edge technology projects including the development of Merrill's corporate intranet. Dr. Ziv received her PhD from New York University in applied linguistics.

Index

A

absenteeism 214
ambient semantics 21
arranged marriage 329, 332, 338
attention phase 282

B

bereavement framework 194
big man 65, 67, 71
business engineering (MBE) 148
Business Engineering Community (BEC) 149

C

character theory 63, 65
chat room Bob 65, 69, 71
Circle of Friends 61, 72, 62, 267, 271, 272, 273
CKP-Net 150, 151, 152, 153, 154, 155, 156
collaborative management 114
Competence Center Customer>
        Knowledge>Performance (CC CKP) 150
computer-mediated communication (CMC) 143
cultural convergence 338
customer-relationship management (CRM) 143, 150
cyberbullying 172, 186, 379

D

Dada 51, 53, 57
Deleting Online Predators Act 173
dowry 332, 333, 334, 348, 354

E

e-dater 293, 304, 306, 307
e-dating services 273
e-venger 68
eHarmony.com 256, 259, 263

emergent semantics 20
employee selection scenarios 217
ethnography 65, 334, 348, 355

F

face-to-face meeting 284
Facebook 1, 2, 3, 45, 56, 59, 95, 163, 164, 165, 166,
        175–199, 200–224, 242, 244, 251, 271, 272,
        273, 286, 309, 353–384
flirt 65, 67, 71, 76, 368
flirtation 76, 281, 285, 289, 365
Friendster 2, 3, 18, 19, 23, 41, 95, 165, 190, 199,
        229, 267, 271, 273, 358
Friendzy 2

G

gender 6, 7, 9, 14, 16, 17, 136, 215, 217, 223, 224,
        257, 309, 310, 322, 327, 328, 339, 347, 365,
        366, 378, 380, 381, 385
gotra 350
groupware 116, 120, 143, 376

I

iconoclast 65, 69, 71
IdentityMirror 18, 21, 33, 35, 36
implicit semantics 20
Indian Diaspora 338
individualism (IDV) 318
interaction phase 283
InterestMap 18, 21, 29, 31, 32, 33, 34, 42, 374
internet self-efficacy 5

K

knowledge management (KM) 143